THE ELECTORAL SYSTEM IN BRITAIN

The Electoral System in Britain

Robert Blackburn
Reader in Public Law
King's College, University of London

St. Martin's Press

First published in Great Britain 1995 by
MACMILLAN PRESS LTD
Houndmills, Basingstoke, Hampshire RG21 2XS
and London
Companies and representatives
throughout the world

A catalogue record for this book is available
from the British Library.

ISBN 0–333–62919–1 hardcover
ISBN 0–333–62918–3 paperback

10	9	8	7	6	5	4	3	2	1
04	03	02	01	00	99	98	97	96	95

Printed and bound in Great Britain by
Ipswich Book Co Ltd, Ipswich, Suffolk

First published in the United States of America 1995 by
Scholarly and Reference Division,
ST. MARTIN'S PRESS, INC.,
175 Fifth Avenue,
New York, N.Y. 10010

ISBN 0–312–12391–4

Library of Congress Cataloging-in-Publication Data
Blackburn, Robert, 1952–
The electoral system in Britain / Robert Blackburn.
p. cm.
Includes bibliographical references and index.
ISBN 0–312–12391–4
1. Elections—Great Britain. 2. Great Britain—Politics and government—1945– I. Title.
JN961.B58 1995
324.6'3'0941—dc20   94–22533
                                               CIP

For Paula, Sophie, Amy and Eden

Contents

List of Tables and Illustrations

Preface

Few subjects in politics are as important as the way in which the people of a country choose those who will govern them. New research and thought on electoral affairs is always to be welcomed. However, when I made the decision to embark on this book, it seemed to me there was now a very distinct need for a comprehensive account and commentary on the state of parliamentary elections in Britain. In part, this was because earlier books have tended to deal only with particular or selected topics in the subject, or else be addressed at some specific discipline or type of reader. Of greater importance, however, was that since the mid-1970s there has been a steady growth in the level of political and public concern about the way in which general elections are organised and regulated in Britain. In recent years, there have been several reports by Commons' select committees on electoral affairs, and two of the political parties have carried out wide-ranging enquiries into the electoral system, the most significant of which has been the Plant Report to the Labour Party in 1993. I have tried, therefore, first, to write a book which is as comprehensive and accessible as possible for the many different kinds of reader who are interested in general elections. Second, I have sought to pay special attention throughout my book to those subjects which have given rise to political concern or controversy in recent times.

The purpose of the book is to offer the reader both a description and an evaluative study of the electoral system. I have regarded it as a necessary and essential part of my work to take my evaluative analysis of the subjects and issues dealt with to its tangible conclusion of offering specific recommendations for reform. It would have been insufficient to my task if I had simply drawn general observations on matters of major political significance, such as the establishment of fixed-term Parliaments, the public financing of political parties, or proportional representation, without proceeding to elaborate in political and legislative detail on how such changes, in my view, are best implemented. The end result is that my book contains an extensive programme for electoral reform. It is offered as my contribution to the present debate on how the electoral system should be developed in the years ahead to improve the quality of representative democracy in Britain.

The term 'Britain' is used informally throughout this book to mean the United Kingdom of Great Britain (comprising Scotland, England and Wales) and Northern Ireland. A few passages are drawn from earlier works of mine: from *The Meeting of Parliament*, on some procedural matters affecting dissolution; from *Rights of Citizenship*, on the right to vote; and from my article in the journal *Electoral Studies*, on the Prime Minister's announcement of the date of a general election. This book is based upon the situation in August 1993, with up-dating on certain details and topics.

ROBERT BLACKBURN

1 Introduction: British Parliamentary Democracy

THE STRUCTURE OF PARLIAMENTARY DEMOCRACY IN BRITAIN

L. S. Amery once described the British system of democracy as one of, 'Government of the people, for the people, with, but not by, the people.'[1] Ideas about what democracy means, and what it involves, are as manifold as the innumerable interpretations that have been placed by different philosophers at different times upon the associated concepts of freedom and equality.[2] Aristotle, writing over 2000 years ago, expressed the basic principle that in a democracy the people are sovereign.[3] Yet the difficulties and complexities that have confronted democratic theory and practice, particularly in modern times, have mostly related to problems of political representation, and to how best the aspirations and wishes of 'the people' can be translated into governmental and legislative action. Few societies, apart from, for example, the ancient Greek city-states, have ever been small enough to be able to practise any form of direct personal democracy, in which all citizens have participated in the governmental decision-making of the community. In the democracies of the contemporary Western world, such as the United Kingdom with over 55 million inhabitants, systems of political representation have evolved over hundreds of years, under which political élites are elected to office in order to make decisions concerning government and to make law on the people's behalf. The crucial democratic link between politicians and people – or government and the governed – is the electoral system. The quality of that electoral system itself determines the quality of our democracy.

Few other countries in the world – and none across Europe, North America and the Commonwealth – possess a form of popular representation that is as concentrated into one set of elections as in the United Kingdom. A general election has a double claim to be regarded as the main political event of British democracy by virtue of performing two separate functions in a single electoral process. The first and most direct of these functions is to determine who will be the 651 persons to represent the different constituencies of the United Kingdom and sit as MPs in the House of Commons. The second function, which is generally uppermost in the minds of the British electorate, is to choose a government and decide which party leader will occupy 10 Downing Street as Prime Minister. In Britain,

1

therefore, a single vote cast by each eligible elector in the country controls both the personnel of Parliament and the personnel of government. In this respect, the British political structure is very different from those of countries that are founded upon the theory of the separation of powers, such as the United States, where different elections are held to decide the composition of the legislature and the composition of the executive.[4] Under the British system of parliamentary government, it is fundamental that members of the government must be appointed from among the ranks of those who are ordinary members of Parliament.[5]

Furthermore, there is no other popular electoral process taking place across the entire structure of central government which in any way serves to challenge or diminish the democratic authority of a general election. Unique in its composition as a parliamentary second chamber, the House of Lords remains in an unelected state (despite a parliamentary declaration of intent as far back as 1911 'to substitute for the House of Lords as it at present exists a second chamber constituted on a popular instead of hereditary basis').[6] The Lords' membership today includes 773 hereditary dukes, earls and barons, together with 374 life peers who have been appointed by the government.[7] All these peers are unaccountable to the people, and hold office until their deaths. The consequence of the second chamber's lack of democratic credibility was starkly seen recently. It enabled Conservative ministers to repudiate the constitutional authority of the House of Lords when they arranged for the War Crimes Bill, which the House of Lords had rejected in two successive parliamentary sessions, to be enacted under the legislative power of the House of Commons and the Queen alone.[8] Of even greater symbolic importance, the office of the nation's Head of State is itself unelected, being occupied by an hereditary monarch. The constitutional theory that reconciles the continuation of monarchy in a political democracy is that the Queen exercises all her public functions, including the Crown's legal prerogative powers, strictly in accordance with whatever ministerial advice is tendered to her by the government.[9] And within the confines of the constitution itself, the democratic authority vested by a general election in the British system of parliamentary government cannot be impugned or restricted in any way under the terms of any body of fundamental or basic law, because the United Kingdom lacks a written constitution. An Act of Parliament is the supreme source of law, and under the ancient judicial doctrine of parliamentary sovereignty, no court or judge will ever question the moral validity of whatever subject matter Parliament chooses to legislate into existence.[10] A general election, we may conclude, is unquestionably the sovereign political act within the functioning of the British system of parliamentary government.

The purpose of any system of democratic elections is to control political power, and render those politicians who govern us accountable for their policies and actions. In terms of affecting the content of government and legislative policy, popular elections impose a powerful incentive upon our rulers to please us, rather than themselves, and to interpret what is in the public interest according to how we, the electorate, perceive our best interests, rather than according to paternalistic notions of what they think is in our best interest regardless of whether or not we agree. The quality of British democracy has always been characterised more by ideas of political responsibility – by government and ministers to Parliament, and by parties and MPs to their electors – rather than by strenuous efforts designed to improve the quality of popular representation. This is one reason why the case for introducing proportional representation into the electoral system has been treated harshly in Britain as being irrelevant to the business of government.[11] Similarly, the right of electors in Britain to express an opinion upon important single issues of public policy via referendums has been widely rejected as being alien to British tradition and its political culture.[12] A constitutional function sometimes specifically attributed to general elections has been that of deciding questions of public policy. In at least three cases this century, a general election has been called by the Prime Minister upon some specific policy issue. This was the purpose of the December 1910 general election called by the Liberal Prime Minister, Herbert Asquith, over the Parliament Bill to curtail the powers of the House of Lords. Asquith's Liberal Party was returned to power, but with a loss of two Liberal MPs in the process. In 1923 the Conservative Prime Minister, Stanley Baldwin, called an election upon the issue of tariff reform, as a result of which his party lost its Commons' majority and went into opposition. Much closer in living memory was the débâcle of the Conservative Prime Minister, Edward Heath, going to the polls in February 1974 over 'who rules Britain' during the miners' strike, only to lose to Harold Wilson's Labour Party. This precedent above all others makes it highly improbable that the present Conservative government would ever seek to call an election in such circumstances or over any single issue, even over such a fundamental matter as the Maastricht Treaty, for the historical record suggests that such general elections are counter-productive for the government and less than popular with the electorate.

In the normal case of a general election, the political parties lay before the British electorate their manifestos containing the parties' whole range of public policies they will aim to implement if elected to govern. Since there are literally hundreds of policies referred to in each of the parties' election manifestos, there is no opportunity for the voter to distinguish between those policies he or she may particularly like and those which he or she may particularly dislike. The political party that wins the general election will claim an electoral mandate for its entire policy programme, but the reality under the electoral system in Britain is that the winning party will never knowingly have received the support of an electoral majority on any individual item of policy.

BRITISH POLITICAL PARTIES

The importance of political parties

'Without party,' Benjamin Disraeli remarked, 'parliamentary government is impossible.'[13] Political parties have a crucial role to play in the performance of the British electoral system. Their most important associated political functions include: (1) providing choice and alternatives at elections; (2) interpreting and representing public opinion, national and local interests, and the needs and aspirations of the electorate; (3) the formulation (and reformulation) of public policy to be adopted by the parties in government and opposition; (4) research and education into public policy issues, and communication of results to the public; (5) providing the contact for popular participation in politics; and (6) supplying individuals for political office, by selecting and supporting parliamentary candidates and party leaders. Whereas the great majority of citizens may have little or no direct interest in politics as such, it is to the respective leading party politicians that ordinary people turn to hear an explanation of the major issues of the day. At election times, the differences and choices to be made, both in terms of social principle and practical policy, are offered to the electorate, along with the reasons why one party's programme for government policy might be preferred over another's. For those more actively concerned, the opportunity for ordinary citizens to become members of the local and national political parties provides the channels for popular participation in policy formulation and the selection of party officials. The all-pervading importance of parties to the British political system has been described in the following terms:[14]

> Effective political parties are the crux of democratic government. Without them democracy withers and decays. Their role is all pervasive. They provide the men and women, and the policies for [government] . . . The parties in opposition have the responsibility of scrutinising and checking all the actions of the executive. Parties are the people's watchdog, the guardian of our liberties. At election times, it is they who run the campaigns and whose job it is to give the voters a clear-cut choice between different [persons] and different measures. At all times they are the vital link between the government and the governed. Their function is to maximise the participation of the people in decision-making . . . In short, they are the mainspring of all the processes of democracy.

Political parties in Britain, as elsewhere among the Western democracies, have become the principal criterion for voter choice at general elections. With rare exceptions, when British voters go into the polling booth to mark a cross on their ballot paper against one of the names of the candidates standing for election as MP within his constituency, they are basing their choice upon which political party's ideas and programme of policies they support and whose leading members they hope will govern the country for the next four or five years. In terms of personality, the typical voter at the last general election will have been thinking of John Major, Neil Kinnnock and Paddy Ashdown as he or she entered the polling booth, rather than the names of the local parliamentary candidates. The truth of the proposition that today electors vote for parties and not for candidates is borne out, first, by the great rarity of successful independent candidates (none were elected in 1992); and second, by the fact that an MP who loses his or her party's whip almost invariably loses the seat at the next election (such as was the case in the 1992 general election with the MPs Terry Fields and Dave Nellist, who had been expelled from the Labour Party a year earlier for alleged links with the Militant Tendency).

The personnel who achieve political office will owe their position to the political party that supports and selects them. Not only is this true of successful parliamentary candidates, but also of the party leaders who are the contenders for the office of Prime Minister at the general election. Unlike constitutional presidencies, as in the USA or France, which are directly voted in by the electorate, a Prime Minister owes his or her position not to the people directly, but to the political party which has selected him or her to lead them. For this reason, a common description of the British political structure is that of a system of party government. That the Prime Minister, the head of government in the United Kingdom, can be toppled by political circumstances outside a general election without a change in the political party holding office, was illustrated vividly in November 1990, when Margaret Thatcher was removed from the premiership and replaced by John Major.[15] Foreign observers, particularly American commentators, looked on in even greater disbelief than they had when Winston Churchill was voted out of office in 1945 just after Britain's victory in the second world war. For in Mrs Thatcher's case, her eleven years in office as Prime Minister was the longest period of any Prime Minister since Lord Liverpool in 1812–27, outdoing even William Gladstone, Disraeli, David Lloyd George and Churchill, and she had taken the Conservative Party to three general election triumphs in 1979, 1983 and 1987. Yet the *coup de grâce* that finished her political career came not from the British voter but from her own political party.

Each British political party has its own elaborate set of leadership rules,[16] that operate either when a vacancy arises (for example, because of resignation, illness or death of the Prime Minister), or at any time if there is dissatisfaction with the current leader and one or more rival candidates are put forward to challenge him or her, which requires a ballot. In the case of the Conservative Party in 1990, it was Michael Heseltine who initiated the challenge to Margaret Thatcher, standing as a candidate against her under the annual procedure for re-election, but following the result of the first ballot under which neither of them won outright, Margaret Thatcher resigned and her Cabinet colleagues, John Major and Douglas Hurd, entered their names for the second ballot, which John Major subsequently won. The consequence of this sensational event upon the outcome of the 1992 general election almost certainly transformed what would have been a Labour victory into the Conservative victory that in fact occurred under John Major's leadership. The Conservative Party electoral process for leader in 1990 rather than the general election in 1992 proved to be the real election that mattered in the parties' struggle for government office.

Despite the great public importance of political parties, it is a striking characteristic of the British electoral system that both its law and its constitutional traditions continue to treat them as purely private, voluntary bodies. As Lord Hailsham once put it, 'Political parties are no part of our constitution, but no part of our constitution can ignore their existence.'[17] Political parties receive no mention in British election law at all. Thus there are no legal controls over the expenditure involved in parties' national election campaigning, analogous to the controls that apply to individual candidates campaigning in their constituencies.[18] The funding of parties and their election propaganda at general elections remains private and unregulated, with no legal requirement even to publish accounts.[19] It is only since 1969 that the name of a political party has been allowed to be placed on the ballot paper given to each voter on polling day, making it clear which candidate is representing which party.[20] This characteristic of the British electoral system might be compared with those other countries (which have written constitutional frameworks laying down the conditions within which democracy is to operate) which give formal recognition to political parties as being vital ingredients in the electoral process. In France, for example, the Constitution of the Fifth French Republic states that, 'Political parties and groups shall play a part in the exercise of the right to vote.'[21] In Germany, the Basic Law of the country declares that, 'Political parties shall participate in the forming of the political will of the people', and there are whole statutes devoted to the conduct of party election campaigning and the financial affairs of the parties.[22]

Conservative, Labour and Liberal Democrat parties

The two largest political parties in the United Kingdom at the time of writing are the Conservative Party and the Labour Party. Their level of representation in the House of Commons currently amounts to 332 Conservative MPs and 269 Labour MPs. These two parties have, at irregular intervals, alternated in occupying the constitutional positions of Government and Opposition during the past fifty years. Other parties represented in Parliament, but with only a very small number of MPs compared to the Conservative and Labour parties, include the Liberal

Democrats (currently with 22 MPs), the nationalist parties in Scotland and Wales (with 3 and 4 MPs respectively), and four locally-based parties in Northern Ireland (holding 17 parliamentary seats between them). The Liberal Democrats have a claim to be regarded as one of the three major national political parties, having polled a substantial proportion of all votes cast at recent elections (17.8 per cent of the poll in 1992), although it (or its predecessor, the Liberal Party) has not now formed a government in its own right since the general election of December 1910. Whereas the Conservative Party and the Liberal Democrats' predecessor, the Liberal Party, have an ancient ancestry going back to the loose parliamentary groupings known as 'Tories' and 'Whigs' in the eighteenth century, the Labour Party is a relatively modern creation dating from the establishment of a Labour Representation Committee (to co-ordinate a campaign for the election of Labour MPs) in 1900, which then changed its name to the Labour Party in 1906.[23] During the 1920s, Labour succeeded in replacing the Liberals as the main opponent of the Conservative Party, and formed its first government in 1924. The two nationalist parties are both twentieth-century creations, the Scottish Nationalist Party being formed in 1928 and winning its first parliamentary seat in 1967, and Plaid Cymru (the Welsh Nationalist Party) being founded in 1925 and gaining its first MP in 1966.

Conservative Party organisation

It is important to appreciate the organisational distinctions between the major British political parties, for they explain a great deal about how the particular parties operate in terms of presenting themselves and their policies to the electorate. The party organisations of the Conservative and Labour parties are very different in their history, character and structure.[24] The Conservative Party was founded upon a parliamentary grouping of Conservative MPs at Westminster, and a national organisation was later developed and attached in support. The Labour Party, in contrast, was founded upon a national organisation formed outside Parliament, and the grouping of Labour members of both Houses of Parliament at Westminster is more properly described as the Parliamentary Labour Party. Conservative MPs, as a group, with the party leader they elect, operate with political autonomy from the national party (although there are procedures for consultation with constituency parties on various matters). The national party is properly known as the National Union of Conservative and Unionist Associations, and constitutes a union of all the local constituency associations around the country supporting the Conservatives. These local parties run their own affairs independently, including in the selection of officers and officials, but receive advice and guidance from the national party headquarters, known as Conservative Central Office, and also from various area councils established around the country (of which there are eleven in England and Wales). The governing body of the National Union is the Central Council, which is a large body with around 3600 members, and includes all members of the Executive Committee of the National Union, all Conservative MP and peers, representatives from each constituency association, and from various advisory bodies and Conservative societies. The Council meets once a year, generally in the spring, to debate motions submitted to it for resolution, and has its annual general meeting in the autumn (during the Conservative Party Conference). An Executive Committee of the National Union meets more regularly, around eight or nine times a year, and prepares recommendations to the Council for election of officers of the National Union, deals with disputes between or within constituency associations, and prepares policy advice for the party. It contains around 200 members, including the leader of the party, the leader of the party in the House of Lords, the party's chief whips in both Houses of Parliament, representatives of the 1922 Committee, and representatives of the provincial area councils. The four-day Conservative Party Conference is held each year in the autumn, which all members of the Central Council may attend, together with two further representatives (one of whom is a Young Conservative) from each constituency association around the country. Conservative Party conferences have no executive authority, nor any power to determine questions of party policy. Any resolutions passed at the Conference will not therefore be binding in any way upon the party leadership in Parliament and government.

Labour Party organisation

The Labour Party is a confederation of different bodies united under a formal, written constitution, including a set of common objects, one of which is 'to organise and maintain in Parliament and in the country a Political Labour Party'.[25] The principal groups in the party organisation are the Parliamentary Labour Party, the National Executive Committee, the Constituency Labour Party General and Executive Committees, and the Labour Party local branches across the country. The National Executive Committee is the central administrative authority in the party, comprising 29 members, including the leader and deputy leader, a young member elected at the National Youth Conference, and a treasurer and 25 members elected at the previous Party Conference (12 being chosen by trade union delegates, 7 by constituency party delegates, 1 by socialist, co-operative and professional organisations, and 5 women members elected by the whole Conference). A range of functions of the National Executive Committee is laid down in the party constitution; these functions amount to supervising virtually all the work of the party outside Parliament, together with formulating policy proposals and making annual reports for the Party Conference. 'The fountain of authority' in the party (quite different from the Conservative Party) is the Labour Party Conference, held annually for a four-and-a-half-day period each autumn. Those who may attend the conference number around 2500, and include all Labour MPs and peers, elected delegates from local constituency Labour parties, affiliated national trade unions, other affiliated groups (such as student organisations and socialist societies), endorsed parliamentary candidates, and members of the National Executive Committee. Motions on party affairs and the policies of the party will be debated and voted upon at the Conference, and those proposals that are adopted by a majority of more than two-thirds of votes cast (on a card vote) are required to be included in the party's official policy programme under the terms of the Labour constitution. The authority of the Party Conference over the political work of the leader and Parliamentary Labour Party is open to different interpretations. Some within the party have claimed that MPs are always morally bound to advocate and carry out the conference resolutions of the national party. However, the reality is that there is no way of enforcing such a claim over the work of parliamentarians, and there have certainly been occasions when Labour MPs, individually or collectively, have adopted a different viewpoint from that contained in Party Conference policy. Furthermore, when the party is in government, the leader is able to claim a higher authority derived from his constitutional office of Prime Minister. The constitution of the party, however, imposes an important restriction upon the party leader, by providing that the election manifesto, written prior to a general election, should be drafted by a joint meeting of the National Executive Committee and the Parliamentary Labour Party. By contrast, the Conservative leader has complete control over the drafting of his party's election manifesto, consistent with his freedom of action generally from the national party.

Liberal Democrats' organisation

The present Liberal Democrat party is the product of a permanent merger which took place in 1988 between the Liberal Party and the Social Democratic Party (SDP), which had emerged in 1981. The formation of the SDP was the result of a number of MPs and four former Labour Cabinet ministers breaking away from their existing parties, and by 1982 the SDP was represented by 29 MPs in the House of Commons. An electoral pact was arranged between the two parties at the 1983 and 1987 general elections, and this SDP/Liberal Alliance succeeded in polling 25.4 and 22.6 per cent respectively of all votes cast in Great Britain (whereas the Liberals alone in 1979 had polled only 13.9 per cent). The decision to form a permanent union between the two parties after the 1987 general election led to the present organisational structure of the Liberal Democrats contained in a formal constitution.[26] The party is a federation of separate regional parties formed in Scotland, Wales and across England. A Federal Policy Committee is responsible for the development and presentation of policy proposals for consideration by the Party Conference. The administrative work of the party is carried out under the direction of the Federal Executive. The composition of the Policy Committee and Executive is determined separately by the Conference each year, and includes certain *ex-officio* members, such as the leader and president of the party and prescribed numbers elected from certain categories of party member. The policy programme of the party is determined by its Federal Conference, which meets twice a year, and is attended by party officials, MPs and peers representing the party in Parliament, and representatives of its local constituency parties.

WINNING AND LOSING THE GENERAL ELECTION

Government formation following the election

The chief political consequence of a general election is to determine which party (or parties) will form the next government. It has been normal in the electoral history of the past fifty years for a single political party to win an overall majority of seats in the House of Commons, and for the leader of that party to be appointed Prime Minister by the Head of State, the monarch, and to form the government. If the party already in power wins the general election, then the incumbent Prime Minister simply remains in office with no further formalities necessary. However, where the government loses, the Prime Minister will immediately resign once the election results are declared, and the leader of the winning political party will be asked by the Queen to form the government. So, for example, on the first day after polling at the 1979 general election, being the most recent time that there has been a change of political party in government, this key moment in British parliamentary democracy came as follows:[27]

> The outcome was accepted tranquilly enough. At 2.30 on Friday afternoon Mr. Callaghan drove to Buckingham Palace to resign. He was followed an hour later by Mrs Thatcher, who kissed hands with the Queen as the first woman Prime Minister of the United Kingdom.

The transfer of governmental power between political parties is less straightforward where the result of a general election shows that no single party has won an overall majority of seats in the House of Commons. Such a situation has arisen on three separate occasions since 1918. On the first of these, in 1923, the Labour Party was in the process of eclipsing the Liberal Party as the second major party of state. The result of the election was that the Conservative Party won 258 seats, the Labour Party 191 seats, and the

Liberal Party 159 seats. The existing Conservative government under Stanley Baldwin, having polled more seats than any of the other parties, did not resign but decided to remain in office. However, when the new Parliament met five weeks later, a resolution expressing No Confidence in the government was passed by the Labour and Liberal MPs voting together, the constitutional effect of which was to oblige Stanley Baldwin to tender the resignation of the Conservative government, and the Labour Party to be invited by King George V to form its first administration. The next hung Parliament to be produced at a general election was in 1929, when the Conservative Party had 260 MPs elected to the House of Commons, the Labour Party 288, and the Liberal Party 59. The existing Conservative government, again under Stanley Baldwin, upon this occasion immediately resigned, and the Labour leader Ramsay MacDonald formed a Labour government. The third and last time a British general election produced such a situation was in February 1974 when the Conservative governing party obtained 296 seats, to Labour's 301, but with the Liberals having 14, the Scottish Nationalists 7, Plaid Cymru 2 and Ulster Loyalists 11. Polling day had been Thursday, 28 February, and by the afternoon of Friday the results clearly indicated that not only the Conservative Party, but also Labour, were short of a majority. The Prime Minister, Edward Heath, did not tender his resignation immediately, but instead entered into negotiations with the Liberal Party leader, Jeremy Thorpe, over the possibility of a governing coalition composed of the two parties. When these talks failed four days later, Edward Heath visited Buckingham Palace to resign at 6.30 pm on Monday, 4 March, and the Labour leader, Harold Wilson, met the Queen at 7.30 pm to be asked to form the next government.

The first task of an incoming Prime Minister is to complete the formation of the new government by selecting which of his or her party's MPs should be appointed as ministers (in the different ranks of Cabinet minister, minister of state, and under-secretary of state) to assume collective responsibility for the public administration of the country in the new Parliament after its first meeting about one week after polling day. Even though a party leader will have contemplated such appointments in advance, in practice in modern times such appointments – numbering about 100 in total – are made with remarkable speed. In 1979, Mrs Thatcher's Complete List of Government was published in a Downing Street Press Notice on 5th May, within two days of the general election and her acceptance of office as Prime Minister.

For the principal losing party, the frustrating task of opposition commences. The British state formally recognises Her Majesty's Opposition, and its Leader will be that person who leads the chief opposition party in the House of Commons. The Leader of the Opposition is entitled to a special salary in addition to his or her normal MP's pay, and is given precedence at state functions. Before the meeting of the new Parliament, he or she will form a 'Shadow Cabinet', comprising leading MPs from the party who will act as opposition spokespersons for the different departments or portfolios of government. The party in opposition, of course, is generally outnumbered by the government and, lacking the capacity to veto measures introduced by the government, has negligible direct impact upon public policy and legislation. However, in constitutional terms, the functioning and importance of the opposition cannot be overestimated.[28] Indeed, throughout the period up to the following general election the most important collective functions of the House of Commons, acting as the watchdog of the Executive and the popular assembly entrusted with the scrutiny of public administration generally, will be orchestrated and performed by the party in opposition. It is the task of the opposition to demand that government ministers articulate and justify the reasons why they are pursuing certain policies and why they are taking certain administrative action. It is their responsibility to seek out and expose any weaknesses in the government's case, and to argue why their own alternative proposals for public policy and legislation should be seen to be preferable. This is a continuing process that shapes the parliamentary consideration of all forms of public business in the House of Commons, whether at any given moment the timetable of the day is concerned with legislative bills, national finance, or opposition motions and adjournment debates. Ministers are obliged routinely to attend the House of Commons and to take part in the rough-and-tumble, abrasive and often rude quality of Commons' debate in the chamber. As such, the work of the opposition also serves constantly to discourage our rulers in government from delusions of grandeur fostered by the power they wield, and to remind them that they are, after all, only ordinary mortals – or a lot of 'jumped-up' MPs, to use Lord St John's expression. This whole process of government and opposition lies at the heart of British parliamentary democracy during the interval between general elections. It is a process rooted in the working of the House of Commons, but perhaps of equal importance is the similar brand of political dialogue that extends beyond Westminster, into the television studios and newspaper columns, and into the country at large. It is against this background that the preparation for each general election campaign takes place and, as Sir Ivor Jennings commented, 'The tactics of the opposition are directed to the conversion not of the government's party but of the electorate outside.'[29]

Past General Election results

The winners and losers at general elections over the past fifty years, together with the parties' respective levels of electoral support, are shown in the table on pages 13–15.[30] The table indicates, first, the number of total votes cast for each political party; second, the share of the total vote which each party

General Election results, 1945–92

	Total votes	Percentage share of votes	MPs elected
1945: Thursday 5 July			
Conservative	9 988 306	39.8	213
Labour	11 995 152	47.8	393
Liberal	2 248 226	9.0	12
Communist	102 780	0.4	2
Common Wealth	110 634	0.4	1
Others	640 880	2.0	19

Result: Labour Government 1945–50
Prime Minister: Clement Attlee

	Total votes	Percentage share of votes	MPs elected
1950: Thursday 23 February			
Conservative	12 502 567	43.5	298
Labour	13 266 592	46.1	315
Liberal	2 621 548	11.8	9
Others	381 964	1.3	3

Result: Labour Government 1950–1
Prime Minister: Clement Attlee

	Total votes	Percentage share of votes	MPs elected
1951: Thursday 25 October			
Conservative	13 717 538	48.0	321
Labour	13 948 605	49.2	295
Liberal	730 556	2.5	6
Others	198 969	0.7	3

Result: Conservative Government 1951–5
Prime Ministers: Sir Winston Churchill (1951–5)
Sir Anthony Eden (1955)

	Total votes	Percentage share of votes	MPs elected
1955: Thursday 26 May			
Conservative	13 286 569	49.7	344
Labour	12 404 970	46.4	277
Liberal	722 405	2.7	6
Others	346 554	1.2	3

Result: Conservative Government 1955–9
Prime Ministers: Sir Anthony Eden (1955–7)
Harold Macmillan (1957–9)

	Total votes	Percentage share of votes	MPs elected
1959: Thursday 8 October			
Conservative	13 749 830	49.4	365
Labour	12 215 538	43.8	258
Liberal	1 638 571	5.9	6
Others	142 670	0.9	1

Result: Conservative Government 1959–64
Prime Ministers: Harold Macmillan (1959–63)
Sir Alec Douglas-Home (1963–4)

Table continued overleaf

	Total votes	Percentage share of votes	MPs elected
1964: Thursday 15 October			
Conservative	12 001 396	43.4	304
Labour	12 205 814	44.1	317
Liberal	3 092 878	11.2	9
Others	347 905	1.3	0

Result: Labour Government 1964–66
Prime Minister: Harold Wilson

	Total votes	Percentage share of votes	MPs elected
1966: Thursday 31 March			
Conservative	11 418 433	41.9	253
Labour	13 064 951	47.9	363
Liberal	2 327 533	8.5	12
Others	422 296	1.2	2

Result: Labour Government 1966–70
Prime Minister: Harold Wilson

	Total votes	Percentage share of votes	MPs elected
1970: Thursday 18 June			
Conservative	13 145 123	46.4	330
Labour	12 179 341	43.0	287
Liberal	2 117 035	7.5	6
Scottish Nat. P.	306 802	1.1	1
Others	596 497	2.1	6

Result: Conservative Government 1970–4
Prime Minister: Edward Heath

	Total votes	Percentage share of votes	MPs elected
1974: Thursday 28 February			
Conservative	11 868 906	37.9	297
Labour	11 639 243	37.1	301
Liberal	6 063 470	19.3	14
Plaid Cymru	171 364	0.6	2
Scottish Nat. P.	632 032	2.0	7
Others (GB)	240 665	0.8	2
Others (NI)	717 986	2.3	12

Result: Labour Government 1974
Prime Minister: Harold Wilson

	Total votes	Percentage share of votes	MPs elected
1974: Thursday 10 October			
Conservative	10 464 817	35.8	277
Labour	11 457 079	39.2	319
Liberal	5 346 754	18.3	13
Plaid Cymru	166 321	0.6	3
Scottish Nat. P.	839 617	2.9	11
Others (GB)	212 496	0.8	0
Others (NI)	702 094	2.4	12

Result: Labour Government 1974–9
Prime Ministers: Harold Wilson (1974–6)
                          James Callaghan (1976–9)

	Total votes	Percentage share of votes	MPs elected
1979: Thursday 3 May			
Conservative	13 697 690	43.9	339
Labour	11 532 148	36.9	269
Liberal	4 313 811	13.8	11
Plaid Cymru	132 544	0.4	2
Scottish Nat. P.	504 259	1.6	2
Others (GB)	343 674	1.2	0
Others (NI)	695 889	2.2	12

Result: Conservative Government 1979–83
Prime Minister: Margaret Thatcher

	Total votes	Percentage share of votes	MPs elected
1983: Thursday 9 June			
Conservative	13 012 315	42.4	397
Labour	8 456 934	27.6	209
Liberal/SDP Alliance	7 780 949	25.4	23
Plaid Cymru	125 309	0.4	2
Scottish Nat. P.	331 975	1.1	2
Others (GB)	232 054	0.7	0
Others (NI)	764 925	3.1	17

Result: Conservative Government 1983–7
Prime Minister: Margaret Thatcher

	Total votes	Percentage share of votes	MPs elected
1987: Thursday 11 June			
Conservative	13 760 583	42.3	376
Labour	10 029 807	30.8	229
Liberal/SDP Alliance	7 341 633	22.5	22
Plaid Cymru	123 599	0.4	3
Scottish Nat. P.	416 473	1.3	3
Others (GB)	151 519	0.5	0
Others (NI)	730 152	2.2	17

Result: Conservative Government (1987–92)
Prime Ministers: Margaret Thatcher (1987–90)
John Major (1990–2)

	Total votes	Percentage share of votes	MPs elected
1992: Thursday 9 April			
Conservative	14 093 007	41.9	336
Labour	11 560 094	34.4	271
Liberal Democrats	5 999 606	17.8	20
Plaid Cymru	156 796	0.5	4
Scottish Nat. P.	629 564	1.9	3
Others (GB)	436 207	1.4	0
Others (NI)	740 485	2.1	17

Result: Conservative Government 1992–
Prime Minister: John Major

Table 1.1

obtained: third, the number of parliamentary candidates from each party who were elected as MPs; and, finally, which political party after the election results were declared proceeded to form a government or to remain in office.

DEMOCRATIC CREDENTIALS FOR AN ELECTORAL SYSTEM

A genuinely free and democratic system of elections can only operate where certain basic elements are guaranteed by law. The most important of these may be categorised as follows. *First*, the elections should be held at reasonable intervals, with the duration between being long enough to permit those elected to public office to carry out their responsibilities effectively, but short enough to ensure that they remain responsive and properly accountable to the opinion of the electorate. *Second*, every adult citizen should possess the right to vote, which must be exercised under conditions that ensure the secrecy of the ballot and are free from intimidation. *Third*, every citizen should be free to belong to, or form, political parties for legitimate political ends, and present their representatives or themselves as candidates for election (subject to such minimum qualifications for public office-holding as may be prescribed by law). *Fourth*, the electoral system should adopt a method of counting votes and determining winning parties and candidates which provides for the fair and accurate representation of the electorate. *Fifth*, the state should ensure the existence of conditions which provide for fair election contests between parties and candidates competing against one another, including freedom from intimidation of parties and candidates, the avoidance of unfair advantages in electioneering founded upon wealth, and reasonable opportunities for the parties and candidates to present their views and policies to the electorate. As expressed in international law, under the first protocol to the European Convention on Human Rights, the British government is pledged to ensure that its election law guarantees the holding of 'free elections at reasonable intervals by secret ballot, under conditions which will ensure the free expression of the opinion of the people'.

The future success of any electoral system will depend upon the institutional and ethical context within which it works. The object of the law must be to create a framework within which free elections and fair electioneering can flourish. The procedures for holding parliamentary elections must be administered by an administrative system which operates impartially between the different parties and candidates competing for office. The state must ensure that the voting citizen receives an informed choice, with adequate opportunities available for candidates and parties to present their cases. The workings of a free and responsible media has emerged in recent years as being of critical importance to the functioning of the electoral system. Complaints of electoral irregularities must be adjudicated by an independent judiciary which possesses sanctions that will be enforced. There must be a system for ensuring the continuous review of the electoral system, allowing it to develop in step with changing social circumstances and patterns of electioneering. This will rely largely upon the integrity and competence of those politicians who are already holding government office, acting with their civil servants, and a preparedness to bring forward legislative proposals for improvements that are needed but which might not always operate in their own partisan, vested interests. In Britain, the House of Commons is the central custodian of the nation's democratic rights, and MPs themselves hold the ultimate responsibility for safeguarding the working and modernisation of the electoral system. Permeating the working of any electoral system will be the culture and ethos which governs a country's political life, shaping its manner of government and the nature of the political conflict between the parties. The essential prerequisites for any modern democracy include a fundamental respect for human rights, above all the political liberties of free speech, the right to hold dissenting political views, and the protection of minorities. And the future stability of the political process must be built upon 'widely diffused habits of toleration' throughout the nation. For, as Professor Harold Laski wrote, 'Men who are to live together peacefully must be able to argue together peacefully. Without this tolerance there is no prospect in the society of compromise; and every subject of division then becomes a high-road to disruption.'[31]

2 The Timing of General Elections

WHEN GENERAL ELECTIONS ARE HELD

The five-year limit

The date of the next general election remains unknown to British voters and opposition parties alike, until it is announced by the Prime Minister approximately five weeks before polling is due to take place. It is the Prime Minister who possesses the constitutional power to select the date for a general election, and he or she formally exercises this power by requesting the Queen to carry out the legal ceremonies involved in dissolving Parliament and causing election writs to be issued to every parliamentary constituency to set the candidature nomination and ballot arrangements in motion. The only legal limitation upon the Prime Minister's freedom of choice is a 1911 statutory provision that a Parliament will automatically terminate exactly five years after the date of its first meeting. The wording of this fundamental provision controlling the frequency of British general elections reads as follows:[1]

> All Parliaments that shall at any time hereafter be called, assembled, or held, shall and may respectively have continuance for [five] years, and no longer, to be accounted from the day on which by the writ of summons . . . any future Parliament shall be appointed to meet, unless . . . any such Parliament hereafter to be summoned, shall be sooner dissolved by His Majesty, his heirs or successors.

A Prime Minister, therefore, must reach a decision on when the date of the next general election should be within this five-year time span.

The prerogative of dissolution

What permits the Prime Minister to determine the timing of elections at his or her own personal discretion is the theory of the royal prerogative. Formally, it is the Queen who calls a general election, since it is she as British monarch who is vested with the legal power to dissolve and summon Parliaments. The prerogative is derived not from any constitutional or parliamentary document, but simply from judicial recognition of Crown activities over many centuries past.[2] The power to dissolve Parliament and determine the timing of elections dates back to the thirteenth century, when Parliaments first came to be assembled at the order of the King or Queen of the day, and served as personal great councils of the monarch to be summoned and dissolved whenever he or she wanted 'advice' (generally, national support for the levying of special taxes). The legal basis of the right of dissolution therefore is the common law, and it is a prerogative right feudal in origin and nature which has remained uncodified to the present day.

The question of the most appropriate length of time between elections was a matter of constant political controversy in the last two centuries. The Septennial Act in 1715 laid down a maximum parliamentary term of seven years, which replaced the three-year term which had operated under the Triennial Acts in the late seventeenth century. The Septennial Act had been brought in as an emergency measure by the Whig government during the first year of the reign of King George I in order to help facilitate popular acceptance of the Hanoverian dynasty on the throne and safeguard the Protestant succession against the claims of the Jacobites who had mounted an armed invasion in Scotland. After the immediate crisis had passed, governments proved reluctant to return to three-year parliamentary terms, which would have had the effect of curtailing the duration of their tenure in office. For the next 196 years the law on election timing was left in a state which was regularly condemned as providing too long a period in which to leave MPs unaccountable to the electorate. Within the House of Commons there were strong partisan lobbies for terms of three, four or five years, and outside Parliament the Chartist movement, more idealistically, pressed the case for annual general elections. By the early years of the twentieth century, most radical reformers, such as the MPs Keir Hardie and Sidney Buxton, were still arguing in favour of a return to three-year terms, but the Liberal consensus which emerged in section 7 of the Parliament Act 1911 preferred the present five-year maximum. The wording of section 7 simply stated that, 'Five years shall be substituted for seven years as the time fixed for the maximum duration of Parliament under the Septennial Act 1715'. This new five-year limit was based upon the idea, as expressed by Herbert Asquith (then Prime Minister) in presenting the Parliament Bill to the House of Commons, that this would 'probably amount in practice to an actual working term of four years',[4] which was regarded as being about the right balance to be struck between the competing interests of political accountability to the electorate and the need for governments to have a sufficient length of time in which to implement their policy programmes. The motives behind the Parliament Act 1911 (together with all of its other statutory provisions apart from section 7) were not in fact inspired by the governing party's desire to reform the law of electoral timing so much as the immediate political necessity to reform the House of Lords' power over legislation from one of veto to that of temporary delay only. As part of a revised constitutional system of checks and balances, a more frequent accountability of the government and House of Commons to the electorate was presented as a 'set-off' against the reduced future power and role of the parliamentary second chamber within the workings of the British constitution.

There is no legal or constitutional reason today why each five-year period allowed for under the Parliament Act should not be served out in full, and a general election held immediately at the end of each term. However this maximum duration has never been allowed by any Prime Minister to be reached. The legal power to dissolve Parliament prior to the end of each five-year parliamentary term has always been exercised by a Prime Minister as the device for setting the date of the next general election. In order to retain the constitutional legitimacy of their power to set the election date, being a right which is based purely on historical precedent, the machinery of dissolution must be kept well-oiled and in permanent, continuing practice. Permitting a termination of Parliament by effluxion of time would give rise to the suggestion that the power of dissolution should only be exercised in special circumstances (such as a censure motion upon the government in the Commons, or where a Prime Minister felt it necessary to gain the electorate's support over some specific matter of government policy). For tactical reasons too, a Prime Minister will prefer to avoid Parliament reaching anywhere near the end of its five-year term (unless an immediate election is likely to bring defeat for the Prime Minister's party, as was the case with John Major between March and December in 1991)[5] because his or her electoral advantage in being able to wrong-foot political opponents by springing an election upon them at minimal notice will diminish as the final months of the five-year parliamentary term approach, with the growing certainty that an election must be imminent.

There is no minimum period of time which must elapse between general elections. Neither is there any minimum period of notice which a Prime Minister must serve to the electorate and political opponents before Parliament is dissolved. The period of time allowed for by a Prime Minister today between the general election announcement and the dates he or she has fixed for the dissolution of Parliament and polling day has become significantly shorter than at the elections held in the 1950s and 1960s. This has been particularly so since Edward Heath abruptly called a general election in February 1974, giving the country just one day's notice before Parliament was dissolved under the prerogative. It had previously been customary to allow between ten and twenty days between the announcement and the dissolution of Parliament. Since 1974 however, Edward Heath's historical precedent has been capitalised upon by successive Prime Ministers, who have been eager to maximise the advantage of surprise over political opponents. Harold Wilson allowed two days before the dissolution in September 1974, James Callaghan nine days in 1979,

Margaret Thatcher four days and seven days at the 1983 and 1987 elections respectively, and John Major five days in 1992.

The nature of the Crown's prerogative powers, including the right of dissolution, has upon occasion been the subject of scrutiny by the judiciary. Although the exercise by government ministers of some prerogative powers may be challenged in courts of law today, it was plainly stated by the House of Lords in the leading administrative law case of *Council of Civil Service Unions* v. *Minister for the Civil Service* (1984),[6] that there could be no grounds whatever upon which the power of dissolution could ever be challenged by way of judicial review proceedings. The common law of Britain, then, allows the Crown an absolute control over the date of the dissolution of Parliament and the timing of the date of an election. Since the Crown exercises this power to dissolve Parliament and set the election date upon the advice of the Prime Minister, it allows the party leader in office at 10 Downing Street an absolute and unfettered control over the timing of the next general election.

Frequency of elections in practice

The principle on democratic voting expressed in the European Convention on Human Rights requires parliamentary elections to be held 'at reasonable intervals'.[7] Britain's 'floating date' system for the timing of its general elections operates very differently from the fixed periods for elections to compose legislatures and heads of government that are laid down in the law of most other European countries and the USA (such as the five-year fixed term for the French National Assembly, the four-year fixed term for the German Bundestag, and the four-year fixed term for the American Presidency).[8] The 'reasonable intervals' between parliamentary elections in Britain, determined politically under the power of the royal prerogative, have been far from regular in duration. The average length of time between parliamentary elections since 1918 has been three years and seven months, but this tells us nothing about the actual duration of any particular Parliament, nor does it help us to predict with any degree of accuracy when the date of the next occasion will be for citizens to cast their votes. The intervals between general elections in Britain have varied widely in practice, from less than one year (1923–4, 1974); to one to two years (1922–23, 1950–51, 1964–66); to two to three years (1929–31); to three to four years (1918–22, 1951–55, 1970–74); to four to five years (1924–29, 1931–35, 1945–50, 1955–59, 1966–70, 1974–79, 1979–83, 1983–87, 1987–92); to over five years (1959–64); and during the Second World War for almost ten years under special prolongation statutes suspending elections (1935–45). Margaret Thatcher happened to call both of her two general elections, in 1983 and 1987, after almost exactly four years for each. In the case of the 1992 election, on 9 April, this came four years and ten months after Margaret

Intervals of time between General Elections, 1918–92

Year	Polling day	Interval		
		Years	Months	Days
1918	Saturday, December 14			
1922	Wednesday, November 15	3	11	1
1923	Thursday, December 6	1	0	21
1924	Wednesday, October 29	0	10	23
1929	Thursday, May 30	4	7	1
1931	Tuesday, October 27	2	4	28
1935	Thursday, November 14	4	0	18
1945	Thursday, July 5	9	7	21
1950	Thursday, February 23	4	7	18
1951	Thursday, October 25	1	8	2
1955	Thursday, May 26	3	7	1
1959	Thursday, October 8	4	4	13
1964	Thursday, October 15	5	0	7
1966	Thursday, March 31	1	6	16
1970	Thursday, June 18	4	3	18
1974	Thursday, February 28	3	8	10
1974	Thursday, October 10	0	7	11
1979	Thursday, May 3	4	6	24
1983	Thursday, June 9	4	1	6
1987	Thursday, June 11	4	0	2
1992	Thursday, April 9	4	9	28

Table 2.1

Thatcher's success on 11 June 1987. The table above includes the dates of all general elections held since the Parliament Act 1911. It gives a picture of great diversity and fluctuation in the constitutional practice of electoral timing in Britain.

It should be observed that the five-year time limit controlling the prerogative is directed at curtailing the duration of a Parliament, rather than specifically at regulating the interval of time between general elections. The periods of time surrounding polling day – when no Parliament is in existence, from the dissolution of the old Parliament to the poll, and from the poll to the date when the new Parliament actually meets – are variables that may have some effect on the precise intervals that occur in practice between general elections. So, for example, at the 1964 general election held on 15 October, the preceding Parliament had been in existence for exactly 4 years, 11 months and 5 days (therefore inside the five-year time limit), but the previous polling day had been held over 5 years beforehand on 8 October 1959. The interval of time between the dissolution of Parliament and polling day is controlled by a statutory timetable for electoral administration, which currently amounts to seventeen working days.[9]

There is no law stipulating when the newly-elected Parliament should meet following the general election, except for an antiquated three-year maximum time limit still in force under the 1694 Meeting of Parliament Act (see page 40). The date for the meeting of the new Parliament is therefore selected under the prerogative by the Prime Minister and will be stated in the Royal Proclamation prior to the election. In practice, since 1945 the period between polling day and the meeting of the new Parliament has never been longer than one month. A timetable of the pivotal events at each general election since 1918 is given below.

General Election timetable, 1918–92

Year	Election date announced	Parliament dissolved	Polling day	Parliament assembled
1918	November 14	November 25	December 14	February 4
1922	October 23	October 26	November 15	November 20
1923	November 13	November 16	December 6	January 8
1924	October 9	October 9	October 29	December 2
1929	April 24	May 10	May 30	June 25
1931	October 6	October 7	October 27	November 3
1935	October 23	October 25	November 14	November 26
1945	May 23	June 15	July 5	August 1
1950	January 11	February 3	February 23	March 1
1951	September 19	October 5	October 25	October 31
1955	April 15	May 6	May 26	June 7
1959	September 8	September 18	October 8	October 20
1964	September 15	September 25	October 15	October 27
1966	February 28	March 10	March 31	April 18
1970	May 18	May 29	June 18	June 29
1974	February 7	February 8	February 28	March 6
1974	September 18	September 20	October 10	October 22
1979	March 29	April 7	May 3	May 9
1983	May 9	May 13	June 9	June 15
1987	May 11	May 18	June 11	June 17
1992	March 11	March 16	April 9	April 27

Table 2.2[10]

PRIME MINISTERIAL CONTROL OVER THE ELECTION DATE

Uppermost in the mind of the Prime Minister in selecting a general election date will be the prospects for his or her party winning or losing the election. Prime Ministers will always be subject to some political factors beyond their personal control. These may increase or decrease popularity and affect his or her party's chances of success in the election. Examples include fluctuations in the international markets affecting the performance of the domestic economy, and how the resolution of international disputes precipitated by foreign leaders affects the standing of the government. Yet ultimately it is the Prime Minister alone who assesses his or her party's electoral prospects and reaches a conclusion on whether to wait until an unfavourable position improves or to bolt while public opinion appears favourable. For the Prime Minister, it is a decision of immense importance. He or she is in the position of trustee for the governing party's electoral prospects and whether or not they will remain in office to implement the range of public policies upon which they believe the national interest depends. For the Prime Minister personally, a general election defeat is likely to lead to his or her removal or resignation as party leader. Of those Prime Ministers who have led their parties to electoral defeat over the past twenty-five years, Harold Wilson managed to survive as leader of the Labour Party following its defeat in 1970, but Edward Heath was defeated by Margaret Thatcher in a leadership contest the year after the election he called and lost in February 1974, and James Callaghan resigned as leader of the Labour Party in the year following its election defeat in 1979.

The roles of Cabinet and Parliament in the decision

The power of the Prime Minister to determine the date of the next general election rests upon the constitutional convention that the Queen will exercise her prerogative of dissolution upon the Prime Minister's sole and exclusive advice.[11] There is no constitutional requirement for the Prime Minister to seek or obtain the approval either of the Cabinet or of Parliament before a general election is called.

Cabinet

The convention that the Prime Minister is free from any formal obligation to secure the agreement of the Cabinet is, in fact, of relatively recent acceptance. In the early decades of the twentieth century politicians and constitutional writers maintained that the Cabinet did and should control the date of elections. For example, Herbert Asquith, Prime Minister between 1905 and 1915 (and during which time two general elections were held), stated in his memoirs *Fifty Years of Parliament* that 'the dissolution of Parliament is always submitted to the Cabinet for ultimate decision'.[12] However since the Second World War our contemporary constitutional law texts have all agreed, to cite the words of Professors Stanley de Smith and Rodney Brazier, 'that the Prime Minister may decide to advise a dissolution without prior reference to the Cabinet'.[13] What has happened here is that constitutional principle has followed *de facto* political practice. Several of the elections held after Asquith left office were caused by pressure of events rather than choice: for example, the end of the First World War in 1918; the collapse of the governing coalition in 1922; the censure motion on the Labour Government in 1924; and the financial crisis and formation of the National Government in 1931. It was Stanley Baldwin, described by Professor Berriedale Keith, a leading constitutional lawyer of the 1930s, as 'a man of autocratic character',[14] who adopted this power over elections. He caused three general elections to be held during his tenure of the premiership, in 1923, 1929 and 1935, and he personally determined the timing of each. Indeed, the decision to call an election in 1923 was despite his colleagues, for he sought a mandate from the electorate on protectionism as a device to silence critics of his policy in his own party. It then simply remained for the Prime Ministers serving immediately after Baldwin (Winston Churchill, Clement Attlee and Sir Anthony Eden) to follow the precedent set by Baldwin, until the point was reached in the 1950s when advisers accepted the Prime Minister's sole control over a general election as 'normal'. As Berriedale Keith noted, what is particularly remarkable of these transition years from the 1920s to the 1950s is that 'the claim to decide a dissolution should have been made and apparently enforced, without effective, or perhaps any, protest' either among ministers or in Parliament.[15]

So politicians now accept that the choice of election date is the Prime Minister's preserve. Writing of the contemporary British constitution in his book *The Governance of Britain*, Harold Wilson, who as Prime Minister called three general elections in 1966, 1970 and 1974, says, 'there is no obligation on the Prime Minister to consult' Cabinet colleagues or anyone else.[16] Indeed of the 1966 general election, called only sixteen months since the previous election, and timed solely to increase the Labour government's slim majority in the Commons, Wilson says, 'I had made up my mind with no consultation whatsoever'.[17] Political colleagues, with only one or two exceptions, now appear to accept completely the legitimacy of this arrangement. Of Margaret Thatcher's power to set the election date in 1983, her close Cabinet colleague Norman Tebbit said it was 'hers and hers alone'.[18] A Prime Minister will generally take some soundings during periods when he or she may be considering an election, from trusted members of his or her inner Cabinet and personal office at 10 Downing Street, as well as from party whips and constituency officials who may have a closer ear to the electoral terrain than sometimes even opinion polls (which in both 1970 and 1992 proved themselves to be seriously at odds with how voters really felt).

Once a provisional decision is reached it is not uncommon for a Prime Minister to go down to Chequers for the weekend before the announcement of the election, inviting a group of his or her most trusted political advisers to attend an election campaign meeting. This was the pattern followed by Margaret Thatcher in both 1983 and 1987. In 1983, for example, the people she invited to this weekend meeting on 7 and 8 May included: from the party staff at Downing Street, David Wolfson, head of her political office, and

Ferdinand Mount, head of her policy unit; from Conservative Central Office, Christopher Lawson, director of marketing, and Anthony Shrimsley, director of press and publicity; Ian Gow, her parliamentary private secretary; and five of her ministerial colleagues – William Whitelaw, deputy leader of the party, Sir Geoffrey Howe, Chancellor of the Exchequer, John Biffen, Leader of the Commons, Cecil Parkinson, the party chairman, and Norman Tebbit, Secretary of State for Employment. Thus fortified in her election campaign plans for a general election on 9 June, a formal meeting of the Cabinet was swiftly organised for the following Monday morning, 9 May, to be informed of the date set for polling day. Within an hour of this meeting, the Prime Minister had an appointment, at 12.20 pm, at Buckingham Palace to tender her constitutional 'advice' to Queen Elizabeth on the dates for the dissolution and general election, and to set in motion the Royal Proclamation to effect the legal formalities. A similar train of events occurred before the 1992 election, with the Cabinet meeting at Downing Street being held at 11 am on the morning of Monday, 11 March, with the Prime Minister, John Major, subsequently being taken by car to Buckingham Palace to see the Queen at precisely 11.50 am for a brief visit of about ten minutes.

Parliament

Parliament – our national democracy assembly – does not have any say over the timing of its own dissolution and the accountability of the government to the electorate. Parliament is summarily dissolved without any prior formal approval or consent in the House of Commons or the House of Lords, and neither is it the custom for the Prime Minister to make an announcement about the pending dissolution and date of the election within the House of Commons. The Commons therefore has no legal control over its own existence, and no opportunity to debate the merits and demerits of the timing of the general election. Instead, once the Prime Minister has reached his decision, he or she will visit the Queen to tender his or her advice at Buckingham Palace, and a simple Press Notice will be issued one or two hours later from 10 Downing Street. Members of Parliament in both Houses are left to hear the news of the pending election through the media, or from one of the Westminster lobby correspondents, like ordinary members of the public. It has been argued by some officials, unconvincingly, that this method of communicating the fact of an imminent general election to those most directly affected, in other words MPs themselves, is justified on legal and constitutional grounds since the announcement being made by the Queen's Government outside Parliament is simply consistent with dissolution itself being a prerogative act which is effected at a meeting of the Privy Council at Buckingham Palace and away from either chamber of Parliament.

The deeper constitutional issue, however, is whether the House of Commons should have a legal right to control the Prime Minister's choice of election date. It has been proposed by some commentators over the past decade that the prerogative of dissolution (along, perhaps, with other Crown prerogative powers) should be made subject to the formal prior consent of the House of Commons. The Labour MP Tony Benn has gone even further, to argue that the Prime Minister should no longer be the public official to tender the advice to the Head of State on the date of the general election at all, and instead it should be for the Speaker of the House of Commons to advise the Queen.[19] The idea of a holding Commons' debate and vote on a proposal to dissolve Parliament and call a general election is not, in fact, a radical suggestion at all. Because, as is explained later in this chapter,[20] earlier in the twentieth century Prime Ministers frequently broke the news of a forthcoming election in the House of Commons in the form of introducing a motion to give precedence to government business for the remainder of the session. This would involve a vote being taken at the end of the debate, notionally on the change of parliamentary procedure, but in substance on the desirability of the general election. Today, therefore, it is very convenient for the government that under House of Commons Standing Order 13 the Leader of the House of Commons (a Cabinet minister) may make a simple statement to rearrange the parliamentary timetable to ensure the passage of all outstanding government business prior to the pending dissolution, and the consent of the House of Commons is no longer needed.

Many constitutionalists think that proper control over the Executive's use of the prerogative power, including the setting of the election date, is already in place, and is inherent in the arrangement whereby the Executive holds office and governs with the confidence of the House. If at any time the Prime Minister and government lose that confidence, then a censure motion can be passed by MPs which by convention will cause the resignation of the government (as in 1923) or a general election to be called (as happened in 1924 and 1979). A leading advocate of this viewpoint is Enoch Powell, the former Conservative MP, Treasury minister and high Tory intellectual, who in a BBC radio broadcast debate with Labour's Tony Benn about the Crown's prerogative powers, rejected out of hand Benn's proposals for parliamentary ratification, saying, 'These are decisions which although they are deeply political are covered by the authority of the House of Commons. They are covered by a majority in that very place'.[21] By the same token, according to this line of reasoning, if ever the majority party in the Commons begins to lose its confidence in its leader as Prime Minister, then the party's leadership election rules provide the annual opportunity for the removal of that person – as indeed happened to Margaret Thatcher in November 1990 at a time when Conservative MPs no longer believed that she could win the forthcoming election for them.

Political factors in the Prime Minister's calculation

A Prime Minister who enjoys a comfortable working majority in the House
of Commons will not under normal circumstances consider a dissolution
and general election within the first three years of a Parliament, and only
exceptionally good electoral prospects will tempt an interruption of its
legislative work in Parliament during the span of the fourth year. Such an
early dissolution would invite the possibility of losing the election. Only a
frustrated government, being one either with a minority in the Commons (as
with the minority Labour government under Harold Wilson in 1974) or with
a tenuous majority which could easily be eroded by a succession of deaths
among its MPs followed by unfavourable by-election results (as with
Labour under Clement Attlee, with a majority of five after twenty months in
1951) may choose to gamble on increasing its parliamentary support
through a dissolution within this period. Normally, then, after a three to
four year interval, the Prime Minister will fix the precise date of a general
election at the time he or she considers the party he or she leads has the best
chance of winning a majority of seats in the House of Commons. As Lord
Poole, a former chairman of the Conservative Party, once put it succinctly,
'The Prime Minister is likely to have a general election at the time when he
thinks he is most likely to win it.'[22] Or, as the constitutional lawyer
Professor Sir Ivor Jennings wrote in his text *Parliament*, 'A Prime Minister
will necessarily choose the moment for dissolution most favourable to his
own party.'[23]

Guiding the Prime Minister's calculation of his or her party's electoral
prospects will be by-election results, local government election results, the
party headquarter's monitoring of views being expressed by party workers
in the constituencies, and, above all, the results of public opinion polling
(both that commissioned confidentially by the parties themselves, and the
polling conducted for the newspaper and television companies by the major
market research companies such as MORI, ICM and Gallup). As far as by-
election results are concerned, being the more ancient barometers of
electoral prospects, a good result will certainly make a general election more
likely, but there may be problems in attaching too much significance to a
governing party victory or defeat either way. Voting behaviour in one
constituency may be highly unrepresentative of the nation or electorate as a
whole, and this will be especially likely if there is a preponderance of one
social group or class in that area making one item of government policy
disproportionately popular or unpopular. Looking at two by-elections lost
by the government in spring 1991, for example, when John Major was
looking actively for indicators of the likely result of an imminent general
election (it being four years since the last election), it was reform of the poll
tax that loomed largest as an issue in Ribble Valley, but a few weeks later in

Monmouth the by-election was lost specifically on changes being made to the National Health Service. In addition, the personalities of the respective party candidates competing for the vacancy are a far greater factor in voting behaviour at a by-election, whereas during a general election it is the personalities of the national party leaders who count most in the minds of the voters. In practice, the real significance of a by-election result is perhaps more important in public relations or presentational terms, whether the party looks to be a winner or a loser, rather than as an accurate barometer of the outcome of a general election. A poor performance by the government party candidate bodes ill for an election because it affects the credibility of the government itself, but a sound victory buoys up morale in the party and confidence in the government as a winning, successful force.

Similar considerations apply to the importance to be attached to local authority elections, which are often described as being mid-term referendums upon the performance of the government in office. Local issues are of much greater significance than at a general election, and the electoral turnout at this 'referendum' is generally around 30 per cent down on a general election. An election for the European Parliament is perhaps of even greater accuracy as a reflection of national opinion about the parties, although the turnout at these elections is also poor (36.5 per cent in Great Britain in 1989). The European elections involve national campaigning, often with sensational claims being made about the future of Europe. At the European elections on 15 June 1989, the Conservatives lost their majority, polling 32 seats to Labour's 45, against a background of Margaret Thatcher's highly controversial manner of diplomacy with other European leaders in the months immediately beforehand, something which proved to be an embarrassment to some of her Cabinet colleagues and contributed to her downfall as party leader the following year.

By far the most important factor in the Prime Minister's equation in calculating when he can win a general election is opinion polling on voting intentions.[24] A Prime Minister is most unlikely to call an election when his or her party is trailing behind the opposition in the opinion polls, unless he or she has no alternative. Government is perhaps an inherently unpopular undertaking, certainly all taxation and restrictive regulations are, and a new administration after an election will invariably enjoy a short honeymoon period with the electorate before a decline in its popularity sets in, as the hopes and aspirations of various interest groups are disappointed, probably through restraints on public expenditure, and shake-ups and strong medicine are meted out by the government in the medium- and long-term interests of its social policies. Similarly, prior to the 1992 general election, John Major, after he succeeded Margaret Thatcher in November 1990, enjoyed a short honeymoon period of popularity with the voting population. The Conservatives, from a dire position prior to Margaret

Thatcher's resignation, when they were trailing by around 12 per cent to Labour in the results of most public opinion polls throughout the whole of 1990 (and by 33 per cent to 49 per cent a fortnight before her departure), leapt into the lead in the last three months of December 1990, and January and February 1991, before slipping back into second place again. The government's successful conclusion of the Gulf War in January 1991 had added to the general expectation that John Major would call an election in the spring of that year, exactly four years after the previous polling day (with four years having been the exact period prior to the 1983 and 1987 general elections which had proved so successful to the Conservative Party). However, while anxious to secure his own mandate from the British electorate, John Major will have been most concerned to avoid going down in history as the shortest serving Prime Minister in history since Bonar Law in 1922. By June 1991 John Major was publicly declaring, 'I am not concerned with opinion polls – just with the economic performance of the country',[25] but few will believe that he did not call an election that year for any reason other than that the Conservatives were consistently running behind Labour in virtually all the public opinion polls taken from March 1991 to the end of the year. The monthly polling on voting intentions carried out by ICM for the *Guardian* in this period is shown in the table on page 31. With only a handful of months left to run before Parliament automatically terminated on reaching the five-year limit under the Parliament Act 1911, almost as soon as the Conservatives went into the lead, a popular Budget with cuts in taxation and interest rates took place in March, and a general election was announced.

The writings and autobiographies of former Prime Ministers and party campaign managers provide some of the most honest and fascinating insights into how election dates have been calculated by political leaders. Lord Hailsham, writing of his period as Conservative Party chairman, working with Prime Minister Harold Macmillan for election victory in 1959, says, 'I watched the opinion polls, together with by-elections and other signs of the political weather, like a lynx.'[26] Some of these personal accounts show that the fine tuning of electoral timing by Prime Ministers can depend upon some totally non-political considerations such as a desire to avoid bad weather, public holidays, local elections, and the national financial year. The view of Clement Attlee recorded in his memoirs *As It Happened* was that,[27]

It is therefore the duty of the Prime Minister to choose the time which, in his view, is the most propitious. In these days the choice is limited. The Budget and the financial year, the local elections and the holiday periods restrict the choice to late autumn, early spring or midsummer. There is always the gamble as to what the weather will be. November and

Electoral support for the parties,1990-92

		Conservative	Labour	Lib Dem
1990	November **John Major succeeds Margaret Thatcher,** (5-year term of Parliament due to expire on 17 June 1992)			
	December	45	43	9
1991	January	43	43	10
	February	44	42	9
	March	39	40	16
	April	39	43	13
	May	37	43	16
	June	34	44	43
	July	37	43	16
	August	36	45	16
	September	39	39	17
	October	41	43	12
	November	41	43	13
	December	39	42	14
1992	January	42	41	12
	February	40	40	16
1992	March **General election announced for 9 April**			

Table 2.3

February are notoriously liable to be foggy. Election work is difficult in winter in rural areas generally, and particularly in the north. I chose February and was very fortunate in that it turned out to be one of the best months in the year.

And in the 1960s and 1970s this is how Harold Wilson analysed the situation, related in his account of *The Labour Government 1964–70*.[28]

There was a lot to think about. There had not been a March election since 1880 (when the government lost). There was a risk of bad weather, as in 1963 – or indeed as there was to be in March 1970 – which not only lowers morale and, therefore, government support, but which also makes many families worse off – building and other outdoor workers are unable to work, an extra bag of coal to buy or, in other cases, more shillings needed in the meter for heating. On the other hand, there is usually a better feeling as the country emerges from winter into spring. These are difficult things to assess in electoral terms.

The timing of Easter was all right: there were no county council elections in early April. When I said on announcing the 1970 election that

I had planned this in 1966, my remark caused some hilarity. But one of my worries in 1966 was that I might limit my freedom of manoeuvre for the succeeding election. I had looked up the 'golden numbers' in Whitaker's Almanac, and found that Easter in 1970 was inconsiderately early, and was followed at the wrong interval by the county and GLC [Greater London Council] elections, with the borough elections and Whitsun following. I was anxious not to be forced into a premature autumn election in 1969, nor to have to leave a decision until late 1970, when, if the omens were unfriendly, we should have to continue through a final, perhaps hard, winter, postponing the election to the very end of the statutory life of the Parliament. I worked out that it would still be possible to go on 19th March, 1st May or late June, the 1st depending on the date of the wakes weeks. So all was well.

Are there any respects in which a Prime Minister's freedom of choice to set the election date is restricted as a matter of constitutional principle? There are only two scenarios when convention dictates a particular course of action. One is where the government is defeated on a Motion of No Confidence in the House of Commons, as on 28 March 1979 (by 311 votes to 310) following the collapse of the Labour–Liberal pact that had sustained James Callaghan's administration in power. Here the convention is that the Prime Minister must either call a general election, which James Callaghan proceeded to do, or resign office and allow the Leader of the Opposition to form a government. The second scenario, which has never arisen in practice, is the extremely improbable situation of an incumbent Prime Minister who has just lost the election going to Buckingham Palace and, instead of tendering his or her resignation, requesting the Queen for a second election immediately, hoping to improve his or her party's results. Such 'advice' from the Prime Minister would be manifestly unconstitutional, and the Queen, of course, would be both entitled and obliged to sack him or her and appoint the Leader of the Opposition as the new Prime Minister.[29] Similar considerations apply under a hung Parliament, where the Prime Minister has first claim on remaining in office, but if the government is subjected to a No Confidence Motion at the Opening of Parliament on an amendment to the Address, as, in fact, happened on 24 January 1924 to Stanley Baldwin's Conservative government, then by analogy with defeat at the polls the Prime Minister must resign and as a matter of convention he cannot call a second general election. However, once a Prime Minister is installed in office for any decent interval of time after an election, he or she appears to be free from any such constitutional restriction, leaving him or her to set the election date as he or she pleases, as Harold Wilson did in setting the election on 10 October 1974 after only seven months in 10 Downing Street, or Clement Attlee, in requesting King George VI to dissolve Parliament and call an election on 25 October 1951, after only eighteen months.

The public announcement of general elections

A forthcoming general election is announced to the world in the form of a Press Notice issued to the media by the Prime Minister's staff at 10 Downing Street. The Press Notice begins by stating formally that the Prime Minister has asked Her Majesty the Queen to proclaim a dissolution of Parliament and that Her Majesty has been graciously pleased to signify that she will comply with this request. Then the dates will be laid out in turn for the dissolution of Parliament, the general election, the first day of the new Parliament, and the State Opening. This public announcement is made less than a week before the Queen's Proclamation, which formally dissolves Parliament and sets in motion the legal procedures for holding the election. Thus in 1987 the Press Notice was issued on Monday 11 May and the dissolution was on Monday 18 May. In 1992 the notice was issued on 11 March and the dissolution took place on 16 March. A novel development in 1992 on 11 March was that the then Prime Minister, John Major, simultaneously with the issue of the Press Notice at 1.05 pm, stepped out of 10 Downing Street to give a personal statement and press conference in front of a battery of television cameras, in which he confirmed the date of the general election and then elaborated on why it was in the national interest that an election be called and why it would be preferable for the public to vote Conservative.[30]

The Press Notice is distributed directly to the media by 10 Downing Street officials, and news of the election is reported immediately in the day's television and radio news bulletins, and in the next editions of all newspapers. As a matter of courtesy a personal letter signed by the Prime Minister, sometimes preceded by a telephone call from an official, will be despatched an hour or so in advance of the Press Notice to the leaders of the other political parties and the Speaker of the House of Commons. This letter will usually have a copy of the Press Notice attached. It will add that in the interval between then and the dissolution, Parliament will transact essential financial and other outstanding business, and finally state that the public announcement will take place before a specified time that day and that the letter is for the personal information of the person to whom it is sent and that its contents are confidential until the announcement is made.

There has been some disquiet about the present method for the public announcement of general elections. The main criticism has been that members of Parliament should be informed in the Chamber first, before the news is given to the media. Indeed, the modern practice is for no announcement to be made in the Commons at all and for the government to assume members have heard the news from the press. For example on the day of the public announcement in the case of the 1987 Election, at 3.30 pm (a little over an hour after the Press Notice had been issued), the Leader of the House of Commons, John Biffen, said he would like to make a brief

Prime Minister's Press Notice announcing the forthcoming General Election

10 DOWNING STREET

Press Notice

GENERAL ELECTION, APRIL 1992

The Prime Minister has today asked Her Majesty The Queen
to proclaim the Dissolution of Parliament. Her Majesty has been
graciously pleased to signify that She will comply with this
request.

Parliament will be prorogued on Monday, 16 March. Dissolution
will take place on the same day. The General Election will take
place in Thursday, 9 April. The new Parliament will be summoned
to meet on Monday, 27 April, when the first business will be the
election of the Speaker and the swearing-in of members, and the
State Opening will be on Wednesday, 6 May.

11 March 1992

Prime Minister's letter to the Leader of the Opposition
informing him of the forthcoming General Election

10 DOWNING STREET
LONDON SW1A 2AA

THE PRIME MINISTER   11 May 1987

Dear Mr. Kinnock,

I am writing to let you know that I have this morning
asked The Queen to proclaim a Dissolution of Parliament. She
has been pleased to comply with this request.

Parliament will be dissolved on Monday 18 May, and the
General Election will be on Thursday 11 June. In the
interval between now and 18 May Parliament will transact
essential financial and other outstanding business.

The new Parliament will be summoned for Wednesday
17 June, when the House of Commons will elect the Speaker and
swear in Members. The State Opening of the new Parliament
will be on Thursday 25 June.

The announcement of the Dissolution and the consequent
Election will be issued before 2.30 p.m. today from
10 Downing Street - a copy of the announcement is enclosed.

This letter is for your personal information, and I
should be grateful if you would treat it accordingly until
the announcement is made.

Yours sincerely

Margaret Thatcher

The Right Honourable Neil Kinnock, M.P.

business statement that 'in the light of the announcement earlier today by my Right Hon. friend the Prime Minister, the business for the remainder of the week will be rearranged'. Not surprisingly, few members had, in fact, heard the news and had to hear the details from journalists at the House or other members who knew. No protest was made about this in 1987, although Sir Kenneth Lewis stood up to say he had not heard the announcement.[31] In similar circumstances before the previous election in 1983, the Labour MP William Hamilton protested in the strongest terms:[32]

On a point of order, Mr Speaker. I thought I heard the Leader of the House refer to an announcement by the Prime Minister . . . This is a gross discourtesy. Are you aware, Mr Speaker, that I first knew of the announcement from a member of the Press Gallery? That was the first indication that I had. What has happened is a gross discourtesy.

Previously, in 1979, several Members criticised the method of public announcement.[33] The Conservative MP Robert Adley suggested that the Leader of the House, Michael Foot, should feel ashamed of himself. Norman St John-Stevas teased Michael Foot for employing a Conservative argument in his defence that he was merely following precedent. This was all Michael Foot could say in justification to the following suggestion from the former Liberal Party leader, Jo Grimond:

Whatever the precedents may be, does the Leader of the House not feel that it would be more courteous to the House of Commons, if it is sitting when a dissolution and general election are announced, if the announcement of the general election were made to the House and not to the press?

Announcement in the House of Commons was, in fact, the customary method earlier in the twentieth century. The method of making an announcement to the press appears to date from 1945 since it has been followed on every occasion since then, although there was an earlier instance in 1922. However, the true break with constitutional practice should more properly be regarded as being in 1966, because before every general election from 1945 to 1964 (as well as in 1922 and later in September 1974) the announcement could not be made to the Commons because it stood in recess. In 1966, 1970, February 1974, 1979, 1983, 1987 and 1992, parliamentary business was in session but the government chose a public announcement to the press instead of the Commons. The new method stands in great contrast to the historic occasions before 1935 when members assembled in anticipation and excitement to hear what was to be the content of a special statement to be made by the Prime Minister. Premiers including Herbert Asquith, Ramsay Macdonald and Stanley Baldwin all did this and set out in speeches their reasons for the election. Sometimes their speeches would be in the form of introducing a motion to give precedence to government business for the remainder of the session, and this would then be debated, not only giving members the news first but also the opportunity to comment.

One may only surmise at the reasons for the change in procedure. No reasons were given by the government in 1966 and no officials or politicians from that period are able to say with certainty why the decision to break with pre-1945 tradition was taken. It is probable that the change was caused by administrative confusion by officials in 1966 as to what was the precise custom – they advised and followed the pattern in the immediately prior elections, forgetting that those had been times of parliamentary recess. Furthermore, since 1945, there has been no need for the Prime Minister to obtain the consent of the Commons that precedence in the Commons' timetable be given to outstanding government business for the last few days of the session, because contemporary Standing Orders now automatically give precedence to government business except where otherwise specifically reserved (for example, private members' business on twenty Fridays in each session). The Prime Minister and other politicians will, of course, not be sorry at the passing of the political practice of making a public announcement in the chamber, and in fact are likely to be very keen to avoid it. The usual reason for electoral timing, namely when it is considered that the governing party has the greatest chance of winning a general election, needs necessarily to be clothed in more respectable terms, such as it being in the national interest to end uncertainty and speculation, whereas opposition politicians in the House of Commons will try to debunk such claims, accusing them of a discreditable, cut-and-run decision.

CEREMONY AND PROCEDURE FOR DISSOLVING PARLIAMENT AND CALLING THE GENERAL ELECTION

The Queen's ceremonial role

In legal procedure the general election is called by way of a Royal Proclamation signed by the Queen at a meeting of the Privy Council. Its ancient, traditional form declares the dissolution of the existing Parliament and the calling of another, and requires writs from the Lord Chancellor's department to be sent out to all parliamentary constituencies for the holding in each of an election to return a Member of Parliament. The Proclamation also states the date upon which the newly constituted Parliament shall meet for the first time. This Proclamation is legally effective immediately it is signed by the Queen, and is authenticated by the Lord Chancellor fixing the Great Seal to the document.[34] Its publication, however, takes place by a curious variety of methods. It has been the standard practice in recent times for the Proclamation to be recorded formally in *The London Gazette*.[35] The form of the Proclamation is as shown opposite.

Ceremonially, there is no announcement of this Proclamation at Westminster, or inside the House of Commons, because technically Parliament has already ceased to exist. But ancient pageantry continues in the form of a bell-ringer and Common Cryer and Sergeant-at-Arms standing on the steps of the Royal Exchange in the City of London to read out the terms of the Proclamation. A separate but similar public reading ceremony takes place in Edinburgh seven days later, being a tradition based upon the length of time it took horseriders to reach the city from London bearing news of the Proclamation.

It is perhaps interesting to note just how personal a ceremonial function the calling of general elections is to the Queen herself. Whereas most Crown prerogatives can be exercised by ministers or civil servants in the name of Her Majesty the Queen, a small number of prerogative powers can only be exercised by the Queen and these, along with the appointment of the Prime Minister and Cabinet ministers and the granting of honours, include the dissolution and summoning of Parliaments and the order to the Lord Chancellor to send out royal writs of election to Parliament. There is no legal mechanism in place to provide for a situation that the Queen might ever refuse to sign the Proclamation, and in law Parliament cannot call itself into existence once dissolved.[36] A statutory framework was laid down in 1641 for other state officials to be authorised to call elections for a new Parliament if King Charles I or his heirs failed to do so, but the royalists under King Charles II insisted upon its repeal in 1660 on the restoration of the monarchy after Oliver Cromwell's death. If the Queen is travelling abroad, she may in fact now delegate her legal ceremonial duties to persons appointed to perform the task in her place as Counsellors of State, authorised by letters patent from her under the Great Seal, as laid down in the Regency Act 1937. Persons who may be appointed Counsellors of State are stated by the Act to include the heir to the throne and the four persons after him next in line of succession to the throne, and the 1953 Regency Act shortly after the accession of the young Queen Elizabeth II specifically added the name of Queen Elizabeth, the Queen Mother. Disqualifications from being a Counsellor are being under 18 years, a Roman Catholic, living abroad or ceasing to be a British citizen. However, even where such delegation of the power to dissolve Parliament does takes place, section 6 of the 1937 Act specifically provides that the dissolution may only be effected by the Counsellors of State 'on the express instruction of the Sovereign'. This situation did, in fact, arise in 1966, when Harold Wilson, the then Prime Minister, wanted an early election in order to increase the size of his party's majority in the Commons. In his memoirs of prime ministerial office he related this particular form of ceremonial ritual as follows.[37]

The Queen's Proclamation for the Dissolution of Parliament, 1987

BY THE QUEEN

A PROCLAMATION

For Dissolving the Present Parliament and Declaring the Calling of
Another

ELIZABETH R.

Whereas We have thought fit, by and with the advice of Our Privy
Council, to dissolve this present Parliament: We do, for that End, publish
this Our Royal Proclamation, and do hereby dissolve the said Parliament
accordingly: And the Lords Spiritual and Temporal, and the Members of
the House of Commons, are discharged from further Attendance thereat:
And We being desirous and resolved, as soon as may be, to meet Our
People, and to have their Advice in Parliament, do hereby make known
to all Our loving Subjects Our Royal Will and Pleasure to call a new
Parliament: And do hereby further declare, that, by and with the advice
of Our Privy Council, We have given Order that Our Chancellor of Great
Britain and Our Secretary of State for Northern Ireland do respectively,
upon Notice thereof, forthwith issue our Writs, in due Form and
according to Law, for calling a new Parliament: And We do hereby also,
by this Our Royal Proclamation under Our Great Seal of Our Realm,
require Writs forthwith to be issued accordingly by Our said Chancellor
and Secretary of State respectively, for causing the Lords Spiritual and
Temporal and Commons who are to serve in the said Parliament to be
duly returned to, and give their Attendance in, Our said Parliament on
Wednesday, the seventeenth day of June next, which Writs are to be
returnable in due course of Law.

Given at Our Court at Buckingham Palace, this eighteenth day of May
in the Year of our Lord One thousand nine hundred and eighty-seven
and in the thirty-sixth year of Our Reign.

GOD SAVE THE QUEEN

In my latest audience with the Queen on 27 January, before she left for her Caribbean tour, I had informally mentioned the probability that I should be recommending a dissolution for the early days of March, by which time she would be back in London. She agreed that the formal recommendation to enable the forthcoming dissolution to be announced could be sent by secure telegram. A fortnight before this was sent I wrote a letter setting out my recommendations, to which the Queen replied in her own hand.

The legal theory is still that the Queen could dissolve a Parliament, and decide whether or not to call elections for a successor, by way of any action or verbal direction which clearly indicates her intention.[38] Before the modern conventions of limited monarchy were complete, kings and queens often effected control over Parliament by entering personally one of the parliamentary chambers at the Palace of Westminster to say that Parliament was dissolved. However, the Prince Regent, later King George IV, was the last monarch to exercise the prerogative over Parliament by appearing in the House of Lords to effect a personal dissolution, and for the past 175 years a Royal Proclamation has been the invariable procedure used in practice.

The anachronism of the 1694 Triennial Act

There remains in force in British law the curious spectacle of the 1694 Triennial Act (now retitled the Meeting of Parliament Act under the Statute Law Reform Act in 1948), which states that the Queen should summon a Parliament and cause a general election to be held within three years of each dissolution of Parliament:

> Within three years at the farthest from and after the determination of every . . . Parliament, legal writs under the Great Seal shall be issued by directions of Your Majesties your heirs and successors for calling assembling and holding another new Parliament.

This means that in strict legal theory general elections only need to be held once in every *eight* years. After a general election there is the five-year limit on the duration of a Parliament, then added to this is a further three years under the Triennial Act before the next general election actually needs to be called in law.

In practice, the constitutional settlement of 1689 following the Glorious Revolution in 1688 ensured the annual meeting of Parliament through, first, providing in the Bill of Rights that express parliamentary approval was required for all government taxation and expenditure, and, second, Parliament limiting most of its financial consents to a cycle of one-year periods. But in the modern political system, even one year would be too long a period of time in which to allow no Parliament to meet and a general election to be held following a dissolution. Parliament's primary function is to keep the workings of government under its constant supervision, and to give vent to public opinion and the views of the government's political opposition. Indeed, in some countries, such as Germany (whose constitutional law Britain helped to construct after the Second World War) Parliament's legal existence never expires, even during the election campaign. When the German election results are declared, the newly elected representatives simply replace outgoing members who have either decided to resign or been defeated. In Britain, the constitutional guarantee that a general election is called immediately a dissolution of Parliament takes place is the unwritten convention that the Queen will simultaneously call a new Parliament and order election writs to be sent out in the self-same Proclamation that dissolves Parliament. The time in which Parliament ceases to exist after a dissolution is therefore in practice kept to an absolute minimum, being only the time in which election campaigning and preparation for the poll takes place. This generally amounts to a period of about six weeks. In 1992 Parliament was dissolved on 16 March and it met again on 27 April, the election being held on 9 April.

Precisely why electoral reformers during the passage of the Parliament Bill in 1911 did not rationalise the Triennial Act while dealing with the frequency of general elections is not clear, but it is as much a mystery why the Home Office when preparing the successive Representation of the People Acts over the period since 1911, particularly in 1983 and 1985, have still thought it best to leave the enactment unchanged. The answer must either be an administrative oversight or else a sentimentality about an historic document that was of political relevance to the seventeenth century, but of none since, coupled with a contentment to leave the fundamental elements that guarantee the calling of general elections in this country – and the existence of our parliamentary democracy – uncodified in law.

The issue of election writs to the constituencies

As soon as is practicable after the issue of the Proclamation summoning the new Parliament, royal writs of election must be sealed and issued by the Clerk of the Crown in Chancery to the returning officers in every constituency in Great Britain. The form of the royal writ is based on ancient precedent, and the statutory specimen currently laid down by the Representation of the People Act 1983 is not greatly different from that used in past centuries. The Great Seal held by the Lord Chancellor, or now more usually a wafer seal which is permitted to be used instead by the Crown Office Act 1877, must authenticate the issue of each writ sent out to the constituencies. The Parliamentary Election Rules contained in the Representation of the People Act 1983 permit the government, by way of Orders in Council, to regulate delivery of the writs, and currently the

Form of election writ

Elizabeth the Second by the Grace of God of the United Kingdom of Great Britain and Northern Ireland and of Our other Realms and Territories Queen Head of the Commonwealth Defender of the Faith to the Returning Officer for the .... Constituency Greeting

Whereas by the advice of Our Council We have ordered a Parliament to be holden at Westminster on the .... day of .... next We Command you that due notice being first given you do cause election to be made according to law of a Member to serve in Parliament for the said .... Constituency And that you do cause the name of such Member when so elected, whether he be present or absent, to be certified to Us in Our Chancery without delay.

Witness Ourself at Westminster the ...... day of .... in the year of Our Reign, and in the year of Our Lord 19....

Label or direction of writ

To the Returning Officer for the .... Constituency
A writ of a new election of a Member for the said Constituency.

Endorsement

Received the within Writ on the ...... day of ...., 19....
(Signed)
Returning Officer

Certificate endorsed on writ

I hereby certify, that the Member elected for the Constituency in pursuance of the within written Writ is ....
of .... in the County of ....
(Signed)
Returning Officer

Parliamentary Writs Order 1983 provides for their conveyance by post. The Post Office is required by law to maintain a 'parliamentary writs list' setting out details of all the returning officers (and acting returning officers if administrative functions have been delegated), together with their addresses, and it is the duty of all returning officers to keep the Post Office informed of the necessary details. The contents of this list, and any alterations made to it from time to time, is relayed to the Clerk of the Crown for use in posting out the writs for a general election. To ensure that the writ has arrived safely, the returning officer has to sign a receipt form which is sent back to the Clerk of the Crown in Chancery, by registered post, by a designated postal official. The returning officer must also endorse the election writ with a statement that it has been received and the date upon which it was delivered. The returning officer then sets the constituency election administrative arrangements in motion. His first important duty is to see that before 4 o'clock in the afternoon of the second day after that on which the election writ is received by him, a notice of the election, which includes the invitation for nominations as parliamentary candidates, is published in the constituency.

The Representation of the People Act 1983 lays down certain essential information that must go into the notice of the forthcoming election that is given to voters belonging to the returning officer's constituency. First, it must specify the date of the election; second, it must state the times and place at which nomination forms for proposing prospective parliamentary candidates may be obtained, and also the time and place for completed nomination forms to be delivered to the returning officer;[39] and third (being of greater importance since the extension of postal and proxy voting by the Representation of the People Acts 1985 and 1989), the notice must state the date by which applications for electors to cast their vote, not in person but by way of using the post or use of a proxy, must reach the returning officer.[40] The obligation upon the returning officer is to 'publish' the notice and he or she has the discretion as to the form the notice takes. Publication of the notice, under the 1985 Act,[41] involves posting the notice in some conspicuous place or places in the constituency and in such other manner as he or she thinks desirable. Because of the speed with which the notice must be published (within two days) it is unlikely that a weekly local newspaper will satisfy these statutory requirements. Public libraries and Post Offices are favourite places in which to pin up notices of the election.

The timetable of key events following the Royal Proclamation up to polling day itself is shown on page 44.

A remote possibility that could affect the date set for a general election would be if the British monarch happened to die during the period between the dissolution of Parliament and the designated polling day.[42] Such an event has never occurred in modern times. However, if it did, the Representation of the People Act 1985 provides that the date fixed for the

Statutory time limits in the electoral administration

Event	Time limit	Day
Issue of writs (from the Lord Chancellor's Dept, House of Lords	As soon as practicable after the issue of the Royal Proclamation dissolving the old Parliament and summoning the new Parliament (usually on the same day)	Day 0
Receipt of writs by returning officers	The day after the writs are issued.	Day 1
Notice of the election	Not later than 4 pm on the second day after that on which the writ is received	Day 3
Postal or proxy voting applications on normal grounds	Not later than noon on the thirteenth day before the date of the poll	Day 4
Delivery of candidates' nomination papers (including appointment of election agent)	Between the hours of 10 am and 4 pm on any day after the date of publication of the notice of the election, but not later than the sixth day after the day of the Proclamation summoning the new Parliament	Day 6
The making of objections to nomination papers	During the hours allowed for delivery of nomination papers on the last day for their delivery and the hour following	
Publication of statement of persons nominated	At the close of the time for making objections to nomination papers or as soon afterwards as any objections are dealt with	
Postal or proxy voting applications by ill persons	Not later than noon on the sixth day before the date of the poll	Day 11
Last day for candidates to appoint their polling and counting agents	Not later than on the second day before the date of the poll.	Day 15
Polling day	Between 7 am and 10 pm on the eleventh day after the last day for delivery of nomination papers	Day 17

Note: In computing any period of time for the purpose of the timetable, the following days are disregarded: Saturdays, Sundays, Christmas Eve, Christmas Day, Maundy Thursday, Good Friday, bank holidays and any day appointed for public thanksgiving or mourning.

Table 2.4

poll should be postponed by fourteen days. In such circumstances the prospect of politicians continuing to attack one another and the carnival atmosphere generated at polling day would be grossly incongruous, and some short delay in holding the election is clearly appropriate to allow time for national mourning and the state funeral for the British Head of State.

SAFEGUARDS AGAINST THE SUSPENSION OR ABOLITION OF ELECTIONS

In what circumstances is it legitimate to suspend general elections altogether and prolong the existence of an elected House of Commons (and the government it supported) beyond its five-year maximum term? British law on this point is contained in section 2(1) of the Parliament Act 1911, which simply provides for the House of Lords to have an absolute veto over legislative measures designed 'to extend the maximum duration of Parliament beyond five years'. This is a special power which the House of Lords possesses over no other item of general public legislation, not even any possible future government Bill to dismantle the structure of the United Kingdom or abolish the monarchy or the House of Lords itself.[43] In the written constitutions of most democratised countries in the world, the law does not permit the Parliament of that state to extend its own tenure, although there are usually legal provisions for amending the constitution, to permit the suspension of elections. Several countries, including the United Kingdom, permit the postponement of their parliamentary elections by way of special legislative process, and in some of them – unlike the United Kingdom – only upon specified grounds. For example, the constitutional law of Canada permits the term of the House of Commons to be extended in times of national crisis if not opposed by more than one-third of its existing members. The Swedish and Italian constitutions permit legislation only in the event of war, as does the Maltese constitution (Malta being formerly a British colony); Malta, in addition, restricts the period of postponement under any such legislation to twelve months, with a maximum figure of five years being imposed upon the total permissible period in which a general election might be suspended under a series of such one-year prolongation statutes.[44]

British law provides equal power to each of the two Houses of Parliament to decide if and when a general election might be dispensed with or postponed, but it does not identify the conditions under which parliamentary elections can be suspended, nor does it specify any circumstances to help us determine the constitutional legitimacy regarding when the power of Parliament to delay or cancel elections might or should be used. In other words, the legitimacy or proper criteria upon which the power is exercised is to be decided *ad hoc* by our parliamentary representatives according to their perception of what is appropriate in any given situation. Whether or not a governing party majority in the House of Commons – the very people who would be perpetuating themselves in political office – together with over 1200 hereditary and life peers in the House of Lords, is a suitable decision-making body to be given a completely free hand over an issue of such constitutional importance is clearly a moot point. There is a powerful case behind the proposition that the cancellation of parliamentary elections except in times of war would be unethical in terms of constitutional convention. But this does not mean that warfare of itself might legitimise the suspension of elections. The putting into abeyance of the normal working of democracy is so fundamental to the political state that only conditions on such a scale of disruption that make it patently impractical to conduct the administrative arrangements for the holding of elections can be tantamount to a genuinely constitutional justification. Among an electorate of about 44 million citizens, the dislocation caused by a British war effort fought exclusively overseas would be unlikely to be on such a severe scale. Parliamentary candidates on military service would be granted leave of absence for campaigning (and discharged if they won their constituency election), and facilities for postal voting would be arranged for the troops. Suppose that a five-year parliamentary term had been approaching its end during the Falklands War in 1982 or the Gulf conflict in 1990, for example. Conditions were certainly less than ideal for holding a general election and for conducting partisan policy campaigns in face of the national interest of supporting the government's military operation; but it is extremely doubtful that these war conditions could legitimately have been used as an excuse to put off a general election that was otherwise constitutionally required by law.

Past episodes of suspended General Elections

In Britain both Houses of Parliament approved Acts to suspend general elections during the two world wars in the twentieth century. The House of Commons elected in December 1910 remained unaccountable to the electorate for eight years, until December 1918. In that period a Liberal Party Cabinet led by Prime Minister Herbert Asquith governed until May 1915, whereupon a coalition was formed to confront the war with Germany, at first under Asquith's premiership, until December 1916, and thereafter under David Lloyd George. In response to the Second World War, which began in 1939, the House of Commons elected in 1935 remained unaccountable for almost ten years, until July 1945. The National Government (which excluded Labour) returned to office in 1935 under Stanley Baldwin (who was replaced as Prime Minister by Neville Chamberlain in 1937) gave way to a coalition of all parties under Winston Churchill in 1940 in order to direct the war effort against Germany. The government and Parliament agreed during both world wars that political partisanship and party electioneering would be detrimental to the overriding public interest of winning the military conflict with Germany that threatened the life of the nation, at a time when national unity was called for, and that in any case all the political parties were represented in the coalition government. As the then Home Secretary, Herbert Morrison, put it in 1943 when speaking to the Commons.[45]

The fundamental reason for the prolongation of the life of Parliament is that [a general election] would be seriously prejudicial to the prosecution of the war. It would be out of tune with the spirit of the nation, which is one essentially of national unity during the war, and . . . it would be difficult to find an issue upon which to fight the election, as we are all united about the war . . . Quite apart from the diversion of labour and materials, the distraction of attention from the primary task of fighting the war and the possible promotion of national disunity make it appear to us that it would be more helpful to the enemy than to this country that this Parliament should come to an end at this point.

The level of physical disruption caused to the country by the two world wars was not identical, and while the mass mobilisation of personnel engaged in fighting the war in Europe between 1914 and 1918 was greater than anything this country has ever known, the nature of the military conflict in 1940–5 more conclusively precluded a general election being held. This was because, in addition to the huge numbers of troops engaged in fighting overseas, the British civilian population was mobilised around the country during 1940–44 in a state of readiness for invasion, and Britain was actively within the theatre of warfare and was subjected systematically to mass aerial bombing. Among Commonwealth countries fighting alongside Britain in 1940–5, Australia, Canada and New Zealand all managed to hold general elections, although they were largely outside the theatre of warfare and not subject to the same scale of internal disruption and bombing which was suffered by Great Britain. Within the British Parliament there were a number of reservations expressed by MPs about the need to cancel elections during 1915–18, whereas there were virtually none in 1940–5, but the truly colossal scale of manpower involved in pursuing the First World War, amounting to some 6,000,000 Britons, of whom 750,000 were killed and 1,700,000 wounded, gave great force to the legitimacy with which the government introduced its Bills to postpone a general election, upon the basis not only that party electioneering would be inappropriate to the need for national unity, but also that it was impractical to conduct a fair election when the massive mobilisation of the population engaged in the war effort meant that the compilation of constituency electoral registers would be flawed and administrative arrangements to receive ballot papers from all eligible voters could not be guaranteed.

Future constitutional constraints

It must be axiomatic in any democracy that the legislative measures postponing parliamentary elections should be supported by public opinion. But the dilemma in this is that, short of a referendum (which for the same reason of disruption it would be impracticable to hold) there is no accurate mechanism for knowing what the electorate thinks. Ultimately the electoral system in Britain trusts those already in positions of political power to apply their own judgement on the postponement of general elections. Perhaps the only real constitutional principle that may be said to apply at present is that the period of postponement specified by a statute prolonging the five-year maximum life-time of Parliament should not exceed one year, so that Parliament has the opportunity to review any suspension of elections on an annual basis. In 1916–18 four statutes were passed specifying extensions of less than one year (specifying eight, seven, seven and eight months respectively).[46] In 1940–5 a similar form of Prolongation of Parliament Act was passed annually, each specifying an extension of exactly one year.[47] These precedents have almost certainly given rise to a convention for any future legislative enactments postponing a general election to comply with. Herbert Morrison, the Home Secretary, accepted this principle of annuality when he told MPs when presenting his Prolongation of Parliament Bill to the House in 1943:[48]

> It is right that this Bill should only last for a year in order that both the government and the House may be required to review the matter year by year and not take any further liberties with the normal workings of the constitution without such a periodical review. This is a constitutional measure, and the government are quite properly required to justify the measure annually to Parliament, so that Parliament may have the opportunity of reviewing the situation in the light of current conditions, and so that if Parliament thought that owing to changes of conditions or other circumstances it was right that it should be brought to an end, it may always be within the power of Parliament itself to secure this.

It should be understood that the veto of the House of Lords over a corrupt use by the government to prolong its own existence, along with the life of a Parliament, is in present circumstances illusory. Constitutional lawyers are virtually unanimous that the Parliament Act procedure may be used to abolish the House of Lords itself, or diminish its legislative power to nothing, in the same way that the power of the Commons to have its measures enacted without the Lords' consent after two years under the Parliament Act 1911 was utilised to railroad the Parliament Act 1949 on to the statute book, which reduced the Lords' power of delay to one year only. And the readiness of the government in power at the time of writing – a

Conservative one whose party defends the claims of the present House of Lords to a continuing role in the British Constitution – to enact the War Crimes Act in 1991 under the Parliament Act procedure, after the Lords had deliberately rejected it upon judicial and constitutional criteria in two successive parliamentary sessions, indicates that a determined government would have little difficulty in circumventing any opposition in the Lords founded upon democratic or any other criteria. The solution to the artificiality of this legislative safeguard is to modernise our second chamber of Parliament by way of reconstituting its composition upon the basis of direct popular elections with two or three members being returned from the current European Parliament constituencies, and with the second chamber being given special responsibilities such as in the field of international treaty ratifications, and over constitutional-type legislation such as the postponement or abolition of elections where it had a genuine veto.[49]

THE CASE FOR FIXED-TERM PARLIAMENTS

Since the mid-1980s there has been a revival of political support for introducing a fixed term for the British Parliament. An earlier supporter was Professor Ramsay Muir who, in giving evidence to a Commons' committee in 1931, described the 'personal prime ministerial prerogative' of calling an election at any time to suit his political convenience as 'an unsound constitutional doctrine'. In 1970 the late Professor Owen Hood Phillips, author of one of the country's principal constitutional law texts, argued in his important monograph, *Reform of the Constitution*, for a fixed-term Parliament. More recently, a similar proposal was included in the Institute for Public Policy Research's programme of constitutional reform, published in September 1991,[50] and was given the personal backing of the then Labour Party leader, Neil Kinnock, at the following month's Party Conference. At the 1992 general election, it was an item of policy included in both the Labour and Liberal Democrat parties' election manifestos.

The arguments for a fixed-term Parliament will now be considered. Taken together they represent a strong case for reform of the law of election timing in Britain. Apart from growing backbench support for the idea at Westminster, indicated by several Private Members' Bills introduced in the House of Common on the subject in the past few years, MORI's extensive opinion polling carried out for the Joseph Rowntree Trust on *The State of the Nation* has shown a very clear popular approval of the principle for a fixed term between general elections.[51] Their 1991 poll showed that over two-thirds of the electorate would support the change, and among the 18–24-years-olds the level of support was over three-quarters. It is a proposal now firmly on the political agenda.

Comparative models

First, one should be aware of how other major Western democracies organise their electoral timing. Most countries of the world have a written body of constitutional law that clearly provides for regular intervals between their popular elections. In these countries, there are usually distinct electoral processes for determining the composition of the legislature and government, and for composing the two chambers of the Parliament.

In America, for example, article II:1 of the 1787 Constitution of the United States of America provides that presidential elections shall be held every four years, and article I:2–3 lays down that the House of Representatives shall be composed of members chosen every second year, and that the Senate shall be composed of senators chosen for six-year terms. In Germany, the largest and most powerful country in Europe, with a parliamentary system of government similar to that in Britain, Parliament (called the Bundestag) is elected for a four-year fixed term under Article 39 of their new Constitution (following the unification of West and East Germany on 3 October 1990). In France (where the duration of fixed terms is currently under review, at present being regarded as too long), under article 6 of the 1958 Constitution of the Fifth Republic, the President holds office for seven-year terms, and under an Electoral Code required by article 25 of the Constitution, the lower House of Parliament (called the National Assembly) is elected for five-year terms, and members of the second chamber (the Senate) serve for nine years.

The democratic arguments

Owen Hood Phillips summarised the British system of parliamentary election timing in the following scathing terms:[52]

> The practice is for the Prime Minister (formerly, as we have seen, the Cabinet) before the end of the statutory period of five years, after consulting his party henchmen and nowadays the public opinion polls, to choose a date for the dissolution – published as short a time as possible beforehand – that he thinks will be most advantageous to the government party and most disadvantageous to the opposition party. Since the Prime Minister and his fellow conspirators alone know when that date will be, they can juggle with direct and indirect taxes and manipulate the economy in such a way as to favour their chances at the general election. Any unpopular measures will have been taken in the earlier part of their term of office. This squalid practice of the leaders of both main parties as it has developed is the least creditable aspect of the British constitution.

No one should imagine that a fixed date for elections will ever take the politics out of electioneering, nor should it aim to do so. The main political parties will do their utmost, as at present, to persuade voters that they are the preferable team for government, the better statesmen, more capable in managing the economy and securing employment and prosperity, and generally improving the quality of citizenship and public services. As at present, government legislation that is likely to be unpopular will be implemented in the first three years of the Parliament, and then (assuming that the fixed term is four years) in the final months before the election date the Prime Minister will almost certainly see to it, on political rather than economic grounds, that his Chancellor presents a popular giveaway Budget in April, that favourable tax concessions are made, and interest rates for home owners and businessmen become significantly lower than in the previous year, in order to give the country a sense of improved financial well-being under the political party in power. A major foreign trip for the Prime Minister, preferably to the USA or Russia, or an important international conference with major foreign heads of government, complete with the media fully briefed on its timing and ample photo-opportunities so that pictures can be relayed back to the electorate via newspapers and television cameras, would continue to be *de rigueur* in the months before polling day, as an electioneering device designed to promote the public image of the incumbent party leader in 10 Downing Street as an authoritative world statesman. The key difference would be that these party political shenanigans would be kept in a proper perspective, because the electorate would know the election date was approaching, and the opposition could more fairly arrange their own election campaign.

At present the governing party has a tremendous tactical advantage in the minimal notice it needs to give to its political opponents. A British general election has been described as 'a race in which the Prime Minister is allowed to approach it with his running shoes in one hand and his starting pistol in the other.'[53] Not surprisingly, victories of the government party are more frequent at parliamentary elections than those by the party in opposition, because the Prime Minister can avoid periods of unpopularity, but make a premature dash for the polls well before the end of the present five-year maximum term whenever public opinion is favourable. And even in those elections where the party in government has lost, in the majority of cases it was only by a small margin, such as Labour's defeat by 43 seats in 1970, and Edward Heath's Conservatives by a mere 4 seats to Labour in February 1974. On the other hand, the party in government that called an election for the first or second time after coming into office have tended to secure massive majorities, such as Margaret Thatcher's Conservative victories of 397 to Labour's 209 in 1983, and 376 to Labour's 229 in 1987. The minimum notice of the election that needs to be given in law by the Prime Minister, is now a mere 17 working days from the time of the Proclamation dissolving Parliament, and the former political custom that the duration of election campaigns should always last for a minimum of four weeks was undermined by Edward Heath in February 1974, when he decided *de facto* to arrange the shortest campaign term in our election history and have a three-week period instead.[54] Lord Hailsham, the former Lord Chancellor, has described this whole system of election timing determined at the whim of the Prime Minister as one whereby an 'elective dictatorship has proved more and more powerful, and more and more liable to perpetuate itself'.[55]

Any election will produce a certain degree of uncertainty and volatility in the running of the country and economy, as there will be speculation about a change of government and consequent public and fiscal policies. But whereas under a fixed date for elections, industry and the City can to some extent plan for possible dislocation of its business, under the present 'floating' date system the period of uncertainty is a prolonged matter, because an election may be sprung at any time, and if and when it occurs at five weeks' notice it may catch many businesses unprepared. As far as the Treasury is concerned, who can doubt that political considerations dominated the Chancellor's fiscal policies from January 1991 onwards in preparation for a snap election at any time, to enable John Major to seek an electoral mandate of his own? Such prolonged uncertainty and speculation about a general election is fed by media speculation, much of which emanates from non-attributable press briefings by politicians and political advisers close to, or inside, the government or 10 Downing Street itself.

It is not only financiers, the market and the world of business that is caused problems by the uncertainty, but also public administration and private individuals. While government politicians are blowing hot and cold over whether a general election is on the horizon or not, the civil service spends a considerable amount of time on contingency plans and ministerial briefings to put before a new, incoming government, in the event that the election is lost. Individuals wanting to buy or move house will be worried by the effect on house prices or mortgage loans of a sudden election. Describing the system as an 'election blight on economic policy', a leader in *The Observer* argued, during a bout of election fever in May 1991:[56]

Our present ramshackle electoral system, which allows a Prime Minister to call an election whenever it suits him within a five year period, is an absurdity in a modern economy and looks more and more out of touch with democratic developments elsewhere in Europe. The case for fixed term Parliaments . . . is a powerful one. If an election has to be held every four years, legislation could be progressed more efficiently. Whitehall, industry and the business community could plan ahead, and – no less important – the electoral field would be levelled.

A case-study of electoral muddle

A study of the twelve-month period between September 1990 and August 1991 serves to illustrate well the prolonged uncertainty endemic in the present system, and the often ridiculous dance performed by politicians in office in raising or lowering expectations of an imminent election. By the autumn of 1990 it was three-and-a-half years since the previous election (June 1987), and the assumption created by there having been elections at almost exactly four-yearly intervals previously (1979–83, and 1983–87) was of a May announcement for a June 1991 poll. However, as 1990 progressed the country was sliding into a deep economic recession, with the poll tax deeply unpopular, and interest rates on home loans soaring to over 15 per cent. Not surprisingly the Conservative government found itself trailing Labour by as much as up to 10 points in the public opinion polls. So, no less surprisingly, just before the October Conservative Party conference, the Conservative Party chairman, then Kenneth Baker, cast doubt on a 1991 election date, and expressly hinted to the public that 1992 was the preferred date. He declared, 'We shall be thinking in terms of 1992. But my task as Party chairman is to have the party ready to fight the election if the Prime Minister decides to have one in 1991.'[57]

The government's fortunes were transformed in November 1990 when John Major replaced Margaret Thatcher as Conservative Party leader and Prime Minister. John Major enjoyed the usual 'honeymoon' period afforded to a new premier, and the government took a modest lead over Labour in the opinion polls. The government's new popularity was further sustained and enhanced by the Gulf conflict in January 1991, when British armed forces took part in the liberation of Kuwait. In January and February the opinion polls put the government ahead of Labour by as much as four points. At worst, ICM's poll for *The Guardian* in January put the parties neck and neck, and in February the Conservatives were two points ahead. But MORI's surveys of 18–26 January listed the Conservatives 46 per cent to Labour's 41 per cent, and between 22 and 25 February 44 per cent and 41 per cent respectively. On 17 February John Major instructed ministers to deliver election manifesto submissions to him the following week, and ordered all Whitehall departments to clear their desks of all but vital business during that month.[58] A bout of election fever broke out, with a rash of media polls indicating a government victory in a spring election, and that voters had no objection to a 'khaki election' and would prefer to give their verdict on John Major and his government before the summer.[59]

In March doubts started to appear. The modest government lead in the opinion polls had slipped, and beneath the general Tory euphoria about victory in the Gulf and an imminent success in a general election, non-attributable briefings to the press began to make it clear that a strong and influential current of Cabinet and backbench Conservative opinion was convinced that a May or June election would be a dangerous and potentially lethal gamble. Despite a spate of interest rate cuts by the Chancellor, in March the Conservatives and Labour stood neck and neck at around 40 per cent in the opinion polls, and then the government suffered a by-election disaster in Ribble Valley. The local government elections on 3 May were looked to as a deciding element in the decision of whether to go for a June election or not. On 7 April the then party chairman, Chris Patten, publicly hinted at a poll in the autumn, stating in a radio interview:[60]

> There may be people on 3 May, after they have helped me look at the computer print-outs, who will suggest we should have an election sooner rather than later. But there will be other people who will be looking at the economy and suggesting the opposite. I do not honestly think that the case for a June election, or the case against a June election, is proven.

The uncertainty continued throughout April on whether there would be an election or not eight weeks later.

But in May it became clear that there would not be an election in June. The local government election results were discouraging for the Conservatives, and the government had fallen even further behind Labour in the public opinion polls (by 6 per cent in a MORI survey of 24–28 May). Was the election to be October or November? The deepening recession and the continuing Labour Party lead in the opinion polls throughout the summer put even that prospect in doubt, although it would leave the Prime Minister trapped in 1992 with far less room for manoeuvre to call an election at a time of government popularity, since constitutionally an election had to be called before 7 July. But John Major's dilemma was that virtually all City analysts and economists did not believe that the national economy could recover before 1992. This dilemma was all too clearly demonstrated by the fact that on 16 May within the same newspaper, *The Times*, directly contradictory hints were published from the two key figures in the Conservative Party, the Prime Minister and the party chairman: on the front page it was reported, 'Major ready to defer [autumn] election to help Lamont [his Chancellor of the Exchequer]'; but inside the newspaper, Chris Patten was said 'to be keen to see early interest rate cuts to bring down mortgage payments and induce a feeling of economic well-being, so keeping open the option of an October election'. By the following month (June), the Conservative Party's rating in the opinion polls had slipped by as much as 10 per cent behind Labour to its lowest point under John Major's premiership. That month the Prime Minister publicly declared there would be no election until he had completed negotiations on the future shape of Europe, the talks on which were due to end in December.[61] In early August, the party chairman, Chris Patten, agreed, saying that there would be no election until the Prime Minister had 'sorted out' the economy.[62] And so the muddle over when a general election should properly take place remained and continued into 1992.

In a parliamentary debate in 1991 on the principle of a fixed-term Parliament, one member commented:[63]

Why does the British electorate have to endure every few years a coy guessing game about the date of the general election? It has become the electoral equivalent of that childish game of peekaboo: 'Now you see it, now you don't!' At least once a month since January of this year, the government's backbenchers have been marched grumbling up to the top of the hill, perched on the verge of a general election, and then marched unceremoniously down the other side of the hill. We know that the opinion polls are scrutinised with all the feverish anxiety of a hypochondriac. The Conservative Party chairman raises and lowers expectations every day like a political barometer.

One might say that that is all good clean fun, and so it would be if it were an obscure private game, but it is not. General elections are about renewing the power and re-establishing the legitimacy upon which democratic government rests. So in a very real sense, elections should belong to the voters rather than in any sense belonging to or being manipulated by the Prime Minister and the government. If that is not so, it is to give to the Prime Minister and his party what, in American politics, is known as an incumbency advantage. It is a travesty of serious democracy when Messrs. William Hill and Ladbroke give odds not just on the result of the election – that is fair enough – but on the date of the general election. One can place a wager on the date upon which the general election will be held as if it had all the unpredictability and charm of a horse race.

Prime ministerial rule

There are other important constitutional arguments in support of the reform of the timing of general elections, apart from ending the uncertainty and democratic unfairness found in existing arrangements. One constitutionally unsound element in the present system is that the prerogative is exercised independently of Parliament whereas, in the view of a succession of authorities and politicians, such decisions or acts should be controlled or subject to prior approval or ratification by the House of Commons. In the words of Alistair Darling, speaking in 1991 as one of Labour's front bench home affairs spokesmen, 'It is essential that when the royal prerogative is to be used, Parliament must be able to give or withold its consent.'[64]

Constitutional writers have for a long time attributed a special importance to the political power of dissolution and calling a general election, as a primary means by which control is exercised over party colleagues and supporters who sit in the House of Commons. Sir William Anson wrote in his leading text on *The Law and Custom of the Constitution* that,[65]

> The weapon by which the Prime Minister or the Cabinet enforces its will upon the Commons is the threat of dissolution. The mere intimation that, if the necessary support is not given to a government . . . its careless or lukewarm supporters may be sent to explain their conduct to their constituents has been known to produce the desired results.

Sir Sidney Low, the constitutional historian at King's College, London, agreed and described the threat of dissolution as 'a kind of penal measure', explaining,[66]

> Whatever motives may have induced a Member to seek a place in the House of Commons, he will usually want to hold it as long as he can, and with as little trouble . . . as possible. Each election means to him a fight . . . and the risk that he may lose a seat which he presumably desires to retain . . . The ministry can often subdue rebellion in its own ranks, and to a certain extent keep its antagonists from going to extremities by allowing it to be known that if things are done, or not done, there will be a general election. 'If you don't vote straight, and vote regularly', says the Leader, through the whips, 'you will have to fight for your seats . . . and risk the loss of your parliamentary salaries, now instead of two, three, or four, years hence.' The hint is, no doubt, carefully and diplomatically conveyed, and is not often made in public.

This sanction over government backbenchers is always present and has regularly been a feature of internal party wrangles over public policy. On several occasions the threat of dissolution has been made expressly. One much-publicised instance was in July 1985, when dissolution was threatened in order to quell government backbench opposition to the recommendations of the Top Salaries Review Boards, involving increases of up to 46 per cent in the pay of senior civil servants and senior members of the judiciary and armed forces, at a time when teachers were locked in a national dispute over being offered only 6 per cent. According to the parliamentary lobby reporters, the government chief whip, then John Wakeham, called potential rebels into his room at the House of Commons in groups of six to twelve, informed them that the Prime Minister, Margaret Thatcher, regarded the matter as a resignation issue, and was paraphrased as telling each, 'If you vote against us . . . you spend your summer not on the beaches but travelling the streets in a general election campaign.'[67] In the event, the government (who held a 140-seat majority in the House) won the vote by 249 to 232.

In contemporary politics, with the power to set the election date by convention now firmly attached to the office of Prime Minister alone, it is a form of pressure that can be applied not only to party backbenchers but equally to ministers and Cabinet colleagues. Previously, Professor Berriedale Keith, a leading constitutional lawyer, wrote in 1936 (at a time when it was still widely understood that a decision on the dissolution of Parliament was for the Cabinet collectively), that,[68]

> It would clearly be a most dangerous increase of the already excessive power of the Prime Minister, were it to be left in his hands to decide on a dissolution over the heads of his colleagues, and even against the wishes of the majority.

Instances of such forms of political blackmail over Cabinet colleagues are hard to be sure of as they will not be documented and would be likely to be communicated via intermediaries. It seems that Harold Wilson made it clear to colleagues that the trade union reforms proposed in *In Place of Strife* were a dissolution issue in 1969, and the extent to which the poll tax was a similar issue under Margaret Thatcher in 1990 is a story for future historians. According to one senior parliamentarian and former Cabinet minister, the threat of dissolution over key policies of importance to the Prime Minister is always implicit in Cabinet proceedings, and is especially potent as a weapon of coercion under a minority government and a hung Parliament.[69]

This prerogative power to control the election date is a most important source of political authority to a strong premier, and together with his or her other prerogative right of appointing and removing ministers, gives great credence to the widely-held thesis that in Britain behind the dignified, ceremonial façade of Cabinet Government, there exists a political reality of Prime Ministerial rule.[70]

Problems concerning the monarchy

A final constitutional advantage of fixed-term Parliaments would be to remove any prospect of the British monarchy becoming the subject of political controversy if some special difficulty over the legitimacy of a dissolution arises. In normal circumstances the Queen plays no political role in the decision on when a dissolution and election should take place, and she simply follows the advice tendered to her by the Prime Minister. But 'normal circumstances' in this respect means the usual situation in the House of Commons of the government holding a majority of seats. It is especially in circumstances of a hung Parliament, with no single party having an overall majority, that controversy might surround a Prime Minister's request for a dissolution, and the Queen might be persuaded to withold her consent and refuse to issue the necessary Proclamation.

Furthermore, some constitutional authorities would even extend the possibilities of royal intervention into certain situations where the government does possess an overall majority. If the monarchy were ever to intervene and block prime ministerial advice, the institution would run the serious risk of meeting hostility from the political party then in government. Such royal intervention would necessarily embroil the Queen in party political controversy and throw the continued existence of the monarchy into doubt. This general danger to the monarchy has been described by the former Conservative Lord Chancellor, Lord Hailsham, as follows:[71]

> The monarchy can survive only so long as the parties who possess a real chance of winning continue to support it. When this ceases to be the case, the pendulum will ultimately swing to the party supporting a republican programme. The monarch, therefore, who ventured to use the prerogative against either of the two major parties of the state would risk either enforced abdication or republicanism, and even if the action of the Crown was confirmed by the electorate, there would be uncertainty and controversy for a long time thereafter.

In order to appreciate the present problems posed for the monarchy, it is necessary to explore the complex theory and practice of the royal power of dissolution. There are no conventions for the Queen's intervention to refuse a dissolution because no precedents exist in modern times. Rather, the whole subject is one of constitutional opinions, and such opinions by constitutional authorities may conflict. In my own opinion, it is in fact most appropriate to regard any power of royal intervention as being obsolete (or limited only to the enforcement of the obvious rule that a Prime Minister who is defeated at a general election cannot ask for a second election – an unreal situation which has never occurred and nor is it ever likely to). Such power to interfere with a Prime Minister's judgement upon when a general election should take place has not been exercised now for over 150 years, and it is clearly against the interests of the monarchy today to wish ever to become involved in such a political minefield. It is far preferable from the Queen's point of view always to allow a request for dissolution and so put the government's case to the people at the general election called for.

However, there remain in existence today the opinions of a substantial body of constitutional authorities to the effect that the monarchy possesses a personal, reserve discretion to overrule prime ministerial advice, although the conditions and criteria for its exercise are not clearly specified. This school of opinion is founded upon our history and a desire to continue traditions from the past. Even following Walter Bagehot's generally accepted synopsis of the Crown's political powers at the end of the nineteenth century, comprising 'Three rights – the right to be consulted, the right to encourage, the right to warn: and a King of great sense and sagacity would want no others',[72] leading constitutional writers continued to maintain the theory of the monarch's personal discretion in dissolution matters. The great lawyers at the turn of the century, A. V. Dicey and Sir William Anson, subscribed to this view, and then Sir Ivor Jennings in the 1930s gave the notion a fresh appearance by describing dissolution as one of the monarch's 'personal prerogatives' which he defined as 'certain prerogative powers which he exercises on his own responsibility'.[73] More recently in the 1980s, the Oxford historian and Conservative peer Lord Blake, an adviser to Buckingham Palace on constitutional affairs, has said in a public lecture on *Monarchy* that, 'The monarch does . . . possess even today some political powers of last resort, very much ones of ultimate reserve'; and elsewhere he has written that, 'There are, and long have been, matters (a few) on which the Crown does not need to take ministerial advice'. Into both categories Lord Blake included a political discretion to refuse or insist upon a dissolution.[74]

Of greater importance is that Queen Elizabeth II (and her father King George VI and grandfather King George V before her) appears to have espoused this doctrine. Such matters are not publicly discussed by Buckingham Palace and its officials, but one expression of a royal view came over forty years ago in the context of public discussion on whether the King might refuse Clement Attlee a dissolution in 1951, being less than two years since he had called the previous election. The royal view was expressed in the form of an anonymous letter sent to and published by *The Times*, under the pseudonym 'Senex', by the private secretary to George VI, Sir Alan Lascelles.[75] Lascelles made plain that the Palace asserted the personal right of the monarch to intervene by opening with a statement of the personal authority and status of the sovereign in the constitution and indicating criteria which a 'wise sovereign' would take into account. These conditions, in fact, simply described the political and financial crisis situation in August 1931 when instead of an election being called upon the resignation of the Labour government, George V presided over an arrangement between the incumbent Labour Prime Minister Ramsay MacDonald and the leader of the Conservative opposition Stanley Baldwin, whereby a coalition National Government was formed until an election could be called in October later in the year.

No wise Sovereign – that is, one who has at heart the true interest of the country, the constitution, and the monarchy – would deny a dissolution to his Prime Minister unless he were satisfied that: (1) the existing Parliament was still vital, viable, and capable of doing its job; (2) a general election would be detrimental to the national economy; (3) he could rely on finding another Prime Minister who could carry on his government, for a reasonable period, with a working majority in the House of Commons.

In the constitutions of Commonwealth countries in the twentieth century, two precedents of rejection of prime ministerial advice by governor-generals have taken place: Lord Byng's refusal to Mackenzie King in Canada in 1926, and Sir Patrick Duncan's refusal of General Hertzog in South Africa in 1939 (at a time when that country retained the British sovereign as its own monarch), and both were justified on the basis of constitutional principles that were argued to exist in Britain. And, more famously, the case in 1975 of the Governor-General of Australia, Sir John Kerr, dismissing Gough Whitlam as Prime Minister despite the latter's majority in the House of Representatives lends still further evidence that the Crown prerogatives might be exercised independently. It should be noted that the sacking of Gough Whitlam was widely condemned in Australian public opinion, and contributed substantially to a wave of anti-monarchist and pro-republican sentiment in Australia, sufficient to prevent the Prince of Wales being appointed Governor-General there in 1982.[76]

Recent political events in Britain have also fuelled the fears about dangers into which the monarchy might become drawn. The growth in the electoral fortunes of the centre party or parties in the 1980s (formerly the Liberal Party and the Social Democratic Party (SDP), now converged into the Liberal Democrats) has given rise to a real prospect for hung Parliaments at recent general elections. Not unnaturally, politicians from the centre party see themselves as holding the balance of power in such a situation and they will be anxious to avoid the risk of losing it by an early second general election, which would then be likely to deprive them of their position, and restore the usual overall majority to either the Conservatives or Labour. Consequently, politicians from the centre party or parties, and their sympathisers, have over the past ten years been at pains to express the opinion in public that the Queen possesses the power to reject a Prime Minister's advice for an election under the circumstances of a hung Parliament. A pamphlet issued for the Constitutional Reform Centre in 1986 drew up a list of situations in which, it was argued, the Queen might intervene.[77] In 1987 the then leader of the SDP, MP David Owen, was openly arguing that if the election that year produced a hung Parliament, the Crown should reject any recommendation for an early dissolution from the Prime Minister of the day, and instead compel both Labour and Conservatives to negotiate an alternative programme for holding office with the Liberal/SDP Alliance.[78] More recently, in 1988, Professor Rodney Brazier, in a book called *Constitutional Practice*, has argued that the Queen is 'ideally placed to moderate between competing wishes of party leaders in a hung Parliament'.[79]

This formidable battery of constitutional opinion may well serve to persuade Buckingham Palace that it is their duty to exercise some personal discretion, independent of a debate and resolution on the matter in the House of Commons, in order to resolve constitutional problems concerning government formation and dissolution affairs. If and when such a situation arises, it will do so simply because of the existing inadequacy in the state of British law and the present vacuum of constitutional rules to address such problems. These persuasive opinions about royal intervention pose a serious danger to the monarchy in practice. Any monarch who allowed him/herself to be persuaded to go ahead and reject the advice of a Prime Minister – instead of allowing an election and putting the legitimacy of an early poll to the electorate to decide by their votes – would be tempting political suicide. The monarch would, in effect, be sacking the Prime Minister, since the latter would then undoubtedly resign. And even if the outgoing governing party was unable to muster a Commons' majority immediately to censure the opposition politicians taking office, one day (possibly at the following election) that party would be returned to power with probably a radical reform of the monarchy in mind. It is therefore very much in the monarchy's own interests to avoid such a situation. Until the law is modernised within a framework of a fixed-term Parliament, the Palace's wisest course of action (remembering always its previously quoted 'three rights – the right to be consulted, the right to encourage, the right to warn') will be always to follow prime ministerial advice on a dissolution.

An Act of Parliament, specifying fixed intervals between elections, and providing clear legal rules for the circumstances and procedures whereby an election might be called before the expiration of the four-year period, would remove any question of the personal discretion of the monarch being used to determine the election date and obviate the problems inherent in the present state of affairs. Far from diminishing the role of the Crown within the constitution, its future would be better protected.

Legislating for a fixed-term Parliament

The first important detail of the proposal to be settled is the question of the most appropriate length of the fixed interval between elections. Elsewhere in the world, as already observed,[80] the tenure of members of legislatures, or of positions in government office, tend to vary, being somewhere between two and seven years. In the USA, members of the House of Representatives (the lower House in Congress) are elected every two years; the President holds office for four years; and members of the Senate (the second chamber of Congress) serve for six-year terms. The Parliaments of both Australia and New Zealand operate three-year terms between elections. French law operates at the maximum end, with the French President being elected every seventh year, members of the French second chamber (the Senate) being elected for nine-year terms, and National Assembly elections being every fifth year. In Sweden, members of the Rikstag serve for three-year terms. But the majority of European countries, including Denmark, the Netherlands, Germany, Norway, Portugal and Austria, all regulate the intervals between their parliamentary elections at the period of four years.

In Britain, there can be little doubt that the period between general elections should be four years. The proposal for fixed-term Parliaments as a whole should fit as closely as possible into existing constitutional expectations, and the idea that four years is about the right length of time between elections is very prevalent. It was the period expressly approved of as being normal in practice, when the Parliament Act set the period of five years as a maximum.[81] In an ideal democracy it may be that there should be elections as frequently as possible – even annually, as supported by the Chartists in the eighteenth century – but a government must be allowed sufficient time to put its programme of public policies into effect before submitting its record of achievement, or otherwise, to the voters. Three full legislative sessions, and certainly four, is sufficient for this purpose.

A second detail of the legislation for a fixed-term Parliament must be to lay down clearly the circumstances in which an earlier election might be permitted within the four-year period. It is important that there is some such safety-valve, as is common in fixed-term arrangements in other countries, to provide for those exceptional situations where the government loses the support of the House of Commons, and no new government can be constructed from the composition of the House as it stands. Essentially, the new legislation should provide for the House of Commons to be able to control whether there should be either a fresh general election, or whether there should simply be a change of Prime Minister and government. The trigger for any such process should be a No Confidence motion in the House of Commons, consisting either of an opposition motion of No Confidence in the government or Prime Minister being passed, or a government motion seeking the formal Confidence of the House being put forward and lost. If any such motion is expressed towards the government as a whole, there should be a general election; but if the motion is expressed towards the Prime Minister, then he should resign office. If it transpires, following a prime ministerial resignation, whether voluntary or through a No Confidence vote, that no Prime Minister is appointed within a prescribed period of time (say, 20 days), for example because no alternative party leader feels able to form a new government, then again there should be a general election.

It is appropriate that the process of Confidence motions is adopted as the only procedure to bring about an early general election, because any other form of Commons' resolution, such as a vote on dissolution itself, would allow the government to remain in full control of electoral timing. Little would change if dissolution was simply put to the vote or confirmed by the Commons, as has been suggested by some,[82] because assuming that the Prime Minister took the usual care through the whips to ensure the loyalty of his or her own party backbenchers, the government's majority in the

House could be relied upon to support the Prime Minister's decision on the timing of the election whenever he or she chose to put the motion before the House. A simple confirmation vote does have one advantage, however, over existing arrangements, in that before putting forward his or her motion, the Prime Minister would be obliged to take soundings of backbenchers and Cabinet colleagues to ensure that the party voted together. But it is only under a fixed-term arrangement subject to No Confidence motions as proposed that one could hope to keep early dissolutions free from political manipulation by the government, and ensure electoral timing was determined by reasons of genuine constitutional need, as opposed to pure party political advantage.

A final legal provision, designed to circumvent the situation where a government might seek to abuse parliamentary procedure and organise for its own party supporters to vote against it when putting forward a motion requesting the Confidence of the House, is that the duration of any Parliament elected following an early dissolution will only be for the remainder of the original four-year term. In other words, if after three years, a government sought to manipulate losing a Confidence vote in order to capitalise on current popularity in the country and spring a general election upon its political opponents, even if that government won the election, they would still have to face the electorate again after a further year.

In practice, a No Confidence motion leading to a change of government or early general election would only take place under a hung Parliament – where no single party has an overall majority of seats in the Commons. A minority government, if it failed to gain consent to any significant part of its legislative programme, might resign and allow another party or combination to form a government, or else opposition parties may choose to unite behind a motion of No Confidence if it suited them. A governing coalition would be secure throughout the four-year term unless it collapsed because one party left the coalition and joined in an opposition vote of No Confidence. The predicament of a hung Parliament is exceptional under the British first-past-the-post electoral system. In only three of the eighteen general elections since 1918 have the results of the poll produced a situation other than that of a single political party possessing an overall majority in the House of Commons – in 1923, 1929 and February 1974. Upon three further occasions, marginal overall majorities were produced. In the 1950–1 and 1964–6 Parliaments, early dissolutions were triggered by the Government losing, or fearing it would shortly lose, its narrow majority because of successive by-election defeats. In the 1974–9 Parliament, the Labour government survived its loss of a majority in 1977 through a parliamentary pact with the Liberal Party. The prospect of a hung Parliament is therefore less rare than is commonly assumed – effectively one-third of general elections since 1918 have been inconclusive in the sense of providing no single political party with a comfortable working majority. Of particular significance here is that reform of the method whereby votes are translated into parliamentary seats under the British electoral system, involving proportional representation, would (in current party political circumstances) make hung Parliaments even more likely. The arguments for a fixed-term Parliament, then, apply regardless of whether or not a new electoral system is adopted. But adoption of a new electoral system – including the proposal suggested in Chapter 8 – makes the case for a fixed-term Parliament, that, in place of the existing, unacceptable constitutional vacuum, states clear legal rules and parliamentary procedures concerning government formation and early dissolutions, all the more important.

The precise details and drafting of the reform legislation need to be tailor-made to the British legal and political context into which the fixed intervals between general elections is to be introduced. Ideally, it would make sense to provide for the continuing existence of Parliament, for modern democratic doctrine requires the constant parliamentary scrutiny of government and the state bureaucracy. Such permanence of existence is provided for in the constitutional law of some other Western democracies, notably those of the USA and Germany. Under the terms of the American Constitution, Congress cannot be dissolved. In Germany, elections take place within the legal lifetime of the Bundestag (during the last three months of its legislative term) and on an appointed day following declaration of the results of the poll, the newly elected members replace those who have been defeated.[83] Adopting this legal structure in Britain would have the advantage of facilitating a separate electoral process for each of the Houses of Parliament, so that a future second chamber (currently the House of Lords) could introduce a rotating system of elections – which in the British political system presents the best way of recomposing and democratising that parliamentary body. Such an electoral process is used in many other Parliaments of the world, including the American Senate where one-third of the membership stands for election every other year.

However, while the second chamber in Britain remains in its unreformed, non-elective state, and the theory of the Crown prerogatives to summon and dissolve Parliaments remains intact, it would be easier simply to regulate the procedures for summoning new Parliaments and calling elections. Mandatory statutory requirements of the Sovereign would be unenforceable in the courts against the monarch personally,[84] but statements of legal rules would make it clear if she ever chose to act unconstitutionally. The new legislation should repeal the 1694 Triennial Act and provide, first, for the summoning of a new Parliament and calling of an election simultaneously on the same day as a Parliament terminates, whether by expiry of the four-year term of by earlier dissolution; and second, it should lay down the general principles that a general election shall be held as soon as is practicable following the Proclamation (say, within three months at the outside) and that arrangements for the newly-elected Parliament to assemble at Westminster should take place at the earliest practicable opportunity thereafter (say, within one month at the outside following the general election).

In conclusion, the form of the new legislation, which might be entitled 'the Parliamentary Assembly Act', should be as follows:[85]

PARLIAMENTARY ASSEMBLY BILL
An Act to provide for a four-year term of Parliament
and related matters.

Four-Year Term of Parliament
1. The House of Commons shall be elected for a four-year term; and the legislative term of Parliament shall end four years after its first meeting or on its dissolution.

Proclamation Causing Parliamentary Elections
2. On the same day that the legislative term of Parliament terminates, whether by expiry or dissolution, a new Parliament shall be summoned by Proclamation of the Sovereign; and a general election of Members of the House of Commons shall be held within three months of every such Proclamation, and the meeting of the newly elected Parliament shall be held within one month of the general election, at such times as the Proclamation shall appoint.

Dissolution Following Confidence Resolution
3. Parliament shall be dissolved by Proclamation of the Sovereign within seven days following there taking place in the House of Commons either a resolution of No Confidence in the Government or the defeat of a Motion for the Confidence of the House of Commons in the Government.

Dissolution Upon Failure to Appoint a Prime Minister
4. If, following the resignation of the Prime Minister or a House of Commons' resolution of No Confidence in the Prime Minister, a new Prime Minister is not appointed within twenty days, Parliament shall be dissolved forthwith by Proclamation of the Sovereign.

Duration of Term Following Dissolution
5. The term of any Parliament summoned following a dissolution shall be the remainder of the term of the previous Parliament.

Citation and Commencement
6. (1) This Act may be cited as the Parliamentary Assembly Act 1995.
(2) This Act shall come into force upon the next dissolution or expiry of Parliament.

3 The Electorate: Voters and Voting

The registered electorate of the United Kingdom at the time of writing comprises a total of 43 724 954 persons. This means that over four-fifths of the entire population of the United Kingdom are eligible to vote at a general election. Most of those remaining are made up of people who are either too young to vote or whose names have been left off the electoral register erroneously. Today we take it for granted that voting at a general election is one of the fundamental rights of every ordinary citizen. But we should always remember that the principle of 'one man, one vote' is of comparatively recent origin, and the notion of 'one woman, one vote' even more so. Political equality in Britain was an ideal that had to be campaigned for over many generations by courageous men and women, often in the face of harsh resistance, and the right to vote was finally won for each adult citizen, regardless of property ownership or gender, only in 1928.

POLITICAL EQUALITY AND THE RIGHT TO VOTE

Earlier in the history of the United Kingdom, political representation was not thought of in terms of counting heads. As the MP and political philosopher Edmund Burke put it in the 1790s, the constitution was 'not a problem of arithmetic'.[1] Even in the nineteenth century the idea of democracy, in the sense of equal political rights and universal suffrage, was still regarded by most respectable people as a dangerous experiment and subversive to any sound system of government. Popular or representative government was fine, so long as only right-minded, educated people had a say in electing MPs, and thus had an influence upon government policy. Government by discussion meant excluding all those whose opinions were not worth listening to. This is reflected, for example, in the writings of the famous political author and journalist Walter Bagehot, who opposed any further extension of the franchise in 1867, and spoke in his book *The English Constitution* of the 'bovine stupidity' of the mass of the working classes, consisting of 'crowds of people scarcely more civilised than the majority of 2 000 years ago'.[2] He went on to say:

> The principle of popular government is that the supreme power, the determining efficacy in matters political, resides in the people – not necessarily in the whole people . . . In plain English, what I fear is that

both our political parties will bid for the support of the working man; that both of them will promise to do as he likes if he will only tell them what it is; that, as he now holds the casting vote in our affairs, both parties will beg and pray him to give that vote to them. I can conceive of nothing more corrupting or worse for a set of poor ignorant people than that two combinations of well-taught and rich men should constantly offer to defer to their decision, and compete for the office of executing it. *Vox populi* will be *vox diaboli* if it is worked in that manner.

The first glimpse of a genuinely popular electoral system came with the 1832 Representation of the People Act, commonly called the Great Reform Act, but even this statute only brought the number of qualified voters up to around 720 000, out of a total adult population of under eleven million.[3] The 1832 Act made some small reduction in the existing property qualifications, and made residency necessary as well, increasing the size of the electorate by 38 per cent. At least as important, the Act also redrew some constituency boundaries in order to remove 'rotten' boroughs (where MPs were returned from locations where virtually no one lived), although glaring inequalities remained: for example Liverpool and Totnes returned two MPs each, but comprised 8 000 and 179 voters respectively. The real significance of 1832 was not so much what it achieved in itself, as the precedent it set for constitutional change and future reform of a representative process that had remained stagnant over the centuries.

The next milestone on the road to democracy came with the 1867 Representation of the People Act, known as the Second Reform Act. This statute further extended the franchise, and out of the British adult population that had by now risen to almost 14 million, two-and-a-quarter million were now eligible to vote. The changes were directed towards constituency boroughs, in other words towns, where the vote was granted to all householders (freehold or leasehold owners who occupied the premises) who paid rates. By the 1884 Representation of the People Act, known as the Third Reform Act, this same provision was applied to the county, in other words more rural, constituencies. Out of a total population of 31 million in 1885, there were around five million qualified electors, of whom 4 380 000 voted in the 1885 general election.[4] The right to vote was now in the hands of 58–60 per cent of the adult male population.

Still no women were thought fit to vote. By the end of the nineteenth century, various women's groups known as 'suffragists' were quietly lobbying for political rights. But the strength and complacency of the reactionary opposition they faced was fierce and very deeply ingrained. Married women had not been allowed to own property in their own name, independently of their husbands, until the 1882 Married Women's Property Act. Quite apart from social tradition, one argument put forward against a female franchise was that there should be 'one family, one vote', and when the man voted he was doing so as head of the household in consultation with its members. If this seems absurd today, then the views of the politician and Cabinet minister John Bright, in the 1880s certainly belong to a different way of thinking:[5]

> To introduce women into the strife of political life would be a great evil to them, and that to our sex no possible good could arrive. If women are not safe under the charge and care of fathers, husbands, brothers, and sons, it is the fault of our non-civilisation and not of our laws. As civilisation founded upon Christian principle advances, women will gain all that is right for them, although they are not seen contending in the strife of political parties. In my experience I have observed evil results to many women who have entered hotly into political conflict and discussion.

In 1903 this political issue was transformed by the establishment of the Women's Social and Political Union under the leadership of Mrs Emmeline Pankhurst. She and her followers became known as the 'suffragettes' and organised mass demonstrations in Hyde Park attended by hundreds of thousands of people, and adopted direct action tactics, involving chaining themselves to the grilles outside Parliament and at the homes of ministers, hunger strikes, arson, wrecking paintings at the National Gallery, and disruption of national events. In 1913 the suffragette Emily Davison was killed by throwing herself into the path of the King's horse in a race on Derby Day. Many have argued that the militancy of the suffragettes proved counter-productive, for it confused opposition to votes for women with opposition to their political tactics, whereas propaganda and lobbying might have better helped the attempts of those parliamentarians prior to the outbreak of the First World War in 1914 who presented draft legislation on the female franchise to the Commons, but which was confounded by furious controversy. For four years, however, this was eclipsed by the terror and slaughter of the war with Germany (in which 750 000 uniformed troops died – one man for every eleven in Britain aged between 20 and 45 years of age was killed – and 1 700 000 were wounded). As one historian of the period has written, 'The First World War had a profound influence upon British society, for quite simply it swept away a whole world and created a new one . . . The war was in fact the greatest watershed of modern British history . . . The effects of total war in the twentieth century has been as much concerned with accelerating as with diverting the course of social policy.'[6] Above all, it was the national acceleration of bringing women into industry and government jobs, as a necessity to help in the war effort, that transformed perceptions of a woman's social role. Throughout the war, 'The Women are Splendid' became a government slogan to encourage and enlist female workers. Prime Minister David Lloyd George's promise of 'A Better World' and reconstruction of 'A Land Fit for Heroes' after the war meant that he could hardly now deny them the vote. Speaking in 1917 in the House of Commons, David Lloyd George declared,[7]

> There is no doubt that the War has had an enormous effect upon public opinion so far as this question is concerned. . . When we come to settle the conditions of labour with hundreds of thousands, running now into millions, of women in work in which they were never engaged before, when we come to recast the whole of our industrial system, are we going to fling them out without giving them a voice in determining the conditions? All I can say is it is an outrage, it is ungrateful, unjust, inequitable . . . .

The statutory foundation of the modern franchise, then, was finally laid by the Representation of the People Act (RPA) in 1918. It followed closely the recommendations of a Speaker's Conference on Electoral Reform which reported in 1917.[8] First, the Act removed all forms of property qualification, and established residence alone as the qualifying basis for the vote; and second, it introduced votes for women – but only at the deferred and discriminatory age of 30 years. The male and female franchises were dealt with in separate sections of the Act, and it was section 4 that contained the historic words: 'a woman shall be entitled to be registered as a parliamentary elector for a constituency'. The statutory differential in ages for voting was a sop to the strong remaining anti-feminist sentiment among a substantial number of MPs in the House of Commons. Indeed, the Speaker's Conference had alternatively considered a higher age limit of 35 years. The Home Secretary at the time, Sir G. (later Viscount) Cave presented the measure to the Commons, not with the Government's wholehearted endorsement, but as a free vote for backbenchers. He called it a 'thorny subject, which I must treat with more reserve, because it is a matter which . . . is to be left to the judgement of the House.'[9] The discriminatory age qualification was heavily criticised at the time, including by most Labour MPs and also the former Liberal Prime Minister, Herbert Asquith, who attacked the 'restricted and illogical form' of the new female franchise.[10] This legal restriction upon female voting became even more ludicrous over the next few years with the lifting of the legal prohibitions upon women holding public office. In particular, only ten months after the 1918 RPA was passed, the Parliament (Qualification of Women) Act 1918 was enacted, which permitted women to become MPs – from the age of 21 years. So between 1918 and 1928 the law permitted women between the ages of 21 and 30 years to stand for Parliament and to become MPs, but it did not allow them to vote. Parity between the sexes was finally attained by the Representation of the People Act 1928 which reduced the female franchise to 21 years.

The original residency qualifications, replacing property ownership as the basis for the franchise, prescribed a minimum period in which the voter must have lived in the constituency. This is in contrast to today (except for the three months required in Northern Ireland) where residence on the specified date (thus possibly a period of only a single day) is sufficient. The Representation of the People Act in 1884 required a full year's residency in the constituency, and the 1918 Act consolidated the principle of a qualifying period while reducing the duration to six months. This requirement of a six-month period of residency before voting rights were acquired in any constituency was only changed in 1949,[11] and some would say for the worse. It might be argued that the effort of travelling to one's former place of residence to vote is much less today than it was in the 1940s, and surely some local knowledge should be acquired before voting in a locality.

Two further features of our recent electoral history are worth recalling, and show that the principle and practice of 'one person, one vote' only dates, in fact, from 1949. A prominent feature of voting in the early part of the twentieth century was that affluent or educated voters were often in possession of a right to vote twice, or even more times, in different constituencies.[12] The 1918 Act allowed all people who occupied business premises worth more than £10 per year an extra vote, so long as the premises were in a different constituency from their residence. Wives of such businessmen were also allowed an extra vote. Women who occupied business premises in their own right were similarly allowed an extra vote, at a reduced valuation of £5 per year, by the 1918 RPA, and in 1928 men were given an additional vote if they were married to such businesswomen. Not surprisingly, the business vote was a controversial subject within the Liberal and Labour parties, for it was clear that the people in possession of these extra votes overwhelmingly supported Conservative candidates. It was eventually abolished by the Labour government in 1949.

Then there was the curiosity of the university constituencies. These were notional, not geographical, bodies of electors, comprising the graduates of particular universities. The first university representation in the Commons had been created by King James I in respect of two seats, for Oxford and Cambridge universities, each returning one MP elected from all their respective MA graduates. In the nineteenth century this principle extended to graduates of the universities of London, Durham, and Trinity College Dublin, and then collectively to the Scottish universities, and to the English universities. Several famous MPs sat in the Commons by virtue of representing the universities, including the Oxford lawyer, Sir William Anson. By the time of their abolition by Labour in 1949, there were 12 MPs in the Commons representing university constituencies. Since their abolition there has been, perhaps somewhat surprisingly, a sustained interest among a small minority of MPs and peers at Westminster in resurrecting the idea of university representation in Parliament. For example, in 1983, Viscount Cranborne introduced a Private Member's Bill into Parliament on the matter, entitled House of Commons (University Constituencies) (Election and Rights of Members) Bill.[13] This Bill failed to receive a second reading, but is recorded in parliamentary papers and now serves as a precedent for future debate.

The ostensible purpose of Lord Cranborne's Bill was to elevate the intellectual quality of debate in the House of Commons. According to the Bill, twelve additional MPs would sit in the Commons, drawn from seven constituencies as follows: Oxford University (1 MP), Cambridge University (1 MP), London University (1 MP), remaining English universities combined (5 MPs), University of Wales (1 MP), the combined Scottish universities (2 MPs) and Northern Ireland universities (1 MP). The Bill mentions no special qualifications or disqualifications for candidates, the final selection of whom would be a matter for the wisdom of the electors. However, an important feature of such candidates and MPs would be that they were independent of political parties. Thus the Bill provides that no candidates shall give any details of his or her political party or affiliation on a ballot paper, and stipulates that MPs elected by university constituencies shall enjoy all the rights and privileges of members of the House of Commons excepting that 'they shall not accept any party whip'. These measures are aimed at guaranteeing they are free from party discipline and may speak according to their conscience alone. Such MPs would also be prohibited from being ministers of the Crown, to ensure that their primary loyalty was to Parliament, and remove any incentive to curry favour with the Executive. Registered voters for such elections would be people who were British citizens, 18 years of age or over, not subject to any legal incapacity, and who held a degree (other than an honorary degree) at the relevant university. Residence therefore would not be necessary to the university franchise, and such voters would retain the right to vote in the constituency where they lived. The idea of direct representation of university opinion in the Commons is no doubt an appealing one to professors and students alike as both categories have in recent times felt themselves to be discriminated against, by government financial policy on higher education. On the other hand, there is no guarantee that graduates in comfortably-paid jobs will be any more sympathetic to the material demands of the universities than the recent Education Secretary John Patten, himself formerly a university don. It might also be noted that several MPs, in addition to the Labour and Liberal Democrat spokesmen on education policy, have taken a special interest in education, for example, the Conservative MP Keith Hampson, and Labour's Jack Straw (a former President of the National Union of Students when studying Law at Leeds University). In the House of Lords there are a number of peers with very definite commitments to representing the universities, such as the hereditary peer Earl Russell (son of the philosopher Bertrand Russell) who is Professor of History at King's College, London, and Lord Jenkins (the former Labour Chancellor of the Exchequer and Home Secretary) who is Chancellor of Oxford University. But above all, however well intentioned, the thinking behind a plan that gives preferential voting rights to a supposedly more intelligent pool of voters by virtue of being university graduates smacks of paternalism and intellectual snobbery, and is very much at odds with the fundamental principle of political equality among our citizens. Such a scheme for special university representation, then, remains a political anachronism.

Tables 3.1 and 3.2 on pages 74–7 provide, first, a summary of the progressive changes made towards universal suffrage over a period of 120 years between 1832 and 1951, enlarging the British electorate by 90 per cent; and, second, a breakdown of the total numbers of parliamentary electors in the different regions of the United Kingdom, as registered upon the electoral roll between 1983 and 1992.

QUALIFICATIONS TO VOTE

The principal elements that determine whether a person may vote at a parliamentary election today are, first, that he or she must be 18 years or over at the date of the election; second, that the person must be resident in the constituency where he or she wishes to vote, and have had his or her residency entered upon the constituency's electoral register; and third, the voter must be a British, Commonwealth or Irish citizen.

Age

The age for voting was 21 years until the Family Law Reform Act 1969 reduced it to 18 years along with the age of majority in general, and thereby added over four million new voters to the electoral roll. Whether or not the voting age should be lowered still further to 16 years has been discussed in several political quarters over the last few years. There is some degree of support for such a change within the Labour Party, including from the veteran socialist Tony Benn who included it in his scheme for wholesale reform of the Constitution published and presented to the House of Commons as the Commonwealth of Britain Bill 1991.[14] It was also an election manifesto commitment of the Liberal Democrats at the 1992 general election, forming part of their Written Constitution proposal published earlier the previous year.[15] The Liberal Democrat MP, James Wallace, has argued that he and his party members,[16]

> hope for greater involvement by young people in decision-making. The young have an important stake in the future, and what they lack in experience may be more than compensated for by the fresh ideas that they can bring forward. A number of causes now coming to the fore in politics – for example environmental concern – were espoused by young people long before they gained political respectability.

The argument against any further age reduction in voting rests simply upon grounds that some arbitrary age limit has to be drawn, and that many 16 and 17 year old people are unlikely to have gained the necessary maturity to be able to express a considered political judgement. At present there is no support for a reduction in the voting age on the government and opposition frontbenches, so there is little prospect of such a change, and little chance either of a parliamentary debate on the issue unless an MP such as James Wallace or Tony Benn comes near the top of the annual ballot of backbenchers for allocation of time in which Private Members' Bills may be introduced, and choose to make it the subject of their draft legislation.

Residency in the constituency

The key concept of the modern right to vote is one of residency in the constituency. Within Great Britain there is no required duration for which the citizen must have lived in the constituency in order to qualify for the vote, simply that he or she was living in the locality on the 'qualifying date' of 10 October.[17] In Northern Ireland, however, where three months' residency is required, a separate qualifying date applies. Residency is established by forms[18] being sent out to the occupier of each household in the United Kingdom by the electoral registration officer for each constituency several weeks before the qualifying date, the main householder entering on the form the names of all people living in their household who will be aged 16 or over on the following 10 October, and returning the form promptly. The results of this annual national exercise are published in lists known as 'electoral registers' in each constituency, drafts being prepared for public inspection between 28 November and 16 December. These are then formalised, with any corrections, on the following 16 February and operative for any election thereafter in the next twelve months.

Today the situation regularly arises that a person may be treated as resident in more than one constituency. This means that he or she has a choice of constituency in which to vote. Section 1 of the Representation of the People Act 1983 makes it plain that 'a person is not entitled to vote as an elector . . . in more than one constituency at a general election'. *Fox* v. *Stirk* in 1970 was the legal case which clarified that a citizen could be 'resident' in two places for voting purposes. In that particular case, students were held to be eligible for registration and voting both in the constituency where they lived during term-time, and in the constituency where their parents lived and to which they returned during vacations. The students in question were at Bristol and Cambridge universities and each had a right to occupy their rooms there for between 26 and 30 weeks in the year. The three general principles on 'residence' under the Representation of the People Acts were laid down by Lord Denning, then Master of the Rolls, as follows:

Principal changes in the electorate, 1831–1951

Date	Title of amending Act	Main classes of population added	Electoral qualifications	
1831			Counties – 40/- freeholders Boroughs – a medley of narrow and and unequal franchises	
1832	Representation of the People Act, 1832, 2 & 3 Will. 4. c. 45 (known as the 'First Reform Act')	Small land-owners owners, tenant farmers and shopkeepers	Counties	40/- freeholders £10 copyholders £10 leaseholders £50 tenants at will
			Boroughs – £10 householders	
1867	Representation of the People Act, 1867 30 & 31 Vict. c. 102 (sometimes called the 'Second Reform Act')	Smaller agricultural owners and tenants; artisans and many town labourers	Counties	£40/- freeholders £5 copyholders £5 leaseholders £12 tenants at will
			Boroughs	All occupiers of dwelling houses rated to poor rates, lodgers occupying £10 lodgings
1884	Representation of the People Act, 1884 48 & 49 Vict c.3 (sometimes called the 'Third Reform Act')	Agricultural and other labourers in country	Counties and Boroughs	A uniform householder and lodger franchise in effect giving a vote to every man over 21 who had a decent settled home
1918	Representation of the People Act, 1918 7 & 8 Geo. 5 c. 64 and Parliament (Qualification of Women) Act, 1918 8 & 9 Geo. 5 c. 47	Women of 30 and over	Counties and Boroughs	*Men* Final assimilation by abolition of property qualification in counties. Qualification now either six months' residence or occupation of £10 business premises *Women* Enfranchised at 30 and over
1928	Representation of the People (Equal Franchise) Act, 1928 18 & 19 Geo. 5. c.12	Women 21 to 30	Women enfranchised at 21. In effect every man or woman of 21 and upwards thereafter entitled to vote	
1948	Representation of the People Act, 1948 11 & 12 Geo. 6 c. 65 (Consolidated in 1949)		University constituencies and all plural voting abolished	

Note:　These figures refer to Great Britain and Ireland until the separation of Eire: thereafter to Great Britain and Northern Ireland only. The available statistics of population upon which the diagrams at the end of this Table are based relate to persons aged 20 years and over and not to those aged over 21. When the relevant allowance is made it will be seen that complete adult suffrage for both sexes has been achieved within a century.

Table 3.1[19]

Remarks	Statistics to show the effect of these changes			
	Before and after the change	Total electorate	Population aged 20 years and over	Electorate as percentage of population over 20 years
Similar Acts which were passed for Scotland and Ireland in 1832 differed in detail from the English Act	Before (1831) After (1832)	509 391 720 784	10 207 000 10 207 000	5.0 ◔ 7.1 ◔
Reform Bills were introduced in the Commons in 1852, 1854, 1859, 1860 and 1866. Similar Acts which were passed for Scotland and Ireland in 1868 differed in detail from the English Act	Before (1864) After (1868)	1 130 372 2 231 030	13 051 816 13 625 658	9.0 ◔ 16.4 ◔
The Ballot Act was passed in 1872. No woman could yet vote	Before (1883) After (1886)	2 955 190 4 965 618	16 426 233 17 394 014	18.0 ◔ 28.5 ◔
Plural voting by University graduates and holders of the business premises qualification was restricted to two votes, including one for residence	Before (1914) After (1921)	7 483 165 19 984 037	24 969 241 26 846 785	30.0 ◑ 74.0 ◕
Male and female adult suffrage achieved	Before (1927) After (1931)	21 895 347 29 175 608	29 654 721 30 096 135	74.0 ◕ 96.9 ●
'One man (or woman) – one vote'	After (1951)	34 915 112	(Dec. 1950) 36 078 000	96.7 ●

Parliamentary electors, 1983–92

	Total	Difference from preceding year	Service voters	Attainers	Voluntary patients	Overseas electors
United Kingdom						
1983	42 703 516	241 200	271 129	739 874	–	–
1984	42 983 727	280 211	275 920	729 656	–	–
1985	43 130 535	146 808	276 699	687 452	3 912	–
1986	43 392 617	262 082	275 194	694 168	–	–
1987	43 666 375	273 758	277 294	708 653	2 870	11 100
1988	43 705 071	38 696	272 928	691 444	2 736	2 092
1989	43 612 826	−92 245	272 680	655 200	2 142	1 836
1990	43 663 423	49 463	266 461	626 858	1 639	1 237
1991	43 556 783	−106 640	271 689	560 893	1 661	34 454
1992	43 724 954	168 171	274 559	551 961	2 387	31 942
England						
1983	35 569 726	205 993	234 301	617 759	–	–
1984	35 800 362	230 636	237 609	605 954		
1985	35 937 374	137 012	237 428	570 649	3 057	–
1986	36 158 417	221 043	235 466	575 955	2 412	–
1987	36 393 203	234 786	236 549	591 490	1 966	9 980
1988	36 448 414	55 211	232 262	576 745	1 776	1 868
1989	36 364 782	−83 632	231 683	542 196	1 441	1 662
1990	36 388 575	22 659	225 460	522 100	984	1 122
1991	36 302 099	−86 476	229 483	466 137	883	31 175
1992	36 435 873	133 774	231 229	456 738	1 127	29 146
Wales						
1983	2 138 385	10 450	10 856	35 546	–	–
1984	2 148 484	10 099	11 264	34 931	–	–
1985	2 142 609	−5 875	11 379	32 320	325	–
1986	2 160 147	17 538	11 569	34 694	272	–
1987	2 175 168	15 021	12 101	34 814	221	250
1988	2 180 269	5 101	12 518	34 233	275	52
1989	2 194 625	14 356	12 970	32 391	168	36
1990	2 207 542	12 917	13 095	30 456	169	29
1991	2 207 283	−259	13 574	26 753	164	910
1992	2 218 551	11 268	14 399	27 408	226	895
Scotland						
1983	3 934 220	20 835	23 175	68 572	–	–
1984	3 957 276	23 056	23 890	68 636	807	–
1985	3 967 943	10 667	24 696	65 940	235	–
1986	3 986 654	18 711	24 762	65 739	201	–
1987	3 994 893	8 239	25 300	61 965	458	800
1988	3 967 377	−27 516	24 802	60 254	521	165
1989	3 932 911	−34 466	24 623	58 618	317	132
1990	3 936 704	3 793	24 581	52 260	338	79
1991	3 914 590	−22 114	25 220	47 275	523	2 172
1992	3 929 064	14 474	25 475	47 732	885	1 750

	Total	Difference from preceding year	Service voters	Attainers	Voluntary patients	Overseas electors
Northern Ireland						
1983	1 061 185	3 922	2 797	17 997	–	–
1984	1 077 605	16 420	3 157	20 135	–	–
1985	1 082 609	5 004	3 196	18 543	295	–
1986	1 087 399	4 790	3 397	17 780	–	–
1987	1 103 111	15 712	3 344	20 384	225	70
1988	1 109 011	5 900	3 346	20 212	164	7
1989	1 120 508	11 497	3 404	21 995	216	6
1990	1 130 602	10 094	3 325	22 042	148	7
1991	1 132 811	2 209	3 412	20 728	91	197
1992	1 141 466	8 655	3 456	20 083	149	151

Table 3.2[20]

The first principle is that a man can have two residences. He can have a flat in London and a house in the country. He is resident in both. The second principle is that temporary presence at an address does not make a man resident there. A guest who comes for the weekend is not resident. The third principle is that temporary absence does not deprive a person of his residence.

Lord Denning also said that, 'a person may properly be said to be "resident" in a place when his stay there has a considerable degree of permanence'.[21]

Students and other people registered in two or more constituencies may therefore prefer to cast their vote in the constituency that is more marginal and more likely to be of some impact on the fortunes of the party they support in winning or losing that seat. The first general election since 1966 to take place in university vacation time was in 1992, and therefore students were freer from their studies to travel between college and home to vote. There was considerable speculation that student opinion and the way that the student population voted would be a determining factor in the outcome of an election which commentators universally agreed would be a closely-fought contest. For those wishing to vote in the constituency away from where they were resident on 9 April, polling day, but save their train fare, they could obtain a form from the local returning officer to register a postal vote. Over 60 000 students registered for a postal vote in the fortnight following the calling of the 1992 election.[22] The National Union of Students encouraged its members to vote in this way, at the same time as publishing the names of seventy marginal constituencies where the student choice of vote might count. The political parties also urged students to take advantage of their voting choice, and cast their vote for them where most favourable. The effect of the student vote at the polls is unclear, and in 1992 seems to have been minimal, with most students tending to favour one of the opposition parties (whose policies on higher education and student grants were closer to student opinion than those of the Conservatives) but against the background of a general public trend of 7 per cent in favour of the Conservative government. As one leading psephologist has put it, 'For a group's vote to be pivotal there have to be certain pre-conditions – the group has to be particularly large, the seat has to be very, very marginal and the group has to swing in a way dramatically different from everyone else.'[23] In 1992 this failed to happen.

Of greater importance, both in principle and numerically, is that dual or multiple registration, and choice of constituency in voting, applies to more affluent citizens by virtue of owning two or more houses. It may be relevant to add, to no great surprise, that according to psephologists there is a close correlation between wealth and voting for the Conservative Party.[24] Affluent voters therefore may travel to, or apply for a postal vote at, a more marginal constituency rather than one where the result is a foregone conclusion.

Should the law require citizens to nominate a 'main residence' for voting purposes? Surely this must be so, and the process of nominating the relevant home would be no more administratively difficult than such nomination for capital gains tax purposes, and no more complex than the concept of 'residence' itself which led to the case of *Fox* v. *Stirk*. Legislation should be passed, or an amending clause inserted in some future Representation of the People Bill passing through Parliament, to require every elector to be treated, for the purposes of the right to vote at parliamentary elections, as resident at his 'main residence' only.[25] This would remove an element of electoral chicanery that has favoured the better-off.

The expatriate vote

Some have claimed that the statutory extensions of voting rights to British citizens not resident at all in this country, but living abroad, have had the effect of maximising the Conservative Party vote. This again assumes that the relatively affluent tend to vote Conservative and that people living abroad tend to be relatively affluent. True or false, it was the Conservative Party in office that extended the right to vote to such people, first by the Representation of the People Act 1985 for up to five years' absence, and then by the Representation of the People Act 1989 for up to twenty years.

This means that an expatriate living hundreds or thousands of miles away, for a period which may exceed a whole generation, carrying memories of British politics of the past and with little or no personal knowledge of contemporary issues in the constituency where he or she used to live, can influence the election of the government of a country to which he or she is not subject and to which he or she may be paying no taxes. Indeed, many such people may have left Britain specifically to avoid paying taxes there, yet since 1989 they have been rewarded with a say in the country's affairs. Each parliamentary constituency's registration officer compiles a list of overseas electors, to whom letters are sent each year reminding the voters of the need to make an overseas elector's declaration in order to remain on the register. This declaration confirms the person's British citizenship and non-residence, and gives the date of his or her last residence in the United Kingdom. The overseas voter can then vote in the constituency in which he resided at some time within the previous twenty years, and may use a proxy for the purpose who may not live in the constituency at all.

This extension of voting rights flouts two important principles of the British electoral system, namely that the basis of the parliamentary system is the representation of constituencies, and that the basis of the right to vote is one of residency in a constituency. It was largely for these reasons that the Home Affairs Select Committee of the House of Commons, in its Report in 1983, unanimously rejected the introduction of giving all expatriates the right to vote, recommending instead that it be restricted to British citizens working or living within the European Community.[26] The view of the Labour opposition, as expressed by Gerald Kaufman, was particularly scathing:[27]

Another example of Tory democracy is undoubtedly the proposal that British residents abroad should have the right to vote in our parliamentary elections for a period of [twenty] years after their exile, which may well be permanent, voluntary and financially rewarding . . . .

Their use of the right will be a farce. They will not be able to meet their candidate, to question the candidate or be canvassed by someone calling on behalf of the candidate. They may not receive any election literature, and they may therefore know nothing of the candidate except his or her name and party. Furthermore, they will have an anomalous status as constituents.

Those absentee voters could have a decisive influence on this country's affairs. In a close election, they could even decide its outcome. In the 1964 general election, 84 such voters, located in three constituencies, could have deprived the properly elected government of their majority. Unless this government change their mind, they could make it possible for tax exiles to decide the taxes that are paid by people living and working in this country. Property speculators living abroad could decide what pension should be paid to people who have worked all their lives in this country. . . The proposal is quite unacceptable and the government would be well advised to withdraw it. It is not only unfair but dangerous.

Government and related personnel working overseas, such as members of the armed forces and embassy officials, have always had the right to vote, however long the absence from home, and special arrangements are made for them. But for other overseas voters, newly enfranchised by the Conservative government, some modification of the law is necessary. It is estimated that some three million people are now eligible as overseas voters, though in 1992 the number of such people who wished to vote, and returned their declarations, was limited to 31 942.[28] Only a small proportion of expatriates, therefore, appear to want to continue to be involved in the political affairs of the country they have left behind.

One suggestion is simply to reduce the qualifying period of absence from the constituency from twenty years to perhaps seven years, as recommended in a recent report from the Hansard Society for Parliamentary Government (although it gave no reasons for choosing the specific length of time),[29] or to five years as in the original 1985 Act which conferred the right to vote upon non-resident British citizens. Two better approaches, aimed at citizens working abroad temporarily, would be either (a) to abolish this novel extension of the 1980s altogether but to reserve the right to vote for those living overseas who owned a house in the United Kingdom and lived in it for part of the year; or preferably (b) to revert to the five-year period of the 1985 Act but at the same time make the right to vote dependent upon a genuine intention to return to this country. Such an intention is expressed in a person's choice of domicile, which is a legal concept used mainly in family law, and is also of some significance for Inland Revenue purposes. Domicile, therefore, should become a principal factor in a British citizen's eligibility to vote. British citizens abroad should be permitted to vote for only such length of time, up to a maximum of five years, that they declare their domicile to be in the United Kingdom and thus retain a firm root in its body of citizenship.

Nationality qualifications for voting

The Representation of the People Act 1983 confers the right to vote upon not only British citizens but also Commonwealth citizens and citizens of the Republic of Ireland. Even before statute controlled the nationality qualifications in 1914, people born within the British Empire and Dominions were at common law regarded as British subjects and therefore entitled to vote, subject to satisfying the property and other qualifications at that time. The 1914 British Nationality and Status of Aliens Act codified that common law rule, which was then refined by the 1948 British Nationality Act to replace the notion of common nationality with a system of reciprocal citizenship. It also provided a system whereby countries such as India and the African republics were still to be regarded, for nationality purposes and the right to vote, as 'British subjects', even though they no longer owed allegiance to the Crown but retained their position within the Commonwealth with the British monarch being recognised as Head of the

Commonwealth. There are about one-and-a-half million citizens from other parts of the Commonwealth resident in Britain today and in possession of the right to vote. There are also about 400 000 Irish citizens resident in the United Kingdom who may vote in British elections, although Ireland is not part of the Commonwealth.[30] This arrangement was provided as part of the settlement in the Ireland Act 1949, and reflects in the words of the British Prime Minister at that time, Clement Attlee, 'our propinquity of Eire, the longstanding relations between our peoples and the practical difficulties that flow from any attempt to treat Eire as altogether a foreign country.'[31]

There are no good arguments for excluding these voting rights now enjoyed by Commonwealth and Irish nationals, and indeed it is important that the franchise should now be extended further to European Union (EU) state nationals who satisfy a main residency or domicile qualification. This, it might be noted, should supersede the basis of Irish voters here, by virtue of their membership of the EU. At present there are about 260 000 non-United Kingdom EU state nationals working and living in Britain.[32] The arguments for conferring voting rights upon EU nationals is strongest for local authority elections, but it is not possible to draw sensible distinctions between different parts of the democratic process. If a French, German or Italian national from within the EU is, on the one hand, being encouraged by the principles of, and mobility offered by, the shared market to work and live here, and on the other hand is subject to United Kingdom law, paying taxes and taking part in the life of the community, he or she has a good claim to exercise a vote in local and national community affairs.

Any attempt to restrict voting rights of Commonwealth citizens, and draw some distinction between citizens of the United Kingdom and citizens from Jamaica, Guyana, New Zealand or any other Commonwealth country would be highly invidious. It would divide families here into voters and non-voters by virtue of the idiosyncrasies of the British Nationality Act 1981 and, given the symbolic importance of the right to vote, those people who had not yet acquired full British nationality would be made to feel that they were second-class citizens. Candidature for public office would presumably also be affected, so not only would Commonwealth state nationals permanently resident in Britain and paying taxes be disenfranchised from voting, they would also be prohibited from playing any active role in the representation and leadership of the community. In constituencies comprising multiracial communities, the insecurities and fears too often present among ethnic minorities would be aggravated, and attempts being made to construct genuinely representative bodies within those communities and across the country would be seriously impeded. There may be a case for introducing a required period of residency within the United Kingdom before eligible non-British nationals (that is EU and Commonwealth state nationals) are allowed to vote, but this should be kept to a minimum – in the case of local council elections for as little as twelve continuous months prior to the residency qualifying date for electoral registration, and in parliamentary elections for a period of four years, being equivalent to the general period of time between general elections.

Legal incapacity to vote

In addition to the age, residency and nationality requirements, the voter must be free from any specific disqualification imposed by law. Peers are disqualified at common law, on the grounds that they have the right to sit in the House of Lords and are therefore already represented in Parliament. Previously, peeresses in their own right did not have the same right to membership of the House of Lords as had men, but when such a right was conferred by the Peerage Act 1963, the Act also expressly extended to peeresses a legal incapacity to vote in parliamentary elections. Both peers and peeresses may, however, vote at local government and European Parliament elections.

The extent to which the Lords Spiritual (in other words, the twenty-six most senior Anglican bishops, including the Archbishops of Canterbury and York) in the House of Lords are to be treated as being similarly disqualified from voting at common law is a moot point that has never been tested in the courts. The titles held by these priests are not peerages as such, but are *ex officio* lordships conferring a right to sit in the parliamentary second chamber. According to *Halsbury's Laws*, 'a peer of Parliament is legally incapable of voting at a parliamentary election', but 'there are Lords of Parliament who are entitled to be summoned and to sit and vote in Parliament but who are not peers, namely the Lords Spiritual'.[33] Robert Runcie, then Archbishop of Canterbury, did cast a vote in the General Election of 1983. In doing so, he chose to rely upon legal advice given to him by the town clerk at St Albans when he was bishop there, and also by a lawyer friend, that he was not technically disqualified from voting as were other peers.[34] In the event, no legal repercussions were forthcoming – although Graham Leonard, then Bishop of London, joked, 'I look forward to visiting him in the Tower in my capacity as dean of the chapels royal.'[35] However, the matter did cause a minor stir in the press and some disquiet in the House of Lords and among other bishops, with the result that the Bishop of Derby announced in Parliament that the Archbishop of Canterbury and the other Lords Spiritual would not vote at a parliamentary election in the future.[36] The view of the then Bishop of Rochester, the most senior and authoritative of the bishops at the time, was that whatever the legal position, the practice had always been for the Lords Spiritual not to vote, and that morally they should indeed refrain from doing so:[37]

> I believe quite strongly that those of us who have the privilege of being a member of the Upper House of Parliament should accept, without

question, that if we can exercise a vote in Parliament itself, we should not also vote for someone to represent us and cast a second vote in the House of Commons.

Two other disqualifications, included in the Representation of the People Act 1983, are that convicted people are unable to vote during the period of their imprisonment; and that people reported by the Election Court to have committed a corrupt or illegal electoral practice are disqualified from voting for a period of five years (the prohibition extending to any constituency in the case of a corrupt practice, and limited to the constituency where the malpractice occurred in the case of an illegal practice).[38] A final disqualification, imposed by the common law, relates to the seriously mentally ill and handicapped. The language of the common law continues to speak in terms of 'idiots' and 'lunatics', being the product of antiquated thought on the subject, and is somewhat imprecise, since these are not clinical terms in use now. However, the simple rule, such as it is, is that 'idiots' cannot vote and 'lunatics' can only do so in their lucid intervals.[39] In practice, seriously mentally ill people are often resident in a psychiatric hospital. In such cases, the Representation of the People Act 1983 provides that the hospital cannot be treated as their place of residence for the purposes of electoral registration.[40] If the person is a long-term, compulsorily-detained patient, then he or she will effectively be disenfranchised. If the person has entered the psychiatric hospital voluntarily (as opposed to being compulsorily detained under the Mental Health Act 1983), then if he or she without assistance files a duly witnessed statutory declaration (on relevant personal matters as laid down under section 7 of the Representation of the People Act 1983) then that person may be registered in and vote at the constituency where he or she would be resident if he or she were not in hospital. Mentally ill people who are only temporary patients may have their name registered as a voter under their home address in the normal way.

THE REGISTRATION OF VOTERS

A person may only vote at a general election if, in addition to satisfying the legal qualifications to vote, his or her name is entered on the electoral register in the constituency where he or she has been living and wishes to vote.[41] The quality and efficiency with which electoral registers are drawn up is therefore crucial to the operation of the British electoral system. Compiling the register in each constituency is the legal duty of an 'electoral registration officer'. These people are officers of the council for the district or London borough in which the parliamentary constituency happens to fall. Sometimes there will be more than one constituency in a local district or borough, or a constituency will straddle two or more of them, in which case the registration officer for each district or London borough will compile a register of persons falling within his area. Registration officers operate independently of one another, and are not local officials of some central unifying agency, although the Home Office supervises registration practice and issues circulars and advice to all officers. The registration officer's duties and powers are laid down in the Representation of the People Act 1983, and begin by requiring him or her 'to prepare and publish in each year a register of parliamentary electors for each constituency or part of a constituency in the area for which he acts'.[42] As was explained in the context of a voter's residency qualification,[43] it is the names of all people who were resident in the constituency on the statutory 'qualifying date' (being 10 October in Great Britain, and 15 September in Northern Ireland) which must be entered in the register, which then becomes operable on the following 16 February for the purposes of any general election held during the next twelve months.

The electoral registration officers' duties involve taking all reasonable steps to obtain the necessary information to enable them to compile a register of all eligible voters within their area. Officers and their staff are authorised by the Representation of the People Act to 'have a house to house or other sufficient inquiry made as to the persons entitled to be registered'.[44] This task of electoral registration is a large and difficult administrative undertaking, which is too often forgotten or not fully appreciated as being of fundamental importance to the voting system. It is generally accepted that, with registration at present being an annual exercise, and with constant population changes, for example from deaths or moving house, to expect perfect accuracy from the electoral register is impracticable. Some commentators, including Dr David Butler and Professor Keith-Lucas, believe as much as a 3 to 4 per cent error is 'acceptable', being the margin of error estimated to exist in surveys conducted by the Office of Population Censuses and Surveys (OPCS) in both 1951 and 1966.[45] However, in 1982 the OPCS published a report entitled *Electoral Registration in 1981* which disclosed a significantly higher level of inaccuracy, calculating that 6.5 per cent of those eligible to vote were not included in the 1981 electoral register at their qualifying address on 10 October 1980, and by the time the register came into force on 16 February 1981 the level had risen to 9 per cent, rightly described as 'an alarming degree of inexactitude'.[46] This meant that out of the total electorate, over three million citizens were effectively disenfranchised from their right to vote.

Parliamentary disquiet over the quality of electoral registration was one of the factors that led to the Home Affairs Select Committee of the House of Commons undertaking an inquiry into the Representation of the People Acts in the 1982–3 parliamentary session. In the course of taking evidence, one of the members of the Committee expressed herself to be 'absolutely dumbfounded' by the 'extraordinarily slip-shod, careless and indeed highly inefficient way in which our electoral registration officers are working'.[47] Even if this may be rather unfair on electoral registration officers as a whole, the Report of the Committee strongly believed that many improvements needed to be made, particularly with respect to greater involvement of the Home Office in supervising registration procedure and acting as the agent for the public accountability of electoral registration officers. Galvanised by this report, the Home Office strengthened its supervisory work, issuing many circulars for the guidance of electoral registration officers, and gathering and disseminating statistical information about working practices of registration officers,[48] aided by annual reports it has commissioned from the OPCS since 1987.

Voting is a voluntary activity, but electoral registration is compulsory. A responsibility lies with the individual citizen to respond promptly to the forms for completion sent from the electoral registration officer, and persons in any doubt should check the published draft register in October. About a third of households fail to respond to these forms[49] (called 'Form A' by officials). Two reminders are usually delivered to non-respondents, and most electoral registration officers have follow-up procedures involving calling personally at the residences. When these local procedures have been tried without success, the electoral registration officer must decide whether to carry forward the names for that address from the previous register. If names are carried forward, there is a risk of a redundant name appearing on the new register; if names are not carried forward, there is a risk of an eligible voter being disenfranchised. A survey carried out by the OPCS for the Home Office on compiling the 1990 electoral register established that 27 per cent of constituencies carried forward all non-responding names (47 per cent in London), and 50 per cent of constituencies carried forward names if there was good supporting evidence. Only 6 per cent of constituencies did not carry forward any names of non-respondents.[50] The House of Commons Select Committee recommended that names of non-respondents should be carried over for one year only, and such advice is repeated in the current Home Office Code of Practice for registration officers, but it seems that in practice only a minority of constituencies follow this recommendation. Traditionally, registration officers have erred on the side of inclusion rather than deletion because of the possibility of depriving people of their right to vote.

In recent years, the local government poll tax registers have provided one source of information to registration officers to assist them in compiling the electoral register. Under the terms of the Local Government Finance Act 1988 – the legislation that brought in the ill-fated 'poll tax', more properly called the 'community charge' – electoral registration officers have a statutory right to inspect the register of names and addresses within each local authority which is gathered in connection with every adult citizen's obligation to pay the poll tax.[51] A Home Office circular to registration officers suggested that 'to ensure maximum benefit' is derived from the electoral registration officer's statutory right to inspect the poll tax register, they 'should exploit all readily available sources of information', and 'the community charges register is likely to include the names of a number of people eligible to vote who do not appear on the electoral register.'[52] This advice went on to say that, 'in addition, some names which are on the electoral register will not be on the community charges register', and there should be 'annual comparison of electoral and community charges registers to identify differences'.

Poor people, and people who did not own freehold or leasehold houses, saw their tax bills rise with the poll tax, but the tax benefited more affluent citizens with big homes. Not surprisingly, therefore, following the introduction of the poll tax in England and Wales in 1990, there were widespread fears that poll tax evasion would lead to the disenfranchisement of a large number of poor people, and this in party political terms was likely to work against the electoral interests of the Labour Party, especially in marginal constituencies. There was indeed a significant fall in voter registration in 1991, when the OPCS calculated there to be over 100 000 fewer eligible voters on the electoral register compared with 1990 and each year since the 1987 general election. The OPCS suggested that not all of this fall could be blamed on the poll tax and that the fall in registration might be due to other factors such as changes in numbers of people eligible to vote, and lack of incentive to register when no election was in prospect.[53] In the twelve months prior to the 1992 general election the impact of the poll tax upon electoral registration appeared to slow down, assisted no doubt by vigorous attempts by registration officers to register adults after the autumn of 1991, when the 1992 election campaign effectively began, and by February 1992 the 100 000 lost voters had 'reappeared'. The political and civil rights implications, and use to electoral registration officers, of the poll tax register for voting purposes ended in 1992 upon the demise of this discredited tax.

Proposal for a rolling electoral register

For the future, there is now a large measure of agreement across the political spectrum about the need for improvements in the efficiency of compiling the electoral register. The first aim must be to make greater efforts to encourage all voters to inform the electoral registration office of their residency in the constituency. Currently this means greater advertising and door-to-door efforts to secure the return of the annual request sent out to all householders, completed with the names of all people resident at each address. At the time of writing, the advertising efforts by registration officers in the weeks preceding the preparation of the draft register are still largely confined to billboards; more extensive press and television campaigns should be undertaken. Greater energy should be devoted to publicity in different languages, and registration officers must identify sizeable ethnic minorities within their constituencies and make arrangements for information leaflets and media advertisements in appropriate languages. The authority to make house-to-house inquiries under section 10 of the 1983 Act should extend to a greater use of personal canvassing than at present, not only to remind householders to complete and return Form A, but also to verify improbable answers, particularly if the address in question is known to be in multiple occupation, or where it is common knowledge that negligent omissions frequently occur, for example in old people's homes where residents are least likely to check the accuracy of the draft register. Registration officials should check automatically with the registrar of deaths. They should also inspect the draft register carefully, to weed out obviously erroneous entries. The London Borough of Richmond was not an isolated example in producing an electoral register for the 1992 general election with the names on it of two babies and a dog, to whom official poll cards were sent.[54]

The public and the government must now confront the problem of providing sufficient finances, personnel and other resources to match the civil importance of the work. Some countries, notably the USA, leave the chasing of voter registration to the political parties, in whose interests it is that supporters are able to vote at the forthcoming elections. But this is certainly not the practice in Britain at the time of writing, where in any event the parties, particularly on the Left, have very restricted financial resources (especially when compared with the huge amounts of political finance involved in American electioneering), and little if any to spare over and above that which they need to perform their basic tasks of formulating public policy, encouraging public awareness and participation in politics, publicising their work, and campaigning for office. At present it is reckoned that the government spends only 1.2 pence per elector towards the national promotion of voter registration.[55] In 1988 the Home Office provided £569 000 for its entire domestic electoral registration publicity and advertising campaign for that year. By contrast, it might be noted that it supplied £750 000 for the one-off campaign to publicise the new voting rights of the relatively far smaller number of overseas voters.[56]

Of more fundamental importance, it seems right that there should be a radical overhaul of administrative responsibility for voter registration. Particularly now that 95 per cent of electoral registration offices have computers installed, a citizen's right to vote should be founded upon the date on which he files his claim in a particular constituency, not on an arbitrary anniversary. In other words, electoral registration should become a rolling exercise, being updated constantly, with the annual issue and return of forms to householders being just one method of verification and accuracy of the register. Such a proposal is now attracting widespread support. Legislation will be needed to implement this new system of electoral registration, and this might adopt some of the drafting from a recent Private Members' Bill presented to the House of Commons on the subject by Harry Barnes.[57] Harry Barnes' Bill failed to secure a second reading only because the parliamentary quorum for a closure motion of 100 was not reached (voting was 78 for the Bill, none against), but the Bill provided a valuable occasion for parliamentary debate on the subject, as part of the political process that will (and certainly should) eventually lead to a change in the law on electoral registration.

The new legislation should begin by creating the requirement for a rolling register, and then proceed to modify the registration officer's duty so that he or she takes all reasonable steps to ensure that the rolling register is accurate at all times. People moving into a new constituency should be placed under a legal requirement to notify the registration officer within three weeks of taking up residence there. Provision should also be made for voters left off the register by accident. It very often happens that voters do not realise their name is missing from the electoral register until a general election is called and they do not receive an official poll card telling them where to vote. Under a rolling register system, provision should be made so that such people can, in fact, vote, assuming they are otherwise legally qualified to do so at the time the general election is called. The new legislation should require returning officers to publish the electoral register and send out the official poll cards to all voters within two days of the dissolution of Parliament. Local advertising and notices in the national and local press should then inform the public that all qualified people who did not appear on the register or receive poll cards should apply to their registration office immediately to be entered on the electoral roll and be permitted to vote. Extra resources for this new system of electoral registration will be needed and must be derived centrally out of money expressly provided by Parliament. In addition, there needs to be created a national agency with a more interventionist role in co-ordinating and supervising the practices of electoral registration officers. Central responsibility for this task might be passed to the Electoral Commission, the proposed new body with responsibility for a range of important electoral matters, which is discussed later in this book.[58]

HOW THE VOTE IS CAST

Polling day arrangements

The voter is sent his or her official poll card about ten days before the general election, and this explains precisely the manner in which he or she is to cast his or her vote. It is the responsibility of the returning officer for each constituency to arrange for the printing and delivery of these poll cards as soon as is practicable after the close of nominations.[59] A standard form for the purpose is prescribed by the Representation of the People Regulations 1986, on which the returning officer fills in the voter's name, address and electoral registration number, the date of polling day and the address of the relevant polling station.[60] It is not necessary to take the official polling card along to the polling station, although the clerks prefer it if people do so because it enables them to locate and cross off the voter's name from the electoral register more quickly. The purpose of the polling card is for information only. On the reverse of the card, there is a statement telling the voter how to proceed.

When you go to the polling station, tell the clerk your name and address, as shown on the front of this card. The presiding officer will give you a ballot paper; see that he stamps the official mark on it before he gives it to you.

Mark your vote on the ballot paper secretly in one of the voting compartments. Put one X in the space to the right opposite the name of the candidate for whom you wish to vote. You may vote for only one candidate. If you put any other mark on the ballot paper your vote may not be counted.

Then fold the ballot paper so as to conceal your vote, show the official mark on the back to the presiding officer and put the paper into the ballot box.

It is remarkable how many people get this simple procedure wrong – or 'spoil' their ballot papers, as it is officially known. Around 40 000 or more voters unintentionally spoil their ballot papers at every general election, by one means or another.[61] The record held is 117 848 spoilt papers at the general election of Thursday 3 May 1979, although on that occasion it is safe to assume that this was caused by local government elections taking place on the same day, and voters being confused by the fact that they could put crosses on the local elections ballot paper against more than one candidate for local councillors, and thinking they could do similarly in the parliamentary election. Most people spoiling their papers do not realise they have done so, but if they are aware of it and it was an accident then they can ask for a second paper to use for voting. The Election Rules in the 1983 Act provide, 'A voter who has inadvertently dealt with his ballot paper in such a manner that it cannot be conveniently used as a ballot paper may, on delivering it to the presiding officer and proving to his satisfaction the fact of the inadvertence, obtain another ballot paper in the place of the ballot paper so delivered, and the spoilt ballot paper shall be immediately cancelled'.[62]

Form of ballot paper

VOTE FOR ONE CANDIDATE ONLY		
1	**BROWN** (John Edward Brown, of 52, George Street, Bristol, Labour Party)	
2	**BROWN** (Thomas William Brown, of 136, London Road, Swindon, Conservative Party)	
3	**JONES** (William David Jones, of High Elms, Wilts., Green Party)	
4	**MERTON** (George Merton, of Park Lodge, Swansworth, Berks., Natural Law Party)	
5	**SMITH** (Mary Smith, of 72 High Street, Bath, Liberal Democrat)	

The 1983 Act expressly states that the voter must place a cross against the name of the candidate he or she supports, but also provides that a vote which disobeys this advice shall not for that reason be void 'if an intention that the vote shall be for one or other of the candidates clearly appears, and the way the paper is marked does not itself identify the voter and it is not shown that he can be identified by it'.[63] Over the years an amusing line of cases has been presented before the courts for a decision upon the legitimacy of how particular voters have expressed themselves. In 1880 Mr Justice Hawkins rejected the suggestion that the cross on the ballot had to be 'of sufficient thickness to make it easily recognisable by a person of weak sight'. In 1886 Baron Pollock permitted a vote to count when a circle was placed against the candidate's name, and in 1908 the placing of a dot was held by Mr Justice Bigham to be sufficient. In 1971 Mr Justice Waller held a ballot paper to be valid where all the candidates' names except one had been crossed out, and in 1982 Lord Denning similarly did so when the voter, in the box to the right-hand side of the name of the candidate 'Ruffle', had written 'Ruffle Liberal'. In 1992, the Divisional Court allowed a vote which had against one of the candidates a 'smiley face' and the words 'yes please'.[64] The one thing that will always invalidate a vote in election law is if the voter signs or initials the ballot paper, or in any other way makes a mark that allows him or her to be identified.[65]

Tellers or checkers

After the voter has placed his cross for the candidate of his or her choice on the ballot paper in the polling booth, he or she folds the paper in half, and places it into one of the black tin boxes to be opened at the count that evening. On the way out of the polling station the voter is then likely to be confronted by a small group sitting or standing just outside the doorway. These people often appear to be, and act like, election clerks (and, indeed, polling officials inside the station have been known to direct voters to them and suggest they give them their names or polling cards). They are known as 'tellers' or 'checkers' and are in fact officials of the political parties whose candidates are standing in the constituency election. The principal task these tellers perform is to determine which eligible voters have voted on polling day. If by the early evening the people whom they think are likely to vote for their party candidate have not turned up to vote, then they or their colleagues will call round at the individuals' residences and try to persuade them to go to the polling booth. Tellers perform a very important political role at elections in producing a good turnout of voters. They and their parties may even offer to drive voters to the polling station personally. They may not, however, organise mass transport facilities hired for the purpose. It is an illegal practice under the 1983 Representation of the People Act for people such as tellers to 'hire, borrow or use . . . public vehicles for the purpose of the conveyance of electors', and it is an offence for people such as taxi drivers and transport companies to 'let, lend or employ' such vehicles. The offer or receipt of money for such purposes is, similarly, an offence.[66]

Armed with the information gained from people leaving the polling station, the tellers check each voter against a copy of the electoral register that shows the addresses of all eligible voters in the area. Canvassers in the local party will over the previous few weeks have called at most doors in the constituency in an attempt to glean voting intentions within each household. Apart from clear declarations of loyalty for or against the party of the canvasser, rough-and-ready calculations are made from people who decline to respond because either they wish to preserve their privacy or they simply 'don't know'. In this way the local parties draw up lists of known or possible supporters (usually held now on computerised data banks) with reference to the local electoral register (copies of which are obtainable on computer disk from local registration officers). This is stored and made available for use by tellers on polling day and also perhaps for other future purposes by the party.

Although most people involved in political and electoral affairs view tellers as part of the polling scenery, and a useful device for chivvying citizens out of their homes and into the polling booths to perform their civic duty, it remains an unacceptable fact that many, if not most, ordinary voters are unaware both that tellers are not in fact election officials, and that voters do not have to give them the personal details requested. In response to a warning published in the *Independent* newspaper on general election day in 1992, that voters need not give their electoral registration numbers to party agents outside polling stations, a voter wrote a letter to the Editor:[67]

> Being only half awake during the early hours of voting day, I inadvertently gave my number to one of these people. It was only a couple of hours later while reading the *Independent* that I discovered my error. On returning to the polling station in the evening to accompany my wife, I learnt that not only were these people conning voters into unwittingly giving their own registration numbers, they were carrying out house calls on those who had not yet voted. I consider this an extreme invasion of people's privacy and feel they should not feel pressurised into disclosing when and if they intend to vote.

Once voters know who the people are in the doorway of polling stations, they sometimes feel intimidated and as if they are running the gauntlet to avoid being pestered by them. Tellers generally restrict their inquiries to establishing the electoral registration number and/or name of the voter. If they seek to discover how a person cast his or her vote, this would certainly become even more objectionable. In the opinion of *Parker's Conduct of Parliamentary Elections*, 'whilst such questioning would not be an offence against the requirements on secrecy in section 66 of the 1983 Act,[68] they might give rise to allegations of undue influence or simply antagonise the voter'.[69]

It would be a simple improvement in the practice of tellers if they were required to maintain a greater distance than at present from the doorways and means of access to the polling station. There should also be some clear notice displayed on or near their desk, or where they are standing, which states the name of their party and the fact that they are acting in a non-official capacity as party checkers of who has, and who has not, yet voted. Returning officers should instruct staff to explain either orally or by clear written notices in the polling station who the people outside are, what they are doing, and above all staff should be advised never to tell voters to give their polling cards to tellers on their way out of the polling station, as has been known to happen in the past. It is often assumed, falsely, that such measures will reduce the effectiveness of the tellers' work (and consequently the electoral turnout), but in fact it might improve their efficiency because voters would probably more readily assist the tellers of the party they support; at present many people are dubious about responding to individuals whose identity and authority is unknown to them. In any event, primacy in polling arrangements should be given to a citizen's individual interests, and his or her right to make a properly informed choice on whether or not to assist the party tellers in their work.

Postal and proxy voting: holiday-makers, the infirm and other absent voters

The Conservative government's Representation of the People Act 1985 considerably extended the provisions whereby eligible electors who are unable to go to their polling station on general election day can none the less cast a vote, either by appointing a proxy to vote on their behalf, or by receiving and returning a ballot paper through the post.

An elector may apply to vote by proxy or by post either for an indefinite period (in other words permanently for all future general elections until such time as the elector may apply to be taken off the proxy or postal voter register), or he may apply for the absent vote in the case of the forthcoming election alone. An elector will be eligible for an absent vote for an indefinite period if he or she falls into one of five categories. These are, (a) if he or she is a service voter (in other words a member of the armed forces away from home); (b) if he or she is no longer resident at his or her qualifying address in the constituency (for example, in the case of a voluntary long-term patient in a hospital); (c) if the voter cannot reasonably be expected to go in person to the polling station or to vote unaided by reason of blindness or other physical incapacity; (d) if the voter cannot reasonably be expected to go in person to the polling station because of the general nature of his or her occupation, service or employment or that of his or her spouse (for example, seamen, lorry drivers or other itinerant workers); and (e) if he or she is an expatriate living abroad and registered as an overseas voter.[70] Proxy voting means that the elector appoints someone (who must also be an eligible voter) to vote on their behalf, either by going personally to the polling booth and marking the elector's ballot paper, or else the proxy (especially if living outside the constituency) may himself vote by post. Proxies may be appointed to act for an indefinite period or for just one election. This is a common method of voting by the elderly and the infirm. Some commentators have suggested that the practice of political activists acting as permanent proxies for elderly citizens is inappropriate and could be open to abuse, particularly where the elderly person signing the proxy form presented to him or her has declining mental faculties and is only half aware of the permanent status of the authority being granted.[71] As postal votes cannot be sent outside the United Kingdom,[72] all overseas voters wishing to vote must do so by proxy.

To be eligible for an absent vote for a single election, the voter must satisfy the electoral registration officer that his or her circumstances on the date of the poll will be or are likely to be such that he or she cannot reasonably be expected to vote in person at the polling station.[73] This covers holiday-makers who, when the election is called, realise that they will be away on the polling day. It would also cover people away by reason of their employment, or because they had recently moved out of the constituency,[74] or if for medical reasons they are unable to leave their home. Such people may apply for an absent vote, by proxy or by post, and the electoral registration officer must receive all such forms of application not later than noon on the thirteenth day before the poll.[75] An absent voters register is compiled, with three special lists containing all those voting by post, all those voting by proxy (with the names and addresses of the proxies), and all proxies voting by post. Upon request, copies of these lists are made available to the election agents of the candidates free of charge, and these may be utilised for canvassing purposes.

Finally, the absent voters' lists will be used by the returning officer in each constituency in order to issue postal ballot papers, and to verify those individuals acting as proxies.[76] No specific time is laid down for sending out postal ballot papers, but it is usually shortly after the twelfth day prior to the poll. The returning officer will send out to the postal voter a ballot paper, a declaration of identity to be signed by the voter, and a ballot paper envelope. Upon receipt, the voter marks the ballot paper according to his or her preference, and returns it (inside the official envelope, together with the completed declaration of identity) to the returning officer to arrive at any time before the close of polling on election day. The returning officer then prepares a postal voters' ballot box into which all postal ballot papers, still in their envelopes, will be placed unopened. After the close of polling this box will be opened in the presence of the candidates or their election agents, before being mixed in with other ordinary ballot papers for the purposes of the count.

PSEPHOLOGY AND VOTING BEHAVIOUR

Precisely how individual electors choose to cast their vote is, not surprisingly, a subject of very great political interest, not only to politicians themselves, but also to journalists, market research companies, and academics and students in university Politics departments. The name that has been coined for research and analysis into voting behaviour and patterns is 'psephology'.[77] This is a line of enquiry which combines the disciplines of both sociology and psychology. Almost by definition it is not an exact science, for if it were, we should always know the result of a general election in advance. As David Butler, one of Britain's leading psephologists, has admitted, 'The reasons why people vote as they do and why they change their allegiance are still obscure, despite an ever-growing body of academic and commercial research.'[78]

At a general election voters are exercising their own rational judgement about the people and policies of the different political parties best fitted to represent them in Parliament and govern the country. It is clear none the less that such subjective voting decisions tend to follow certain sociological patterns. The effect, for example, of the voter's class, region of the country where he or she lives, occupation, sex or age, all serve to condition voting preferences. The principal social factor in conditioning voting behaviour today is still class. It is widely held that the poor, unemployed or less affluent members of society, viewed as belonging to the solid or upper working class, are more likely to vote for candidates of the Labour Party, whereas affluent or wealthy citizens belonging to the middle or upper classes are considered to be more likely to vote Conservative. Other widely established patterns of voting behaviour are sometimes interwoven with class factors, such as regional and demographic considerations. The electorate in the prosperous South of England vote far more heavily in favour of Conservatives than do these in Scotland and the North, where Labour has most of its constituency strongholds. Similarly, most electors within a common occupational group tend to vote for one particular party, for example, company directors favour the Conservatives, while manual workers predominantly favour Labour (though to a lesser extent since the 1970s, according to recent research). There is also a significant correlation between people working in the public sector voting Labour (whose social ideology supports greater state ownership of essential utilities and industries) and people working in private businesses voting for Conservative policies (which reflect the virtues of minimal state intervention and the free market).

On the relevance of the elector's sex, it has been claimed that women tend to be more Conservative in their political orientation than men. According to the Oxford University political scientist, Peter Pulzer:[79]

There is overwhelming evidence that women are more conservatively inclined than men, as in most other countries . . . Sex is the one factor which indubitably counter-balances class trends: working-class women are more right-wing than working-class men, middle-class women are more right-wing than middle-class men. In certain Continental European states religion, especially Catholicism, plays an important part in making women more right-wing. In Britain, where this factor is less influential, the 'sex gap' is correspondingly smaller.

Public opinion polling in the periods around each of the three most recent British general elections would seem to support this Conservative trend, although an extraordinary feature in 1992 was that women voters within the

18–24-year-old age group preferred the Labour Party over the Conservatives by 43 per cent to 30 per cent.[80] It always used to be said that electors were very likely to follow the pattern of the party allegiances of their parents, but since the 1960s it is probably truer to say that young electors will in some way react to the political attitudes of their parents, and are as likely to rebel against them as to support them. Most people become more conservative in their politics as they get older, and at any given time there is a tendency for electors within a particular age band to vote for one particular party. Teenage and young voters are more intuitive of political image[81] and more likely to conform to the prevailing fashionable social attitudes within the youth culture of the day. Thus, an age factor appears to have been important in the 1970 and 1974 general elections. It is said that the number of newly-enfranchised 18–21-year-olds in 1969 effectively halved the overall majority that Edward Heath's Conservatives would otherwise have received (from 60 to 30 MPs) at the 1970 general election, and that this age group was the decisive factor in giving Harold Wilson's Labour Party its narrow victories in the two 1974 elections. However, this predisposition towards Labour had declined by the early 1980s, and at the 1983 election people aged under 30 years were supporting Margaret Thatcher's Conservatives by around 10 per cent over the Labour Party.

A social portrait of the electorate at each of the three most recent general elections (1983, 1987 and 1992) is given on pages 97–8, together with the results of a professional opinion poll indicating voting tendencies within each category. This provides a description of just some of the tendencies that can be drawn from voting behaviour in recent years.

The criteria upon which voters rationalise their choice are usually ones of material self-interest or moral principle, or perhaps most commonly a mixture between the two forged in terms of the national interest. Vested interest factors have been of paramount importance in recent British elections, the citizen primarily being swayed by a calculation regarding under which party in government over the following few years he or she is likely to be financially better-off. Crude appeals by electioneering politicians to this voting instinct are now commonplace, but in fact their prevalence is a relatively recent campaign phenomenon, and they were given a tremendous boost by Harold Macmillan's successful political slogan of 1959: 'You've never had it so good!' The 1992 general election was largely and fought won on competing party claims about which set of politicians would offer the citizen the larger net income after tax, the accuracy of such claims being often highly dubious. Electoral behaviour otherwise may be guided more by matters of social or moral principle, with voters looking for a brand of political leadership that will reflect their own political values. The ideology and priorities underlying the parties' general programmes of public policy as published in their manifestos, especially on such matters as unemployment and state intervention in industry, will be important criteria for these

A social portrait of voters and voting at the
1983, 1987 and 1992 General Elections

Percentage of 1992 voters		1983 vote			1987 vote			1992 vote		
		Con	Lab	L/D	Con	Lab	L/D	Con	Lab	L/D
100	Total	44	28	26	43	32	23	43	35	18
49	Men	42	30	25	43	32	23	41	37	18
51	Women	46	26	27	43	32	23	44	34	18
14	18–24	42	33	32	33	40	21	35	39	19
19	25–34	40	29	29	39	33	25	40	38	18
33	35–54	44	27	27	45	29	24	43	34	19
34	55+	47	27	24	46	31	21	46	34	17
23	Pensioner	51	25	23	47	31	21	48	34	16
19	AB–Prof	60	10	28	57	14	26	56	20	22
24	C1–white collar	51	20	27	51	21	26	52	25	19
27	C2–skilled	40	32	26	40	36	22	38	41	17
30	DE–skilled	33	41	24	30	48	20	30	50	15
67	Owner occupier	52	19	28	50	23	25	49	30	19
23	Council tenant	26	47	24	22	56	19	24	55	15
7	Private tenant	41	33	23	39	37	21	33	40	21
7	Men 18–24	41	35	21	42	37	19	39	35	18
7	Women 18–24	42	31	25	31	42	24	30	43	19
9	Men 25–34	37	34	28	41	33	24	40	37	17
10	Women 25–34	42	25	30	37	33	27	40	38	18
16	Men 35–54	42	29	27	42	32	24	40	37	19
17	Women 35–54	46	24	28	47	27	25	46	32	19
17	Men 55+	45	28	25	45	31	23	43	38	17
17	Women 55+	49	26	24	46	32	20	49	32	17
9	Men 65+	50	25	23	47	30	22	44	38	16
9	Women 65+	51	25	23	46	33	20	51	31	17
4	Unemployed (m)	25	49	24	21	56	20	24	52	17
3	Unemployed (f)	32	41	24	23	54	19	26	51	16
17	North (m)	35	39	24	34	42	20	33	46	14
19	North (f)	40	33	25	33	41	22	36	43	15
13	Midland (m)	43	31	23	46	34	19	44	38	16
13	Midland (f)	46	27	24	45	29	24	46	36	16
19	South (m)	48	23	28	49	22	28	46	29	22
20	South (f)	51	19	30	51	24	24	50	27	22
	HOMEOWNERS									
36	Middle-class	58	12	29	57	15	26	56	21	20
31	Working-class	46	25	27	43	32	23	41	39	17

Percentage of 1992 voters		1983 vote			1987 vote			1992 vote		
		Con	Lab	L/D	Con	Lab	L/D	Con	Lab	L/D
	COUNCIL TENANTS									
2	Middle-class	32	39	25	28	41	24	34	40	18
21	Working-class	25	49	24	21	58	18	22	58	15
	TRADE UNIONS									
23	Members	31	39	29	30	42	26	30	47	19
15	Men	29	41	28	31	42	25	30	48	18
8	Women	34	34	31	29	41	27	31	44	21
3	18–24	31	34	23	29	46	23	30	42	20
5	25–34	29	37	32	28	47	23	28	49	19
10	35–54	30	40	29	29	40	29	31	45	20
5	55+	32	40	26	36	37	24	33	49	16
10	ABC1	38	27	33	37	30	30	36	36	24
8	C2	27	44	27	28	47	24	27	52	17
5	DE	25	50	24	22	56	19	24	59	13
9	North	26	44	28	25	50	21	25	53	14
6	Midlands	32	40	25	35	39	24	32	49	18
8	South	35	32	32	33	34	32	35	38	26

Table 3.3[82]

electors in choosing between two or more of the parties. Exceptionally, there may be individual policies of the parties which prove particularly attractive or worrying to voters concerned with the national interest, one recent example being the unilateralist nuclear defence stance of Labour in the 1983 election which proved to be a definite vote loser.[83] Occasionally, there may also be special constituency reasons for voting in a particular way. A voter may be particularly troubled by some local consideration, such as a planning matter or threat to a local industry where he or she works, or alternatively he or she may personally know or have been helped by one of the candidates, and this sways him or her to disregard party considerations in favour of a particular person viewed as being the best for the local job.

One variable factor that psephologists have said may influence voting behaviour is the current state of national morale. A general election called immediately following the successful conclusion to an international military conflict has been known to produce a strong pattern of electoral support for the government (known as a 'khaki election'), but while this was certainly the case in 1983 following Margaret Thatcher's successful conclusion of the Falklands War, on the other hand Winston Churchill lost the general election in 1945 just after gaining a far greater victory in the Second World War. There is a myth in the Labour Party that bad weather tends to affect their electoral prospects adversely (the so-called 'feel-wet factor'). The general election of 1970 was held four days after England were knocked out of the football World Cup, and the outgoing Prime Minister, Harold Wilson, partially attributed his party's unexpectedly poor performance at the polls to the depressing effect this defeat had upon the country's morale.[84]

Clearly, the success and impact of the political parties in projecting themselves and their policies is of great importance, although research indicates that remarkably few electors in fact change their voting intentions during the election campaign period. Graham Wallas, a political scientist at the London School of Economics, was an early pioneer of the study of electoral behaviour, and in his book *Human Nature in Politics*, published in 1908, he stressed the great importance of 'political image' in influencing voters – a factor that has become of even greater significance with the advent of television. Wallas emphasised that in the minds of voters, 'Emotional reactions can be set up by the name [of the political party] and its automatic mental associations.'[85] Connected with this is voting behaviour influenced by culture or status. There will always be those who like to be seen as supporters of, for example, the Conservative Party (but equally so for the other parties) because it is fashionable in the social circle to which they belong (or aspire to belong) to be of this political persuasion. Such voters tend to identify with the archetypal party figure, and are particularly useful to constituency parties as local volunteer leaflet distributors, workers or officials. These image or status factors are again in many respects associated with social class (or perhaps more accurately, self-assigned class).

Many electors vote for the same party through the whole of their lives, or will do so predominantly with just one or two lapses. General elections are fought and won not so much upon the support of the broad mass of the electorate, but by one of the parties successfully winning over a majority of floating voters. The average nationwide swing between Conservatives and Labour over the past fifty years has been less than 3 per cent.[86] This means that the number of crucial votes at any election is, in fact, relatively very small. Peter Pulzer has argued that there are four types of floating voter: 'Those whose involvement with the party of their choice is low and who therefore hesitate between voting and abstention; those who experiment with alternative allegiances but generally return to the party of their first choice at election time; those who support a minor party but may be deprived of a candidate of their highest preference; and those who experience a genuine conversion and transfer their allegiance.'[87] But the analysis and prediction of what finally prompts each floating voter to make his final choice at an election is most difficult of all. As another psephologist, Professor Jean Blondel, has observed:[88]

The floating vote is a very complex reality. In a straight fight, in two successive elections, there are three possibilities open to each elector: he can vote Conservative, vote Labour, or abstain. Since he can have voted

Conservative, have voted Labour, or abstained at the previous election, there are nine possible courses open to the electors of the constituency. All these courses are in fact taken.

There is some evidence that many floating voters do not in fact know how they will vote until they are inside the polling booth. Such complexities of psephology are likely to grow in the future, because it is clear that the British electorate as a whole has become increasingly volatile since the 1960s and less predictable in its voting patterns. There are many reasons for this new volatility in the British electorate. According to the Labour MP, Austin Mitchell, the 'volatility is partly a product of the steady erosion of traditional allegiances on both sides of the electorate, and partly a product of economic failure which has led to comparative and now absolute decline. The electors have expected to become better off, but governments have failed to deliver and the result has been increasing alienation'.[89] It is also no doubt the result of a better-informed and better-educated electorate, the arrival of television and a more sophisticated style of political marketing, the loosening of British class structures giving greater mobility between the middle and working classes, and more recently the emergence of substantial third-party forces, notably the Liberal Democrats and the Scottish Nationalists.

Whatever the pitfalls and difficulties in theorising about psephology and voting behaviour, it will continue to be an important part of political analysis in the media when considering future and past elections, and within the political parties themselves for the purposes of campaigning. There is some irony in the fact that after all the efforts that have been made in our history to secure and maintain the secrecy of the ballot, tremendous efforts are made today by academics, politicians, journalists and polling companies to discover precisely how and why the British elector votes as he or she does.

COUNTING THE VOTES

After the polling stations have closed at 10 pm on general election day, arrangements are made for collecting all the ballot papers together and counting up the votes cast for each candidate in the constituency. Only in a small minority of constituencies (about 30 of them) is it the practice to wait until the following morning to begin counting votes. In the great majority of the remaining constituencies, the count begins straight away and usually means that the question of which political party will be forming the next government is decided by dawn the next day. Considering the huge numbers of votes involved, returning officers and their clerks at recent general elections have managed to process the counts and declare the winners in a remarkably short space of time. In 1992 the first result was declared in Sunderland South at precisely 11.06 pm on election day, just one hour and six minutes after the close of polling. By 5 am the following morning, all the overnight results had been completed, with the Conservatives having 321 seats, Labour 269 and the Liberal Democrats 17. At 5.28 am the Labour Party leader, Neil Kinnock, appeared on the steps of the Labour HQ in Walworth Road, London, to concede defeat.

Following the close of the poll, the presiding officer at each polling station seals up each ballot box that has been filled, and delivers them together with the marked electoral registers and other documentation to the place where the count is to be held. A suitably large location needs to be chosen by the returning officer for the count, such the main public meeting room at the Town Hall, to house all the people entitled to be present when the counting is under way. It is normal practice to hold the count in a single location, although two or more places may be selected for the task, and it is also usual for the place for the count to be selected from within the constituency which is the subject of the election, although again there is no legal requirement to do so. The people who may be present include not only the returning officer's staff who count the ballot papers and perform the administrative work involved, but also the candidates and their spouses, and the candidates' election agents and counting agents.[90] The counting agents supervise the manner of the count to ensure that everything is carried out properly. The returning officer restricts the number of agents as he or she thinks fit, generally allowing the candidates a similar number each. Other people may attend only with the permission of the returning officer, and under such conditions as he or she demands, and this includes the media. Television cameras and journalists are usually allowed into the place where the counting is being held, but remain at a distance from the count, such as in a public gallery overlooking proceedings.

The counting of votes cast for each candidate takes place manually. The returning officer's staff follow a number of procedures for uniformity, such as leaving each ballot paper counted lying face upwards, and putting to one side those papers which might be open to challenge for being invalid. The counting clerks will reject any ballot paper which does not bear the official mark, or on which votes are given for more than one candidate, or on which anything is written or marked by which the voter can be identified, except the printed number on the back, or which is unmarked or deemed by the returning officer to be void for uncertainty.[91] The decision of the returning officer on any question about the validity of a ballot paper is final, and cannot be challenged by the candidate in any way (apart from later issuing a petition to review the officer's decision in the Election Court).[92] In the future, pressure is bound to grow for electronic vote counting to replace the present manual method. Electronic counting of votes is already used in some elections in other countries, including Germany, Portugal and in 31 states of the USA. Computers are also used in some European countries, including Denmark and Spain, for calculating electoral results under their schemes of proportional representation. There are obvious administrative advantages in using computers. The clerks would be relieved of what some might regard as a boring and tedious job. In the words of Robert Maclennan MP, for example, 'It might cost a bit to install but once installed it would almost certainly be cheaper and more efficient.'[93] Computer experts, however, disagree on the issue of efficiency. The Home Affairs Committee of the House of Commons has been inquiring into this issue, and has recommended that trials of electronic counting should be held.[94] (The Committee was also interested in the idea of electors voting not by crosses on a ballot paper, but by pressing an electronic button in the polling station.) An experiment with electronic counting took place on a local referendum held in Bognor Regis, West Sussex, where the first results were announced eight minutes after the ballot boxes were delivered to the location for the count. It is certainly likely to be true that in general machines will count more accurately and serve to eliminate human error. But on the other hand, even if only very rarely, there will be exceptional situations where a computer behaves in a rogue fashion for no apparently explicable reason (attributable perhaps to some undetected new computer virus or theoretically, even because of a fluke beam of ultra-violet light striking the system). The American aphorism, 'if it ain't broke, don't fix it', should be applied to our method of counting votes. Existing arrangements work extremely well, and such an important matter as the outcome of our democratic elections should be left in human hands. However, as with most things, it is probable that the interests of administrative convenience will prevail, and that electronic counting will be introduced in the not too distant future.

At every general election, there will be a very close result in some of the constituencies, and in such cases a recount is very likely to take place, involving all the ballot papers being counted for a second time. A candidate or election agent, if he or she was present when the counting was completed, is entitled to require the returning officer to perform a recount, and even a second or third recount, unless in the opinion of the returning officer the request is unreasonable.[95] In the extraordinary event of there being an equal number of votes cast for two candidates, then the Representation of the People Act 1983 provides that the returning officer shall decide the result 'by lot'.[96] No particular method of lottery is prescribed, so the returning officer could choose to determine the political fortunes of the candidates and constituency simply by tossing a coin in the air.

THE SECRECY OF THE BALLOT

One of the fundamental assumptions about democracy today is that the citizen has the right to vote by way of a secret ballot. Great importance has been attached to this principle in Britain, largely for historical reasons. In the eighteenth and nineteenth centuries electoral bribery and intimidation were rife. This is a feature of British electoral history, incidentally, which explains the large number of books written about election law in the nineteenth century. The demand for these books arose because of the huge number of court actions involving disputed elections, ballot rigging and corruption. (By contrast, only one new book on election law has been written in Britain since 1945[97] – apart from *Parker* and *Schofield* which are essentially manuals written for electoral administrators.) One of the first books written by Herbert Asquith in 1884, as a barrister before entering politics and later becoming Prime Minister between 1906–15, was *An Election Guide*, which provided an analysis of the proper conduct of elections. The problem of bribery was dealt with by Parliament in a series of statutes designed to circumvent and punish offenders, notably the Corrupt Practices Prevention Act 1854 and, most successfully, the Parliamentary Elections (Corrupt and Illegal Practices) Act 1883.

The essential component in the process of cleaning up electoral corruption and intimidation, however, was put into place by the Parliamentary and Municipal Elections Act 1872, commonly known as 'The Ballot Act'. Previously, voting had taken place by way of a public show of hands or else a public ballot. The old procedures for parliamentary voting were once memorably recalled by Lord Denning in the following terms:[98]

> The common law method of election was by show of hands. But if a poll was demanded, the election was by poll. . . A poll was taken in this way: the returning officer or his clerk had a book in which he kept a record of the votes cast. Each voter went up to the clerk, gave his name, and stated his qualification. The clerk wrote down his name. The voter stated the candidate for whom he voted. The poll clerk recorded his vote. . . Such was the method of election at common law. It was open. Not by secret ballot. Being open, it was disgraced by abuses of every kind, especially at parliamentary elections. Bribery, corruption, treating, personation were rampant.

The Ballot Act did away with the traditional, open method of voting, and instead introduced the modern system whereby no one except the voting citizen him or herself need know how he or she in fact voted. As a direct and immediate result, intimidation and fear of reprisals were radically undermined. The historic principle declared in the Ballot Act 1872 (now no longer in force but re-enacted in greater procedural detail in the Representation of the People Act 1983) was as follows:

> In the case of a poll at an election the votes shall be given by ballot. The ballot of each voter shall consist of a paper . . . showing the names and

descriptions of the candidates. . . At the time of voting, the ballot paper shall be marked on both sides with an official mark, and delivered to the voter within the polling station . . . and the voter having secretly marked his vote on the paper, and folded it up so as to conceal his vote, shall place it in a closed box in the presence of the officer presiding at the polling station after having shown to him the official mark at the back.

After the close of the poll the ballot boxes shall be sealed up, so as to prevent the introduction of additional ballot papers, and shall be taken charge of by the returning officer, and that officer shall, in the presence of such agents, if any, of the candidates as may be in attendance, open the ballot boxes, and ascertain the result of the poll by counting the votes given to each candidate.

Other European countries experienced similar problems of corruption and intimidation in earlier voting practices, and have in modern times universally incorporated the principle of a secret ballot into their constitutional law. Thus Article 2 of the French Constitution (the 1958 Fifth French Republic) proclaims that voting 'shall always be universal, equal and secret'. Article 38 of the German Constitution provides for 'general, direct, free, equal and secret elections.' Under international law, the United Kingdom, along with other Council of Europe states, is signatory to the First Protocol of the European Convention on Human Rights which upholds the principle of 'free elections at reasonable intervals by secret ballot'.

British regulations concerning the secrecy of the ballot are now to be found in the Representation of the People Act 1983. The Act specifies that 'votes at the poll shall be given by ballot',[99] and lays down a wide range of stipulations for maintaining the secrecy of how electors have voted. Returning officers are obliged to ensure that every person attending the polling booth (apart from voters and the constable on duty) is to be handed a written copy of the appropriate sections of the Act so as to ensure they are aware of their obligations of secrecy.[100] (An earlier rule, repealed in 1987, additionally required all officials to swear declarations of secrecy.) The 1983 Act states as a general principle that all officials and other persons allowed to attend the polling station 'shall maintain and aid in maintaining the secrecy of voting', and then proceeds to lay down detailed requirements. Thus under section 66 (3),

No person shall –
(a) interfere with or attempt to interfere with a voter when recording his vote;
(b) otherwise obtain or attempt to obtain in a polling station information as to the candidate for whom a voter in that station is about to vote or has voted;

(c) communicate at any time to any person any information obtained in a polling station as to the candidate for whom a voter in that station is about to vote or has voted, or as to the number on the back of the ballot paper given to a voter at that station;

(d) directly or indirectly induce a voter to display his ballot paper after he has marked it so as to make known to any person the name of the candidate for whom he has or has not voted.

There are strict rules governing who is and who is not allowed to be present inside the polling station, designed to avoid voters feeling that they are being watched. Presiding officers have a duty to regulate the number of voters who are admitted to the polling station at one time, and to exclude all other people except the candidates and their election agents, one polling agent per candidate appointed to attend the polling station, the official clerks appointed to attend, constables on duty, and companions of blind voters.[101] Several other rules in the Act serve to promote a high standard of secrecy, even detailing the procedures to be adopted on how the ballot boxes are to be sealed up. The rigour of the theory behind the secret ballot in British contemporary law has been taken so far (perhaps excessively so) that now even if a citizen wishes to identify himself and write his name or initials on his ballot paper, the effect of this will be to invalidate his vote altogether.[102]

This great stress in the 1983 Act of Parliament on the secrecy of the ballot stands at some odds with the obvious flaw in the modern British practice of ballot voting. Casting one's vote in the polling booth in circumstances of privacy is to be sharply distinguished from the equally important matter of maintaining the secrecy of how each citizen actually voted. In this second respect, there is not and never has been a secret ballot in Britain, because the way in which individual citizens vote can be traced from each ballot paper used. The ballot paper given to the citizen who is voting contains a serial number, which is also printed on the counterfoil retained by electoral officials. Before a ballot paper is handed to the citizen, he is asked for his name and address (or, preferably, asked to show the clerk his official poll card which shows his name, address and electoral registration number on it). The polling clerk then traces the person in the copy of the electoral register that he has on the table in front of him, and ticks the voter's name off the list. The clerk tears one of the ballot papers out of the book of papers printed for the purpose, hands it to the voter and directs him or her to the private booth. And then the clerk writes the electoral registration number of the voter on the counterfoil to the ballot paper just issued.

This means that after the election, documentary information is in existence which will disclose who voted for which particular party in the constituency. The count by the returning officer's officials leaves all votes for each candidate in separate bundles, which are then placed in paper sacks with special labels and seals supplied by Her Majesty's Stationery Office and forwarded to the Clerk of the Crown in London. It is possible for the serial numbers of these ballot papers to be matched against those retained on the counterfoil stubs which disclose the electoral registration number – and therefore also the name and address of citizens and how they voted – which are similarly forwarded to the Clerk of the Crown in London.[103] Copies of electoral registers are already available on computer disk, and in the future computerised counting of ballot papers by means of electronic vote-counting machines is likely to replace manual counting.[104] If computers now in existence are able to read numbers on stacks of papers, then the technology for speedy cross-referencing in the making of such political inquiries is already with us. It seems that computerised matching and print-outs of entire lists of voters for each party is now perfectly possible. It may or may not be far-fetched to conjecture that at some point in the future an oppressive government might surreptitiously wish to find out the name and address of all 'dissidents' who voted against them at a general election, but if so the bundles of ballot papers and counterfoil stubs retained by the Clerk of the Crown are available for analysis to produce the necessary information. The law, of course, prohibits such inquiries, but compliance with and enforcement of the law ultimately depends upon the government itself.

The current legal regulation against breaches of secrecy on how any particular citizen has cast his or her vote is contained in the Representation of the People Act 1983. First, there are the general obligations upon all people attending polling stations not to disclose any personal details about voters. Section 66 provides that:

(1) The following persons –
(a)   every returning officer and every presiding officer or clerk attending at a polling station,
(b)   every candidate or election agent or polling agent so attending, shall maintain and aid in maintaining the secrecy of voting and shall not, except for some purpose authorised by law, communicate to any person before the poll is closed any information as to –
(i)   the name of any elector or proxy for an elector who has or has not applied for a ballot paper or voted at a polling station;
(ii)   the number on the register of electors of any elector who, or whose proxy, has or has not applied for a ballot paper or voted at a polling station; or
(iii)   the official mark.
(2) Every person attending at the counting of the votes shall maintain and aid in maintaining the secrecy of voting and shall not –

(a) ascertain or attempt to ascertain at the counting of the votes the number on the back of any ballot paper;

(b) communicate any information obtained at the counting of the votes as to the candidate for whom any vote is given on any particular ballot paper.

Second, the Act provides for the protection of the documentary information whereby it might be discovered how individual electors cast their votes. Following the count and the declaration of the result, returning officers are under a legal obligation to forward to the Clerk of the Crown all documents relating to the election, notably the packets of ballot papers, the packets of counterfoils, and the packets containing marked copies of registers.[105] The Clerk of the Crown is then directed in law to retain these documents for the period of one year, and then 'shall cause them to be destroyed'.[106] The Act lays down the lawful circumstances in which access may be granted to the election documents, which is confined to situations where an order is made by the House of Commons or by a court of law in proceedings such as prosecutions for election offences. The Act stipulates that 'in making and carrying into effect an order for the opening of a packet of counterfoils or for the inspection of counted ballot papers, care shall be taken that the way in which the vote of any particular elector has been given shall not be disclosed until it has been proved – (i) that his vote was given; and (ii) that the vote has been declared by a competent court to be invalid'. The vital general principle on disclosure is expressed in terms that, subject to such orders of the House of Commons or court of law, 'No person shall be allowed to inspect any . . . counted ballot papers in the possession of the Clerk of the Crown or to open any sealed packets of counterfoils.'[107]

The ostensible argument for putting the voter's electoral registration number on the counterfoils of ballot papers is said to be that it facilitates investigations into alleged electoral offences, such as multiple voting and impersonation, so as to decide whether a fresh election needs to be ordered by the Election Court. However, vote-tracing hardly helps in the detection and prevention of any offence in itself, for there is no way that the identity of the impersonator can be discovered from the ballot paper. Investigations of such electoral fraud, involving voters finding out when they arrive at the polling station that their name has already been ticked off the electoral register by the clerk, can rely upon the evidence of the polling clerk that a ballot paper has indeed already been handed to some impersonator – tracing the ballot paper itself is not essential. Where impersonation occurs, it would only be if the number of such instances was very large, and the margin of victory by the winning candidate very small, that a fresh election would be necessary. In most constituencies it would require thousands of electoral impersonations to change the result, whereas the number of allegations of voter impersonation in Britain is negligible,[108] and no fresh election has been ordered at any time in the twentieth century.

The case for recording voters' registration numbers on the ballot counterfoils is, therefore, a weak one, and cannot outweigh a growing public concern at the risk to the secrecy of the ballot. The regulations contained in the Representation of the People Act limiting the legal circumstances in which the information may be retrieved may be sufficient as rules themselves, but compliance with the rules raises more complex questions and while the information allowing the discovery of how individual citizens voted continues to be stored, the potential for abuse remains. The practice of writing voters' electoral registration numbers, and therefore noting their personal identity, on the counterfoils of ballot papers should be abolished by law. If combating the potential for voter impersonation needs to be strengthened, two measures would considerably improve current practice. First, voters throughout the United Kingdom might be required to produce identification to the polling clerk (being one of a list of specified documents: for example, passport, birth or marriage certificate, driving licence or National Health Service card) before being ticked off on the electoral register and given a ballot paper.[109] Second, by making citizens eligible to vote in only one constituency, being (as suggested earlier)[110] their main place of residence, the potential for dual or multiple registration and therefore for voting more than once would be much reduced.

Some people, however, would argue that it is weak of citizens – or even wrong in principle – to want to vote by way of a secret ballot. John Stuart Mill was opposed to the secret ballot and believed the voter has a duty to participate in the political process by proclaiming what he or she believes to be right. In other words, voting is essentially a public act. In his *Considerations on Representative Government,* Mill wrote,[111]

> In any political election ... the voter is under an absolute moral obligation to consider the interest of the public, not his private advantage, and give his vote to the best of his judgement, exactly as he would be bound to do if he were the sole voter, and the election depended upon him alone. This being admitted, it is at least a *prima facie* consequence that the duty of voting, like any other public duty, should be performed under the eye and criticism of the public; every one of whom has not only an interest in its performance, but a good title to consider himself wronged if it is performed otherwise than honestly and carefully.

In the case of the ordinary voter, very often he or she will indeed publicise his or her voting intentions by way of party posters or candidate stickers facing out of the windows of his or her home, and politically active citizens will already be participating in their party meetings and canvassing other voters. But a great many people less involved in political discourse will prefer to make up their minds quietly, in their own time, by absorbing what information they receive from the media and parties, and by entering into discussions with close friends and relatives. In Britain especially, as with its religious culture, the greatest tendency is for individuals to want to keep their conscience and moral beliefs a relatively private affair. Neither should the potential for intimidation or reprisals be forgotten, though the electoral corruption of the nineteenth century is thankfully a long way behind us. A public ballot opens up the possibility of people in authority over the voter, for example at work, disapproving of how he or she casts his or her vote, and then being able to exercise such discretionary power over that person whose political judgement is disapproved of in ways such as being discriminated against upon grounds of political opinion at job interviews, or if already at work, then not being chosen for promotion, or being selected for dismissal in redundancy situations.

In the theory of elections generally, a distinction must be made between voters and the people on the one hand, and the elected representatives on the other. It is fundamental that the ordinary citizen is entitled to the secrecy of how he or she votes; but, by contrast, the political representative conforms to Mill's obligation to act and vote in public in the performance of his or her political duties. Members of every Parliament in the EU exercise their voting rights over parliamentary motions or legislation in public, and usually (as in Britain) in person. Arguably, too, British MPs when voting for a new party leader should record their votes in public. Conservative MPs, when voting in their leadership contest in November 1990 that led to Margaret Thatcher's resignation as Prime Minister and John Major being selected in preference to Michael Heseltine or Douglas Hurd, proceeded by a method of secret ballot, when many believed that they should have been recording their votes in public for their local constituency parties and parliamentary colleagues to see.

PROPOSAL FOR COMPULSORY VOTING

Should voting be made compulsory in the United Kingdom? This would be consistent with the legal compulsion in the first place to register one's name and address as a voter at the local Town Hall. Several countries abroad have introduced compulsory voting, including Australia, Belgium, Greece, Luxemburg and Italy, and the obvious result is a far higher turnout of the electorate (even if 100 per cent is never, in practice, attainable), and therefore a more comprehensive expression of public opinion at the polls. The turnout of electors at general elections since 1945 has been as shown in the following table:[112]

Electoral turnout in General Elections, 1945–92 (per cent)

1945	72.8
1950	83.9
1951	82.6
1955	76.8
1959	78.7
1964	77.1
1966	75.8
1970	72.0
1974 (Feb.)	78.8
1974 (Oct.)	72.8
1979	76.0
1983	72.7
1987	75.3
1992	77.7

Table 3.4

A MORI public opinion poll, commissioned by the Rowntree Reform Trust and published in 1991, rather surprisingly disclosed that a majority of people in the United Kingdom in fact favour compulsory voting. The precise response was 49 per cent in favour, 42 per cent against, and 9 per cent undecided.[113] However, this proposal has never received any substantial degree of support in British politics. It was one of the issues raised for inquiry by the Home Affairs Select Committee examination of the Representation of the People Acts in 1982–3, but was not dealt with in any depth in its discussions, and was not an issue mentioned in its final report. The general, traditional view on compulsory voting is, first, that it is an infringement of civil liberty: that politics is essentially a voluntary exercise (hence also the lack of public regulation and provision for political parties), and people should be left alone to decide for themselves how and whether to vote. In other words, a great many British people instinctively feel that there is something rather totalitarian about being forced to vote. Many also feel that it is no bad thing if the country as a whole is relatively depoliticised, and this is simply reflected in a number of citizens not being sufficiently interested in turning up at the polling station to vote on election day. Second, it is often argued that compulsory voting is unnecessary in Britain and as a principle of election law tends to be resorted to only in states with a weak democratic culture or a fragile national identity. Third, it is sometimes said that compulsory voting produces a highly undesirable 'donkey vote'. This was an expression used by the Liberal Party in giving evidence to the Home Affairs Select Committee in 1982,[114] presumably meaning that compulsory voting would mean hordes of politically mindless voters being dragged along to the polling booth. A final reservation has been the alleged impracticality of enforcing such an obligation. This is a factor that has especially troubled those who might be expected to enforce it. A memorandum by Rochdale Borough Council to the Select Committee mentioned that it would result in tens of thousands of prosecutions and clutter up the courts, and in the view of the Association of District Councils, there would be 'severe enforcement problems, and there would be the problems created by electors who could not vote on account of sickness'.[115]

These arguments when looked at closely are rather weak. There are very few practical problems attached to compulsory voting in Australia. Easier voting arrangements, such as greater use of postal voting or (as in Australia) centres in each constituency where voters from other constituencies might vote, would alleviate any hardship on voters with physical disabilities or with travel commitments, and for the ordinary voter a walk to the local ballot station is hardly a taxing exercise. The 'donkey vote' argument is highly suspect if it assumes that people not voting are likely to be any weaker in their mental faculties than people who do vote. Neither is any draconian enforcement of compulsory voting more likely than the prosecutions presently in force for householders failing to complete and return the annual forms sent out each year by the electoral registration officer, for which there were just three prosecutions in 1979, one in 1980, and four in 1981.

The real issue is a constitutional one, and whether it is a citizen's duty, as well as a right, to vote. It seems to me that there is unquestionably a moral obligation to cast one's vote, and that the arguments of principle against such a duty are no more democratic than those than can be mustered by an anarchist. The 'voluntary' argument, which relies upon a moral right not to vote, or 'optional democracy' as it might be called, is essentially anti-social in nature. There are also good reasons to suppose that a duty to vote would tend towards a better informed electorate as a whole. Certainly, compulsory voting would transform the work of party workers and canvassers away from 'getting out the vote' (in other words, persuading people to go to the polling station) and allow them to concentrate more on talking with voters about the issues and policies that are represented by their party. At present, local party electioneering concentrates almost entirely on canvassers identifying where their party's support is the greatest, so that their colleagues acting as tellers waiting outside ballot stations on polling day can try to calculate which of their supporters have voted, and then instruct other party colleagues to call at non-voters' homes to try to persuade them to vote. There is also some reason to suppose that if people know they have to vote, they are more diligent in taking the trouble to find out more about what the parties and candidates stand for and what their policies are. Generally, therefore, compulsory voting is likely to lead to more discussion and understanding of what elections are all about.

Whether or not the moral duty to vote should be crystallised into law confronts traditional British feelings about encroaching upon a citizen's 'right to be left alone'. Legislation that introduced a legal duty upon all our citizens to vote might allow for people who consciously wished to cast no vote, by providing that all ballot papers should contain a box in addition to the names of the candidates against which the voter could signify an abstention. And if general election day was made a national public holiday or else held on a Sunday, as is the case in many other countries such as in France and Germany, then there could be no reason whatsoever why those who now possess the fundamental political right to vote should not equally be called upon to express their opinion on whom should represent them in government and Parliament over the following four years. This question of compulsory voting, then, raises issues which are of great symbolic and practical political importance. It is a proposal which the next Speaker's Conference on Election Law should consider far more seriously than it has in the past.

4 Parliamentary Constituencies

Determining the precise boundaries of parliamentary constituencies across the United Kingdom, and therefore the number of voters in each, is a matter of very great importance in electoral affairs. A healthy parliamentary democracy must aspire in its elections not only to 'one person, one vote', but also to the representative principle of 'one vote, one value'. If, as a result of constant shifts in population, one constituency comes to contain 101 492 voters, whereas another one has only 42 845, then the combined political representation of these constituencies is contradicting a very basic tenet of electoral equality. These numbers were in fact those in the constituencies of the Isle of Wight and in Surbiton respectively at the time of the 1992 general election. Such wide divergences between the sizes of the electorates in different constituencies across the United Kingdom have been far from uncommon at recent general elections (see the table on pages 114–15).

It is the responsibility of the Boundary Commissions to supervise and keep up to date the electoral parity and boundaries of parliamentary constituencies. Their reviews, and the redistribution of parliamentary seats that they recommend, are always a political minefield. For each set of changes made in the boundary lines dividing the country up into parliamentary constituencies will favour one political party's electoral prospects of winning or losing the next general election over the others. It is generally reckoned that every boundary review over the period since the Second World War has favoured the Conservative Party, principally because population shifts tend to be away from the urban centres where Labour support is traditionally strongest, and towards growing suburban areas which possess a marked propensity for Conservatism. In total, a redistribution of parliamentary seats in the United Kingdom has taken place on only eight occasions in our history, and there is to be one in 1995. Each episode in the past has aroused fierce political controversy, accompanied by claims of political chicanery and gerrymandering by the opposition parties in the House of Commons against the party which is in government.

CONSTITUENCIES IN THE UNITED KINGDOM

The law controlling the number of constituencies, and therefore the size of the membership of the House of Commons, is now contained in the Parliamentary Constituencies Act 1986. The main features of the relevant

113

Parliamentary constituencies with the largest and smallest electorates at the 1992 General Election

	Constituency	Electors	Constituency	Electors
	Largest number of Parliamentary electors		**Smallest number of Parliamentary electors**	
United Kingdom	Isle of Wight	101 492	Western Isles	23 015
	Huntingdon	94 077	Caithness and Sutherland	31 173
	East Hampshire	93 393	Orkney and Shetland	31 837
	Eastleigh	92 851	Meirionnydd Nant Conwy	32 779
	The Wrekin	92 037	Glasgow, Provan	36 986
	East Berkshire	91 504	Tweeddale, Ettrick and Lauderdale	39 907
	Swindon	91 002	Glasgow, Garscadden	41 675
	Devizes	90 882	Montgomery	41 842
	Cirencester and Tewkesbury	89 320	Kensington	42 327
	Peterborough	88 702	Chelsea	42 549
	Westbury	88 417	Surbiton	42 845
	Ryedale	88 120	Roxburgh and Berwickshire	44 001
	Wokingham	87 815	Glasgow, Cathcart	45 149
	Dudley West	87 633	Edinburgh East	46 157
	North Colchester	87 556	Glasgow, Govan	46 199
	South Colchester and Maldon	87 456	Glasgow, Springburn	46 216
	North Wiltshire	86 922	Glasgow, Pollok	46 655
	South Suffolk	86 034	Newham North West	46 855
	Bridlington	85 930	Paisley North	46 867
	South West Cambridgeshire	85 645	Caernarfon	46 977
England	Isle of Wight	101 492	Kensington	42 327
	Huntingdon	94 077	Chelsea	42 549

	Constituency	Electorate	Constituency	Electorate
	East Hampshire	93 393	Surbiton	42 845
	Eastleigh	92 851	Newham North West	46 855
	The Wrekin	92 037	Hammersmith	47 468
	East Berkshire	91 504	Greenwich	48 225
	Swindon	91 002	Hendon South	48 816
	Devizes	90 882	Coventry South East	49 249
	Cirencester and Tewkesbury	89 320	Knowsley North	49 373
	Peterborough	88 702	Walthamstow	49 603
Wales	Pembroke	74 077	Meirionnydd Nant Conwy	32 779
	Carmarthen	69 711	Montgomery	41 842
	Clwyd North West	68 145	Caernarfon	46 977
	Vale of Glamorgan	67 558	Cynon Valley	50 264
	Delyn	67 386	Islwyn	51 502
Scotland	Gordon	81 097	Western Isles	23 015
	Inverness, Nairn and Lochaber	70 164	Caithness and Sutherland	31 173
	East Lothian	67 588	Orkney and Shetland	31 837
	Kincardine and Deeside	67 216	Glasgow, Provan	36 986
	Ayr	66 284	Tweeddale, Ettrick and Lauderdale	39 907
Northern Ireland	South Down	77 371	Belfast South	52 556
	East Londonderry	77 371	Belfast East	53 375
	Foyle	75 970	Belfast West	55 280
	Lagan Valley	73 688	Belfast North	55 587
	Fermanagh and South Tyrone	71 472	East Antrim	63 739

Table 4.1[1]

provisions are first, that they allow for some overall fluctuation in the number of constituencies, rather than fix a precise figure; and second, that different rules apply for the regions of England, Scotland, Wales and Northern Ireland. Across Great Britain (England, Scotland and Wales together), the Act provides that the number of constituencies 'shall not be substantially greater or less than 613'. It then prescribes minimum numbers for Scotland and Wales respectively: 'the number of constituencies in Scotland shall not be less than 71'; and 'the number of constituencies in Wales shall not be less than 35'. Finally, in Northern Ireland the number of constituencies 'shall not be greater than 18 or less than 16, and shall be 17 unless it appears to the Boundary Commission for Northern Ireland that Northern Ireland should for the time being be divided into 16 or (as the case may be) into 18 constituencies'.

So there is no minimum number for English constituencies, whereas there is for each of the other regions of the United Kingdom. This operates somewhat to the disadvantage of the English electorate in terms of its representation in the House of Commons, and the impact in practice has been that England receives fewer parliamentary seats in terms of numbers of voters than do the other regions. The average number of voters per constituency at the time of the last Boundary Commission report were 54 642 voters in Scotland, 56 273 voters in Wales, 62 697 in Northern Ireland, and 68 010 voters in England. The case for removing this disparity was put by Sir John Wheeler MP, the former chairman of the Home Affairs Select Committee, in a House of Commons debate on the subject in 1992, as follows:[2]

I contend that it is inconsistent with the existence of the Union of the United Kingdom and our system of parliamentary democracy that the votes of electors in two of the constituent parts should, as a matter of course, carry greater weight than those of the electors in the remaining parts – England and Northern Ireland. That is the position under existing law and, as far as I can judge, that disparity is likely to continue. Most people in the different parts of the United Kingdom are of mixed descent and I can see no validity for such disparities to continue.

Those differences cannot be justified by geographical considerations. As a matter of common sense, relatively isolated areas, such as Orkney, the Shetlands and the Western Isles, can be overrepresented, but the exception cannot apply, in this age of modern communications, to the whole of Wales and Scotland. There is no moral justification why a vote cast in a Welsh constituency should be worth more than one cast in England or Northern Ireland or why a vote cast in Glasgow should be worth more than one cast in Manchester.

The number of parliamentary constituencies has steadily grown this century from 615 in 1918, to 625 in 1950, 630 in 1955, 635 in 1974, and 650 since 1983. At the time of writing there are 651 constituencies, following the division of Milton Keynes in 1990. This cumulative increase in the number of seats should not be allowed to go on, above all because there must be a limit to the number of MPs who can belong to and participate in the proceedings of the House of Commons. The Commons Home Affairs Select Committee recommended in 1987 that the then existing number of 650 should be 'stabilised' and the 1986 Act amended so that maximum figures were imposed for the purposes of future boundary changes.[3] Their view was that England should be allocated 'not substantially more than 523', Scotland 'not substantially more than 72', Wales 'not substantially more than 38', and Northern Ireland 'not substantially more than 18'. These rules would be an improvement on the existing written provisions, but they allow for a total figure that is still too high and far exceeds most legislatures in the Western world. For example, in the USA there are 435 seats, and in France 577. An excessive number of MPs diminishes the importance of the individual Westminster politician, and reduces the impact of general debates in the House when there are so many participants who may wish to speak, and from whom the Speaker has to make a very restricted choice in the time available. Calls for a reduction in the number of MPs and parliamentary constituencies have recently come from the Institute for Public Policy Research,[4] the Liberal Democrats,[5] and even some items of backbench draft legislation in the Commons itself. A Representation of the People (Amendment) Bill introduced by the MP Robert Rhodes James in 1986 wished to enact that 'there shall not be more than 500 constituencies in the United Kingdom as a whole',[6] and in March 1991 Sir Peter Emery presented a Private Member's motion in the Commons that the number of constituencies be reduced by 100.[7] Clearly, a reduction in numbers means effectively some redundancies among MPs, many of whom therefore can be expected not to welcome such proposals. None the less, it would be an improvement if an Act of Parliament was passed providing that, 'The House of Commons shall be composed of not more than 525, and not less than 475, members.' The Parliamentary Constituencies Act 1986 should be amended accordingly to reflect these maximum and minimum numbers of constituencies, allowing constituency reviews a limited but perfectly sufficient discretion for fluctuation within a margin of fifty seats across the United Kingdom.

An essential characteristic of the British electoral system is that each parliamentary constituency returns a single MP. This rule is contained in section 1 of the Parliamentary Constituencies Act 1986. It is often forgotten today that two- or multi-member constituencies were, in fact, common in the United Kingdom until relatively recently.[8] Fifteen such constituencies still existed at the time of the 1945 general election, being Blackburn (one of whose two Labour MPs returned was Barbara Castle, a leading Cabinet minister in the 1960s), City of London, Brighton, Bolton, Derby, Norwich,

Oldham, Preston, Antrim, Down, Fermanagh, Southampton, Stockport, Sunderland and Dundee. Throughout the country's history up to the 1885 Representation of the People Act, single-member constituencies had been very much the exception, with two-member constituencies being normal. In them, electors cast two votes and the two candidates who came first and second by simple majority voting were returned to the House of Commons. In this way it might be said that Britain's earlier voting practices promoted a greater degree of proportional representation than does the electoral system today.

THE BOUNDARY COMMISSIONS

A permanent machinery exists for the purpose of the continuous review of the distribution of seats at parliamentary elections. This was first established in the 1940s, by the House of Commons (Redistribution of Seats) Acts 1944 and 1949, and with later amendments is now consolidated in the Parliamentary Constituencies Act 1986. Four Boundary Commissions were created, one each for England, Scotland, Wales and Northern Ireland, and since they came into existence they have jointly undertaken three general reviews and produced three reports, all of which resulted in a substantial redrawing of constituencies and redistribution of parliamentary seats. These were in 1955, 1974, and – most radical of all – in 1983. Before this permanent statutory machinery was set in place, there were five occasions when a redistribution of seats took place: 1832, 1867, 1885, 1918 and 1948, and each was the product of an *ad hoc* inquiry being set up by the Prime Minister or Home Secretary, and the boundary changes being put into effect legally by primary legislation. The present system is that the Boundary Commissions' recommendations, together with any modifications by the Home Secretary, are presented to Parliament in the form of draft Orders in Council which then require the approval of both the Commons and the Lords.

The Boundary Commissions undertake their general reviews of the distribution of seats once every eight to twelve years. This, in fact, is a new, shorter time limit introduced by the Conservative government in the Boundary Commission Act 1992. The Act is also retrospective in that it specifies a precise date, 31 December 1994, for the submission of the next recommendations of the Commissions. This will ensure that the forthcoming boundary changes, which most psephologists estimate will lose the Labour Party around twenty parliamentary seats, will be made in time for the next general election.[9] This new eight-to-twelve-year period in which reviews must be conducted replaces the earlier statutory interval of ten to fifteen years that applied from 1958 to 1992. There had been a far shorter period of three to five years laid down in the 1949 Act, which required the

Boundary Commissions essentially to effect changes within the lifetime of each Parliament, and meant that an MP and his local party might be organising and fighting an election campaign in a changed constituency at every general election. Once the political implications of this were fully realised in 1955, with many sitting MPs representing different constituencies at both the 1950 and 1955 general elections, and some losing their seats as a result of a changed local electorate making it a marginal instead of a safe electoral prospect, there was strong all-party criticism that frequent boundary changes were disruptive and caused serious problems for constituency affairs. As a consequence the 1958 Act tripled the duration in which the redistributions were to take place. Although party leaders believe their party as a whole may benefit from new boundary changes, individual MPs regard the process with great trepidation. As one MP said during the debates on the 1983 changes, at which only sixty-six constituencies were left unaltered:[10]

Boundary changes always cause enormous heartache for Members of Parliament and constituents. Not only do Members of Parliament who have represented a constituency for a long time move areas and lose their political supporters, they lose constituents who may have become personal friends. Moreover, there are battles for nomination between members of the same party. There can be enormous difficulties when sitting Members from the same party have an equal claim to a new constituency. Someone once said that civil war is the nastiest of all wars as it sets brother against brother. The same applies to politics. Some of the squabbles have caused enormous bitterness. I speak with some feeling because I was involved in that type of battle during the previous boundary changes. That was the nastiest period of my political life. Nevertheless, it gave me an insight into the types of problems that Hon. Members on both sides of the House now face over the English Boundary Commission's report.

In addition to their general reviews, each Boundary Commission may also from time to time submit to the Home Secretary a special report with respect to any particular constituency or constituencies into which they recommend that an area should be divided. This became an urgent necessity in 1990 in the case of Milton Keynes, for example, whose constituency population had expanded rapidly to 109 839, and was divided into Milton Keynes North East and Milton Keynes South West.

The timing of the Boundary Commissions' general reviews is of immense political significance. Not only are the careers of individual MPs at stake, but constituency changes are always likely to favour the electoral prospects of one party over another, and therefore a report of the Commission and its implementation can play a decisive role in the winning or losing of a general election. The political manoeuvres that have taken place upon virtually every occasion by the political party in government either to speed up or to delay the work of the Boundary Commissions ready for an election have become a degrading political fact of life. It is highly unsatisfactory that uncertainty should be allowed to linger over the timing of the reports of the Commissions. Consideration is given later in this chapter, under a general programme for the reform of constituency review, to replacing the provisions on variable timing in the 1992 Boundary Commissions Act by a prescribed fixed interval of twelve years between each redistribution of parliamentary seats.

The commissioners

Each of the four Boundary Commissions consists of a chairman, a deputy chairman and two other members. The chairman is *ex officio* the Speaker of the House of Commons.[11] However, in practice the Speaker never participates in the Commissions' proceedings. During his term of office as Home Secretary, Kenneth Clarke referred to the present incumbent Betty Boothroyd as follows: 'Madam Speaker, like her predecessors in office, is indeed chairman of the Commissions and, like her predecessors, she will take no active part in their work.'[12] The point of the Act prescribing the Speaker as a member of the Commissions and thereby giving him or her nominal overall supervision, and the right to chair proceedings if he or she ever believed it to be necessary, is to consecrate an official link with the House of Commons consistent with the traditional constitutional principle that the House should have ultimate control over its own composition. The Speaker also encapsulates the political impartiality which is essential to the task of constituency review,[13] and it is the role of the Speaker to represent the interests of all members in the House. However, for reasons which are explained later,[14] the nominal presence of the Speaker on the Commissions has come to detract rather than to promote parliamentary control over constituency review. For the same ostensible reason of political neutrality and independence, a member of the judiciary is selected to serve as deputy chairman. In the case of the English Commission and the Welsh Commission, two separate High Court judges are appointed by the Lord Chancellor; for the Scottish Commission a Court of Session judge is appointed by the Lord President; and for the Northern Ireland Commission, a judge of the High Court of Northern Ireland is appointed by the Lord Chief Justice of Northern Ireland. By virtue of the Speaker's actual non-participation, then, the judge who is appointed deputy chairman is the most important figure in the working of the Boundary Commissions. When presenting the Boundary Commission Bill in 1992, the Home Secretary, Kenneth Clarke, described the Commission in glorious terms: 'I have never heard it seriously suggested that the work of the Boundary Commissions is anything other than impartial. Our system must be the envy of many of the major democracies of the Western world. It is implemented by a High Court judge and I do not think that there can be any claim of partiality.'[15] It is interesting to contrast in juxtaposition the view of a former Labour Home Secretary, Merlyn Rees, who during his tenure of office had cause to remove a judge from the Boundary Commission, that, 'The House [of Commons] should examine the way that redistribution is handled in other countries. We should not pat our backs and clap ourselves to death for being impartial.'[16]

The two other commissioners appointed will be people not involved in party politics, and under the terms of the House of Commons Disqualification Act 1975 cannot be MPs.[17] Although no legal qualification is necessary, it is regular practice for another judge or else an eminent barrister or solicitor to be selected for the job. Their selection will be made by government ministers, generally the Home Secretary and Environment Secretary appointing one each; usually after consultation with the other political parties, more recently by way of a letter with the suggested name being circulated to the parties inviting their comments.[18] The personnel of the Boundary Commission for England that reported in 1983, apart from the Speaker, comprised Sir Raymond Walton as deputy chairman, Mr Harold Marnham QC (until 14 December 1976), Mr John Muir Drinkwater QC (from 8 July 1977 to 31 December 1979), Judge John Newey QC (from 21 February 1980), and Mr William Willis Ruff (a solicitor). Every single member was, therefore, a lawyer. Neither the chairman nor deputy chairman is paid for this work: the Speaker receives no extra salary, and nor does the judge appointed by the Lord Chancellor, who instead will simply release the judge from his Court duties as necessary. The terms of service of the two other ordinary commissioners are not standardised or protected in the 1986 Act, so there is no security of tenure as such and no prescribed duration of service. The Act simply says that the commissioner 'shall hold his appointment for such term and on such conditions as may be determined before his appointment by the person appointing him'.[19] Previously, no salary was payable, but the Boundary Commissions Act 1992 now provides that the two ordinary commissioners may be paid at a level determined by the minister with the approval of the Treasury.[20]

The 1986 Parliamentary Constituencies Act gives the Home Secretary the power, exercisable at the request of the Commission, to appoint any number of assistant commissioners 'to inquire into, and report to the Commission upon, such matters as the Commission think fit',[21] and such people are in practice appointed for the purpose of chairing and reporting on local public inquiries into provisional recommendations. Fifty-four such assistant commissioners were appointed in this way for the 1976–83 review of the English Commission. It is a remarkable fact that although the Act does not mention legal qualifications for the post, every one of them was a barrister (one of whom was the London University Professor of Public Law, Jeffrey

Jowell). One MP who was somewhat aghast at this information commented, 'As they have gone around the country conducting their local inquiries we have had the veritable rule of judges and lawyers. There has been nothing quite like it since the days of Joshua in the Old Testament.'[22] Secretarial and administrative support staff are provided, generally being seconded civil servants appointed by the Home Secretary. For expert advice on population statistics and geographical surveys, the Registrar General for England and Wales and the Director General of Ordnance Survey serve as assessors to the English and Welsh Commissions, and their counterparts in Scotland and Northern Ireland similarly serve in respect of the Scottish and Northern Ireland Commissions.

Very little is known or publicised, even from the Boundary Commission reports, on how the deputy chairmen and other commissioners are selected, or what the internal working practices of the Commissions are, or what these three principal figures in each of the four Commissions, who are charged with the responsibility for one of the most important tasks connected with our parliamentary democracy, do in relation to the work and how long they spend on it. For this reason the House of Commons Home Affairs Select Committee in 1986 was anxious to question some commissioners about it, and the few responses made were particularly illuminating.[23] Sir Raymond Walton explained how he came to be appointed deputy chairman of the English Commission as follows: 'May I say that as far as I was concerned, I was hauled in by the Vice Chancellor, the head of my division, and told, "You're the youngest judge. This job has come up. Would you like to take it?", and I took it.' When asked by the Select Committee whether, when members are appointed to the Commission, it is known whether they have had any political involvement in the past, and if so whether it was a bar, Sir Kenneth Jones, deputy chairman of the Welsh Commission, emphasised that 'the most careful inquiries were made, so far as I can see, to ensure that I had had no political past, even going back to the days when I was at university'.[24] Sir Raymond Walton commented, 'That happens now, but it did not happen when I was appointed.' When the Committee asked how much time is devoted by the commissioners to Boundary Commission work, according to the English commissioner Judge Newey, 'On time spent, I did keep a rough record, just out of interest. During the general review I think we met once a month for a full day's meeting, and I found I spent between five and six evenings a week reading the papers.'[25] Mr McLaggan of the Welsh Commission said, 'My experience is that during the general review we had perhaps half-a-dozen meetings a year, something of that order, and each of those would involve me in somewhere between two and three days (the day of the meeting, then certainly one day and possibly two days examining the papers beforehand).' Perhaps at least as revealing was that the deputy chairman of the Welsh

Commission, Sir Kenneth Jones, did not know. The exchange with the MP David Winnick went as follows:[26]

Mr Winnick: I wonder if I might ask you a few questions regarding personnel? Sir Kenneth Jones, you are Deputy Chairman. Is that a full-time position?
Sir Kenneth Jones: You are asking me?
Mr Winnick: Yes, I am.
Sir Kenneth Jones: No. I am a High Court judge, the same as Sir Raymond [the English Commission's Deputy Chairman].
Mr Winnick: Could I ask what time is actually devoted by you to the Boundary Commission?
Sir Kenneth Jones: That is a difficult question, because obviously the amount of time would differ as to whether it is during the currency of a general review or between general reviews. I am in the unfortunate position of not having joined the Commission until after the last review was complete, so I cannot really answer as to how much time would have to be spent on that at the time when really a lot of work is being done by the Commission.

So the principal working boundary commissioner had no clear idea of the work involved and how much of his time it would take, even over a year after he had been appointed to the post. The real answer, perhaps, was provided by one of the other Welsh commissioners, Mr J. Long: 'I think we ought to make the point that the real work, of course, is done by the Secretaries of which we have the benefit. It takes us a day or two to read through what they produce for us before each meeting. However, the number of meetings is very small.'[27] There are two joint secretaries for each of the Commissions, including at the time of the 1983 reports and the 1986 Commons Select Committee hearings, Mr Geoffrey Barnes and Mr Andrew Pickersgill, although in giving evidence to the Committee Mr Barnes appeared with the commissioners invited, and Mr Pickersgill had earlier given evidence on behalf of the Home Office. Both served not only as joint secretaries of the English Commission, but also the Welsh Commission: the offices of both Commissions are at the same address, St. Catherine's House in London. The secretariat of the Northern Ireland Commission is housed in the Northern Ireland Office in Whitehall, and that of the Scottish Commission at St. Andrew's House in Edinburgh. These secretaries to the Commissions, then, are in a very important and powerful position, despite being individuals who go largely unnoticed by parliamentarians and the public alike. It is they who effectively supervise and co-ordinate the full-time operation of the Commissions, and the enormous administrative under-taking involved in each general review.

THE CONDUCT OF BOUNDARY REVIEWS

The rules for redistribution of seats

How each Boundary Commission is to set about its task is prescribed in the 1986 Act, and published as Schedule 2 are the very important 'Rules for Distribution of Seats'.[28] Rules 1 and 2 recite the numbers of constituencies allowed, and declare the fundamental principle that each constituency shall return a single member. Rule 3 makes special provision for the City of London: 'there shall continue to be a constituency which shall include the whole of the City of London and the name of which shall refer to the City of London'. Then there follow rules 4 to 8, which contain the vital criteria upon which the Commission must base its judgement. What these rules amount to may be said to enshine two different aspirations for the Boundary Commissions in undertaking their work: first, they try to achieve electoral parity in terms of similar numbers of voters within each constituency; and second, they attempt to draw boundary lines around each constituency in such a way as to respect and foster coherent political communities and existing local authority boundaries. Rules 5 and 8 deal with equal electorates and the electoral quota. The expression 'electoral quota' means a number obtained by dividing the electorate for that part of the United Kingdom (for example, England as a whole for the English Boundary Commission) by the number of constituencies in it. So at the start of the third general review of boundaries by the English Commission in 1976, the current number of registered electors was 33 928 554, and the number of constituencies then in existence was 516. This produced an electoral quota of 65 753 upon which the Commission proceeded to base its work. Rule 5 declares the important principle that in reviewing the parliamentary representation for the part of the United Kingdom for which each Boundary Commission has responsibility, 'the electorate of any constituency shall be as near the electoral quota as is practical'. The discretion this allows the Commissions in practice has meant variations from the quota up to and beyond 20 per cent (see the table opposite).

The total electorates and numbers of constituencies in England, Scotland, Wales and Northern Ireland are different, so different electoral quotas will be established for each of the four Boundary Commissions. It has already been commented upon that the rules relating to the number of constituencies within each region operate to the disadvantage of some regions, notably England, over others with a significantly lower electoral quota. Attention should also be paid to the effect of rule 8, that the number of parliamentary electors on the register at the time of the start of each new Commission's general review will form the basis of their recommendations. As each review takes several years to complete, this means that boundary changes are always effected on out-of-date information. Thus the 1983

Deviations of more than 20 per cent from electoral quota

England (1976 electorates; quota 65 753)	
Isle of Wight	88 460
Hornsey and Wood Green	84 401
Sunderland North	81 189
Crosby	80 213
Harrow East	79 705
Feltham and Heston	78 810
Surbiton	46 493
Old Bexley and Sidcup	49 739
Milton Keynes	50 408
Staffordshire South East	51 602
Berwick on Tweed	51 714
Walthamstow	51 763
Blyth Valley	51 785
Copeland	51 805
Morecambe and Lunesdale	52 154
Barnsley East	52 368
Hexham	52 429
Scotland (1978 electorates; quota 53 649)	
Dundee West	64 500
Western Isles	22 700
Orkney and Shetland	28 307
Caithness and Sutherland	30 100
Tweeddale, Ettrick and Lauderdale	36 299
Cumbernauld and Kilsyth	39 700
Roxburgh and Berwickshire	41 766
Wales (1981 electorates; quota 58 753)	
Meirionydd nant Conwy	30 413
Montgomery	37 421
Caernarfon	43 813
Brecon and Radnor	46 800

Table 4.2[29]

boundary changes were based on the 1976 electoral register, that being the year in which the Commission announced its intention to commence its next review and began its work. As the English Commission itself commented in its final report in 1983, 'the 1976 electorate on which we were required to base our general review became less realistic as the task proceeded'.[30] Over the six-year period of the review the English electorate in fact increased by 1 435 178 (4.2 per cent) to 35 363 732 in 1982. Some of the rapidly growing or shrinking individual constituency populations were markedly different. For example, the constituency of East Berkshire, with 66 489 votes in 1976, had grown to an electorate of 82 502 by 1983. In seventeen separate constituencies there was a difference of over 10 000 voters between 1976 and 1983 (see the table below). Unless, as is considered later in this chapter under my reform proposals,[31] changes in the law are made so that the Commissions should always use the most recent electoral register for their assessments, and ways are found of ensuring that the Commissions complete their work within a much shorter period than recent general reviews, then boundary changes will continue to be made in many cases upon grossly out-of-date figures.

Electorate change of more than 10 000 in England
during period of boundary review, 1976–82

	1976	1982
Increases		
Houghton and Washington	63 314	74 526
South West Bedfordshire	65 921	76 418
East Berkshire	66 489	81 226
Aylesbury	61 981	73 049
Milton Keynes	50 408	76 548
Peterborough	63 526	78 585
Warrington South	59,630	73 149
Billericay	64 699	74 751
Basingstoke	60 414	71 473
East Hampshire	67 352	78 654
Eastleigh	70 021	82 197
Mid Worcestershire	57 376	73 447
The Wrekin	64 964	76 569
South East Staffordshire	51 602	63 660
Horsham	67 575	79 791
Decreases		
Vauxhall	75 037	64 437
Liverpool Riverside	73 708	63 615

Table 4.3[32]

Alongside the aim of mathematical equality of voters within constituencies is that of communal representation, and the protection of local political identities. The Home Secretary at the time of the 1983 boundary changes, William Whitelaw, said,[33]

Implicit in any system of redistributing seats is the idea that a vote should be worth just as much in one sort of constituency as in another, and each redistribution has tended to iron out the differences between urban seats and rural seats. At the same time, we have never entirely lost hold of the idea that constituency boundaries should so far as possible reflect those of natural communities. In entrusting an independent commission with the task of drawing up new boundaries, Parliament has repeatedly taken steps to ensure that fair and equal representation is considered alongside local ties.

Rule 4 provides that so far as is practicable English and Welsh constituencies are to be contained within the areas of counties or London boroughs, Scottish constituencies within local authority areas, and Northern Ireland constituencies within wards. However, the Commission may depart from the strict application of this rule if it appears to them that a departure is desirable to avoid an excessive disparity between the electorate of a constituency and the electoral quota of a neighbouring constituency, or if there are special geographical considerations including the size, shape and accessibility of a constituency. Special geographical considerations are also cited in rule 6 as a ground for departing from a strict application of equal electorates and the electoral quota in a particular constituency. In the 1983 English boundary review the Commission used this exception in three counties, Cumbria, Lancashire and Northumberland, to justify allocating one more constituency in each. Finally there is a general and supplemental provision contained in rule 7 which perhaps detracts from rather than adds to the clarity of the rules taken together. It gives the Commissions a wide discretion to depart from the other rules, and then as a proposition in itself is further qualified. Its existence is explicable historically in that it was introduced in 1958 in the parliamentary context of a backlash of opinion against the rigid application of the electoral quota in 1954. It reads, 'it shall not be the duty of a Boundary Commission to aim at giving full effect in all circumstances to the above rules, but they shall take account, so far as they reasonably can (a) of the inconveniences attendant on alterations of constituencies other than alterations made for the purposes of rule 4 [equal electorates], and (b) of any local ties which would be broken by such alterations'. Not surprisingly, virtually every objector to any of the changes being recommended in 1983 claimed that the new parliamentary constituency boundary proposed upset existing local ties. Other objections were that the Commission possessed a discretion to take into account some element of special weighting in certain areas on a variety of grounds, such as failure of some of the population to register as electors although eligible to do so; projected increases of population and therefore of electorate attributable to housing development; the problems of inner city areas which produced heavy caseloads for MPs and, conversely, the difficulties of local political organisations in rural areas. The English Commission's view was that they possessed no authority under the rules to take such factors into account.[34]

The existing rules for the redistribution of seats contained in the 1986 Parliamentary Constituencies Act have with some justification been described as 'convoluted, ambiguous and imprecise'.[35] Their lack of clarity and cross-qualification, combined with their status in law (in the opinion of the Court of Appeal)[36] as being mere guidelines, results in too wide a discretion being left to the commissioners, which in practice means that of each of the fifty or so assistant commissioners operating within different areas. There are a number of inherent defects in the way the rules are legally drafted, which serve to confuse the paramount purpose of general reviews and also allow for an ever-increasing number of constituencies. Their rationalisation is considered below under the suggested programme for reform.[37]

Procedure for the reviews

The first step in the Boundary Commission procedures is the decision to begin a new general review. This involves an estimate of the length of time the review is likely to take, so as to complete its report and recommendations within the statutory period. Clearly, the government (and in particular the Home Secretary) plays a leading role in this respect, not least because it appoints the commissioners. In the case of the third general review completed in 1983, the English Commission announced its intention to commence its work on 17 February 1976, and this was formally published in *The London Gazette* on 5 March.[38] The report of the preceding second general review had been submitted in 1969, though for reasons explained later in this chapter[39] its recommendations were not implemented until 1974. The Home Secretary informed the House of Commons on 11 March 1976 of the Commission's decision to proceed to a third general review, in the form of a reply to a parliamentary question. At that point the Commission felt three years would be needed to complete their work, but in the event this took seven years.[40]

The next stage is for the commissioners to formulate provisional recommendations. In order to be able to do this, they first gather all necessary information concerning registered electors across the country, which is supplied by the Registrar General, and concerning administrative and electoral areas which is supplied by the Director General of Ordnance Survey. The Department of the Environment will also supply details of any plans for major development in the counties. Whether or not the Commissions should at this stage be involving itself in consultations with other interested bodies is a point of some controversy. Any views of the Home Office are extremely likely to be given in any event, and of course some support staff are on temporary secondment from that department of state. In fact it has been a regular cause for complaint that the working relationship between the personnel of the Home Office and the Boundary Commissions, described by one MP as 'far too intimate and too incestuous',[41] undermines the genuine independence of the Commissions' reports. Discussions with the political parties, and more particularly the opposition parties, since the party in government is already additionally represented by the Home Secretary, do take place from time to time throughout the course of the review. Five such meetings took place during the course of the English Commission's last review, and in its report it commented that they had 'adopted the practice of meeting the representatives of the party organisations together, sometimes at their request, and we found our discussions most informative and helpful'.[42] This may be being rather polite. In the view of one former Labour Home Secretary, Merlyn Rees, 'What is said by representatives at the Labour Party's headquarters, the Liberal Party's headquarters or at Conservative Central Office is interesting but no more than that. The job of the Home Office and of the Commissions is to implement the law and not to listen to party functionaries.'[43] None the less, consultation with the parties is to be encouraged, and the willingness of the Commissions to meet them and listen to their views is extremely important to the political acceptability of their work. It is revealing to see the interchange with the parties from the following extract from the English Commission's report on the question of crossing London borough boundaries:[44]

We discussed the situation with the representatives of the political parties. They were of the unanimous opinion that none of the constituencies in London should cross a borough boundary, despite the disparities which currently resulted from this arrangement. Similarly they were opposed in all circumstances to the crossing of any county boundary. We were asked to give an assurance that we would only recommend a constituency which crossed a county or London borough boundary in the most exceptional circumstances.

One might have thought that local authorities would be consulted extensively at an early stage of the review, since they directly represent the local communities and areas which the Commission must respect under rule 4, and they will be most aware of local developments and peculiarities. However, the English Commission explained in their 1983 report that they had decided not to invite such suggestions for changes but rather 'that we should take the initiative in formulating provisional recommendations from our position of neutrality. Only in this way would it be clear that we had not been influenced by any particular viewpoints.'[45]

The Commissions' provisional recommendations for boundary changes are calculated over a period of time, and are then required to be published under the terms of the Parliamentary Constituencies Act 1986, with a view to holding local inquiries if there is sufficient popular demand or good reason to hear representations from interested persons or organisations within the affected constituencies.[46] On the level of publicity to be given to proposed boundary changes, the Act states that they shall publish in at least one newspaper circulating in the constituency a notice which states, first, the effect of the proposed recommendations and (unless no changes are proposed) where a copy of the recommendations can be found open to inspection at a specified place within the constituency; and, second, that representations with respect to the proposed recommendations may be made to the Commissions within one month after the publication of the notice.[47] Letting everyone within the constituency know about the proposed boundary changes in just one local newspaper, the circulation of which will be a small fraction of the total local electorate, is clearly inadequate publicity for this important purpose. In the case of the English Commission's third general review (1976–83), it decided which newspapers to select for advertisements, and in which public offices or libraries to display the information about proposed changes, after consultation with the relevant local authorities. Additional measures adopted by the English Commission were to circulate in advance of publication copies of the notices to the headquarters of the major political parties, and to inform individual MPs of recommendations affecting their particular constituencies. Copies of the notices and maps were placed in the Library of the House of Commons, and arrangements were made with the Central Office of Information and the Home Office Public Relations Branch for news releases to be issued to the national and local press and the radio and television organisations. It is then open to journalists to develop news items and features on the proposed changes to increase public awareness of them.

The Boundary Commissions are required by law to 'take into consideration' any representations made as a result of the publication of their proposals, and they have a general power to hold a local inquiry whenever they think fit. In addition they *must* hold a local inquiry into their proposed changes if they receive representations objecting to the proposals from one hundred or more electors in the constituency, or else from one of the local authorities wholly or partly within one of the affected constituencies.[48] These local inquiries are public hearings where any interested person may attend and present their views. Their purpose is to solicit and hear opposing or supporting views and arguments regarding the recommendations, and to take these into account when reaching a final decision. In other words, local inquiries generally should be understood as being part of the administrative decision-making process, and they are used extensively in town and country planning affairs. In the case of Boundary Commission local inquiries, the organisation of each event is under the control of a chairman who controls proceedings, and who, after receiving all the views expressed, will prepare a report and conclusion on the recommended boundary changes going ahead in the light of what he or she has heard. If the Commission decides not to revise its recommendations at all, copies of the report of the local inquiry are distributed to the people who have made representations to them. If it decides to revise its recommendations in the light of the inquiry and other representations made, the new proposals are published in the same way as the original provisional recommendations. In the event that a large number of objections are then received to the second proposal, they need not hold any further inquiry if 'after considering the matters discussed at the local inquiry, the nature of the representations received on the publication of the notice and any other relevant circumstances, [they] are of the opinion that a further local inquiry would not be justified'.[49] The effect of these provisions is that interested parties may have no chance at all to comment on the final outcome. Thus at the third general review, the MP for Leeds South complained:[50]

I attended an inquiry at the Civic Hall, Leeds. It appeared that my constituency had been left alone in the Commission's provisional report. I learnt that a part of the constituency of my Hon. friend the Member for Normanton was to be added to it. The addition of that one ward would have made Leeds South a large constituency. There were 84 objections to the wider scheme. Only two of those objections concerned Leeds South and only about the addition of Rothwell. I sat in the Civic Hall for two days listening to the inquiry and the issue of my constituency was not raised. When the final report appeared three months later, I found that the Commission had split my constituency down the middle. My criticism is that my constituency has been broken in two in the daftest way with no mention of it in the public inquiry.

A great many changes to the provisional recommendations of the Boundary Commissions are made as a result of the local inquiries. During the third general English review completed in 1983, nearly half of the constituencies were modified in some way, either by redrawing the boundary lines or by changing the constituencies' names. The inquiry in Gwynedd, for example, led to the withdrawal of the original proposal to unite Welsh-speaking Meirionydd with the English-speaking Aberconwy, and instead the Commission retained a small, separate Welsh-speaking constituency named Meirionydd nant Conwy. Four new seats were added directly as a result of county inquiries, within West Yorkshire, Strathclyde, Gwynedd and Powys. The only provisional recommendation in Britain to cross county boundaries, between Gwent and Powys, was withdrawn after local feelings were expressed at the ensuing inquiry.

There is no statutory prescribed procedure for the conduct of these local inquiries. The Commissions issue for public use brief explanatory booklets explaining the purpose of the inquiries as being to ascertain local opinion, to hear criticisms of the provisional recommendations, to receive counter-proposals, and to enable everyone who wishes to comment on these or on the Commission's proposals to do so. It says that the Commission will not be represented at the inquiry, although a member of the secretariat may be present as an observer, and that those who wish to express views may do so in person, or through a representative, even though they may not have filed a written representation leading to the inquiry. Otherwise the chairmen themselves will determine how the inquiry is to be conducted. As noted,[51] it has become standard practice to select barristers for this work, and such people will bring, no doubt for better or worse, ideas of courtroom legal procedure and natural justice to the public hearings. The reports of these chairmen, who are appointed as assistant commissioners for the purpose by the Home Secretary at the request of the Commission, submit their report to the three working boundary commissioners to decide upon. During the third English review, ninety-five such local inquiries were held, including three second or reopened inquiries. The notices and recommendations were not all published at the same time, but county by county. Thus following the decision to begin the review in February 1976, the first published proposals were in Nottinghamshire in September 1976, the first recommendations for thirty-one of the boroughs in Greater London were in June 1979, and the last was for Manchester in June 1981.

In the overwhelming majority of cases, the conclusions of the chairmen of the local inquiries are simply adopted by the three working commissioners at their 'one day a month' meetings. In their 1983 report the English Commission said:[52]

When the assistant commissioner's report on the inquiry was received, we considered his recommendations together with all the representations received. We set out with the view that if the assistant commissioner's recommendations were in accordance with the statutory requirements and carried local support then we would accept them. We have consistently applied this policy. In those cases where we have found ourselves unable to accept the assistant commissioner's recommendations, the reasons have varied. Just occasionally we have considered that some facet of the recommendations was not sufficiently brought to the consideration of those who attended the inquiry; sometimes there was a recommendation that a ward should be divided, which clashed with our settled policy; and sometimes the assistant commissioner himself, whilst recommending a particular solution, recognised that we might not regard it as fully compatible with the statutory rules, and suggested an alternative which we did in fact prefer. We never differed from the recommendations of an assistant commissioner save after anxious consideration.

This 'hands-off' approach by the Commission to the individual work of the fifty-four different assistant commissioners may explain the apparent lack of consistency, where similar problems in two constituencies were often treated in very different ways. The conclusions of one of Britain's leading political geographers, Robert Waller, on the 1983 boundary changes was that, 'Overall the most prominent impression left by the commissioners' policy is one of inconsistency.'[53] For example, a common problem confronted by the Commissions was where a city had grown in population and become too large for one parliamentary seat. This, in fact, had happened in both the ancient English university cities of Oxford and Cambridge. The conclusion reached by the Commission for Oxford was to cut it in two, divided by the rivers Thames and Cherwell, and add suburban and rural wards to it from outside the city. In Cambridge, on the other hand, they decided to maintain a distinct Cambridge seat, but transfer two wards away from it into adjoining constituencies. The City of York survived intact, with an overblown electorate of 77 693, but Colchester and Reading were, like Oxford, chopped in half. Another type of inconsistency was that in some areas the Commission recommended crossing metropolitan borough boundaries to establish constituencies of more equal size, as in Newcastle–Gateshead, Manchester–Trafford, Oldham–Rochdale, Stockport–Tameside, Leeds–Wakefield and Salford–Wigan. But in other areas where similar or stronger cases could be made for doing so, notably South Yorkshire and the West Midlands, the Commission decided not to do so. On the question of names, which aroused more passionate feelings in the 1980s review than on any earlier occasion, sometimes existing old constituency names were carried over to a redistributed seat (such as Colne Valley) yet elsewhere district names were adopted instead (such as Waveney rather than Lowestoft, or Gravesham rather than Gravesend). Several famous names were allowed to lapse altogether, including Ebbw Vale, which had been represented by leading Labour politicians, first Aneurin Bevan and later Michael Foot.

CHALLENGING THE BOUNDARY COMMISSIONS' RECOMMENDATIONS

Challenges in Parliament

The permanent statutory machinery for constituency review, now re-enacted in the Parliamentary Constituencies Act 1986, provides for the redistribution of parliamentary seats to be put into legal effect by way of delegated legislation. Once the Boundary Commissions have completed a general review, they are required by law to deliver their reports to the Home Secretary, with recommendations for constituency changes. The Home Secretary is then under a responsibility to react to their proposals, and present draft Orders in Council to Parliament for approval. Assuming the votes in both Houses support the draft Orders, it is submitted to the Queen for signature at a meeting of the Privy Council. The changes will then come into force at whatever date is specified in the draft Order.

A cardinal feature of this process of parliamentary review is that the government has the power to make amendments to the Commissions' proposals, but Parliament does not. Parliament is powerless to do otherwise than accept or reject the Orders as a whole. This is because it is a fundamental rule of parliamentary practice that amendments can only be made during the passage of primary legislation (Acts of Parliament) and cannot be tabled or proposed to delegated legislation (known as statutory instruments).[54] It would only be possible for MPs to propose and vote on modifications to the Boundary Commissions' conclusions if the parent statute, here the Parliamentary Constituencies Act 1986, expressly conferred power upon Parliament to do so. This power of amendment over statutory instruments has historically only ever been granted on eighteen occasions, and it was not included as part of the statutory machinery for the redistribution of parliamentary seats despite the constitutional principle that Parliament should have ultimate control over its own composition. The Home Secretary, on the other hand, is granted express power under sections 3 and 4 of the 1986 Act to make any changes he or she likes to the Commission's recommendations and incorporate these into the draft Orders in Council presented to Parliament. The only proviso in the Act is that the Home Secretary should let Parliament know why he or she has made the amendments: 'Where any such draft gives effect to any such recommendations with modifications, the Secretary of State shall lay before Parliament together with the draft a statement of the reasons for the modifications.'[55]

So the fate of the recommendations of the Boundary Commissions lies effectively in the hands of the political party that forms the government of the day. For not only may the Home Secretary modify the Commissions' recommendations in advance of their being presented to Parliament, but within the House of Commons the government may rely upon its party majority to get its own way. The events of 1969 provide a good illustration of how the existing legal framework for redistribution allows the government, if it wishes, to frustrate the work performed by the Boundary Commissions. After the Commissions had submitted their 1969 reports to James Callaghan, who was Home Secretary at the time, the government decided that the recommendations were inconsistent with the major reform of local government boundaries planned as a result of the Report of the Royal Commission on Local Government,[56] which had been chaired by Lord Redcliffe-Maud and published in June. However, critics of the government claimed that the real reason for obstructing the Commissions' proposals was that if implemented they would have lost the Labour Party between ten and twenty seats at the next general election. James Callaghan proceeded to present the Commissions' reports to Parliament, by having them deposited in the Votes and Proceedings Office at the Commons, but declined to prepare draft Orders in Council to put into effect any boundary changes. Instead, a House of Commons (Redistribution of Seats) Bill was introduced, which would implement the Commissions' proposals within Greater London (where local government reforms had already taken place) and elsewhere in selected, very large constituencies. However, the Bill was wrecked by the

Conservative majority in the House of Lords, via a series of major amendments, and eventually withdrawn by the Government.

Meanwhile a Conservative supporter and voter in one of the affected constituencies, Ross McWhirter, applied to the High Court for an order of mandamus directed to the Home Secretary requiring him to comply with the statutory provision in the Act that 'as soon as may be' after receipt of the Commissions' reports, he should lay draft Orders in Council before Parliament.[57] *R. v. Secretary of State for the Home Department, ex parte McWhirter* (1969)[58] was a remarkable case for a number of reasons, but in the event it was defused by the Home Secretary announcing that he did intend after all to present the draft Orders before Parliament and that he would make an *ex gratia* payment to cover the legal costs of the applicant. The case was heard before the Lord Chief Justice Lord Parker, sitting with Mr Justice Ashworth and Mr Justice Cantley, with the Attorney-General Sir Elwyn Jones (later Lord Chancellor) and Mr Gordon Slynn (now a Law Lord) appearing on behalf of James Callaghan. Ross McWhirter's counsel, Mr Raymond Sears, opened by arguing that 'the only object of my client in seeking this order is to ensure that no man, whatever power he wields, however high a position he holds in this country, is in a position to bend the law to suit his own wishes'. Sir Elwyn Jones in defence argued alternatively that Ross McWhirter lacked *locus standi* to bring an application for mandamus, and/or that the case was premature since the Home Secretary did not need to present the Orders until such time 'as soon as may be' and that time had not passed while the Bill to put into effect part of the Commissions' proposals was before Parliament, and/or that the Home Secretary's duty under the Act was to the Crown or to Parliament and could not be enforced by a claim for mandamus in the courts, and/or that the legal proceedings were misconceived and doomed *ab initio*, amounting to an impeachment of 'proceedings in Parliament' and a breach of parliamentary privilege.[59] Perhaps unhappily for scholars and students of Britain's idiosyncratic constitution, for whom the boundary lines between the sole jurisdiction of Parliament to determine its own affairs and the extent of judicial review into such matters are sometimes as much in conflict as the principles upon which the Boundary Commissions operate, the judicial resolution of such lofty arguments of high constitutional law were lost when Ross McWhirter withdrew his application in consideration of James Callaghan's declaration that he would duly proceed to lay draft Orders in Council before the Commons.

James Callaghan then embarked on a highly original episode in the United Kingdom's parliamentary history. He came to the House of Commons on 12 November 1969, put the affirmative resolutions on the Commissions' recommendations before the House, and then promptly advised the House to reject those very same orders. The official record of parliamentary debates, *Hansard*, records:[60]

The Secretary of State for the Home Department (Mr James Callaghan): I beg to move that the Parliamentary Constituencies (England) Order 1969, a draft of which was laid before this House on 28th October, be not approved.

The Conservative opposition were outraged that the Boundary Commissions' proposals would not be implemented in full, and accusations of gerrymandering have continued from that day to the present. The then Conservative leader, Edward Heath, replied to the Home Secretary's motion in very strong language, condemning the government's tactics as 'politically and morally wrong', and 'against the traditions of the House and the interests of democracy'. He continued:[61]

The real reason why [the Home Secretary] is behaving in this shabby fashion and why the government are rejecting the recommendations of the Boundary Commission [is that] the Right Hon. Gentleman believes that the recommendations have an in-built bias against his own party. This is the real reason, and that has emerged without any shadow of doubt. . . [This motion is] unique in substance in rejecting four years' work by independent Boundary Commissions and rejecting changes affecting, as the Right Hon. Gentleman said, more than 400 constituencies. They are unique in form in that the Home Secretary is rejecting Orders which he has laid. They are unique in the brazen effrontery with which the Right Hon. Gentleman overthrows the established means of demarcating boundaries in our parliamentary democracy. They are unique in modern times in the shameless demonstration . . . of government manipulation for seats for their own advantage.

A three-line Whip had been imposed by the government on its backbenchers in the House of Commons, and the draft Order in Council was duly rejected on the vote at the end of the day's debate.

The political controversy created by this incident is still not forgotten at Westminster. When introducing the Boundary Commissions' Act 1992, the then Home Secretary, Kenneth Clarke sought to pre-empt accusations that he himself was bringing forward boundary changes to suit Conservative electoral prospects at the next election, by referring to the 'gerrymandering' of Labour in 1969.[62] Kenneth Clarke also revealed that if the Boundary Commissions' recommendations had been implemented by Labour in 1969, instead of after the Conservative election victory in October 1970, he himself would have been one of the MPs who lost their seats (along with his neighbouring MP, Sir Norman Fowler: 'In 1969 the then Home Secretary, now Lord Callaghan, went to considerable lengths to avoid implementing the boundary changes before the 1970 general election. My position is slightly ambiguous because had it not been for Lord Callaghan's gerrymandering on that occasion I probably would not have been elected to the House in 1970.'

Challenges in the courts

Challenging the recommendations of the Boundary Commissions in the courts has a very restricted potential. In theory, the inherent supervisory jurisdiction of the High Court over all statutory bodies exists to redress any error of law.[63] But so far as the Boundary Commissions are concerned, there will always be formidable obstacles in the way of any application for judicial review. The first limiting factor is that any legal proceedings must be brought at a time before the recommendations have been implemented in an Order in Council duly approved by Parliament and signed by the Queen. This is because the Parliamentary Constituencies Act 1986 contains an 'ouster clause', excluding the jurisdiction of the courts: 'The validity of any Order in Council purporting to be made under this Act and reciting that a draft of the Order has been approved by resolution of each House of Parliament shall not be called in question in any legal proceedings whatsoever.'[64] A second limiting factor is that in practice there is very little opportunity to challenge a report of the Boundary Commission as a whole. This is because in recent practice the government moves very quickly between receiving the Commissions' reports (which are only then published and made available to the public) and the Order in Council being presented to Parliament (a period of less than three weeks between 11 February and 2 March in the case of the third general review's constituency changes in 1983). It then need only be a matter of days before the Order in Council passes into law. The opportunity to mount a legal challenge to Boundary Commission conclusions is best directed at individual constituency changes, the results of which will have been known publicly from the provisional changes deposited for public inspection, or the modifications to them as a result of a local inquiry being similarly deposited in accordance with the provisions in section 6 of the Parliamentary Constituencies Act 1986. The position concerning legal challenge to the findings of the Boundary Commissions must now be gleaned from the Labour Party's attempt more than ten years ago, *R.* v. *Boundary Commission for England, Ex parte Foot and others* (1983),[65] against the background of one earlier important legal challenge brought by the Mayor of Manchester, *Harper and another* v. *Secretary of State for the Home Department* (1954).[66] Both these legal actions were spectacular failures for the complainants.

It needs to be clearly understood that there is no appeal as such from the decisions of the commissioners to the courts. Such a right of appeal would only exist if it was expressly provided for in the Parliamentary Constituencies Act, and it is not. An application to the courts for judicial review of the commissioners' decisions is a very different type of legal action, and in theory it simply involves the courts ensuring that the commissioners have complied with their legal duties as laid down in the Act creating them and have exercised their powers as intended by Parliament. The courts in a judicial review action can never substitute their own decision for the one challenged, in the way that where a right of appeal exists the appellate body can. In the *Ex parte Foot* case, the then Master of the Rolls, Lord Donaldson, stated the general role of the courts in judicial review cases in the following way:[67]

It is important that everyone should understand what is the function and duty of the courts. Parliament entrusted the duty of recommending changes in English constituency boundaries to the Commission. It could, if it had wished, have further provided that anyone who was dissatisfied with those recommendations could appeal to the courts. Had it done so, the duty of the court would, to a considerable extent, have been to repeat the operations of the Commission and see if it arrived at the same answer. If it did, the appeal would have been dismissed. If it did not, it would have substituted its own recommendations. Parliament, for reasons which we can well understand, did no such thing. It made no mention of the courts and gave no right of appeal to the courts.

There are some who will think that in that situation the courts have no part to play, but they would be wrong. There are many Acts of Parliament which give ministers and local authorities extensive powers to take action which affects the citizenry of this country, but give no right of appeal to the courts. In such cases, the courts are not concerned or involved so long as ministers and local authorities do not exceed the powers given to them by Parliament. Those powers may give them a wide range of choice on what action to take or to refrain from taking and so long as they confine themselves to making choices within that range, the courts will have no wish or power to intervene. But if ministers or local authorities exceed their power – if they choose to do something or to refrain from doing something in circumstances in which this is not one of the options given to them by Parliament – the courts can and will intervene in defence of the ordinary citizen. It is of the essence of parliamentary democracy that those to whom powers are given by Parliament shall be free to exercise those powers, subject to constitutional protest and criticism and parliamentary or other democratic control. But any attempt by ministers or local authorities to usurp powers which they have not got or to exercise their powers in a way which is unauthorised by Parliament is quite a different matter. As Sir Winston Churchill was wont to say, 'That is something up with which we will not put.' If asked to do so, it is then the role of the courts to prevent this happening.

This branch of jurisprudence is termed administrative law, and a feature of its operation within the United Kingdom has been that there is no special framework within which litigation between individuals and public bodies takes place, whereas many other countries, France and Germany for example, have a separate system of administrative courts with distinct principles of law applicable to complaints by individuals against state officials and administrative agencies.[68] In the absence of such a framework, the courts themselves have developed a variety of administrative law principles upon our common law case-by-case method, such as the requirement of 'rationality' by a decision-maker, sometimes called 'the reasonableness test'. According to this principle of law, no administrative body such as a minister, local authority or the Boundary Commission must exercise a legal discretionary power given to them by Parliament 'unreasonably' – or, more precisely, in a way in which no reasonable similar body can reasonably be expected to act. The classic exposition of this principle was enunciated by a former Master of the Rolls, Lord Greene, in *Associated Provincial Picture Houses Ltd.* v. *Wednesbury Corporation* (1948):[69]

> It is true that discretion must be exercised reasonably. Now what does that mean? Lawyers familiar with phraseology used in relation to exercise of statutory discretions often use the word 'unreasonable' in a rather comprehensive sense. It has frequently been used and is frequently used as a general description of the things that must not be done. For instance, a person entrusted with a discretion must, so to speak, direct himself properly in law. He must call his own attention to the matters which he is bound to consider. He must exclude from his consideration matters which are irrelevant to what he has to consider. If he does not obey those rules, he may truly be said, and often is said, to be acting 'unreasonably'. Similarly, there may be something so absurd that no sensible person could ever dream that it lay within the powers of the authority. Warrington L. J. in *Short* v. *Poole Corporation* (1926) gave the example of the red-haired teacher, dismissed because she had red hair. This is unreasonable in one sense. In another it is taking into consideration extraneous matters. It is so unreasonable that it might almost be described as being done in bad faith; and, in fact, all these things run into one another.

The court in the *Ex parte Foot* case specifically accepted that this reasonableness argument might apply to decisions of the Boundary Commissions. Lord Donaldson said that the principle 'would or might in our opinion entitle the court to intervene if it was satisfied that the Commission had misdirected themselves in law, or had failed to consider matters which they were bound to consider or had taken into consideration matters which they should not have considered'.[70] However, no hypothetical examples of manifest irrationality were given. Upon the facts of both these cases, the legal arguments put forward on behalf of the applicants, that the Rules for Redistribution of Seats had been misconstrued and misapplied by the Commission in a matter which constituted an irrational exercise of their discretion, did not succeed.

The problems in challenging the Boundary Commission in this way are far greater than in respect of normal administrative bodies. This is because a fundamental approach of the courts in judicial review cases is to construe statutory powers in accordance with what the apparent or supposed intention of Parliament was in establishing the administrative body and its powers in the first place. As a leading administrative law professor, John Griffith, has put it, 'At its simplest, judicial review is the means of ensuring that the will of Parliament is obeyed. It is an essential corollary of parliamentary supremacy.'[71] In both the *Ex parte Foot* and *Harper* cases, the courts were clearly of the opinion that Parliament must have intended the Boundary Commissions to have a very wide discretion in preparing their recommendations. In support of this view, the judges pointed out that the Commissions were not themselves executive decision-making bodies, but merely advisory bodies set up by Parliament in order to give Parliament and the Government the benefit of the Commissions' advice in deciding for themselves whether, and how, to make changes in parliamentary constituencies. It is well settled in law that administrative decision-makers may in any event arrive at different conclusions without being in breach of administrative law for 'irrationality'.[72] In other words, the Labour Party and the Boundary Commissions might reach different conclusions on how the Rules should best operate in any particular area, but both would be 'reasonable' in the context of judicial review principles. In Lord Donaldson's view, 'There being more than one answer, Parliament has asked the Commission to advise on which, in their judgement, should be adopted . . . [The Commission] is intent on giving the Secretary of State and Parliament their advice – not ours or that of the political parties – and that is what they were instructed to do.'[73]

The courts see the legal status of the Rules for the Redistribution of Seats laid down in the Act not as prescribed, mandatory criteria which the Commissions must scientifically apply, and which, therefore, the court will enforce if the Commission fails to do so, but instead as merely guideline criteria to assist the commissioners in drawing up their opinion or advice for Parliament and the Home Secretary. Indeed it was part of the central *ratio decidendi* of *Ex parte Foot* that although the Commission's duty 'to give effect to the Rules' (now in section 3 of the 1986 Act) was mandatory, the discretion provided by the Act (particularly that 'it shall not be the duty of a Boundary Commission to aim at giving full effect in all circumstances to the above rules' now in rule 7) was to be construed broadly, and as a result the Rules, while remaining very important were reduced to the status of guidelines. Much discussion of the status and application of the Rules took place in *Ex parte Foot*, because the main complaint of the Labour Party was that the Commission had failed to give primacy to its statutory obligation to ensure equality of electorates both within counties and between seats in different counties and London boroughs. This legal action brought by the Labour Party was fought in the name of its leader, Michael Foot, and three other party officials, but was prepared with legal advice largely supplied by Dr Edmund Marshall, MP for Goole, and Gerald Bermingham, a prospective parliamentary candidate for St. Helens and also a practising solicitor. Arming themselves with a mountain of statistical information about wide disparities in constituency electorates, the Labour complainants argued before the court that the Commissions' conclusions across the country had been inconsistent, had failed to give effect to the object of equal electorates which, they asserted, was the paramount purpose of the Rules, and that they had refused to consider the possibility of crossing county boundaries. The court rejected each of these arguments as a misconceived reading of the purpose of the Act for which the Commissions were created:[74]

Undoubtedly the Commission could have made different recommendations which would have produced constituencies whose electorates were more equal in size, but then they could have been criticised on grounds of a failure to take account of other factors, such as geographical considerations and the need to respect boundaries . . . It is important to realise that Parliament did not tell the Boundary Commission to do an exercise in accountancy – to count heads, divide by a number and then draw a series of lines around each resulting group. It told it to engage in a more far-reaching and sophisticated undertaking, involving striking a balance between many factors which can point in different directions. This calls for judgement, not scientific precision.

It is fundamental to the judiciary's attitude in these cases that constituency review is essentially the business of Parliament, and not that of the courts. In this assumption they are undoubtedly being politically correct, even if it means that complaints from individual citizens and MPs belonging to the opposition, who will be voted down by the government, are thereby left with no real form of redress at all. The constitutional basis for the distribution and redistribution of constituencies is the authority of Parliament, and what it enacts. The theory is that the Home Secretary is accountable to Parliament, which has the final say and ultimate control over the recommendations of the Boundary Commissions and what constituency changes should be made. This was forcefully stated by the most senior civil judges of the day, the Masters of the Rolls, in both the *Ex parte Foot* and *Harper* cases. Lord Donaldson MR put it thus in 1983, 'The Commission's task is ancillary to something which is exclusively the responsibility of Parliament itself, namely, the final decision on parliamentary representation and constituency boundaries.'[75] And according to Lord Evershed MR earlier in 1954:[76]

My reading of these Rules and of the whole Act is that it was quite clearly intended that, insofar as the matter was not within the discretion of the Commission, it was certainly to be a matter for Parliament to determine. I find it impossible to suppose that Parliament contemplated that, on any of these occasions when reports were presented, it would be competent for the court to determine and pronounce on whether a particular line which had commended itself to the Commission was one which the court thought the best line or the right line – whether one thing rather than another was to be regarded as practicable, and so on. If it were competent for the courts to pass judgements of that kind on the reports, I am at a loss to see where the process would end and what the function of Parliament would then turn out to be.

AN ELECTORAL COMMISSION AND A PROGRAMME FOR REFORM

(a) Proposed Electoral Commission

There is a strong case for the United Kingdom now setting up an Electoral Commission. This would be created by Act of Parliament for the purpose of supervising electoral affairs throughout the country, and among its most important responsibilities would be the task of the review of parliamentary constituencies and to take over the existing work of the four Boundary Commissions. Another important responsibility of the Commission would be to keep under review the practice and working of political campaigning affecting elections, including matters of finance, broadcasting and advertising.[77] The new establishment of a single, independent body for these purposes would be a recognition of the completely different era in which we now exist in contrast to the political and electoral context existing when the Boundary Commissions were first created in the 1940s. More rapid population movements, new technology and changes in recent political opinion now require a highly professional agency, under the control of a board of full-time commissioners who are chosen from a pool of candidates with high-level political and managerial experience, to prepare recommendations on constituency review in a politically acceptable manner. This, combined with the transformation since the 1970s in the nature and practice of political campaigning in this country, which is self-evident to anyone over the age of 40 years, certainly justifies the establishment of an Electoral Commission analogous to similar bodies operating in other democracies, notably the Federal Election Commission in the USA. The creation of this new administrative machinery would provide the occasion for a much-needed rationalisation of law now regulating the Boundary Commissions.

One fundamental administrative rationalisation of the existing rules must be to replace the four Boundary Commissions with just one unified Commission, which would then apply similar working practices and criteria across the whole of the United Kingdom. At present, although there is some limited degree of *ad hoc* informal co-operation between the four separate bodies, there is no statutory requirement for the synchronisation of their reviews, nor that their recommendations and reports are to be published simultaneously, nor even that they discuss and consult together on producing guidelines for common policies on similar practical problems. This single Commission should be comprised of eleven commissioners, who receive salaries, and office and administrative facilities appropriate to the full-time performance of their responsibilities. They might continue to be appointed by the Prime Minister or Home Secretary, or perhaps nominated and approved within the House of Commons. They should be given some limited security of tenure, to protect their impartiality and independence from political interference, in the form of fixed five-year appointments. These fixed appointments would be renewable for a second term, but otherwise a commissioner could only leave office by way of removal for misconduct or incapacity or else by resignation or attaining a retirement age of 65 years. As with the two members of the European Commission at present appointed by the Prime Minister, a convention should arise that the Leader of the Opposition might nominate one of the two people invited to serve. This analogy with the European Commission is a worthwhile one in one further respect also. For in the same way that, for example, Roy Jenkins and Leon Brittan, both former Home Secretaries for Labour and Conservatives respectively, gave up their work as MPs to serve as members of the European Commission, so experience of political life in the composition of the Electoral Commission should certainly not be a bar to people appointed, in the way that it is at present in the selection of people to serve on the Boundary Commissions. On the contrary, knowledge and experience of political affairs would be an asset on the Commission, although, of course, there must be a prohibition that commissioners could not at the same time be members of or candidates for election to Parliament, the European Parliament or local authorities.

The disadvantages of the Speaker of the House of Commons continuing to act as *ex officio* chairman for the work of constituency review have already come to outweigh the advantages, and the chairman of the new Electoral Commission should simply be appointed by the Commission itself from among its members. The Speaker would in any event become an inappropriate choice as an absentee chairman in a full-time working agency, and also it would compromise his traditional political distance from the political parties to too great an extent, while other functions of the Electoral Commission might involve inquiries and disputes with one of the parties

over their campaigning practices or financial affairs. But the greatest
problem in the past with the Speaker being chairman has been that it
interferes with rather than promotes the accountability of the Boundary
Commissions. As the Labour Party discovered in its legal challenge to the
validity of the English Commission's decisions in 1983, the courts are going
to be particularly reluctant to entertain any judicial review proceedings of
the Commission if the chairman of that body is the Speaker of the House of
Commons. Instead, the courts will give greater emphasis than normal to the
proposition that the Commission is responsible to Parliament for its
decisions. But, of course, the Speaker's presence on the Commission is an
illusion. As one senior Labour MP said to the Speaker during the 1983
debates, 'I hope that I can say this with deference to you, Mr Speaker, but
you should not be the chairman of the Boundary Commission. That leads to
people outside and the judiciary to believe that, although you are described
as *ex officio*, you play a part in the procedure in the neutral way in which
you act as Speaker of the House. The Speaker plays no part in the
Commission's work and it is phoney to put the name of the Speaker at the
head.'[78] At Westminster the Speaker's presence on the Commission serves to
inhibit free parliamentary discussion, together with possible criticism, of the
Commissions' decisions and reports, for in theory the Speaker as chairman
has already been representing the views of MPs and protecting their interests
within the workings of the Commission. Once the decisions of the
Commissions are published, MPs have often been reluctant to express any
harsh criticism, not only out of respect for the Speaker, which is likely to be
both personal and professional (in that the Speaker holds a great deal of
power over individual members including the selection of who shall speak in
future debates), but also for procedural reasons of parliamentary law. Thus
during the Commons' debate on one Boundary Commission report, the
Speaker told MPs, 'So far as my own part in the Commission is concerned, I
must remind the House of the ancient and salutary rule, that any criticism,
implied or expressed, of the Chair should be put down in the form of a
Motion.'[79] Any criticism of the Commissions, then, might be interpreted as
a criticism of the Speaker. Jeff Rooker recently complained about this in the
debates on the Boundary Commissions Act 1992:[80]

> The fact that the Speaker of the House is the chair of the Boundary
> Commission prevents Hon. Members from criticising the Boundary
> Commission in a serious and hard-headed way, simply because it may be
> misconstrued as an attack on the Speaker. The fact is that the Speaker
> plays no role in the Commission and does not attend the meetings. I
> believe that the Speaker should have no role and should not be the chair
> of the Boundary Commission. The Boundary Commission should be up
> front with a positive role. If it did things with which the House disagreed,
> we should not then be prevented from complaining about it.

The presence of the Speaker as the Commission's chairman in the law currently constituting the Boundary Commission, then, serves to obstruct parliamentary accountability rather than promote it, and this is all the more untenable since the Speaker does not, in fact, participate in the Commissions' work at all. For all the reasons given, the Electoral Commission responsible for redistribution of parliamentary seats should choose its own chairman from among its members; someone who is likely in practice to be one of their more experienced members, having been reappointed for a second term of office.

The political independence of the Commission should be made more secure, and for this reason they should be placed in charge of their own budget and permitted to recruit their own staff. A long-running complaint about the Boundary Commissions' work in the past has been that it has been insufficiently independent of the Home Office, and that the administrative process of the Commission is too influenced by informal direction from the Government. In the view of some critics, this is facilitated precisely because of the interchange of administrative staff between the two bodies. Dr Edmund Marshall told the Home Secretary, then William Whitelaw, during the 1983 parliamentary debates:[81]

> There is far too intimate and too incestuous a working relationship between the Boundary Commission and the Home Office for the Commission to be described as in any way independent of the Government . . . Great difficulty arises because the joint secretaries, and, possibly, other staff, of the Boundary Commission are in post on secondment from the Home Office. The Prime Minister's claim that the Boundary Commission is independent of the Home Office seems strange when there seems to be an overlapping and a going to and fro of staff between the two Departments. We have further evidence of that today as yet again we see at least one of the secretaries of the Boundary Commission present with Home Office civil servants to advise Ministers on the nature of the debate.

As mentioned earlier in this chapter, the central part of the controversy over the 1983 Boundary Commission proposals was born from the assessment of psephologists that the electoral consequences of these constituency changes would benefit the Conservative Party. Robert Waller calculated that if an assessment was made of the notional results for the 1979 general election as if it had been fought on the new boundaries, the results for the main parties would have been: Labour 257 seats (11 less than they actually won), Conservatives 360 (21 more seats), and the Liberals 10 (1 less).[82] In other words, based on 1979 voting patterns, the Conservatives stood to win 32 extra seats from the boundary changes recommended. There was some suspicion that it was the likely outcome of the Commission's recommended changes that led to the Labour Party's ill-fated judicial review challenge, which sought an order prohibiting the English Commission from submitting its report to the Home Secretary, and if this had been successful it would have had the effect of either postponing a general election at a time when Labour was well behind the Conservatives in the public opinion polls, or else delaying implementation of the changes recommended until after an election had taken place. The challenge was heard and dismissed by the Court of Appeal in January 1983, prior to the election that was eventually called the following June. However, on the other hand, there was also a strong suspicion that the way in which the Boundary Commission's recommendations were organised displayed a policy reflecting Conservative desires to rush them into law in the minimum time possible so as to be effective for a general election immediately if the public opinion polls remained favourable to the government. Extra staff were provided by the Home Office to the Boundary Commission to speed up the review, and the government's printers (Her Majesty's Stationery Office) were prematurely ordered on 21 December 1982 to print the English Boundary Commission's report even though it had not at that time been submitted to the Home Secretary and this did not take place legally until 11 February 1983. The view taken by then Labour deputy leader, Roy Hattersley, was that the Home Secretary's enthusiasm for the Boundary Commission's recommendations 'is demonstrated by the allocation of extra staff to the preparatory work in the Right Hon. Gentleman's Department, his encouragement to the Commission to surge ahead, his anticipation of the formal receipt of the report, his ignoring of the court's enjoinder and his decision to send the report to the printers before he had lawfully received it and before the House of Lords had decided whether it was right for him to receive it'.[83]

Clearly, the Home Secretary at present is in a somewhat ambivalent position within the House of Commons in that it falls to him to present the Commissions' recommendations to the House, and although the work is not presented as that of his Department, he or she generally explains and defends the conclusions. An important part in promoting the independence of the Electoral Commission's work from government, and promoting the Commission as an independent impartial agency established for the purpose of making recommendations to the House of Commons, will be to strengthen the existing procedures for parliamentary scrutiny over proposed constituency changes.[84]

(b) Rationalisation of the rules

The statutory provisions laid down to guide the Commissions' work in the redistribution of parliamentary seats need to be reformed quite substantially from those existing at present within the Parliamentary Constituencies Act 1986. The rules need to be clarified and refined to resolve the inherent conflict within them, to redress the practical defects in the existing legal drafting, and to replace the present unacceptably broad degree of discretion left in the hands of the Commission as a result. The rewritten rules should have the purpose of specifying the paramount purpose of redistribution of seats, fixing and keeping down the overall number of seats within the United Kingdom, securing parity between the different regions, replacing the present enumeration date for calculating local electorates and electoral quotas from the start of the review to the annual electoral register prior to the Commission's final report, and instituting a maximum toleration limit away from the electoral quota, which in no circumstances may be departed from.

The legal provisions controlling the number of parliamentary constituencies must be changed and, as suggested earlier in this chapter,[85] should be confined within the range of 475 to 525, with a median figure of 500 seats being aimed at by the Commission. The new provisions must ensure that there is a stop to the creeping growth in numbers that has taken place since the Boundary Commissions were established, which is the inevitable consequence of the poor legal drafting of the existing rules. The critical defect at present is that under rules 5 and 7 the Commission begins its allocation using an electoral quota based upon the existing number of constituencies, but then is given both a general and specific discretion to add to that number under rules 6 and 7, on grounds such as special geographical considerations, preserving local ties or any other inconveniences attendant on alterations to particular constituencies. Such a system is bound always to produce a growth in the number of constituencies. Instead the electoral quota upon which the Commission should aim at equal electorates should be calculated upon the minimum figure of 475 constituencies, and not any higher figure of constituencies that may in fact be in existence. This in itself will terminate the present assumption in rules 5 and 7 that there should never be fewer than the already existing number of constituencies, but further new drafting of the rules should ensure there are clear restrictions to the discretion to add further seats. The rule dealing with equal electorates, currently rule 5, should clearly state that the paramount purpose of the redistribution of seats is to maintain equal electoral sizes between parliamentary constituencies, and that the work of the Commission is to respond to growing or diminishing electorates across existing constituencies, and where necessary to recommend changes to compensate for these shifts in the voting population.

How the Commission does its sums in calculating how many voters there are in any given constituency must surely be based upon the electoral register of the year immediately preceding the final Report of the Commission or, more precisely, upon the exact date of publication of the most recent electoral register. At present, as seen,[86] the enumeration date is the commencement of the Commission's review, and the glaring differences between the size of the local electorates at the beginning and end of the most recent Commission's review is evidence enough that this existing practice is highly inefficient. The rule dealing with local government boundary lines, currently rule 4, should certainly be preserved as the principal ground for departure from mathematical equality, but a maximum tolerance limit of 15 per cent from the electoral quota should be imposed upon its application. Similarly the exceptional ground of special geographical considerations may be retained, currently rule 6, but confined within an exceptional toleration limit of 25 per cent. Under no circumstances should the number of constituencies be permitted to exceed 525, and this would pose no more problems than would be the case with fixing the number of constituencies at a precise figure, which is already done electorally in this country in the case of the 81 European Parliament constituencies.

(c) Fixed twelve-year reviews

The reduction made by the Conservative government through the Boundary Commissions Act 1992 in the statutory intervals between general reviews was certainly an improvement in the timing of boundary changes. A maximum period of twelve instead of fifteen years is more appropriate to modern conditions, which involve the population of the country in being far more mobile than before, and the shifts that take place in local areas often being very rapid. But there is a still greater problem over the timing of reviews which the Act failed to address. This is the floating date allowed for when reviews are to be completed, and the uncertainty for all concerned over when the Reports of the Commissions will be submitted. As a result, no one knows precisely when the changes in parliamentary constituencies will be made, and this can have a chaotic effect on political planning for general elections. It poses great difficulties for individual politicians and political parties alike, especially in the important process of selecting constituency candidates and arranging the campaign to help promote their candidate and win them the support of constituency voters. That the government itself fully appreciates this problem is evident from the fact that it had no wish for any uncertainty itself over whether the changes to be made by the current review would be implemented in time for the next general election, and so in the 1992 Act it additionally imposed a prescribed date for completion of this particular review of 31 December 1994.[87] It is to a large extent this feature of a floating date in the present review machinery – that a Commission's recommendations are to be submitted at some time, unknown to electors and the political parties in advance, on some date within the very wide margin of four years (formerly five until the 1992 Act)[88] – that has led to claims of gerrymandering, and the political and legal shenanegans to either postpone or speed up the Commissions' recommendations, on each of the occasions that Boundary Commission reports have been submitted under the permanent statutory machinery. It was wholly unacceptable that at the review completed in 1983, the House of Commons passed the Orders in Council redistributing parliamentary seats in March, and the general election was called in April. This allowed no proper time for local constituency parties to reorganise themselves, as it necessitated rushing through the selection and confirmation procedures on whom they wished to represent them, and did not allow sufficient notice for proper campaigns to be put before the constituency voters.

The present system should be replaced by the legal requirement for twelve-year fixed reviews. The Commission should commence its general review at the end of ten years from its previous Report, against a background of constant information gathering on population and geographical factors, and electorate statistics, by the staff and secretariat to the Commission. It would then complete its provisional recommendations, its consultation and local inquiry work, and finalisation of recommendations within a two-year time span. The prescribed period should not be reduced below twelve years, at least in the circumstances existing at the present time, for a balance must be struck between fostering the cohesion and identity of constituencies and the life of the political community within them. For parliamentary purposes, considered below,[89] there should then be a period of six months between publication of the Commission's Report by the Home Secretary and the draft Orders in Council being laid before Parliament to put the recommendations with any modifications into legal effect. Finally, there should be a minimum period of one year between the Orders in Council being approved and the changes in parliamentary constituencies coming into effect at the following general election.

Some have argued that a preferable approach is to have a 'rolling review' of constituency boundaries. This would involve the Commission dividing the country up into a number of designated review areas (often counties), and at least one of these areas would be subject to a review by the Commission each year. Michael Steed of Manchester University has for some time been arguing for this system of continuous, ongoing reviews, and it is significant that the English Boundary Commission, when giving evidence to the House of Commons Home Affairs Select Committee in 1986 said that they approved of the idea in principle.[90] According to the scheme, no review area would be subject to more than one redistribution of seats within the lifetime of each Parliament, but at least one review would take place within each twelve-year period. There are clearly some merits in using a 'rolling review' as a means of targeting and dealing with those areas with the greatest population changes, and keeping those constituencies within them as up-to-date as possible. It would also be possible to incorporate the two statutory periods proposed above, a 'cooling off' period of three months between Report and draft Orders in Council, and a year between the Orders and an election, into legislation to give effect to a 'rolling review'.

But the scheme is questionable in that it permits a very large degree of discretion in the hands of the Commission, and makes even more uncertain the precise timing of reviews for any particular constituency within each twelve-year period. From a broader perspective, it is right that every redistribution of parliamentary seats should be a national event which everyone concerned in British politics should be well aware of and paying close attention to. A rolling enterprise would too easily become part of the political 'wallpaper', and devalue each individual constituency review's political importance as a notable event for Parliament and the media to focus attention on. Too frequent redistributions would pass as a largely unnoticed activity, becoming just one more facet of the bureaucratic structure of this country to be taken for granted.

(d)   Constituency consultation

The working procedures relating to local consultation might be improved in a number of ways. First, the level of publicity at present required under section 5(2) of the Parliamentary Constituencies Act 1986 to be given to the Commissions' provisional recommendations on boundary and name changes in a constituency is clearly inadequate if, in fact, the majority of local voters are to be made aware of what is going on. The stipulation for an advertisement in one local newspaper should be extended further to public information broadcasts in local radio and regional television stations. Attention to the proposed changes should also be advertised on appropriate billboard posters. Second, the period of notice described in section 5(2) of one month between the initial advertisement and lodging of the detailed recommendations in a specified public office is too short a period of time for voters to hear about and read what is being recommended, and then prepare any representation they may wish to make. Three months would be a more appropriate period. Third, where a second report and proposal is drawn up for a constituency, there should be a requirement for a mandatory local public inquiry in the same way as for the first proposal. This must be so, since the second proposal is often very different from the original one, yet the evidence given at the first inquiry will have related only to the first proposal and not necessarily to problems or difficulties raised by the later scheme. Several MPs, as indicated above,[91] were surprised at the final changes made in their constituency, which were not those that had been discussed at the inquiry; and even if they had been made aware of the fresh subsequent plans, they felt there had not been an adequate opportunity for constituents to express their views. And finally, while it may be expecting too much for a member of the Commissions' staff to attend local inquiries to explain and defend the proposals that are being made, at the very least local voters are entitled to an explanation of the reasons for the recommendations being put forward for consultation. A statement of the reasons for the changes proposed should always accompany the report made and lodged within the constituency concerned.

(e) Parliamentary review

On 2 March 1983 the draft Parliamentary Constituencies (England) Order, giving effect to the recommendations of the Boundary Commission that would affect 468 of the 516 English MPs, was laid before the House of Commons for its approval. The quality and extent of the House of Commons' control over its own composition was limited to seven hours' discussion at an unsocial time of day at the end of which the government majority approved the changes without modification. Between teatime and bedtime, or more precisely 3.44 pm and 11.30 pm, an often ill-tempered debate took place, with fiercely contested opinions being expressed from all sides of the House. Control over the parliamentary timetable is delegated to the government through Standing Orders, and the Leader of the House, who is a Cabinet minister, simply announces at the beginning of each week what public business will be dealt with and when. Neither does an Order in Council have to pass through different stages of progress (unlike a Bill, which has three separate Readings, a Committee and Report Stage, all offering occasions for parliamentary scrutiny), with opportunity to amend at Committee and Report Stage), but instead is passed complete in one sitting. The view of the opposition spokesman on electoral affairs about the way in which the government presented the Boundary Commissions' recommendations to the House of Commons for their consideration was as follows:[92]

> It really is too much for these proposals, with all their imperfections, to be foisted on the House in one great block. When one considers the parliamentary importance of these proposals, it is constitutionally draconian for the future composition of this House to be decided by a Boundary Commission with discretion so wide that it cannot be challenged in the courts and then by a Government unwilling to take account of suggested modifications and with sufficient Lobby fodder to force their will upon the House.

There are fundamental questions of accountability at issue here. Are the Commissions at present supposed to be independent bodies set up to make constituency changes free from the hands of politicians? Or are the Commissions to be understood as being accountable for their recommendations to the House of Commons, which then makes the final decisions? Or is it right to see the Commissions as an extension of the government, to whom they submit their advice, and the minister is then responsible to Parliament in the normal way? At present there is a confusion of all three of these perfectly legitimate, but very different, constitutional principles. It helps to remember that at law the British Parliament is sovereign in all things and, traditionally, its control over its own composition and proceedings has been a particularly important principle following the constitutional conflicts with the Crown in the seventeenth century. But it also needs recalling that one political purpose of setting up the permanent statutory machinery in the 1940s was not simply to establish an efficient method of periodic constituency review to keep matters up to date, but to try to find a way of cooling down the ferocious political controversy between the parties, and avoiding the extraordinarily protracted parliamentary proceedings that had always accompanied the redistribution of parliamentary seats when made previously by way of primary legislation. The result was a sort of halfway house between an impartial machinery for making the changes, and the final decision being left to Parliament, with ministers in the middle being left with responsibility for drafting the changes and making any necessary modifications. Not surprisingly, therefore, clarity of constitutional principle behind the statutory machinery was somewhat lacking in the ministerial statements to Parliament in the parliamentary debates leading to the Boundary Commissions being set up. But in 1983 the then Home Secretary, William Whitelaw, made a passing reference to the issue of accountability, when he said:[93]

> Implementation through an Act of Parliament [would bring] the recommendations of an impartial Commission right into the political arena. There was always the chance that Parliament might decide to alter the Commission's proposals to suit, not the electorate, but party advantage. The problem was to devise a procedure which allowed a democratically elected Parliament to retain the ultimate control of the redistribution of seats without overwhelming the House with detail or endangering the independence of the Boundary Commission's recommendations.

The situation at the time of writing has moved too far in the opposite direction from parliamentary involvement in constituency affairs, and it is right that MPs should now be given a greater opportunity to scrutinise the work of the Commissions and the recommendations for change that are made. Furthermore, the intermediary position of the Home Secretary is an anomaly. Normal constitutional wisdom would certainly require the most important element of the Commissions' independence to be freedom from interference by government ministers. Yet members of the government have the power to amend the Commissions' proposals, while MPs do not. As the Labour MP, John Maxton, has said, 'If it is wrong for the House to have the power to amend Boundary Commission Reports, it is equally wrong for members of the government to have that power. We should explore how to make Boundary Commissions organs of the House rather than organs of the Home Office.'[94] Symbolically, an important part of this would be to provide for new commissioners to be appointed by way of nomination and approval within the House of Commons. The other ways of improving the quality of parliamentary control lie in the development of existing parliamentary procedures, and this depends upon the willingness of backbenchers at Westminster to assert their authority and right to inquire into and supervise the recommended constituency changes.

The general purpose of such improvements should not be designed to substitute changes and modifications preferred by MPs, but for MPs to be far better informed about what is going on, how the Commissions are operating, and whether the rules and stipulations laid down in the Act are being complied with in the way intended. At present the independence of the Commissions seems almost to be synonymous with the government not letting Parliament know why or how it is operating. Independence means impartial decision-making and freedom from political interference, not secrecy in decision-making and freedom from supervision and criticism. It is essential that Parliament should supervise the efficiency of the agency which performs this vital role in our parliamentary democracy. Yet far from knowing the precise reasons why particular decisions were reached in particular constituencies, very little is even known about the office of the Commissions. We have already seen that the Home Affairs Select Committee had to inquire of commissioners how they were appointed, whether it was on a full-time basis or not, and how often they met. This lack of knowledge was frequently complained about during the 1983 debates. One MP said:[95]

My Hon. Friend the Member for Manchester, Central [Mr Litherland] described the Boundary Commission as a farce. Although I hesitate to use such a word about it, that word does come to mind. Without blaming any one individually and collectively, there are so many and such massive irregularities in its findings that, no matter how the Commissioners try to do their job, especially with the criteria they use, all types of wrongs emerge that are bound to make Hon. Members think more deeply about this. When one thinks about the size of the Commission and the unknown people who work for it, one is bound to conclude that it cannot possibly do a proper job. Even we politicians do not know how many people work for the Commission, how they go about their work and how they come to their conclusions. We do now know whether any form of democracy is involved or whether their decisions are completely arbitrary. We do not know how decisions are made by these powerful individuals who, in their normal lives, probably have nowhere near the same power as they have on the Boundary Commission. . . Virtually no one, even the Chamber, apart from those deeply involved, understands exactly how the Commissioners arrive at their conclusions.

The apparent inconsistencies of policy on the part of the Commissions towards different constituencies around the country in their 1983 recommendations might have been perfectly justifiable and each case might have been founded on good reason. Or the Commissions might have been operating in an erratic fashion, allowing each of the different assistant commissioners too much discretion, and without sufficient central guidance and leadership to pull the general review together as a whole. In either case, Parliament has a right to know. It has a right to understand the detailed reasons why changes are made, and a right to know if the Commissions are operating inefficiently and if they are, how this can be rectified. This is not only essential to avoid unjust criticism of its work, and to increase the level of confidence which MPs and public have in the Commissions, but it is the proper constitutional function of Parliament to be the national body for overseeing and scrutinising all our national administrative bodies.

The first object of reform upon which all parliamentary review should be founded is to secure both the independence and the efficiency of the Electoral Commission's work. Efficiency will be improved by a rationalisation of the rules for redistribution of seats, more specific provisions on timing, and the changes in staffing and working procedures considered earlier. The independence of the Commission would be damaged if Parliament were to be given the power to modify and amend parts of the Commission's proposed changes, and, as in the days when primary legislation was the legal means for effecting constituency changes, months of acrimonious parliamentary debates would ensue if amendments could be tabled by every MP who disliked some section of the draft Order. Parliament should possess, however, the power to veto the Commission's recommendations as a whole. In such a case, it should then be incumbent upon the Commission to resubmit revised recommendations within a specified period of time. Second, the Commission should clearly be seen to be the independent agent of the House of Commons, to whom it should report, and the power of the government to modify recommendations, as in 1948 and 1969, should be abolished. As already suggested, commissioners might be formally appointed by Parliament, and the independence of the Commission's operation otherwise will be considerably improved by the establishment of fixed twelve-year reviews, thus avoiding what has effectively become party political control over the date of implementing the present-day Commissions' report. The third and final component of reform is to improve the quality with which Parliament performs its crucial role in scrutinising and monitoring the work and efficiency of the Commission. If and when Parliament considers improvements are needed in the way the Commission operates, it can enact statutory changes.

The channels of accountability can be strengthened in a number of ways. An important initial reform is that the Commission should be required to give reasons for its proposed changes. At present, a Report of the

Commission gives a brief two or three page account of particular problems faced in each county or similar area containing many different constituencies. The Commission should be required to explain the reasons that led it to its conclusions with respect of each constituency. The Home Affairs Select Committee, composed of eleven MPs drawn from different political parties, should build on its work on electoral affairs carried out over the past ten years, and Standing Orders should specifically make it responsible for examining the expenditure, administration and policy of the Electoral Commission. As with the other departmental Select Committees, created in 1979 and still establishing themselves, this Committee should take a more proactive view of its responsibilities and be prepared to examine administrative problems confronted by the Commission as they arise rather than after the event. The Select Committee's own periodic reports will be submitted to the Commons as a whole for discussion and action if necessary. The Joint Statutory Instruments Committee should continue to scrutinise and advise Parliament on the form of the draft Orders in Council which are submitted every twelve years to give effect to the Commission's proposals.

The nature of parliamentary scrutiny of proposed constituency changes will always be coloured by two realities of life at Westminster. The first is that the government will always be able to control questions of constituency boundary changes, as with all other matters, while it can rely upon a party majority in the House of Commons. Second, the opinion of any individual MP or political party as a whole upon any set of proposals for constituency redistribution is apt to be interpreted according to the vested political interests of that individual or his or her party and the impact the changes will make on political fortunes. As the former Labour deputy leader, Roy Hattersley, has put it:[96]

A Boundary Commission debate offers the House an almost irresistible temptation to behave and speak with a wholly bogus and equally incredible air of purity and objectivity. If we are to have a serious debate on Boundary Commissions, their history and their work, I believe we ought all to begin with an admission. Most politicians' enthusiasm for or antipathy towards a Boundary Commission report is at least influenced by the effect that that report has on the prospects of his or her party . . . I make no allegations or accusations about the Home Secretary. He and I are joined by the mutual attitude of politicians in that we are inclined to look at the Boundary Commission's reports according to whether in our judgement they assist or work to the detriment of our parties. That is our partisan reaction. It is a natural and perhaps proper reaction. I make that admission at once because I believe that if the debate is to have any purpose, it should be honest and serious. It cannot be serious unless it is honest. The honest point is the political bias of all of us as we discuss the report.

None the less it remains one of the House of Commons' most fundamental functions to supervise and protect the working of our democratic process, and this involves a duty to ensure the impartiality and efficiency of the constituency review machinery that Parliament has established. The adoption of the improvements suggested in this chapter will offer backbench MPs in the House a far greater opportunity to oversee this process of the redistribution of parliamentary seats, while preserving the means to challenge the recommendations of the Commissions where a genuine sense of injustice or inappropriate delineation of parliamentary constituency boundaries has been proposed.

5 Parliamentary Candidates

The quality of the work performed by the institutions of Parliament and Government can be no better than the quality of the personnel who fill the places within them. Precisely who is able and willing to stand for Parliament, and whom we choose to elect to political office, raise questions which determine the entire running of the British state. A fundamental principle of parliamentary candidature is that the electorate should be as free as possible to choose whomsoever they wish to represent them. Accordingly, there are no statutory qualifications or requirements as such for a parliamentary candidate to satisfy, simply an ancient legal presumption of the courts that he or she should be of full age and a British subject. However, there are a number of legal disqualifications upon specific grounds, ranging from the holding of a public office deemed incompatible with membership of the House of Commons (such as a civil servant or a judge) to being a person suffering from severe mental illness. So far as legal requirements are concerned, then, it is easy to become a candidate for Parliament in Britain.

But to be a successful candidate requires considerably more. There are a range of political, social and personal qualifications which in practice a candidate will need if he or she is to win the right to sit in the House of Commons. The person concerned must have the support of one of the political parties, and he or she must possess the necessary personal attributes for the job. Not one independent MP was elected from among the 2946 candidates who were legally nominated at the 1992 general election, and minor parties (including the Green Party) failed not only to achieve any seats for their candidates but also polled considerably less than even 1 per cent of the total national votes cast.

To have any real prospect of success at an election, a person must first be adopted as the official candidate of one of the three main national political parties, namely the Conservative Party, Labour Party and the Liberal Democrats (or by the Scottish Nationalist Party, Plaid Cymru or one of the Northern Ireland parties operating regionally). He or she will have to persuade the party selection committee not only that he or she is a good representative of the brand of political opinion within the local constituency association and the national party, but also that he or she is a vote winner and can attract the necessary level of popular support within the constituency to win the seat. If the candidate is the sitting MP seeking re-election, he or she will be judged by the local party selection committee and the local voters upon how he or she has performed over the previous four or

157

so years. The political party selection process is often the most gruelling and testing time for prospective parliamentary candidates in the whole business of reaching Westminster, especially if the constituency he or she wishes to represent is a safe seat in the hands of the party to which he or she belongs. There are many political autobiographies giving vivid accounts of the political intrigue and in-fighting that can take place within a local constituency party going through its procedures for selection (and in the case of the Labour Party, mandatory reselection). After the general election is called, the process of nominating the candidate, appointing an experienced election agent to act on the candidate's behalf with respect to financial matters, arranging a deposit of £500 with the constituency returning officer, together with all the professional skills entailed in launching and maintaining an effective electioneering campaign to win over voters, makes the backing of an established party machinery virtually essential today to a would-be MP.

The person wishing to become an MP must have a formidable array of personal qualities. He or she must possess the necessary personal skills and abilities to sustain the confidence and trust of party colleagues who have selected him or her as their candidate. The candidate must be able to speak effectively at public meetings, and even more importantly perform on radio and television to win over the voters. He or she must be quick thinking, and excel at combating interviewers and debating the details of public policy issues with other candidates. The successful politician must be psychologically tough; sensitive people who are easily offended or angered will not survive long in the bearpit of parliamentary debate, which is well-known for its robust form of verbal attack and criticism. The quality of public comment broadcast across Britain in the media is likely to be even rougher. In all, the successful candidate must have the personal qualities necessary to fulfil a wide variety of different kinds of work and responsibilities expected of a MP, both at Westminster and within his or her constituency. In addition, for those parliamentary candidates who aspire to the top, up to 95 MPs will be chosen by the Prime Minister to work as government ministers. To reach the top of the 'greasy pole' of Westminster politics, therefore, the parliamentary candidate must have the necessary managerial skills to take control of a large department of state, while at the same time representing the political party at a national and international level as one of Britain's foremost public spokesmen and leaders.

ELIGIBILITY TO STAND FOR ELECTION

One might have expected that such an important aspect of our constitutional law as parliamentary candidature would be contained in a single Act of Parliament, readily accessible and intelligible for all. But this is not the case. There is no statute prescribing eligibility to stand for Parliament as such, in the way that the Representation of the People Act 1983 provides for who can vote. Instead, the question of what qualifications are required of a parliamentary candidate by law needs to be answered in the reverse – in other words, who cannot be a candidate? The relevant law is comprised of a plethora of legal disqualifications that have been laid down progressively (and in some cases regressively) over the past three hundred years or more. So a feature of the law on who may and may not become an MP is that, without the help of books such as this volume which look at the whole subject, the legal provisions themselves are extremely difficult to know about and to find. The sources of law on the subject lie scattered across the common law, the law and custom of Parliament, and in many different Acts of Parliament.

Another important feature of the law on candidature is that generally the disqualifications relate not to parliamentary candidacy *per se*, but to membership of the House of Commons. Accordingly, the returning officer who organises the electoral arrangements within the constituency at a general election is not under any general duty to establish whether or not a prospective candidate is, in fact, qualified to stand for election or not. His duty extends only to establishing that the proper procedures for nominating the candidate have been complied with and that the nomination papers which have been delivered are valid.[1] If it happens that a person who is disqualified is elected, then either (a) his or her election can be challenged by one of the other candidates in the Election Court;[2] or (b) the elected candidate may be prevented from taking up his seat at Westminster by a motion initiated inside the House of Commons itself. Such a situation has arisen only very rarely in Britain's history. The precise consequences of a disqualified person being elected depend upon the circumstances. Where a disqualifying factor is unknown to the voters in the constituency, then a by-election will be held for a fresh contest. But if it is established that the local electorate were well aware that the candidate was disqualified, then the runner-up will be declared the lawful Member of Parliament for the constituency. This turn of events happened in the 1960s, in the famous case concerning the Labour MP Tony Benn, following the death of his father, Viscount Stansgate, in 1960 and Mr Benn thereby succeeding to his father's hereditary peerage – a disqualifying factor which meant that he could no longer continue to serve as a member of the House of Commons. Following his Bristol South-East seat being declared vacant, a by-election was held to elect a new MP, at which Tony Benn none the less proceeded to stand as a parliamentary candidate. Despite receiving a resounding majority of the votes cast at the election, winning by 23 275 to his Conservative rival's 10 231, the Election Court declared the Conservative runner-up duly returned as the constituency's lawfully elected MP.[3] Tony Benn's campaign to change the law so that people succeeding to an hereditary peerage can choose to relinquish their title, and thereby become eligible for election to the House of Commons, was eventually successful and enacted in the Peerage Act 1963.

The legal disqualifications

The different categories of legal disqualification will now be identified and explained.

Aliens

As is usual with legislatures around the world, there are nationality restrictions upon becoming an MP. Aliens are disqualified – the term 'alien' being the official legal term for any person who is not a British citizen, a Commonwealth citizen, or a citizen of the Republic of Ireland. Under the ancient common law, only British subjects could stand for election, and this was then confirmed in the Act of Settlement 1700 which provides that, 'No person born out of the kingdoms of England, Scotland or Ireland or the dominions thereunto belonging . . . shall be capable to be . . . a member of either House of Parliament.'[4] In this century, the Ireland Act 1949 specifically retained Irish candidature upon the independence of that country, for reasons similar to those for retaining the right to vote for Irish nationals.[5] And again, similar to franchise arrangements, the right of Commonwealth citizens to stand for election was expressly confirmed and provided for in the Nationality Act 1981.[6]

In juxtaposition, given the apparent similarity of voting and candidature qualifications, it is perhaps remarkable that a candidate does not in fact need to be a British voter in order to stand for election to Parliament. Nor does the candidate have to satisfy any residency qualification in British law, as is common in many other countries, including Canada or Australia, where the person seeking election must have been resident in the country for a minimum period of three years. Certainly, a candidate does not have to live within the constituency where he is standing for election in order to become its MP, although this may prove a factor to be taken into account by local selection committees of the political parties in selecting their parliamentary candidate. Most past and present MPs have not lived within their constituency prior to their adoption as their party's candidate, but subsequently it has been common for them either to move house to that locality or at the very least to buy or rent some *pied-à-terre* there in order to lend credibility to their claims that they keep in close touch with the opinions and interests of the local community.

No provision is made for nationals from other member states of the EU to be eligible to sit in the British Parliament.

Persons under twenty-one years of age

This legal disqualification, which is separately considered later in this chapter, in the context of possible reform, was expressly preserved when the age of majority was otherwise reduced in 1970 to eighteen years of age.[7]

Peers and peeresses

People who are peers or peeresses in their own right, holding titles connected to England, Scotland, Great Britain or the United Kingdom, are disqualified.[8]

This means, in effect, that membership of one of the two Houses of Parliament disqualifies a person from membership of the other. This is a principle followed in virtually all other bicameral legislatures in the world. The second chamber of the British Parliament – the House of Lords – is, however, a rather different kind of legislature from all other Western parliamentary second chambers. It is a non-elected body consisting of 1 202 earls, dukes, viscounts, barons and bishops who, by virtue of their titles, have an automatic and exclusive membership of the House of Lords. With the exception of the twenty-six Lords Spiritual (the Archbishops of Canterbury and York, the Bishops of London, Durham and Winchester, and the twenty-one Anglican bishops who have served longest in their sees) who sit in the House of Lords *ex officio*, all peerages and rights of membership in the House of Lords are permanent – being either hereditary or for life – and there can therefore be no question of retirement from membership of the Lords, except in the single case of a person disclaiming an hereditary title succeeding to him or her within twelve months under the terms of the Peerage Act 1963. Similarly, any member of the House of Commons is effectively disqualified from membership of the parliamentary second chamber – unless and until the Queen, acting on the advice of the Prime Minister, might confer the honour of a peerage upon him or her.

Ministers of religion

All those who have been episcopally ordained to the office of priest or deacon are disqualified. In practice, this means that some types of Christian priest are disqualified, but not others. The disqualification extends to clergy of the Church of England and the Church of Ireland (House of Commons Disqualification Act 1801), and Roman Catholic priests (Roman Catholic Relief Act 1829), but not nonconformist Christian priests (being people who are not episcopally ordained), or clergy of the Church of Wales (Welsh Church Act 1914), or ministers of the Church of Scotland (Presbyterian). Priests of non-Christian faiths are not disqualified. These rules have very little contemporary logic to them, and are further considered in detail later in the chapter,[9] together with recommendations for reform.

Severe mental illness

The common law has always regarded severe mental illness as a disqualifying factor, formerly describing the condition as idiocy or lunacy. More recently, under the 1983 Mental Health Act,[10] there is a special procedure to deal with a situation where an MP is compulsorily detained (or 'sectioned') in a psychiatric hospital upon being certified by a doctor as suffering from severe mental illness. The Speaker of the House of Commons must be informed of the detention, and is empowered to send specialists to review the condition of the MP. There is then a statutory procedure for vacating the MP's parliamentary seat six months later, causing a by-election to be held.

It is worth adding that there are no good grounds today for maintaining that physical disability is a disqualification from candidature or membership of the Commons. Certainly blindness is no bar: the Labour MP David Blunkett sits and participates in the Commons as an opposition front-bench spokesman. There used to be a recognised common law principle that deaf and dumb persons were ineligible, but few would support such a disqualification if it was asserted today. *Schofield's Election Law* still maintains it is a disqualification,[11] but the better view is that of *Parker's Conduct of Parliamentary Elections* which states that, 'In the absence of decided cases, it may be unwise to assume that a court would hold the election of such a candidate to be invalid.'[12] The former Labour MP Jack (now Lord) Ashley was re-elected to the House of Commons after he had become completely deaf, and he proceeded to serve with distinction assisted by a device to help him follow proceedings, later regaining his ability to speak.

Bankruptcy

People declared bankrupt by a court are disqualified from election to Parliament during the period until their bankruptcy is discharged. The current legislation on this ancient rule is contained in section 427 of the Insolvency Act 1986.

Corrupt electoral practices

Those who are reported by the Election Court to have committed a corrupt electoral practice will be disqualified from parliamentary candidature. Corruption was always a disqualifying factor at common law, but now the Representation of the People Act 1983 defines more closely the range of activities which may be held to be a corrupt practice, such as undue influence, bribery or impersonation of voters.[13] A constituency election won by a candidate who is found to have committed a corrupt electoral practice will be declared void, and the candidate will be disqualified from standing again in that constituency for ten years, and in any other constituency for five years. He or she is also disqualified from voting or being registered as an elector for five years. Similarly, any other person who commits a corrupt electoral practice is barred from candidature or voting in any constituency for five years. Candidates are always held responsible for corrupt practices indulged in by their election agents, and in such situations the candidate is disqualified for a period of seven years from standing again for election in the constituency he or she was contesting.

Inherent power of the House of Commons to expel its own members

The House of Commons possesses the inherent power to control its own composition and proceedings.[14] This means that a majority in the House can resolve to expel a member of whom it disapproves, whether for reasons relating to his or her conduct, or any other matter. This power has been exercised only very rarely in recent British history: in 1922, when it was used to remove an MP who was guilty of fraudulent conversion of property; and in 1947 to remove Garry Allighan who had given false answers to an inquiry of the Privileges Committee. Further back in Britain's past, however, it was a power used regularly to get rid of members regarded as unfit to sit in the Commons, on a wide variety of grounds ranging from being guilty of fraud, perjury and libel, to rebellion, or simply conduct unbecoming of an officer and a gentleman. However, if a Commons majority does choose to eject an MP in this way, the expulsion only has the effect of vacating that person's parliamentary seat, and it does not disqualify him or her from standing for election again at the subsequent by-election. The radical John Wilkes in the eighteenth century was expelled and re-elected three times in this way before the House of Commons decided to tolerate his presence. Similarly, just over a hundred years ago, when the militant atheist Charles Bradlaugh was expelled but re-elected, no question was raised of the legal validity of his membership of the House as a result of the fresh election.

Sitting member

There is nothing to prevent a parliamentary candidate standing for election in as many constituencies as he or she wishes. There might, in fact, be some advantage to a political party if their most prominent figures did so, in order to be sure that they were elected and could therefore serve in the government. In modern times, however, quite rightly, it is not regarded as ethical for political leaders to do this, although in the past it was not uncommon. In 1880, for example, the two leading Liberal statesmen, William Gladstone and Lord Hartington, were each elected in two constituencies, and Charles Parnell was elected in three Irish constituencies. The record number of candidacies held by one person seems to have been held by T. L. Keen and Harold Smith, who between them at the

October 1974 general election contested twenty-nine constituencies (losing their deposits in all of them).[15] Where such a candidate wins in more than one constituency, then he or she has a free choice as to which of them to represent in the House of Commons, and a by-election will be held in the other constituencies.

Representation of the People Act 1981

This Act disqualifies any person who has been sentenced to more than one year's imprisonment from being elected during the period in which he or she is in prison. It was passed as a direct result of an Irish Republican Army hunger-striker, Bobby Sands, being elected MP in an April 1981 by-election in the Northern Ireland constituency of Fermanagh and South Tyrone while he was serving a long term of imprisonment.

House of Commons (Disqualification) Act 1975

This Act disqualifies a wide range of public office holders. It is the single most important legal measure affecting eligibility for parliamentary candidature, and as such is considered at length separately later in the chapter.[16] In outline, it lays down six classes of office holders who are disqualified, namely: (1) holders of certain judicial offices including High Court and Court of Appeal judges (Law Lords are already disqualified by virtue of being peers); (2) civil servants, whether established or not, and whether full or part time; (3) members of the regular armed forces; (4) full time police officers; (5) members of the legislature of any country outside the Commonwealth; and (6) holders of any of the offices listed in the Act. This list, laid out in schedules to the Act, is a very lengthy one. The Act enables the government to add to or vary the list from time to time by way of parliamentary resolution and an Order in Council. The Act also lays down the important rule that no more than ninety-five people holding ministerial office are entitled to sit and vote in the House of Commons.

The main principle guiding these provisions, therefore, is that the holding of paid employment in the service of the government is incompatible with the work of a parliamentarian, whose constitutional task it is to maintain a close scrutiny over the affairs of public administration. It is interesting to note that British law has not developed any analogous prohibition upon paid employment being accepted by MPs in the private sector, where the nature of the work might be incompatible. Some believe there should be a disqualification of this kind. In 1987 Dennis Canavan presented draft legislation into the Commons which was designed to 'disqualify from membership of Parliament people with pecuniary interests which are incompatible with proper representation of the people'.[17] The object of the legislation would be to ensure that MPs were not distracted by paid outside employment from their parliamentary duties, and to ensure that no conflicts of interest arose. In some countries, including the USA, there are constitutional laws of this nature which limit the percentage of outside income that a member of the legislature may earn. Dennis Canavan proposed that a ceiling of 5 or 10 per cent of their parliamentary salary be imposed, together with mandatory disclosure of all financial interests of MPs, and a code of practice to regulate the type and performance of work that MPs might undertake, to ensure compatibility with the work of an MP. In the event of these restrictions being broken, the MP would be disqualified from the House and his or her seat declared vacant. Despite the merits and serious issues raised by this measure, it received very little support among MPs and was not allocated time by the government for a full debate.

Bailiff or steward of the Chiltern Hundreds or the Manor of Northstead

Acceptance of one of these two ancient offices automatically disqualifies a person from membership of the House of Commons. This was so under the old law disqualifying people from holding an office of profit under the Crown, and they are expressly among the disqualifying public offices in the House of Commons Disqualification Act 1975. They are in reality only nominal public offices, which specifically serve the purpose in practice of operating a legal fiction whereby an MP may resign his seat if he or she so wishes. There is otherwise no legal procedure whereby an MP can quit the job since, in *Erskine May's* words, 'It is a settled principle of parliamentary law that a Member after he is duly chosen, cannot relinquish his seat.'[18] In the relatively few cases when an MP wishes to resign, therefore (recent cases being Stuart Holland in 1989 and Leon Brittan to become a European Commissioner in 1988) he or she simply applies to the Chancellor of the Exchequer for one of these two offices, a request which is almost automatically granted, and, in effect, the MP is then voluntarily disqualifying himself. A by-election will need to be held in his or her constituency to fill the vacant seat in the Commons.

Timing of the disqualifying factor

Curiously, there is no clear legal statement on the precise time at which the disqualifying factor applies. At what exact time does a disqualifying factor end or begin for the purposes of standing as a parliamentary candidate? Is it the time of nomination, or the date of the general election, or the date when Parliament first meets after the election? Clearly, if a person is free from disqualification at nomination time, and also on the day of the election, but then he or she becomes disqualified at or following the time when Parliament first convenes, then his or her seat in the House of Commons becomes vacant, and a by-election must be held. But what happens if a person is disqualified in the period due for receipt of nomination papers, but he or she knows that he or she will *become* eligible about ten or twelve days later, when the election actually takes place? For example, what if a candidate's twenty-first birthday falls between these two dates, or a legal impediment such as bankruptcy or holding an office of profit under the Crown is discharged? It is highly unsatisfactory that there is no clear statutory provision on this issue.

Neither is the common law of any real assistance, as in practice disputes over the right to be a candidate are few and far between. The principal legal authority is the case of *Harford* v. *Linsky*[19] in 1899, which suggests that nomination is the crucial time. *Harford* v. *Linsky* involved a dispute dealing with the analogous situation of a local authority election. The question was whether or not a person was disqualified by reason of his interest in a commercial contract with the local corporation (not, of course, a legal impediment applicable to a parliamentary election), despite the fact that he could have assigned his interest before the date of the election. Holding that this person was indeed disqualified from candidature, Mr Justice Wright in the Queen's Bench Division said he thought it 'safest' that 'a person, who at the time of the nomination is disqualified for election in the manner in which this petitioner was disqualified, is disqualified also for nomination'.[20] The judge made the point that nomination is an essential part of the election process, illustrated best in his view by the legal rule (which is applicable also in modern parliamentary election law) that if there are no other competitors, the statement of the returning officer showing only one nomination shall also declare that candidate elected and no poll is necessary.[21] The judge also maintained that any other construction of the timing of disqualification would lead to much confusion:[22]

> What is to be the effect if the disqualification continues until the poll begins, or until the middle of polling day, or until the close of the poll? Will votes given before the removal of the disqualification be valid? If not, how is the number of them to be ascertained? It seems to us unreasonable to hold that the [law] means to leave the matter in such a state of uncertainty.

For these reasons he thought the effective moment for disqualification must be the time for nomination.

There is a major distinction, however, to be drawn between disqualifications which may be removed before the poll, and those which necessarily will be. In *Harford* v. *Linsky* there could be some uncertainty about whether the disqualification would be lifted in time, but in the case of a person being nominated on the last day of his twenty-first year it is certain the restriction relating to age would no longer apply at the date of the poll. Similarly, where there is a fixed disqualification period of time, imposed, for example, upon individuals guilty of corrupt electoral practices, it will be known for certain if the disqualification is to end on a date before polling day.

Unfortunately, Mr Justice Wright declined to give an opinion of the law on such cases, or to say whether the conclusion he reached on the facts of *Harford* v. *Linsky* would also apply.

British election law should not be uncertain on this detail concerning the timing of the disqualifying factor, however rare it might be for the issue to arise. Accordingly, a provision that clarifies the position should be inserted in the next Representation of the People Bill to be presented to Parliament. Certainty is more important than the choice between the various options when discussing the time for disqualification. Thus either nomination should be taken as the time for the disqualifying factor generally, or else an authoritative statement distinguishing between the different disqualifications might be put into statutory writing.

We shall now consider in greater detail some special problems relating to the eligibility of parliamentary candidates in three of the categories outlined above. These concern, first, the age for candidature; second, the way in which public officials are prohibited from standing for election under the House of Commons Disqualification Act 1975; and third, the archaic rules for proscribing certain ministers of religion from entering Westminster.

SPECIAL PROBLEMS IN DISQUALIFICATION

The age limit for candidature

Those people who have not yet reached their twenty-first birthday are disqualified from election to the House of Commons under the terms of section 7 of the Parliamentary Elections Act 1695:

> No person hereafter shall be capable of being elected a member to serve in this or any future Parliament who is not of the age of one-and-twenty years and every election or return of any person under that age is hereby declared to be null and void. And if any such minor hereafter chosen shall presume to sit or vote in Parliament he shall incur such penalties and forfeiture as if he had presumed to sit and vote in Parliament without being chosen or returned.

This age limit was recognised in the courts before the Act, including in one case heard by Sir Edward Coke in 1623.[23] That case dealt with the fact that in practice some members were being elected to the House of Commons, and speaking and voting there despite being under 21 years of age. Coke held that these members were indeed disqualified under the law and custom of Parliament, but that several sat 'by connivancy, but if questioned would be put out'. Even following the 1695 Act some under-age members sat 'by connivance' and are recorded as participating in parliamentary debates, including some who later became famous, such as Charles James Fox and

Lord John Russell. There are no reported instances of disqualified minors being tolerated in this way after the greater rationalisation of political representation made in the 1832 Reform Act.

Why has the age for candidature remained at 21 years, and not been reduced to 18 years? In the late 1960s the Labour government under Harold Wilson decided to grant full citizenship to all people at the age of 18. By section 1 of the Family Law Reform Act 1969, which came into force on 1 January 1970, 'A person shall attain full age on attaining the age of eighteen instead of on attaining the age of twenty-one.' People aged 18 were now to be entitled to equal civil rights as with any other adult, including freedom from restrictions on property ownership, the right to marry, the right to bring legal actions, and the enjoyment of a host of other basic rights of citizenship. It excluded voting,[24] but separately in the same year a Representation of the People Act was passed, lowering the right to vote from 21 to 18 years, taking effect from publication of the new annual electoral register on 16 February 1970 and therefore for any general election that year. It had in fact been the intention of the government to reduce the age for voting to 20 years, as recommended by the final Report of the Speaker's Conference on Electoral Law begun in 1965 and published in February 1968. But, as the then Leader of the House of Commons, Richard Crossman, recorded in his *Diaries of a Cabinet Minister*, from that time, 'It was obvious that if you reduced the age for everything else it was impossible to keep voting at twenty so . . . we now had to recommend votes at eighteen.'[25] For some extraordinary and unclear reason, this sentiment did not extend to the other crucial exception to the Family Law Reform Act, namely the age for parliamentary candidature. The Representation of the People Act 1969 simply ignored the remaining candidature exception. The Cabinet failed to consider the matter at all,[26] and throughout the parliamentary debates in both Houses during the passage of both Acts in 1969, not a single mention was made of the candidature age and its omission from the terms of the new legislation.

There remains today this inconsistency in our election law, between being an elector at 18 but not being electable until 21. At one end of the political process, the exercise of the vote, the age of maturity is set at 18; but at the other, receiving end – candidature – a different level of maturity is prescribed. Arguments for this discrepancy might include that 18 year olds are too immature and inexperienced to be working at Westminster and representing the nation, as opposed to expressing a political opinion through the vote. Some would say there is no reason why voting and candidature ages should automatically be identical, and it is true that some other countries have disparate ages. In the USA voting is from the age of 18, but candidature to the House of Representatives is limited to 25 year olds and upwards (and 30 years in the case of their second chamber, the Senate). In France, voting is at 18, but people must be 23 before standing for election to the National Assembly (and 35 years old for their Senate). On the other hand, it is precisely upon the principle that adults should assume equal civil responsibilites at the same time, and that only the electorate can pass any further judgement on a candidate's suitability for political office, that many other countries including Australia, Canada and Germany make 18 years the age for both voting and candidature.

Some will also argue that reducing the age for candidature will make negligible difference in the number of candidates coming forward, and so it is not worth the bother of drawing up the necessary legislation or amending the clause in the next Representation of the People Act. It is again true that in practice few people between the ages of 18 and 20 will wish to start a professional political career, and it is very rare for a local party association to wish to select someone at that age to be their official candidate, especially as there is always stiff competition from experienced party members and campaigners, as well as former MPs defeated at the previous election looking for a new constituency. None the less, the law governing our democracy should reflect points of rational principle, not anachronisms that Parliament has overlooked to debate, or finds inconvenient to consider. Even if only one person is blocked from becoming a parliamentary candidate by this antiquated 1695 law, in the absence of a sound constitutional basis it is an unjustifiable restriction upon the electoral process. Over the past twenty-five years there have been many parliamentary candidates in their early twenties, most beginning their political careers in unwinnable seats for their parties, but also some who have won and been elected to the House of Commons. Such people include the former Cabinet minister Paul Channon at the age of 23 in a 1969 by-election, Charles Kennedy at the age of 24 in the 1983 general election, and Matthew Taylor at the age of 23 in a 1987 by-election. There have been seven MPs during the twentieth century who have been elected at exactly 21 years of age.[27] And there have certainly been instances of MPs who had to wait until they were 21 to be adopted as a parliamentary candidate, including Sir Richard Body, the present Conservative Member for Holland with Boston constituency and a leading supporter of a reduction in the candidature age to 18.[28] Only a parliamentary debate on the issue can determine the matter, but the signs are that there is in fact strong cross-party support for reform. Many Labour MPs support the idea, the Liberal Democrats included it in their 1992 election pledges, and in 1985 a group of Conservative backbenchers tabled a Members of Parliament (Minimum Age) Bill but this failed to receive time for consideration.[29] It must be hoped that time can be found at some point in the near future for the reintroduction of this draft legislation. The 21 years age restriction upon candidature is anomalous, and should be reduced to 18 years, consistent with the right to vote. After a person has reached adulthood at eighteen for virtually all other civil purposes, he or she should be free to offer himself for election to Parliament, and the law should not restrict the choice of local voters to decide for themselves the suitability of the particular candidate, and whether or not he or she is the best person to be representing them.

Public officeholders and the House of Commons Disqualification Act 1975

The widest category of exclusion from parliamentary candidature is that of those who work for the state or otherwise in the public sector. The constitutional principle that state officials and other public officeholders should be banned from sitting in Parliament needs to be understood from our history, and in particular parliamentary concern to prohibit all those who held 'offices or places of profit under the Crown', which arose originally in the seventeenth century from the need to prevent placemen of the King swamping the House of Commons, thus putting it effectively under the Crown's control. From the seventeenth century to 1957, a great many parliamentary resolutions were passed on the matter, and around a hundred statutes enacted at different times, perhaps most importantly the Succession to the Crown Act 1707, the 'Place Act' of 1741 and the House of Commons (Disqualification) Act 1801. By the middle of the twentieth century the law was in a highly unsatisfactory state, not only because the political context within which the various resolutions and statutes operated had become something quite different, with Britain having evolved from a monarchic to a Cabinet system of government, but because the proliferation of legal rules on the subject had left the the law on public officeholders muddled and uncertain. Parliament in 1957 updated and codified the law in a single statute, and this is now re-enacted in the House of Commons Disqualification Act 1975.

According to a parliamentary committee which examined the subject in 1941, there are three guiding principles underlying the law concerning public officeholder restrictions on becoming an MP:[30]

There can be traced the genesis and gradual development of the three chief principles which by the beginning of the eighteenth century had become, and have since been, and should still be, the main considerations affecting the law on this subject. These, in the order of historical sequences, are:

(1) Incompatibility of certain non-ministerial offices with membership of the House of Commons (which must be taken to cover questions of a Member's relations with, and duties to, his constituents),
(2) The need to limit the control or influence of the executive government over the House by means of an undue proportion of officeholders being Members of the House, and

(3)   The essential condition of a certain number of ministers being Members of the House for the purpose of ensuring control of the executive by Parliament.

The first principle is one often adopted by legislatures around the world to distinguish between questions of eligibility for membership, and questions of incompatibility of certain individuals to serve as an MP by virtue of other work they do. There may be different reasons for the incompatibility, but they will usually involve practical conflicts of interest, or else ideas of constitutional wisdom such as the desirability of maintaining the separation of powers between executive, legislature and judiciary. The second and third principles spoken of by the committee specifically concern the relations between ministers and members of the government – in other words political officeholders – and the House of Commons. There is as much reason today as there was under King James II to ensure that members belonging to the executive branch of state do not dominate the legislature, or else parliamentary control and scrutiny of the government would be under-mined. Under the British political system there is no strict separation of powers between executive and legislature, in that ministers are appointed from the membership of the House of Commons and thus there is an overlap of personnel. On the contrary, the idea that ministers should sit in Parliament and be directly answerable to MPs is fundamental to the British method of political responsibility. The 1975 Act reflects the need to strike a balance between executive dominance of, and ministerial responsibility to, the House of Commons. The law relating to non-political officeholders, and ministers or political officeholders, must be considered separately in turn.

All civil servants are disqualified from becoming MPs.[31] This restriction on all civil servants is consistent with the strong constitutional principle that the civil service should be politically neutral and impartial. As part of the permanent machinery of state civil servants are expected to serve governments of any political persuasion, and while individuals will always hold their own private political views, the preservation of confidence in the system requires civil servants to be excluded from all active or public participation in party politics. The usual formal definition of a civil servant is that he or she is a Crown servant, other than the holder of a political or judicial office (or a member of the armed forces), who is appointed directly or indirectly by the Crown, paid wholly out of funds provided by Parliament, and employed in a central government department of state. The Act makes it clear that part-time as well as full-time civil servants are disqualified, and that the civil service of the Crown includes the civil service of Northern Ireland, the Northern Ireland Courts Service, Her Majesty's Diplomatic Service and Her Majesty's Overseas Civil Service (but not the Royal Observer Corps).[32] Employees of nationalised industries, and local government workers, are not civil servants and are therefore not precluded from standing for Parliament.

Similarly, members of the armed forces are disqualified.[33] This means all regular members of the Army, the Royal Navy and the Royal Air Force, and also members of the Women's Royal Naval Service, Queen Alexandra's Royal Naval Nursing Service, and the Ulster Defence Regiment. Members of the Territorial Army, non-commissioned members of the reserve forces, and people on the retired or emergency lists of any of the armed forces, are not disqualified, because they do not fall within the definition of regular members of the armed forces.[34] The titles of Field Marshal, Admiral of the Fleet and Air Marshal are personal to the recipients, and such people would only be disqualified if they in fact hold regular appointments within the armed forces. There used to be a custom within the armed forces that any member who stood for election to Parliament would automatically be released from the Service. No doubt this is largely derived from the fact that many military people in the past have gone into politics, both professions being linked by being thought of as particularly suitable for gentlemen from upper-middle-class families. However, in the 1960s, the existence of this custom was exploited by a large number of recruits who had signed their lives away to the armed forces for a number of years and were refused an early discharge on any other grounds. The successful pioneer of this wheeze was Malcolm Thompson in 1962, who, having had his application for demobilisation turned down when he wanted to go to university, then stood as an Independent parliamentary candidate at a by-election in Middlesbrough and as a result was granted a discharge.[35] To deal with this situation now, an advisory body of two senior barristers and six former MPs is established by the Home Secretary, with responsibility for vetting regular servicemen standing as parliamentary candidates, and only recommending discharges for those few who in their opinion have a serious wish and prospect of a political career.

For reasons of judicial independence and maintaining the credibility of the political neutrality and impartiality of the administration of justice, most members of the judiciary are disqualified, as are full-time members of the police.[36] It is clearly vital that full-time judges, who are regularly called upon to decide cases where a government minister or department is one of the litigants, are free from any party political ties. Law Lords are already ineligible to stand for election to Parliament, by virtue of being life peers sitting in the parliamentary chamber of the House of Lords. The 1975 Act prohibits circuit judges, and judges of the High Court and Court of Appeal, and similarly judges of the Court of Session, the High Court of Justice of Court of Appeal in Northern Ireland, the Courts-Martial Appeal Court, and the Scottish Land Court. Other prohibited judicial officeholders are stipendiary magistrates, Social Security commissioners, Sheriffs in the Sheriff Courts in Scotland, and income tax commissioners. Ordinary magistrates or Justices of the Peace, and Recorders, are not included in the list, so are able to stand as parliamentary candidates. The disqualification of the police extends only to full-time members of any police force maintained by any police authority, so special constables (who are part-time) are not disqualified and neither are constables who work for other authorities such as the railway bodies and London Underground police. Members of the legislature of any country or territory outside the Commonwealth are also stated by the Act to be disqualified.[37] As non-Commonwealth citizens are already disqualified for candidacy, with the exception of citizens of the Republic of Ireland, the main effect of this provision is to disqualify members of the Seanad and the Dail of the Republic of Ireland. The principle that a member of one legislature should not be a member of any other is surely a good one, upon grounds of possible conflict of interest, and that both positions are likely to require full-time attention. At present there is no restriction upon a person standing and being elected to both the House of Commons and the European Parliament, and as the future workload and importance of the European assembly continues to grow, the case becomes stronger for excluding Members of the European Parliament from parliamentary candidature.

There is, then, a provision in the 1975 Act banning from membership of the House of Commons any person who holds any one of a huge number of specified particular public offices. All such positions are non-political and range in nature of responsibility from membership of the Independent Broadcasting Authority to the British Railways Board, and the University Funding Council. The list of prohibited offices is contained in a schedule to the Act which, as new public posts are created, may be, and often has been, added to from time to time without the need for fresh primary legislation, under a procedure explained below. The strong view of the Report of the Commons' Select Committee which preceded the legislation in 1957 that reformed and codified the law on offices and places of profit under the Crown, was that,

> Electors should be allowed as wide a field as possible from which to select their representatives . . . It is for constituents to decide whether or not a person is suitable to represent them in the House of Commons in view of his other occupations or of any office he holds . . . There are several classes of non-ministerial officeholders whom there is no good reason for excluding from membership . . . It is therefore important to see that such persons are not inadvertently or unnecessarily disqualified. Provided that such an office is not incompatible with membership of the House, does not substantially interfere with performance of a Member's duties, and is not of such a nature as to increase the influence or control of the executive government, there would seem to be no good reason for the House to exclude holders thereof.

Readers may decide whether all of the offices listed on pages 175–81 are disqualifications that are essential upon grounds either of incompatibility or executive domination.

The most controversial feature of the House of Commons Disqualification Act is the great length of this list of non-ministerial offices whose occupants are excluded from parliamentary candidature, accompanied by the rather nebulous and arbitrary criteria upon which the offices appear to be selected under a power conferred in section 5 of the Act. Such disqualifications are legally effected by way of simple resolution of the Commons in response to a Treasury minister's motion, then legitimised in an extra-parliamentary Order in Council. The section reads:

> If at any time it is resolved by the House of Commons that Schedule 1 to this Act [that is offices disqualifying from membership] be amended, whether by the addition or omission of any office or the removal from one Part of the Schedule to another, or by altering the description of any office specified therein, Her Majesty may by Order in Council amend that Schedule accordingly.

In 1985 for example, this matter of some constitutional importance was dealt with in twenty-four minutes, from 7.29 to 7.53 pm, with a very low attendance in the Commons' chamber. There was no statement or elaboration given by Mr Barney Hayhoe, the proposing government minister, of the reasons for adding further job titles to the list of excluded people, but just a reference to a brief explanatory note deposited in the Vote Office of the House, which included *inter alia* the rather engaging phrase – 'the need to disqualify has only just been recognised'.[38] New officials suffering erosion of their political liberty included a Member of the Trinity House Lighthouse Board, the Chairman of the Northern Ireland Tourist Board, the Chairman of the Red Deer Commission, and a director of any company in receipt of financial assistance under section 5 of the Films Act 1985. In all, nineteen such additions were made, together with several other amendments. Was it really constitutionally vital that all these new people, mainly part-time public workers, earning little over £4 000 a year from the state, should be prohibited from membership of the Commons, if their local electorate wished to support them? Possibly so, but this procedure for parliamentary scrutiny and control over loss of political rights to stand for election to the Commons is very inadequate. As the MP Douglas Hogg, later a Minister of State at the Foreign and Commonwealth Affairs office, commented at the time, 'We as the legislature should not entrust to ministers and officials the right to enfranchise or to disqualify.'[39] The practice of the House of Commons should be changed and the 1975 Act amended, so that proposals to exclude further public officeholders are always referred to a special Select Committee established by standing orders for the purpose,

Public offices disqualifying holders from membership of the House of Commons

(A) DISQUALIFYING OFFICES

Additional Commissioner of the Commission for Racial Equality.

Additional Commissioner of the Equal Opportunities Commission.

Additional Commissioner of the Equal Opportunities Commission for Northern Ireland.

Adjudicating medical practitioner or specially qualified adjudicating medical practitioner appointed under or by virtue of Part III of the Social Security Act 1975 or Part III of the Social Security (Northern Ireland) Act 1975.

Adjudicator appointed for the purposes of the Immigration Act 1971.

Advocate Depute (not being the Solicitor General for Scotland) appointed by the Lord Advocate.

Ambassador or Permanent Representative to an international organisation representing Her Majesty's Government in the United Kingdom.

Assessor of Public Undertakings (Scotland).

Assistant Commissioner appointed under Part IV of the Local Government Act 1972.

Assistant Commissioner appointed under Part II of the Local Government (Scotland) Act 1973.

Attorney General of the Duchy of Lancaster.

Auditor of the Civil List.

Auditor of the Court of Session.

Boundary Commissioner or assistant Commissioner appointed under Schedule I to the Parliamentary Constituencies Act 1986.

Certification officer or assistant certification officer appointed under section 7 of the Employment Protection Act 1975.

Chairman of the Advisory Board for the Research Councils.

Chairman or Vice-Chairman of the Advisory Committee on Distinction Awards.

Chairman of the Agricultural and Food Research Council.

Chairman or member of a panel of deputy-chairmen of an Agricultural Land Tribunal.

Chairman or Director-General of the British Council.

Chairman of the British Library Board.

Chairman of the British Overseas Trade Board.

Chairman of the Business & Technician Education Council.

Paid Chairman of the Central Transport Consultative Committee for Great Britain established under section 56 of the Transport Act 1962.

Chairman or Deputy Chairman of the Civil Service Appeal Board.

Chairman of a consumers' committee appointed under section 2 of the Electricity Act 1989.

Chairman of the Council for the Accreditation of Teacher Education.

Chairman of the Countryside Commission for Scotland and any other member of the Commission in receipt of remuneration.

Chairman, Deputy Chairman or Managing Director of the Crown Agents for Overseas Governments and Administrations.

Chairman of a customer service committee maintained under section 28 of the Water Industry Act 1991.

Chairman or Vice-Chairman of the Dental Practice Board or member of that Board appointed at an annual salary.

Chairman of a designated agency within the meaning of the Financial Services Act 1986 if he is in receipt of remuneration.

Chairman of the Distinction and Meritorious Service Awards Committee for Northern Ireland.

Chairman of the Economic and Social Research Council.

Chairman of the English National Board for Nursing, Midwifery and Health Visiting.

Chairman of Enterprise Ulster.

Chairman of the Fire Authority for Northern Ireland.

Chairman or other full-time member of the Forestry Commission.

Chairman of the Gas Consumers' Council.

Chairman or Deputy Chairman of the General Consumer Council for Northern Ireland.

Chairman or any member, not being also an employee, of a Health Board constituted under the National Health Service (Scotland) Act 1978.

Chairman of the Health and Safety Agency for Northern Ireland.

Chairman of the Health and Safety Commission.

Chairman or any member, not being also an employee, of a Health and Social Services Board established under Article 16 of the Health and Personal Social Services (Northern Ireland) Order 1972.

Chairman or non-executive director of a Health and Social Services trust established under the Health and Personal Social Services (Northern Ireland) Order 1991.

Chairman or Deputy Chairman, in receipt of remuneration, of the Historic Buildings and Monuments Commission for England.

Public offices disqualifying holders from membership of the House of Commons (*contd.*)

Chairman or Vice-Chairman of the Home-Grown Cereals Authority.

Paid Chairman of an Industrial Training Board constituted under the Industrial Training Act 1964 or the Industrial Training Act 1982 or of a committee appointed under either of those Acts or paid Deputy Chairman of such a board.

Chairman of the Inland Waterways Amenity Advisory Council.

Chairman or Deputy Chairman of the Langside Corporation.

Chairman of the Land Authority for Wales.

Chairman, Vice-Chairman or member of the executive committee of the Land Settlement Association Limited appointed at a salary.

Chairman of the Legal Aid Board.

Chairman of the Letchworth Garden City Corporation.

Chairman of the Livestock Marketing Commission for Northern Ireland.

Chairman of a local flood defence committee for any district in England and Wales.

Chairman of the Local Government Staff Commission for Northern Ireland.

Chairman of the London and Metropolitan Government Staff Commission.

Chairman in receipt of remuneration of the London Regional Passengers' Committee.

Chairman or any member, not being also an employee, of the Management Committee of the Common Services Agency for the Scottish Health Service constituted under the National Health Service (Scotland) Act 1978.

Chairman of the Mental Health Commission for Northern Ireland.

Chairman or any member, not being also an employee, of a committee constituted under section 91 of the Mental Health (Scotland) Act.

Chairman or Deputy Chairman of the National Consumer Council.

Chairman of the National Council for Vocational Qualifications.

Chairman of the National Enterprise Board.

Chairman or non-executive member of a National Health Service trust established under the National Health Service and Community Care Act 1990 or the National Health Service (Scotland) Act 1978.

Chairman of the National Research Development Corporation.

Chairman of the Natural Environment Research Council.

Chairman of the Northern Ireland Central Services Agency for the Health and Social Services.

Chairman of the Northern Ireland Civil Service Appeal Board.

Chairman of the Northern Ireland Tourist Board.

Chairman of the Northern Ireland Training Authority.

Any Chairman of the Plant Varieties and Seeds Tribunal.

Chairman or Vice-Chairman of the Police Authority for Northern Ireland.

Chairman of the Post Office Users' National Council.

Chairman of the Prescription Pricing Authority.

Chairman of the Probation Board for Northern Ireland.

Chairman of the Public Health Laboratory Service Board.

Chairman of the Red Deer Commission.

Chairman of a regional flood defence committee for any area of England and Wales.

Chairman or any member, not being also an employee, of any Regional Health Authority, District Health Authority, Family Health Services Authority or special health authority which is a relevant authority for the purposes of paragraph 9(1) of Schedule 5 to the National Health Service Act 1977.

Chairman of the Science and Engineering Research Council.

Chairman of the Scottish Dental Practice Board or a member of that Board appointed at an annual salary.

Chairman of the Scottish Legal Aid Board.

Chairman or Vice-Chairman of the Scottish Sports Council.

A regional or other full-time Chairman of Social Security Appeal Tribunals, Medicine Appeal Tribunals and Disability Appeal Tribunals.

A full-time chairman of Social Security Appeal Tribunals and Medical Appeal Tribunals for Northern Ireland.

Chairman of a special health and social services agency established under Article 3 of the Health and Personal Social Services (Special Agencies) (Northern Ireland) Order 1990.

Chairman of the Special Hospitals Service Authority.

Chairman or Vice-Chairman of the Sports Council.

Chairman or Vice-Chairman of the Sports Council for Northern Ireland.

Chairman or Vice-Chairman of the Sports Council for Wales.

Chairman of the Standing Advisory Commission on Human Rights constituted under section 20 of the Northern Ireland Constitution Act 1973.

Chairman of the Training Enterprise and Education Advisory Group for Wales.

Chairman of a transferee body within the meaning of Schedule 11 to the Financial Services Act 1986 if he is in receipt of remuneration.

Chairman of the tribunal constituted under section 706 of the Income and Corporation Taxes Act 1988.

Chairman of the United Kingdom Central Council for Nursing, Midwifery and Health Visiting.

Chairman of the Wine Standards Board of the Company of the master, wardens and commonalty of Vintners of the City of London.

Chairman of the Women's Royal Voluntary Service.

Chief Electoral Officer for Northern Ireland or any whole time officer appointed under section 14A(I) of the Electoral Law Act (Northern Ireland) 1962.

Chief executive of the National Enterprise Board.

Chief executive of the Simpler Trade Procedures Board.

Chief Scientist of the Scottish Home and Health Department.

Clerk or deputy clerk of a district council in Northern Ireland.

The Commissioner for Local Administration in Scotland.

Commissioner or Assistant Commissioner appointed under section 50(1) or (2) of, or Schedule 4 to, the Local Government Act (Northern Ireland) 1972.

Commissioner or Assistant Commissioner of Police of the Metropolis.

Commissioner of the City of London Police.

Commissioner for the Rights of Trade Union Members.

Commons Commissioner.

Comptroller and Auditor General.

Comptroller and Auditor General for Northern Ireland.

Controller of Audit appointed under section 97(4) of the Local Government (Scotland) Act 1973.

Controller of Audit appointed under paragraph 7(1) of Schedule 3 to the Local Government Finance Act 1982.

Counsel to the Secretary of State under the Private Legislation Procedure (Scotland) Act 1936.

Crown Solicitor for Northern Ireland.

The Data Protection Registrar.

Delegate for Her Majesty's Government in the United Kingdom to the Central Rhine Commission.

Director of the British Aerospace Public Limited Company appointed subject to the approval of a Minister or government department.

Director of British Nuclear Fuels p.l.c.

Director of British Telecommunications p.l.c. nominated or appointed by a Minister of the Crown or government department.

Director of Caledonian MacBrayne Limited.

Director of Citybus Limited.

Director of the Commonwealth Institute.

Director of a company for the time being holding an appointment under Chapter I of Part II of the Water Industry Act 1991 or of such a company's holding company, being a director nominated or appointed by a Minister of the Crown or by a person acting on behalf of the Crown.

Director of any company in receipt of financial assistance under the Local Employment Act 1972, Part II of the Industry Act 1972 or Part III or section 13 of the Industrial Development Act 1982, being a director nominated by a Minister of the Crown or government department.

Director nominated by the Secretary of State of any company in respect of which an undertaking to make advances has been given by the Secretary of State under section 2 of the Highlands and Islands Shipping Services Act 1960 and is for the time being in force.

Director of Flexibus Limited.

Director of International Military Services Limited.

Director of Northern Ireland Airports Limited.

Director of Northern Ireland Railways Company Limited.

Director of the Northern Ireland Transport Holding Company.

Director of Nuclear Electric p.l.c.

Director, or Deputy Director, of Public Prosecutions for Northern Ireland.

Director appointed at a salary of Remploy Limited.

Director of Scottish Nuclear Limited.

Director of the successor company (within the meaning of the British Steel Act 1988) being a director nominated or appointed by a Minister of the Crown or by a person acting on behalf of the Crown.

Director of the successor company (within the meaning of the British Technology Group Act 1991) being a director nominated or appointed by a Minister of the Crown or by a person acting on behalf of the Crown.

Public offices disqualifying holders from membership of the House of Commons (*contd.*)

Director of a successor company (within the meaning of Part II of the Electricity Act 1989), being a director nominated or appointed by a Minister of the Crown or by a person acting on behalf of the Crown

Director of Ulsterbus Limited.

Director General of Electricity Supply.

Director General of Fair Trading.

Director General of Gas Supply.

Director General of the National Economic Development Office.

Director General of Telecommunications.

Director General of Water Services.

The Governor or Administrator of a dependent territory within the meaning of section 50(1) of the British Nationality Act 1981.

Governor of the British Broadcasting Corporation.

Governor, Deputy Governor or Director of the Bank of England.

Governor, Lieutenant Governor and Secretary, or Captain of Invalids of Chelsea Hospital.

Governor, Medical Officer or other officer or member of the staff of a prison to which the Prison Act (Northern Ireland) 1953 applies.

Health Service Commissioner for England.

Health Service Commissioner for Scotland.

Health Service Commissioner for Wales.

High Commissioner representing Her Majesty's Government in the United Kingdom.

Judge Advocate of the Fleet.

Judge Advocate General, Vice Judge Advocate General, Assistant Judge Advocate General or Deputy Judge Advocate.

Lay observer appointed under Article 42 of the Solicitors (Northern Ireland) Order 1976.

The Legal Services Ombudsman.

Liquidator appointed under section 2 of the Licensing (Alcohol Education and Research) Act 1981.

Lyon Clerk.

Lyon King of Arms.

Managing director of the National Research Development Corporation.

Medical Officer for Complaints appointed for Wales by the Secretary of State.

Member of an Agricultural Marketing Board appointed by the Minister under Schedule 2 to the Agricultural Marketing Act 1958.

Member of an Agricultural Marketing Board appointed under section 3 of the Agricultural Marketing Act (Northern Ireland) 1964 or Schedule 2 to the Agricultural Marketing (Northern Ireland) Order 1982.

Member appointed by a Minister of the Crown of the Agricultural Wages Board for England and Wales.

Member appointed by the Secretary of State of the Scottish Agricultural Wages Board.

Member appointed by the Head of the Department of Agriculture for Northern Ireland of the Agricultural Wages Board for Northern Ireland.

Any member of the Audit Commission for Local Authorities in England and Wales in receipt of remuneration.

Any member in receipt of remuneration of the British Tourist Authority, the English Tourist Board, the Scottish Tourist Board or the Wales Tourist Board.

Any member of the Countryside Commission in receipt of remuneration.

A member of the Curriculum Council for Wales established under section 14 of the Education Reform Act 1988 who is in receipt of remuneration.

Any member of the Education Assets Board in receipt of remuneration.

Any member of the Financial Services Tribunal in receipt of remuneration.

Member appointed by the Secretary of State of the Horserace Betting Levy Board.

Any member, in receipt of remuneration, of a housing action trust (within the meaning of Part III of the Housing Act 1988).

Any member of the Insolvency Practitioners Tribunal in receipt of remuneration.

A member of the Interim Advisory Committee on School Teachers' Pay and Conditions appointed under section 2 of the Teachers' Pay and Conditions Act 1987 who is in receipt of remuneration.

Member of the Legal Aid Board.

Member of the Local Enterprise Development Unit.

Member of a Medical Appeal Tribunal appointed under paragraph 2(2) of Schedule 12 to the Social Security Act 1975.

Member of a Medical Appeal Tribunal for Northern Ireland appointed under paragraph 2(2) of Schedule 12 to the Social Security (Northern Ireland) Act 1975.

Any member of the Mental Health Act Commission in receipt of remuneration.

Member of the staff of the National Audit Office.

A member of the National Curriculum Council established under section 14 of the Education Reform Act 1988 who is in receipt of remuneration.

Any member of the Nature Conservancy Council for England, the Nature Conservancy Council for Scotland or the Countryside Council for Wales in receipt of remuneration.

Member of the staff of the Northern Ireland Audit Office.

Member of a panel of persons who may be appointed to consider representations in accordance with section 3(4)(b) of the Employment Agencies Act 1973.

Member of a panel of persons appointed under Schedule 10 to the Rent Act 1977 to act as chairmen and other members of rent assessment committees.

Member of a panel of persons appointed under Schedule 5 to the Rent (Northern Ireland) Order 1978 to act as chairmen and other members of rent assessment committees.

Member of the panel of persons appointed under Schedule 4 to the Rent (Scotland) Act 1984 to act as chairmen and other members of rent assessment committees.

Member of the panel of chairmen for Social Security Appeal Tribunals for Northern Ireland appointed under section 97(2D)(a) of the Social Security (Northern Ireland) Act 1975, or of the panel of chairmen for Medical Appeal Tribunals for Northern Ireland appointed under paragraph 2(4)(a) of Schedule 12 to that Act.

A member of a panel appointed under section 7 of the Tribunals and Inquiries Act 1971 of persons to act as chairmen of Social Security Appeal Tribunals, Medical Appeal Tribunals and Disability Appeal Tribunals.

Member of a panel of persons who may be appointed to serve on a Vaccine Damage Tribunal.

Any member of the Polytechnics and Colleges Funding Council in receipt of remuneration.

Any member of a residuary body established by Part VII of the Local Government Act 1985 who is in receipt of remuneration.

Member, in receipt of remuneration, of the review body appointed under section 1 of the School Teachers' Pay and Conditions Act, 1991.

A member of the School Examinations and Assessment Council established under section 14 of the Education Reform Act 1988 who is in receipt of remuneration.

Any member of the Universities Funding Council in receipt of remuneration.

Any member, in receipt of remuneration, of an urban development corporation (within the meaning of Part XVI of the Local Government, Planning and Land Act 1980).

Member of a Wages Council appointed under paragraph 1(b) of Schedule 2 to the Wages Act 1986.

Member of a Wages Council appointed under paragraph 1(b) of Schedule 2 to the Wages (Northern Ireland) Order 1988.

Northern Ireland Commissioner for Complaints.

Northern Ireland Parliamentary Commissioner for Administration.

Officer or servant employed under the Commissioner of Police of the Metropolis or the Receiver for the Metropolitan Police District.

Officer or servant of the Crown Estate Commissioners.

Officer, clerk or servant appointed or employed under section 20 of the Greenwich Hospital Act 1865.

Officer of the Supreme Court being the holder of any office listed in any Part of Schedule 2 to the Supreme Court Act 1981 or a district registrar, or assistant district registrar, of the High Court.

Parliamentary Commissioner for Administration.

Person appointed under section 3(1) of the Local Government and Housing Act 1989 to carry out functions relating to the political restriction of posts under local authorities, within the meaning of Part I of that Act.

Person appointed to hear and decide appeals under the Trade Marks Act 1938.

Person holding a politically restricted post, within the meaning of Part I of the Local Government and Housing Act 1989, under a local authority, within the meaning of that Part.

President, or member of a panel of chairmen, of industrial tribunals established under section 12 of the Industrial Training Act 1964.

President, or member of a panel of chairmen, of industrial tribunals established under Article 30 of the Industrial Training (Northern Ireland) Order 1984.

President of Social Security Appeal Tribunals, Medical Appeal Tribunals and Disability Appeal Tribunals.

President of Social Security Appeal Tribunals and Medical Appeal Tribunals for Northern Ireland.

President or Vice-President of Value Added Tax Tribunals or full-time chairman of value added tax tribunals.

Public Works Loan Commissioner.

Receiver for the Metropolitan Police District.

Registrar or Assistant Registrar appointed under section 6 or section 7 of the County Courts Act 1984.

Public offices disqualifying holders from membership of the House of Commons (*contd.*)

Registrar or Assistant Registrar of Friendly Societies.

Registrar of the Privy Council.

Registrar of Public Lending Right.

Registration Officer appointed under section 8(2) or (3) of the Representation of the People Act 1983.

Rent officer or deputy rent officer appointed in pursuance of a scheme under section 63 of the Rent Act 1977.

Rent officer or deputy rent officer nominated under Schedule 5 to the Rent (Northern Ireland) Order 1978.

Returning Officer under Section 25(1) of the Representation of the People Act 1983 and any Deputy Returning Officer appointed by him.

Scottish legal services ombudsman appointed under section 34 of the Law Reform (Miscellaneous Provisions) (Scotland) Act 1990.

Social fund Commissioner.

Solicitor in Scotland to any department of Her Majesty's Government in the United Kingdom.

Standing Counsel to any department of Her Majesty's Government in the United Kingdom.

Statutory officer appointed under section 70 of the Judicature (Northern Ireland) Act 1978.

Traffic commissioner for any area constituted for the purposes of the Public Passenger Vehicles Act 1981.

Traffic Director for London.

(B) BODIES OF WHICH ALL MEMBERS ARE DISQUALIFIED

The Aircraft and Shipbuilding Industries Arbitration Tribunal.

An Arbitration Tribunal established under Schedule 3 to the Industry Act 1975.

An Area Electricity Board in England and Wales.

The Attendance Allowance Board.

The Attendance Allowance Board for Northern Ireland.

The Authorised Conveyancing Practitioners Board.

The British Board of Agrément.

The British Coal Corporation.

The British Railways Board.

British Shipbuilders.

The British Steel Corporation.

British Telecommunications.

The British Waterways Board.

The Broadcasting Complaints Commission.

The Broadcasting Standards Council.

The Building Societies Commission.

The Cable Authority.

The Central Arbitration Committee.

The Central Electricity Generating Board.

The Civil Aviation Authority.

The Civil Service Arbitration Tribunal.

Comataidh Telebhisein Gaidhlig.

The Commission for Local Administration in England.

The Commission for Local Administration in Wales.

The Commission for Local Authority Accounts in Scotland.

The Commission for the New Towns.

The Commission for Racial Equality.

The Commonwealth Development Corporation.

The Copyright Tribunal.

The Council of the Advisory, Conciliation and Arbitration Service.

The Council on Tribunals.

The Covent Garden Market Authority.

The Criminal Injuries Compensation Board.

The Crofters Commission.

The Crown Estate Commissioners.

A Dairy Produce Quota Tribunal constituted under the Dairy Produce Quotas Regulations 1984.

The Data Protection Tribunal.

The Development Board for Rural Wales.

The Development Commission.

A Development Corporation within the meaning of the New Town Act 1981 or the New Towns (Scotland) Act 1968.

A Development Council established under the Industrial Organisation and Development Act 1947.

The Disability Living Allowance Advisory Board.

The Electricity Council.

The Employment Appeal Tribunal.

The English Industrial Estates Corporation.

The Equal Opportunities Commission.

The Equal Opportunities Commission for Northern Ireland.

The Fair Employment Commission for Northern Ireland.

The Fair Employment Tribunal for Northern Ireland.

Food from Britain.

The Football Licensing Authority.
The Foreign Compensation Commission.
The Gaming Board for Great Britain.
The Health and Safety Executive.
The Highlands and Islands Development Board.
Highlands and Islands Enterprise.
The Housing Corporation.
Housing for Wales.
The Human Fertilisation and Embryology Authority.
The Immigration Appeal Tribunal.
The Independent Broadcasting Authority.
The Independent Commission for Police Complaints for Northern Ireland.
The Independent Television Commission.
An Industrial Court established in Northern Ireland.
The Industrial Development Board for Northern Ireland.
The Industrial Injuries Advisory Council.
The Intervention Board for Agricultural Produce and every committee of the Board performing functions of the Board.
A Joint Planning Inquiry Commission constituted under Part III of the Town and Country Planning (Scotland) Act 1972.
The Labour Relations Agency.
The Lands Tribunal.
The Lands Tribunal for Northern Ireland.
The Lands Tribunal for Scotland.
The Law Commission.
The Local Government Boundary Commission for England.
The Local Government Boundary Commission for Scotland.
The Local Government Boundary Commission for Wales.
London Regional Transport.
The Lord Chancellor's Advisory Committee on Legal Education and Conduct.
The Meat and Livestock Commission.
A Medical Practices Committee constituted under section 7 of the National Health Service Act 1977 or section 3 of the National Health Service (Scotland) Act 1978.
The Medicines Commission and any committee established under section 4 of the Medicines Act 1968.
A Mental Health Review Tribunal constituted or having effect as if constituted under the Mental Health Act 1983.
The Mental Welfare Commission for Scotland.
The Monopolies and Mergers Commission.
A National Broadcasting Council.
The National Bus Company.
The National Development Team for People with a Mental Handicap.

The National Radiological Protection Board.
The National Rivers Authority.
The North of Scotland Hydro-Electric Board.
The Northern Ireland Economic Council.
Northern Ireland Electricity.
The Northern Ireland Housing Executive.
The Occupational Pensions Board.
The Oil and Pipelines Agency.
The Parole Board constituted under section 59 of the Criminal Justice Act 1967.
The Parole Board for Scotland constituted under section 59 of the Criminal Justice Act 1967.
A Pensions Appeal Tribunal.
The Planning Appeals Commission established under Article 88 of the Planning (Northern Ireland) Order 1972.
A Planning Inquiry Commission constituted under Part III of the Town and Country Planning Act 1990.
A Planning Inquiry Commission constituted under Part III of the Town and Country Planning (Scotland) Act 1972.
The Police Complaints Authority.
The Post Office.
The Radio Authority.
A regional water authority established in accordance with section 2 of the Water Act 1973.
The Restrictive Practices Court.
The Review Board for Government Contracts.
A Rural Development Board.
The Scottish Committee of the Council on Tribunals.
The Scottish Conveyancing and Executry Services Board.
The Scottish Development Agency.
Scottish Enterprise.
Scottish Homes.
The Scottish Land Court.
The Scottish Law Commission.
Scottish Natural Heritage.
The Scottish Transport Group.
The Sea Fish Industry Authority.
Sianel Pedwar Cymru.
The Social Security Advisory Committee.
The South of Scotland Electricity Board.
The Transport Tribunal.
The Tribunal established under the Interception of Communications Act 1985.
The Tribunal established under the Security Service Act 1989.
The United Kingdom Atomic Energy Authority.
The Water Appeals Commission for Northern Ireland.
The Welsh Development Agency.
The Welsh Water Authority.

which can then examine and comment on the proposals in some detail, and publish a report to be circulated to all MPs for a properly informed debate and decision.

How does the law regulate the disqualification of political officeholders, in other words government ministers? On the one hand the law must prevent government ministers from dominating Parliament, but on the other, ministers must be present in the chamber to present and answer for government policies and measures. The House of Commons Disqualification Act imposes an upper limit of ninety-five government ministers who may sit as MPs in the Commons.[40] If ever the number of MPs appointed to ministerial office exceeds this number, then those ministers appointed after the limit was reached would be legally disqualified from sitting or voting in the House, until such time as the excess was reduced by death, resignation or by some other means to the maximum permitted number. So, out of the total membership of 651 MPs, just under a sixth, or 14.6 per cent, of the Commons may be composed of members of the government. There are certain British constitutional conventions, in other words non-legal rules of political practice, which are none the less regarded by British politicians as being binding. Known collectively as the doctrine of 'ministerial responsibility' this regulates the relationship of government ministers to one another, and also individually and collectively to Parliament. One of its rules is that all government ministers must have a seat in Parliament, predominantly in the Commons (where the Prime Minister and Chancellor of the Exchequer must sit) but otherwise in the House of Lords.[41] Thus following the general election in 1992, there were eighty-eight ministers in the Commons and twenty-five in the House of Lords. If one valued minister loses his seat in the Commons at the general election, then the Prime Minister can arrange for him or her to be given a life peerage and sit in the House of Lords so as to satisfy constitutional convention. Thus Lynda Chalker became Baroness Chalker in 1992 when her local electorate in Wallasey rejected her. Now she need never face the voters again and remains Minister for Overseas Development. Another basic convention of ministerial responsibility is that government ministers are expected always to speak and vote for government policy with unanimity. This means, in effect, that the Prime Minister, after appointing all his ministers, can rely absolutely upon a bedrock of support in the House of Commons to back government motions and legislation, even when difficulties are met with the party's own backbenchers. A minister who broke this rule would be obliged to resign (or else be sacked).[42] For this reason, a Prime Minister (especially one with a minority or small overall majority in the Commons) will sometimes particularly want to appoint influential backbench party members as ministers of his or her government, who, if they spoke their own mind in the Commons, might cause trouble during the passage of government resolutions and legislation. As the former American President Lyndon B. Johnson once put it, it is better to have such troublemakers 'on the inside pissing out, than on the outside pissing in'. It is likely that James Callaghan, Prime Minister of the Labour minority government during 1976–9, included Tony Benn in his Cabinet against his own personal preference for this reason;[43] and similarly at present John Major may privately view some members of his Cabinet as 'bastards' but he tolerates them in preference to the problems they could cause him if, free from collective ministerial responsibility, they publicly aired dissatisfaction with government policy from the Commons' backbenches.

The precise political or ministerial offices to which the maximum number of ninety-five MPs limit applies are listed in the 1975 Act.[44] The list includes the Prime Minister and First Lord of the Treasury, Lord President of the Council, Lord Privy Seal, Chancellor of the Duchy of Lancaster, Paymaster General, any secretary of state (the title of most heads of a government department), the Chancellor of the Exchequer, the Minister of Agriculture, Fisheries and Food, the President of the Board of Trade, any Minister of State, the Chief Secretary to the Treasury, any minister in charge of a public department of Her Majesty's Government in the United Kingdom (if not within the other provisions of the 1975 Act), the Attorney General, the Lord Advocate, the Solicitor General, the Solicitor General for Scotland, the Parliamentary Secretary to the Treasury, the Financial Secretary to the Treasury, any Parliamentary Secretary in a government department other than the Treasury or without departmental responsibilities, the Junior Lord of the Treasury, the Treasurer of Her Majesty's Household, the Vice-Chamberlain of Her Majesty's Household, and any assistant government whip. At the time of writing, eighty-eight MPs fill the politicial offices mentioned, which represents the highest number of political offices ever appointed from among the ranks of the House of Commons. Over the twentieth century the number of MP-ministers has increased remorselessly as follows: 1900, 33; 1910, 43; 1917, 60; 1920, 58; 1930, 50; 1940, 58; 1950, 68; 1960, 65; 1970, 85; 1980, 86; and 1992, 88.[45]

It should be remembered that there is an additional block of MPs from the government side of the House who effectively increase further the voting strength and influence of the government in the Commons, namely the parliamentary private secretaries (PPSs). These are MPs who are selected and invited by individual ministers to act as their personal assistants. Whereas holders of ministerial office receive a government salary in addition to their MP's pay, these private secretaries are unpaid, but none the less perform an important political service as a minister's confidential adviser. They also gain a foothold on the 'greasy ladder' towards ministerial office for themselves. Their position was described by the Commons' Select Committee on Offices or Places of Profit under the Crown as follows:[46]

The PPS has no recognised official position: he acts as the confidential friend and assistant of his minister and necessarily enjoys in very large measure the confidence not only of the minister personally, but of the minister's department and the officials in it. Thus he must necessarily be to some extent imbued with the 'team spirit' which is part of the life blood of the ministry; thus, too, his independence as a member of the House must be liable to be impaired to a somewhat greater degree than that of an ordinary member of the party.

Virtually all aspiring Cabinet ministers begin their government careers by acting as a PPS to a prominent minister, and the work is generally regarded as an invaluable apprenticeship in terms of gaining experience of the ways of government business.[47] The issue here is that these additional MPs are involved in government, and are bound ethically by the convention that demands unanimity of political officeholders in support of government policy, or else resignation. Thus a PPS can be relied upon always to vote in favour of the government in any vote that takes place in the House of Commons (and if he or she feels unable to do so will resign). Yet they fall outside the net of the House of Commons Disqualification Act as political officeholders disqualified from membership of the Commons. At the time of writing there are twenty-eight PPSs in the Commons, bringing the total number of MPs involved in government up to 116: between a fifth and a sixth of the entire body of the Commons.

It is worth recalling that it was the law until 1926 that whenever an MP was appointed as a government minister, his or her seat in the House of Commons would immediately be vacated, and the minister had to be re-elected as an MP via a fresh electoral contest being fought in his or her constituency.[48] In other words, newly-appointed government ministers were conditionally disqualified from membership of the Commons until such time as they were specifically elected in their ministerial capacity by their constituents. This provided a mechanism for electoral approval of ministerial appointments. To avoid the need for a series of by-elections immediately after a general election, when new ministerial appointments are common, often an incumbent Prime Minister would appoint any new intended ministers in advance of the general election, so that the consequent vacation of seats and legal requirement for re-election would be satisfied by the general election itself. The first modification of the rule came with the Re-election of Ministers Act 1919, which made re-election unnecessary if the minister was appointed to office within nine months after a general election, then the Re-election of Ministers Act 1926 abolished the old legal requirement altogether. Some have regretted the passing of these ministerial elections; for example, complaints were put to a parliamentary committee in the 1940s that, 'Now that this necessity for re-election has been done away with, there is no such reason for [the Prime Minister] appointing members of his intended government until after the general election is over; thus the electorate may have to cast its votes in ignorance of what will be the composition of the government if the Prime Minister obtains a majority.'[49] The transition of this law has formed just part of the general process in the twentieth century towards a more presidential system of government in the hands of the Prime Minister, allowing him or her a greater freedom of action to appoint the political personnel of his or her administration.

Finally, one feature of the old law on offices and places of profit under the Crown has been retained specifically as a convenient legal fiction in parliamentary practice to permit the possibility for an MP to resign. At common law there is no method whereby an MP can resign and so voluntarily relinquish his or her seat in the Commons. But since the appointment of an MP to an office of profit under the Crown would disqualify him or her from membership of the Commons, from 1750 until the present, the offices of Steward of the Chiltern Hundreds and of Steward of the Manor of Northstead have been retained specifically as disqualifying offices for the purpose of an MP's resignation, although no profits are derived from holding either post, neither are there any duties involved. The official view is that, 'The appointments and their profits came to be one of the many "legal fictions" which have been of practical use. This method of enabling a Member to vacate his seat with the approval of the executive has such a long tradition behind it that there is much to be said for preserving it, not merely as an interesting historical relic enshrining the principle of disqualification by reason of acceptance of office under the Crown, but as a useful incident of parliamentary procedure.'[50] The two stewardships were specifically excepted from the operation of the 1919 and 1926 Re-election of Ministers, and are mentioned in section 4 of the main text of the 1975 House of Commons Disqualification Act, to be treated in law as one of the number of public offices cited in the schedules to the Act that disqualify individuals from membership of the Commons.

Politics and religion: the clergy

It has been argued in this chapter that the law relating to the qualification of parliamentary candidates should be as clear, intelligible and easy to find out about as possible. Nowhere in British election law is this further from the case than concerning the position of priests and ministers of religion. It is hardly an exaggeration to say that the law in this respect is incoherent, illogical and virtually impossible for anyone except a legal expert to discover. For anyone seeking a simple answer to the question 'Can a priest stand for Parliament?', reading the legal sources on the subject requires burrowing away in collections of parliamentary statutes to find at least nine separate legislative acts on the subject stretching back to the sixteenth century. The short answer is that some priests are disqualified, and others are not; and some priests can relinquish their ministry to become an MP, but others are unable to do so. The following generalisations may be said to apply. Only certain *Christian* priests are disqualified, whereas ministers of all other religious faiths, such as Judaism, Islam and Buddhism, are all eligible. All episcopally ordained priests of the Anglican Church are disqualified, but not in Wales. All Roman Catholic priests are disqualified. Non-conformist clergy (being priests not ordained episcopally, in other words not made a priest by a bishop) are not disqualified, but they are in Scotland. A fuller exposition of these curious rules on disqualification is provided below, after first considering the religious disqualifications which operated in previous times that largely explain the state of affairs today.

Earlier in our history it was not only priests but anyone belonging to a religious faith different from that of the Church of England who could not sit in Parliament. The legal reasons for this were derived essentially from the requirement for a new MP to take a particular form of parliamentary oath. In the sixteenth century, as a result of the Reformation and break with the Roman Catholic Church, when the British monarch became Head of the Church of England, all MPs were required before taking up their seat in the House of Commons to take the oath of supremacy – to 'swear that the King or Queen is the only supreme governor of this realm as well in spiritual as in temporal causes, and that no foreign person or potentate has any authority ecclesiastical or spiritual within this realm'. This effectively prohibited all those who were not members of the Established Church in Britain from parliamentary candidature, including even Quakers and Jews. Roman Catholics were the particular object of exclusion in the period up to the eighteenth century, because of the political links between Roman Catholicism and treason, fuelled by the attempts from Catholic Spain and France sanctioned by the Pope to invade the country, and the claims of the Stuart kings and (after 1688) the Old and New Pretenders to the Throne. In 1689 MPs were required additionally to swear that they 'abhorred as impious and heretical the damnable doctrine' of the Pope in issuing renewed excommunication threats against British Anglicans, and for a time voters were also required to take oaths of allegiance, thus disenfranchising Roman Catholics from the electoral process altogether.[51] But by the middle of the nineteenth century, the political and religious climate had completely changed, and a series of statutes relaxed the terms of the parliamentary oath, culminating in 1888 with a legal provision permitting as an alternative to the normal oath a simple affirmation of loyalty to the Crown without reference to any religious authority. Under the Oaths Act 1978, the usual form of parliamentary oath is that while holding a copy of the New Testament (or, if a Jew, the Old Testament), an MP, before taking up his seat in a new Parliament, will say, 'I swear by Almighty God that I will be faithful and bear true Allegiance to Her Majesty Queen Elizabeth, her heirs and successors, according to law. So help me God.' Non-Christians take a similar oath but substitute their own holy book for the Bible, so that a Moslem would hold a copy of the Koran (in an envelope, to avoid it being touched by one not of the faith), or a Sikh a copy of the Granth.[52] For other situations where it is not reasonably practicable without inconvenience or delay to administer an oath in the manner appropriate to his or her belief, the MP may take an affirmation in lieu: 'I do solemnly, sincerely and truly declare and affirm that I will be faithful and bear true allegiance to Her Majesty Queen Elizabeth, her heirs and successors according to law.'[53] So there are today no legal disqualifications upon grounds of religious belief *per se,* unless the person concerned happens also to be a priest and is within the category of Christian churches whose clergymen are prevented from membership of the Commons.

When the terms of the parliamentary oath were changed in the nineteenth century to allow members of religious faiths other than Anglicanism to sit in Parliament, and also to vote in parliamentary elections, it was decided none the less to maintain for the time being the legal disqualification so far as religious officials of the Roman Catholic Church were concerned. Under the terms of the Roman Catholic Relief Act 1829:[54]

Be it enacted, That from and after the commencement of this Act it shall be lawful for any . . . Roman Catholic . . . to sit and vote in either House of Parliament.

And be it further enacted, That *no person in Holy Orders in the Church of Rome shall be capable of being elected to serve in Parliament as a member of the House of Commons*; and if any such person shall be elected to serve in Parliament as aforesaid such election shall be void; and if any person, being elected to serve in Parliament as a member of the House of Commons shall, after his election, take or receive Holy Orders in the Church of Rome, the seat of such person shall immediately become void; and if any such person shall, in any of the cases aforesaid, presume to sit or vote as a member of the House of Commons, he shall be subject to the same penalties, forfeitures, and disabilities as are enacted by an Act passed in the forty-first year of the reign of King George the Third, intitled 'An Act to remove doubts respecting the eligibility of persons in Holy Orders to sit in the House of Commons'; and proof of the celebration of any religious service by such person, according to the rites of the Church of Rome, shall be deemed and taken to be *prima facie* evidence of the fact of such persons being in Holy Orders within the intent and meaning of this Act.

The parliamentary statute which disqualifies the widest range of Christian priests today is contained within the House of Commons (Clergy Disqualification) Act 1801. This measure was passed as a direct result of there then sitting in the Commons as the member for Old Sarum the Rev J. Horne Tooke, an ordained priest of the Established Church. Parliamentary law appeared sufficiently uncertain on the subject for there to be needed lengthy debates among MPs and an Act of Parliament to settle the matter. The terms of the Act are as follows:

> Whereas it is expedient to remove doubts which have arisen respecting the eligibility of persons in Holy Orders to sit in the House of Commons, and also to make effectual provision for excluding them from sitting therein: Be it enacted . . . that *no person having been ordained to the office of priest or deacon, or being a minister of the Church of Scotland, is or shall be capable of being elected to serve in Parliament as a member of the House of Commons.*
>
> And . . . if any person, having been ordained to the office of priest or deacon or being a minister of the Church of Scotland, shall hereafter be elected to serve in Parliament as aforesaid, such election and return shall be void: and . . . if any person shall . . . presume to sit or vote as a member of the House of Commons, he shall forfeit the sum of five hundred pounds to any person . . . who shall sue for the same in any of His Majesty's courts at Westminster . . . and be henceforeth incapable of . . . holding . . . any living . . . or office of honour or profit . . . Provided also that no person shall be liable to any forfeiture or penalty . . . unless a prosecution shall be commenced within twelve calendar months after such penalty shall be incurred.
>
> And . . . proof of the celebration of divine service according to the rites of the Church of England, or of the Church of Scotland, in any church or chapel consecrated or set apart for public worship, shall be deemed . . . *prima facie* evidence of the fact of such person having been ordained to the office of a priest or deacon, or of his being a minister of the Church of Scotland.

On the face of it, the meaning of this Act seems fairly clear: ordained priests in the Church of England, and ministers of the Presbyterian Church of Scotland, both being Established Churches of the British state, were legally disqualified. But in February 1950, the case of the Rev J. G. MacManaway who had been elected in the general election as Ulster Unionist member for Belfast West threw the meaning and application of the Act into confusion. Mr MacManaway had been ordained a priest in 1925 by the Bishop of Derry and Raphoe, a diocese in the province of Armagh in the Church of Ireland. A dispute as to his right to sit in the Commons begged a consideration of the 1801 Act, and also the Irish Church Act that had been passed later on in the nineteenth century in 1869 and provided that, 'The union between the Churches of England and Ireland shall be dissolved, and the Church of Ireland . . . shall cease to be established by law.' The House of Commons referred the disputed election to the Judicial Committee of the

Privy Council for a legal ruling on the case, and the Court gave this response:[55]

> Their Lordships answer the questions of law referred to them as follows. They will humbly advise His Majesty:
>
> (1) That the provisions of the House of Commons (Clergy Disqualification) Act 1801, so far as they apply to persons ordained to the office of priest or deacon, do not disable from sitting and voting in the House of Commons only persons ordained to those offices in the Church of England as by law established;
>
> (2) That those provisions disable from so sitting and voting all persons ordained to the office of priest or deacon, whether by a bishop of that Church in accordance with the form of making and ordaining priests and deacons according to the order of the Church of England, or by other forms of episcopal ordination;
>
> (3) That the Reverend James Godfrey MacManaway is disabled from sitting and voting in the House of Commons by reason of the fact that, having been ordained as a priest according to the use of the Church of Ireland, he has received episcopal ordination.

The legal arguments in the case revolved around the meaning of the words 'ordained to the office of priest or deacon' in the 1801 Act. The judicial principles of statutory interpretation as they now exist have rarely been very helpful for deciding points of political common sense, and Mr MacManaway's position is a good case in point. Their Lordships applied the 'literal rule' or no-nonsense approach of statutory interpretation to this uncertain provision – in other words, they simply took these words at their face value. Anyone, anywhere, belonging to any church at all who had ever been ordained a priest by a bishop was disqualified. So now all persons who were, or who had once been, a priest of any one of an enormous number of churches around the world were deemed legally prohibited from parliamentary candidature. This therefore includes all the following churches, and any others which episcopally ordain entrants into their priesthood: the Church of Ireland; the Episcopal Church in Scotland; the Church of India, Pakistan, Burma and Ceylon; the Church of England in Canada; the Church of England in Australia and Tasmania; the Church of New Zealand; the Church of South Africa; the Church of the West Indies; the Japan Holy Catholic Church; the Protestant Episcopal Church in the United States of America; the Roman Catholic Church; and the Greek Orthodox Church.

The alternative interpretation that might have been taken of the words in the 1801 statute was that the disqualification related only to priests of the Established Church. This was clearly the purpose of the prohibition two hundred years ago, when not only were the Anglican clergy regarded as a fourth estate of the realm, but their religious posts were in the grant of the

Crown and they were therefore in a directly analogous position to other holders of public offices or places of profit under the Crown. Mr Chancellor Addington made this very point during the House of Commons debates during the passage of the 1801 Act. His view was that, 'As a great part of the benefices of the clergy were in the immediate gift of the Crown, the inclusion of the clergy would tend to diminish the independence of the House by increasing the influence of the King.'[56] This factor could only apply to priests of the Established Church, because elsewhere the Crown did not make the appointments. Furthermore, if all episcopally ordained priests were meant to be disqualified, as the court ruled, this clearly included all priests of the Roman Catholic Church, yet the Roman Catholic Relief Act of 1829 (considered above) was passed a few years later to cover their situation. This 1829 Act can only be explained if Parliament at the time intended the 1801 Act to apply only to the Established Anglican Church. Mr MacManaway was unfortunate, therefore, in losing the legal right to sit in the Commons, after his local electorate had given him the political right to do so. The more appropriate interpretation of the 1801 Act, after the Church of Ireland was disestablished in 1869, was that ordained priests in the Church of Ireland were no longer disqualified. This would also have been in tune with the general political feeling that the ancient statutes prohibiting priests or former priests standing for Parliament had become antiquated and anachronistic, that it should be the internal rules or ecclesiastical law of the churches concerned to regulate whether or not it is suitable for a priest to stand for Parliament, and if so, in what circumstances, and that any development in our parliamentary or judicial law should move in the direction of relaxing rather than increasing the extent of this statutory disqualification.

It was precisely in line with this better political view favouring relaxation of restrictions that when the Welsh Church Act was passed in 1914, with the purpose of disestablishing the Church of England in Wales, express provision was made in the Act that ordained priests in Wales would no longer be disqualified from parliamentary candidature. After declaring that the Church of England in Wales 'shall cease to be established by law', the Act provides that:[57]

> No person shall be disqualified or liable to any penalty for sitting and voting in the House of Commons by reason of having been ordained to the office of priest or deacon if the ecclesiastical office he holds is an ecclesiastical office in the Church of Wales, or if he does not hold any ecclesiastical office, if the last ecclesiastical office which he held was an ecclesiastical office in the Church in Wales.

When a Select Committee of the Commons decided to undertake an inquiry into clergy disqualification following the MacManaway case, they were somewhat perturbed at the incoherence of the law generally on the subject, but none the less rejected sound arguments put to them that the disqualification statutes still in existence might simply be repealed, and recommended instead that no changes whatsoever were necessary. During the course of their deliberations, however, they came near to rendering the law more consistent but more restrictive by seriously considering a proposal to reimpose a legal disqualification upon Welsh priests. In this they were encouraged by views expressed by the Archbishop of Canterbury to them, who incidentally in his opening sentence asked the Committee to explain to him what the clergy disqualifications were: 'I ought to know, but I have forgotten what the law is.'[58] Later, he turned his considered thoughts on the whole subject to the idea of reform:[59]

If you finally reported that it would be much better to leave the thing alone, I should not doubt that you might very well have taken the course of wisdom . . . The only anomaly in the present situation is that the Church in Wales should be exempted from this disqualification. I have never spoken to the Archbishop or any of the Bishops of the Church in Wales on this and I have no notion what their feeling is, but I would strongly imagine that if they were asked they would say they had no objection, in principle, to their clergy being treated on all fours with clergy of the Church of England. That, I think, really covers all I have got to put before you.

Are there any legal means whereby someone who has been a priest, but no longer wishes to work as such, can effectively divest him or herself of the legal disqualification so as to start a political career and become an MP? After all, if a civil servant working in the Foreign Office wishes to stand for Parliament, all he or she has to do is resign from the job. (The present Foreign Secretary, Douglas Hurd, was himself formerly legally disqualified from parliamentary candidature by virtue of being a career diplomat in the Foreign Office.) The answer is, as might be expected in clergy disqualification law, that some priests can but some priests cannot. The general position is that once a person has been an ordained priest they can never in the future be an MP, unless they fall within the provisions of the one statute on the subect applicable to ministers of the Church of England only. This is the Clerical Disabilities Act 1870:[60]

An Act for the relief of persons admitted to the office of priest or deacon in the Church of England . . . . Any person admitted to the office of minister in the Church of England may, after having resigned any and every preferment held by him, . . . execute a deed of relinquishment . . . . There upon . . . He shall be incapable of officiating . . . as a minister in the Church of England . . . [and] . . . He shall be . . . free from all disabilities . . . to which, if this Act had not been passed, he would, by

force of any . . . Act or of any other law, have been subject as a person
who had been admitted to the office of minister in the Church of England.

A priest who wishes to take advantage of this statute must first draw up the
deed of relinquishment in a prescribed form, then officially deposit it in the
Chancery Division of the High Court. He must deliver a copy of the deed
together with proof of deposit in the High Court to the bishop of his
diocese, or the one where he formerly worked as a priest, and give notice
that he has done so to the Archbishop of Canterbury or York, depending
upon in which ecclesiastical province of England he worked. For people
who later on in their life change their mind again, and wish to work once
more as an Anglican priest, the Clerical Disabilities Act 1870 (Amendment)
Measure 1934 enables ministers to resume the position of officiating
ministers in a limited capacity for two years, and thereafter to hold any
religious office subject to the consent of their bishop. The term 'minister' in
the 1870 Act is defined as 'a priest or deacon', and a 'bishop' it says 'shall be
construed to comprehend archbishop'. This makes it doubtful that bishops
of the Church of England, who are the Church's most articulate and best-
known figures, could ever take advantage of the 1870 Act and stand for
Parliament.

So, at the time of writing, only priests of the Established Church of
England can resign to become parliamentary candidates. All other ordained
priests are disqualified by British law for life, and it makes no difference that
they might have given up working as a priest, or lost their faith, or even
become a member of some completely different faith, such as Buddhism;
they can never be MPs. Into this very wide group of former Christian priests
who are treated differently from those in the Church of England are, of
course, those who have been ministers of the Church of Scotland, or
ordained into the Roman Catholic Church. Bruce Kent, the former Roman
Catholic priest who resigned his ministry to lobby for nuclear disarmament
and enter politics, stood as a parliamentary candidate at the 1992 general
election for the constituency of Oxford West and Abingdon, but it is unclear
whether he knew he was in fact disqualified for life from ever becoming an
MP. If he did, he would be right in thinking that the disqualification was
grossly unfair. There is, in fact, one legal method of circumventing the
lifetime disqualification of non-Anglican priests, which has largely passed
unnoticed. This is that if the politically aspiring priest can apply successfully
for a position in the Church of England in Wales, then he can take
advantage of section 2(4) of the Welsh Church Act 1914 which says that
ecclesiastical officeholders there are not disqualified. In Bruce Kent's case,
however, this would mean disavowing Catholicism for Protestantism. The
better way forward is to lobby for a reform of the law, analogously perhaps
with the position of Tony Benn who, as described earlier in the chapter,

found himself disqualified from membership of the Commons for life by virtue of succeeding to his father's hereditary peerage in 1960.[61]

Reference has already been made to the Select Committee on Clergy Disqualification which was set up by the House of Commons in the wake of the MacManaway case, and reported to MPs in 1953 that, 'On the basis of the evidence which they have heard, your Committee recommend that no change in the law be at present made.'[62] In fact, the oral and written evidence submitted to the Committee, with one or two notable exceptions, was of an excellent quality, and many of the witnesses called by the Committee strongly argued the case for removing all clerical disabilities in relation to membership of the Commons, including the Secretary of the Diocesan Chancellors' Committee ('in modern times it is wrong to have a disqualification attaching to clergymen'),[63] the Procurator of the Church of Scotland ('civil disability is obsolete'),[64] and the Roman Catholic Archbishop of Westminster ('it ought not to be for Parliament to debar people from becoming candidates as far as the church is concerned; that ought to be for the internal discipline of each church').[65] Reading between the lines, it seems clear the Committee in fact became progressively more exasperated at having to try to grasp what the overall state of the law was, became riveted by diversions such as trying to establish a technical meaning for 'episcopal ordination' and to know precisely what would happen if someone claimed that a parliamentary candidate had once been ordained by a bishop in the Church of South India which was no longer in communion with the Anglican Church, and the prospect of having to prepare a rational exposition for the House of Commons simply confounded them. Instead, they produced a two-and-a-half page report, with no exposition of the law, pointing out that there were some anomalies, that logically either all priests should be disqualified or else all entitled to stand for election to Parliament, but concluding with the moral support of the Archbishop of Canterbury that nothing need, in fact be done: MPs did not even bother debating the Report in the House of Commons.

What are the present-day arguments that priests and ministers of religion should not be allowed to stand for election as members of the House of Commons? There are two principal arguments that can be identified. One is particularly addressed towards Church of England clergy, and emphasises, on the one hand, that the Church already has adequate parliamentary representation in the House of Lords, and on the other, that any closer links between priests and Parliament might cause undesirable political and religious controversies. Ever since the Reformation under King Henry VIII, statutory provision has been made that Anglican bishops should sit in the House of Lords. Currently those entitled to do so comprise the archbishops of Canterbury and York; the Bishops of London, Durham and Winchester; and twenty-one other bishops of the Church of England according to seniority of appointment to diocesan sees. It can be argued, in resistance to the idea of Anglican priests in the Commons, that the Church of England is already represented in Parliament. Indeed, it is said that the bishops jealously regard their position in the Lords, which provides them with a valuable source of authority and status within and outside the Church. If Anglican clergy were ever to be elected to the Commons, which in modern times is by far the most important of the two parliamentary chambers, such priest-MPs would steal the bishops' thunder in the Lords and effectively overshadow whatever the bishops were saying in the second chamber. It would also, of course, pose internal difficulties as to how the leadership of the Church of England was presented to the public, given that it is the bishops who are the spiritual leaders of the Church, and that Anglicanism is structured hierarchically under them, in a manner more similar to the Roman Catholic Church than to most other Protestant religions. It is predictable therefore that the Anglican authorities would not favour their priests entering the House of Commons. The continuation of the bishops in the House of Lords is a separate matter, and begs future reform of the composition of the second chamber. Establishment certainly gives the Anglican Church a preferential position within Parliament, whereas no other religious faith has a right to sit and speak upon an *ex officio* status. Even Welsh, Scottish and Irish Anglican bishops are not included among the Lords Spiritual who sit in the House. A Conservative backbench MP, Richard Holt, introduced an Amendment of the Constitution of the House of Lords (Bishops) Bill in 1986, but this proceeded no further than a First Reading for reasons of lack of time. Richard Holt wanted to render the present contingent of religious leaders in the Lords more representative of the range of churches that exists generally within the United Kingdom. He said, 'I want to strengthen the House of Lords, and I think one way to do that is to ensure that it reflects the more ecumenical society in which we live and is a true reflection of the nation.'[66] Under his scheme, twelve of the Anglican bishops would be replaced by nominees thought suitable, including the Moderator of the Church of Scotland, the Archbishop of the Church of Wales, the Primate of All Ireland and Bishop of Armagh, four Catholic cardinals, archbishops or bishops, the Methodist Chairman, and the Chief Rabbi.

Many government politicians fear interventions from religious spokesmen, and particularly the Church of England, for the political embarrassment priests can cause by raising grounds of conscience to condemn particular policies or decisions being taken. In the 1980s there were several episodes when even relatively mild criticism by Anglican clerics of the moral ethic of market forces, or suggestions that more might be done for the homeless and poor, were met by furious attacks and personal abuse being directed at the priest concerned by members of the government. This is likely to be explained, at least in part, by fears of what such criticism might stir up in public opinion. In 1987, for example, when the Bishop of Durham questioned government social policy, the government's Lord Chancellor, Lord Hailsham, delivered a speech which was reported in the press to have been previously approved by the then Prime Minister, Margaret Thatcher, to the effect that:[67]

> It would be better if priests and bishops approached the subjects on which they desire to pontificate to the laity with more humility and possibly more charity than they are apt to do. It is likely that the laity are better informed than they on secular subjects. And on moral issues I have never seen the smallest evidence that the intelligent laity require instruction on moral principles from persons of the intellectual limitations of the Bishop of Durham, which cannot equally be acquired by reading and reflection.

A major argument against priests standing as parliamentary candidates, then, is that it will politicise religion, and embroil them in party politics, which is not the proper role of priests. It seems likely that the added moral authority a priest can bring to political discourse will be resisted by many politicians.

The other principal argument against relaxing the clergy disqualification laws is that the business of party politics is simply inappropriate in tandem with the pursuit of a priest's vocation. The business of politics is highly materialistic and involves the constant compromise of principles in a manner incompatible with spiritual values and doctrinal matters of conscience. Furthermore, it is argued that the overriding responsibility of a minister of religion is to his or her parish and parishioners, many of whose feelings about what a religious minister should be doing might be offended, and their confidence in their priest damaged if the priest became embroiled in political controversy, especially so if the controversy were of a party political nature and this would be extremely likely if the priest represented one of the national parties. On a more practical note, some would argue that an individual cannot do two jobs at the same time, and in the case of a minister of religion more so than perhaps any other form of work, apart from perhaps being an MP itself, a priest's life in devotion to God and the parish is full-time, if not wholly absorbing. For all these reasons the Pope has ordered Roman Catholic priests involved in party politics and government throughout the world to withdraw. Amongst the views expressed to the Commons' Committee on the subject, it was said:[68]

> They have a parish, they have a mission, they have the cure of people's souls in their particular areas, and whilst as normal citizens they ought to be quite free, it might be a breach of good taste as far as the community was concerned if people who were still occupying those positions were to become centres of political controversy.

And elsewhere a question and answer session between the Committee and one of the bishops was as follows:[69]

> MP's Question: 'Is your objection to a clergyman being a member of the House of Commons based primarily on the fact that he would be faced with a conflict of loyalties, loyalty to his religion and loyalty to his constituents, and is it also based on the fact that in any form of legislation, either in the House of Commons or in the House of Lords, he would also have work that would take him away from his real vocation. Is that it?'
>
> Rt. Revd Edward Williamson: 'Yes, that is so . . . The point is that he has a cure of souls in his parish and he could not be in London by the midnight train from Monday till the midnight train on Friday and adequately execute his cure of souls. There is also another objection – and I hope you will not think this is in any way meant offensively – and that is that in order to be elected he must come out as an avowed member of one party or the other. By becoming a candidate he signalises his adhesion to a particular political party. In that case you are bound to lose the confidence of some of the souls whose cure is committed to your charge, and that is one of the objections which I am sure are felt.'
>
> MP's Question: 'There would be a conflict of loyalties between their cure of souls and their duty to their constituents?'
>
> Rt. Revd Edward Williamson: 'Yes.'
>
> MP's Question: 'Would you say that was the gravest objection, or should I put first the fact that it is a question of taking a man away from his vocation, his cure of souls, in order to come up here for other purposes?'
>
> Rt. Revd Edward Williamson: 'I think that they are both grave; I cannot say which is graver.'

Many people will believe that there are indeed one or more good reasons why, as a general principle, it is preferable that active ministers of religion do not stand as parliamentary candidates. But it is important to emphasise that this does not mean automatically that the state should ban them by law from doing so. The original reasons for the ancient clergy disqualification statutes have long since ceased to exist. Roman Catholic priests are no longer seen as potential subversives, and the Anglican clergy no longer represent a fourth estate of the realm. Still less should the state use the law of the country to disqualify clergy in such an inconsistent and illogical fashion, so that the Reverend Ian Paisley can be an MP by virtue of being a non-conformist but other priests who are Anglicans or Roman Catholics are subject to legal prohibition. Perhaps most objectionable of all is that only Anglican religious ministers can choose one profession or the other, and relinquish religious office for a new career as an MP, but all other ordained priests cannot do so. One simple reform that would be a definite improvement would be simply to extend the terms of the Clergy Disabilities Act 1870 to cover all disqualified priests. But more generally it is wrong for the state today to be regulating a matter that should more properly be for internal church discipline to decide. The objections to priests standing for Parliament are canonical ones, not constitutional, and it should be ecclesiastical law, not the state, that imposes disqualifications upon the individual's political liberties. It is for the individual churches concerned to decide whether or not to impose restrictions as a matter of religious ethics, or incompatibility of the two professions, as a necessary condition of the priest's particular work. And just as a civil servant can resign to go into politics so too should a minister of religion be free to do so. Ultimately the question of the individual's suitability for politics should be left to the local electorate to decide, and it is fundamental that there should be as few restrictions as possible upon the right of the voters freely to decide who they wish to represent them. There are basic principles of political liberty involved here, about which British public policy as enshrined in its law is muddled and which the government and Parliament seem reluctant to confront and prefer to ignore. In recent years there has been growing support within the Anglican Church for reform of clergy disqualification. In November 1982 its General Synod carried a motion by 181 votes to 147 that 'this Synod believes that clergymen of the Church of England should be free like other citizens to take their seats as elected Members of Parliament'.[70] It is time for the clergy disqualification legislation simply to be repealed.

SOCIAL BACKGROUND OF SUCCESSFUL CANDIDATES

There are three particularly important social conditions which in practice tend to promote successful parliamentary candidates: these concern the upbringing, education and occupation of the aspiring parliamentarian.[71] The family or personal environment in which a person grows up and spends his or her formative years is likely to assist or hinder his or her desire and aptitude to enter professional politics. An MP is far more likely to come from a family where politics is part of everyday discussion – especially if it is a direct part of its life, such as where one or both parents are politicians or working for a trade union – and/or had a school or university environment in which he or she happened by design or chance to flourish in social or student union events of a political nature. Not only will this early conditioning have shaped the political will and culture which attracts the prospective candidate into putting his or her name forward, but it is very likely to have opened up the necessary awareness of how the political system operates, as well as given him or her the personal contacts that are invaluable in terms of receiving advice and in helping his or her potential candidacy along.

The type and quality of education a person has received makes a marked difference to their political prospects. Completion of a secondary school education followed by a university education, will encourage and train the necessary mental skills and abilities, as well as giving confidence and articulacy, to a person later competing in politics. Although notable exceptions can be named – Sir Winston Churchill did not go to university, and John Major did not complete his secondary education (but did complete his professional accountancy examinations) – generally a university degree would seem greatly to enhance a candidate's prospects. Education is a distinctly more important factor for candidature within the Conservative Party than within Labour. The majority of Conservative candidates at every election this century have held university degrees. For the Labour Party the number has steadily grown, from just 19 per cent at the last general election before the Second World War, rising to a majority of successful candidates at every election since 1966. At the 1992 general election, a strong majority of all parliamentary candidates representing all three main political parties had been to University (see the table opposite).

Most public schools have an in-built advantage over state schools in terms of the quality of general education and training they offer, because the private fees they receive from affluent parents means they can afford to finance better facilities for use by students and employ more staff to give the students closer personal attention. Of all the successful parliamentary candidates from the three main parties who were elected at the 1992 general election, 258 had been to a public school. The top public schools are well represented in this figure: thirty-four are Old Etonians, nine Old Rugbeians, and seven Old Harrovians. It is particularly within the Conservative Party that the social status and class *mores* inherent in the public school sector have proved a strong advantage throughout this century. Despite its recent claims to be the party of opportunity and classlessness, the percentage of successful Conservative candidates at the 1992 general election who went to public school was still at a level of 62 per cent. Although there is now some small decline on the former proportion of public schoolboys who have traditionally dominated the party (in the 1960s accounting for as many as 80 per cent of Conservative MPs), it still accounts for an astonishingly socially unrepresentative body of people (see the table on page 200). It certainly lends credence to those who claim that Britain's old class structure of party politics is in reality still with us today.

The previous occupation or professional background of a person may improve or detract from his or her chances of becoming a successful parliamentary candidate. Some types of work or profession share similar skills to those needed by the politician. Some jobs will provide or foster an environment in which a person's awareness and interest in practical politics thrives. Whether or not some people are willing to stand as parliamentary candidates may depend upon whether or not their occupation is one that is

Education of candidates in the 1992 General Election

Type of education	Conservative		Labour		Liberal Democrat	
	Elected	Defeated	Elected	Defeated	Elected	Defeated
Elementary	–	–	2	–	–	–
Elementary +	–	–	7	–	–	1
Secondary	19	40	34	60	2	79
Secondary + poly/college	28	53	61	93	2	152
Secondary + university	81	100	127	173	6	257
Public school	28	11	–	3	–	11
Pub sch + poly/college	16	11	2	3	1	12
Pub sch + university	164	83	38	31	9	100
Total	336	298	271	363	20	612
Oxford	83	24	28	23	4	40
Cambridge	68	23	16	9	2	31
Other universities	94	136	122	172	9	286
All universities	245 (73%)	183 (61%)	166 (61%)	204 (56%)	15 (75%)	357 (58%)
Eton	34	9	2	–	–	5
Harrow	7	2	–	–	–	3
Winchester	3	–	1	–	–	–
Other public schools	164	94	37	37	10	115
All public schools	208 (62%)	105 (35%)	40 (14%)	37 (10%)	10 (50%)	123 (20%)

Table 5.1[72]

capable of being carried on part-time while serving as an MP (and resumed altogether in the event of losing a future election). It will come as no surprise to discover that those professions which involve a great deal of public speaking and discussion feature on the top of the list for professional people who become MPs. Barristers – professional advocates – represent the established profession which features most strongly among Conservative MPs. The former Conservative Prime Minister, Margaret Thatcher, was a barrister, and so too is the Labour leader, Tony Blair (and indeed his immediate predecessor, John Smith). Being a solicitor, whose work involves constant negotiating with other lawyers and also some limited advocacy, is also a common professional background for MPs. Among other professional talkers and thinkers, university or Polytechnic lecturers are most numerous within the Labour Party (at present thirty-eight MPs compared to

Successful candidates from public schools, 1918–92 (per cent)

	Conservatives	Labour
1918	81	3
1922	78	9
1923	79	8
1924	78	7
1929	79	12
1931	77	8
1935	81	10
1945	85	23
1950	85	22
1951	75	23
1955	76	22
1959	72	18
1964	75	18
1966	80	18
1970	74	17
1974 Feb.	74	17
1974 Oct.	75	18
1979	77	17
1983	70	14
1987	68	14
1992	62	14

Table 5.2[73]

only six Conservatives) and, similarly schoolteachers (thirty-eight Labour MPs and sixteen Conservatives). Working environments that foster a political career may include journalism specialising in political and current affairs, and the civil service. Of particular importance inside the Labour Party are the occupations of trade union officials and employees, or manual workers associated with unions which will sponsor and support the manual worker through the party selection and candidature process. In 1992, fifty-nine Labour MPs were manual workers who had followed this route. But far and away the highest category of occupational background throughout Westminster within the Conservative Party is that of being a private business-person – a company director or executive. One hundred and twelve Conservative MPs are business-people, the great majority of whom continue their business interests part-time while serving as MP, unless and until they are appointed a minister in the government.

It goes without saying that none of these 'social qualifications' concerning a person's family life, education or occupation are in themselves essential, and certainly a great many examples of successful candidates may be found who do not conform to them. The talent or genius for political leadership and the work of a constituency MP may well be innate. But it is irrefutable

Occupation of candidates in the 1992 General Election

Occupation	Conservative Elected	Conservative Defeated	Labour Elected	Labour Defeated	Liberal Democrat Elected	Liberal Democrat Defeated
Professions						
Barrister	39	26	9	9	5	13
Solicitor	21	18	8	11	1	18
Doctor/dentist	4	6	2	5	–	13
Architect/surveyor	3	6	–	6	–	9
Civil/chartered engineer	3	4	–	9	–	23
Accountant	12	14	2	6	–	29
Civil servant/local govt	10	5	16	21	–	20
Armed services	14	3	–	–	1	1
Teachers:						
University	4	3	14	6	1	13
Polytechnic/college	2	4	24	33	–	46
School	16	16	38	73	3	103
Other consultants	2	2	–	1	1	3
Scientific/research	1	–	2	8	–	12
Total	131 (39%)	107 (36%)	115 (42%)	188 (52%)	12 (60%)	303 (50%)
Business						
Company director	37	30	1	–	–	20
Company executive	75	73	8	13	2	88
Commerce/insurance	9	15	1	5	–	22
Management/clerical	4	5	11	14	–	20
General business	3	8	1	12	–	22
Total	128 (38%)	131 (44%)	22 (8%)	44 (12%)	2 (10%)	172 (28%)
Miscellaneous						
Miscellaneous white-collar	9	11	36	64	1	69
Politician/political organiser	20	17	24	17	2	10
Publisher/journalist	28	9	13	14	3	19
Farmer	10	15	2	–	–	8
Housewife	6	7	–	4	–	9
Student	–		–	–	–	6
Total	73 (22%)	59 (20%)	75 (28%)	99 (27%)	6 (30%)	121 (20%)
Manual workers						
Miner	1	–	12	1	–	–
Skilled Worker	3	1	43	27	–	15
Semi/Unskilled Worker	–	–	4	4	–	1
Total	4 (1%)	1 (–)	59 (22%)	32 (9%)	0 (–)	16 (2%)
Grand Total	336	298	271	363	20	612

Table 5.3[74]

that in practice one or two of these factors, and especially where all three are operating together, constitute the ingredients that tend overwhelmingly to produce a successful parliamentary candidate. It is not difficult to discern the essentially middle-class, or upper middle-class, nature of many of these ingredients, since a middle-class upbringing is likely to produce better educational opportunites and onward entry into the professions such as law, lecturing or private business from which parliamentary candidates are often drawn. It may be the case, as the politics professor, Jean Blondel, once wrote: 'Whether one likes it or not, politics is a middle-class job and the training appropriate for middle-class jobs is also a training for politics. The dice are loaded by the present structure of society as well as by the natural conditions which govern the job of politics in any society.'[75]

Twenty-two ethnic minority candidates stood at the 1992 general election (a decrease of six from the number at the previous general election), of whom six were elected to the House of Commons. At the 1987 general election, four of Labour's Asian or Afro-Caribbean candidates were successful: Bernie Grant (Tottenham), Diane Abbott (Hackney North), Paul Boateng (Brent South) and Keith Vaz (Leicester East), and all of them received increased majorities in 1992. Ashok Kumar joined them in the Commons in 1991, following his by-election victory for Labour in Langbaurgh, but he then lost his seat in the following year's general election. Among Labour's overall number of nine ethnic minority candidates in 1992 (three of whom lost), there was one new successful candidate, Piara Khambra, who had been selected to fight the safe Labour seat of Ealing Southall and which he duly won. The Conservative Party was represented by an ethnic minority candidate in seven constituencies. Six of these candidates lost, including John Taylor, who had been selected to defend the Conservative seat of Cheltenham. However, Nirj Joseph Deva at Brentford and Isleworth became the first Asian Conservative MP to be elected this century.

Finally, the great majority of successful candidates across all three main political parties at the 1992 general election were in their forties or fifties. Their average age in the Conservative, Labour and Liberal Democrat parties respectively were 48, 49 and 45 years (see the table opposite).

WOMEN CANDIDATES

The small number of women elected to Parliament

The results of the 1992 general election were that 592 successful candidates were men and fifty-nine were women. This means that women comprise just 9 per cent of the total membership of the House of Commons. This statistic clearly points to the fact that it is very much more difficult to enter

Age of candidates in the 1992 General Election

Age on 1 Jan. 1992	Conservative		Labour		Liberal Democrat	
	Elected	Defeated	Elected	Defeated	Elected	Defeated
20–29	–	40	–	23	1	63
30–39	47	114	34	131	3	165
40–49	129	93	115	153	9	215
50–59	112	43	82	44	7	128
60–69	46	8	40	12	–	41
70–79	2	–	–	–	–	–
Total	336	298	271	363	20	612
Median age						
1992	48	39	49	42	45	43
1987	48	36	51	38	–	–

Table 5.4[76]

Parliament if you are a woman. If the present number of women MPs seems low, it in fact represents the highest-ever level of female composition in the Commons. At the 1987 general election only forty-one women MPs were returned, and before that in 1983 a mere twenty-three. Women have had the right to vote and stand for election to Parliament now for over seventy years, but the rise in the number of female MPs since Lady Astor first took her seat in 1919 has proved remarkably slow. Until the last general election, there was little difference between the Labour and Conservative parties in terms of the number of women MPs representing each of them in the Commons, but in 1992 Labour was the party which contained most of the additional new women members. Of the women candidates who were successful in 1992, thirty-seven were Labour, twenty Conservative, two Liberal Democrat and one Scottish National (see the table on page 204).

That less than one-tenth of British MPs are women represents an extremely low ratio, if the country is genuinely committed to the principle of sexual equality. Parliament is responsible for the nation's public policy and administration, including the creation of new laws, yet there is a very wide discrepancy between the national influence of men and women who hold positions of power inside government and Parliament. The issue is not that women have an equal right to a place in Parliament, which is undeniable, but that arrangements should ensure that the interests and attitudes of women are properly represented in Parliament. No one denies that men are capable of understanding women, or vice versa, and that an MP of either sex can represent all types of people in a general way. But the essential point is that women by virtue of their gender have distinct and separate concerns, and also tend to prioritise policy and administrative matters of public and national importance in a different way from men. The special role of women

Women candidates and MPs, 1918–92

	Conservative		Labour		Liberal/ Lib. Dem.		Other		Total	
	Cands.	MPs	Cands.	MPs	Cands.	MPs	Cands.	MPs	Cands.	MPs
1918	1	–	4	–	4	–	8	1	17	1
1922	5	1	10	–	16	1	2	–	33	2
1923	7	3	14	3	12	2	1	–	34	8
1924	12	3	22	1	6	–	1	–	41	4
1929	10	3	30	9	25	1	4	1	69	14
1931	16	13	36	–	6	1	4	1	62	15
1935	19	6	35	1	11	1	2	1	67	9
1945	14	1	45	21	20	1	8	1	87	24
1950	28	6	42	14	45	1	11	–	126	21
1951	29	6	39	11	11	–	–	–	74	17
1955	32	10	43	14	12	–	2	–	89	24
1959	28	12	36	13	16	–	1	–	81	25
1964	24	11	33	18	25	–	8	–	90	29
1966	21	7	30	19	20	–	9	–	80	26
1970	26	15	29	10	23	–	21	1	99	26
1974 Feb.	33	9	40	13	40	–	30	1	143	23
1974 Oct.	30	7	50	18	49	–	32	2	161	27
1979	31	8	52	11	51	–	76	–	210	19
1983	40	13	78	10	115	–	87	–	280	23
1987	46	17	92	21	106	2	84	1	328	41
1992	59	20	138	37	144	2	213	1	554	59

Table 5.5[77]

with respect to children is the most obvious example. Men can look after children too, but they do not go through pregnancy and labour, nor do they have to take leave from work to give birth, and the most common social pattern of domestic life strongly continues to be one where the mother takes ultimate responsibility for the care of the child. There is a close connection between the fact that Britain has one of the lowest number of women MPs of any Parliament in Europe, and also has among the worst public provisions for maternity pay, child care facilities and taxation policies that help women to return (if they wish) to work after giving birth. There is a very wide range of other national issues upon which men in general can have had little or no direct experience. At the very least, when legislation is passed, a significant proportion of the people making and approving the law should be women. Whether the subject is the criminal law of rape or abortion, or licensing and gambling regulation, or legislation on sex discrimination and promoting equal opportunities at work, it is clear that women tend to have a different perspective from men. It is the combination of public opinion from both sexes which should be reflected in the body that passes our national laws and holds government to account.

Reasons for the low representation of women MPs

The reasons for this bias against women within the parliamentary electoral system are not hard to identify. One major obstacle is the nature of the House of Commons itself and the way it works. Spectators in the public gallery overlooking the chamber have often commented on its atmosphere being very similar to that of a men's club (some have said a 'public schoolboys' common room'). Such an impression is reinforced by the manners of the chamber, which regularly include, for example, male ministers propping their feet up on the despatch box and packs of male MPs ritualistically howling down whatever a prominent member of the opposite party has to say. The Commons is male-dominated in many different respects. It has seven different drinking bars, but claims to have no room in which to start a crèche. It starts work in the chamber at 2.30 pm (most young children finish school and need to be collected at 3 pm), and the business of members voting on legislation continues until at least 10 pm. These hours may suit MPs who are also busy businessmen or barristers who rarely attend to the domestic needs of their children, but they virtually preclude the attendance of anyone who has primary responsibility for children and/or wishes to maintain some semblance of normal family life. The work of an MP will always be a demanding and time-consuming one, but there is no good reason why the structure of a normal business working day cannot be used as the basis for the parliamentary timetable. The traditions of the Commons always contain a heavy inertia against change of any sort. (It now seems astonishing, for example, that the élitist arguments against allowing television cameras into the Commons' chamber succeeded time and again until as recently as 1987, when the democratic arguments that ordinary voters across the country should be allowed to see what was going on in their name were at last accepted as irrefutable.) Opponents of the modernisation of the parliamentary timetable say that it would be 'a charter for the castration of the opposition',[78] because MPs could not hold up government business by employing the tactic of going on talking all night. But nothing will challenge the government's ability to pass its measures through Parliament if it has the necessary majority. Others have suggested that the work of the Commons' select and legislative committees, which at present generally begins at 10.30 am, would be disrupted by frequent demands made by party whips on committee members to attend the chamber, particularly when voting took place. However, committee work can easily be scheduled on to one afternoon each week set aside by standing orders for the purpose, extended as each committee thinks fit to occasional *ad hoc* early morning or evening sessions, as is normal in any line of work.

The second major obstacle is that too few women are selected as candidates to represent local constituency parties. The total number of women candidates fielded by each of the main parties shows a marked disparity between the sexes. In 1992 the Labour Party fielded 138 women candidates (its largest ever number), with the Liberal Democrats selecting 144, but the Conservative Party putting forward only fifty-nine. Both the Labour Party and the Liberal Democrats now have policies whereby there must be women's representation on all constituency party shortlists of candidates, but still the number of women candidates is in a substantial minority.[79] Part of the reason for this is simply that at the time of writing there are significantly fewer women than men who are interested in being an MP. The working conditions at Westminster are one major factor, and research also indicates that there are particular characteristics of the British electoral system that operate as a disincentive to women. The first-past-the-post method of election encourages a peculiarly combative type of approach in the selection process, because each party only fields one candidate within each constituency. According to Lesley Abdela of 'The 300 Group' (a campaigning organisation for increasing female representation in the Commons), 'The sheer nastiness of all too many of the selection races' is off-putting for many women, and 'I have heard a lot of women saying they really do not want the sneering and character assassination that goes on in the effort to push them aside.'[80] The first-past-the-post system is also directly conducive to Britain's two-party, adversarial style of politics at Westminster and in national debate, which is confrontational and abrasive in nature. There is evidence from opinion polling that women in general prefer a softer, more compromising approach to politics. A recent poll disclosed that almost 70 per cent of women thought it preferable that two or more parties should work together to provide a government.[81]

Since under first-past-the-post voting only one candidate is fielded by each political party in each constituency, the likelihood of bias towards men is more acute. By contrast, under multi-member constituency or party list electoral systems, parties field teams of candidates, the effect of which upon selecting bodies is to choose 'balanced tickets' of men and women or at least avoid choosing all the candidates of the same sex. As a recent Hansard Society report on the low representation of women generally in the upper reaches of life in this country put it:[82]

The first-past-the-post electoral system is likely to be one of the main reasons for the low representation of women in the House of Commons. Under proportional representation, it is the multi-member and/or party list element that favour women. In single-member constituencies, selection committees often hesitate to choose women candidates, while in constituencies with more than one member or a party list, there will be concern to secure a 'balanced ticket'. The absence of a woman from a list is seen as being likely to cause offence and narrow the party's appeal ... It is the unanimous finding of all studies of the legislative representation of women that systems of proportional representation favour the election of women.

This handicap against women candidates inherent in the present British single member/first-past-the-post electoral system goes some way to explain why Britain compares so badly in terms of its number of women MPs with other countries in the EU – the great majority of whom have electoral systems with proportional representation. Thus, in contrast to Britain's paltry 9 per cent of women MPs, Denmark has 33 per cent of women MPs in its Parliament, the Netherlands 24 per cent and Germany 22 per cent.

There is widespread opinion that the majority of voters think that men make better MPs than women, and that this explains the low number of successful women candidates at the polls, and why party constituency selection committees may be either actively or subconsciously prejudiced against them. Such a view, however, is wrong and misleading. While there certainly exists some prejudice about the relative roles of men and women generally in society, this does not appear to extend to voting behaviour in the election of an MP. All empirical research by psephologists and opinion-polling companies on the effect of a candidate's sex upon the voting preferences of electors shows only a very marginal inclination in favour of male candidates. Curiously, perhaps, such minimal bias as does exist is more pronounced among women voters rather than men. A recent investigation found that 90 per cent of men and 83 per cent of women say that the sex of the candidate makes no difference at all to how they vote. (Of the small minority who say it does, the results showed that men prefer men by two to one, and women prefer men by four to one.)[83] Easily the overriding criterion for voter choice is the identity of the political party to which a candidate belongs – not the gender of the particular candidate who is representing the party.

But attitudes about sexual roles are undoubtedly a part in the whole process of why there is a gender problem in parliamentary candidature. The origin and problem of sexual prejudice in politics does not begin and end with party selection committees and at Westminster. It is simply a reflection of British social attitudes that permeate the country in general. One problem is getting many men to take the gender problem issue seriously. For example, in a newspaper article on the aims of 'The 300 Group', Bernard Levin was moved to write:[84]

If women, solely because of their numbers, ought to be half of Parliament, what about homosexuals? I don't know what the latest imaginary figure for the proportion of homosexuals in the population is supposed to be – I last saw it passing the 20 per cent mark and for all I know it may be approaching 120 by now – but if sex is to decide the way we elect our MPs the 'third sex' can surely claim treatment as fair as that which is to be meted out to women when the 300 Group has its way. And what about race, religion, and other important qualifications? There is a real case to be made out, if we are going to abandon the purely political nature of candidate selection, for a fixed proportion (indexed to allow for changes in the population) of coloured MPs, Jewish MPs, disabled MPs, drunken MPs (already, as a matter of fact, represented far more numerously than their boozy brothers and sisters in the population at large) and mad MPs.

Another major obstacle to increasing the number of women MPs is that power, and the positions of power, whether in politics or in industry, is still strongly associated with sexual masculinity. This at the same time tends to inhibit women and aggravates a patronising attitude towards them by men. One does not need to look far for examples of this. The view of the Conservative MP and former Scottish Solicitor-General, Sir Nicholas Fairbairn, on women MPs is:[85]

I'm delighted to have more of them in the House of Commons, but they certainly don't give me feelings of femininity – and by that I don't mean beddable. They lack fragrance on the whole, they're definitely not desert island material. Maybe, in this day and age with all these hang-ups, they deny their femininity. Why has womankind given up the exaltation of herself, that attempt to attract, to adorn, to glint? They all look as though they're from 5th Kiev Stalinist machine-gun parade.

Yet another factor that operates against women in politics is that women tend to be socialised in their upbringing to be less assertive and selfish in their career aspirations, particularly once they are married. Professor Elizabeth Vallance sees it like this:[86]

Women are socialised both positively and negatively in ways which conspire to dampen both their general aspirations of achievement and the specific political abilities which they might develop. Positively, girls are brought up to believe that their role is different from that of boys (separate but equal, so the story goes). They have a role as wife and mother to look forward to and their education, although formally often similar to that of their brothers, is to this end . . . Positively girls are encouraged, not just in school, in formal education, but in the attitudes they take from home, the media etc, to aspire and conform to certain standards of passivity, softness, domesticity and above all perhaps, maternal feelings, the dispensation of care and comfort. Negatively, the encouragement to femininity means the discouragement of the masculine virtues. Girls who are too self-opinionated or articulate are 'brash'; those who flaunt their logicality are 'cold'; those who have qualities of leadershiip are 'hard', or just generically 'lacking in femininity'. Again, there is discouragement of the woman who looks outside the traditional maternal role for her fulfilment.

For similar reasons, women are seriously under represented in terms of equal numbers with men in rising to top positions, not only in politics, but also in the civil service, the professions, industry and commerce, trade unions and academia.[87] In the media too, men tend to dominate the ownership and editorial management of newspapers and television companies. For this reason women's policy issues are the hardest upon which to campaign. According to the Labour MP, Harriet Harman, 'One of our difficulties in getting our message across to women is the male domination of the media. Getting uncomprehending male journalists and reporters to cover child care sometimes feels like asking them to file a report in a foreign language.'[88]

Finding out the actual extent of unspoken discriminatory attitudes within selection committees that work against the interests of more women parliamentary candidates being adopted is very difficult to discover, because only a very few beyond-the-pale male chauvinists would ever openly admit to it. Professor Elizabeth Vallance's research had to conclude that, 'The extent of actual discrimination – at the selection stage, say – is almost impossible to establish. The women MPs do not complain of it, but then they are the successful products of the system. They made it, so it can't be totally discriminatory'.[89] In fact, since her research was published in 1979, some of the new women MPs who have entered the Commons, such as Harriet Harman, Teresa Gorman and Clare Short, have been far more critical of the inherent sexism of much of the way politics operates than were the more prominent female MPs of the 1960s and 1970s, perhaps most notably Margaret (now Baroness) Thatcher herself, who defied the sexual mould of Westminster to become Britain's first woman to be leader of one of the major political parties, and then Prime Minister. Earlier in Margaret Thatcher's career, when she was Education Secretary in Edward Heath's 1970–4 Cabinet, she said she did not believe there would be a female Prime Minister in her own lifetime. Her eventual success in reaching the top job in British politics represented a very significant landmark for the cause of women in Parliament.

Sociological dynamics tend to be self-perpetuating, and the best way of undermining the various factors discussed above that militate against women entering politics is simply to get more women in the Commons by whatever means necessary. Once this has been achieved, a successful 'feminine' culture will *de facto* have to be recognised in the House of Commons. It is very likely that if there is a substantial number of women MPs, they will insist on changes to the timetable and facilities of the Commons to accommodate their own family lives and those of others who wish to go into politics. Above all, they will serve as role models for young women to follow if they choose. Part of the present socialisation process that holds women back from career success is often the lack of role models upon which to base their lives. It remains of particular importance, then, to work towards increasing the number of women MPs at Westminster, for reasons of proper representation of public opinion on the wide range of social issues that are of direct concern to women, and also for symbolic reasons. A society committed to sexual equality should be seen to have a more equal number of men and women as its political leaders.

Proposed measures to increase female representation

One proposed reform, which has the great advantage of simplicity, but otherwise at present appears to have little chance of gaining broad political support, is simply to legislate for parity between the sexes in the membership of the House of Commons. Teresa Gorman, the Conservative MP for Billericay, put forward this proposal in a draft Representation of the People (Amendment) Bill introduced into the Commons under the Ten Minute Rule procedure on 21 January 1992. Her plan was to halve the number of constituencies by merging neighbouring seats together, and then provide that each of the 325 new constituencies returned two MPs each, one being a man and the other a woman. At all general elections, the voter would be presented with two lists, one of male names and one of women, and he or she would have a vote on each. Pointing to the fact that voters in Germany have two votes (one for the constituency MP, the other for a Party List MP) and that in the USA two Senators represent each State, Teresa Gorman went on to argue:[90]

> I do not seek special privileges for women. I simply seek to redress an anomaly in our legislative procedure . . . The House should be a mirror reflecting all aspects of society. It should reflect the ambitions, aspirations and concerns of the majority of electors who are women. Although I do not deny that under the Conservative Party of the last decade women have made enormous strides, it is still a contentious issue that every time there is an election we have to have special women's areas and policies . . . I am not seeking to promote any advantage for women; I simply seek equality. A woman is regarded by many selection committees, for better or worse, as not being the typical Member of Parliament. The image of a Member is still that of a man. We have to overcome that prejudice.

Her Bill was supported by Edwina Currie, Clare Short and David Amess, and received a formal First Reading but proceeded no further for lack of parliamentary time being made available. The only speaker in the ten minute debate who voiced opposition was Patrick Cormack, a fellow Conservative, who attacked the measure as 'nonsense' and 'just plain daft'. He said, 'In 22 years in the House I have never heard a more silly proposition'.[91] Similar sentiments had earlier been voiced against another plan for securing equal representation of women in the Commons, put forward by Tony Benn in his Commonwealth of Britain Bill printed in 1991.[92] Clause 10 of his Bill simply provided that, 'Half of the members of the House of the People [his new name for the Commons] shall be women and half shall be men', and the details of the changes to existing electoral law would be settled by subsequent legislation operating within this principle. 'This would rid us once and for all,' he wrote in a pamphlet later that year, 'of the scandal, to which both major parties contribute, of the tiny representation of women'.[93]

Although there is no endorsement by Labour or by any of the other parties for legislation of the kind drafted by Teresa Gorman or Tony Benn, the Labour Party at its conferences has backed resolutions laying down the principle of aiming towards equal numbers of men and women MPs. In 1990 the Party Conference agreed to 'a phased programme over the next 10 years or three general elections so that at least half the parliamentary party shall be women'. On precisely what new rules or procedures are needed to secure the objective of equal representation, there has been a great deal of discussion and conflict of opinion. Recently in the Labour Party, the greatest attention has been paid to the drawing up of short lists by constituency parties. Under existing party rules, there must be at least one woman on every constituency party's short list where a woman has been nominated.[94] If, after the short list has been drawn up in the normal way, (and taking into account the respective number of nominations), it transpires that there is no female on the list, then the final name on the list is eliminated, and a ballot is held to decide whom out of the women nominated has the highest level of constituency party support, and this name will be substituted on the short list. A more radical and controversial step took place at Labour's 1993 Conference, when a resolution was passed which (while lowering its sights 'at achieving 40 per cent of women as MPs for Labour by 1999 or two elections' time') proclaimed that, 'The only realisable way of achieving this aim is to implement women-only shortlists in 50 per cent of the seats where a sitting Labour MP is not standing for re-election.'[95] In response to this resolution (which was actively supported by the then party leader, John Smith), women-only short lists will now be prepared for the selection of the Party's parliamentary candidates in half of all seats where a Labour MP is retiring and half of all marginal seats where the Labour candidate has a good prospect of being elected successfully to Parliament. At the last general election there were twenty-six retiring Labour MPs (of whom three were in fact replaced by women), so the effect of this measure in those twenty-six constituencies in 1992 could have been to add up to thirteen extra female MPs. The impact of women-only short lists in marginal seats, however, has the potential to prove of far greater significance, especially if the Labour Party performs well at the polls. If Labour win the next general election, it could result in around a quarter of the members in the House of Commons being women.

The adoption of all-women short lists has been strongly criticised by a vocal minority of Labour members, including the former deputy leader of the party, Roy Hattersley.[96] Critics have predicted that there will be practical difficulties in carrying out the 1993 resolution on all-women short lists, particularly in the process of choosing precisely which constituencies are to be subject to the women-only short lists. It has been said that the process may stir up resentment within local parties at the regional or central office's interference with their freedom of choice to select their own candidate, generating division within the Labour Party and a distraction and electoral liability to voters throughout the country. Another damaging claim made by some civil rights and employment lawyers has been that the rule change is in breach of the Sex Discrimination Act 1975. In the opinion of David Pannick QC, publicised by *The Times* on its front page in December 1993, the new rule 'may be politically correct, [but] it is legally incorrect'.[97] However, even assuming David Pannick is himself legally correct (which is debatable) the issue is largely academic, since the question would only arise in legal proceedings if a Labour member was so incensed that he was prepared to take his own party to the Industrial Tribunal. The political criticisms that have been made of the policy have so far proved to be unfounded, and the process of deciding which constituencies will have all-women short lists has proceeded by internal party consultation and consent. The procedures followed have been that, 'In pursuance of the party's objective of considerably increasing the number of women candidates in winnable seats, the regional secretary shall convene "consensus" meetings of CLPs [constituency Labour parties] from vacant Labour and the most winnable seats to agree which constituencies will comprise the 50 per cent quota of all-women short lists.' However, Labour's Rule Book does go on to say that, 'In the event of no agreement being reached by such consensus meetings, the NEC [National Executive Committee] may determine which constituencies shall have all-women short lists.'[98]

Politically, it is difficult to see how the Labour Party (in present circumstances) can even begin to make substantial strides towards its legitimate objective of half of the House of Commons being women without resort to some measure at least as radical as the temporary imposition of all-women short lists as resolved at its 1993 Conference. Meanwhile, other organisational changes that are now taking place within the Labour Party, notably (under an earlier 1991 Conference decision) that by 1995 40 per cent of the posts at all decision-making levels in the Party are required to be occupied by women, represents another significant advance. Furthermore, if the Labour Party is returned to government, it is committed to establishing a new, special department of state which will concentrate on promoting sexual equality, called a Ministry for Women, and the Party will have the power to press ahead with the changes it believes are necessary to facilitate the careers of women in public affairs and in industry.[99]

Apart from the advances that may be made within each of the political parties in their selection procedures, any further genuine progress towards a substantially greater number of women MPs will depend on three developments. The first and most immediate way in which a substantially greater number of women MPs can be achieved is by adoption of the additional-member system of elections, coupled with a determination of the parties themselves to promote sexual equality in their parliamentary representation. This proposal to modify the present electoral system is explained and argued for elsewhere in this book, and entails the allocation of parliamentary seats partly through single-member constituency elections as at present, and partly through allocating additional seats to the political parties by reference to the proportion of total votes received by each.[100] This would inject not only a greater degree of proportional representation into our electoral system, but also provide a simple device whereby the parties can ensure that greater numbers of women enter Parliament. In their selection of parliamentary candidates to go on to the Party List from which the additional members are drawn, the parties can write in the names of an equal and fair number of women – or even give women candidates a greater priority if required. Second, a far more radical reshaping of the timetabling, facilities and working methods of the House of Commons should be introduced, specifically taking into account the requirements of female MPs who have children or other dependent relatives to care for. The guiding principle, which might be contained as a section in any future sex equality legislation, should be that 'Standing Orders of the House of Commons shall ensure that the time and hours of their sitting have regard to the needs of all persons who are eligible to be Members'.[101] The unnecessary conditions of work at Westminster which at present operate as barriers to put women off a career in politics must be removed. Finally, and perhaps most important, is simply that attitudes must change, so that it is generally regarded as important that there should be greater numbers of women MPs, and that something must be done to ensure that this happens. This means that a great deal of talking and public discussion must go on in order to raise the public's consciousness that the 'gender problem' is a genuine national issue which must be tackled. One part of this might be to set up a Speaker's Conference to consider the ways in which parliamentary and party practices and procedures place women at a disadvantage.[102] The appointment in 1992 of one of the women MPs at the House of Commons, Betty Boothroyd, as Speaker of the Commons makes such a Conference all the more appropriate. Whatever its recommendations, the Conference would help to draw political and public attention to this issue, and prove a valuable part of raising political and public concern that the present very low number of women MPs sitting in Britain's national legislature is simply not acceptable if the country aspires to be a modern democracy.

THE POLITICAL PARTIES' SELECTION OF CANDIDATES

Not a single candidate who was independent of a political party was elected at the 1992 general election, and not a single candidate who did not represent the Conservative, Labour and Liberal Democrat Parties was elected in England. Membership of a party is essential if a parliamentary candidate is to have any real chance of winning an election in his or her constituency. This will always be so, not just because the candidate needs a campaign team and workers to canvass for him or her, but because at the heart of our system of parliamentary democracy is the political organisation of popular participation and public opinion. There have in Britain's political history been a handful of successful independent MPs, generally defectors from one of the major parties, perhaps because they had been removed by their local party association as the party's choice of candidate for the coming general election, such as Dick Taverne in Lincoln, who was rejected by his Labour association and then stood as Democratic Labour candidate in the February 1974 election. But Dick Taverne, as with most party defectors, only enjoyed a temporary success as an independent, losing the seat to the official Labour candidate at the second general election held in October of the same year. At the 1992 election, rejected MPs from both Conservative and Labour Parties failed to keep their parliamentary seats by standing as independents: for example, the former Conservative John Browne at Winchester (polling only 3 095 votes to his successor, Peter Malone's, 33 113); and the former Labour MP, Dave Nellist, at Coventry South East (who precipitated one of the closest contests in the election, polling 10 551 votes, to the Conservatives' 10 591, and his Labour successor as MP, Jim Cunningham's, 11 902). Regional-based parties dominate the electoral politics of Northern Ireland, and in 1992 the Ulster Unionists, Democratic Unionists, Popular Unionists and the Social Democratic and Labour Party (SDLP) won all seventeen of the parliamentary seats between them. In Scotland and Wales the nationalist parties had some success. The Scottish National Party fielded a candidate in each of the seventy-two constituencies in Scotland and won three seats; and Plaid Cymru in Wales fielded a candidate in each of the thirty-eight constituencies in Wales and had four MPs returned (but with twenty-three of their candidates losing their deposit). But with the exception of these twenty-four MPs representing regional parties, the big three political parties – the Conservative Party, the Labour Party and the Liberal Democrats – won the parliamentary seats in every other United Kingdom constituency.

So, at the time of writing, the Conservative Party, Labour Party and the Liberal Democrats account for 96.3 per cent of all MPs. Omitting the Liberal Democrats, with the far smaller number of 20 MPs, the Conservative and Labour Parties account for 93.2 per cent between them. The political importance of these parties' selection of their parliamentary candidates, then, can hardly be over-emphasised. Their selection procedures will determine the effective choice that is put to all local voters at election time, and between which precise persons electors will be able to express their view and cast their vote. And then in turn, from the pool of those political party candidates who win and sit as MPs in the House of Commons, ministers and the composition of the government of the country will be decided.

The selection processes of the political parties

Each of the political parties has its own distinct set of rules and procedures for choosing its prospective candidates in advance of a general election.[103] The common pattern across the three main parties, however, is for the local association within the constituency to handle the actual selection from nominations put forward, and then for the central headquarters of the political party concerned to endorse the local party's selection (thereby reserving a power of veto over a candidate the party leadership regards as being wholly unsuitable). Selecting a parliamentary candidate is the most important political act of a local party association, and it is the time at which they exercise their own greatest influence upon the political process. Not surprisingly, therefore, party members within the local constituency associations take the selection process very seriously, and differences of opinion can give rise to some extremely heated and acrimonious meetings. Local associations are very jealous of their power over the selection, and will bitterly resent any heavy-handed interference from the central party headquarters seeking to impose upon the local selection committee a favourite of the national leadership's own choice.

The distinctive systems of each of the three major political parties in their selection of prospective parliamentary candidates are now explained.

The Conservative Party

When a new Conservative parliamentary candidate needs to be chosen, the executive council of the local association will first establish a selection committee. This selection committee will then set about the task of gathering together nominations, considering the names put forward and preparing a short list of around three to six candidates. This short list is then submitted to the executive council, who will conduct personal interviews with the people concerned, and decide upon a recommendation to put before a general meeting of the constituency party. The names on the short list from the selection committee are usually accepted by the executive council, and the general meeting will almost always endorse the recommendation of the executive council, but in both cases there is a power to refer back. It is possible for the executive council to put before the general meeting more than one name, and in fact in recent years there has been a growing tendency to do so. When this occurs, the final selection will be made by a ballot being taken of all paid-up local members of the party attending the meeting (and if there are more than two candidates, by way of the exhaustive ballot method). After the selection has been made at the general meeting, whether by way of endorsement of a single name offered by the executive council, or by way of the result being declared of the ballot on a choice of names offered by the council, the meeting will pass a formal resolution, generally supported by a unanimous vote,

> That this general meeting of members of the [name] Conservative and Unionist Association hereby adopts [name] as prospective Conservative candidate for the [name] constituency and pledges its wholehearted support to secure his/her return to Parliament at the next Election.

The Liberal Democrats

Within the Liberal Democrats, the executive committee of the local party is charged with responsibility for initiating the selection process, and for appointing a selection committee which will scrutinise all the nominations and prepare a short list of between three and seven names. The final selection from this short list is then determined by all paid-up members of the local party, using a secret ballot and single transferable method of election. Details of the people on the short list are distributed in advance to the local party members, and a series of hustings meetings held, at which short listed members present themselves and votes are cast.

The Labour Party

In the Labour Party, it is the task of the local association's executive committee to receive nominations, put forward by the local party branches within the constituency and affiliated trade unions, which in practice amounts to no more than about twenty names. After detailed consideration (and possibly personal interviews) they will produce a short list of five or six names for recommendation to the local party's general committee.[104] The general committee has the power to accept, amend or reject this short list before submitting it to the final decision of all paid-up Labour Party members registered within the constituency. Before individual members cast their votes, all party branches across the constituency will have had the opportunity to interview the short listed candidates, and an all-member constituency meeting will be held at which all eligible members must be invited. At the meeting, candidates' election addresses will be distributed, and each nominee will speak to the meeting and answer questions. Finally, voting takes place, 'on the basis of one member, one vote' by secret ballot. the voting continues in order of preference until one nominee has received 50 per cent of the votes cast.[105]

Selection of the candidate upon the basis of 'one member, one vote' was established as a new principle in 1993. Formerly, it had been a running controversy that the final decision was reached under a complex electoral college system which allowed for trade unions to account for up to 40 per cent of the college's vote (the precise proportion depending upon the number of affiliated unions within the local constituency), accompanied by block-voting by the unions so that each vote cast by an affiliated trade union was multiplied by the size of the union's membership. This system was heavily criticised for giving an often wholly disproportionate influence to trade unions over ordinary party members. Other common complaints were that within the union section of the college there was no requirement for union branches to ballot their members, and that eligibility for a union to affiliate and receive a vote in its share of the electoral college could be claimed if only one member of the local trade union lived within the constituency. Reform had been stymied for many years, due principally to opposition from the trade union element at Labour Party Conferences, but in 1993 the then Labour leader, John Smith (supported by his predecessor Neil Kinnock) confronted the issue head-on. In a day of high drama on 29 September passionate speeches were made on all sides (most famously by John Prescott, who is widely credited with having swayed the final decision) and individual voting by trade unionists – or OMOV ('one member, one vote') as it is now called – was finally introduced.[106]

Central party control over constituency party choice

All the parties have some system whereby the national central headquarters maintains lists of potential candidates who have been vetted and approved as suitable for consideration by local associations in drawing up their short lists. The local associations are not compelled to draw names from these lists, and their main significance is to advertise the interest of those individuals who appear on them.

In the Conservative Party, there is a 'list of approved candidates' which is the responsibility of a Standing Advisory Committee on Candidates, first established in 1935 and subsequently endorsed by resolution of the Party Conference at Brighton in 1948 and by the Report of the Maxwell Fyfe Committee on Party Organisation accepted by the Central Council of the party in 1949. The Advisory Committee is composed of senior members of the party, including the party chairman, the three vice-chairmen, the chairman of the Executive Committee, the chairman of certain groups within the party (including the Conservative Women's National Committee), the chief whip in the House of Commons, and the chairman of the 1922 Committee of backbench MPs. Those who wish to have their name placed on the Approved List will normally have to attend a Parliamentary Selection Board organised by one of the vice-chairmen of the party. This is a 24-hour residential meeting at which assessors and group leaders from Central Office look closely at the individuals concerned via discussions, written projects, group tasks, debates and interviews. As a result of what the Central Office staff see and hear, the vice-chairman will make a recommendation to the Standing Advisory Committee before it agrees to place the candidate's name on the approved list or not. The committee will also consider the qualifications and record of others not on the list, whom the constituency party wishes to consider for a vacancy. Local associations are urged to consult the nationally approved list of candidates before they start drawing up their own short list, although adoption by the local party of a candidate on the approved list does not mean that the committee will automatically endorse his selection for that particular constituency. The selection of a prospective parliamentary candidate by a local party always has to be approved by the Standing Committee, which retains a power of veto.

In the Labour Party, central headquarters at Walworth Road holds the names of those people whom the local constituency parties may wish to consider for nomination. Under model rules dating from 1929–30, there are, in fact, two lists maintained for this purpose: List A, which has the names of people sponsored by a trade union affiliated to the party and who have been approved by the National Executive Committee; and List B, which contains the names of other individuals who have made known their wish to serve as parliamentary candidates. The executive committee of a constituency party is not bound to draw names from these nationally-approved lists in preparing its short list, but others included will eventually have to be endorsed by the National Executive Committee at headquarters. The power to nominate prospective candidates, as observed above, is vested in the party branches within the constituency, and in affiliated trade unions, and individuals cannot submit themselves of their own volition. Eligibility as a candidate is generally restricted to those who have been members of the party for at least two years, and who undertake to accept and act in harmony with the standing orders of the Parliamentary Labour Party. The rules of the party expressly state that the selection of Labour candidates for parliamentary elections shall not be regarded as being complete until the name of the person selected has been placed before a meeting of the National Executive Committee, and his or her selection has been endorsed.[107]

Sitting MPs as party candidates

All sitting MPs will need to be readopted by their political party as official candidates of that party before contesting a general election. However, while it is always possible for the local association to remove the official party candidature from a sitting MP, and especially so in the Labour Party where there is a full reselection procedure, all the party rules put the sitting MP in a favoured position and in practice very few fail to be readopted for the forthcoming election.

Within the Conservative Party, the local association's executive may recommend the reopening of the selection process, and this will then need to be confirmed by a full general meeting of local party members. The national party's adoption rules state that in those circumstances where other potential candidates are being considered by a Conservative executive council, the name of the sitting member must be included automatically in the list to be considered by them.[108] Prior to the 1992 general election, there were four serious attempts within local Conservative associations to remove their MP as the official party candidate, three of which succeeded, with Sir Trevor Skeet (objected to by some local Conservatives on grounds of his advanced age) surviving the challenge in his North Bedfordshire constituency. One of the three deselected was Sir Anthony Meyer, who achieved national prominence in 1989 for putting himself forward in a party leadership contest against Margaret Thatcher (a year before she was removed in another leadership contest), as a result of which two months later he was censured by 206 votes to 107 within his Clwyd North-West constituency. The other two cases included a former minister, Sir John Stradling-Thomas in Monmouth, who after failing to be recommended by his executive council (upon grounds of neglect of his parliamentary duties) announced that he would not be seeking readoption; and John Browne in Winchester, who had survived a deselection motion at the 1987 general election, but in the face of an executive reselection resolution in 1991 (following his suspension from the Commons for a month for non-disclosure of financial interests) decided to withdraw – although subsequently he fought and lost the election as an Independent candidate.

The Liberal Democrats' rules on the matter state that if a sitting MP informs the chairman of his or her local party in writing that he or she wishes to stand at the next general election, then a general meeting of the local party shall be called and if the MP is endorsed at the meeting by a majority of those members present and voting by secret ballot, the MP shall thereby be reselected. If the resolution is defeated the MP may request a ballot of all the members of the local party, the meeting shall appoint a returning officer to conduct the ballot and the MP shall be reselected if the proposition is supported by a majority of those voting.

Of the three main parties, only Labour has an automatic, mandatory reselection procedure. This means effectively that the normal procedures applicable where there is no sitting MP are to be followed, involving nominations for prospective parliamentary candidates being invited and sought. The sitting Labour MP is to be treated like any other possible candidate to be selected, with the exception that he or she must be included in the short list prepared by the local executive committee.[109] In practice, many sitting Labour MPs will have the overwhelming support of their local parties, in which case a short list of one (the MP) may be drawn up, for onward transmission and approval by the general committee and the electoral college. Mandatory reselection of MPs was only introduced into the Labour Party in 1981, and was the product of a widespread feeling across the party that MPs in the 1960s and 1970s were failing to represent rank and file opinion within their local parties properly in carrying out their parliamentary and governmental duties. It was introduced at the same time as other important constitutional matters aimed at extending party democracy, most notably the change in the method for electing the party leader, from one in which MPs alone cast a vote to one in which an electoral college was created. Between 1981 and 1986, fourteen MPs were removed under the new reselection procedures. Prior to the 1992 general election, there were 229 Labour MPs needing to be reselected, and around a quarter of them (fifty-nine) faced a serious contest. Only five were in fact removed, and still fewer (only two) went through a normal local association reselection procedure, namely John Hughes (aged 67 years) in Coventry North-East, and Syd Bidwell (aged 74 years) in Southall. Ron Brown, who had recently been suspended from the Commons for a month and had the Labour whip withdrawn from him for three months for damaging the Mace in the House, was removed under a special procedure in his Leith constituency, approved by the National Executive Committee, that reopened his earlier selection and barred him from the contest. The two other deselections, Dave Nellist in Coventry South-East, and Terry Fields in Liverpool Broadgreen, were removed by virtue of the fact that the National Executive Committee expelled them from the Labour Party in December 1991 on grounds of being linked with the Militant Tendency. Prior to their expulsions, they had, in fact, both been reselected by their local associations. Labour's procedures for dealing with sitting MPs are now being reviewed. While the principle of mandatory reselection will undoubtedly remain, many sitting MPs have complained that the present procedure is very time-consuming for them and results in repeated absences from the House of Commons to attend constituency meetings connected with the selection process, and if and when Labour is next elected to power, those MPs who are also ministers will find this drain on their time even more of a problem. What is being suggested is a modification of the procedures, so that especially in the case where there is a short list of one (the MP), the full selection procedures might be by-passed by a ballot of all local party members.

Criteria for selection of party candidates

Ideas about what makes a good parliamentary candidate will vary from constituency to constituency, as well as from party to party. The party rules themselves do not lay down criteria, although the common concern to see more women MPs has led to formal means to encourage the consideration of women candidates. As considered earlier in this chapter, under Labour Party rules there must be at least one woman on each short list prepared by a local association. For the Liberal Democrats, there must be at least one man and one woman on any short list of under five names, and at least two men and two women on a short list of over four. The Conservative Party's notes on procedure state that, 'From time to time the Party has passed resolutions urging the need for more women and more trade unionists to be adopted. There is no doubt that our Party wants more women MPs and more MPs with varied backgrounds and selection committees should endeavour to include them in short lists.'[110]

In all other respects, it is left to the judgement of the local party to decide who is the best person to represent the party in their constituency. Where nominees of equal merit in terms of their intellect and speaking ability present themselves, the attraction of any one from a range of different qualities may prove conclusive to a local association's decision. An experienced and well-known politician (especially a former government minister) offering him or herself, as a result of losing his or her seat either at the most recent election or through a constituency boundary review, will always be an advantage and will bring kudos to the constituency itself. Some local party members will place a high premium on the candidate's knowledge of local matters, so that he or she may better understand the feelings and problems of constituents being represented in Parliament; but, on the other hand, some local politicians may be associated with old local controversies or political factionalism within the constituency party which are best avoided or forgotten. There will always be flexibility in the proximity of political opinion between the views of the candidate and local party members, in the same way that local party members among themselves will often disagree with one another on a range of matters, but local associations will need to know that the candidate has a broadly similar brand of politics to that prevailing within the constituency party, and also that he or she can relate to a wide spectrum of opinion within the party and across the constituency – not least because as a candidate he or she will need to appeal to a majority of the local electorate. The guidance of national headquarters in the selection process is always available, and, not surprisingly, they give their highest priority to a nominee who looks to be a 'winner' in the forthcoming general election, who will help increase the representation of the political party as a whole in the House of Commons, and who also possesses the potential skills to serve, if called upon, as a government minister.

For the nominee who succeeds in being selected as the party's prospective parliamentary candidate, the whole selection process will have been an enormous ordeal. He or she will have been subjected to a degree of detailed scrutiny and cross-examination, sustained over a period of many months, which will make the forthcoming election campaign itself seem positively enjoyable by comparison. Furthermore, adoption in a 'safe' seat where the party is defending a large majority means that the main political hurdle for getting into Westminster is over. The successful candidate will not forget the selection experience, nor the possible question of readoption at the next election, and will therefore always do his or her best to treat members of the general committee as friends, helped along by small personal gestures such as sending them individual greetings card at Christmas. The veteran Conservative MP Julian Critchley, once memorably described the whole selection process as follows:[111]

> Adoption is hell for the candidate, pure joy for those that select him. The choice of a candidate is for the constituency party worker the reward of many years of hard, unglamorous work. It is a pleasure to be savoured. Whereas he would normally 'look up to' his candidate, and will tend if not to praise at least to justify him, it is at the selection conference that he comes briefly into his own. Then it is 'they' who are the suppliants, he who calls the tune.

NOMINATION AND THE DEPOSIT

The formal means by which a person submits his or her parliamentary candidature is by lodging with the returning officer for the constituency a nomination paper, duly completed, together with a deposit of a sum of money. Nomination papers must be delivered to the returning officer within six working days after the Royal Proclamation calling the general election, and must be in a prescribed form, signed by ten registered voters in the constituency, two of whom formally propose and second the nomination, with the other eight assenting.[112] The only personal details of the candidate required to be placed on the nomination paper are his or her names in full, and home address in full. In addition, a description of the candidate may be included, up to a maximum of six words. For official party candidates, this description will refer to their political party. The individual nominated must give his or her own written consent to the returning officer, which must be attested by one witness, and this form must also notify the returning officer of the candidate's date of birth, and state that the candidate is aware of the provisions of the House of Commons Disqualification Act 1975 and that to the best of his or her knowledge and belief he or she is not disqualified from membership of the House of Commons.

Candidates will not be validly nominated unless the sum of £500 (at the time of writing) is deposited by them or on their behalf with the returning officer during the time for delivery of nomination papers. The money may be handed over in cash (with only notes or one-pound coins being acceptable), or by banker's draft, or any other manner acceptable to the returning officer. This £500 will be returned to the candidate after the general election if he or she manages to collect at least 5 per cent of the total votes cast in the constituency, but if the candidate polls less than 5 per cent then he or she loses the money, which then goes to the Treasury. The pattern of lost deposits across the political parties over the period since 1918 is indicated in the table on page 224. The two major parties of the day, therefore, tend to lose only a small number of deposits. The Liberal Party (now the Liberal Democrats), as the smaller centre party, have had fluctuating fortunes since the 1970s: at that time they lost a large number of deposits, which proved very expensive for them, but since then have not lost more than eleven upon any occasion.

Proposal for abolition of the deposit

The principal issue concerning the nomination of candidates in Britain is whether this requirement of a financial deposit is consistent with the democratic right of every citizen to stand for election if he or she wishes, regardless of the availability of capital or financial status. The deposit was first introduced by the Representation of the People Act in 1918 at a time when the property qualifications required for electors and candidates had only just been removed. Previously, candidates had been nominated without any need to deposit sums of money with the returning officer. The Home Office's invention of the deposit in 1918 was hardly mentioned, let alone properly discussed, during the otherwise very lengthy debates on the parliamentary passage of the Act, but a tacit acceptance seems to have existed at the time that some capital requirement was a good idea in order to keep out unsuitable candidates. Undoubtedly there were many within the political élite at the time who regarded the fledgling Labour Party and its trade-union and working-class candidates, who would be hardest hit by the requirement of a deposit, as less than top-class parliamentary material and a potential threat to the good government of the country.[113] The original amount of the deposit when introduced in 1918 was £150 (at 1994 values,

Forfeited deposits at general elections, 1918–92

Election	C	Lab	L	Com	NF	PC	SNP	Green	Others	Total	Percentage of total opposed candidates
1918	3	6	44	—	—	—	—	—	108	161	10.6
1922	1	7	32	1	—	—	—	—	11	52	3.8
1923	0	17	8	0	—	—	—	—	2	27	1.9
1924	1	28	30	1	—	—	—	—	8	68	4.9
1929	18	35	25	21	—	1	2	—	11	113	6.6
1931	5	21	6	21	—	1	2	—	29	85	6.9
1935	1	16	40	0	—	1	5	—	18	81	6.2
1945	6	2	76	12	—	6	6	—	74	182	10.8
1950	5	0	319	97	—	6	3	—	31	461	24.7
1951	3	1	66	10	—	4	1	—	11	96	7.0
1955	3	1	60	15	—	7	1	—	13	100	7.1
1959	2	1	55	17	—	14	3	—	24	116	7.6
1964	5	8	52	36	—	21	12	—	52	186	10.6
1966	9	3	104	57	—	18	10	—	36	237	13.9
1970	10	6	184	58	10	25	43	—	72	408	22.2
1974 (F)	8	25	23	43	54	26	7	—	135	321	15.0
1974 (O)	28	13	125	29	90	26	0	—	131	442	19.6
1979	3	22	303	38	303	29	29	53	221	1 001	38.9
1983	5	119	11	35	60	32	53	108	316	739	28.7
1987	0	0	1	19	—	25	1	133	110	289	12.4
1992	4	1	11	—	—	23	0	253	609	901	32.7

Note: Abbreviations for names of political parties: C=Conservative; Lab=Labour; L=Liberal; Com=Communist; NF=National Front; PC=Plaid Cymru; SNP=Scottish National Party; Green=Green Party (formerly Ecology Party).

Table 5.6[114]

around £2 500); this was forfeited unless 12.5 per cent of votes were received by the candidate. It remained at that level until a review was conducted in the early 1980s, as a result of which the sum was increased in 1985 to the current figure of £500, with the threshold for forfeiture being lowered to 5 per cent. The Conservative government (who introduced the legislation in 1985, supported by a report of a Conservative-dominated Home Affairs Select Committee of the House of Commons two years earlier) had originally wanted to raise the deposit to £1 000, and had been urged by some commentators, including Dr David Butler (the psephologist) and Sir Robin Day (the television interviewer) to go for an enormous increase, even up to £2 000.[115] From a comparative perspective, the present deposit system – and the desire in some quarters to push the sum of money involved even higher – is an extraordinary state of affairs. Only four other states in Europe (France, Ireland, Greece and the Netherlands) and none in the USA have deposit systems, and even in the four states listed the sums required are far lower than the £500 at present demanded of a parliamentary candidate in Britain.[116] Many will agree that 'The deposit system appears grossly unfair to those public spirited citizens who have a real desire to place themselves and their opinions before the electorate. Therefore, to further diminish their democratic right to participate in parliamentary elections is to diminish democracy itself.'[117]

The principal argument in support of the deposit has been that it is the best deterrent that can be found to put off people from standing who are not serious parliamentary candidates. As the then Home Secretary, Leon Brittan, said in defending the Representation of the People Bill in 1985:[118]

I think that the deposit is a perfectly respectable parliamentary barrier founded in principle. It is not just a financial barrier erected to make it more difficult for those who do not have the necessary money. The deposit is founded in principle because the essence of election to Parliament is the contest between people who have serious aspirations to represent a constituency.

Or, in the words of Dr David Butler, when advocating large deposits for candidature to the Home Affairs Committee, 'It does seem to me that the democratic discourse ought to be confined to people who are serious candidates.'[119] According to this argument, parliamentary candidates have rights, privileges and advantages conferred upon them, such as the right to free postage of election addresses, the right to free use of publicly-maintained buildings for public meetings, the right to veto broadcast transmission of material relating to the constituency election, and in addition, considerable publicity. An unrestricted exercise of the freedom to stand for election is therefore open to abuse.[120]

The problem here is a lack of any clear distinction, both in the analysis of the problem and in the application of the law on nomination procedure, between (a) the joke candidates who, by their own admission, are out to make mischief for one or more of their fellow candidates, or who are otherwise standing for amusement or seeking self-publicity for some selfish reason; and (b) candidates who stand no serious chance of winning the parliamentary seat, but who quite legitimately wish to draw attention to their views, contribute to political debate, and display what level of popular support they possess. Of the first kind of candidate, there is no doubt that such people can be irritants to other candidates, and occasionally disruptive.[121] The former Prime Minister, Margaret Thatcher, always had to put up with a battery of around eight frivolous or crank opponents in her Finchley constituency, all of whom were validly nominated but each of whom received barely a handful of votes. In 1957 there was a case of a crooked property developer who stood as a parliamentary candidate, saying, 'Don't vote for me, but I can build a house cheaper than anyone else.' He regarded the financial loss of his deposit as well worth the accompanying publicity.[122] A well-known veteran among joke candidates is Screaming Lord Sutch, leader of the Monster Raving Loony Party. At the 1992 general election he stood in three constituencies, losing his deposit in each. Such mischievous characters are, in fact, far more in evidence at by-elections (when the national press is focused exclusively upon the contest in which they are standing) rather than at a general election, when a few may stand in the constituencies of the Prime Minister or some other prominent politician, but otherwise the normal pattern across the constituencies of the United Kingdom is simply for the contest to be between three to five representatives from the main parties operating in the locality.

Even if the law should indeed aim to discourage frivolous or mischievous individuals from being nominated as parliamentary candidates, defenders of the deposit tend to exaggerate the negative impact of these fringe candidates. Some will admit to feeling a sneaking regard for some of the impudent candidates such as Lord Sutch, and occasionally finding the quality of their electioneering endearing and humorous. None the less, it remains the view of the government and some commentators, such as David Butler, that, 'Oddball candidates do impede the democratic process . . . They cause confusion to the electorate.'[123] The principle of the deposit is therefore supported as a device for weeding out people who are not regarded as being serious parliamentary candidates.

Quite apart from the fact that the deposit does not seem to operate very effectively towards this end (since any crank with £500 can put himself up as a candidate), at any general election there is a far greater number of the quite distinct category of candidates who may be independents or belong to some minor political party but who most certainly regard themselves as serious in their purpose. These parties include Plaid Cymru, the Green Party, the National Front, the Natural Law Party, and the Communist

Party. Independents are a declining type of candidate in modern times and largely confined to defectors, or those expelled, from one of the major parties. However, there have been some very distinguished independent MPs this century, including the writer and law reformer A. P. Herbert, whose own view of the deposit system was vividly described in an introduction to a book entitled *The British Political Fringe* in 1965:[124]

> If you do not get one eighth of the votes polled you must forfeit that to the State . . . Why on earth should I, or anyone else, be fined £150, for failure? It is like hitting a man when he is down, is it not? And why is he down? Because he sought to serve the State. It is like the Umpire saying to a cricketer: 'You are out, Sir. May I add that you are out for a duck. And now you will be hit on the head with a bat.' Now this undemocratic nonsense does not affect the supporters of the 'great parties', which have huge funds and insurance schemes. It does affect the independent and fringe candidates very much . . . I do not call this 'tolerance'.
>
> The object of the deposit was to discourage freaks . . . but what is a freak? You might describe so a man who wanted to introduce a Bill to assert that the earth was flat. But Plaid Cymru, for example, have a perfectly serious and comprehensive plan to take over Wales and let the Welsh govern it. You may not agree, it may never happen: but no man has a right to call them 'freaks'. A Liberal member said well in 1917: 'It seems to me that if a man can get one vote he is justified in testing the opinions of the electorate.'

No doubt many people see some of the fringe parties, notably the Communist Party and the British National Party, as extremist groups who should in some way be excluded and given no encouragement. But this may be short-sighted, and by positively discouraging them from presenting their policies in a democratic manner, may serve to aggravate their tendencies towards extra-parliamentary tactics. Thus Matthew Parris, then a Conservative MP and now a feature writer for *The Times,* said to the Home Secretary during passage of the 1985 Act, which raised the size of the deposit,[125]

> Contesting seats when there is not a ghost of a chance of winning them is one of the ways in which a small party shows that it is serious. The Bill will stop small parties from doing just that. If the Bill is enacted, small parties will be able to say with some justice that they are not fielding a credible spread of candidates because we passed a law that prevented them from doing so. That argument and that sense of grievance, which I believe will sustain the argument, will prove a moral weapon in the hands of minority parties that my Right Hon. and learned Friend will be unwise

to ignore. He is giving fringe movements a better case for extra-parliamentary action than they have ever been able to make for themselves.

I do not know whether my Right Hon. and Hon. Friends see this as I do, but I have always felt it a cause for satisfaction that in this country the Communist Party, the National Front or the Socialist Workers' Party can and do field candidates. A cause for even greater satisfaction is that they regularly and visibly fail to attract much support. No longer will we be able to say that. Their spokesmen will be able to say that their parties are not rich enough to test the electorate's support or to get their message across.

It is the newer, fledgling parties who suffer most disproportionately under the present system. One of the most important objections to the deposit is that it penalises financially the serious minority parties and independents, who are least able to afford to put forward sizeable sums of capital, especially when added to their expenses in financing their election campaign, such as printing election addresses and posters. At the 1992 general election, for example, the Green Party fielded 253 candidates, which necessitated a capital investment of £126 500, and every single candidate lost his or her deposit by polling below 5 per cent of the local votes, though 170 047 electors across the country voted for the party. Were the Greens therefore not serious candidates? Did they detract from the seriousness of the general election? Or did they constructively participate in the election debate by putting serious environmental issues across to the voting public? Again, in the words of Matthew Parris during the 1984 House of Commons debates on raising the level of the deposit:[126]

The Ecology Party [later renamed the Green Party] fielded 109 candidates at the 1983 general election. It hopes to field 300 at the next general election. It will lose a fortune. I ask my Right Hon. and learned Friend whether we need to do this to small parties. I cannot speak for organisations, such as the [Green] Party, but I imagine that they hope to move from being single-issue organisations, which attract a small but respectable following because of public feeling on those single issues, to becoming broader parties with fuller manifestos. It is not uncommon or wrong to enter politics on the back of one central issue and to mature and evolve from that. The first stage is inevitably a minority one. My Right Hon. and learned Friend will, perhaps unwittingly, kill such movements at birth. It is neither wrong nor unhelpful to field candidates on one issue as an end in itself, as a way of testing and demonstrating public feeling on that issue, and not so much as a launching pad. It is a way of showing the mainstream parties that they should take an issue more seriously, and they do so in the hope that they will.

The aim of the law should certainly encourage individuals and small parties to think seriously before putting their candidature forward, but to use a financial hurdle as an obstacle is not an appropriate test. Not only does the deposit penalise and suppress the valuable contributions that can be made by minorities and independents who have every right to put their policies before the public at election time, it also does nothing to prevent affluent eccentrics or troublemakers who have no serious intention at all. The requirement of a deposit is indefensible in principle and should be abolished. The nomination procedure should be amended so that, instead, a candidate must have a much larger prescribed number of local electors nominating him or her. An appropriate number of such nominators would be 200. Each person putting their name to the nomination should be required to sign the paper, and add in a clear, legible form their full name and electoral registration number. The statutory provision should permit the list of nominations to be drawn up at any time within one year prior to the election date, so that proper care and consideration can be given to the matter (and avoid a rush in the six days following the Royal Proclamation). The lists of nominators for each candidate should be displayed in a public place, and published in at least one local newspaper. The fact that a nominator's electoral registration number must be stated would avoid petition-like gatherings of names for frivolous candidates in town centres, since the person approached would need to have time to find out his electoral number and this would ensure a period of serious reflection. On the other hand, established parties, whether one of the three major parties or a smaller organisation such as the Green Party, would have no difficulty in arranging for a sufficient number of local party members to sign the nomination papers.

The objections to such a system were put forward by the Conservative government in its White Paper prior to the Representation of the People Act 1985. It said:[127]

A requirement of this kind would greatly increase the work of the acting returning officer, who would have to check the signatures on each nomination paper against the electoral register in the busy period before nominations close, and it would increase the risk of a nomination being held invalid on purely technical grounds. But the main objection, in the government's view, is that a candidate's ability to produce signatures is no test of the number of votes he or she will receive in the election.

There are therefore three objections being stated here. First, it 'would greatly increase the work of the acting returning officer'. To use the word 'greatly' here is a complete exaggeration. It has been calculated reliably that it would take one minute on average to check each signature.[128] In other words, all the nomination lists could be checked within one working day by a competent official, and even if in the planning of resources allowance was made for an extra working day to deal with exceptional cases where an allegation of impersonation needed to be investigated, the total work involved would still be only two working days for one official, at a total cost of around £200. Second, the government says that this procedure 'would increase the risk of a nomination being held invalid on purely technical grounds'. This is a very weak argument. Good planning by the candidates' organisations would always ensure that there was a small number of signatories in excess of the 200 required, say 225, so that in the unlikely event that one or two of their supporters proved ineligible (for example, by not in fact being registered on the electoral roll) there would still be the statutory number required. And finally the government says that, 'a candidate's ability to produce signatures is no test of the number of votes he or she will receive'. This, as the political editor of the *New Statesman* commented at the time, is 'the worst argument of all. The point of setting any hurdles is not – or should not be – to block serious minority candidates, but to block frivolous ones.'[129] Certainly, people nominating a candidate do not necessarily undertake to vote for him or her (although in the overwhelming majority of cases they will in fact do so), but this misses the whole point of the proposed reform. What is being suggested is a requirement for the judgement of a substantial number of local electors on the suitability of the person concerned to replace the invidious barrier existing at present, whereby any person can stand as a parliamentary candidate, however frivolous, so long as he or she can afford to lose £500, regardless of whether or not there is any substantial support for his or her nomination.

Especially if the recent cost-cutting in appointing returning officers, whereby they may be required to serve in more than one constituency, were reversed, a single returning officer and staff for each constituency will have no difficulty at all in supervising and, where necessary, verifying two hundred voters' nominations for each candidate. If any vestige of the deposit is allowed to remain, it should be translated into a non-returnable fee of £100 paid by all candidates upon lodging their nomination papers. This fee would serve to reinforce the purpose of making joke candidates think twice before standing, even if (in the unlikely event) they are able to find the required number of signatories to their nomination, and in addition the major political parties can be regarded as making a contribution towards the election services they enjoy (such as postage and meeting halls) provided free from the state, and which are made use of by the larger parties to a considerably greater extent than by other candidates.

In the meantime, and until better arrangements are introduced to modify the existing law on the nomination and deposit requirements for parliamentary candidature, for the observer outside Britain there is perhaps something quintessentially British about the by-election result in

1984 shown below, which featured one of the most remarkable line-ups of parliamentary candidates in British contemporary political history, when Tony Benn first won his present parliamentary seat:

CHESTERFIELD
Electorate 69,892
Turnout 76 per cent

A. WEDGWOOD BENN (Lab.)	24 633
G. PAYNE (Lib./SDP Alliance)	18 369
N. H. BOURNE (C.)	8 028
W. MAYNARD (Ind.)	1 355
D. SUTCH (Monster Raving Loony Party Last Stand)	178
L. BENTLEY (Four-Wheel Drive Hatchback Road Safety)	116
J. DAVEY (No Increase in Dental Charges)	83
T. LAYTON (Spare the Earth Ecology)	46
H. ANSCOMBE (Death off the Road; Freight on the Rails)	34
J. JIM BARDWAJ (Yoga and Meditation)	33
D. BUTLER (Buy your Chesterfield in Thame)	24
P. NICHOLLS-JONES (Ind. – The Welshman)	22
S. SHAW (Elvisly Yours Elvis Presley Party)	20
C. HILL (Prisoner – I am not a Number)	17
G. PICCARRO (The Official Acne Candidate)	15
D. CAHILL (Reclassify the Sun Newspaper as a Comic)	12
J. CONNELL (Peace Candidate)	7

6   Election Campaigns: Publicity and the Media

MODERN ELECTIONEERING

The style of political campaigning at general elections in Britain has dramatically altered in recent times. The single most important feature of modern electioneering has been the arrival of television broadcasting technology, so that today the overwhelming majority of families throughout the country possess a television set in their home which they regularly watch in the evening for entertainment and news bulletins. Following only a short time after radio broadcasting itself had transformed electioneering methods in the 1920s and 1930s, the new technology of television in the 1950s rapidly eclipsed radio as the most popular source of political information and became the primary focus for electioneering by the political parties, not least because it was quickly realised that the visual impact of this medium was at least as important as (and indeed frequently more important than) words alone. As one leading market research company chairman, Robert Worcester, has stated:[1]

> There is no question that the main message that television news during an election campaign gets across is visual. The thing that sticks in people's minds is what they saw, not what they heard.

Meanwhile, the advent of radio and television caused the newspaper industry to lose its earlier position as the main vehicle through which ordinary men and women received their information about political events. Indeed, the very nature of the newspaper business has been revolutionised by broadcasting, for the very reason that nowadays, by the time a newspaper is bought its front-page stories will contain the previous day's news, which the reader will already know about from the previous evening's television reports. As a result, a strong tendency throughout the newspaper business as a whole has been to concentrate upon what is sensational or entertaining about what has happened, and otherwise to diversify the contents of what is published by way of feature articles and commentaries. These may none the less prove to be a significant influence in swaying voters, particularly so because, unlike television which is under a duty to report the news impartially and provide political balance in its contents,[2] newspapers are under no such restrictions and most of them do in fact openly and rampantly support one party and oppose the rest.

The traditional methods of campaigning by candidates and parties, aiming at maximising personal contact with the voters by way of canvassing, election meetings and open-air hustings, have gone into a marked decline, together with the degree of personal dialogue and debate that used to be a feature of the packed halls and market-place meetings where politicians practised their oratory. Instead, today, the emphasis in election campaigns has shifted to how most effectively to 'sell' the party's political image to voters through the media. This whole marketing process was foretold by Graham Wallas at the London School of Economics early in the twentieth century, in his classic book *Human Nature in Politics*, where he described the importance that would come to be attached to political image in the new era of democratic politics:[3]

Emotional reactions can be set up by the name [of the party] and its automatic mental associations. It is the business of the party managers to secure that these automatic associations shall be as clear as possible, shall be shared by as large a number as possible, and shall call up as many and as strong emotions as possible.

For the parties' campaign strategists, this means that the most important work to be done during the campaign is to try to manipulate television facilities and broadcasting so as to project the party's message and image in the best possible light. Direct political advertising on television paid for by the parties remains prohibited by law in this country,[4] in contrast to the USA, where unrestricted fee-paying propaganda broadcast on any of their huge number of private television companies has come to dominate presidential elections. Political access to television in Britain essentially takes two forms. Most directly, the main political parties are allocated free party election broadcasts on television and radio during the period of the general election campaign. But, of equal importance, the main daily work of the parties at campaign time has come to be focused on staging media events which will present the party and its leaders in the best light when reported on the news. Television, and the deliberate orchestration of the party's daily campaigning for the benefit of television, has come to be of pivotal importance to party campaign managers in recent years. As the journalist, Robert Harris, has said, 'In the end it is on television that the election is decided. If the cameras ain't there, it ain't happening.'[5]

The central political controversies affecting electioneering in the late twentieth century are ones which concern national campaigning by the parties, involving the publicity of the campaign generally and relations with the media in particular, coupled with the question of each party's financial resources and capacity to campaign effectively. British election law has been rather slow to catch up with the reality of modern electioneering, and statutory provisions regulating election campaigns are still aimed mainly at personal methods of constituency campaigning. Most of the minutiae of legal rules touching on the election campaign are concerned with matters such as potential bribery or coercion of individual voters, or unfair election expenditure by individual candidates. These are matters still of great importance in principle, but are predominantly re-enacted legal provisions passed long ago in response to the widespread electoral corruption in the nineteenth century. Similarly, it is a striking anomaly that, whereas it is well known that the great majority of electors in recent times cast their vote according to the national party they favour (some voters even being unaware of the names of the individual candidates standing for election within the constituency), British election law on the one hand continues to apply rigourous legal controls over the financial expenditure that can be incurred by individual candidates campaigning within their local constituencies. On the other hand, however, it has failed to impose any analogous limits upon the expenditure which may be incurred by political parties in the course of their national electioneering. Fundamental questions of political finance are not addressed by British law at all, including whether the parties have adequate financial resources upon which to draw to present their election campaigns. There is no public contribution made to the expenses of the parties for their electioneering, and in the past this has bred an unhealthy institutional dependency in the case of the Conservative Party on big business and in the case of the Labour Party on the trade unions. In matters of broadcasting, even the very important matter of the criteria on which party election broadcasts are to be allocated between the political parties has not been put into formal legal effect, and instead the BBC and independent television companies follow an informal system of consultation between themselves and the major parties, often producing a result that outrages the Liberal Democrats, Greens and nationalist parties.

PARTY ELECTION BROADCASTS

History of party election broadcasts

The foundations of the present system for party election broadcasts were laid in the 1920s in the particular fashion in which the British Broadcasting Corporation and its first general manager Sir John Reith, later Lord Reith, pioneered political broadcasting. When the BBC was created in 1922 to take charge of radio broadcasting, John Reith himself had a clear vision of the great public service to which radio could be put in informing and educating the community, including the political affairs of the country. However, concerning the content of what radio might broadcast, Reith came under heavy pressure in the early days to limit broadcasting to light entertainment

– music and drama. The pressure came from newspaper proprietors who were worried about the effect of broadcasting on sales, and from the government, who laid down a number of restrictions relating to any broadcasting materials which might be considered 'controversial'. The BBC in its early years broadcast news bulletins, but these did not contain independently produced material; instead the broadcasters simply used summaries of reports received from the press news agencies. In the original licence under which it operated, the BBC was required to 'provide a programme of broadcast matter to the reasonable satisfaction of the Postmaster-General'.[6] Reith's invitation to the government during the 1923 election campaign to broadcast three speeches by the party leaders was turned down, but at the general election held in the following year the Postmaster-General, Vernon Hartshorn, finally lifted his prohibition on party election broadcasts. For the first time, the leaders of the three main parties gave election broadcasts over the radio, each lasting for twenty minutes: Ramsay MacDonald for Labour on 13 October; Stanley Baldwin for the Conservatives on 16 October; and Herbert Asquith for the Liberals on 17 October.

There is some significance in the way in which the Prime Minister, Ramsay MacDonald, chose to make the first party election broadcast. The content and style of the broadcast was a speech delivered live from a packed meeting at the City Hall in Glasgow. In choosing this format, he was simply extending to radio what was then normal electioneering oratory. This was quickly realised to be a mistake, as noted by a BBC spokesman:[7]

He raised his voice to its highest pitch and he dropped it to a whisper. He turned to the right and to the left, and even behind him, and spoke to all parts of the hall. He strode up and down the platform and was at varying distances from the microphone all the time. This is extremely effective for those who are present in the hall, but very detrimental for broadcasting.

Whereas a requirement for skill in oratory, especially at election campaigns, was formerly virtually a prerequisite for political leadership, today such skills are no longer at a premium. Few would say that the present Conservative leader John Major is a great orator, nor the Labour leader Tony Blair. The coming of television, even more than radio, has caused skills in personal communication to decline, and skills in image and visual presentation in the media to be of much greater importance.

The manner in which party election broadcasts came to be put out on television followed a rather similar pattern to radio. As with radio, the BBC had initially been granted a broadcasting monopoly of television (which it continued to enjoy until 1955).[8] In 1950 the BBC invited the parties to make one broadcast each on television, which was declined. At the election the following year, however, a similar invitation to fill three 15-minute programmes was accepted and the first televised party election broadcasts took place. The first broadcast consisted of a rambling talk by the elderly Lord Samuel, who forgot to look into the camera as he was speaking, and was then cut off mid-stream through inadvertently giving the cameraman the prearranged signal to end. The second broadcast was a little more modern in tone, with the handsome and distinguished-looking Anthony Eden being fielded by the Conservative opposition speaking in conversation with the BBC presenter, Leslie Mitchell, both of them reading from a prepared script. Being programmes broadcast by the BBC, which was financed through a licence fee being paid by viewers on the television sets they owned or rented in their homes, and not by way of commercial advertising, the principle of free party election broadcasts was established, with no question ever arising of payment being made by the parties for use of the broadcasting facilities.

Allocation between the parties

Following the BBC being reconstituted under the terms of a Royal Charter in 1926, the future arrangements for allocating radio broadcasts between the parties was left to the initiative of the BBC within the confines of its general legal duty to operate with political impartiality.[9] No specific legal obligation has ever been introduced to require or compel the broadcasting authorities to carry party election broadcasts. What emerged initially was a *de facto* administrative practice of the BBC putting forward a proposal, following which soundings were taken from the political parties, with the general aim of securing agreement across the political parties for a schedule of allocations. The way in which this informal system operated at the first election with party election broadcasts, dealing with radio in 1929, was that, first, the BBC suggested that the Conservative government be offered broadcasting space after each broadcast made by the Labour and Liberal parties, and then after adverse representations were received from the opposition parties, this plan was amended so that the government had an equal number of broadcasts as the opposition parties combined, but the government was to make the first broadcast and one of the opposition parties was to make the last. In 1947 this process of proposal and securing agreement was institutionalised further by the creation of a Committee on Political Broadcasting, composed of representatives of the political parties and the broadcasters. When election broadcasts on television arrived in the early 1950s, they were made subject to similar informal arrangements. Then, finally, when commercial television companies started broadcasting in 1956 (who were also subject to a legal duty of political impartiality), their controlling body the Independent Broadcasting Authority[10] (IBA, now replaced by the Independent Television Commission (ITC) after the

Broadcasting Act 1990) simply followed the pattern, and joined in with the practice of the BBC, with its representatives sitting on the Committee on Political Broadcasting.

The Committee on Political Broadcasting remains a rather secretive body with no legal status of its own, whose broad terms of reference are to be found in an aide-memoire dating from 1969, and whose proceedings are never published.[11] Originally only the Conservative, Labour and Liberal parties were represented on the Committee, but now the Scottish and Welsh Nationalist parties are represented as well. Its chairman is the Lord President of the Privy Council and Leader of the House of Commons (a government Cabinet minister), and membership of the Committee from the other political parties includes the opposition party's shadow leader of the House and senior representatives from the Liberal Democrat and nationalist parties. Representing the BBC and the ITC is their Director-General or some other senior management official. However, the normal working of this Committee is that it does not in fact meet, but instead agreed proposals from the broadcasters are delivered either to the Leader of the House of Commons or the government chief whip, and then it is the task of the government chief whip to liaise with the chief whips of the other parties, each consulting within their own particular party. After the parties' chief whips have completed their negotiations, the Leader of the House of Commons returns an agreed response to the broadcasters. This process of negotiation between the political parties is part of the normal parliamentary practice whereby difficult or sensitive matters between the parties are settled through 'the usual channels' – the euphemistic expression for parliamentary wheeling-and-dealing behind the Speaker's chair between the whips' offices. Only if there is some extraordinary difficulty or new problem to be encountered will the Committee on Political Broadcasting physically come together. The last time such an event occurred was in 1983, with problems caused by the formation of the Social Democratic Party.

From recent decisions made on broadcast allocations, coupled with what is publicly stated about the operation of the Committee, there are some recognisable conventions upon which the Committee operates. Outside periods of general election campaigns, the Committee decides upon the number of normal party political broadcasts to be offered to parties on an annual basis. The Committee reaches its decision on a formula of 10 minutes' time for each 2 million votes cast for the party at the previous general election. Since 1962, this has been subject to the important qualification that, regardless of the difference in votes cast or parliamentary seats won at the previous election, the party in government and the party in opposition will always have an equal number of broadcasts. Special arrangements operate concerning the nationalist parties, providing for broadcasts restricted to a particular region of the country. Thus the formula for the allocation of time to the Scottish National Party is 10 minutes for each 200 000 votes cast for the party in Scotland, and time is allocated to Plaid Cymru on the basis of 10 minutes for each 100 000 votes cast in Wales.

By contrast, the series of broadcasts allocated by the Committee on Political Broadcasting before a general election, known as party election broadcasts, are not subject to such precise mathematical formula. The main conventions of current practice are for there to be a maximum of five party election broadcasts for any single party, that the party in government and party in opposition should be given parity in allocation, and that any political party fielding over fifty parliamentary candidates is entitled to a 5-minute television broadcast. It was on the basis of this 'fifty candidates' rule that not only the Green Party but also the Natural Law Party qualified for national television broadcasts during the 1992 general election. Otherwise, as far as possible, the discretion and agreement of the Committee is relied upon for a fair judgement. It is, of course, the small parties, and also the Liberal Democrats (or previously the Liberal Party and the Social Democratic Party) who stand to gain or lose by such judgement. The number of seats won at the previous election might be a factor, but will not necessarily preclude access to broadcasting. For example, at the time of the 1983 general election the new Social Democratic Party had not existed at the time of the previous election in 1979, but was included in the broadcasting allocation because of its recognised level of political support in the country as witnessed at by-elections. Allocations of broadcasts restricted to particular regions of the country are made, notably to the Scottish National Party and Plaid Cymru. Concerning Northern Ireland, at general elections, the Committee has allocated party election broadcasts to parties operating there under special principles whereby only those parties which field a minimum number of candidates, and who won a minimum number of votes at the previous election, are allocated broadcasting time.[12]

If the Committee on Political Broadcasting fails to secure agreement across the parties represented in its membership, then the broadcasters could in theory decide not to transmit any broadcasts at all. Politically, however, the parties in government and opposition would never allow this to happen. If the broadcasters took this line, no doubt legislation would be passed on the matter, imposing a mandatory obligation and setting the Committee and the criteria upon which it operated on a statutory footing. There would in fact be some virtue in such public clarification of this 'quasi-constitutional' task[13] performed by the Committee. Alternatively, if the Committee members fail to agree upon allocation of broadcasts, the broadcasters may impose their own decision. This is realistically the only choice the broadcasters have, its only possible problem for them being the likelihood that one (or more) aggrieved political party may launch legal proceedings against them by way of judicial review in the High Court, on the basis that the particular decision on allocation they had reached constituted a breach of their duty of political impartiality. Unless the broadcasters acted wholly unreasonably, it is unlikely that the courts would choose to interfere with the discretion of the broadcasters.[14] Failure to reach an agreement between members of the Committee has only occurred once, in 1983 when the Liberal/SDP Alliance would not agree any allocation that did not give them parity in broadcasts with the Labour Party. The response of the broadcasters was to impose the allocation they believed fair, which was that the Alliance received four broadcasts, and five each were offered to the Conservative and Labour parties.

From the outset, there has always been criticism of the system for allocating party election broadcasts. Most obviously, the third and minor parties tend always to feel aggrieved that their allocation is unfair. The Liberal Party was deeply unhappy with the very first allocation made concerning radio in 1929, and put out a statement that it accepted the broadcasting allocations 'only under protest . . . against the partial action of the government in the matter'.[15] An important factor which feeds the discontent among Liberal Democrats and the minor parties today is that the quantity of television news and programme coverage of each political party broadcast by the television companies generally throughout the election campaign period is also subject to a scheduled quota which is calculated in direct proportion to the allocations worked out for the party election broadcasts. This aggravating factor serves to reinforce the prominence of the major parties in the eyes of television viewers, and explains much of the strong language used by Liberal Democrats and the minor parties in criticising the working of the present allocation system. In 1979 the allocation of television broadcasts was 5:5:3 between the Labour government, Conservative opposition, and the Liberal Party, then in 1983 the allocation was 5:5:4 between Conservative government, Labour opposition and Liberal/SDP Alliance – which Liberals and the SDP called a 'monstrous' injustice.[16] In 1987 the Alliance was content with its parity of five 10-minute broadcasts with the other two major parties, but three years previously the smaller Green Party had been sufficiently infuriated by not being allocated a single political broadcast during the European Parliament election campaign to commence judicial review proceedings (later withdrawn) against the BBC and independent television companies. During the 1992 general election campaign, the Liberal Democrats were again furious at being relegated to a 5:5:4 allocation, and their campaign manager, Des Wilson, wrote strong letters of complaint to the BBC and ITV claiming that the broadcasters had 'abandoned their responsibility for fair coverage'.[17] In so far as some parties will always receive less broadcasting attention than others, yet will argue for more, such criticism is, perhaps, inevitable. None the less, it is true that the effect of the present system is that it 'helps tilt the balance of visible power towards Parliament and the existing parties'.[18]

Political content of the broadcasts

The content of party political and election broadcasts is a matter for the parties themselves, and they can transmit whatever programme they choose to make to promote themselves, free from any editorial interference by the television companies. The material the parties choose to broadcast is, naturally, pure party propaganda and designed to influence electors to vote for them. Initially, these political broadcasts often consisted of the leader, or another senior member, of the party delivering a monologue to the television audience, often with background charts to help illustrate generalisations being made about the national economy or standard of living. However, since the 1959 election, party managers have used marketing and media consultants to advise the parties. The 1979 election proved to be a landmark when such professionals were used for the first time in a major way to help orchestrate the Conservative election campaign. Margaret Thatcher hired her own personal media adviser, Gordon Reece, and in 1978 the advertising agency Saatchi and Saatchi took responsibility for all Conservative political advertising and broadcasting leading up to her 1979 election triumph. Not only matters of visual design in media presentation, but also market research on what political subjects mattered most to voters, together with the invention of effective political slogans, became specialist tasks for advertisers and communications experts as much as for the politicians themselves. Within the Labour Party, their disastrous election campaign under the leadership of Michael Foot in 1983 was followed rapidly by their new leader, Neil Kinnock, paying much closer attention to how to project the party to greatest effect over the television broadcasting medium, with the result that the Labour Party's campaigning style and media presentation was transformed for the 1987 and 1992 elections.

Media and advertising consultants have, in turn, advised party politicians that the most effective way of selling themselves to voters is to concentrate upon how they appear and how they look. An overriding objective for party strategists in modern electioneering is to make voters 'feel good' about their party, and 'feel worried' about the other party coming to power. The style of the party election broadcasts in 1992 was dominated by such attempts at projecting positive and negative visual images on television, utilising a sophisticated blend of happy or grim film clips, accompanied by rousing or gloomy background music, interspersed with platitudes spoken by actors, or hand-picked party supporters saying how terrible or marvellous things were.

So, in 1992, with little for the Conservative government to boast about in terms of social policy and the economy (which was sliding into recession with unemployment rising), coupled with recent memories of the débâcle of the poll tax, and widespread fears about the future of the National Health Service, the best argument for voting for the government was that Labour would make things even worse. This was pointed out on the front of *The*

Economist in the week of the election with a feature headed 'May the Worst Lot Lose'.[19] The way in which the Conservative election broadcasts presented this train of thought effectively was by, on the one hand, fiercely attacking Labour as a backward-looking, irresponsible party that would raise taxes, cause inflation, bring about strikes, and fail to defend the country properly, and on the other hand presenting the Prime Minister, John Major, as a nice, smiling, dependable statesman in whom the country could trust.

Thus Conservative broadcasts devoted considerable attention to the person of John Major. Their opening broadcast was made by the film director John Schlesinger, and consisted principally of Mr Major travelling back to where he spent his childhood in Brixham in south London, recounting memories of his family, and revisiting places such as the market where he used to buy kippers. It then moved on to a talk by Mr Major expanding on the opportunity and individualism he wished to see opened up to all in the country, and ended with a stream of film clips showing Mr Major shaking hands with or being greeted by other world leaders. The final broadcast also centred on the personality of the Prime Minister, with a succession of testimonials from other Conservative ministers, before a final talk about the type of country John Major wished Britain to be.

PRESIDENTIAL-STYLE CAMPAIGNING

From: Fifth Conservative broadcast, 1992

John Major:	I hope in the next few years that we will carry on with much of the work that has been done in the last few years. In particular I want to see us build a country that is at ease with itself. I will fight for my belief, and my belief is a return to basics in education.
Virginia Bottomley:	We visited a hospital together, and it is a great event a Prime Minister visiting a hospital. And what is so remarkable is John Major's ability to put people at their ease, to make them feel he understands, to touch people. He knows what it is all about.
[*Pictures of John Major, addressing British troops in the Gulf*]	Thank you very much for what you've done over the last few months. It has been an absolutely fabulous job.
Chris Patten:	The people said that he was a rookie Prime Minister who wouldn't be able to tackle the international side of things, well look – Gulf War, Kurds, Maastricht – extraordinary piece of negotiating skills: calm, courteous but tough as old boots as well.

Tom King:	I saw at first hand the courage and resolution of John Major in the most immediate way because at the very start of the Gulf War, [the] War Cabinet met and at that moment a mortar bomb landed ten yards outside the Cabinet Room and the windows were shattered, there was smoke in the room and the smell of explosive. I was incredibly impressed by the determination and resolution he showed. He just said, 'Why don't we go to another room?'
Douglas Hurd:	We had a fairly rough second day at the summit in Maastricht in December because John had, I suppose, forty – perhaps more – points that Britain had to insist on and the other countries had maybe four or five each. And the one in particular at the end which needed everyone to agree to, everyone agreed to it around the table, and finally Britain and John said, 'I don't agree.' Chancellor Kohl laughed at his bravery at doing this, but we won the point and afterwards another big delegation said, 'Thank God you did that. We didn't quite have the nerve to say that'.
Chris Patten:	I remember him once pushing a piece of paper across to me. It said, 'Do you want to come to Stamford Bridge on Sunday?' So I passed it back and wrote on it, 'Yes, but who's playing?' He sent it back. He'd just written on the top, 'If you don't know, you can't come!'
[Two photo sequences of John Major, addressing the previous Conservative Conference]	'During the summer, Mr President, I did quite a bit of travelling: Headingley, Edgbaston . . .' 'I've got it, I like it, and with your help, I'm going to keep it!'
David Mellor:	It's never any effort for him to talk to anyone, not in a sort of 'I'd better do this 'cos that's what politicians are supposed to do' kind of way, but just out of a natural interest in people.
[Pictures of John Major, addressing a general election meeting]	'What we want is a better Britain, a country which is strong in the world. A country where the individual counts, a country of real opportunity where every one of her people is free to choose. A country with a head and a country with a heart, and on April the 9th I have no doubt it is for our kind of Britain that the people of Britain will make their choice'.

One Conservative broadcast, the second transmitted, simply attacked the Labour Party and sought to raise public fears that Labour would reduce voters' incomes and make a mess of the economy. The visual and emotive impact of this broadcast was transmitted by way of a dark, steamy room in which a blacksmith was hammering shackles and tying down voters using three iron balls (revealed at the end to represent 'Taxes Up', 'Prices Up' and 'Mortgages Up'), accompanied by a doom-laden soundtrack and the ominous tones of the anonymous narrator (who was, in fact, the actor Robert Powell). The third broadcast was devoted to national defence and sought to play on viewers' worries about international conflict and nuclear bombs falling into the hands of our enemies, maintaining that Labour 'which has at least a hundred MPs who are members of the CND' and has 'pledged to cut defence' could not be trusted to protect the country properly. The visual image on the broadcast again contained no politician, but featured two young children getting out of bed to play with their computer war-games, with occasional flashes of film showing international armed conflict. Although the intellectual content of what is said in such broadcasts would appear to be considerably less influential in shaping individual impressions about a party, and therefore voting preferences, than the visual manner of its presentation, the extract given below from the Conservative broadcast on Labour and the economy captures the flavour of the negative electioneering methods regularly used today by the parties.

NEGATIVE TELEVISION ELECTIONEERING

From: Second Conservative television broadcast, 1992

Voice over: March 1992. Labour are so keen to get into power that they have been making lots of promises. They would have to increase taxes far beyond the levels they have already admitted. They would have to hit the average taxpayer with an extra £1250 a year tax bill. Last week, Labour's Mr Smith said that he wanted the biggest increase in taxes on incomes since the war.

Labour also plan a minimum wage, which would push up industry's costs. That means lost jobs and higher prices.

So Labour would push up taxes and prices. And there's more. According to City forecasts, Labour would have to push up interest rates by two-and-a-half per cent. That would add £40 a month to the average mortgage, so Labour would push taxes up, prices up and mortgages up. Could you face five years' hard labour? Could you pay £1250 more tax a year?

Woman 1:	'If Labour do get in and my husband's taxes go up, I mean it would be devastating in our household'.
Woman 2:	'If we have a big increase in taxation then the chances are we might have to think about selling the house'.
Voice over:	Last time Labour were in power, they taxed people so hard it hurt.
Man 1:	'If they increase income tax I can't think of a more direct disincentive to people not to work harder'.
Man 2:	'Oh yes, I've no doubt at all that we'd have much higher tax rates, both business-wise and personally'.
Voice over:	Could you get along with Labour's high prices?
Man 3:	'Prices will go up, I'm certain of that, because taxes are going to go up, National Insurance contributions go up, people will look for more money to pay for it, salaries go up. What happens then? Prices go up'.
Woman 3:	'Prices – I hate to think – they would go sky high'.
Voice over:	According to independent City analysts, Labour's plans would virtually double inflation.
Man 4:	'People are paying more and more and more for less and less and less'.
Voice over:	How would you feel about £40 a month on your mortgage bill?
Woman 1:	'Yes, if Labour got in and taxes on my husband's wages, he had to pay more tax, it would cripple us, with a mortgage'.
Voice over:	So under Labour you're taxed more, you pay more, and your mortgage costs you more. Last time the only way people thought they could break out of it was through strikes, strikes and more strikes. No wonder 86 per cent of businesses say that Labour would be bad for the economy. Of course, this need not happen.
	The Conservatives have cut taxes. The basic rate is lower than at any time since the war and they're still going down, so the incentive is there. And because the Conservatives have the determination to keep prices down, Britain has lower inflation than even Germany. And because the Conservatives have cut inflation, interest rates are now down, taking £80 a month off

the average mortgage. And because the Conservatives have broken the grip of the unions, strikes are down to the lowest level for a hundred years. Even through an international slow down Britain's share of world trade has steadily grown. No wonder Japanese and American companies invest more money in Britain than in any other country in Europe. For Britain to grow when the world economy bounces back, the last thing we need is five years' hard Labour!

The efforts by Conservative strategists at pushing John Major to the forefront of their election campaign in 1992 (as, indeed, had been done at earlier elections with his predecessor, Margaret Thatcher) at times made the general election look very much like a presidential-style contest for the office of Prime Minister. During the 1987 election, the Labour leader, Neil Kinnock, had similarly been presented prominently in the Labour campaign generally and during election broadcasts, most famously in the programme directed by Hugh Hudson (maker of the film *Chariots of Fire*), scored by Michael Kamer (responsible for the soundtrack in the film *Mona Lisa*), and written by the playwright and actor Colin Welland. This election broadcast showed Neil and Glenys Kinnock walking hand in hand across the countryside in the sunshine, accompanied by the voice of Mr Kinnock explaining his social convictions, followed by a number of testimonials from senior Labour figures such as Jim Callaghan, Denis Healey and John Smith, before closing with film of Mr and Mrs Kinnock again, then the Houses of Parliament, the Labour rose logo, and finally the single word transmitted on the screen: 'Kinnock'. Although controversial within parts of the Labour Party for its presidential-style political imagery, it was generally viewed by the party campaign managers as a tremendous success in impressing the voters favourably, and Neil Kinnock's personal popularity in the country was reported to have risen by 16 per cent.[20]

However, during the 1992 election campaign, Labour's broadcasts emphasised its leading politicians as a youthful, modern team who would bring about a more equal and fair society. Two of Labour's broadcasts particularly projected the team nature of Labour's leadership, including the first programme which included John Smith, Gordon Brown, Tony Blair, Jack Straw, Bryan Gould, Ann Taylor, Margaret Beckett, Harriet Harman and Robin Cook as well as Neil Kinnock, and the third broadcast which concentrated on 'Labour's economics team'. A central feature in the political content of the Labour series lay in aiming to project a feeling about it being 'a time for change' and making a fresh start. This is something the opposition, comprising whichever party, always suggests to voters at election time, and it was certainly a strong theme of Margaret Thatcher's election campaign in 1979.

TIME-FOR-A-CHANGE TELEVISION ELECTIONEERING

From: First Labour broadcast, 1992

Neil Kinnock: We live in a country rich in heritage, in natural resources, and of course, most of all, rich in the quality of the people. But when you know that the potential is not being used properly, it really makes you ask, what has happened in these last years? Why has life become so bleak, narrow, insecure for so many of our people? Why has a country that has so much ability to do well not been doing better?

We've got to see a Britain that makes the most of people's vitality, people's creativity. We've got to ensure that every man and woman, every child gets the chance to bring out the best in themselves. That means making real changes to improve child care, schools, hospitals, training. It means making basic changes to get jobs, to build houses and see the streets are clean and safe.

That's the kind of change people want. Everybody knows it. It is time for that change now.

John Smith: Labour's economic policy starts from one simple common-sense fact: the only way to build a strong economy is to make the goods and services that people at home and abroad want to buy. That is how to bring down unemployment. That is how to create the wealth to pay for a top-class National Health Service and higher living standards. That is how it is done in Germany and Japan and other successful economies. It's time to pull Britain out of recession and to start to build a strong and prosperous economy.

Gordon Brown: For more than a century 'Made in Britain' has been the guarantee of quality right across the world. But now, as British manufacturing declines, it is becoming harder and harder to buy British. It's time that 'Made in Britain' becomes the basis of economic success again.

To manufacture much more that's made here, we will start by introducing immediate incentives for industrial investment that will help lift us out of recession, and lay the foundations for a British prosperity that lasts.

Tony Blair:　　And it is time to make Britain the best educated and trained nation in Europe, raising school standards by cutting class sizes, making sure every teacher is qualified in the subject they teach, getting every company to invest in training, and giving all young people the opportunity to learn a skill. A workforce of quality – that's the way a modern economy succeeds, where you, your children, everyone can develop their potential to the full.

Margaret Beckett:　　It is time Britain's families got a better deal. Labour will start by investing at least an extra billion pounds in the National Health Service over the next two years as well as an extra six hundred million in our schools. We'll help working mothers by giving tax relief on employer-assisted child care and increasing nursery places for three- and four-year-olds. We'll increase child benefit by £127 a year for a family with two children. We'll raise pensions by an extra £8 a week for a couple, £5 a week for a single person, and we'll abolish the poll tax – the tax on families. Under Labour's Budget proposals, eight out of ten families will be better off. Labour will put families first, and about time too.

Robin Cook:　　If you elect a Labour government, we'll end the privatisation of the National Health Service, and we'll bring back to it the hospitals that opted out. We'll modernise our hospitals and we'll start by investing at least an extra billion pounds. Labour created the National Health Service; we need Labour now to save it. It is time for a strong National Health Service, one that we can all rely on. It is our right.

Ann Taylor:　　It is about time we improved the quality of all our lives. That is why we will make sure that every local community gets first rate local services, and why we're committed to a safer Britain with more police officers on the beat and a transport system we can rely on. And we must improve our environment, cut down on air pollution, ensure our rights to safe drinking water. We will set up an independent green watchdog to cut pollution, clean up our rivers and beaches, anticipating future problems, to make Britain and our world a cleaner, safer place in which to live.

John Smith: And can we afford this? Well, as the economy starts to grow again, there'll be more money to invest and that money must be invested in our industrial base, in our hospitals and schools and in our social services. A Labour government will introduce a fair system of tax and national insurance. More money needs to be raised to help pay for much-needed increases on retirement pensions and in child benefit. We will introduce a new top rate of tax at 50 per cent which will apply to incomes over £40000 per year. And the unfair upper limit on National Insurance contributions will be removed. But our reforms of tax allowances and of National Insurance will mean that every taxpayer with an income of up to £22000 per year will pay less than now. And 740000 taxpayers will be taken out of paying tax completely. And, of course, families with children and pensions will gain more. Labour's tax reforms, unlike those proposed by the Conservatives, will not be paid for by borrowed money.

Tony Blair: It is time for a Britain where the best values count again.

Ann Taylor: And it is time for a leader whose values are the values of the British people.

Neil Kinnock: I work to ensure that Labour is forward-looking and fit to provide good government for our country, now I know that we have the talented people and the practical policies needed to deal effectively with the challenges and with the opportunities of the 1990s. This country has enormous strengths. We have got some of the world's best companies and most committed workforces, some of the greatest scientists and investors, some of the most outstanding artists and sports people. By electing Labour you'll be electing a government to build on those strengths. You'll be electing a government that really believes in Britain and the people of Britain, a government that will invest in Britain and the British people.

It is time for a new leader in our country. It is time for a new government with people of energy and vision to bring out the best in Britain. That means making real changes to improve child care, schools, hospitals,

> training. It means making basic changes to get jobs, to build houses, and see the streets are clean and safe.
>
> That's the kind of change people want – everybody knows it. It's time for a change. It's time for Labour.

The final broadcast transmitted by the Labour Party in 1992 was significant because it included a large number of famous personalities from the arts and professions indicating both their concern for the future and their support for Labour's policies. Among them, for example, were the playwright and novelist, John Mortimer QC; the director and actor, Sir Richard Attenborough; the comedians Ben Elton and Stephen Fry; the writer and mathematician, Professor Stephen Hawking; and the lawyer and broadcaster, Helena Kennedy QC. The popular benefit of associating with actors and personalities is a well-known American technique in electioneering and looks set now to take root in this country. Meanwhile, Labour's most controversial broadcast in 1992 was one which aimed to exploit public concern about the future of the National Health Service. This programme, which came to be known as 'Jennifer's ear' told the story of two little girls who suffered from 'glue ear', and contrasted starkly the plight of one who could be treated quickly by private medicine with the unhappy state of affairs for the other girl, whose parents could not afford the operation and had to suffer a protracted wait for treatment under the NHS. This programme took the form of a drama, using actors, with emotive background music provided by B. B. King, and no narration until the end, when Neil Kinnock told viewers, 'On April 9, the choice is between recession and recovery, between privatisation and modernisation. It is a choice between fear and hope. It's time for a change. It's time for Labour.' This new technique of taking a basically true story and turning it into a drama using actors has been given the name 'faction'. It is now regarded by media specialists as a highly effective and sophisticated use of the television medium to communicate a powerful emotive message to the viewer. We can therefore expect to see its further development in the electioneering of the future.

How true are the claims and allegations made by the parties in their electioneering? No doubt voters generally take what politicians say with a large measure of cynicism, but it is characteristic of modern election campaigns – and perhaps political discourse generally – that generalisations and statistics are produced casually by politicians in purported verification of how things would be better under their party or worse under the other. It is clearly a matter of some public concern that, within the law of libel, electioneering and the presentation of the political choice being put before the electorate does not lapse into false claims and deceitful statements, whether made recklessly or intentionally. For the 1992 election, a leading Sunday newspaper published a series of articles devoted to the factual analysis of the claims being made by the political parties in their election broadcasts. Its conclusions were that a substantial number of assertions being made were either erroneous or misleading. On some of the principal economic claims made, for example, during the second Conservative broadcast and the first Labour broadcast (see extracts above at pages 243 and 246) the opinion of this independent factual analysis was as shown below.[21]

FACTUAL ACCURACY OF CLAIMS MADE IN PARTY ELECTION BROADCASTS

Conservative Party Claims

CLAIM: *'Independent City analysts say that Labour plans would virtually double inflation.'*
FACT: This claim is based on a document *The City in London* which included assessments of inflation under Labour by seven City forecasters (Phillips & Drew, James Capel, Daiwa, Credit Lyonnais, Kleinwort Benson, Nomura, and Hoare Govett) and three non-City forecasters (the London Business School, Liverpool University, and the National Institute). James Capel . . . says inflation would be 1.5 per cent higher under Labour, while Phillips & Drew says that there would be little difference if John Smith maintains his commitment to sterling's membership of the European exchange-rate mechanism. Only one City forecast, that by Daiwa, came close to the Tories' claim, with an estimate that inflation would be 3.5 per cent higher after three years. But Daiwa said yesterday that the figures were illustrative and had been taken out of context. In practice, Daiwa said, ERM membership would keep inflation low under Labour.
CONCLUSION: **False.**

CLAIM: *'Under the last Labour Government, tax bills doubled, prices doubled.'*
FACT: Prices rose by 112 per cent under the 1974–9 Labour Government. But it is misleading to say that tax bills doubled because of higher inflation, any more than it would be to say that tax bills have more than trebled under the Tories. Labour inherited a basic rate of income tax of 30 per cent in 1974 and left office with a basic rate of 33 per cent, as well as a reduced rate of 25 per cent on the first £750 of taxable income.
CONCLUSION: **False.**

CLAIM: *'Under the last Labour Government an average of over 7 million days a year were lost through strikes.'*
FACT: This is the first example so far of a party political broadcast 'own goal'. In its previous broadcast on tax and the economy, on January 22, the Tories claimed that 29 million working days a year were lost through strikes. Since then the figure has been dramatically revised. Unfortunately, the

Tories have gone too far. Under the 1974–9 Labour Government, 9.6 million working days a year were lost through strikes. The figure of 7 million working days a year applies to the Tories over the 1979–91 period, when an annual average of 7.15 million days were lost.
CONCLUSION: **False.**

CLAIM: *'Britain's taxes are down, so the incentive is there to work harder.'*
FACT: The overall level of taxation has increased since 1979, from 34.25 per cent to 37.25 per cent of gross domestic product, in spite of a reduction in income tax rates.
CONCLUSION: **False.**

CLAIM: *'Strikes are down – to the lowest level for 100 years.'*
FACT: Last year 759 000 working days were lost due to industrial disputes, the smallest annual total since records began in 1891.
CONCLUSION: **True.**

Labour Party Claims

CLAIM: *'Under Labour's budget proposals 8 out of 10 families will be better off.'*
FACT: The independent Institute for Fiscal Studies says that 80 per cent of families would gain from the shadow budget relative to a neutral budget. However, in comparison with Norman Lamont's actual budget, only 48 per cent of families would gain and 17 per cent would be worse off.
CONCLUSION: **Only partly true.**

CLAIM: *'Every taxpayer with an income of up to £22 000 will pay less than now.'*
FACT: Many self-employed people earning less than £22 000 will not benefit from Labour's budget proposals. Unlike employed people, they do not pay the so-called 'entry fee' into the National Insurance system and so do not benefit from Labour's proposed abolition of it. In addition, some taxpayers earning less than £22 000 will be hit by the abolition of the 2 per cent National Insurance rebate for personal pensions.
CONCLUSION: **False.**

CLAIM: *'Labour's tax reforms, unlike those of the Conservatives, will not be paid for by borrowed money.'*
FACT: The shadow budget did not feature any additional borrowing, sticking to Lamont's £28 billion target for the public-sector borrowing requirement. Labour cut taxes in its shadow budget by increasing the main personal allowances by 10 per cent and abolishing the 2 per cent entry fee in the National Insurance system. But overall, the tax package took £1.89 billion away from the personal sector through higher taxes on upper income earners, even allowing for increases in pensions and child benefit.
CONCLUSION: **True.**

The precise timing of party election broadcasts, which may affect their political impact, is in the hands of the television companies. This in fact emerged as an issue in 1992, and novel scheduling by the broadcasters caused a furious row between some politicians and broadcasters. There used to be a convention that all television channels issued the political broadcasts simultaneously, maximising their audience because reluctant viewers could not immediately turn over to watch something else. Although this ended after 1983, the television channels had all broadcast the programmes at around 9 pm – 10 pm. For 1992, however, the BBC chose to transmit the election broadcasts slightly later than usual, showing them on BBC1 after the extended Nine O'Clock News at around 9.50 pm or 9.55 pm, and on BBC2 at around 10.30 pm. But what infuriated some politicians most was the decision of ITV to bring forward its scheduling for the election broadcasts to 6.55 pm, and even worse, Channel 4 postponing transmission until after midnight. Des Wilson, for the Liberal Democrats described this as 'sheer cynicism', and expressed 'outrage' at the way 'broadcasters are marginalising' the political broadcasts.[22]

THE CONDUCT OF THE MASS MEDIA

Television and radio

Television and radio broadcasting companies in Britain have always been expected to operate with political impartiality. Conventions about what exactly impartiality and balance meant in the practice of preparing political news, in the making of programmes on political subjects, and in interviewing party politicians, were developed by the BBC, and many of its procedures have been in due course adopted by the independent television companies. The BBC is legally established under the terms of a special Royal Charter issued under the Royal Prerogative, the original Charter being made in 1926 and the current one in force being dated 7 July 1981.[23] This Charter lays out the objects of the BBC, which include *inter alia*, 'To provide, as public services, broadcasting services of wireless telegraphy by the method of telephony for general reception in sound, by the method of television for general reception in visual images and by the methods of television and telephony in combination for general reception in visual images with sound, in Our United Kingdom.'[24] The Charter also provides for the constitution and organisation of the BBC, and for advisory councils, and that the BBC shall be further regulated by licences issued by the government 'for such period and subject to such terms, provisions and limitations as [the Home Secretary] may prescribe'.[25] The current licence is dated 2 April 1981,[26] and its most important regulation on political impartiality reads: 'The Corporation shall at all times refrain from sending any broadcast matter expressing the opinion of the Corporation on current affairs or on matters of public policy.'[27] There is in addition a clause dealing specifically with the reporting of parliamentary debates, which says, 'The Corporation shall broadcast an impartial account day by day prepared by professional reporters of the proceedings in both Houses of the United Kingdom Parliament'.[28]

This means that the BBC may not hold any corporate political views of its own, nor may its employees who are the makers, producers and broadcasters of any particular programmes, express their own political opinions. Such programmes may be full of opinions of outside experts, such as party politicians or university professors, but its overall presentation of the political arguments involved must be impartial and fair. Viewers and listeners should not be able to gauge from BBC programmes the personal views of presenters and reporters.[29] Specialist correspondents may be interviewed on the programme, but the opinions they express should be limited (as suggested in the BBC's internal guidelines for factual programmes) to using their own personal experience to explain, interpret or summarise complex situations, or to give an informed assessment of the likely course of future events. Fundamental to the political impartiality of the BBC is its own broadcasting freedom – meaning the freedom of BBC producers and editors to make programmes on subjects of their own choosing, and the independence of the BBC from the government. One of the most difficult and controversial aspects in achieving political impartiality lies in the term 'balance', and what it means to work towards achieving a political balance in broadcasting programmes which involve competing arguments. The actors or advocates in any political debate will always tend to demand a tit-for-tat or mathematically-calculated allocation of time in a programme for their views, especially if they feel that their views have been given less prominence than those of their opponents, and there may be some situations (such as over the allocation of party election broadcasts) where such quotas of broadcasting time are appropriate. But, generally, the editor of any individual programme will have to weigh the strength and extent of political opinion behind one set of claims made about a subject of current interest, and whether or not to give those claims greater stress and broadcasting exposure over a second or third set of rival claims. As a former Director-General of the BBC, Sir William Haley, wrote in 1945, 'Impartiality does not mean so artificially "balancing" the speakers that the listeners can never come to a conclusion on the basis of the argument.'[30] Furthermore, the political impartiality of the BBC's television broadcasting does not depend upon every individual programme achieving a perfect balance but rather that the general spread of programmes over a period of time is broadly equal between the different partisan perspectives operating within the world of British politics. In the view of another Director-General,

Sir Hugh Carleton Greene, 'We have to balance different points of view in our programmes but not necessarily within each individual programme. Nothing is more stultifying than the current affairs programme in which all the opposing opinions cancel each other out. Sometimes one has to use that method but in general it makes for greater liveliness and impact if the balance can be achieved over a period, perhaps within a series of related programmes.'[31] These principles upon which BBC political impartiality are based in the late twentieth century have evolved with experience over time, and are currently committed to writing within the BBC's advisory guidelines issued to its employees.

Public service broadcasting in the field of public affairs since the earliest days of John Reith has been founded upon a sense of mission to explore what is going on and to explain it to the people. In the BBC's own words:[32]

Impartiality lies at the heart of BBC programme making. The BBC must serve the nation as a whole. This means recognising the differing tastes, views and perspectives in millions of households. They have to be served through a very diverse range of programmes. This requires effort and imagination . . . The makers of objective factual programmes need to be most scrupulous. News judgements should be informed by the best expertise. Treatment of a story must involve depth of inquiry. Beware of easy and prevalent assumptions. It is often necessary to report the opinions of institutions and major participants in a dispute or story, but good reporting should go beyond that. It should offer the audience an intelligent and informed account which enables them to form a view.

In 1986, at a time when the BBC was coming under attack from members of the Conservative government for allegedly unsympathetic coverage of its policies and arguments, David Dimbleby, the broadcaster and son of Sir Richard Dimbleby (one of the great political broadcasters in the early days of the BBC), delivered an important lecture defending the BBC from such allegations of bias and making some important points about the nature of political impartiality within television.[33] The professional job to be done by broadcasters, he said, 'is to examine fairly and equally the political proposals put forward for Britain's proper government, and for solving the problems we face. A broadcaster has to see a political argument from all sides, otherwise he is failing in the job.' He went on to point out the perennial problem of television broadcasting in its relations with the government, which explains why successive governing political parties, including particularly Labour in the 1960s and Conservatives in the 1980s, have felt that their reforming zeal has been unfairly attacked in the media. He said, 'Like any institution the BBC takes its tone from the society it springs from and therefore tends to reflect the consensus of which it is part. If a political party or a government comes to power believing that the consensus needs shifting, that the country as a whole needs to change its way of looking at itself, adjust its view, adopt different attitudes, it will see an organisation still rooted in the centre as its enemy.' Finally, David Dimbleby pointed to the mounting problems facing standards in television broadcasting which had been brought about by the remorseless financial pressures forcing it to produce ever more popular and lower-budgeted programmes, and that these were eroding the very ethos and sense of public mission upon which British broadcasting in its political and current affairs programmes had been founded. 'The massive expansion of television has put that ethos at risk. My fear is that the battle for ratings and the proper coverage of news and current affairs are incompatible ambitions.' The expansion of the television network in the 1980s and arrival of satellite television have now considerably exacerbated these worries.

The conduct of broadcasting by television companies other than the BBC, commonly known as the commercial or independent television broadcasting companies, is currently controlled by the provisions of the Broadcasting Act 1990. The Act established an Independent Television Commission to regulate and license these television companies, and provides that, 'The Commission shall do all that they can to secure that every licensed service complies with the following requirements, namely . . . that any news given (in whatever form) in its programmes is presented with due accuracy and impartiality; [and] that due impartiality is preserved on the part of the person providing the service as respects matters of political or industrial controversy or relating to current public policy.'[34] The Commission is required under the Act to draw up a code of guidance for the conduct of broadcasting by the licensed companies, aimed particularly at preserving due impartiality, indicating what due impartiality does and does not require (both generally and with respect to particular situations), and the ways in which due impartiality may be achieved.[35] The final version of the impartiality guidelines issued by the Independent Television Commission was published in February 1991, and began with the declaration that, 'Broadcasters licensed by the ITC are free to make programmes about any issue they choose. This freedom is bounded only by the obligations of fairness and a respect for truth, two qualities which lie at the heart of impartial broadcasting. Impartiality does not mean that broadcasters have to be absolutely neutral on every controversial issue, but it should lead them to deal even-handedly with opposing points of view in the arena of democratic debate.'

The obligations upon commercial television broadcasters under the Broadcasting Act and the ITC's code of guidance is fairly similar to the way that political impartiality has been construed within the BBC. Thus the problems inherent in achieving political balance, referred to above, are explained in the code. In interpreting what 'due impartiality' means under the Act, the ITC says:[36]

The term 'due' is significant: it should be interpreted as meaning adequate or appropriate to the nature of the subject and the type of programme. While the requirement of due impartiality applies to all areas of controversy covered by the Act, it does not mean that 'balance' is required in any simple mathematical sense or that equal time must be given to each opposing point of view. Nor does it require absolute neutrality on every issue or detachment from fundamental democratic principles. Judgement will always be called for.

Similarly, both the Act and the ITC code make it clear that impartiality may be achieved over a period of time, even if individual programmes may be relatively partisan, especially so if the programme is one within a series presenting a number of different political perspectives. But the code warns that, 'There are times when the principal opposing viewpoints should be reflected in a single programme or programme item, either because it is not likely that the licensee will soon return to the subject, or because the issues involved are of current and active controversy.'[37] So far as subjects or news dealing with political dissent between the parties are concerned, this will virtually always be the case during a general election campaign.

Not surprisingly, during the election campaign period the BBC and commercial television companies adopt a far narrower interpretation of impartiality than is normally the case.[38] In particular, broadcasters move much closer than at any other time towards trying to achieve a fair balance in terms of broadcasting time in representing the policies and personalities of the different political parties. The broadcasters accept not only an obligation to achieve balance between the parties over the whole period of the election campaign, but also to be close to it within its news and programme output each day. What falls into the melting-pot constituting contributions from each party towards this political balance are extracts from political speeches, sound recordings, studio contributions and live appearances from politicians. News bulletins, and also feature programmes on current affairs topics, will work towards achieving such political balance in its coverage of each day's events, although news values will still continue to determine the final presentation and content of what is broadcast. On 11 March 1992, the day that the 1992 general election was announced, John Birt, at the time of writing the BBC's Director-General (in 1992, the Deputy Director), sent a letter to all BBC journalists offering some general advice, from which the following is an extract:[39]

This will be a close-fought election. The BBC has a special responsibility during these next weeks to inform the choice our viewers and listeners will soon make. That means: providing a clear and comprehensive exposition of the policies of the parties; offering a proper opportunity for politicians to set out their stalls for the voter; and testing the policies of the parties in an even-handed but rigorous fashion.

We should give due weight to all of the parties contesting the election; and to the perspectives of the whole of the United Kingdom. We should try to bring coherence and perception to our reporting of the campaign as well as communicating the flavour and the fun of it. We should provide a meticulous and impartial assessment of the whole range of issues aired at the election; and draw in a full spectrum of informed and independent opinion from outside the parties to comment on these issues.

At all times we should act with a manifest sense of fairness to different shades of opinion and to those seeking election.

The most important issue which then arises in practice is the question of precisely what is the balance between the different political parties. What broadcasting time should be allocated to the Conservative Party, the Labour Party and the Liberal Democrats, in order for the television companies to be operating with political impartiality and to be striking a fair balance in the presentation of the parties' respective policies and representatives before the viewers and electorate? Any mathematical allocation aiming to achieve such a balance will always be a matter of profound political interest – and deep controversy. The present basis for the balance between the major parties is the formula also used in the allocation of party election broadcasts,[40] a matter settled by the judgement of the Committee on Political Broadcasting. Between the Conservatives, Labour and the Liberal Democrats (or their predecessors) respectively in 1992 the ratio was 5:5:4; in 1987, was 5:5:5; in 1983, 5:5:4; and in 1979, 5:5:3. This system has produced a tendency towards television broadcasting by 'stopwatch' during election campaigns or, more accurately, for politicians to complain that they have been unfairly treated if they can show that they have received anything less than their 'mathematical share' of air time. However, this method of calculating a balance of political coverage of the different parties was never intended to be applied literally, nor to take away the freedom of media journalists to report on election news as they believed to be most consistent with their general duty concerning newsworthiness and impartiality. When the television companies announced their intention prior to the 1992 election campaign not to follow a rigid 'stopwatch' approach in their political programmes and news, the Conservative and Labour parties did not complain, but the Liberal Democrats were furious. Des Wilson, the Liberal Democrat campaign manager claimed that, 'These television companies are putting themselves in a position where they can affect the result. News values are an instinct of a particular editor on a particular day . . . I have looked at every possibility and you cannot beat stopwatching.'[41] But the views of the television companies were unanimously to the contrary. Glyn Mathias, Head of Public Affairs at ITN, said, 'There is no intention of squeezing the Liberal Democrats. We will maintain the stopwatch as one measurement of impartiality. We will obviously take note of how much time each party is getting among many and varied programmes.'[42] At the BBC, their chief political adviser, Margaret Douglas, commented, 'Clockwatching does not determine the news agenda. It is useful to keep a note of the time given simply because everyone else is doing it and it can be a useful defence against charges that one has failed to represent parties fairly, but news judgements are not substantially warped in any way by the need to adhere to some false stopwatching procedure.'[43]

The Representation of the People Act 1983 imposes some important restrictions upon political broadcasting during the election campaign. Section 92 prohibits any unlicensed broadcasting taking place from outside the United Kingdom which is intended to influence voting at elections. Anyone doing so commits an illegal election practice. This prohibition was introduced in 1969 against a background of the innovation of pirate radio stations (such as Radio Caroline) broadcasting pop music from ships outside British waters. The current section in the 1983 Act reads, 'No person shall, with intent to influence persons to give or refrain from giving their votes at a parliamentary or local government election, include, or aid, abet, counsel or procure the inclusion of, any matter relating to the election in any programme service (within the meaning of the Broadcasting Act 1990) provided from a place outside the United Kingdom otherwise than in pursuance of arrangements made with (a) the British Broadcasting Corporation, (b) Sianel Pedwar Cymru, or (c) the holder of any licence granted by the Independent Television Commission or the Radio Authority, for the reception and re-transmission of that matter by that body or the holder of that licence'.[44]

Section 93 of the Representation of the People Act

Far more controversial in the 1990s is the effect of section 93 of the Representation of the People Act 1983, which restricts significantly the freedom of television and radio broadcasters to make programmes on constituency elections if any of the parliamentary candidates standing for election in the constituency which is the subject of the programme object. Unless every candidate not taking part in each particular broadcast gives his consent to the programme, it cannot be shown. The purpose of this provision was to prevent candidates gaining unfair advantage over their rivals through access to broadcasting. It has turned out in practice to offer a legal right of veto to a calculating politician who wishes to prevent television or radio coverage of his or her opponents. Originally, it was conceived to protect the rights of minority candidates, but in practice it can be and has been used to interfere grossly with the general broadcasting obligation of balanced political reporting. Any candidate, even one with the most negligible of political support, such as the representative of the Monster Raving Loony Party, has this power of veto. As one member of the Association of British

Editors has put it, 'Mischievous, misguided or malicious candidates have been deliberately sabotaging broadcasts by refusing to take part or to let their opponents take part. The losers are the voters, who are denied the full story.'[45] In rather convoluted legal drafting, the precise wording of this highly unsatisfactory legal provision reads as follows:

Pending such an election it shall not be lawful for any item about the constituency or electoral area to be broadcast from a television or other wireless transmitting station in the United Kingdom if any of the persons who are for the time being candidates at the election takes part in the item and the broadcast is not made with his consent . . . Where an item about a constituency or electoral area is so broadcast pending such an election there, then if the broadcast either is made before the latest time for delivery of nomination papers, or is made after that time but without the consent of any candidate remaining validly nominated, any person taking part in the item for the purpose of promoting or procuring his election shall be guilty of an illegal practice, unless the broadcast is so made without his consent.

A few expressions used in the Act need clarification. An election becomes 'pending' from the moment the Prime Minister gives the public announcement of the forthcoming general election.[46] The term 'candidate' includes not only a person who has lodged his or her nomination papers with the returning officer, but also anyone who upon common-sense grounds is holding him or herself out as a potential or likely candidate. The 'consent' of a candidate may be given orally, and is sufficient where all candidates agree to take part, but in a situation where a candidate declines to take part but agrees to allow the other candidates to take part without him or her, it is wise for journalists and broadcasters to have the candidate sign a written form of consent referring to the particulars and date of the programme in case any later dispute arises. It may be helpful to restate the effect of section 93 in more intelligible language than that used in the Act.[47]

(1) The first legal requirement is that, between the start of the pending period and the close of nominations, no candidate may take part in any broadcast about the constituency or electoral area.
(2) The second legal requirement is that, after nomination day and up to the declaration of the poll, no candidate may take part in a broadcast about a constituency or electoral area without the consent of all candidates.

Precisely what is meant by 'taking part in' a broadcast? This expression is not defined in the Act, and in the past it has posed some uncertainty. Is it limited to studio discussion with the candidates, or other circumstances where the candidate is an active participant in the programme, or does it extend also to any programme whenever film of the candidate is being shown: for example, talking to constituents? The question arose in the 1979 case of *James Marshall* v. *BBC*,[48] where James Marshall was fighting the constituency seat of Leicester South for the Labour Party against three other candidates – Conservative, Liberal and National Front. During the general election campaign in April 1979, the BBC sent out a camera crew to film all the candidates. They told James Marshall they wished to film all the candidates for a programme they were making, but he said he would not take part in any such programme if the National Front candidate was also permitted to take part. The BBC proceeded with the preparation of the programme, and without his consent took photographs of James Marshall as he was going about his campaigning in Leicester. He protested that the camera crew were violating his rights as a candidate, and when they continued filming him, he issued a writ against the BBC. The Court of Appeal decided that Mr Marshall could not prevent the programme being broadcast, because he had not been 'taking part' within the legal meaning intended by section 93. The Court believed that, having regard to the importance of freedom of communication on political matters during an election campaign, the section was to be construed as only conferring a right of veto on a candidate in respect of the broadcasting of an election item if the candidate participated actively in the item. Since James Marshall had merely been shown, and had not actively participated in the programme, it did not require his consent before it was broadcast. In the view of Lord Denning, then Master of the Rolls:[49]

> It is important to observe that the BBC has accepted a duty to be impartial in their programmes. This is especially important during an election campaign. They are not to favour one candidate or party more than another candidate or party. Take this very case. If Mr Marshall is right, he can say: 'Film of the National Front candidate is not to be shown in this review of the constituency at all.' If he can say that about the National Front, he can say it about any other opposing party. He could say to the BBC: 'Either them or me, but you have to choose between us.' If they have to choose between two parties, they are ceasing to be impartial. If Mr Marshall's claim were correct, it would mean that the BBC would no longer be impartial. They would be forced by this veto to become partial.
>
> The words 'takes part in' do not mean 'is shown in'. They do not even go so far as to mean 'co-operates in'. They apply only when the candidate actively participates in the item. If he actively participates in the item, then he has a veto: and the item is not to be shown except with his consent. The BBC should be free to present an impartial account or film of an election campaign.

Only broadcasting of an 'item about a constituency' is caught by the terms of section 93. It has no effect therefore on programmes about the policies or personnel of the parties generally, or on reporting the national campaigning. A person who is a parliamentary candidate cannot be vetoed from appearing in programmes by the other candidates in his constituency if he or she is participating in the programme as a party spokesperson and the focus of the broadcast is not about the constituency where he or she is standing for election. Prominent national or regional politicians, then, even if they face a difficult opponent who vetoes his or her appearance on television and radio programmes under section 93, will have no difficulty in gaining access to broadcasting programmes during the election campaign in order to publicise and promote themselves so long as they stick to party policy, and not constituency matters.

It is impartial broadcasting of constituency elections, raising matters of local democracy, that suffers most under section 93, rather than the national battle between the parties for government office. By the same token, it is local radio and television that suffers rather than the national broadcasters. Quite apart from the practical difficulties the broadcasters encounter in having to trace and contact all the candidates every time they wish to make a programme about a constituency (made worse in 1992, for example, by the arrival of over 300 Natural Law Party candidates across the country), it is hardly fair or balanced reporting of election campaigns for the benefit of the electorate if a veto on candidates or political parties can prevent an opponent taking part in a programme (or if, as the BBC's chief political adviser has claimed, parties may use the section to 'keep off the air a candidate from their own side who is not thought to perform well').[50] In conclusion, the prohibition upon candidates having access to broadcasting until the close of nominations might remain in place, but the separate requirement that 'after nominations no candidate may take part in a broadcast about a constituency without the consent of all candidates' should be repealed. Section 93, therefore, needs to be rewritten (preferably in clear, intelligible English) and re-enacted. As long as television and radio broadcasting remains, in theory and practice, impartial, this effective right of veto by candidates is an unnecessary restriction upon the communication of political information to local electors.

Newspapers

In striking contrast to the way in which television and radio broadcasting has been expected to report the news and comment upon it in an impartial manner, historically it has been regarded as a vital principle of any country's democracy that its press (like individual politicians and voters themselves) is given the widest possible freedom to express whatever opinions its publishers, editors and journalists please. The press is under no legal obligation to provide objective or impartial news reporting or comment, and the extent of its freedom of expression is constrained only by the limits of the ordinary law (most notably, on points of factual accuracy, the law of defamation; and on points of government conduct, the Official Secrets Act 1989). At various times in our modern history, the press has been described as 'the fourth estate' of the realm, embedded within the political structure of the country, performing an essential role of scrutinising the work of government and Parliament, and representing an independent political balance against the power of politicians within the community. The level of constitutional importance attached to press freedom, however, has never been quite as high in the United Kingdom as that recognised in the USA, and, equally, the law relating to the press generally has not been developed in Britain in such an advanced manner as it has in the United States, (for example, in their common law development of principles protecting personal privacy, and in their statutory creation of rights of access to official information).[51] None the less, the concept of press freedom was pioneered in Britain, as shown in these words of the famous eighteenth-century jurist, William Blackstone:[52]

> The liberty of the press is indeed essential to the nature of a free state; but this consists in laying no previous restraints upon publications, and not in freedom from censure for criminal matter when published. Every free man has an undoubted right to lay what sentiments he pleases before the public; to forbid this, is to destroy the freedom of the press; but if he publishes what is improper, mischievous or illegal, he must take the consequences of his own temerity.

Press freedom means that individual newspapers may express highly subjective opinions in reporting political news, and in commenting on the personalities and policies of the political parties. Individual feature writers within a newspaper may be as subjective and partisan as they wish, and each newspaper may (and generally does) possess a distinct editorial political bias of its own. Collectively, of course, the press embraces a wide range of styles of reporting and commentary, from the cooler and more detached analysis within the *Financial Times* or the *Independent* to the openly biased and partisan *Sun* or the *Daily Mirror*. It has already been observed that the arrival of radio and television broadcasting transformed the newspaper business, by transmitting political news and events to people immediately as they occurred, so that newspapers have become less genuine bearers of news *per se*, although they still aim to provide a more comprehensive and more detailed version of the previous day's news than do the broadcasters. More particularly, all newspapers in the 1980s and 1990s have been distracted as never before by a fierce battle between one another to raise circulation and sales, and in turn advertising. Newspapers are not charitable, public-service organisations; they exist to make money for their proprietors. This means publishing subject-matter that is interesting to the public, and the overwhelming majority of readers are stimulated to buy a particular newspaper at least as much for its entertainment value as for the purposes of being educated and kept informed. There have been two marked tendencies in the British press over recent years. One of these, seen typically in the broadsheet or 'quality' end of the market (for example, the *Daily Telegraph*, the *Guardian*, *The Times*, the *Financial Times* and the *Independent*), is to offer much bigger newspapers than before, including a greater range and level of detail in its news items. The other tendency, seen typically among the 'tabloid' newspapers (for example the *Sun*, *Today*, the *Daily Mirror*, and the *Daily Express*), is to concentrate more than ever before upon pure entertainment for its readers. Alongside summaries of political and social news they provide distinctive publishing attractions within their pages such as bingo games, ongoing stories about the private lives of the rich and famous (especially members of the royal family) and photographs of naked or semi-naked women and men. At the same time, particularly within the tabloid press, the commercial emphasis on news reporting has come increasingly to rest upon its sensational and entertainment value. Indeed, editorials and newspaper headlines are often constructed specifically to be as sensational as possible in themselves, and by rampant political bias provoke a reaction and discussion, and further stimulate sales.

During general election campaigns most newspapers will be urging their readers to vote for or against a particular political party. The election result preferred by the great majority of newspapers in recent times has consistently been in favour of the Conservative Party. Amongst the daily national press, only one newspaper (the *Daily Mirror*) consistently supports the Labour Party, whereas six or seven newspapers regularly support the

Partisanship and circulation of national daily newspapers, 1992

Name of paper	Preferred result	Circulation (000s)	Readership (000s)
Daily Mirror	Labour victory	2903	8035
Daily Express	Conservative victory	1525	3643
Sun	Conservative victory	3571	9857
Daily Mail	Conservative victory	1675	4303
Daily Star	No endorsement	806	2628
Today	Conservative victory	533	1408
Daily Telegraph	Conservative victory	1038	2492
Guardian	Labour victory (with more Liberal Democrat MPs)	429	1214
The Times	Conservative victory	386	1035
Independent	No endorsement	390	1083
Financial Times	Not a Conservative victory	290	668

Table 6.1[53]

Conservative Party. In terms of national circulation, around 70 per cent of the national press is anti-Labour. This alignment of the press towards the right wing of British politics is remarkable in itself, but what is all the more striking, and makes the press in Britain without parallel in the Western world, is its lack of political diversity. The following is a sample from the leading tabloids on polling day in 1992. The headlines and editorial in the *Daily Mirror*: THE TIME IS NOW – VOTE LABOUR ('"X" marks the spot. The moment today in the polling booth when we can discard the failures of the past and seize the opportunities of the future . . . USE your vote. Use it for a brighter future, a future with real hope. Yes, it IS time for change. The time is NOW. Vote LABOUR'.) The headlines and editorial in the *Sun*: IF KINNOCK WINS TODAY WILL THE LAST PERSON TO LEAVE BRITAIN PLEASE TURN OUT THE LIGHTS ('It's D-day folks – the day you make the big decision about who you want to run the country. You know our views on the subject but we don't want to influence you in your final judgement on who will be Prime Minister! But if it's a bald bloke with wispy red hair and two K's in his surname, we'll see you at the airport'.) The 'quality' broadsheet papers are more analytical in their support for a particular party, and generally are more independent-minded and detached than are the tabloids. Thus, the *Daily Telegraph* and *The Times* in 1992, continued their support for the Conservative government as usual, but the *Guardian* supported Labour (with more Liberal Democrats being elected to Parliament), and the *Independent* throughout the election campaign held itself out as being non-politically aligned ('The only paper that will bring you unbiased reporting'). The greatest surprise of all, however, in the press coverage of the 1992 election campaign was for the *Financial Times* (traditionally a bastion of Conservative support) to encourage voting against the Conservative government: 'If this Election were solely a choice between party leaders, Mr Major would be preferable. But it is not. The dangers of perpetuating in power a weakened and uncertain Conservative Party, set alongside the progress Labour has made in modernising itself, justify by a fine margin the risks of a change.'

What is the impact of press bias upon the outcome of general elections? The reasons for voting behaviour, as we considered in Chapter 3, are easy to speculate about but notoriously difficult to define. Firstly, we might observe the correlation between a citizen's choice of newspaper and how he or she votes (see table 6.2 opposite).

Does the high level of Conservative voters reading the *Daily Telegraph* and *Daily Express*, or of Labour voters reading the *Daily Mirror* and the *Guardian* mean that these newspapers are influencing their voting behaviour? It is generally argued that statistics on such associations are meaningless, because a reader will tend to choose a newspaper that reflects his or her own political preference in the first place. Furthermore, the most rampantly Conservative newspaper, the *Sun*, does not have a proportio-

Correlation between a reader's choice of newspaper and
choice of party to vote for, 1987 and 1992

Newspaper		Party supported by readers		
		Conservative	Labour	Lib. Dem.
Daily Telegraph	1992	72	11	16
	1987	80	5	10
Daily Express	1992	67	15	14
	1987	70	9	18
Daily Mail	1992	65	15	18
	1987	60	13	19
Financial Times	1992	65	17	16
	1987	48	17	29
The Times	1992	64	16	19
	1987	56	12	27
Sun	1992	45	36	14
	1987	41	31	19
Today	1992	43	32	23
	1987	43	17	40
Daily Star	1992	31	54	12
	1987	28	46	18
Independent	1992	25	37	34
	1987	34	34	27
Daily Mirror	1992	20	64	14
	1987	20	55	21
Guardian	1992	15	55	24
	1987	22	54	19

Table 6.2[54]

nately huge predominance of Conservative-voting readers: in 1992, there
was only a 9 per cent difference between *Sun* readers voting Conservative or
Labour. Meanwhile, readers of the *Financial Times* in 1992 voted by 65 per
cent to 17 per cent in favour of Conservatives over Labour, despite the
leading articles of that newspaper prior to polling day advising readers
against voting Conservative. The rejection of this correlation between
newspaper reading and voting, however, misses the important point that
whereas most people's party allegiances remain settled throughout their
lives, it is the small proportion of floating voters who, in fact, determine the
result of a general election. It is the floating voter who is most likely to be
influenced by the political bias of the newspaper he or she reads. This is even
more likely to be the case if the reader is unaware of the bias of the
newspaper he or she is reading. In a famous *New Statesman*/MORI opinion
poll published during the course of the 1979 general election campaign,

respondents were asked to state the bias of the newspaper they read (see below). It disclosed that only 28 per cent of *Sun* readers recognised that their newspaper was biased towards the Conservatives, and 41 per cent did not think the paper was politically partisan at all. Even more surprising were the perceptions of *Daily Mirror* readers: while 38 per cent did not believe the newspaper was biased at all, most of those who thought it was politically partisan believed it preferred the Conservative Party.[55]

Perceptions of newspaper partisanship, 1979 General Election (%)

Readers of	Conservative	Labour	Unbiased	Don't know
Daily Express	44	5	33	9
Daily Mail	45	9	34	12
Sun	28	9	41	22
Daily Mirror	24	19	38	18

Table 6.3

Lack of awareness of a newspaper's partisan support for one of the parties might be taken to signify that the reader was particularly receptive to whatever political information was being fed to him or her. Academic research on the association of newspaper readership and voting behaviour, most recently in William Miller's *Media and Voters* (1991), has indicated that, particularly over a period of time, newspaper readers are quite clearly influenced by the politics of the publication they are reading. Furthermore, according to Professor Patrick Dunleavy of the London School of Economics:[56]

> The liberal arguments about downgrading press influence are contra-dictory. It cannot simultaneously be true that people pay little attention to the political news and comment in their newspaper, *and* that they select which paper to read partly to fit in with their political views. If the first argument is correct, then partisan self-selection in newspaper readership will be quite rare, and any correlation between readership and voting patterns needs to be taken seriously. On the other hand, if people do select a paper to read on partisan grounds, presumably they will go on to take a great deal of notice of what that paper says on political issues. There can be no *a priori* grounds for discounting press influence.

It was claimed by many Labour politicians after the 1992 general election campaign, including both the former Labour leader, Neil Kinnock, and the deputy leader, Roy Hattersley, that it was the aggressively Conservative and anti-Labour bias in the news reporting of sections of the tabloid press, notably the *Sun*, the *Daily Mail*, the *Daily Express* and the *Evening Standard*, that effectively caused them to lose the election. In his resignation speech outside Labour's Walworth Road headquarters in the early hours following polling day, Neil Kinnock said, 'I express no bitterness when I say that the Conservative supporting press has enabled the Tory Party to win yet again when the Conservative Party could not have secured victory for itself on the basis of its record, its programme or its character.' A few weeks later, on television, Roy Hattersley gave the following details of the ways in which he believed the press had helped the Conservatives to win:[57]

> On the day before the election, the *Sun* printed nine pages under the headline 'Nightmare on Kinnock Street'. Of course, those nine pages were intended to sway votes. That is why nine pages were devoted to propaganda instead of the usual stuff – stories about soap stars and so-called revelations about the Royal Family. Of course, in a free society Tory newspapers have an absolute right to support the Tory party, but the way in which the *Sun* and the *Daily Mail* and the *Daily Express* gave their support over the last three or four months raises real and serious questions about democracy in this country . . . Some people pretend that saying newspapers influence votes is the same as saying that readers are stupid. That is just not true. No matter who you are, no matter how clever, sophisticated, educated, if you get the drip, drip, drip of propaganda every morning, sooner or later it is going to influence your opinions and it is going to influence your vote. With the *Sun*, it was not so much drip, drip, drip, as a positive deluge. During the four weeks before polling day, it ran story after story damning Neil Kinnock and Labour policies.

Equally, it was the view in some Conservative and newspaper quarters that the Conservative victory was a triumph for the Conservative tabloid press. The next day, Lord McAlpine, the former Conservative Party Treasurer, declared that 'the heroes of the campaign' had been 'Sir David English [*Daily Mail*, knighted by Margaret Thatcher], Sir Nicholas Lloyd [*Daily Express,* knighted by Margaret Thatcher], Kelvin Mackenzie [*Sun*] and the other editors of the grander Tory press. Never in the past nine elections have they come out as strongly in favour of the Conservatives. Never has their attack on the Labour Party been so comprehensive . . . This was how the election was won.'[58] The *Sun* itself, two days after polling, broadcast across its front page the headline, 'IT'S THE SUN WOT WON IT!' Opinion polling evidence by MORI (based on a large sample of 22 700 voters), published on 12 April, suggested that there was indeed a swing towards Conservative support within the ranks of the tabloid press. There was a 4 per cent swing to the Conservatives among *Sun* readers in the last week of the election campaign, and similarly a 3 per cent shift among *Daily Express* readers, and 2 per cent among readers of the *Daily Mail*. Yet, on the other hand, the poll also contained evidence that this swing was just part of a national trend, for 2.5 per cent of *Daily Mirror* readers also switched to the Conservatives. After the dust of the general election had settled, several senior newspaper figures rebutted the notion that the press could bring about an election result, one way or another. The view of Sir Bernard Ingham, Margaret Thatcher's former press secretary, was that politicians always need a scapegoat:[59]

> If they lose, oh dear me, they by no means were to blame, their policies were never to blame, it is somebody else. And who the hell else is there these days other than the media. And therefore you had to look at that bit of the media that was against you, and therefore inevitably caused trouble. But the facts don't bear it out.

Or as Andrew Knight, the chairman of News International (publishers of *The Times, Today* and the *Sun)* put it:[60]

> Did the newspapers have an influence? Of course. So did television. So did the next door neighbour. So too perhaps the vicar's sermon, and who knows, possibly the bank balance. In the end it was the voters who decided, not the Tory tabloids, the BBC, or any other single news outlet. Labour lost the election with a gap of eight points behind the Tories. To blame such a crushing defeat on the tabloids is simply sour grapes.

Whatever effect partisan support in the newspapers for one party or another has on voting behaviour in modern times is perhaps tempered in the overall process of election campaigning by the growing techniques used by the political parties to manipulate the day's news as it is fed to the media generally. This new, very important component of national electioneering by the parties is described later in this chapter. Two remaining matters of growing public importance in the workings of the press during election campaigns are also dealt with in separate sections in this chapter. One is the far greater use of political advertising space being bought from newspapers, and the other the now widespread practice of newspapers commissioning and reporting on the results of public opinion polling on voting intentions, as a device to report on which parties are winning or losing the campaign.[61] There are advantages that the press should be free to express differing, subjective opinions, and so contribute to the public debate on political matters. The crucial practical problem with the role of the press during election campaigns, however, lies in the important distinction to be drawn between a newspaper offering subjective political opinions in its articles and commentaries, from the quite different journalistic responsibility to communicate to readers objective and truthful political facts. It would now appear to be a depressing reality that many readers in Britain have little confidence in the truthfulness of what their newspapers are telling them. An opinion poll by NOP in February 1992 revealed that only 29 per cent of readers of tabloid newspapers trust their own paper 'a great deal' or 'a fair amount' to tell the truth about the election. The proportion of readers of the tabloids who do not trust their own paper 'at all' totals 35 per cent. The relative credibility of television, party politicians, and the press – distinguishing between the broadsheet and tabloid newspapers – is shown below.

Popular credibility of the media and politicians (%)

		Party support			Newspaper readers	
	All	Con.	Lab.	Lib.Dem.	Broadsheet	Tabloid

Q. How much do you trust each of the following to tell the truth in the coming general election campaign?

Independent Television News

A great deal/a fair amount	67	73	65	65	69	67
A little	21	17	23	23	22	21
Not at all	9	6	10	9	7	10
Don't know	3	4	2	3	2	2

BBC News

A great deal/a fair amount	66	69	66	68	73	63
A little	19	18	18	21	18	20
Not at all	12	10	13	8	8	13
Don't know	3	3	2	4	1	3

The Liberal Democrats

A great deal/a fair amount	36	34	32	66	42	33
A little	35	39	37	21	35	36
Not at all	25	22	27	12	19	17
Don't know	4	5	3	1	3	7

The Labour Party

A great deal/a fair amount	32	19	54	19	28	32
A little	35	40	28	39	40	32
Not at all	32	40	17	40	30	34
Don't know	1	1	1	1	1	1

The Conservative Party

A great deal/a fair amount	31	68	6	20	30	31
A little	29	21	32	34	29	27
Not at all	39	11	61	46	39	41
Don't know	1	1	1	0	1	1

Your daily newspaper(s)

A great deal/a fair amount	29	39	28	25	53	29
A little	32	32	30	35	27	35
Not at all	32	24	35	30	19	35
Don't know	7	6	6	10	1	1

Table 6.4[62]

There would appear, therefore, to be a widepread feeling among voters that many newspapers, particularly among the tabloids, regularly confuse fact and opinion, and simply offer political propaganda. Roy Hattersley's view on this is that:

> There are bigger issues at stake than even the outcome of a general election. Without an honest press there cannot be real democracy in this country. How are the voters to make up their minds about the best government, if what they get from so many papers is prejudice and bias and slanted news? How can the electors make an informed choice if what they are being told day after day is not what is best for the country, but the choice of most newspapers and most newspaper proprietors?

LOCAL CAMPAIGNING BY THE CANDIDATES

The campaign team

The most important figures in local electioneering at a general election, after the parliamentary candidates themselves, are election agents. Every candidate must appoint an election agent who becomes responsible for the proper conduct and financial affairs relating to the campaign. He or she is required by law to take 'all reasonable means for preventing the commission of corrupt and illegal practices at the election', and if any irregularities or breaches of election law are found to have occurred in the course of the candidate's campaign, it is very likely that the election agent will be held personally liable, as well as the irregularity causing the election of the candidate to be declared void.[63] The most important function of the election agent, however, in the eyes of the law, is to act as the cipher through whom legitimate financial campaign expenditure can be made. The law places a limit on the total expenditure that can be paid out on a candidate's campaigning efforts, and the enforcement of this rule is facilitated by providing that such expenses can only be incurred and paid by (or only with the express authorisation of) the election agent, with no other person being permitted to pay out money in promoting a candidate's election.[64] In this way, the law seeks to ensure that the payment of expenses is not left, in the words of one Election Court judge, to 'uncertain bodies of people . . . whose acts no one would be responsible for or know anything at all about'.[65]

A parliamentary candidate should therefore appoint as his or her election agent someone who has experience and a very good knowledge of local election campaigning and the legal regulations relating to it. Notification of the person appointed as a candidate's election agent must be given in writing to the returning officer for the constituency, together with that person's address and acceptance that he or she agrees to act, which is then publicised by the returning officer. The election agent's legal tenure of the post will last until after the election result has been declared and until he or she has delivered a return of the candidate's full election expenses in statutory form. Until 1950, most local constituency parties maintained a permanent, full-time party agent, who became virtually the automatic choice for election agent at general elections. But because of a steady decline in the frequency and attendance at local party political meetings and other activities, caused in turn by national or general party publicity and propaganda playing a far greater role in both long-term and short-term election campaigning, fewer constituency parties now have a party agent – in less than half of the country's constituencies in the case of the Conservatives, and in less than one constituency in ten in the case of Labour.[66] The Representation of the People Act states that an election agent must be appointed by the candidate, but it is possible for the candidate to appoint him or herself as the election agent, and if a candidate has not appointed anyone within a time limit specified, the Act automatically stipulates that the candidate will be treated as his or her own election agent.[67] It is highly unusual for a candidate from one of the major parties to act as election agent, however, not simply because of the advantage of sharing the workload involved, but because the candidate as election agent adds to his or her liability for the proper conduct of the election campaign as a whole. Both the candidate and the election agent may be liable for electioneering irregularities committed by party workers or supporters in the course of the election campaign, unless they did not consent and had no knowledge of them,[68] but it is always far harder for the election agent (who is legally responsible under the Act for supervising the campaign) rather than the candidate to prove that he or she did not know what was going on.

Local parties generally form a campaign committee of full-time workers to take charge of the organisation of the election campaign, acting under the authority of the election agent. Their primary functions and division of labour will be directed to organising election meetings and the personal schedule and public appearances of their candidate, and then they will supervise party members and volunteers in such matters as canvassing, the setting up of posters, delivering mail and notices, assisting electors who are their supporters with postal or proxy vote arrangements if they need them, and organising an election appeal for funds. The election agent must select an official location for the candidate's campaign headquarters, which must be within or immediately adjacent to the constituency being contested, and inform the constituency returning officer of its address, so that any official communications for the agent can be sent there.[69] If the local party has permanent premises of its own that are sufficiently large for the task, then these will be selected, otherwise the election agent will need to hire offices specially for the purpose.

Throughout the election campaign, local constituency parties will be guided by the national party campaign headquarters. The party's central office will be orchestrating the itineraries of prominent members of the party and directing in which constituencies they will be appearing to speak and to help canvass. The national party chairman or campaign co-ordinator will take a particularly close interest in the work of those local constituency parties which are marginal and where a small electoral swing will win or lose them the seat. Apart from supplying the manifesto upon which all party members will campaign, each party will usually have had printed and distributed well in advance of the general election booklets containing detailed advice on all electoral matters and how to campaign effectively. Thus in 1991 in preparation for the imminent general election, the Conservative Party national office published the sixteenth edition of its *Parliamentary Election Manual* and the Labour Party published *The Way to Win: Labour's Campaign Handbook for the 1990s*. More detailed supplementary publications were issued on such matters as public speaking, dealing with the media, canvassing and campaign organisation. Cohesion and unity on public policy is always important for a political party during election campaigns, and for guidance on policy matters all the parties will have produced documents of a more detailed nature than that contained within the party's manifesto, for local workers to consult. The main Labour policy document for 1992 was still *Meet the Challenge: Make the Change*, which had been prepared by Neil Kinnock as a result of his radical internal policy review initiated immediately after the 1987 general election defeat. That was published in 1989, and had been followed by several more specialist policy documents, for example *The Charter of Rights* in 1990. In fact, his successor, John Smith, believed that Labour made a mistake in completing its policy review too early, nearly three years before the 1992 election and before the economy went into recession, and under his leadership the National Executive Committee laid down a strategy for a series of annual reviews on separate subject areas (beginning with Europe, the constitution and an interim economic policy statement in 1993 and foreign and security issues, the environment, health and education in 1994) leading up to the Party Conference in October 1995 when 'all the component parts of the party's rolling programme of policy will have to be completed' for the imminent election.[70] Perhaps most impressive of all as a campaign tool for local party activists is *The Campaign Guide*, published by the Conservative Party. Editions of this have been produced for general elections since 1892, with the 1991 edition running to 790 pages. Complete with a Foreword by the Prime Minister, this publication provides a comprehensive account of Conservative thinking on virtually all matters of public policy. It also includes politically slanted summaries and caricatures of the policies and ideas of the other main parties, spelling out the arguments that can most effectively be employed by party workers against them. Local party workers, then, will consult and refer to these national party documents in the course of their canvassing or for any other purposes of party political dialogue in the course of the election campaign.

Canvassing and electioneering methods

Corrupt and illegal practices

Election campaign law in Britain is largely founded on nineteenth-century electioneering pretexts. In the nineteenth century, before the advent of broadcasting and mass circulation newspapers, election campaigns were almost exclusively conducted personally at constituency level, with voters being concerned with a choice between the individual candidates standing in their local community, and intimidation and bribery of electors was rife. Following the progressive extensions of the franchise in the nineteenth century, most notably in 1832 and 1867, a Corrupt and Illegal Practices Act was passed in 1883 in an attempt to eradicate electoral corruption and to regulate the more extensive local campaigning practices that had become necessary to influence the growing number of local voters. The fundamental purpose of this statute was to provide a framework through which fair election campaigns could be fought between those standing as parliamentary candidates in each constituency. Two important ways in which it sought to achieve this was by identifying and making illegal many inappropriate or unfair electioneering practices of the late nineteenth century, and by imposing limits upon the amount of money that each candidate could spend in financing his campaign. This approach to the regulation of election campaigns has been followed and developed ever since the late nineteenth century, through several modernising statutes in the twentieth century up to and including the Representation of the People Act 1983. Contemporary British law on election campaigning is designed essentially to regulate local rather than national election campaigns, and the detail and complexity of the Act's provisions dealing with local electoral campaigns by candidates stand in stark contrast to the paucity of close controls over national campaigning by the political parties, most notably in financial affairs.

The Representation of the People Act 1983 contains a mass of detailed regulations governing constituency election campaigns running to over a third of its 200 pages. A breach of any of these election campaign regulations means that a 'corrupt or illegal practice' will have occurred. Some corrupt or illegal practices may be committed by any person, and some may only be committed by either or both the candidate and his or her election agent. Most obviously, it is an offence to seek to bribe a voter. The 1983 Act has a special section providing that it is a corrupt practice to offer or accept a bribe, which is defined as including any 'money, gift, loan or valuable consideration, office, place or employment', in order to influence how an elector will cast his or her vote.[71]

Similarly, a corrupt practice is committed where a person is guilty of undue influence of a voter, meaning where a person physically threatens or intimidates a voter, or where 'by abduction, duress or any fraudulent device or contrivance he impedes or prevents the free exercise of the franchise of an elector'.[72] The ancient common law offence of 'treating' is also codified in the Act. A person is regarded as committing the offence of treating where he or she gives or offers to an elector food, drink or entertainment in order to influence how the elector will vote.[73] Bribery of a parliamentary candidate is expressly declared an election offence too. The Act states that any person who corruptly induces or procures any other person to withdraw from being a candidate in consideration of any payment or promise of payment is guilty of an illegal payment, and so too will be the person withdrawing his or her candidature in consequence of the bribe.[74]

A host of other corrupt or illegal practices are mentioned in the Act, including, for example, personation (voting in the name of another person), tampering with nomination papers, false declarations being given to the returning officer, breaching the secrecy of the ballot regulations, non-compliance with certain legal restrictions upon broadcasting (such as a candidate's veto over programmes in which other candidates appear), and illegal and excessive financial expenditure on local election campaigning. Penalties are prescribed for each particular corrupt or illegal practice. The individuals concerned, who may include candidates and election agents, are liable to be fined or imprisoned, and have their right to vote and stand as a parliamentary candidate taken away for a period up to ten years, depending upon the nature of the particular election offence.

The finding of a corrupt or illegal practice may also invalidate the election in the constituency itself.[75] If the parliamentary candidate him or herself is personally guilty or guilty through any of his or her agents of any corrupt or illegal practice, then election will be declared void. An agent, for this purpose, includes not only his or her election agent but any person at all who is authorised to work on the candidate's election campaigning, such as a canvasser. In other words, even though the candidate may have known absolutely nothing about the corrupt or illegal practice (and even if it was committed in direct contradiction to clear instructions from the candidate or his election agent) the election may still be declared void. This very strict rule shows just how important it is for the election agent to scrutinise closely the legitimacy and propriety of the local campaigning methods of party workers. There are, however, some tightly-drawn statutory grounds upon which a blameless winning parliamentary candidate may obtain relief from an order of the court cancelling the election, depending upon the nature and circumstances of the particular corrupt or illegal practice (for example, where an illegal payment is made inadvertently or from an accidental miscalculation and the court believe it was just to grant relief).[76] An election may also be invalidated where on an election petition it is shown that corrupt or illegal practices committed by anyone with the purpose of promoting the election of any particular candidate have so extensively prevailed that they may be reasonably supposed to have affected the result.[77]

The body that will decide such legal proceedings brought by way of an election petition, is the Election Court. This is a body constituted by the Representation of the People Act specifically for the purpose of resolving disputes arising from election campaigns, and in England and Wales comprises two judges of the Queen's Bench Division of the High Court. Election petitions founded upon campaigning irregularities were common in the nineteenth century, but since the 1930s have become rare occurrences. In 1991 there was a successful case brought, alleging that a political leaflet issued by one party, purporting on its face to come from another party, was a corrupt and illegal practice contrary to section 115 of the Act and constituted a fraudulent device which impeded the free exercise of the franchise of an elector.[78] However, that case dealt with the election of local government councillors in Tower Hamlets, London. As far as parliamentary elections are concerned, no election has been invalidated since 1923 in Oxford because a corrupt or illegal practice was committed. Apart from the very high costs involved in bringing petitions to court, there is a general view that each political party has as much to lose as the others if they start challenging every election where there might be some evidence of a trivial election offence committed. As one senior party official said in 1959:[79]

> If we lost a seat by one vote and I could clearly prove illegal practices by the other side I wouldn't try . . . They might be able to show that our man had slipped up in some way. But worse than that, it might start tit-for-tat petitions and no party could afford a lot of them. On the whole, we're both law-abiding and it's as well to leave each other alone.

Canvassing

One of the most important tasks in local constituency campaigning is canvassing. The primary purpose of canvassing is to establish the political sympathies and voting intentions of all electors within the constituency. This is essential preparatory work in advance of their polling day efforts, when the local parties will be checking which electors have and have not voted, so that late in the day they can do all they are able, telephoning or calling personally at the homes of those who are known supporters or sympathisers to encourage them to go to the polling station – if needs be even offering them transport. Canvassing is therefore part of the whole process whereby local constituency parties aim to 'get out the vote'.

Canvassing also presents the opportunity for a public relations exercise with the local electorate, with a view to influencing voting intentions. Relatively few canvassers in fact set out to enter into political discourse with voters on their doorsteps, but they will be rehearsed in what to say if people put questions to them about their party and its policies. An important secondary purpose of canvassing is to identify political waverers or the 'floating vote', the names of whom will then be fed back to local and/or national party headquarters. They will then have been identified as suitable people to receive a personal follow-up visit from a party member practised in political persuasion, and/or direct-mail letters or other party propaganda encouraging them to vote for the party at the forthcoming election. Where canvassers have established that individuals are committed supporters of one of the other parties, no further time will be wasted on them.

There are three different ways in which canvassing may take place. The traditional method is door-to-door. Here the party canvasser simply calls round at the homes of local residents in order to ask them if they will be voting on polling day, whether they will be supporting the canvasser's party, how they voted at the previous election, and whether there is any prospect of them changing their minds on how they currently intend to vote. Members in a household do not always vote the same way, so similar responses should be elicited from or about other people living there. Electors who are committed supporters will be asked to display party posters in their windows, and might also be invited to volunteer for canvassing activities themselves. A second method of canvassing, which has grown in popularity, especially within the Conservative Party, is for a similar questioning of electors within the constituency to be undertaken by telephone. This has obvious attractions and advantages for the canvasser, not least in terms of physical effort, especially on days with uncomfortable weather or on dark evenings. It also means that less experienced canvassers can follow a standard form of introduction and dialogue taken from a pre-written script placed in front of him or her when telephoning. A final and more sophisticated form of canvassing, which is now becoming common, is questionnaire canvassing. This, in fact, is most useful if conducted in advance of the election campaign starting. Its object is to ask local residents a range of questions drawn from a standard party questionnaire about what they believe are the most important issues of the day, and also to gather personal information about the voters' ages, gender, occupations and so on. This information will then be of use during the campaign, not only if the elector is a political sympathiser or floating voter, in knowing how best to present party policy to him or her personally, but also in order to build up a collective profile of the voters within the constituency (or particular areas or even streets within the constituency) as to the key issues on which to present and fight the election campaign most effectively.

Most information gathered from canvassing is nowadays placed directly on to the party's computer data-bank. The electoral registration officer for the area will provide local parties with a copy of the local electoral register on a computer disk, complete with the names and addresses of all electors in the constituency, and party workers can then use this to start placing against each name the information gleaned from canvassing. Entire political profiles of individual voters across the country are now therefore held by the political parties, each containing various pieces of personal information including previous voting history and voting intentions. It is likely that people might feel uneasy about responding to canvassers (and very possibly refuse to answer questionnaire canvassers entirely) if they realised that what they were saying was going to be recorded on permanently held, computerised information-retrieval systems, to which any member of the political organisation concerned had access. There is no obligation at present upon local party canvassers to inform people that a personal political profile is being compiled about them, and canvassers rarely mention it in case it diminishes the prospects of the person canvassed offering the information sought. None the less, on personal privacy grounds it would be good practice if in advance of soliciting answers, canvassers were required to inform electors of the purposes to which the information sought will be put, and to state that the information will be stored on a computer for campaigning purposes in the future. The normal provisions of the Data Protection Act 1984 at present apply to canvassing information stored in this way, and the public official responsible for supervising the principles and procedures under which such information is obtained and kept is the Data Protection Registrar, currently Eric Howe, at offices in Wilmslow, Cheshire. The general principles of the Act include that such personal data shall be obtained fairly, that the personal data shall be accurate and kept up to date, that it shall not be kept for longer than is necessary for the purpose of its collection, and that security measures shall be taken against unauthorised access to the personal data. Any individual has the right to ask a data user, and be informed truthfully, whether personal information is being held on him or her, and if so the individual has the right to see the personal data and the power to have any erroneous information corrected or erased.[80]

Election meetings and speaking to the voters

The electioneering value of local public meetings has steadily declined over the period since the 1950s, with the arrival of modern mass media. In 1951, 30 per cent of the electorate attended election meetings, whereas in 1987 a mere 3 per cent did so.[81] The era of the hustings in the market square and town hall, with huge numbers of ordinary men and women coming to hear the oratory of rival politicians, has long since passed into history. None the less, it should not be forgotten that while the television screen and national campaigning through the media is of greatest importance to the electoral success or failure of a political party's chances of forming the next government, personal contact between politicians and local electors within each constituency may yet still count for winning or losing a significant enough number of votes in a parliamentary seat with a volatile electorate, or one where the electoral support for two or more of the parties is very narrow. Long in advance of the general election being called, national party strategists will already have clearly identified the crucial 'marginal constituencies' so as to plan and focus their greatest personal efforts within those localities, arranging for senior party figures to visit and speak there. The local party campaign team will have a programme of meetings planned, and, especially in marginal seats, the parliamentary candidate can expect to be campaigning with little relief.

In England, Wales and Scotland, parliamentary candidates have the legal right under the Representation of the People Act 1983 to use rooms in any state school or public hall at reasonable times 'for the purpose of holding public meetings in furtherance of his candidature'.[82] There is no limit to the number of election meetings that can be held, and the frequency with which this legal right may be taken advantage of by a candidate. If other locations are hired for election meetings, the fee will constitute an election expense counting towards the maximum expenditure that may be incurred by each candidate. However, because of the small number of voters who are likely to attend nowadays, only a handful of proper election meetings is held by each candidate, where he or she with guest speakers will formally address an audience of electors and answer questions. There is no point in ordinary local candidates holding public meetings or rallies for only party members to attend, as this will not win any extra votes. By contrast, the party leaders and other top politicians may give speeches at large party rallies, but these will have been designed for the benefit of the television cameras transmitting the speeches to a national audience. The routine method of personal campaigning by parliamentary candidates in modern times takes the form of itineraries around the constituency. Sometimes this takes the form of a motorcade or procession travelling around the constituency, with the candidate or a party member speaking on his or her behalf, addressing the populace through a loudspeaker and urging local residents to vote. Generally more effective is a schedule of personal appearances at prearranged locations, for the candidate or guest politician to shake hands and speak informally with local people in shopping centres, markets, clubs and pubs, health centres, and local factories or offices. One of John Major's electioneering stunts in 1992 when visiting marginal constituencies was to bring a soap box along with him, upon which to stand in a few selected public places and speak through a microphone to local people walking by. Most of the personal campaigning outdoors by the candidates or fellow party politicians are 'whistle-stop' appearances, forming part of a campaign tour, which moves on to a different location in the constituency after twenty minutes or so.

Campaign communications and publicity

Traditionally, each parliamentary candidate prepares a formal written statement of his or her political views and intentions, known as an election address, which is sent out to every elector in the constituency. By law these can be sent free of charge to each elector within the constituency, the Representation of the People Act 1983 specifically providing for the Post Office to deliver 'one postal communication containing matter relating to the election only and not exceeding 2 ounces in weight'.[83] Despite this state subsidy, the typesetting and printing costs of the address still represent one of the highest election expenses of the local campaign. An increasing percentage of the content of election addresses in recent years has simply reiterated the claims or policies of the national political party to which the candidate belongs, adopting text prepared by the party central office, and the proportion of space devoted to the more individualistic views of the particular candidate has diminished. In the 1992 general election, 41 per cent of Conservative candidate election addresses contained a photograph of the party leader, John Major, as well as the face of the parliamentary candidate.[84] This no doubt is simply reflecting perceived campaigning wisdom, that parties matter more than individuals in attracting votes, and that party unity in fighting election campaigns is extremely important. Individualistic or idiosyncratic views of candidates, possibly at odds with official party policy, might be exploited by political opponents as signs of disunity, which is an electoral liability and loses votes. None the less, it is up to the local candidate to decide for him or herself the precise contents of the address, and it remains the most widely read form of local campaigning literature of an election campaign. Further party notices or leaflets may be hand-delivered by party workers to electors later in the campaign, as well as special election editions of local party newsletters which have become popular in recent years, especially with the Conservative and Liberal Democrat parties. A very visible and useful form of free publicity is for members and supporters of a particular political party to accept and display these on their private premises. Posters and notices will routinely be placed by supporters in the windows of their homes facing outwards for all passers-by to see, and larger posters may be positioned on shops, hoardings or other buildings owned by supporters. The Representation of the People Act 1982 specifically prohibits any payment being made to electors for exhibiting party notices or posters.[85] All firm supporters will be asked by canvassers if they are prepared to display posters, and sometimes a separate campaign team is organised by the local party specifically for the task of distributing them to residents in the area. A successful local poster campaign not only serves to convey an impression of strong support within the constituency, but it is often the most effective way of publicising and reminding local voters of the name of their parliamentary candidate.

The campaigning tool at both local and national level which looks set to become increasingly important in the future is 'direct mail'. This is the practice of the parties mass-producing letters personally addressed to each elector, beginning with 'Dear Mr/Mrs/Ms' and ending with a colour-photocopied signature of the local candidate or party leader. It emerged as a novel feature of electioneering in the 1980s, made available by new computer technology which allows party workers to store all the names and addresses of electors on a word processor. As a method of persuasion, it is, of course simply following marketing techniques being used by commercial companies, such as banks bombarding their customers with personalised letters seeking to persuade them to utilise their insurance and other financial services. It has been used extensively in fundraising efforts as well as in campaigning. At general election time, the party campaigners will not waste time and money in sending out direct mail to everyone, but will concentrate on certain constituencies and voters, with the benefit of the personal profiles compiled from electoral registers and the political information gained from canvassing efforts. Marginal constituencies will be the target of most direct-mail activity, and the types of elector identified as particularly suitable for a letter will be all new voters and floating voters, and those who are only lukewarm (or 'soft') supporters of their own party, and similarly people identified as being lukewarm supporters of other parties. Certain electors may also be targeted because of their occupation, notably those regarded as opinion-formers such as teachers, local councillors, religious leaders, publicans and doctors. With the benefit of the personal profiles maintained on electors, it is also possible to modify the subject matter of letters being sent out, to give emphasis to those issues which the letter's recipient is known or calculated to be most concerned about. Ever more sophisticated and glossy techniques of direct mail to market the parties are bound to be a part of future electioneering within this country. At present the parties are in a state of flux in the division between providing the direct mail locally and centrally; and where used centrally, between performing the work in-house or deciding to contract out the work to agencies specialising in direct mail services. At the time of writing, during election campaigns the Labour Party organises most of its direct mail locally. The Conservative Party is most advanced in its central office direct mail activities, and there is little doubt that during the next general election even more British voters can expect to receive a personalised letter from the Prime Minister.

Controls upon campaign expenditure

Local campaign expenditure is controlled in three different ways: first, by specifying that certain types of campaigning expenditure are illegal; second, by placing a maximum figure on the total sum of money that may be spent by a parliamentary candidate in financing his or her constituency campaign; and third, by providing that no expenditure on constituency campaigning may be incurred by anyone apart from a candidate or his or her election agent.

Prohibited expenses

The following types of financial expenditure are completely prohibited in constituency campaigning. One of the most important principles is that the parliamentary candidate and election agent are not permitted to hire anyone to canvass on their behalf. Only volunteers may canvass. The Act reads:[86]

If a person is, either before, during or after an election, engaged or employed for payment or promise of payment as a canvasser for the purpose of promoting or procuring a candidate's election –
(a) the person so engaging or employing him and
(b) the person so engaged or employed, shall be guilty of illegal employment.

Another prohibited form of election expense is that premises in schools may not be hired for use as the candidate's election campaign headquarters (or 'committee room' as it is called) during the campaign.[87] Nor may candidates and their agents pay electors in the constituency where they are standing to display or exhibit election addresses, bills or notices unless the electors involved happen to be professional advertising agents.[88]

It is an old restriction that candidates and their agents may not pay any money for the purpose of transporting voters or their proxies to or from polling stations. Section 101 of the 1983 Act now controls this, and reads:[89]

(1) A person shall not let, lend, or employ any public vehicle for the purpose of the conveyance of electors or their proxies to or from the poll at an election . . . [and]
(2) A person shall not hire, borrow or use for the purpose of the conveyance of electors or their proxies to or from the poll at an election any public vehicle the owner of which he knows to be prohibited by subsection (1) above from letting lending or employing for that purpose . . . .

This means that while commercial dealing for transport services is prohibited, candidates and their constituency parties may still provide such transport as a means of 'getting out the vote' but only using motor vehicles belonging to themselves or other supporters. The restriction now contained in section 101 was first introduced in 1883 as an appropriate device for promoting fairness between the parties in campaigning, but in modern circumstances it has become an anachronism. Formerly, when transport generally was far more difficult and expensive, wealthy Conservatives in the late nineteenth and early twentieth centuries might take considerable advantage of offering such facilities to voters, especially in rural areas. In fact, in 1948, the Labour government restricted the overall number of supporters' vehicles that could be used for transporting voters, upon the basis that Conservatives owned far more cars than did Labour supporters. This restriction was, however, repealed by the Conservative government in 1958. With many people owning their own cars today, and transport generally being more readily accessible and less expensive, this campaigning device of helping sympathetic voters to get to the polling booth is no longer a separate, major issue. If a candidate's campaign team wishes to spend its money on hiring transport as well as freely offering its own supporters' vehicles to take electors to the polling booths, it should be allowed the freedom to do so. The money it decided to spend, of course, would be added to the total sum of election campaign expenditure allowed in the constituency campaign.

Maximum limit upon a candidate's election expenditure

A legal maximum limit on the total amount of money that a parliamentary candidate and his or her election agent may choose to spend on publicity and other campaigning devices aimed at promoting his or her election is contained in section 76 of the Representation of the People Act. This section prohibits the spending of any money in excess of the maximum amount, and makes it an offence for the candidate and election agent intentionally to do so:

> No sum shall be paid and no expense shall be incurred by a candidate at an election or his election agent, whether before, during or after an election, on account of or in respect of the conduct or management of the election, in excess of the maximum amount specified in this section, and a candidate or election agent knowingly acting in contravention of this subsection shall be guilty of an illegal practice.

The precise figure of the maximum limit is subject to variation from time to time, in practice generally increasing in line with inflation.[90] These changes are legally effected under the authority of the Act by way of the Home Secretary presenting a draft statutory instrument to Parliament, which must be approved by the House of Commons and the House of Lords. The limits distinguish between urban and rural constituencies, and between sums allowed in a general election campaign and at a by-election.

The present maximum amount that can be spent at a general election, is (a) for town ('borough') constituencies, £4 642 plus an additional 3.9 pence for every registered elector in the constituency, and (b) for country ('county') constituencies, £4 642 plus an additional 5.2 pence for every registered elector in the constituency. The total amount in any particular constituency therefore depends upon the number of electors there, and also the belief that campaigning in rural areas is more difficult and more expensive than in urban areas. Significantly higher sums are allowed at by-elections in a constituency, which is the subject of Appendix 2, and this reflects the relatively greater national importance and therefore extra campaigning efforts expected of such parliamentary elections outside general election time.

Prohibition upon publicity or campaign advantages being paid for by anyone else

The Representation of the People Act further prohibits any money being spent by anyone apart from a candidate or his or her election agent on activities which are designed to promote the election of the candidate. Such payments will only be permissible if they are made with the written approval of the candidate's election agent, in which case the money will be deemed to form part of the total sum of the candidate's expenditure, which is subject to a statutory limit. Anyone who spends money contrary to this restriction is guilty of a corrupt practice. The exact wording of this legal provision, defining the campaign activities included within the financial prohibition, is in section 75 of the Act and is as follows:

> No expenses shall, with a view to promoting or procuring the election of a candidate at an election, be incurred by any person other than the candidate, his election agent and persons authorised in writing by the election agent on account –
> (a) of holding public meetings or organising any public display; or
> (b) of issuing advertisements, circulars or publications; or
> (c) of otherwise presenting to the electors the candidate or his views or the extent or nature of his backing or disparaging another candidate.

The clear purpose of this restriction is to avoid the campaign expenditure limits imposed upon candidates being rendered illusory by the candidates' political friends or associates being able to spend money on additionally publicising and promoting the candidates.

The flaw in the expenditure controls

The fundamental weakness of the provisions that place a maximum ceiling upon the financial expenditure of a parliamentary candidate, and disallow anyone else from paying for electioneering benefits in his or her campaign, is that they relate exclusively to local constituency campaigning. So far as general or national political campaigning for or against one or other of the parties is concerned, there are no financial limits at all upon the huge sums of money which the parties (to whom virtually all candidates belong) may spend in promoting, publicising or advertising themselves across the country as a whole. Financial expenditure is only caught and limited by the Representation of the People Act if it relates specifically to a particular constituency and to particular constituency candidates. If, by contrast, the expenditure is made on publicity or propaganda simply for or against the political parties or the party leaders, without reference to any particular constituency, then the financial limits and restrictions do not apply. The national political parties may therefore pay out during election campaigns as much as they can afford to spend from the total amount of money they have been able to raise from donations and income. If the purpose of the expenditure restrictions in the Representation of the People Act has been to maintain a legal framework in which fair political campaigns can be presented to the electorate (as was clearly the intention when they were first laid down in the Corrupt and Illegal Practices Act 1883) then the modern extent and drafting of these legal provisions in carrying out this purpose have become seriously out of step with developments in modern electioneering. Nowadays it is national campaigning efforts by and on behalf of the political party to whom an individual candidate belongs which have by far the greater influence in swaying voters for or against the candidate within his or her constituency. Instead of recognising that parliamentary elections are now fought between national political parties waging national campaigns, the law continues to treat the financial regulation of election campaigns during a general election as nothing more than 651 separate elections being carried out in individual constituencies across the country. This legal vacuum between, on the one hand, tightly controlled expenditure limits on local constituency campaigning by candidates, and on the other, the absence of any expenditure controls at all on national campaigning by the political parties, is perhaps the most striking anomaly in British election campaign law today.

This anomaly also applies whenever a commercial company, trade union, wealthy individual or any other body wishes to purchase advertising space or otherwise pay for political publicity to help persuade electors on how to cast their vote. The prohibition on all people other than candidates and their agents incurring expenses in promoting or procuring the election of candidates at an election has been held not to apply as long as the campaigning involved does not refer to any particular candidate nor to any particular constituency. This was shown in the landmark case of *R*. v. *Tronoh Mines Ltd* (1952),[91] which involved a dispute over the meaning of the statutory provision as it appeared in the earlier Representation of the People Act 1949. Six days prior to the 1951 general election, a company took out a full-page advertisement in *The Times* newspaper condemning the Labour government's socialist policies. The advertisement concluded with the words:[92]

> The coming general election will give us all the opportunity of saving the country from being reduced, though the policies of the Socialist government, to a bankrupt 'Welfare State'. We need a new and strong government with ministers who may be relied upon to encourage business enterprise and initiative, under the leadership of one who has, through the whole of his life, devoted himself to national and not sectional interests.

The court was asked to decide whether this constituted spending money aimed at 'promoting the election of a candidate at an election' and/or 'in disparaging another candidate'. The judge in the case, McNair J., accepted that there was an ambiguity in the legal drafting of the section, and that it was arguable that the meaning of the word 'candidate' in the section included any or all candidates across the country. However, he declined to give the statutory provision this meaning and chose to rely instead upon the legal maxim that 'a man should not be put in peril upon an ambiguity'. He decided that the prohibition related only to advertisements encouraging electors to vote for a particular candidate in a particular constituency and not to political propaganda in general, even if the advertisement had the effect of encouraging electors to vote for particular candidates in their own particular constituencies. He declared that, 'The section is not intended to prohibit expenditure incurred on advertisements designed to support, or having the effect of supporting, the interest of a particular party generally in all constituencies, at any rate at the time of a general election.' As the advertisement placed by the directors of Tronoh Mines Ltd did not refer to any particular candidate or constituency, it fell outside the restrictions placed upon campaign expenditure in the Act.

NATIONAL CAMPAIGNING BY THE POLITICAL PARTIES

Winning a general election is a marathon rather than a sprint. As soon as one general election is over, the long-term planning and preparation for the next one begins almost immediately. After three years has passed since the previous election, all the parties will be in a state of perpetual readiness for the next election campaign proper starting at any time. Such planning, of course, is much easier for the party in government, with the Prime Minister holding the personal discretion to decide exactly when the election will be.

The springboard for national party campaigns is often the previous annual party conferences which take place in the months of September and October and are subject to extensive television coverage. Certainly, this was true of the conferences held in 1992, with John Major having no choice but to call a general election before June 1993. The party leaders always give long keynote addresses at these conferences, which serve both as rallying cries to the party faithful present at the conference and also as major opportunities of free television broadcasting time in which to persuade voters of the merits of themselves and their political party. One episode during the party conference season in 1992 serves to illustrate the link between election timing and longer-term party campaigning. On Tuesday, 1 October, the Labour leader, Neil Kinnock, was due to make his keynote speech at the Labour Conference, and as usual on such occasions his party could expect to receive massive press coverage of the contents of his speech the following morning. However, in what was widely regarded as an attempt to overshadow the day's events, the Conservative campaign team decided to leak a decision by the Prime Minister, John Major, to rule out holding a general election in the following month (November), preferring the election to be held instead sometime early in 1993. In consultation with other members of the Conservative campaign team, the Conservative Party's information co-ordinator, John Wakeham, telephoned editors and political editors at five Conservative-supporting newspapers (the *Sun*, *Daily Mail*, *Daily Express*, *Times* and *Daily Telegraph*) to tell them this news just before Neil Kinnock's speech.[93] In the event, this ruse largely backfired, because a journalist on one of those papers passed on the news to the Labour Party campaign team by contacting Labour's then shadow Chancellor, John Smith, for a comment, and Neil Kinnock in his speech was able powerfully to accuse the Prime Minister, John Major, of unprincipled tactics ('It does British democracy no good when government manipulates things in this fashion') and being afraid of a general election ('You can run, but you cannot hide').

Election manifestos

The principal campaigning document for each political party is its election manifesto. This is the document which contains the official programme of public policies of the national party, and the policies themselves constitute pledges as to what the party would do if elected into Government. The foreword of the manifesto will be written by the party's leader, and a large photograph of the leader will also feature prominently inside the document or on its front cover. Party candidates around the country will be expected to campaign during the election upon the policies that are included in the manifesto, and during the campaign party solidarity is at a premium, since any signs of disunity or division within the party erodes voters' confidence in the party leadership and will be seized upon and attacked by political opponents. The general shape and content of party manifestos is usually prepared several months in advance of the general election being called, from the time it is first anticipated, but the final presentation and wording will be approved at short notice at or around the time of the Prime Minister's decision about the date of polling day being made publicly known. In 1992, for example, the Conservative manifesto was agreed by the Cabinet on 12 March, the day after the election had been announced by John Major, and the Labour manifesto was finalised at a joint meeting of the shadow Cabinet and National Executive Committee on 16 March.[94] The physical quality and design of the manifestos has dramatically improved since the early 1980s. Previously they were small, cheaply-produced booklets, simply laying out the policies, but in 1987 and 1992 they were turned into attractive, glossy brochures. The Conservative document had a laminated cover photograph of John Major smiling, entitled 'The Best Future for Britain'. Labour's manifesto made extensive use of photographs conveying images of the type of society they wished to create, entitled 'It's Time to Get Britain Working Again'. And the Liberal Democrat manifesto was a huge, square, coffee-table-type document, featuring a determined-looking Paddy Ashdown, and entitled 'Changing Britain for Good'. In 1992, in proportion to the greater visual impact of the manifestos, efforts were made by the parties to distribute and sell them through major bookshops including W.H. Smith (retailing at £1.95, £1 and £1.50 for the Conservative, Labour and Liberal Democrat documents respectively). None the less, it seems that well under 200 000 copies of each party manifesto were printed and sold, and there has not been any substantial increase in circulation over the period since the 1983 general election, when 90 000 Conservative, 100 000 Labour and 65 000 Liberal/SDP Alliance manifestos were printed. This is substantially fewer copies than any of the national broadsheet newspapers sells in just one day (and nowhere near the 4 million or so sales each day of the *Sun* and the *Daily Mirror*). The direct electoral impact of party manifestos is currently, therefore, rather small, with copies in circulation either being distributed free to party workers or purchased by party members. Their real significance is to put on record the party's proposals for the future, and during the election campaign to serve as both a source of inspiration and a work of reference for candidates and other party workers.

Political advertisements

One of the most important components of a political party's strategy to win a general election is its political advertising campaign. The slogans and images used in these advertisements will set the tone for their election campaign generally. The parties are at liberty to advertise themselves and their campaign messages as freely as a commercial company marketing and selling its product. The single exception is that, by law, political advertising is prohibited on television and radio,[95] although, of course, the party election broadcasts that are allocated free of charge are, in effect, the same as advertising. The most common types of advertisement used during an election campaign are notices placed in the newspapers or on billboards in streets around the country, or in films shown at cinemas.

Parties at recent general elections have spent huge sums of money on their political advertising. For the 1992 election, it is estimated that total outlay exceeded £30 million, two-thirds of which was spent by the Conservative Party.[96] As there is no legal limit to the amount of money that may be spent on political advertising during an election, a party's advertising campaign will be restricted only by the extent of its financial resources and by its spending priorities during the campaign. Similarly, supporters of a particular party may give direct or indirect financial assistance towards advertisements, such as offering the party the use of their billboard sites.[97] Other supporters may take out their own political advertisements in the press aimed at influencing voters, such as the Institute of Directors in support of free enterprise, or the trade union NALGO (National Association of Local Government Officers) in support of more public money being spent on the National Health Service. During the 1987 and 1992 general election campaigns, the Labour Party took 102 and 65 pages of advertisements respectively in national and Sunday newspapers; the Conservatives 217 and 48 pages; and Liberal Democrats 17 and 6.5. The Green Party could afford just one small advertisement in 1987, but none in 1992. Supporters and pressure groups placing political advertisements in 1992 ranged from NALGO (73 pages) and the Institute of Directors (18) to the National Union of Teachers (4), Charter '88 (1) and the London University Student Union (0.1). The Conservatives put up 4 500 posters, Labour 2 200 and the Liberal Democrats 500.[98]

The importance of billboard posters in a party's propaganda campaign has increased recently, and far greater emphasis was given to them over newspaper advertisements in 1992 than ever before. This is because the range of their impact is considerably greater than just reaching people walking or driving past the poster in the street. It has been realised by party campaign planners that the launching of a new billboard poster constitutes a highly effective media photo-opportunity. As one member of the media put it during the run up to the 1992 campaign.[99]

The name of this particular game isn't advertising at all, it's PR. The party does a poster, sticks it up, Chris Patten or Roy Hattersley is photographed in front of it with a Caesar-like gesture towards the unveiled (unveiled!) poster, television news films it, newspapers reproduce it and, hey presto, half a million quid's worth of free advertising. Can't be bad, can it?

Sites for posters have to be booked weeks or months in advance, yet the opposition parties do not know the starting date of an election campaign until one week before. Their campaign managers therefore have to balance on the one hand not being able to find sufficient available sites in time, against on the other hand making a number of speculative bookings only to find they have wasted their money. In the case of the sites for the Conservative Party's posters, most of these were booked by the party's advertising agents three weeks before the election was announced by the Prime Minister, with the bookings being made in the name of commercial products so as not to alert the other parties of when the election would be held.[100] As the agent used by Labour for booking their billboard sites commented, 'It's an incredibly unfair system in which one party can buy thousands of sites weeks ahead under a code name, while the other parties have no idea of the election date.'[101]

The content of political advertising is often highly controversial, especially when factual claims are made about what the other parties' policies are, or what the effect of electing them into government would be. Recent general elections, especially in 1992, have resorted to highly negative campaigning tactics, like those that have been common in the USA for some time, making the potential for falsification of the opposing party's policies all the greater. It is a matter of some concern that political advertising is not bound by any rules at all that provide for the truthfulness or accuracy of claims made in the advertisements. The normal rules that apply to advertisements generally are contained in the British Code of Advertising Practice. This lays down the standards by which the British professional advertising business regulates itself, and provides machinery for complaints about inaccurate or misleading statements. 'The essence of good advertising,' the preamble to the Code states, is that, 'all advertisements should be legal, decent, honest and truthful', and 'all advertisements should be prepared with a sense of responsibility both to the consumer and to society'.[102] On any advertisements which contain assertions of fact, the Code stipulates that as a general rule, 'No advertisement, whether by inaccuracy, ambiguity, exaggeration, omission or otherwise should mislead consumers about any matter likely to influence their attitude to the advertised product.' However, the Advertising Standards Authority has seen fit to exempt political advertising from all its requirements regarding truthfulness. It says at B6.1 of the Code:

To the extent that any advertisement:
- expresses an opinion on a matter which is the subject of controversy; and
- that controversy involves issues within the areas, broadly defined, of public policy or practice,

then neither that opinion, nor any evidence which the advertisement may include in support or explanation of it, is subject to the provisions of this Code on truthful presentation.

There is a strong case for establishing some machinery to avoid the worst excesses of political advertisements which contain downright untruths. Part of the role of a new Election Commission, described elsewhere in this book,[103] might be to lay down a special Code for Political Advertising as part of its general scrutiny of fair electoral campaigning practice in future. This Code should follow the normal requirement for basic truthfulness in advertising, allowing for a wide measure of political interpretation and bias, but not so strong as to constitute a lie. Similarly, a mechanism for receiving complaints and enforcement by the Commission should be laid down in the Code.

Finally, there are some more unusual forms of advertising undertaken by zealous supporters of a political party. An increasingly common form of activity that effectively constitutes media advertising is for supporters to write letters to newspapers explaining the virtues of one party, or the evils of the other. Indeed, party campaigners actively encourage their supporters to do this. A prominent and successful example was a long letter to *The Times* published on 17 March 1992 by Sir Allen Sheppard, supported by forty-two other prominent industrialists from large commercial companies, concluding that, 'We believe businessmen should support the party which, since 1979, has been actively and successfully promoting the renewed spirit of enterprise in the British people. This spirit will bring growing prosperity to Britain in the 1990s.' A more eccentric initiative in political advertising by a supporter in 1992 was an aeroplane-trailed message in the sky greeting Neil Kinnock as he arrived at Blackpool Airport, which read, 'Get Stuffed Boyo'.

The parties' manipulation of the media

The main effort of the political parties' strategists throughout the election campaign is directed towards the manipulation of the media, and of television broadcasting in particular. Such manipulation is designed to maximise the quantity of favourable media reporting about the party, to control precisely what news or information is fed to the media, and to present to voters through the medium of television the most beneficially persuasive images of the party and its prominent figures. The current wisdom of the 'spin doctors' of all parties advising on electioneering methods is to concentrate upon the visual impact of the party and its members at least as much as upon what is said by them, and then to restrict what is said to carefully managed performances, and as far as possible avoid impromptu interviews or journalists' unrestricted questions. Finding the right photo-opportunities for the cameras is perhaps the most important of all tasks for campaign strategists. One novel feature in this respect, at the outset of the 1992 general election, was for the Conservative campaign team to utilise the announcement of the election itself, which was guaranteed to be the main news item on all television news channels, and effectively turn it into a free party political broadcast for John Major and the Conservative Party. On 11 March, all television companies were advised in the morning by the Prime Minister's office to set up their cameras outside 10 Downing Street for an important announcement by John Major. At 1.05 pm Mr Major duly stepped outside to give details of the general election date and then went on to say to the cameras:

> There will be a particularly clear choice at this general election: a Conservative Party committed to low taxation, greater individual choice, greater independence with a clear view of Britain's position in the world, or a principal opposition party committed to higher taxation for the high paid, committed, I now understand, to higher taxation for the low paid, the return of more trade union power and the return of the many policies that proved so disastrous in years gone past.

The principal method used by the national party campaigners for feeding news and information to television and newspaper journalists, in an attempt to set each day's political agenda, is the early-morning press conference held daily by the three main political parties. The institution of such party press conferences dates from Labour's first use of them in 1959, and they are now highly organised. The timing of each conference, by mutual arrangement, does not overlap. In 1992, the order of the conferences was Liberal Democrats, Labour, then Conservatives. The Liberal Democrats' conferences began at 7.15 am, then special buses were arranged to ferry journalists and cameramen to special rooms rented in Millbank by the Labour Party for the purpose, after which the media convoy took a three-minute walk round the corner to Smith Square for the Conservative conference, which generally ended around 9 am. At the conferences, a small, select group of senior party politicians face the media and deliver statements under the chairmanship of the chief campaign organiser – in 1992, Jack Cunningham for Labour, Chris Patten for the Conservatives, and Des Wilson for the Liberal Democrats. In attendance on the floor among the journalists are other party workers, activists and MPs, the presence of whom lends moral support to whatever is said by colleagues at the conference and guarantees a sympathetic audience. The fruits of these press conferences are then relayed on the day's news, especially in the morning and midday television news programmes. The rest of the day's campaigning efforts by each national party are devoted to selected senior figures appearing in different parts of the country, with transport facilities provided for journalists and camera crews, for arranged photo-opportunities and speeches, which appear on the evening news programmes.

As part of their overall attempt to control the political information and images that are fed to the electorate at campaign times, the national parties in recent years have made great efforts to curtail the freedom of press and television journalists to seek answers from candidates and MPs to questions of the journalists' (or their television companies' or newspapers') own choice. Campaign strategists in each party may also aim to control which of their party members are to be made available to the media for interview on party policy, and who will thereby be seen to be most closely associated with the image of the party in the eyes of the electorate. David Lloyd, the senior commissioning editor for news and current affairs at Channel Four, commented after the 1992 general election on the 'insidious' practice of the parties' campaign managers only allowing politicians of whom they approve on to the programmes that matter: 'In my view, the public has a right to expect that it is the broadcasters, rather than the political managers, who construct the guest list.'[104] Not surprisingly, journalists across the media have become increasingly perturbed since 1979 that they are, in fact, losing control over independent political reporting, because the parties are gaining the capacity to decide what and who should be covered as campaign news. After the 1992 general election, a report was commissioned from the International Press Institute on the views of senior media executives and political journalists; it condemned election news being controlled by the parties. In it, David Seymour, the executive editor of *Today* newspaper, said:[105]

> The problems faced during the 1992 election were similar to those of the 1987 campaign, only more so. Both Labour and the Conservatives were interested only in photo-opportunities and television 'sound bites'. No attempt was made to allow proper discussions and interviews with leading figures other than on television and, far more significantly and worryingly, there was virtually no real politics. That cannot be the way to conduct a democratic election.

The manner in which the daily press conferences have been organised in recent elections by the party organisers is symptomatic of this media complaint. The greatest source of discontent among political journalists has been the recent tendency for party chairmen or co-ordinators at the press conferences to refuse to allow supplementary questions from journalists. In other words, after the party politicians on the platform had delivered their prepared statements for the day, the chairmen then controlled tightly the questions that were permitted from the journalists in the audience, first by choosing which journalists were allowed to speak, and then usually allowing them just one question – without the opportunity to respond to or to criticise the answer given. Robin Oakley, the political editor of *The Times*, wrote in the International Press Institute report on the 1992 Election:[106]

> At the press conferences, normally chaired by Jack Cunningham for Labour and by Chris Patten for the Tories, journalists were rarely allowed supplementary questions. Any politician can fluff and bluff his way through a single awkward question with no follow-up . . . Both Mr Patten and, even more ruthlessly, Dr Cunningham, suppressed supplementaries. It was particularly irritating at the Labour press conferences, which opened with up to five statements read out by front bench spokesmen, sharply limiting the question period and allowing Dr Cunningham the excuse that it was 'selfish' for any journalists to seek to come back on an unanswered question in the limited time.

Michael Brunson, the political editor for Independent Television News, agreed, protesting also about the antisocial hours of the press conferences for journalists:[107]

> The organisation of the parties' press conferences this time around was disgraceful. The 'race to be first', which had us all turning up for the Liberal Democrats at 7.15 in the morning may have been part of Paddy Ashdown's 'healthy mind in a healthy body' approach to campaigning, but, in my view, it was an unnecessary extra burden during a very busy time . . . Labour tried, and by and large succeeded, through Jack Cunningham's chairmanship, to restrict the questioning so that no supplementaries were allowed. This in my view was totally unacceptable, especially after Labour usually insisted on their team reading out lengthy, and time-consuming, policy statements. Not allowing supplementaries meant that Labour spokespeople could get away with anodyne answers. Attempts at follow-ups were very occasionally successful – indeed Mr Kinnock himself seemed willing to take them. But more often than not such attempts brought complaints about journalists' behaviour from Dr Cunningham. The Tory press conferences were rather more relaxed, but here again, a considerable amount of time was used up with the reading out of statements. Once again, supplementaries were generally discouraged, though not with the same ruthlessness as at Labour's event, and ministers would sometimes linger for off-the-record conversations afterwards.

For the regional press, Ewen MacAskill, the political editor of the *Scotsman*, made a similar complaint, and protested further that some politicians did not even-handedly invite questions from across the spread of journalists present:[108]

The morning press conferences, particularly the Conservative one, were loaded even more in favour of the politicians than they were in 1987. The main complaint, and this applies to Labour as much as to the Conservatives, is that journalists were not allowed supplementaries. Attempts to come back at politicians when they completely ignored the original question were ruled out of order (except on those rare occasions when the politician judged the supplementary question innocuous and was happy to answer it).

Another complaint, one aimed entirely at the Conservatives, was the way that the party chairman, Chris Patten, morning after morning chose questions from a handful of select journalists – mainly ITN, the BBC, Sky [Satellite TV company] and the Fleet Street qualities – and, for the most part, ignored the rest.

Another significant way in which party campaign leaders have sought to influence media output on political reporting is to issue strong protestations about unfairness, bias or distortion in their reporting. In individual cases, no doubt, there may be some truth in the suggestion that the conclusion or effect of a particular programme offered greater exposure or perhaps a more favourable impression of one or other of the parties. But since the early 1980s the television companies have been bombarded by such claims in a calculated manner, which suggests that it is now a deliberate campaign tactic of all the main parties to remind, forcefully and constantly, television companies of the wrath that will be incurred if the companies are overly critical of the party involved, and that they are being scrutinised very closely for any indications of lack of political impartiality. The most heated attack on television bias, referring particularly to the BBC, came shortly after Norman Tebbit's appointment as Conservative Party chairman in the 1980s, the most memorable complaints being made over the reporting of the bombing of Libya by the Americans with Margaret Thatcher's assent. Undoubtedly, the effect of such attacks has been to produce a new era of self-censorship and caution in many of the BBC current affairs and news programmes,[109] as well as in the independent television companies. The salutary effect produced by threats of complaints and constant cajolery from party campaign managers therefore looks set to continue. In advance of the 1992 election, the former Conservative Party chairman, Kenneth Baker, warned in February of that year that 'the BBC has got to be very careful over the next eight to ten weeks', Jack Cunningham, Labour's campaign director, admitted that 'it's a rare day when we don't complain about radio or television', and Des Wilson was constantly complaining, from January onwards about insufficient news coverage of Liberal Democrat policies and personalities.[110]

It is certainly untrue that television and radio broadcasting as a whole has been rendered incapable of initiating unexpected issues or surprising politicians during the campaign, because of the efforts by the parties to manipulate the media. The most potent types of programme for producing surprises or upsetting politicians in elections nowadays are the live, unedited participatory studio or 'phone-in' television and radio programmes, where ordinary members of the public are given the opportunity to present questions or views to parliamentary candidates and party leaders. The television broadcaster, Peter Sissons, has said, 'What politicians fear more than anything else is a simple question from an ordinary person.'[111] One of the most famous episodes, when a senior politician was visibly rattled and caught off-guard by a simple question from a member of the public was on 24th May 1983 during a live participatory programme on the 'Nationwide' programme, on which the then Prime Minister, Margaret Thatcher, was appearing.[112]

> *Sue Lawley*: Let's go to Mrs Diana Gould in our Bristol studio. Mrs Gould, your question please.
> *Mrs Gould*: Mrs Thatcher, why when the *Belgrano*, the Argentinian battleship, was outside the exclusion zone, and actually sailing away from the Falklands, did you give the orders to sink it?

Margaret Thatcher had to suppress her evident anger at this question being posed so directly, as she was talking to an ordinary voter, rather than a member of the opposition, with millions of other ordinary voters looking on. Mrs Thatcher remarked, 'I think it could only be in Britain that a Prime Minister was accused of sinking an enemy ship which was a danger to our navy, when my main ambition was to protect the boys in our navy.' Members of the public on such programmes usually have just one simple question to ask, and they are looking for a straightforward answer. They are therefore not easily put off, and while they can be as direct or hostile to the politician as they like, the politician cannot afford to be rude back, or to tell them they do not know what they are talking about. In this case, the questioner continued:

> *Mrs Gould*: Mrs Thatcher, I am saying that it was on a bearing 280, which is a bearing just north of west. It was already west of the Falklands and therefore nobody with any imagination can put it sailing other than [away] from the Falklands.
> *Mrs Thatcher*: Mrs . . . I'm sorry, I forgot your name.
> *Sue Lawley*: Mrs Gould.
> *Mrs Thatcher*: Mrs Gould, when orders were given to sink it, and when it was sunk, it was in an area which was a danger to our ships. Now you accept that, do you?

Almost as memorable, during the 1992 campaign period, was the sight of Neil Kinnock on the 'Granada 500' programme refusing to give a straight answer to the question of whether he supported proportional representation or not. This led to the embarrassing scene at the end of the programme of him being booed and jeered by members of the audience. Also on the 'Granada 500' in 1992, the Prime Minister, John Major, was presented with the question, 'Do you seriously expect us to forgive and forget the inhumanity of the poll tax?' During the BBC's 'Election Call' he appeared to admit to one questioner that the forthcoming general election might actually lead to a hung Parliament, something the Conservative campaign team had otherwise been at pains to say would not happen and they would not contemplate. On the Liberal Democrat side, their party president, Charles Kennedy, was forced on an 'Election Call' programme to admit that their policy of raising petrol prices might create inflation.[113] While television has undoubtedly helped to bring about a more informed electorate on the political events and issues of election campaigns, it is also the case that modern electioneering has meant that there is far less direct personal contact between party politicians and the broad mass of British voters. These participatory television and radio programmes have therefore become the modern hustings of our media-dominated general election campaigns: 'They are spontaneous and unpredictable. They are the last resort of the heckler, booer and whistler . . . Their contribution to this election campaign has been to make politicians wriggle. That is democracy at work.'[114]

For many general elections past, the main party leaders have been personally cross-examined on television by a senior professional interviewer, such as Sir Robin Day (now retired), Jonathan Dimbleby, Sir David Frost and Brian Walden. In 1992, there were six different series of political interviews with John Major, Neil Kinnock and Paddy Ashdown, broadcast on the television programmes 'Panorama', 'This Week', 'Walden', 'Frost On Sunday', 'Newsnight' and 'On the Record'. However, despite the range and depth of these interviews, particularly in the last two elections, the leaders concerned were noticeably very carefully rehearsed in what they said, as well as being well-trained in avoiding difficult or embarrassing lines of inquiry. These election interviews have therefore largely lost their power to reveal anything new. To date, all attempts by broadcasters to hold a full-scale television debate between the leaders of the three main parties, in the manner of United States presidential debates since the 1960s, have been turned down by one or more of the figures involved. On 12 March 1992, at the last Prime Minister's question time in the House of Commons before the dissolution of Parliament for the election campaign, Neil Kinnock told John Major that the government's failed economic policies warranted a televised election debate, and Paddy Ashdown (understandably attracted by the prospect of equal billing on such a programme) strongly supported the idea. Amid uproar in the chamber, John Major met the suggestion with ridicule, dismissing it as a time-honoured trick of 'every party politician that expects to lose', and offering a Shakespearian quotation that 'the thread of your verbosity' was such that Mr Kinnock would let neither him nor Mr Ashdown get a word in edgeways.[115]

The efforts made by politicians to stage-manage press conferences and campaign events, concentrating upon a slick delivery of rehearsed political statements and the broadcast transmission of favourable photo-opportunities of their leaders, may be resented by some journalists in the media, but it is currently the most professional way that a party can sell itself successfully to the national electorate. Commenting on the 1987 election campaign, Patricia Hewitt, Neil Kinnock's press secretary at the time, said:[116]

> About ten days into the campaign one of the television reporters said, 'We have just realised what you are doing. You are completely manipulating us. You are stopping us writing any other story. You are dictating the agenda.' And we said, 'Well, we are doing what we think we need to do to get across our story, our message. We want to talk about health, we want to talk about the state of the economy and industry and so on.'
>
> So I do not think we were in any way stopping television from doing their job. In fact, if anything, we were making their job easier, because we made sure they got the pictures on time, of the right quality, and we made sure they got the interviews and access to Neil Kinnock and the other campaigners.

Modern general elections are fought and won through the media. The campaigning efforts of politicians will continue to be television-orientated, and it is doubtful whether journalists, however independent, should be any more free than our politicians to set the political agenda during election campaigns. A balance has to be struck between fair electioneering by the parties, allowing for accurate and impartial reporting by the broadcasters, and fair reporting and election programmes by broadcasters, allowing for the politicians and candidates themselves to present and highlight what they believe are the important political issues of the general election to put to the electorate. As far as the partisan press are concerned, the individual parties are most likely, as at the time of writing, to lobby and co-operate most closely with those newspapers who are either their supporters or else politically independent. There is little electoral capital to be made from any dealings with newspapers who are conducting their own rampantly partisan campaign in opposition to them.

THE PUBLICATION OF OPINION POLLS

The single most prominent subject for media reporting during British general election campaigns is public opinion polling on voting intentions. The practice of newspapers publishing the results of 'straw polls' on public opinion during elections can be traced back to the nineteenth century in America, one of the first known of such instances being during the 1824 presidential elections when journalists belonging to the *Harrisburg Pennsylvanian* took to the streets to question random members of the public as to which of the candidates they supported. Such polling during American election campaigns was always highly unreliable and never taken with any degree of seriousness. It was only much more recently in the USA that Dr George Horace Gallup, a professor of journalism and advertising, became the founder and pioneer of modern scientific methods of opinion polling, which have proved themselves to be highly accurate. In 1935 Dr Gallup joined the advertising agency of Young & Rubicam to apply his academic work to commercial practice, and a year later successfully predicted Franklin D. Roosevelt's victory as presidential candidate. This led to associated polling organisations being established in other countries, and in 1937 the British Institute of Public Opinion (since 1952 renamed Social Surveys (Gallup Poll) Ltd) was founded under Dr Henry Durant of the London School of Economics. This Gallup organisation's first political opinion poll was published in the *News Chronicle* on 9 March 1939. The first general election campaign where an opinion poll was published was in 1945, when Gallup, in the face of prevailing press opinion that Winston Churchill was unbeatable after winning the Second World War as Prime Minister, correctly predicted a sizeable Labour victory instead. Ever since that time, public opinion polls have been a central feature of election campaigning news. Other polling companies soon followed Gallup, notably National Opinion Polls (NOP) in 1957, Marplan Ltd in 1959, Opinion Research Centre in 1965, Market and Opinion Research International (MORI) in 1968, and Harris Research Centre in 1969.

The number of polls that have been conducted and published during election campaigns in Britain has continued to increase remorselessly. In the 29 days of the campaign in 1992, there were 57 national polls conducted by eight different polling companies and published in eighteen different newspapers or television programmes. In other words, the results of two new opinion polls were published every day of the campaign. This is the highest-ever number in any British election, and is more than double the frequency of polls taken in the 1960s. Britain is, in fact, unique among Western democracies for the saturation polling to which readers or viewers of the media are subjected.[117] This is mainly the result of the large number of mass-circulation newspapers and current affairs programmes on television in Britain, all of which feed off one another during an election campaign. Individual newspapers and television programmes will commission a number of their own political opinion polls during the campaign. This ensures them an exclusive item of news, but otherwise they will report the findings of polls commissioned and first published elsewhere. Details of the major polls during the 1992 campaign are given on pages 300–1.

From the opinion polling company's viewpoint, political polling about voting intentions is essentially the same as any other form of market research. Only around 2 per cent of Gallup's work today is taken up with political polling, which, as a commercial enterprise, is more valuable for advertising the name of the polling company than for the revenue it generates. Market research generally, of course, is all about selling commercial products, and the major clients of most of the political polling companies are private manufacturing companies and advertising agencies. Such polling routinely undertaken by polling companies is concerned with establishing levels of market demand, perceptions about leading brand names, and the impact of advertising campaigns. More recently, the parties have undertaken their own private opinion polls to gauge the effectiveness of their own political campaigns, and in what ways they could be strengthened to appeal more to voters.[118] Companies such as Gallup and Harris have a commercial vested interest in the quality of their polling during election campaigns being as accurate as possible, for it is high-profile work which will seriously affect their credibility with commercial clients if their results are seen on election day to have been in error. When the 1992 campaign was under way, Robert Waller, the research director at Harris, commented that, 'It's nerve-racking. It's commercial suicide if we're wrong.'[119] The main political polling organisations including MORI, Gallup, Harris, NOP and ICM, belong to the Association of Professional Opinion Polling Organisations (APOPO), which has a code of practice to which all members agree to conform.

Opinion polling companies now generally maintain that their findings in any particular poll will be accurate to within a margin of 3 per cent at most. The methods used in public opinion polls during election campaigns are similar to one another, although the size of the sample of people interviewed may vary, and the period of time over which interviews take place may be either one or two days. Opinion polling over two days used to be standard at election campaigns, but the number of one-day polls is steadily increasing. As Robert Waller has explained:[120]

> I am very wary of polls conducted in one day, especially for a client who demands the results by early evening. If interviewing is not conducted in the evening, how are full-time workers contacted? The 'man in the street' is not typical, but more pro-Labour than average – less likely to be in a full-time job or using private transport. Home interviewing is superior, but in the daytime a very strange sample can be drawn in-home, except at weekends.

Selecting people at random for a poll is generally based upon quota sampling of individuals drawn from across Britain. This means that if the total sample taken is 1 500, then a certain proportion of that number approached must come from around 100 different locations and be of a

Public opinion polls on voting intentions during the 1992 election campaign

Opinion polls	Date pub.	Sample size	Field dates	Con. (%)	Lab. (%)	Lib. Dem. (%)	Con. lead over Lab.
NOP/Mail on Sunday	15.3	1054	11.3	41	40	15	1
MORI/The Times	13.3	1054	11/12.3	38	41	16	−3
Harris/LWT	15.3	2186	11/12.3	37	41	17	−4
Harris/Observer	15.3	1054	11/12.3	40	43	12	−3
MORI/Sunday Times	15.3	1544	11/12.3	40	39	18	1
Harris/Express	14.3	1086	11/13.3	39	40	16	−1
NOP/Sunday Independent	15.3	2153	12/13.3	40	41	14	−1
ICM/Sunday Express	15.3	1086	13.3	39	40	16	−1
Harris/Express	17.3	1081	15/16.3	41	38	17	3
MORI/The Times	18.3	1099	16.3	38	43	16	−5
ICM/Guardian	18.3	1100	17.3	38	43	16	−5
Gallup/Daily Telegraph	19.3	984	17/18.3	40.5	38.5	18	2
NOP/Independent	19.3	1262	17/18.3	38	42	17	−4
MORI/Sunday Times	22.3	1257	18/20.3	38	41	19	−3
Harris/Observer	22.3	1096	19/20.3	40	39	17	1
ICM/Sunday Express	22.3	1115	20.3	37	42	16	−5
NOP/Sunday Independent	22.3	1004	19/21.3	38	40	16	−2
NOP/Mail on Sunday	22.3	1085	20/21.3	39	41	15	−2
Harris/Express	24.3	1077	21/23.3	43	38	15	5
Harris/ITN	24.3	2158	22/23.3	38	42	16	−4
MORI/The Times	25.3	1109	23.3	38	41	17	−3
ICM/Guardian	25.3	1096	24.3	39	40	17	−1
NOP/Independent	26.3	1326	24/25.3	39	42	14	−3

Gallup/Daily Telegraph	26.3	1092	24/25.3	40	40.5	16.5	−0.5
NMR/The European	26.3	1105	24/25.3	38	39	19	−1
MORI/Sunday Times	29.3	1292	25/27.3	38	40	20	−2
Harris/Observer	29.3	1057	26/27.3	40	38	17	−2
ICM/Sunday Express	29.3	1136	27.3	36	38	20	−2
NOP/Sunday Independent	29.3	1000	26/28.3	39	40	16	−1
NOP/Mail on Sunday	29.3	1099	27/28.3	37	41	18	−4
Harris/Express	30.3	1108	28/30.3	40	39	17	1
MORI/The Times	1.4	1126	30.3	35	42	19	−7
Harris/ITN	31.3	2152	28/31.3	35	41	19	−6
ICM/Guardian	1.4	1080	31.3	37	41	18	−4
Gallup/Daily Telegraph	2.4	1095	31.3/1.4	38	37.5	20.5	0.5
NOP/Independent	2.4	1302	31.3/1.4	37	39	19	−2
Gallup/Sunday Telegraph	4.4	1043	2/3.4	37.5	37.5	22	0
MORI/Sunday Times	4.4	1265	1/3.4	37	39	21	−2
Harris/Observer	4.4	1090	2/3.4	38	40	17	−2
ICM/Sunday Express	4.4	1139	3.4	37	39	19	−2
NOP/Sunday Independent	4.4	1006	2/4.4	38	41	17	−3
NOP/Mail on Sunday	4.4	1104	3/4.4	35	41	20	−6
ICM/Press Association	6.4	10460	31.3/3.4	36	39	20	−3
Harris/Express	7.4	1093	4/6.4	37	38	21	−1
Harris/ITN	7.4	2210	4/7.4	38	40	18	−2
MORI/'First Tuesday'	7.4	1065	6/7.4	37	40	20	−3
Gallup/Daily Telegraph	9.4	2478	7/8.4	38.5	38	20	0.5
MORI/The Times	9.4	1731	7/8.4	38	39	20	−1
NOP/Independent	9.4	1746	7/8.4	39	42	17	−3
ICM/Guardian	9.4	2186	8.4	38	38	20	0

Table 6.5[121]

certain sex, age and social class. So, most obviously, as the voting population is 48 per cent male, and 52 per cent female, these percentages should be represented in the quota. The results from these interviews across the country are fed into a central computer with reference to each interviewee's sample classification, and any gaps in any of the quotas will either need to be filled before the poll is complete or else compensated for in the weighting attributed towards the result. The polling companies aim to present their questions to members of the public in a politically neutral way, to avoid any bias towards one particular answer, and in a form of words that minimises the number of 'don't knows'. The question, 'If there was a general election tomorrow, which party would you vote for?', would appear to be less successful in obtaining a response than, 'Which party would you be most likely to vote for?' The order in which a series of questions is asked may be of importance in keeping the sample free from elements of bias. For example, it would appear that it is always best to ask the question on voting intentions before other more particular questions, so that how the respondent feels about the competence of the party leaders, or the tax policies of the parties, or more funding for the National Health Service, is not left lingering uppermost in the respondent's mind so as to prejudice his or her answer to the key question on how they will vote.

The accuracy of opinion polls

The overall level of accuracy in political opinion polling in predicting the outcome of general elections, taken as a whole since 1945, has been very high. In 1979, 1983 and 1987 the average of the final polls was comfortably within the 3 per cent margin of error.[122] However, there have been some famous cases where the opinion polling companies wrongly predicted an election result. In the USA, the pollsters suffered a huge setback in their credibility in 1948 when they consistently predicted a victory for the Republican candidate, Thomas E. Dewey, over the Democratic President, Harry S. Truman, who was seeking re-election. In 1970 in Britain, four of the five major polling companies predicted a narrow Labour Party victory, whereas in fact, Edward Heath's Conservative Party gained a 30-seat overall majority. At the 1992 general election, the polling companies had their worst day ever. All the polls throughout the campaign had consistently underestimated the level of electoral support eventually won by the Conservatives. Only one of the fifty-seven opinion polls taken over the four-week period of the election campaign put the Conservative level of support at the 43 per cent they in fact won. Of the four final polls published on general election day, one of them (ICM) predicted that the two main parties were exactly level, two (MORI and NOP) predicted a Labour lead of 1 per cent and 3 per cent respectively, and only one (Gallup) showed any

Accuracy of final opinion polls, 1945–92

Election year	Outgoing government	Number of final polls[1]	Deviation of mean estimate from share of vote (GB)					Mean errors for	
			Con.	Lab.	Lib.	Others	All parties	Con./Lab. parties	Gap between 1st and 2nd parties
1945	Coalition	1	+2	–	+1	–1	1.5	2.0	–4
1950	Labour	2	+1	–2	+2	–	1.3	1.5	–3
1951	Labour	3	+2	–4	+1	+1	2.3	3.0	–6
1955	Conservative	2	+1	–1	+1	–1	1.0	1.0	–
1959	Conservative	3	–	+1	–1	–	0.3	0.5	–1
1964	Conservative	4	+1	+1	–1	–	1.0	1.0	–
1966	Labour	3	–1	+3	–1	–	1.3	2.0	+4
1970	Labour	5	–2	+4	–1	–1	2.0	3.0	–6
Feb. 1974	Conservative	6	–	–2	+2	–	1.0	1.0	+2
Oct. 1974	Labour	5	–2	+3	–	–1	1.5	2.5	+5
1979	Labour	5	–	+1	–	–	0.3	0.5	–1
1983	Conservative	7	+3	–2	–	–1	1.5	2.5	+5
1987	Conservative	7	–1	+2	–2	–	1.3	1.5	–3
Mean 1945–87		4	+0.3	+0.2	0.0	–0.3	1.3	1.7	3.1
1992	Conservative	4	–5	+4	+1	–1	2.8	4.5	–9

Note: A final poll is defined for 1959–87 as 'any published on polling day', and for earlier elections, as any described as such. Fieldwork dates vary slightly, but for elections since February 1974 are almost always the Tuesday and/or Wednesday immediately before election day.

Table 6.6[123]

sort of Conservative lead at all, which was put at 1–2 per cent. But the level of votes cast in the polling booth on 9 April 1992 amounted to an 8 per cent margin of lead for the Conservatives over Labour. Robert Worcester said it was 'the worst result for the opinion polls since they were invented'.

Precisely how and why the opinion polls in 1992 ended at such divergence with the final result was the subject of intense speculative controversy. In the wake of the election result, all Britain's leading psephologists such as Professors Ivor Crewe, Anthony King, Dennis Kavanagh and David Butler rushed into print, producing a series of articles on how and why it happened.[124] A stunned market research industry conducted its own cantankerous post-mortem, with the aim of producing coherent reasons why opinion polls should be believed again in the future.[125] Some said that normal sampling error probably accounted for at least half the discrepancy.[126] Others believed that non-registration of voters, together with pollsters not including overseas voters in their samples, distorted their results.[127] Perhaps most controversially, the report of the Market Research Society in June 1992 argued that opinion polls have been consistently biased towards Labour for more than thirty years.[128] It gave no reasons why this should have been the case, except to speculate that the minority of people who refuse to talk to poll interviewers, or who refuse to disclose their voting intentions, are more likely to be Conservative supporters than Labour ones. The most straightforward explanation for 1992 is simply that there was a late swing of support towards the Conservatives. Certainly the opinion polls taken during the last few days of the campaign showed some decline in Labour support and a shift towards the Conservatives. But such movement was in the order of 1–2 per cent, and to account for the serious discrepancy between the opinion polls and the result on election day there would have to have been a massive 8 per cent swing during the final thirty-six hours before the voting booths closed. In an effort to gauge the extent of the late swing, the Market Research Society received evidence from ICM, MORI and NOP about their re-interview surveys (where the companies go back to people who were previously asked about their voting intentions, to question them about how they did, in fact, vote). This evidence taken together indicated a late gain for the Conservative Party of around 1.5 per cent, and a lead of 2.5 per cent over the Labour Party.[129] Even if such re-interview polls can themselves be relied upon, the late swing theory still only accounts for a quarter of the discrepancy between the opinion polls and the election result.

A single rogue opinion poll result is perfectly understandable, but what is so extraordinary about 1992 is that all the opinion polling companies, consistently throughout the campaign period and to a serious extent, pointed to a lower level of Conservative vote than that which the party went on to receive on election day. The most convincing reason for the polls' failure to predict the eventual result in 1992 is one for which the polling companies cannot wholly be blamed. It is that there was a far wider feeling of uncertainty than ever before within the country on which of the two parties was best fitted to govern, and this uncertainty was not reflected in the answers being given to the opinion poll interviewers. The British electorate nowadays, largely as a result of the mass media, is known to be far more volatile in its voting behaviour than previously.[130] Against this background, one of the most interesting opinion polls during the campaign asked its respondents not only which party they were most likely to support, but whether they had in fact yet made up their minds on which way to vote. This *Observer*/Harris poll, published on 5 April, only four days before the election, disclosed that almost a third of all voters (29 per cent) were still undecided. It seems that many such voters had supported the Conservatives previously, but now felt a distaste for the social attitudes and policies of the government. Such disenchanted Conservatives may have wished to register with the interviewer a note of protest by suggesting that they were likely to support one of the other two parties. Non-aligned moderates too may have felt ashamed at admitting they would give their electoral support to the Conservatives. Some Conservative strategists themselves suggest that, 'There is a spiral of silence, in which a crucial 2 or 3 per cent of Conservatives are reluctant to reveal their allegiance because they feel it is unfashionable.'[131] Such a tendency towards being politically correct with friends and with interviewers, but then voting according to one's pocket, might also explain why even the exit polls taken from people leaving polling booths on election day still significantly underestimated the true electoral support for the Conservatives. That voters across the country were all receiving their annual tax returns in the week prior to the general election will have helped to galvanise their minds on the impact of a new government. When it came to the critical point, therefore, it seems that a large number of these uncertain voters gave their vote to the Conservative Party, because on the one hand they believed they would receive higher tax bills and be financially worse off under Labour, and on the other hand felt that the Liberal Democrats could not possibly win the election, so a vote for them would be wasted. However, although no doubt certain theories will linger longest in the psephology textbooks to explain 'the Waterloo of the polls' in 1992, no single scientific explanation is possible. The exasperating fact is that no one will ever really know for certain the exact reasons for the extraordinary divergence between the opinion poll indications and the voting in that election campaign.

Media reporting of opinion polls

Even more important than the sheer number of opinion polls conducted and published during the election campaign, is the degree and style of prominence which is attached to them in the media's reporting of the campaign news. As far as newspapers are concerned, opinion polls were regarded as *the* most newsworthy item to be reported, more than any other topic throughout the campaign. The precise number and proportion of front-page stories in the national press devoted to opinion polls is shown below.

Front page lead stories about the General Election in daily newspapers, 1992

Topic	Number of stories	Percentage of stories
Opinion polls	35	18
Taxation/public spending	31	16
Party strategies and prospects	28	15
Party election broadcasts	18	9
PR/hung Parliament	8	4
Exhortation to vote	7	4
Fitness to govern	6	3
Challenge of Liberal Democrats	6	3
Budget/shadow budget	6	3
Health	5	3
Mortgages	4	2
Devolution	4	2
Trade unions	3	2
Tone of campaign	3	2
City opinion	3	2
Defence	–	–
'Scandal' stories	–	–
Other	24	12
Total	191	100

Table 6.7[132]

The quality of much of the newspaper reporting of the polls panders to the readers' basic sporting instinct which treats elections like a horse race and wants to know who is in the lead. On general election day in 1992, two broadsheet newspapers had identical headlines: 'POLLS PUT PARTIES NECK AND NECK'. The style of the tabloids is even racier, the following example being typical of the daily diet of campaign journalese: 'LABOUR HAS COME ROARING BACK INTO THE GENERAL ELECTION – SLASHING THE TORIES' LEAD BY MORE THAN HALF'. Opinion polls therefore are pre-eminently newsworthy items for the media. They help to sell newspapers and boost television audience ratings. As Professor Ivor Crewe has said, 'However static public opinion is, the polls enable the media to give an impression of flux, change and excitement. The more polls there are, the more true this is.'[133]

The way in which public opinion poll results are presented in television and radio news programmes, however, is substantially different from that in the press. The legal requirements upon broadcasters to be impartial and objective in reporting the election campaign has led to a more cautious and objective evaluation of the political significance that newscasters should attribute to any particular opinion poll results. The BBC guidelines for factual programmes state that, 'Opinion polls are a relevant and important factor in reporting an election campaign. The BBC's use of them must be guided by the intention not to give any party an unfair advantage.' More particularly, each poll must be placed in the context of opinion poll trends generally, and the different ways in which the result of a poll might be interpreted should be pointed out to viewers:[134]

Polls must be seen in relation to earlier published polls: they are most valuable when seen as part of a trend, a dot on the graph. The perspective should go back over the longest relevant period; in elections at least to the beginning of the campaign.

Polls which diverge sharply from a previous trend might have detected a sharp change, or they might be wrong. The audience should be apprised of both possibilities.

Prior to election campaigns, a special circular will usually be distributed to broadcasting journalists and producers, laying down a number of important ground rules for reporting opinion poll results. So in 1992, for example, the BBC circular directed newscasters not to give too much prominence to individual polls, on the basis that results are not reliable enough in detail. The importance of polling trends was emphasised, so that the report of any individual poll should be placed in the general context of what other poll results have been. Similarly, the reporting of any poll result should refer to the 'poll of polls' being maintained, being the average of all the polls taken in a given period. One controversial episode arose during the 1992 campaign, on the degree of prominence which the BBC's 'Nine O'Clock News' should give to its reporting of three new public opinion poll results issued on 31 March, all of which showed that Labour had gone into a strong lead of between 4 to 7 per cent ahead of the Conservatives. But when the BBC programmers referred the matter to John Birt, then the Corporation's Deputy Director-General, he ruled that the general guideline about avoiding prominence being given to poll results should apply, and that this Labour lead in the polls should not be the top item of the news that day. In contrast, ITN's 'Ten O' Clock News' had no such qualms and ran it as their main story. Their campaign executive producer said, 'The real test is – is it news? And without any doubt three polls showing a significant Labour lead was the big news.'[135]

Proposal for prohibition at election times

The question of whether the publication of opinion polls should be banned during election campaigns is one that has been raised regularly since the 1950s. When Labour began to conduct its own private polling to test the impact of its campaigning tactics, Aneurin Bevan accused them of 'taking the poetry out of politics'. A Speaker's Conference on Electoral Law in 1968 believed that there should be some modest restriction upon the polls, and recommended that:[136]

> There should be no broadcast, or publication in a newspaper or other periodical, of the result of a public opinion poll or of betting odds on the likely result of a parliamentary election during the period of seventy-two hours before the close of the poll.

Others have gone further, to suggest that no opinion polls should be published in the final week before the election day, or even throughout the entire four-week period of the election campaign. The Labour MP, Ray Powell, has tried to introduce several Private Members' Bills into Parliament, designed to prohibit polls being held at election time. On 24 February 1987, he received the support of a majority of MPs in the House for a First Reading of his Public Opinion Polls (Prohibition at Election Times) Bill, but no further time was allocated by the government for its discussion.[137] Several other countries, including Australia, France and Portugal, have legislated against the rising tide of public opinion polls that have otherwise engulfed contemporary Western democratic elections.

There are basically three lines of argument behind the proposal to ban opinion polls during elections. First, it has been said that they are essentially unreliable sources of information. Errors can be made in the conduct of the poll, and a distorted interpretation is too readily placed upon them in the press. As Ray Powell put the point in presenting his Bill, shortly before the 1987 election campaign began:[138]

> In recent weeks we have been subjected to all sorts of political fortune-telling which is about as accurate as the palmist on the pier. Is it too much to ask that for just three or four weeks we should be spared the peddling of those pointless predictions? Opposition to the Bill and the protestations that I have received have come mainly from interested parties, press barons and pollsters who obtain rich pickings from attempting to predict the results. It is all too easy to manipulate random sampling to ensure that the result is one that will boost circulation or stimulate further interest and assignments for the pollster. Nevertheless, we all appreciate that on many occasions it is the press which deliberately distorts some of the fair and reasonably conducted polls.

The second objection to the opinion polls is the impact they are believed by many to have in shaping voting behaviour. People vote in the context of which party they believe will win the election, and within their constituency in the context of which of the three main parties stand a realistic chance of winning the seat. Certainly, floating or tactical voters are likely to be deterred from voting for a candidate they would otherwise support if they are convinced that person does not stand any chance at all of winning. This may or may not be regarded as a poor way of exercising a democratic preference, even if the opinion polls relied upon were accurate. But if voters are being influenced directly by erroneous information, as proved to be the case in 1970 and 1992, then this might be considered doubly corrupting to the electoral system. In Ray Powell's view, the publication of opinion polls is increasingly not just predicting the results of general elections, but determining them:[139]

> The problems of reliability and validity of polls would not have any wider political significance if there were not compelling evidence to suggest that polls directly influenced the election results in 1983. The system of tactical voting needs special consideration. It is highly likely that opinion poll results could persuade voters not to cast a vote for the favourite party but to use it to produce the most desired or least objectionable outcome. If we are to preserve the true democratic process of electing a government by the majority accepting the presentation of political parties' policies, we must ensure that pollsters are not the deciding factor and that they are not allowed to sway electors to vote for a party, the policies of which are not liked, just to keep out another party that is liked even less. Tactical voting is encouraged by the present applied system. Until the electorate votes according to conscience, principle and the policies presented, uninfluenced by bizarre pollster predictions, we are allowing the franchise won for us after a considerable struggle by former generations to be lost to the fancies and favourites of the few large influential pollster organisations.

The final and most powerful argument against opinion polls during a campaign period is that they distract the media's attention away from the proper issues they should be reporting, namely the range of public policies being advocated by the respective parties, and the differences between the personnel and policy programmes of the parties upon which electors will be asked to choose a preference on the day of the general election.

Resistance to any such reform restraining the media's reporting of public opinion polls is founded upon concepts of freedom of expression, the freedom of the press, and the fundamental right of all citizens to impart and receive information. Such sentiments were voiced in the House of Commons against Ray Powell's Bill; for example, by the Conservative MP, Colin Moynihan, later a government minister, who said that:[140]

The banning of polls would be deeply detrimental to the freedom of the press . . . Such a ban would treat the electorate like sheep. Ultimately, it must be for the electorate to decide how to use the information available to them. To ban opinion polls during election would be a fundamental move away from freedom of information in our society.

Many opponents of the proposal say that a prohibition on publishing opinion polls would be impracticable and ineffective. It is argued that the press would still make claims about who appeared to be winning the election, but on the basis of guesswork or information considerably less reliable than the opinion polls. The press might compensate for the loss of reporting direct poll findings by relying on the results of the parties' canvass returns. Unless the holding as well as the publishing of opinion polling was prohibited, the media and politicians might still commission their own polling and insert their findings into the innuendo of their reporting or political rhetoric (and the media in other countries would be free to hold and publish poll findings around Europe and the USA which could be read by British travellers abroad). But prohibiting even the holding of opinion polling would mean a deeper in-road into civil liberty, and also serve to deprive the parties themselves of the principal means by which they at present gauge the impact and success of their own election campaigning, and make calculations about how best to adapt the effectiveness of their political campaigning.

The banning of opinion polls at election times therefore runs contrary to the freedom and independence of the press and broadcasters to report what they believe is newsworthy and important, and neither would such a prohibition necessarily be in the political interests of politicians. Added to this, most voters find the poll results to be very interesting, and would disapprove of not being allowed to read them. The MORI 'State of the Nation' poll in March 1991 showed that only 21 per cent of respondents supported banning opinion polls during election campaigns, with 74 per cent being opposed to this. Against such a background, it is hard to maintain that it would be in the public interest to bring in legislation to effect a ban at election times. A Hansard Society report in 1991 unanimously opposed any restriction on opinion polling,[141] and in 1985 an international Council of Europe inquiry on the same issue, whose report was accepted by the Parliamentary Assembly in Strasbourg, had concluded that no controls of polls at election times were desirable, appropriate or workable.[142] We may conclude that public opinion polls have become a nuisance and a distraction at election times, but they are just one part of the technological revolution used by the media and in modern electioneering which has transformed the type and quantity of political information that is fed to the voters. The way forward is to encourage the efforts of the market research and opinion polling professional bodies to ensure that polling methods are upheld to their highest standards, and for the media watch-dogs to maintain and keep under review their codes of practice and guidelines for the manner in which the results of opinion polls should be properly reported. Only if the opinion polling companies fail to regain their credibility after the 1992 débâcle, and if the media come to be perceived as abusing poll results in performing their crucial role of reporting the election campaign, will any experiment in the prohibition of opinion polls become likely.

7 The Financial Affairs of the Political Parties

PARTIES, MONEY AND ELECTIONS

Money is of crucial importance to the election campaigning efforts of the political parties. Not only are there the permanent costs involved in maintaining the central and regional party organisations, but modern methods of political campaigning and election propaganda have become increasingly expensive. Fighting a successful general election campaign in the late twentieth century means spending huge amounts of money on matters ranging from employing the best public relations and marketing agencies, to buying massive quantities of advertising space in the national press and on public billboards, to hiring top film directors and camera crews in the production of party election broadcasts. Political parties in the United Kingdom derive the finance for their work outside Parliament, including that used for their election campaigning expenses, almost exclusively from membership fees and voluntary donations. Clearly, a party which is better funded than its rivals has a considerable advantage at general elections. The more money a political party has at its disposal, the more staff can be hired in organising and administering the election campaign; more and better office facilities and technology can be used in planning the campaign and for special electioneering efforts such as direct-mail canvassing; more and better advertising space can be bought; more and better public relations, marketing, advertising and media agencies and staff can be hired; and more and better transport and communications systems can be used to advantage during the election campaign. In short, a rich party has a greater purchasing power over the means of political persuasion which serve to influence how electors may cast their votes. It is well known that throughout the twentieth century the Conservative Party has been substantially better off financially than any of the other political parties. During the period between the two general elections in the 1980s, the Conservatives received a total of £42.6m compared to Labour's income of £31.4m, giving the Conservative Party an advantage of £11.2m to spend on election propaganda. At the 1987 general election, the Conservatives were able to spend £9m on their campaign (£2m of which was devoted to a final bombardment of national advertising in the week before polling day), with Labour spending £4.2m on its campaign expenses and the Alliance £1.9m. At the 1992 general election, the Conservatives were able to spend £10.1m, Labour £7.1m, and the Liberal Democrats £2.1m.[1]

Despite the public importance of political parties, no legislative framework has ever been established in Britain to regulate their financial affairs. There is no legal obligation upon the parties to publish accounts showing details of their income and expenditure, and there is no law requiring the parties to disclose the names of the individuals and companies who give them large gifts of money. There are no public subsidies of money given to the parties to help them in the performance of their work outside Parliament. The parties are free from restrictions on donations coming to them from abroad, and there is no limit on the size of a donation which any individual person or company may choose to make. This vacuum of legal principle regulating political finance in Britain has, not surprisingly, led to a number of major controversies. Both the major parties have regularly accused one another of being institutionally beholden to special interests. The Conservatives claim that the Labour Party is in the pocket of the trade union movement, which provides the majority of its funding; and Labour accuses the Conservative Party of being the stooge of big business, whose companies and wealthy industrialists within Britain and abroad provide most of the Tory central office's finances. Many have argued that it is unfair that the Conservatives have the greatest financial resources with which to mount their election campaigns. The Labour Party always has less funds at its disposal than do the Conservatives, and the Liberal Democrats are severely financially disadvantaged in competing at elections, with the newer parties such as the Greens being barely able to survive. All the opposition parties currently advocate a system of state funding of political parties to help promote a fairer electoral contest, and there has been mounting concern in the 1990s about the propriety of some very large donations being made to the Conservative Party from abroad. All this has contributed to a general level of public disquiet about the financial affairs of political parties, giving rise to a number of important proposals for reform being put forward by parliamentarians and independent committees of inquiry.

THE FINANCIAL RESOURCES OF THE POLITICAL PARTIES

Although there is no legal requirement for the parties to produce financial accounts regarding their income, they do voluntarily publish descriptions of their finances each year. The table on page 314 gives an indication of the general level of total income received by each of the three main political parties over the period since 1975. The form of the financial accounts published by each of the political parties differs considerably. The Labour Party produces its financial affairs for public inspection in the form of a detailed Statement of Account presented by the National Executive Committee to the annual Party Conference each September. This is generally around eighteen pages in length, and includes a balance sheet

Total income of the main political parties, 1975–92 (£m)

Accounting year	Conservative	Labour	Liberal
1975–6	1.9	1.4	0.1
1976–7	2.1	1.5	0.1
1977–8	2.8	1.5	0.2
1978–9	3.4	2.1	0.2
1979–80	5.6	3.1	0.6
1980–1	3.2	2.8	0.2
1981–2	4.1	3.7	1.2
1982–3	4.8	3.9	1.8
1983–4	9.4	6.2	2.4
1984–5	4.3	4.2	1.3
1985–6	5.0	4.9	1.5
1986–7	8.9	6.1	1.6
1987–8	15.0	10.1	3.0
1988–9	8.6	6.2	1.5
1989–90	9.1	7.9	1.1
1990–1	13.0	9.3	1.0
1991–2	22.0	12.2	0.9

Table 7.1[2]

showing the assets and liabilities of the party, a statement of income and expenditure for the accounting year, and a breakdown of how the money has been spent on the party's different activities. The Liberal Democrats make a financial statement publicly available at the end of each calendar year, of a similar length and degree of detail to that contained in the Labour document. The Conservative Party published no accounts at all between 1979 and 1984, since when they have made available a 3-page memorandum simply outlining general income and expenditure for the year, but without a balance sheet. The lack of detailed information in the Conservative accounts provoked fierce criticism from individuals within the party as well as from Labour and Liberal Democrat opponents, and has resulted in a longer report being produced.[3]

A breakdown of the different kinds of income received by the Labour and Conservative parties immediately prior to the 1992 general election campaign is given in Tables 7.2 and 7.3 opposite. The figures for the Labour Party are condensed from the published details contained in their financial statement to the 1992 party conference. This shows that their money is held in three different accounts, being a general fund, a general election fund (since 1987 mainly being financed from a proportion of trade union affiliation fees being transferred to it) and a business plan (established in 1988 to develop fundraising and membership initiatives). The Labour Party's own estimate in 1993 of its expected recurrent total annual income during the 1990s is approximately £12.75m.[4]

Labour Party income, prior to General Election, 1992 (£000s)

	1991	1990
General fund income		
Trade union affiliation fees	4 321	4 176
Constituencies affiliation fee	613	737
Parliamentary grant	338	300
Donations and fund-raising	917	901
Other	749	383
Total	6 948	6 497
Total income: all funds		
General fund total	6 948	6 497
General Election fund (incl. mainly trade union affiliation fees)	3 532	1 915
Business plan fund	1 692	930
	£12 172	£9 342

Table 7.2

The breakdown, such as it is, of income received by the Conservative Party in the year immediately preceding the 1992 general election is given below. Their income account is shown exactly as published.

Conservative Party income, prior to General Election, 1992 (£000s)

	1991/2	1990/1
Donations	19 070	10 556
Constituency contributions	1 288	1 281
Other income	1 651	1 205
	£22 009	£13 042

Table 7.3

The financial accounts of the Liberal Democrats show that they receive a very much lower income than either the Conservative or Labour parties. In non-general election years their income is currently a little over £1m, but this was boosted by donations in 1992 prior to the election to a figure of around £2.5m. The majority of the Liberal Democrats' income is derived from its membership, through subscriptions and donations. In 1991 the membership fees contributed £901 691 of income, with other sources of income including donations adding up to £697 753, plus an additional £444 551 being paid directly into a special election fund.

Labour Party funding

The principal source of funding for the Labour Party comes from the trade unions. Throughout the twentieth century, trade unions have regularly contributed sums of money amounting to between 50 and 90 per cent of the Labour Party's finances every year, including special donations being made towards Labour's general election campaign.[5] The bulk of this income is received by way of fees that are paid to the party's head office by all trade unions affiliating themselves to the Labour Party. In 1991, the affiliation fees paid by trade unions amounted to £4 321 000 being paid into their general fund, and £3 168 000 going into Labour's general election fund. Another important form of party income from the trade unions is through the financial support that individual unions may choose to give to particular constituency parties. This perhaps means that a substantial part of the affiliation fees paid by all constituency parties to head office may, in fact, be coming indirectly out of trade union funds. The sponsorship of parliamentary candidates is a widely practised form of financial assistance to the party. At the time of writing, 152 Labour MPs in the House of Commons are sponsored by a trade union, the level of financial sponsorship typically comprising a grant of between £2 000 and £3 000 towards the MP's general election expenses, plus £600 being paid annually direct to his or her constituency party.

There has been a long history of controversy surrounding trade union funding of the Labour Party. The Conservatives have always been alarmed at the organised machinery of the trade unions enabling mass individual donations to be used to support the political and election campaign expenses of their Labour opponents, and have equally harboured the suspicion that individual trade union members do not in all cases want to donate their money to Labour politicians but are pressurised into doing so. That the trade unions have always wished to fund the Labour Party is, however, natural, since the very origin of the party (founded in 1900 as the Labour Representation Committee) stemmed from a resolution of the Trades Union Congress that there should be a group of political representatives of the trade union and labour movement sitting in the House of Commons.[6] The increasing success with which their candidates were elected to the Commons in 1903, 1906 and 1910, followed by their participation in the wartime coalition government under David Lloyd George during 1915–18, caused the party to adopt its Labour Party constitution in 1918, with a purpose broadened from that of being essentially a pressure group within the legislature, to being a genuinely national party seeking to form the government. Within Labour's federal organisational structure, the trade unions have continued to play an important, sometime decisive, role in helping to select candidates and leaders to sit in the House of Commons, and in helping to shape the national policies of the party within the National Executive Committee and at the annual Party Conferences.

The legal principles and procedures that govern trade union donations to the Labour Party have had a chequered history. The party was dealt a devastating blow in 1910 when the legality of the arrangements whereby trade unions financed Labour MPs – by compulsory levies upon all members of the union – was challenged in the courts in the case of *Amalgamated Society of Railway Servants* v. *Osborne*.[7] The House of Lords held unanimously that collecting and administering funds for political purposes were *ultra vires* the power of trade unions. Herbert Asquith's Liberal government facilitated the return of trade union donations to Labour in its historic Trade Union Act 1913. A new restriction, however, was placed upon trade union financing arrangements, through the Act's requirement for a special political fund to be created by each union, into which the levy from each member would go, and from which payments for political purposes would be made. The Act also made it possible for individual members of the union to 'contract out' of the political levy, if they so wished. Shortly after the return of a Conservative administration in the 1920s, an amending Trade Disputes and Trade Union Act 1927 made union arrangements for collecting the political levy from members much more difficult, by requiring that all members of the union must expressly agree to contribute (or 'contract in') to the scheme for political donations. As a result, the proportion of union membership contributing to political funding dropped from 75 per cent in 1925 to 48 per cent in 1938. The next Labour government, formed after the 1945 general election at the end of the Second World War, immediately abolished this Conservative procedure, restoring in 1946 the former system of 'contracting out' which has remained the basis of union political contributions ever since.

The Trade Union and Labour Relations (Consolidation) Act 1992 now regulates the legal controls over trade union donations to the Labour Party. This Act consolidates two significant new provisions originally created by Margaret Thatcher's administration in the Trade Union Act 1984. The first is that the resolution for the existence of a political fund in any trade union must be confirmed by a ballot of all union members at least once every ten years. If the resolution lapses without renewal, or is otherwise defeated, no further collection of a political levy from union members can be made.[8] Second, trade union spending, which is to be treated as political objects expenditure (and which must therefore must be met from the political fund of the union), has been broadened. It now includes not only spending incurred in connection with parliamentary candidature, the maintenance of an MP or the holding of events or production of advertisements, the main purpose of which is intended to persuade people to vote for a political party, but also any 'expenditure of money on any contribution to the funds of, or on the payment of expenses incurred directly or indirectly by, a political party' and 'on the provision of any service or property for use by or on behalf of any political party'.[9]

The size of financial donations made by individuals and commercial companies to the Labour Party is limited. Precisely who are the people or companies making over such gifts of money is not revealed in the party's accounts, as with the practice of the Conservatives and Liberal Democrats. However, party officials have said that up to 1992 only fifteen people had contributed more than £10 000 each, with only one person donating over £40 000.[10] Robert Maxwell, the businessman and *Daily Mirror* proprietor, gave the Labour Party a donation of £31 000. He handed over this cheque publicly in front of news television cameras, as a gesture to match the voluntary collection that had just been made at the annual Party Conference.[11] Donations made by boards of directors of commercial companies to the Labour Party would appear to be very small. A recent analysis of company political donations showed that not a single company had donated in excess of £200 to Labour between 1 January 1991 and 31 March 1992, being the period immediately prior to the general election.[12]

The proportion of Labour's total income derived from trade union sources has been in marked decline for many years. In 1973, trade union affiliation fees still amounted to 80 per cent of the Labour Party's total income, but by 1982 this proportion had dropped to 72 per cent, and in the accounting year prior to the 1992 general election, trade union fees accounted for just 54 per cent of Labour's income.[13] The principal reason for this decline has been the fall in the level of trade union affiliations, reflecting a fall in the number of trade union members generally across the country. It seems certain that the Labour Party of the future will never again be able to rely upon trade union funding to the same extent as it has in the past. As a result, the national party has had to make efforts to increase its individual membership and expand its fundraising activities. The party established a business plan in 1988 with the specific objective of broadening the income base of the party by developing fundraising, membership initiatives and financial services, and other initiatives, to pay for the party at the time of general elections and to provide a continuous stream of income to the party thereafter. Money held in the business fund account is used to set up new fundraising initiatives, the income from those projects being recycled so that a broader base of fundraising is built up to be utilised at general election time. Much of the present work under Labour's business plan is devoted to direct-mail appeals, telephone fundraising, and fundraising dinners and social events. Shortly before the 1992 general election a high-profile fundraising campaign was launched by the national office, involving the distribution of leaflets to as many homes around the country as possible, and placing notices in the press, as part of a nationwide appeal for people to join the party as members and give a donation to help towards the Labour Party's chances of victory at the coming election. More ambitious fundraising dinners have been organised, such as the £500-a-head Spring Gala Dinner in 1992 held at the Park Lane Hotel in London, which was attended by a large number of celebrities and businessmen, who were able to mingle with the then Labour leader, Neil Kinnock, and many other Labour politicians. This event alone raised in excess of £200 000 towards funding Labour's 1992 general election campaign, and while controversial in certain quarters (some accusing the organisers of being 'champagne socialists'), is very likely to be repeated. Under Labour's business plan, the party is also selling financial services, including credit card facilities and insurance policies, and a football pools project is being set up.

Conservative Party funding

From the minimal detail made available publicly by Conservative Central Office, it is difficult to be precise about the sources of financial donations which are made to the party. The official explanation for Conservative funding given by party officials has always been, and continues to be, that the backbone of the party's finances comes from voluntary fundraising activities within the constituencies. The Conservative chairman, Sir Norman Fowler, in 1993 described the sources of Conservative funding to a House of Commons Select Committee in the following terms:[14]

The greatest part of the funding of the Conservative Party is raised from voluntary donations to Constituency Associations ... Unlike other parties, there is no minimum contribution for joining the Conservative Party. Members are encouraged to give according to their means. There is no national membership list for the party, but it is generally agreed that the total individual membership of the Conservative Party is larger than that of the other political parties combined. That in itself is a key reason for the party's success in fundraising and elections.

The traditional picture painted by the party, therefore, is one of an essentially membership-driven form of party funding, where Conservative supporters within each constituency meet to organise summer fêtes, and wine and cheese parties, with participants contributing what they can to the Conservative cause.

The reality, however, is that the Conservative Party has always relied heavily on substantial funding from commercial companies, together with large personal gifts from wealthy industrialists. The Conservatives' published accounts do not distinguish between income from individuals and companies, making it difficult to know the extent of their financial reliance upon public corporations. But it is possible to discover when the directors of a company have donated more than £200 to a political party out of company assets because the directors are obliged under the terms of the Companies Act 1985 to declare such a gift in their annual report to shareholders.[15] From a scrutiny of Company House records, where annual shareholders' reports are filed, it seems that between 1983 and 1987 around a half of the Conservative Party's income was derived from company donations.[16] More recently, between 1 January 1992 to 31 March 1993, including the period of the 1992 general election campaign, there were 240 company donations of £200 or more given to the Conservative Party (compared with two to the Liberal Democrats, and none to the Labour Party). The top eleven donations made by commercial companies in this period were £130 000 by United Biscuits; £124 500 by Taylor Woodrow; £115 000 by Hanson; £102 000 by Glaxo; £100 000 by P&O; £100 000 by Rothmans International; £80 500 by Forte; £80 000 by Allied Lyons; £79 000 by Caledonia Investments; £70 000 by Barings; and £70 000 by Scottish & Newcastle Breweries. The largest-ever corporate donation given to a political party is believed to be the £200 000 given in 1991 by the Midlands property developer V & P Midlands to the Conservative Party. The previous largest corporate donation given to the Conservatives was the sum of £167 000 received from by the Yorkshire-based Hartley Investment Trust. Additionally, the Conservative Party has often received assistance towards their election campaigns in non-monetary ways, such as the use of advertising sites, or secondment of company staff, such as that provided prior to the 1992 general election by the public relations group Shandwick, headed by Peter Gummer, the brother of the Cabinet minister and Secretary of State for the Environment, John Gummer.[17] The direct cost of Shandwick's secondment of two executives in the run up to the 1992 general election was calculated to be £101 000 in the company's annual report.

The proportion of the Conservative Party's annual income that is derived from company donations appears to have dropped significantly over the early 1990s. Total donations to the party in the four years prior to the 1992 general election, according to Conservative accounts, came to £6.7 million in 1988/89, £7.1 million in 1989/90, £10.6 million in 1990/91 and £19.1 million in 1991/92. Yet contributions of £200 or more from commercial companies over the same period, it has been calculated from Companies House records, amounted to £3.5 million in 1989, £2.9 million in 1990/91, £2.8 million in 1991 and £2.9 million in 1992. This means that there is now a markedly widening gap between donations coming from British commercial companies and from other sources. Undoubtedly the reason for the relative decline in company donations over this period has much to do with the economic recession, making it much more difficult for businesses to justify gratuitous donations to political causes. Many companies that have previously given substantial sums of money to the Conservatives, such as Peter Palumbo's property development company Rugarth Investment Trust, which donated £156 000 prior to the 1987 general election, failed to make financial donations in 1992.[18]

During much of 1993, a heated controversy raged in Parliament and in the press surrounding the undisclosed sources of Conservative funding. If company donations had gone into a relative decline, from where were the unaccounted-for millions being given towards the Conservative general election campaign coming? The legitimate curiosity of opposition politicians and the national newspapers (as well as some dissident Conservatives)[19] was further aroused by a series of disclosures about a number of very large individual donations that had been made to the Conservative Party in recent years, including some from overseas.[20] Perhaps most sensationally, the party is alleged to have received £440 000 from the Cypriot businessman, Asil Nadir,[21] and the huge sum of £2 million from John Latsis, a Greek shipping and oil magnate.[22] The investigations by the House of Commons Home Affairs Select Committee[23] into the funding of political parties raised the political temperature even higher, and on 22 June a deeply acrimonious debate took place in the Commons on the subject of political finance, in which Labour's then deputy leader, Margaret Beckett, accused the Conservative government of exuding an 'atmosphere of sleaze' and 'odour of corruption',[24] with the Conservative Cabinet minister, David Hunt, accusing the Labour Party of 'hypocrisy' and being 'a parasite living off trade union funds'.[25] Financial magazines such as *Business Age* sought to know the answer to the 60 per cent and rising discrepancy between company and total donations, which was described as 'the black hole at the heart of Tory Party finances – a gap in the accounts that remains inexplicable even to senior Party members'.[26] It was further estimated in the press that the Conservative Party must have received as much as £7 million of its income in the year 1991/2 from overseas sources.[27] If correct, then two-thirds of Conservative Central Office's money spent on the 1992 general election campaign came from unidentified foreign sources.

What is the motivation behind large donations made by boards of directors or rich industrialists to a political party? The Conservative leadership maintains that the reason is simply that their party is a good cause, and that the money is handed over in the same spirit as with any charitable donation. Directors may want to contribute to Conservative funding, according the party chairman, Sir Norman Fowler, 'because of the beneficial effects to the economy, and to their company, of the re-election of a Conservative government.'[28] A typical company director's justification for making donations to the Conservative Party out of company's assets might be taken from Sir Derrick Holden-Brown comments in 1990:[29]

> The key criteria is the long term interests of our shareholders . . . Now, we believe that the Conservative Party policies offer the best chances of an economic climate in which our business can prosper. And that is why we have supported the Conservative Party.

Looked at another way, many commercial companies are most concerned that the Labour Party does not win a general election. According to the former Conservative treasurer, Lord McAlpine, 'They do not give to the Tories because they love them. They hate the Labour Party – they just think they are an absolute disaster.'[30] The Cabinet minister, David Hunt, during the Commons debate on party funding in June 1993 said that, 'It is striking that there is no obvious queue of enterprises or entrepreneurs waiting to fund the Labour Party.'[31]

However, apart from any affinity of general principle and outlook between big business and the Conservative Party, there may be further business and personal attractions in making large donations to the party in government. People who make very large donations can expect to be courted by party officials, whose fundraisers will be working on extracting further gifts for the party's accounts. Such donors might hope for, and receive, personal access to top members in the party, including Cabinet ministers and even the Prime Minister himself. At the very least, donors of large sums will be invited to lunches and dinners, where they can meet leading figures in the party, and personal interviews and meetings may follow. The opportunity for a businessman to make personal representations to influential politicians who exercise governmental decision-making powers affecting national industries is highly attractive, even if it is accepted that British ministers will not allow themselves to be influenced by the corporate or vested interests of individual donors. Whether or not individual governments or ministers have been influenced in this way is a subject of much party political rhetoric. Labour's Margaret Beckett argued in the Commons debate on party funding in June 1993 that 'the influence that such secret donations buy on the policy of the British government' was 'a minor scandal'. By way of example, she alleged, first, that the Conservative government's generous tax treatment of offshore trusts had some connection with the fact that it was through such trusts and accounts that money was being channelled into Conservative Party funds from overseas, and, second, that the government's refusal to ban tobacco advertising, against all medical advice, had some connection with large donations being received by the Conservative Party from tobacco companies.[32]

A different motivation behind some donations may be to favour the chances of a member of the board of the donor company receiving one of the top honours of a knighthood or peerage, grants of which are in the personal gift of the party leader in office at 10 Downing Street.[33] Such honours and titles are not only highly gratifying personally for the individual recipient, but they may also carry some commercial value for the company, in that they clothe the knight or peer in question with the aura – particularly to foreign businessmen – of being regarded officially in Britain as a very important person, close to and influential in the corridors of power, and therefore a desirable person with whom to do business. During the House of Commons debate on party funding in 1993, the Margaret Beckett asserted that, 'There is a remarkable coincidence in the placement of honours and donations to the Conservative Party.'[35] She went on to list the top ten company donors to the Conservative Party since 1979, and show the level of coincidence over that period with titles, 7 peerages and 8 knighthoods, being awarded to directors of those companies.[34] It was further calculated by the Labour Party, in giving evidence to the House of Commons Home Affairs Committee, that between 1979 and 1993 there were 18 peerages and 82 knighthoods given to industrialists connected to 76 companies which had given money totalling over £17 million to the Conservative Party or related bodies.[35] Few can doubt that there is indeed a high correlation between those companies that gave large donations to the Conservative Party and honours which are distributed to one or more of the directors of the company. Earlier in Britain's history, honours were openly sold by the Crown as a source of revenue, and even during the twentieth century, David Lloyd George, during his premiership between 1916 and 1922, is known to have arranged, via his accomplice Maundy Gregory, for the sale of hundreds of honours for financing his political fund, the going rate for the top honours being £20 000 for a knighthood; between £20 000 and £40 000 for a baronetcy; and up to £100 000 for a peerage. Within the six years up to 1922, he awarded 25 000 OBEs, 481 knighthoods, 130 baronetcies and 26 peerages.[36] This scandal led to a Royal Commission and the Honours (Prevention of Abuses) Act 1925 which made it an offence either to solicit or to offer for sale any honour or title. Critics of the operation of the modern-day honours system do not suggest that open arrangements are made for the sale of honours, but it is widely accepted that substantial political donations buy goodwill and substantially enhance the likelihood of being considered for an honour, and the overall prospects of receiving one. The Labour MP, Robin Cook, expressed this view, when arguing the connection between honours and political donations with a Conservative opponent in the House of Commons:[37]

> Let us be clear and fair to the Right Hon. Gentleman. The charge that he must answer is not that he ever arranged with the noble Lords to meet around the back of a motorway service station to pick up his bung and hand over the gong. The charge is much more urbane. Word gets around that the chances of a peerage or knighthood are generously multiplied by generous donations to the Conservative Party.

The *Times* newspaper in 1992 contained a leading article on the honours system entitled 'Baubles and Bribes'. It attacked the honours system for being 'a parody of honour and an insult to those members of the community who truly merit national recognition', adding that among its multifarious purposes, 'Party funds need replenishing other than from taxes, and the *de facto* sale of honours achieves this.'[38] Even more powerfully, an earlier commentary on the honours system, by Adam Raphael, expressed the opinion that:[39]

> The rates may have changed with inflation, but in essence not much else has. Of course, the award of honours is nowadays conducted with slightly more discretion. But the correlation between those who give large sums of money and those who receive high political honours remains disturbingly close. The whiff of corruption is such that it is now acknowledged at the highest levels in Whitehall that the current procedures are unsatisfactory and will have to be changed.

These aspersions that have been cast upon the funding of the Conservative Party, or the purity of donors' intentions in making gifts of money, have been robustly cast aside by Conservative spokesmen. The Conservative chairman, Sir Norman Fowler, said in a debate on party funding in the House of Commons that, 'In the Conservative Party, no donor – large or small – receives any influence or favours in return for a donation.'[40] Addressing the Home Affairs Select Committee in 1993, he referred to four principles which guided the terms upon which the Conservative Party accepted financial gifts:[41]

> We have very strict rules that we refuse to accept any donations with strings attached. We refuse to accept any donation which we have a reason to believe contains illegally maintained monies. We refuse to accept money from a foreign government. We refuse to accept any donation of which we do not know the source.

THE REFORM OF FINANCIAL DONATIONS TO THE PARTIES

Statutory accounting and the public disclosure of large donations

There is a powerful case behind the suggestion that the financial affairs of political parties should be open to public inspection. Currently the accounting practices of the three major parties differ widely, and there would be a considerable benefit to the public's understanding of their finances if annual accounts were required to be drawn up in a prescribed statutory form, fully audited and covering a similar financial year. An essential component in any reforming legislation in this area would need to be the requirement that the parties disclose in their accounts the sources of all large donations made to them over the year.

Such legal requirements for disclosure of sources of party funding are common among Western democracies.[42] In Germany, each party is required to publish annual financial reports, and to deliver a copy to the President of the Bundestag (the federal Parliament).[43] The names of all individual donors who contribute DM20 000 (£8 000) or more must be disclosed. In the USA, a register of all political contributions has to be drawn up and made open to public inspection. In Canada, there is an obligation to reveal income and expenditure details, together with the names of all sources of donations in excess of Can $100.[44] France, the Netherlands and Greece all have Acts of Parliament requiring the publication of annual financial accounts by political parties. In Australia, all election contributions and expenses must be accounted for publicly, and annual accounts must be published, together with a list of all donations over A$100.[45]

The constitutional logic behind public disclosure laws in the world, of course, is that political corruption thrives on secret financial gifts. Political donations are not in themselves corrupt, but they may be corrupting. Politicians who receive a large donation for electioneering purposes from an individual or company may be tempted to treat that person or business differently from others, both out of gratitude and in the hope of further gifts of money. Britain is fortunate in possessing among the highest levels of integrity in public affairs of any democracy in the world, and its political life has been spared the corruption scandals that have so regularly occurred elsewhere, even within Europe. Nevertheless, Britain's past and present good fortune in this respect is not a reason against establishing constitutional safeguards preventing a possible future decline in public integrity. The principal advantage in Britain of new legislation requiring disclosure would be to remove any suspicions or unfounded allegations about improper influences operating in public life, and thus help to maintain the public credibility of the political and electoral system in the eyes of the voters.

A second principle supporting disclosure is that if voters are to exercise an informed choice at elections, they have a legitimate right to know who is financially underwriting the political parties competing for political office. For most observers, the association between politician and financial supporter is clearly not of inconsiderable significance in terms of possible degrees of influence and formulation of policy by the parties. Party politics is all about pressures and influences, members and supporters. Everyone accepts that individual parties will tend to advance the interests of special groups and interests within the community with whom similar economic and social objects are shared, particularly where the proximity of interest is such that financial and other support is given to the party. Electors cast their votes in the light of these associations, and in the knowledge that the party that wins the general election is likely to promote those interests and be generally more indulgent and responsive to its own supporting individuals and organisations. The important point here is that pressures and influences on political parties, particularly those that are born of financial interest, lose their claim to be democratic and a legitimate part of the political process if they operate secretly, without the knowledge of the ordinary men and women who are being asked to vote for the party at a general election. Furthermore, party accounting and the disclosure of all large financial donations would simply be consistent with the existing principle and practice of MPs declaring financial interests on a Register of Members' Interests, required by standing orders in the House of Commons to be updated and published annually.[46] An exception should be made to preserve the privacy of relatively small donors, so that only sums of money in excess of £1 000 need legally be disclosed in the parties' accounts.

There is already wide support across the political spectrum for reform of the law on political donations. Both the Labour Party and the Liberal Democrats pledged in their election manifestos of 1992 to introduce legislation that required donations to political parties to be declared in a public register and the accounts of political parties to be published. At the time of writing, every political party represented in Parliament – except the Conservative Party – supports the case for public accounting and disclosure of large financial donations. The Labour Party recently made it clear that they will name all donors of above an agreed amount (which they have suggested might be £5 000) if the other parties will do similarly.[47] However, the Conservative government defends vigorously the confidentiality of people making political donations.

The basis of the Conservative argument is that the privacy of donors should be respected. According to the former Conservative Lord Chancellor, Lord Hailsham, 'It is the most basic right that what a man does with his money, like what he does with his vote, is a private affair. We defend it.'[48] The matter was hotly debated in the House of Commons in June 1993, when Sir Norman Fowler, the Conservative chairman, reiterated

Lord Hailsham's sentiment, saying, 'I make no bones about the fact that we remain wedded to the principle that where individuals make donations for political or, for that matter, charitable purposes, they are entitled to the right of privacy if that is what they wish.'[49] Sir Norman Fowler's evidence on behalf of the Conservative Party to the Home Affairs Select Committee inquiry into party funding was that:[50]

Donations from private individuals to the Conservative Party's central funds are from personal resources, and are made freely, in much the same way as individuals choose to give to many other voluntary organisations. That individuals choose to give financial support to a political party is, in our view, entirely a matter of private choice. Donors assist the Conservative Party because of their support for its policies. We do not publish details or comment upon the names of donors. That is a matter for donors themselves.

Practical reasons for confidentiality have also been given by Conservative MPs. For example, Henry Billingham, the Conservative MP for Norfolk North-West, has said that the real problem for generous donors whose names are made publicly known is that they are then flooded with letters and telephone calls from other bodies and charities seeking gifts. He said that he has suffered the same fate himself:[51]

I feel very strongly that if someone makes a donation to a political party, to a charity or to any other organisation, he is entitled to total anonymity, because if it is revealed that he made a large donation that individual will be inundated with other requests.

I have made a few small modest contributions to charities in my constituency. On one occasion, although I requested anonymity, the charity gave my donation publicity. Some 40 or 50 other organisations then wrote to me asking for a similar contribution. That is why I feel very strongly that, if any individual makes a donation, it must be up to that person to decide whether that information should be made public.

A more interesting line of argument has come from Sir Ivan Lawrence, the Conservative chairman of the Commons' Home Affairs Select Committee, who has referred to abuses of disclosure regulations he encountered when examining the American experience of party funding. His observation is that in practice the only people who inspect the public registers of financial donors in the USA are political campaigners hoping to find an individual contributing to the funds of their opponent who might prove an embarrassment: 'The only people who go to those offices where about 120 people work at state cost are the researchers for the candidates standing against the incumbent congressman to see what dirt they can churn out. For my part, I do not think that the British taxpayer wants to spend that kind of money on that kind of research in order to pretend that there is open disclosure of contributions to parties.'[52]

Factors of political self-interest are bound to play their part in shaping party attitudes to the issue of disclosure. There is some reason to suppose that the public disclosure of donations might have the effect of reducing the level and overall amount of income received by the Conservative Party, and if Conservative fundraisers and campaigners believe this to be true then they will hardly welcome the change. Greater publicity for a decision by a board of company directors to make a substantial gift of money to the Conservative Party might aggravate problems over making the donation with both shareholders (concerned at loss of profits) and employees of the company (particularly at a time of annual salary negotiations). If individual donors of large sums of money really do wish to remain anonymous, as Sir Norman Fowler has suggested, then they are likely to be put off making such a donation altogether.

Not all Conservatives, however, agree with their leaders on this issue, and there are some party members who are calling for much greater openness about the party's affairs. The Charter Movement, a group of Conservative members campaigning for democracy within the party, in May 1993 published a report on party central funds, in which it was said that,[53]

> Conservative Party members have to face the fact that not only are they denied access to *information* about Central Office finances (let alone proper democratic *accountability* for them) but, far worse, their party actually depends financially upon the goodwill of foreigners. The position of party members is degraded by the revelation that a goodly number of donors had no interest as voters in April 1992 and for them to read allegations that even foreign government interests may have been involved is far worse. Who are these donors and do they get anything in return?
>
> Central Office have always made a virtue of the secrecy they afford to their donors. It has been made to seem a dignified thing, something to respect as gentlemanly conduct. What now transpires is that many of these donors may have special interests to promote . . . It is bad enough that party *members* have no influence on party policy, but it would be intolerable if large donors were better placed . . . The central funds of the Conservative Party are still in private hands. There is still no democratic accountability for the stewardship of those funds. With money goes power and it cannot be right that so much money and so much power are free from any democratic, constitutional constraint.

Some Conservative parliamentarians would also seem to share some of these reservations. The MP Richard Shepherd's view is that, 'As long as things are done clandestinely and anonymously there is always a suspicion that they are done for motives that are not appropriate.'[54] He has said in the House of Commons:[55]

> I, like every other Hon. Member and certainly like every Conservative Member, wish to defend the integrity of my party. I am unable to defend it, because I cannot point to any published list of where the funds come from which would exorcise the malignity of the charges . . . . Political funding or contributions to funding are not, as the former Chancellor Lord Hailsham said, a matter merely of privity or the fact that we have a right to dispose of our money as we wish. I accept that it may be true of charities in general: charities such as the Red Cross and a number of others actively seek funds. The motives of the givers in all instances can be questionable. They may be honourable; many people give to charities in the hope of aggrandising themselves in the eyes of the community. The givers may subtly be trying to reach for honour and recognition. Many give for honourable reasons, but political parties are different because they are contending for the government of the country. They therefore hold public policy decision in their hands . . . As long as donations are hidden and screened by the arguments that the right of privacy gives us the right to donate very large sums to political parties, there will always be a question mark. Public policy should dictate that large sums of money should be identifiable in the accounts of a party.

The arguments and rhetoric of Labour and Liberal Democrat MPs in support of reform have emphasised strongly the constitutional need for the party in government to be open about its large individual and corporate financial supporters. During a Commons debate on the subject, Margaret Beckett complained that, 'There is in all this a terrible danger for the health and well-being of democracy in Britain.'[56] Chris Mullin has made the point that this subject is now of greater concern than ever before because of the growing importance of money in general election campaigns: 'It is regrettable that, in our political life, money is now a greater feature of how a general election or by-election campaign is run, or how a party is funded. The more money that is required, the more dubious those resources become.'[57] Archie Kirkwood, for the Liberal Democrats, believes that, 'It is a fundamental element of a democratic process that the way in which parties finance themselves and the uses and sources of that money are transparent.'[58] Similarly, in the words of the Labour MP Donald Anderson:[59]

> In a democracy, transparency is very important. The Right Hon. Member for Sutton Coldfield [the Conservative chairman Sir Norman Fowler] asserted that, in a democracy, citizens have a right to make voluntary

contributions. Some people may give to Oxfam, some to the National Society of the Prevention of Cruelty to Children, and others to the Conservative Party. But surely it is naïve and simplistic to suggest that there is no difference between giving voluntarily to a charity with a specific objective and giving to a party which, in government, can – in many cases does – adopt policies that may flow from such contributions .... There will always be temptations. The best guarantee against politicians falling into those temptations is openness. I commend to the House the dictum of the Supreme Court Justice Brandeis that sunlight is the best disinfectant. I hope that in all our political funding for all the parties we will be prepared to let in as much sunlight as possible in the hope that those who might otherwise be tempted will draw back and remember the fine political culture within which we have all been brought up.

It may be that over the next few years all the political parties, including the Conservative Party which at present reveals least about its income, will move voluntarily towards a greater openness in their financial affairs. None the less, legislation should control the conduct of annual audited accounting, and settle a common standard for the disclosure of large donations. As well as having the backing of all the parliamentary opposition parties, and also some Conservative members, this proposal in recent years has received considerable support from independent inquiries into party funding and in public opinion generally. A Hansard Society report on the subject in 1981 recommended statutory accounting and disclosure of large donations, as have two leading public law professors at London University, Keith Ewing and Dawn Oliver.[60] When a public opinion poll was taken on the issue and published in June 1993, its results indicated overwhelming popular support within the country for such a reform.[61] To the question, 'Should political parties be legally obliged to disclose the source of large donations from individuals?', 71 per cent said yes and 20 per cent said no (with 10 per cent undecided). To the question, 'Should political parties be legally obliged to disclose the source of donations from foreign nationals?', 77 per cent of persons said yes and 13 per cent said no (with 10 per cent undecided). Even among Conservative voters, 71 per cent supported compulsory disclosure of overseas donations, and 58 per cent backed compulsory disclosure of all large donations. A consensus of opinion is emerging outside Conservative Central Office that the law on political finance needs modernisation, and that a general rule should be implemented requiring all political parties to publish annual audited accounts, listing all donors who in any year have contributed large sums of money exceeding a specified limit, which might be fixed initially at £1 000. Until then, in the words of one leading Labour MP, 'The danger of secret donations is that they leave public government under private obligation.'[62]

A prohibition on foreign donations

In Britain, much of the controversy over the sources from which the Conservative Party has received its funding has been associated with huge gifts coming from people who are foreign nationals or from overseas companies. The Conservative Party opposes all legal controls upon the sources of donations.[63] Foreign gifts are defended on international free market principles, as illustrated in the following sentiments of the Conservative MP Henry Bellingham:[64]

> If foreign donors want to donate money to a political party, why should they not do that? If they feel that our free market system and policies on employment law and trade unions will benefit their corporation and trade, why should those foreign donors not give money to the party that is likely to form a government who will further the system of free enterprise that will benefit their companies?

However, a broad range of politicians and commentators now disagree fundamentally with this viewpoint. Many MPs have been publicly critical of foreign donations, and both the Labour Party and the Liberal Democrats have said that they would prohibit foreign donations by law.[65] The Labour frontbench spokesman, Robin Cook, recently told the Conservative government in a Commons debate that, 'Britain has no right to interfere in the elections of foreign countries, and foreigners have no right to interfere in the elections of this country.'[66]

There can be no doubt that money is hugely important in today's election campaigns, and the idea that foreign sources should be allowed to fund substantial quantities of election propaganda seeking to persuade electors how to vote is subversive to any genuine concept of national self-government. Already, legal restrictions on foreign donations operate in several major western democracies, notably the USA where the acceptance of any foreign donation is banned. The reason for prohibiting foreign donations in Britain, then, is that those who are not members of British society should not be allowed to influence the political process by which ordinary British voters choose their political leaders. Still less should foreign companies or other bodies, especially governmental or quasi-governmental agencies, be permitted to do so. A prohibition upon foreign donations to political parties in Britain is an important political reform which commands strong support across the political spectrum and should be introduced at the earliest opportunity.

A limit to the size of individual donations

The question of whether some maximum figure should be placed on the amount of any financial gift that any individual or organisation can give lawfully to a political party is one that has received little political support in Britain. Legal restrictions on total sums offered in any year operate in the USA, where there is a limit of $1 000 on individual contributions to candidates and $25 000 to political action committees. In France there is a legal limit of £3 000 on donations from individuals and £5 000 from companies.[67] The constitutional logic underlying these restrictions is, as with the prohibition of foreign donations, the preservation of the integrity of the political process.

The argument for placing a legal limit on the size of donations that come from any individual source over any annual period is that it goes against the principle of political equality for any single wealthy person or company to have a disproportionate advantage over ordinary members of the community in influencing the political process and the outcome of election campaigns. It is only the very large donations made by individuals to candidates' and parties' political funds which create the danger that special favours might be sought from or offered by party politicians in office – also, in Britain there is the suspicion that it produces favourable prospects for receiving a knighthood or peerage. A suitable initial threshold in Britain at the time of writing might in theory be in the region of £10 000.

However, such a proposal is not within the bounds of practical politics in the present circumstances, because its effect would be to prejudice the financial prospects of the major political parties. A ceiling on funding received from individual sources would have the effect of reducing company donations received by the Conservative Party, and would similarly adversely affect the quantum of funding received from trade union donations by the Labour Party. None the less there are good arguments of constitutional principle behind the proposal, and changing patterns of funding and other events in the future might one day raise the proposal to a level of serious practical consideration.

The regulation of company donations

Currently there are negligible legal controls on the power of company directors to make gifts of money to political parties out of company funds. The only statutory stipulation concerning company donations is the requirement in the Companies Act 1985 that if such a financial gift is of £200 or more, then it must be declared in the annual report of the directors to the company's shareholders.[68] This requirement for disclosure of payments to political parties amounts to an obligation to inform shareholders of how a proportion of company assets has already been spent. It is not a requirement to seek the approval or consent of shareholders as to whether they agree with the directors that the profits of the company should be donated to politics. The directors' gifts may be made from the normal assets of the company, and there is no statutory requirement for the creation of a separate political fund from which directors who wish to fund a political party should make their payments. Certainly, there is no obligation to consult, inform and secure the agreement of the workforce of the company, or to discover their opinions about the directors giving financial assistance to one or other of the political parties.

This freedom of company directors to donate large sums of money to political parties is stoutly defended by Conservative MPs – who represent the only party that is effectively in receipt of such donations. Meanwhile, at the opposite end of public opinion on this matter, many people believe that directors of companies should not be allowed to spend company funds for political purposes at all. Thus in the view of the industrialist, Sir John Harvey-Jones, 'It is quite wrong. I do not think it is the business of companies to decide to try and influence the democratic system.'[69] For this very reason, in some countries the amount that can be given to a political party by a commercial company is strictly limited by law, such as the £5000 limit now applicable in France, and elsewhere company donations have been prohibited completely, as in Belgium. Some British lawyers have, in fact, tried to argue that donations to political parties may already be *ultra vires* the normal powers of company directors as a matter of the common law,[70] but whatever the moral proprietary rights involved, it seems highly improbable that such an established *de facto* corporate practice by some of the country's top commercial companies would now be struck down as unlawful by the judiciary.

What has infuriated the Labour Party particularly about company donations is that the freedom of directors to make gifts of money to the Conservative Party stands in such stark contrast to the battery of legislative restrictions that have been imposed by successive Conservative governments on trade union funding of the Labour Party. More generally, many politicians and commentators believe that the law is seriously failing to protect the rights of shareholders, by not requiring directors to obtain shareholders' approval before making substantial gifts of money to political parties from company assets. A joint report by the Hansard Society and Constitutional Reform Centre in 1985 supported this view and said:[71]

A formal and retrospective notification in the annual accounts no longer seems adequate . . . Shareholders should consent to company political donations. We do not think it right that company funds should be disbursed for a purpose not central to the company's trading operations without the consent of shareholders. A decision to make a political donation should not be treated as though it were exactly comparable to questions of good commercial management.

There is indeed a marked anomaly in current legislation governing company and trade union donations, which is regarded as unacceptable by virtually everyone outside the Conservative Party. The Labour Party's own proposals for reforming the law on company donations were presented to the Home Affairs Select Committee inquiry into party funding in 1993. The Committee was told that the objective of the Labour Party in this area was to achieve a 'level playing field' between the institutional backers of the various parties. There were two options, they said, as to how this could be done. One option was to change the law on trade union funding, allowing unions to be able to use their money for any purpose they chose to further the interest of their members, subject only to *post facto* reporting in their annual report. In other words, trade union donations would be placed on a similar legal footing to company donations. Alternatively, the Labour Party submission argued, similar rules to those which now controlled trade union political donations should be extended by law to apply equally to public companies, employers' associations, partnerships and private companies. The Labour Party proposal elaborated:[72]

> This new even-handed legislative approach would need to ensure the following:
> 1. A requirement for companies, friendly societies, trade unions, employers' associations and partnerships all to establish a separate political fund before making any political payments within the meaning of the 1913 [Trade Union] Act, as amended by the 1984 [Trade Union] Act.
> 2. A requirement of a vote of individual members/shareholders to establish such a fund if such a vote has not taken place in the last ten years.
> 3. Political donations for expenditure on political activity within the meaning of those Acts by organisations without such funds would from a given date be illegal.
> 4. Once established, the existence of such a political fund could be challenged only if, say, 10 per cent of the members of shareholders of an organisation requested a ballot on the continuation of the fund. Such ballots would then not be required more than once every 10 years.
> 5. Donations from companies should be deducted from shareholders' dividends, and shareholders could 'contract out' of that contribution.
> 6. Included in the accounts for the political funds of trade unions, companies etc. would be any significant donation 'in kind' during an election campaign.

Other proposals for reforming company political donations have been put forward in recent years. A scheme proposed by the Hansard Society was for a voluntary code of practice to be followed by all company directors wishing to make political donations.[73] They believed this code should begin by stating that validation of political payments should be by the shareholders (not employees) at an annual general meeting. Second, the code should require the board of directors to prepare a statement giving its reasons why it believes that such political donations are in the interests of the company, and this statement should then be the subject of approval by the shareholders at the annual general meeting. Third, the size of any political donation by a company should be in proportion to its turnover and profits. And, finally, the code should emphasise the principle that companies making political donations should do so openly, not by channelling the money surreptitiously through other companies or conduits. There would certainly be some value in a voluntary code of practice, which might be drawn up and issued under the auspices of the Department of Trade or the Confederation of British Industry, detailing good practice to be followed in the making of financial gifts to parties. However, in the hard commercial world of company transactions, any effective implementation of changes in company conduct in the practice of making political donations would need to be established by an Act of Parliament.

To this end, several measures of draft legislation have been presented to the House of Commons in recent years but, confronted by the opposition of the Conservative government, all have failed. The most important legislative attempt was in the form of an amendment to the Companies Act 1989 being tabled in the House of Lords as the Act was passing through Parliament. The amending clause sought to introduce the requirement that donations for political purposes should be proposed at annual general meetings of a company. The amendment passed the Lords but was then rejected in the House of Commons. Defending the amendment before it was voted down by the Conservative Party, the then Labour MP, Bryan Gould, argued that, 'What is particularly worrying about company donations is that a small group of people make donations of other people's money.'[74] The Conservative view on the amendment was expressed by Tim Smith, who said, 'I believe that it would be wrong in principle to clutter the agenda of annual general meetings in this way.'[75] Another recent item of draft legislation was the Political Parties (Income and Expenditure) Bill presented by the Labour MPs Marjorie Mowlam, David Winnick and Tony Banks in 1990.[76] The relevant part of the Bill provided for all companies wishing to make political donations to follow a broadly similar pattern of consents as required for trade union donation. The consents required for establishing a political fund from which donations to parties might be made included those of the employees of the company as well as the shareholders. The Bill would also allow shareholders to opt out of the donation to the political party, so that their dividends would be higher than those issued to individual shareholders who agreed with the gift proposed by the board of directors:

1. (1) No company shall make donations of a political nature, including donations to a political party, except from a political fund established under subsection (2) of this section.
   (2) A company shall not establish a political fund unless both a majority of shareholders in, and a majority of employees of, that

> company have approved of the establishment of such a fund, by
> means of a ballot held for that purpose.
>
> 2. When a company makes a political donation from its political fund, it
>   shall inform every shareholder, and any shareholder who objects to
>   the donation may so inform the company and shall thereupon be
>   entitled to an additional dividend from the company in lieu of such
>   proportion of the donation as the nominal value of his shareholding,
>   regardless of the class of his shares, bears to the nominal value of the
>   company's share capital.

While the precise drafting of this Bill requires some perfecting in terms of company law, the principles themselves declared in the document have a wide degree of support across the Labour Party.

The democratic argument that members of any organisation should give their consent before large financial donations are distributed for political ends carries with it an irresistible logic. The principles of consultation and approval have been extended to the practice of trade union funding of the Labour Party, and now it should be applied to the practice of company donations being made to the Conservative Party. It is likely that a significant proportion of individual shareholders of a company begrudge cash payments being handed over out of shareholders' profits to Conservative politicians in the same way and at least as much as some individual trade unionists might prefer their union not to pass donations on their behalf to the Labour Party. Whatever their preferences, it is the individual membership of both trade unions and companies who should decide the matter.

THE CASE FOR STATE FUNDING OF POLITICAL PARTIES

Existing state aid to political parties

The parties already receive various kinds of public assistance with their political work during general election campaigns. The most valuable of these are the arrangements made with the BBC and the independent television companies for the parties to use the television and radio networks to make party election broadcasts, for which no charge is made.[77] The commercial rate for buying such advertising time would be very great indeed. The financial benefit to the Conservative and Labour parties at the 1992 general election was worth £10m per party. Two other free services provided under the authority of the Representation of the People Act 1983 are, as discussed earlier, the free postal communication which parliamentary candidates may use to send out their election addresses to every elector in the constituency,[78] and a candidate's right to the free use of council halls and state school rooms to hold election meetings.[79] The Post Office is reimbursed by the Treasury for the postal service, which in 1992 amounted to over £3m. Some regard the state's supervision of electoral registration as another form of indirect state subsidy for the political parties, since in some other countries (notably the USA) it is the parties and not public authorities who publicise and ensure that eligible people enter their names on the electoral roll in order to be able to vote on polling day.

On a continuing basis, political parties represented in the House of Commons may receive an annual grant towards their expenses incurred in the course of their parliamentary work. The party in government (which receives the huge benefit of Treasury support in publicising its government-related work while in office) is not eligible under this parliamentary grant scheme – known as 'Short money' (after Edward Short, the leader of the House of Commons at the time the scheme was introduced in 1975) – and in order for any other party to qualify for financial assistance it must at the previous general election have had at least two of its members elected as MPs, or one member elected and 150 000 votes cast nationally for all the party's candidates. The amount of money that can be claimed by each opposition party is calculated with reference to the results at the previous general election, in terms of the number of seats won in the Commons and the number of votes cast nationally. The amounts paid annually to the parties during the 1987–92 Parliament were Labour £839 709, Liberal Democrats £187 176, Ulster Unionists £29 993, Scottish National £18 278, SDLP £11 577, Plaid Cymru £10 796 and Democratic Unionist £9 832. Under a revised formula approved by the House of Commons on 4 November 1993, the amounts payable have been uprated by 35 per cent with provision for annual upratings linked to the retail price index, and in addition £100 000 is to be made available towards the travel expenses of opposition parties' frontbench spokesmen.[80] In the Labour Party the money received from the parliamentary grant has been spent principally on the leader's private office and in employing support staff for its shadow Cabinet members and specialist working groups of MPs. The fact that a full-time salary is paid to MPs out of public funds is also of continuous benefit to the parties, particularly when it is considered in contrast to the position prior to 1911, when no parliamentary salaries were paid and MPs had to finance their political career from private means or (particularly in the case of Labour) from party funds. An MP's annual salary is, at the time of writing, £31 687 per annum, and each may claim up to £41 308 per annum on office costs. In addition, the person who is Leader of the Opposition receives an additional annual salary, currently £32 200.

Overall, however, the form and level of public assistance given to political parties in Britain compares unfavourably with many other advanced Western democracies. In some countries, the income tax system is used to encourage donations to political parties from individuals, by making the amount of the sum paid deductible from the donor's liability to tax on their annual earnings. But, as yet, there are no such income tax incentives offered in Britain. The only tax concession offered in Britain, incidents of which are extremely rare and effectively limited only to the wealthy, is that political gifts or bequests of capital are exempt from death duties.[81] In some other ways the British electoral system actively penalises political parties, sapping their financial resources, most notably through the invidious practice of requiring a financial deposit of £500 to be paid on behalf of each parliamentary candidate standing for election to the House of Commons.[82] But most conspicuous of all by its absence, is any system in Britain whereby some measure of public funding is granted to political parties towards their national work of policy-formulation and research, organisation and representation within the community, and political campaigning at election time. Public funding of political parties is the normal practice elsewhere in Europe. France, Germany, Denmark, Sweden, Austria, Spain, Portugal, Italy and Greece all possess well-established public-funding systems, and in those countries political parties and the national election campaigns they organise are recognised formally as playing a vital role in the constitutional process, more than justifying the expenditure of the relatively small sums of public money paid to them.[83] The case that there should now be a new legislative framework introduced in Britain to provide for some modest extension of public financial assistance offered to political parties has emerged as one of the most heated controversies in party politics today.

Support among British politicians, for or against the proposal for state funding of parties, has crystallised almost entirely along party political lines. Virtually all members of the Conservative Party – the richest of the British parties, and with the most to lose from such a scheme – vehemently oppose the introduction of any state funding. And virtually all members of the other parties – who stand to gain from such a scheme – favour the proposal very strongly. Both the Labour Party and the Liberal Democrats promised to introduce a system of state funding for parties in their 1992 general election manifestos. There have been two important independent inquiries on the subject, both of which supported the principle of state funding. These were the Report of the Committee on Financial Aid to Political Parties in 1976 (known as the Houghton Report after its chairman, Lord Houghton) established by the Labour government in the last year of Harold Wilson's premiership, and the Report of the Commission upon the Financing of Political Parties in 1981, established by the Hansard Society. More recently, in 1993 and 1994, the Home Affairs Select Committee in the House of Commons inquired into the general question of party funding, but predictably (its chairman being a senior Conservative backbencher and a majority of MPs on the committee being Conservatives) its majority report on the subject rejected any suggestion of state funding for political parties.[84]

Opposition to public funding

The principal argument employed against state funding of parties in Britain is that, 'Direct state aid would breach the established British constitutional practice that organisation for political ends is a strictly voluntary exercise.'[85] According to this view, state funding would introduce a compulsory element into the political process by virtue of all citizens being compelled to contribute towards the public subsidies, by virtue of a proportion of their taxes being devoted to the purpose. For this reason, according to the minority, dissenting opinion in the Houghton Report of 1976, state aid would be utterly alien to modern British political culture and a 'dangerous and irreversible departure from British constitutional practice'.[86] This minority report went on to say, 'Even voting is not yet compulsory, and to compel taxpayers to finance political parties with which they have no sympathy would undoubtedly antagonise a large number of citizens', and, 'The very activity of raising money has always been recognised as one of the cohesive forces holding parties together.'[87] The Conservative Party evidence to the Home Affairs Select Committee on the subject in 1993 followed similar lines:[88]

> The Conservative Party supports the established British practice that participation in political activity is voluntary in character and that this extends to membership of, and offering financial support to, political parties. The voluntary character of Conservative Party funding and membership is a substantial source of its strength. It is a guarantee of the Party's responsiveness to a broadly-based and active membership drawn from all parts of the United Kingdom and all sections of the community . . . In this country, individuals are not forced to take part in the political process. We do not require people to vote, still less should we require them to give money to parties for their organisation and campaigning.

Shortly afterwards, the Cabinet minister, David Hunt, again repeated such a belief in the House of Commons, saying, 'I believe that the principle of voluntary funding underpins the strength of our democracy and the party political system in this country, and we destroy it at our peril.'[89]

Opponents of state funding argue that a number of adverse and undesirable consequences would follow upon the introduction of public subsides. Among those cited in the Conservative Party evidence to the Home Affairs Select Committee in 1993 were that it 'would either unduly favour established parties or encourage the formation and growth of extremist parties'. The same Conservative paper warned that 'It would give a party with a parliamentary majority control of the funding of political parties, bringing the danger of self-serving legislation.'[90] Any state legislation relating to political parties is regarded by most Conservatives as being highly undesirable, and this is supported by Michael Pinto-

Duschinsky in his book *British Political Finance 1830–1980* where he argued that, 'The law is an uncertain, blunt, and dangerous weapon'.[91] One of Dr Pinto-Duschinsky's main criticisms of public subsidies is that they would have the effect of strengthening the party central office, because it would become less dependent upon local constituency financial support. He argues that, 'An injection of state aid would be likely to diminish fund-raising activities by party organisations and to foster undesirable reliance on the public purse.'[92] He goes on to say that, 'The danger of public funding is that it makes popular backing unnecessary and creates a gulf between the professional staff and the ordinary members.'[93] Most dramatically of all, Dr Pinto-Duschinsky has gone so far as to suggest that public grants to the parties would turn their headquarters into quasi-government departments of state:[94]

> Public funding would almost certainly increase the bureaucratic tendencies of party organisations. There would be pressure to gain for party officials the various advantages enjoyed by civil servants – security of tenure, inflation-proofed pension rights, and so on. It is, of course, wholly understandable that the permanent employees of party organisations should seek these benefits. But, if granted, they would insulate the party machines from ordinary party members and would, to all intents and purposes, make the party headquarters like government departments.

A more potent line of argument that has been levelled against state funding is that it would tend to weaken the links between the political parties and their traditional sources of support. This view challenges the suggestion that there is anything regrettable about the large measure of institutional dependency of the Labour and Conservative parties upon the trade unions and commercial companies. The dissenting conclusions in the Houghton Report found no evidence that this institutional dependency upon special interests within the Labour and Conservative parties had distorted their overall political direction. On the contrary, they suggested that the two parties existed to represent these legitimate interests, among others, and that they attracted the financial support of industry and the trade unions precisely because they do so. By tampering with traditional party alignments, at the same time as assisting the work of minority parties, the British two-party system might come under strain. On this point, the minority view in the Houghton Report was that:[95]

> Any tampering with traditional party alignments, even by accident, would be profoundly mistaken. The existing alignments reflect a degree of actual conflict in society, and to that extent any attempt to distort it would threaten to drive those left wing and right wing elements which currently stay within the mainstream of party politics into extra-parliamentary activity of a potentially dangerous kind. It is almost certainly true that the

existence of the Labour Party as a broad alliance covering the whole territory from the centre leftwards has protected Britain from any significant Communist or ultra-left challenge on the French or Italian pattern. It is probably also true that the breadth of the Conservative Party appeal has had a similar influence on the right.

A favourite argument employed by Conservative MPs in parliamentary debate is to say that the existing system of financing parties is perfectly satisfactory, and that the proposal for state funding is simply a Labour and Liberal Democrat ruse to compensate for their lack of popular support, reflected in the relatively poor income they receive through membership income and voluntary donations. Thus the Conservative Cabinet minister, Tony Newton, recently commented in the House of Commons that, 'It is typical of the Labour Party that when it cannot get people to dig into their own pocket voluntarily to fund it, it wants to introduce a law to make them do so.'[96] Similar sentiments were expressed by the Conservative chairman, Sir Norman Fowler, when he said, 'Unlike the Labour Party we do not believe that the taxpayer should be forced to bail out political parties.'[97]

Reasons why public funding is necessary

The general objectives in granting political parties some measure of financial subsidy out of public funds would be to reduce their dependency upon special interests, to improve the general performance of their work, and to enable all parties to compete at general elections on a more equal footing. It should be remembered that what is being envisaged here is not huge sums of money covering all the campaigning and other running expenses of the parties, but instead a modest supplement to the parties' own membership subscription fees and fundraising.

The most straightforward, practical argument for public funding of political parties is simply that the extra resources provided would improve the general performance of their work. Virtually all supporters of public funding would agree that the present level of financial resources raised from private means by the opposition parties is utterly inadequate for the tasks the parties now seek to perform. In the Houghton Committee's expression, the state of party organisation throughout the United Kingdom is 'pitifully inadequate'.[98] Certainly, people visiting the offices of any of their constituency parties cannot fail to notice the abysmal office facilities at the premises, and lack of staff. Even if they travel to the London headquarters of the parties (the Liberal Democrats at 4 Cowley Street; the Labour Party at 150 Walworth Road; and the Conservative Party at 32 Smith Square) they will find that there resides behind the dignified façade of the building a small number of rather cramped offices housing a workforce no larger than that of a medium-sized London firm of solicitors. There are around twenty employees working at the Liberal Democrats' national office, 110 at the Labour national office, and 140 working for the Conservatives, representing and serving a population of over 65 million citizens. Problems of resources affect all the political parties, although of the three main parties, the Labour Party, and particularly the Liberal Democrats are worst affected. According to the Houghton Committee:[99]

> The evidence we have gathered in this country shows that party organisation is in a number of cases weak at national level, and at local level generally exists on a pitifully inadequate scale of accommodation, equipment, trained staff and resources. Membership fees are low; fund-raising takes up too much time; organisation is frequently inadequate; and the level of political activity is far below what is needed to gain the attention and interest of the general body of the electorate, especially the young. Our considered view is that British political parties frequently operate below the minimum level of efficiency and activity required.

Or as Dick Leonard, former Labour MP and one of the earliest lobbyists for public subsidies, has described the present lack of resources:[100]

> The consequences of the parties being ill-equipped to fulfil their necessary functions can easily be identified, though it is difficult to measure them precisely. What can be asserted is that, in large part, it is not the members of political parties but the general public which suffers when they are not able to perform their roles satisfactorily.
>
> The most immediate effect is that the parties cannot afford to employ sufficient staff and those who are on party payrolls tend to be underpaid, overworked, and – with numerous individual exceptions – of poor calibre. Political parties which win power at general elections, or in elections for county and district councils, tend to take office with ill-thought-out programmes because their research capacity has not been sufficient to enable them to be properly prepared. The cost is seen in avoidable mistakes made by ministers of every incoming government and, inevitably, in the fact that many ministers are more dependent than they should be on civil servants for advice on policy decisions. At constituency level the poverty of political parties leads to their being housed in drab, or often non-existent, premises, to a low level of administrative efficiency and to their often presenting an unattractive and unwelcoming face to their potential supporters ... All these factors contribute to the general lowering of the reputation of party politics which should be a matter of concern to all who cherish our democratic traditions.

Connected with this argument that the parties are unable to perform their existing work as effectively as they might, is the comment that poor financial resources has meant that political parties in Britain have barely begun to perform certain important political functions required in a contemporary democracy. The most obvious example lies in the field of political research and education. In some other European countries there are well-established research and education institutes related to the political parties, which receive substantial public funding direct from the state, most notably in Sweden and Germany, or distributed through the parties. This was a point emphasised to the Home Affairs Select Committee by representatives of the Labour Party in 1993, who said, 'One of the serious problems of the functioning of our democracy is the lack of effective political education in any of the political parties or other institutions in this country.' They went on to argue, 'The continuation of a healthy democracy in this country requires some resources spent on the education, research and communications areas, and the funding or part-funding of activities of institutions related to the political parties, or to political parties themselves undertaking such work.'[101]

One of the other major arguments for public funding is that it would reduce the present unhealthy degree of institutional dependency of the parties upon special private sectional interests, and enable them to represent more freely the community as a whole. This argument applies particularly to the Conservative and Labour parties, with their heavy financial reliance upon political donations received from big business and the trade unions. It was a problem of special concern to the Hansard Society Commission in 1981, which emphasised that in their view democracy could not work fairly 'if the sources of party finance lead to the overrepresentation of some interests and underrepresentation of others'.[102] Their report went on to itemise the different ways in which the financial relationships between the two main parties, business and the trade unions adversely affected the political process. Their view was that:[103]

(a) It distorts electoral choice by stressing a class polarisation which may well not be desired by the voters.

(b) It offers great privileges to certain interests in the representative process, while allowing other interests – perhaps equally important – to be 'organised out' of the political system.

(c) It gives certain interests excessive weight in the policy-making process, and in the selection of candidates.

(d) It militates against popular participation in politics.

(e) It handicaps parties, such as the Liberals or the SNP, which cannot command institutional finances.

(f) It results in some trade unionists and company shareholders contributing to causes with which they did not agree or even actively oppose.

Some of the arguments for public funding take the form of flat rejections of the criticisms that have been levelled against the proposal. Opposition to public subsidies to the parties, particularly from Conservative MPs, has stressed the importance of donations being given voluntarily by individuals, and that this is a great virtue of the present private system of funding. The reality is, however, that the number of voluntary acts of political contribution occurring in the 1990s is extremely small. The donations coming from trade unions (derived from the pockets of workers paying their union subscriptions) and companies (derived from the pockets of shareholders) are determined principally by the decision of trade union leaders and company directors. The Hansard Society Commission stressed this point on the subject when it said:[104]

> Much of this money is not given 'voluntarily' by the donors, but simply as a result of the fact that the donors happen to own shares in a company or belong to a trade union. It could be argued, therefore, that the parties are financed privately, but by no means wholly voluntarily.

Another criticism of public funding, that it would cause parties to lose interest in their membership because they would no longer need the fees and voluntary donations, is soundly rejected as being unrealistic. The case for public funding is a case for a supplementary, rather than an alternative, source of income. Whereas the level of state funding available to each party for their work would be restricted to a maximum amount (analogous in principle to the ceiling of £840 000 imposed upon the annual parliamentary grant payable in 1987–92 to opposition parties), it would be entirely self-defeating for political parties in any way to diminish their source of income from private, voluntary means. On the contrary, it is likely that additional resources will enable the less affluent parties to prepare more effective voluntary fundraising activities, such as better publicity and direct-mail canvassing of donations.

Supporters of state funding also reject the notion that there is anything subversive to political liberty about the state, and parliamentary legislation, making provisions for political parties. Opponents of public subsidies make much of the need to preserve Britain's past 'constitutional practice' or 'tradition' that parties are not provided for or regulated in British law. It can be argued, on the other hand, by supporters of public subsidies that the only reason for this practice or tradition is the backward-looking institutional inertia that continues to dominate Conservative thinking on the British political system. While other European democracies over the course of the twentieth century have not only caught up with but have overtaken Britain's pioneering parliamentary election law enacted in the late nineteenth century, British public policy on national campaigning and political parties has progressed remarkably slowly, leaving non-statutory arrangements to govern party political broadcasts and only belatedly (in 1969) allowing the names of parties to be stated on the ballot papers of candidates. Whether or not political parties in Britain in the past have been recognised as public bodies in law, throughout the twentieth century they have had a very obvious and important *de facto* national political existence which is now fundamental to election campaigning and the operation of government and opposition throughout the United Kingdom as well as inside Parliament. Under the British system of an unwritten constitution, many of our other public institutions are not recognised or provided for in law, even the Cabinet and the office of Prime Minister itself. Lack of legal recognition does not diminish the importance of such institutions to the operation of the British political structure, nor does it signify that they should be immune from public regulation and support when circumstances demand it. The Conservative Party had no difficulty about expressly referring to political parties in its legislation on political funding in the Trade Union Act 1984, when it wished to further restrict trade union payments to the Labour Party out of union political funds.[105]

A general sentiment shared by supporters of public funding of political parties is that the British state has certain fundamental obligations to safeguard the operation of its political democracy, and among a growing number of derogations from its duties in this respect since the 1950s has been its failure to provide a proper structure for the financing of political parties and their parliamentary election campaigns. The relative resources of the parties have quite clearly failed to keep pace with the newer demands imposed upon them by modern political circumstances. The scale and extent of public administration for which political parties are responsible both in terms of policy formulation and in terms of scrutiny and accountability is vastly changed from the early years of the twentieth century and, as a direct consequence, the financial needs of political parties are greater today than ever before. On this aspect of the debate, the Houghton Report commented:[106]

What some sections of public opinion may not have fully realised is that the manifold tasks and responsibilities of political parties are very much more demanding on physical and material resources today than they used to be. And they are more demanding because of the enormous expansion in the functions of government. A century ago the tasks of government were mainly passive and regulatory. Now they involve a much more active and positive engagement in our affairs. The government's traditional regulatory functions have multiplied and greatly broadened in scope. This has been particularly marked since the Second World War. The role of government now embraces responsibility for the maintenance of full employment and the provision of comprehensive social services; and such general economic aims as a satisfactory rate of growth, stable prices and a healthy balance of payments . . . It is against this changing background that we must measure the performance of our political parties. Everything that government is nowadays concerned with should also be the concern of the political parties. But whilst the bureaucracy and powers of the state have been greatly expanded to carry out its greatly enlarged responsibilities, our political parties have lagged behind. To be effective in the context of the vastly expanded role of modern government, the parties need to raise their sights, widen their vision and greatly expand their efforts and resources.

Similarly, the financial needs of the parties with respect to general election campaigns are greater than ever before. It is important to appreciate the huge impact of modern technology upon the modern forms of mass media campaigning and election propaganda, particularly since the 1970s. This new technology has brought with it rapidly escalating costs, and the danger that only those parties that are backed by wealthy sponsors or powerful vested interests will have access to the contemporary, highly sophisticated forms of political persuasion. The argument, then, is that public subsidies have become a necessity in order to sustain the quality of our general election campaigns, and to promote a genuinely fair contest between the political parties. It would help to remove the present glaring inequalities in the resources of the different parties, and enable them to compete with one another upon a more equal and fair basis. As a recent Council of Europe report stated:[107]

> If a pluralist democracy is to operate satisfactorily, it is necessary to establish conditions that ensure that the political parties can be compared and can compete on an equal footing. Systems for financing parties are designed primarily to strike a balance in this respect.

In practice, the parties in Britain will always be unequal in their resources, and the Conservatives are likely always to remain financially better off than the rest. But individual parties – and particularly those which command a substantial body of popular support in the country – should not be greatly disadvantaged compared to others through lack of financial resources. A new system of public funding, designed to supplement the private and voluntary donations parties have traditionally been exclusively dependent upon, would be conducive not only to a fairer electoral contest between the parties but also to an electorate that was better informed and better able to choose between them.

Proposals on the form of the public grant

The Report of the Houghton Committee published in 1976 still stands out as the main work of reference on the subject of state aid to political parties in Britain.[108] Its ministerial terms of reference were to consider 'whether in the interests of parliamentary democracy provision should be made from public funds to assist political parties in carrying out their functions outside Parliament', and the Committee embarked upon a very substantial inquiry which examined the resources and needs of the political parties in the United Kingdom and how best they might be supported in their work. The conclusions of the Committee were presented in a detailed 360-page report which backed public funding of political parties in the United Kingdom, and recommended that such financial aid should take the form of:[109]

(1) Annual grants to be paid from Exchequer funds to the central organisations of the parties for their general purposes, the amounts being determined according to the number of votes cast for the party at the previous general election.
(2) Reimbursement of the election expenses of parliamentary candidates up to a limit of a half of his or her legally permitted maximum expenditure.[110]

The annual grant was to be calculated under the original proposals upon the basis of 5 pence for every vote cast for one of the candidates of the party which, substituted for mid-1990s values might be regarded as equivalent to a figure of 20 pence. In order for a political party to qualify for receipt of any annual grant, under the Houghton proposals, at the previous general election it must have either:

(a) Saved the deposits of its candidates in at least six constituencies, or
(b) Had at least two of its candidates returned as MPs, or
(c) Had one of its candidates returned as an MP and received as a party a total of not less than 150 000 votes.

This is a similar qualification to that required for receipt of the existing 'Short money' scheme of parliamentary grants to opposition parties.[111] In order for a parliamentary candidate to qualify for a grant for limited reimbursement of his or her election expenses, the candidate must have received at least one-eighth of the votes cast in the constituency. The total annual cost of the state aid payable under the Houghton Report proposals was estimated at about £1.5m for the annual grant to the party headquarters, and £360 000 on reimbursement of parliamentary candidates' election expenses. At mid-1990s values the overall cost to the Exchequer would be in the region of £8m.

A different form of public grant to political parties was proposed in the Report of the Hansard Society Commission in 1981.[112] While supporting the proposal that state aid should be paid to the parties, the Commission rejected the particular scheme recommended in the Houghton Report. In particular, the Hansard Commission did not agree that the money should be made available to the parties on an unconditional basis, because the Commission was concerned about the decline in number of members in the parties. They believed that unconditional state aid would not only fail to stimulate greater public participation in politics but might actually discourage it (because, they thought, the parties might have less incentive to recruit new members). The Hansard Society Commission's recommendation was that the level of state funding for any particular party should match the amount of voluntary donations given to the party. For every £2 contributed to the party, an additional £2 would be payable from the Exchequer. For a party to be eligible to receive state funding under this scheme, it would have to satisfy similar conditions to those required under the earlier Houghton Report. Finally, the Hansard Society Commission proposed that a total sum of £5m per annum (at mid-1990s values, worth around £12m) should be made available from public funds towards the scheme, and that no more than £2 (at mid-1990s values, around £5) should be payable from public funds to match each individual political donation made:[113]

> Our scheme provides the parties with aid only if they succeed in persuading individuals to contribute. It is these subscribers who 'trigger off' the public expenditure. No money can be disbursed by the state except by the wish of individual contributors. Our scheme encourages the parties to seek a large number of small donations rather than a small number of large donations. We would hope that, by facilitating contributions to the political parties, we would also encourage contributors to participate in politics, and join the political party of their choice.

The Houghton Report proposals for unconditional state grants have received a far wider degree of support among those who favour state funding of political parties rather than the Hansard Society scheme for state matching of individual donations. In fact, a leading member of the Hansard Society Commission, Dick Leonard, dissented from the report, expressly stating his own preference for the Houghton model of unconditional state aid (which he himself had urged upon the Houghton Committee in a powerfully argued pamphlet in 1975 entitled *Paying for Party Politics: The Case for Public Subsidies*). In 1987, more authoritative support behind the Houghton Report proposals came from Keith Ewing, then at Cambridge University and now Professor of Public Law in London, in his book *The Funding of Political Parties in Britain*. Professor Ewing argued that the Hansard proposals were 'neither persuasive nor convincing', and said that while in principle any mechanism for stimulating greater popular participation in politics might be welcome, on a practical level it was difficult to see why matching aid would in reality stimulate donors to participate in party politics if they did not do so already.[114] The result of the Hansard Society proposals, if ever implemented, would be to generate a great deal of paperwork and make access to the public subsidies a less than straightforward affair.

It is important to understand Labour Party policy on state funding of political parties, for if and when such a scheme is implemented it is almost certain to be under a Labour government. It was a Labour government in the 1970s which established the Houghton Committee's inquiry into financial aid to political parties, but despite the public importance of the subject as well as the importance to its own party, the government did not make time available in the House of Commons for the Houghton Report even to be debated. The failure of the Labour government to bring forward legislation to give effect to the Houghton proposals in the late 1970s has to be explained in the political context of the government's minority in the Commons at that time. Its reasons for not doing so were a mixture of ministerial concern about how the public would perceive public grants being handed out to politicians at a time of national wage restraints and public expenditure controls, coupled with the whips' view that if a Bill was introduced, twenty or more Labour backbenchers might refuse to support the measure and would vote with the Conservative opposition. Even the scheme for public grants for the parliamentary work of opposition parties (Short money) which had been introduced in March 1975, had met with some controversy in the House of Commons, with several Labour MPs including William Hamilton, Dennis Skinner and Audrey Wise voting against the government.

After losing the 1979 general election, however, the Labour leadership firmly embraced the Houghton proposals as items of party policy. A report of an internal inquiry into the finances and organisation of the party in 1980 urged:[115]

> The introduction of state aid is now essential for the continued functioning of our political parties and therefore for the health of our democratic system. Lack of finance by the party has meant that the party has been unable to employ sufficient agents and its organisation has not had the resources to operate as effectively as it would like . . . There must be a commitment to introduce state aid for political parties as a piece of priority legislation.

The proposal for state funding of political parties appeared in each of Labour's manifestos at the 1983, 1987 and 1992 general elections. Its policy document *Meet the Challenge, Make the Change* preceding the 1992 election stated:[116]

> Democracy requires efficient, effective and well funded political parties at both national and local level. We will introduce a system of state financial aid for political parties as recommended by the Houghton Committee. The funding will take the form of annual grants from the Exchequer to national parties, based on the level of electoral support, and limited reimbursement of expenses incurred at local level.

The Liberal Democrats, who have more to gain from state funding than have the Labour Party, also firmly stated their support behind the principle of unconditional state funding along the lines recommended in the Houghton Report.[117]

A more recent version of the Labour Party's policy relating to the form that public funding of parties should take emerged in 1993, when its General Secretary, Larry Whitty, presented the views of the party on the matter to the House of Commons Home Affairs Select Committee.[118] The party continues to endorse the Houghton Report proposals for annual grants for the ongoing expenses of the parties, and for grants to parliamentary candidates at general elections of up to half of their election expenses. But in addition, the Labour Party now believe that at general elections there should be grants paid to each eligible political party towards their national campaign expenses. The amount paid to the party for national election expenses would be subject to a limit of £2.5m.[119] While not ruling out the Houghton Report formula for laying down the conditions for a party's eligibility to receive public funding, and while agreeing that 'the key essential qualification ought to relate to the level of electoral support', its more recent view is that the 'simplest qualification would be based on obtaining at least 5 per cent of the vote' at the previous general election. The party has similarly suggested that reimbursement of a parliamentary candidate's election expenses should depend upon him or her polling at least 5 per cent of votes within the constituency.

Prospects for state funding in Britain

There seems to be little doubt that public funding along the lines proposed in the Houghton Report will be introduced in Britain at some point in the future. The present purely private and voluntary arrangements for party funding, particularly while conducted in secret, have been widely condemned as a very unsatisfactory basis on which politicians can operate in the national interest with complete integrity. There would be a considerable advantage to the British voter in terms of the quality and balance of political information available to him or her nationally over the course of the election campaign, if the new scheme of subsidy adopted included not only an annual grant and reimbursement of 50 per cent of candidates' election expenses (as recommended by the Houghton Report), but also a limited grant available to each qualifying political party which was aimed specifically at alleviating the huge costs of modern electioneering (such as the scheme for reimbursement of a certain amount of party campaign expenses currently supported by Labour). The principle of targeting subsidies at a proportion of the political parties' election expenses has been accepted elsewhere in Europe, where it is perceived to be both necessary and desirable in order to safeguard and foster a fair election contest.[120] The form of future funding of political parties in Britain should depend on efforts to extend the mass memberships of the parties, generating fees and donations from individual members, and introducing a limited scheme of public subsidies to assist the parties to perform their functions – especially in Opposition and during election campaigns – more effectively.

None the less, there will be political difficulties in establishing a scheme of public grants to the parties. Conservative Party opposition is likely to be entrenched, fearing for a decline in its financial advantage over other parties, especially the Liberal Democrats. Times of economic depression make any proposal for a new item of public expenditure less palatable, even if few items of public expenditure can rank higher in importance than protecting the quality of our political and electoral system. And political acceptance of the need for public funding of political parties is handicapped by the lack of enthusiasm for such a proposal in popular opinion. An opinion poll conducted in June 1993 showed that only 13 per cent of voters supported public money being used to finance political parties, with 79 per cent being opposed.[121] Even when the attitude of voters for different parties was compared, the poll indicated that the levels of opinion were fairly similar, with 77 per cent and 82 per cent of Labour and Liberal Democrat voters respectively unfavourably inclined towards the idea of state aid being paid to the parties. However, such opinion poll results are hardly surprising, given that very few ordinary men and women will tell an opinion pollster that they support measures of higher public expenditure and taxation if they can see no immediate benefit to themselves. No doubt public opinion does not look particularly favourably upon any expenditure for political expenses incurred by British politicians, but the reality is that the country accepts such expenditure as being a necessary alternative to politicians becoming beholden to voluntary gifts and the special interests behind them. Parliamentary allowances were never supported enthusiastically by public opinion, yet since 1969 each MP has been able to claim a secretarial and research allowance (up to a maximum of £41 308 per annum), and since 1975 opposition parties have been eligible to receive 'Short money' for reimbursement of their parliamentary work (in 1987–92 up to a maximum of £840 000 per annum). There has been no sign of any public criticism or disquiet following the introduction of these public subsidies, and there is no reason to suppose that the public's attitude to modest grants being paid for the work of parties outside Parliament would be received any differently.

PROPOSAL FOR EXPENDITURE LIMITS UPON PARTY CAMPAIGNING

The principle of ensuring that the wealth of an individual candidate does not give him unfair electoral advantage over opponents was one that was pioneered in Britain in its election law reforms of the late nineteenth century, which established strict limits upon the amount of money that parliamentary candidates may spend on their campaign expenses. But despite the changing political conditions in modern electioneering, such that national party campaigning today has become far more important than local campaigning in determining how local voters choose between their constituency candidates, no analogous expenditure limitation has ever been imposed upon the sums of money which individual political parties may spend during the course of their national campaigning. At Westminster, the policies of the political parties are divided on this issue, along similar lines to that over state funding. All the opposition parties favour national expenditure limitation, including the Labour and Liberal Democrat parties, both of whom have said they will introduce legislation on the matter if elected to government.[122] It was a legislative proposal included in the Political Parties (Income and Expenditure) Bill 1990 introduced as draft legislation into the Commons by Labour MPs David Winnick, Marjorie Mowlam and Tony Banks.[123] Meanwhile, the Conservative Party leadership continues to defend robustly the existing freedom from expenditure controls.

Opposition to national expenditure limits

Defence of the present absence of controls is founded upon the preservation of our existing electoral structure, and freedom of expression by those who wish to campaign upon political issues at elections. It is suggested by opponents that there would be practical problems in drafting the legislation, including on the definition of a political party. Thus the Conservative Party has argued:[124]

> In our opinion there is no anomaly in controlling strictly the expenditure of individual candidates while allowing national campaigning to continue during an election without such controls. National political parties and other organisations should continue to be allowed to promote and explain their policies and viewpoint by all possible means, provided that in doing so that do not directly promote the election of any particular candidate ... Controls over such national campaigning would be quite new to British law and would raise a number of significant questions, of which the salient one would be how to define the organisations on whose behalf the campaigns were conducted. In the case of political parties it would be unavoidable to give these bodies a statutory existence which they at present lack.

A Hansard Society Commission on election campaigns, chaired by the former Conservative MP and minister, Christopher Chataway (and largely written by the Oxford psephologist, Dr David Butler), has now strengthened the arguments against national expenditure controls by producing a report which concluded with its opposition to such a reform. The reasoning of the Commission was that there was no danger of escalating election spending by the parties, nor a worrying imbalance in the campaigns of one major party over another. It said that while spending by the two major parties at general elections was on the increase, the amounts were not excessive by comparative standards. Furthermore, the Commission believed, 'Such restrictions in practice could be easily evaded by sympathetic non-party organisation and by editorial material in the Press', with the result that 'it would be futile to restrict expenditure by the parties if sympathetic groups and individuals could continue to perform the same function unrestricted'.[125] Suggesting that public funding of parties was a more important issue than expenditure controls, the report argued:[126]

> The danger, if there is one, does not seem to us to rest in expenditure imbalances between the major parties or in the fact that they are spending to excess so much as in the risk that other parties and candidates may be unable to put their case to the electors in the same way owing to the cost of modern campaigning methods. We are therefore not attracted to the concept of national party expenditure limits or restrictions on sympathetic advertising.

Support for national expenditure limits

The main argument for expenditure limitation is that it serves to equalise the electoral contest between participants. It is a simple and straightforward device for ensuring that wealthy participants, through their capacity to purchase and produce more electioneering propaganda, are able effectively to buy more votes than are less affluent opponents. This, of course, is the principle adopted in the election law instituted in the nineteenth century, which sought to control local campaign expenses. It is argued that Britain has allowed the state of its election law to become seriously out of date, and that analogous limits should now be imposed upon national party campaigning. Another commission of the Hansard Society, chaired by the former Labour minister, Edmund Dell (and largely written by the Oxford political scientist Vernon Bogdanor), which had earlier reported in 1981 on the financing of political parties, supported national party expenditure controls, saying:[127]

> We believe that there is a strong case for limiting the amount which political parties can spend at national level during an election . . . In the nineteenth century, a general election was seen largely as a contest between individual candidates, and spending by party headquarters was a

comparatively negligible factor. The law restricting the expenditure of individual candidates controlled, therefore, virtually all election spending. Today it controls only a relatively small part of such spending . . . We believe the law in this sphere to be seriously out of date and therefore propose a statutory limitation upon election expenditure by the national political parties.

A different argument for expenditure controls on the political parties is simply to avoid any further downward spiral in the conduct of election campaigning into an endless flood of party propaganda emanating from parties' headquarters. It is argued that voters, in order to form an opinion upon which to base their vote, need sufficient but not excessive electioneering material laid before them by the parties. What voters do not need, and what all contemporary electoral systems are in danger of degenerating into, is an ever-growing, mindless flood of negative campaigning propaganda. This view rejects the 1991 Hansard Society Commission's belief that there is no danger of such excess, pointing to the remorseless increase of election campaign expenditure at every recent general election, to a point which nearly bankrupts each party. Even allowing for monetary inflation, these figures show a dramatic growth in expenditure on electioneering propaganda since the end of the 1970s (see below).

Supporters of national spending limits point to the fact that the absence of controls at the national level is now undermining the purpose and effect of the expenditure restrictions on constituency campaigning under Britain's existing election law. Money from the central party is used to promote the election of particular candidates – the party's candidates – within each constituency, by way of advertisements, direct mail and other propaganda promoting the political party. Indeed, the major events in constituency

National party campaign expenditure at General Elections, 1955–92 (£m)

	Conservative Party	Labour Party
1955	00.14	00.07
1959	00.63	00.24
1964	01.23	00.54
1966	00.35	00.20
1970	00.63	00.53
1974 Feb.	00.68	00.44
1974 Oct.	00.95	00.52
1979	02.33	01.57
1983	03.80	02.30
1987	09.00	04.70
1992	11.20	07.20

Table 7.4[128]

campaigns today are usually orchestrated out of resources from the central parties, such as the transporting of prominent party figures into marginal constituencies to speak and canvass with the local candidate. As the Labour MP David Winnick argued in a House of Commons debate in 1993:[129]

> The amount spent on behalf of a candidate at a general election is tightly controlled. If a candidate exceeds that sum and wins, he may appear before a court and can be disqualified. That is right and nobody is suggesting that that rule should be altered. Nobody would suggest that it should be possible to buy votes. Control exists to ensure fairness.
>
> If that is the case on the local scene, why should the political parties at a general election be able to spend as much as they like? There is no limit. The fact of there being no limit in that case undermines what we are trying to establish locally.

Proponents of expenditure limits can point to an extensive and growing body of opinion both abroad and within Britain which believes that national party expenditure controls have now become vital to protect the political process. Several countries around the world, including in Europe and North America (notably in Canada) have recently established national expenditure limits on party campaigning.[130] In Britain, where every political party in Parliament except the Conservatives supports the proposal, there is overwhelming popular support for a limit being placed upon the parties' campaign spending. Over 80 per cent of respondents supported the proposal (including 79 per cent of Conservative voters) in the most recent poll taken on the subject.[131]

Drafting the new legislation

Three important details will need to be addressed in any future legislation that imposes a national expenditure limit. First, there is the question of whether in the drafting of new legislation there is a need to define what is a political party. As has already been explained, this is a term which has never yet been used in British election law. The issue is considered later in this chapter under electoral administration and enforcement, where a definition is offered that adopts the Canadian test of whether a prime purpose of an organisation is the nomination and support of candidates at elections.[132] Of course, where the organisation in question already has a number of MPs in the House of Commons, no problems would be likely to arise as to whether or not the organisation is covered by the legislation. A second important detail is the precise campaign expenditure limit to be imposed upon the political parties. This must be a matter for political agreement between the parties, but if the spirit of the Act is to be followed, then initially it should represent a figure which calls a halt to existing electioneering practice, and which therefore should certainly be no greater than £12m. This figure might then be made subject in the controlling Act of Parliament to amendment by way of statutory instrument laid before the House of Commons. Under current electoral timing arrangements, the period covered by the expenditure restriction might be similar to that currently applicable to the expenses of parliamentary candidates, namely the four or five week duration from the commencement of the election until polling day. For clarity, the commencement of the election campaign might be specifically stated to be the date on which the general election was publicly announced, or in default of such announcement, then when the royal proclamation dissolving Parliament was issued. However, election campaign propaganda in practice begins significantly earlier than this, particularly by the party in government, whose leadership holds the knowledge of when the general election will in fact be called. If fixed-term Parliaments were introduced, as discussed and recommended in chapter 2, so that the date of the next general election was known by all in advance, then it would become easier to draft a longer and more definite period of, say, three months prior to the election.

A third important component in the legislation will be that if the spending controls are to be effective, they will need to provide not only for campaign expenses of the party itself, but also expenses incurred by other individuals and organisations campaigning on their behalf. In other words, the spending limit should not be circumvented by outside supporters of the party advertising or otherwise spending money lobbying for electors to vote for the party. The Representation of the People Act already prohibits the spending of money by anyone other than a candidate and his or her election agent on promoting or procuring his or her election, and it would be necessary to extend this restriction to apply to expenditure that was shown to be intentionally incurred with a view to promoting the electoral prospects of any party or parties whose candidates were standing for election. Thus the necessary legislation might adapt the present provision in the Representation of the People Act 1983, which prohibits campaign expenses not authorised by candidates' election agents.[133] The relevant provision might then read:

No expenses shall, with a view to promoting or procuring the election of members of a particular political party, or the non-election of members of a particular political party, be incurred by any person or organisation other than the national agent for the party in question and persons authorised in writing by the national agent on account –
(a) of holding public meetings or organising any public display; or
(b) of issuing advertisements, circulars or publications; or
(c) of otherwise presenting to the electors a political party and its members or its views or the extent or nature of its backing or disparaging another political party and its members.

Those campaign expenses that are authorised by the party's national agent will, of course, be treated as falling within the amount of money allowed to be spent on the overall party campaign. The effect of this provision would be that expenditure incurred, similar to that in the *Tronoh Mines* case in 1952 when the Tronoh–Malayan Tin Group of Companies bought a full page advertisement in *The Times* in which to publish its condemnation of Labour Party policies during the 1951 general election campaign, would be unlawful.[134]

Clearly it will always be impossible to control all forms of political assistance to the parties at election time, even some which quite clearly carry some financial benefit. Benefits in kind given to political parties towards their campaign expenses, such as free use of communications systems or advertising hoardings, should be dealt with by other legislation dealing specifically with donations to political parties. Thus benefits in kind offered to parties by individuals would be subject to any new law on disclosure of sources of income over a specified sum of money (suggested earlier to be initially £1 000);[135] trade union benefits in kind offered to the Labour Party might be covered by the trade union legislation on political funds and members' rights of consent and opt-out; and company benefits in kind offered to the Conservative Party should be regulated by new provisions concerning the creation of political funds within the company, similarly made subject to shareholders' approval and opt-out arrangements.[136]

Would this legal restriction on individuals, organisations and pressure groups campaigning for particular political parties and their policies constitute an unwarranted interference with a citizen's fundamental right to freedom of expression? The drafting of campaign expenditure limits in other countries has indeed led to complications under their constitutional civil liberties provisions, but these are not likely to be followed under Britain's legal system. On the moral arguments involved, it is difficult to see why such a restriction should now be regarded as a breach of freedom of expression, when an identical restriction upon promoting the electoral prospects of individual politicians has already been in force under the constituency expenditure limits since the beginning of the twentieth century. Furthermore, there is nothing in this proposal that will affect the complete freedom of all individuals and organisations during general elections to express themselves in any voluntary way – other than through advertising and publicity that is purchased with money. Certainly the freedom of the press will not be diminished, and individual newspapers will no doubt continue to present their partisan viewpoints through their leading articles and reporting.

One of the principal objects of British election law should be to provide a framework in which a fair contest between candidates and parties can take place, with voters receiving a balanced and accurate flow of information upon which to base a choice between the different people and programmes of public policy for the future government of the country. Ensuring that parties which enjoy substantial public support have the minimum necessary financial resources from which to present their election campaign to the people is one way of helping create the appropriate conditions in which free elections can take place. Imposing an expenditure limit on the amount of money that may be spent on campaign advertising and other political propaganda at general elections is its necessary corollary, and represents a direct and simple device for facilitating fair election contests. The control of national election expenses would help to ensure that the present tendency towards an increasing mass of party propaganda is resisted. This in any event is subject to a diminishing impact, whereas from the point of view of informing the voter, the improvements that are crucially needed lie in the arena of quality rather than quantity. In so far as one or more parties may be richer than others, by capping the sum they are allowed to spend at a level perfectly adequate for efficient publicity and promotion purposes, they would not be able to enjoy an unacceptably great advantage based purely upon the wealth of their supporters. Such a limit, plus ensuring that the prohibition on political advertising on television remains in place, should serve to resist any further downward slide into the generally regarded mayhem and excesses of American-style electioneering.

ELECTORAL ADMINISTRATION AND ENFORCEMENT

Earlier in this book, when considering the existing arrangements whereby the boundaries of parliamentary constituencies are reviewed periodically, it was suggested that a single official agency – an Electoral Commission – should be created, with responsibilities covering a number of important aspects of the electoral system.[137] It was envisaged that this new body would be established by Act of Parliament, laying down provisions governing the composition and independence of the commission.

The central functions of this Electoral Commission should be first, the determination of parliamentary constituency boundaries (superseding the work of the current Boundary Commissioners); second, electoral administration (including electoral registration and the work of returning officers at parliamentary elections); and third, a reviewing and advisory function (including the preparation of annual reports to Parliament upon the conduct and administration of electoral matters within its field of responsibility). The case for having an Electoral Commission would be further strengthened if in the future, as seems likely, some or all of the reform proposals on political finance considered in this chapter are adopted. For example, the introduction of expenditure limits upon party campaigning expenses at general elections will require financial accounts to be drawn up and lodged with an appropriate official body. Similarly, there will be a need for official responsibility for the distribution of public grants under any new scheme of subsidies for the political parties. If statutory accounting by the parties is to be introduced, together with any new requirements or restrictions placed upon financial gifts paid to the parties, then an official body will need to supervise, administer and enforce the new arrangements. Since government ministries are subject to the political control of party politicians, it would be wise for the official responsibility for any or all of these statutory innovations to be placed firmly in the hands of a politically impartial body rather than the Home Office. To these functions concerning the supervision of political finance might be added further functions concerning the operation of the electoral system as and when they arise. For example, if and when allocation of party political broadcasts between the parties is based upon some statutory rather than informal basis, responsibility for carrying out the allocation might be handed to the Electoral Commission. Any future regulation of party electioneering (for example in the standards of political advertising), or concerning the media during the election campaign (for example in following codes of practice governing the publication of opinion polls) might also be matters referred to the Commission for supervision and enforcement. Finally, the Commission should be empowered to launch its own independent inquiries into complaints of electoral maladministration or misconduct by officials or politicians, and where appropriate bring legal proceedings.

The creation of a national independent agency such as the proposed Electoral Commission, vested by law with responsibility for a range of electoral matters, has become a modern constitutional feature in several Western democracies. Australia established its own Electoral Commission in 1983 to take charge of all aspects of electoral administration, even for employing returning officers.[138] In Canada, there is a Chief Electoral Officer who is responsible for electoral administration, the control of election expenditure, the registration of political parties, and appointing and receiving reports from both the Commissioner of Canada Elections, who enforces Canadian election law, and the Broadcasting Arbitrator, who regulates political broadcasting. It is likely that this trend towards unifying administrative responsibility for the electoral system will continue in Europe, North America and in Commonwealth countries, as the conduct of parliamentary elections becomes ever more sophisticated and the law and practice governing elections requires a closer degree of attention than before. In terms of public accountability, it is extremely likely that a single, unified body will be a considerable improvement in the quality of information and reporting it gives to MPs and others, rather than the existing state of affairs in Britain, where the various officials charged with responsibility for diverse aspects of the electoral system are spread across the whole terrain of Whitehall and local government. It is significant that those who work in electoral administration, as represented by the

Association of Electoral Administrators, themselves believe that the establishment of an Electoral Commission would improve the quality and efficiency of their work, and 'enable . . . electoral administrators to be seen to perform their duties independently'.[139]

Implementation of several of the reforms discussed in this chapter, particularly those concerning the regulation of the income and expenditure of the political parties, would require the recognition of parties in British law. This would be a relatively new phenomenon in Britain, where parties are not yet part of election law at all, although they have been referred to in at least three Acts of Parliament, namely the Trade Union Act 1984[140] (dealing with trade union political funds), the Companies Act 1985 (concerning disclosure of political donations over £200 in reports to shareholders) and the Inheritance Act 1984 (exemption of political donations from death duties). The regulation of party income and expenditure would be most easily administered through a system of voluntary registration of political parties. Voluntary registration, carrying with it an undertaking to comply with specified obligations such as the filing of annual financial accounts and returns of election expenses, would be the price to be paid by any party that wished to apply for and receive a public grant under any new scheme of state funding of parties. This proposal for voluntary registration has recently been supported by both the Institute for Public Policy Research in its written constitutional proposals, and by the Labour Party in giving its views to the House of Commons Home Affairs Select Committee on party funding.[141]

However, enforcement of expenditure limits on party electioneering expenses at general elections, and also the legal requirement for public disclosure of large donations, would require a legal definition of a 'political party' to cover the unlikely event that a party had sufficient private funding of its own to be able to avoid voluntary registration because it did not need or want any public money. The form of future British legislation on political finance will have many precedents to draw upon from other parts of the world, particularly those where political parties are expressly provided for already in the constitutional law of the state, such as in Germany and France. Under one election finance law in Canada, for example:[142]

> Political party means an association, organisation or affiliation of voters comprising a political organisation whose prime purpose is the nomination and support of candidates at elections.

For all practical purposes, whether or not a political organisation is to be regarded in law as a 'political party' falling within the terms of the legislation can be assumed from its *de facto* existence within the House of Commons. Its status as a party will be self-evident if it is in receipt of 'Short money' from the Accounting Officer at Westminster. In the unlikely situation of a political party which lacked any representation in Parliament spending in excess of the national expenditure limit allowed for in the legislation, the High Court would have no difficulty in establishing whether the organisation was a 'political party' by reference to its members standing as parliamentary candidates at the general election. So, in reality, there is nothing that is very new, and no legal difficulties of definition, in the drafting of new legislation which seeks to overhaul and modernise the British electoral system in respect of the financial affairs of the political parties.

8 Arguments about Proportional Representation

THE PRINCIPLE OF PROPORTIONAL REPRESENTATION

Proportional representation is not in itself a system for elections, but rather a criterion upon which to evaluate the working of any one of a range of electoral systems which can be used for voting purposes. It is a principle or yardstick by which to test the degree of representative proportionality between citizens' votes and successful party candidates. More precisely, what is looked for is the percentage equivalents between the total national votes cast for the respective parties' candidates, and the number of seats won by the parties in the House of Commons. Proponents of proportional representation believe that there should be a direct and close correlation between total votes cast for each party across the country at a general election, and the number of seats won by each party in the House of Commons. Under a pure application of the principle, if half the voters in the country vote for the Conservative Party and one-third vote Labour, then half the membership of the House of Commons – 326 MPs – should be Conservative MPs and one-third of the House – 217 MPs – should be Labour. By contrast, in Britain, as Sir Ivor Jennings once succinctly put it, 'Our system of representation produces the result that the size of a majority in the House of Commons may bear little resemblance to the size of the majority in the country.'[1] No one in British politics today is advocating a scheme of electoral reform that is completely proportional between votes and seats (which would require what is called a national list system) and only two countries in the world (the Netherlands and Israel) possess such a method of voting. But what has precipitated the contemporary controversy over proportional representation in Britain is that of all the different methods of election used in the Western democracies, the existing British system – popularly known as the first-past-the-post system, and more properly called a simple plurality system – is the one that least conforms to the principle of proportional representation. First-past-the-post voting is peculiarly disproportionate in its translation of votes into parliamentary seats, and this has a number of highly significant ramifications with regard to the composition and operation of Britain's Parliament and political leadership in government.

362

Under the British method of first-past-the-post voting, on general election day separate electoral contests are fought within each of the 651 parliamentary constituencies, and the person who achieves the highest number of votes cast is the winner in each constituency. In typical British legal style, this fundamental rule of British political democracy is not prominently declared in section 1 or anywhere near the beginning of the Representation of the People Act 1983, but instead it is buried away in small print at the back in Schedule 1, Rule 18. This pivotal article of our constitutional law is drafted to read:

> The votes at the poll shall be given by ballot, the result shall be ascertained by counting the votes given to each candidate and the candidate to whom the majority of votes have been given shall be declared to have been elected.

So first-past-the-post voting means that if the candidate for party *A* gets 10 883 votes, the candidate for party *B* 13 255, the candidate for party *C* 14 883, the candidate for party *D* 3 108, and others jointly 851, then the candidate for party *C* is returned as MP. This is so despite his percentage support among voters being only 33.7 per cent, and the fact that 66.3 per cent of the local electorate – two out of every three local citizens – voted against him or her. As it happens, these figures represent the precise election result in Conwy, won by Sir Wyn Roberts for the Conservatives in 1992. And such an election result is certainly not unusual: in fact, the majority of constituencies are won on a minority vote. Magnified to a national scale, on 9 April 1992 the Conservative Party won a 21-seat overall majority in the House of Commons on the basis of a clear minority – 41.9 per cent – of the votes cast. So 58.1 per cent of the British electorate voted against the Conservative government, but none the less it was returned to office with the power in Parliament to outvote all other political parties combined. No government since 1935 has taken office with the electoral authority of a majority of the citizens' votes. Even the former Prime Minister, Margaret Thatcher, at the height of her political triumph after the 1983 election, with a huge Commons majority of 397 seats to Labour's 209, had, in fact, been rejected by 57.6 per cent of all voters in the country. With a Commons' majority of over 150 Conservative MPs, her government could legislate freely in Parliament, even on some matters deeply opposed by public opinion such as the poll tax, by reference to the dubious moral authority of just 42.4 per cent of voters in the country.

It is easy to see why the British electoral system has been strongly criticised, not only by those politicians who lose out under the existing system, but also by many leading political scientists such as the late Professor Ramsay Muir, whose view was that 'the existing electoral system is a distortion and a falsification of democracy',[2] and by many leading constitutional lawyers such as Professor Sir William Wade at Oxford

University, who has said, 'If it is accepted that a democratic Parliament ought to represent so far as possible the preferences of the voters, this system is probably the worst that could be devised.'[3] By wrapping up the election of our national Parliament and government into 651 local, separate and self-contained parcels, it distorts popular representation across the country in terms of the proportionality of national preferences. And because of the huge number of 'wasted votes' of ordinary citizens in every constituency – in the Conwy example above amounting to 66.3 per cent, or 28 097 electors, being left unrepresented in the composition of Parliament – it can also be claimed that the British electoral system in reality disenfranchises many millions of voters within the country. In fact, about half of all the votes cast at a general election count towards the election of nobody.

The degree of variation between total national votes cast for each of the three main parties and the number of parliamentary seats each party received after applying the first-past-the-post British method, can be seen from the table on page 365, which shows the general election results over the period since the Second World War. Later in this chapter, we shall see the effect that alternative methods of election used in other countries, might have had on the results of recent elections.

THE DIFFERENT METHODS OF ELECTION

If the existing first-past-the-post method of election used in Britain was ever to be replaced, the serious contenders to take its place would be one of the following: the alternative vote, or a variant of it known as the supplementary vote system; the single transferable vote; or the additional-member system. These are the different electoral models that have been most widely supported and canvassed in Britain in the context of reform. Precisely how each of these electoral systems works will now be considered.

The alternative vote

The alternative vote is the least radical of the different proposals for electoral reform that have been put forward. It would retain the constituencies of the United Kingdom as they stand, and each would continue to return a single MP, as before. The difference, however, and the chief object of this method, is to ensure that each winning candidate receives an overall majority of votes from electors within the constituency. In other words, in contrast to the existing first-past-the-post system where, as has been seen, a winning candidate may, in fact, poll well under half of the votes

Proportionality between votes and seats, 1945–92

		1945	1950	1951	1955	1959	1964	1966	1970	Feb. 1974	Oct. 1974	1979	1983	1987	1992
Conservative	Votes	39.6	43.5	48.0	49.7	49.3	43.4	41.9	46.4	37.8	35.8	43.9	42.4	42.3	41.9
	Seats	32.8	47.7	51.3	54.8	57.9	48.3	40.1	52.4	46.6	43.5	53.4	61.1	57.9	51.6
Labour	Votes	48.0	45.1	48.8	46.4	43.9	44.1	48.1	43.0	37.1	39.2	36.9	27.6	30.8	34.4
	Seats	61.4	50.4	47.2	44.0	41.0	50.3	57.8	45.6	47.4	50.2	42.2	32.2	35.2	41.6
Liberal Democrat	Votes	9.0	9.1	2.6	2.7	5.9	11.2	8.5	7.5	19.3	18.3	13.8	25.4	22.5	17.8
	Seats	1.9	1.4	1.0	0.9	0.9	1.4	1.9	1.0	2.2	2.0	1.7	3.5	3.4	3.1

Table 8.1[4]

cast at the constituency election, and quite often little more than a third, the alternative vote ensures that through a system of preferential voting one candidate always ends up being regarded as having over 50 per cent of popular support. It is a majoritarian system for electing each MP. When the voter goes into the polling booth, he or she is required to place a number against the different candidates in the order of his or her personal preference: his or her favourite candidate being numbered '1', the next preferred candidate '2', and so on. As only one MP is being returned from each constituency, each of the political parties fields only one candidate, of course, so effectively the voter is placing his or her vote in terms of party

Specimen ballot paper: the alternative vote

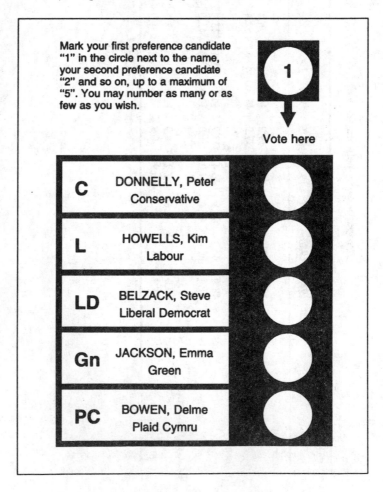

preference. (Note, by way of contrast, that in multi-member constituencies, such as under the single transferable vote, each political party will field several different candidates – up to the number of parliamentary seats to be returned by the constituency – and this allows voters to distinguish between different candidates belonging to the same party.) After the close of polling, the returning officer will count up the numbers of first preferences and see what result this produces. If, as will often be the case, no single candidate has polled over 50 per cent of all votes cast, then the lowest-placed candidate drops out, but the second preferences of that lowest placed candidate are then transferred to the other candidates. This process of removing the bottom candidate and spreading second preferences around the remaining candidates continues until one emerges as the overall majority winner, who will be declared returned as the constituency MP.

The alternative vote system is used for elections to the Australian House of Representatives, and was nearly introduced into British elections to the House of Commons in 1918 and 1931.[5] It is not a system that accords closely to the principle of proportional representation, because in determining the composition of the House of Commons it takes no account of the wasted votes cast towards losing candidates, nor does it include any element whereby voters' regional or national party preferences might count towards overall parliamentary representation. A common criticism of the alternative vote is that it would tend to promote the least disagreeable candidate, rather than the person whom most people felt most strongly should be their MP. One might have thought that this system would particularly operate to the advantage of the Liberal Democrat party, because it often happens that its candidates come in at second place, and they are widely perceived to be the centre party in British politics, lying between the Conservatives on the right and Labour on the left. However, the Liberal Democrats would benefit very little from the alternative vote, which may in part explain why the party has rejected this system as its preferred scheme for electoral reform, and instead strongly support the single transferable vote. Research on the result of the 1992 general election, had it been conducted under the alternative vote, indicates that the Liberal Democrats would have won only ten more parliamentary seats.[6] Indeed, the projected results from this research show that the alternative vote would have made remarkably little difference at all to the result of the 1992 election, and John Major's Conservative Party would still have formed the government.

The advantage of the alternative vote is that it would involve only a very easy modification of elections to introduce it into Britain, above all because it would maintain the same constituencies (and therefore the system of constituency review), and the tradition of a single parliamentary representative for each seat. And the winning MP, and by the same token the government as a whole, could claim to be representing the majority view of the nation. The disadvantage, however, is that the quirks of the system across the whole country can lead to almost as much distorted representative proportionality, in terms of the levels of public support for the different political parties, as under the existing first-past-the-post system in Britain.

Supplementary vote system

The supplementary vote system is a very recent, custom-made electoral system, designed by some contributors to the recent Labour Party's internal Plant Report.[7] It is essentially a modification of the alternative vote, in that it retains the existing single-member constituency structure, and allows for preferential voting in determining the winning candidate. Its differences from the alternative vote are first, that voters may choose only two preferences; and, second, that the eventual winner must be one of the two candidates who scored highest from adding up the first preferences. At the count, the returning officer's staff would add up all the first preferences cast towards all the candidates, and if any candidate had gained over 50 per cent of the votes then he or she would be declared the winner. If there was no overall majority for one of the candidates, then all the candidates except the two who scored the highest number of first preference votes would be eliminated, and a new count would take place. At this count, the second preferences on those ballot papers which expressed a first preference for one of the eliminated candidates will be added to the first count totals of the top two candidates competing for final victory. (Second preferences cast in favour of an eliminated candidate are ignored.) Whichever of the two candidates receives the most votes in total will be declared the winner.

Under this method of election, a British voter would be handed a ballot paper to complete which took the form of that shown on page 369.

The strengths and weaknesses of the supplementary vote system are very similar to the alternative vote. As with the alternative vote, it contains no mechanism for ensuring proportionality, and its impact upon recent general election results is unlikely to have been significantly different from that under the alternative vote. Its chief architect, the MP, Dale Campbell-Savours, maintains that in 1992 it would have produced no more seats for the Labour Party, but would have redistributed 32 seats won by the Conservatives across the Liberal Democrat and nationalist parties.[8] Neither is the supplementary vote a strictly majoritarian system within each constituency. Under this method, the winner may not necessarily secure an overall majority of final votes cast because there may be voters who cast neither a first nor a second preference towards either of the final two candidates. It is a system whose invention has been influenced by, and has close similarities to, the second ballot method used in determining who will

Specimen ballot paper: the supplementary vote system

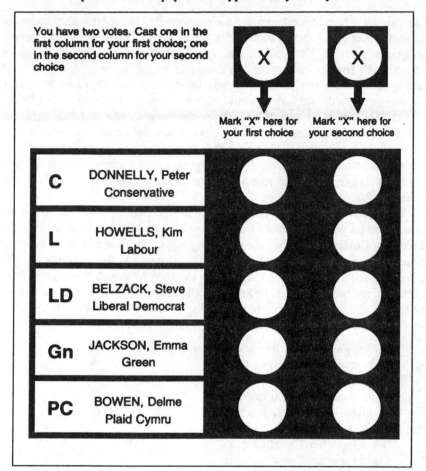

You have two votes. Cast one in the first column for your first choice; one in the second column for your second choice

Mark "X" here for your first choice   Mark "X" here for your second choice

C	DONNELLY, Peter Conservative	
L	HOWELLS, Kim Labour	
LD	BELZACK, Steve Liberal Democrat	
Gn	JACKSON, Emma Green	
PC	BOWEN, Delme Plaid Cymru	

be the President in France, where after a first count of all the votes cast for the respective presidential candidates, if no overall majority winner emerges, then the top two candidates will go through to a final contest.[9] However, in this French election two separate ballots take place, a week apart from one another, for the two respective counts. Only a first preference is stated at the first ballot, and if there is no overall winner, then all French voters return to the polling booths a week later to decide between the two final presidential contestants. Under the supplementary vote system advocated for Britain, the voters would vote twice on the same day (without knowing who the top two candidates are going to be), instead of a week apart.

The single transferable vote

The single transferable vote (STV) would transform the existing constituencies of the United Kingdom into far fewer and larger geographical units. Each of the new constituencies would elect a group of several MPs (normally four or five), instead of the present single-member arrangement. Each party would field up to as many candidates as there were MPs to be elected, and voters would indicate their preferences on the ballot papers. The count by returning officers determining the winning group of MPs is a complicated matter, but involves successful candidates achieving a set quota of votes, above which number second or next preferences are cast among the other candidates. It is recognised as an electoral system that produces a high level of proportional representation between votes for and seats won by political parties.

The precise number of MPs to be elected within each of the new constituencies would be prescribed by law and reviewed periodically by the Boundary Commissions, but the great majority of them would have between three and six MPs. This was the scheme contained, for example, in the detailed proposal for STV designed by the Liberal/Social Democrat Commission on Electoral Reform in the 1980s,[10] which recommended redrawing the United Kingdom into 143 parliamentary constituencies, with the number of members in each of the different constituencies being:

One-member Constituencies	4
Two-member Constituencies	9
Three-member Constituencies	25
Four-member Constituencies	29
Five-member Constituencies	48
Six-member Constituencies	23
Seven-member Constituencies	3
Eight-member Constituencies	2

The most common constituency would be one in which five MPs represent an area with approximately 300 000 citizens. In urban centres, for example, instead of the present single-member constituencies of Bristol East, Bristol North West, Bristol South, Bristol West, and Kingswood, there might be a single, new five-member constituency of 'Bristol'. In larger, more rural areas, for example in north Wales, the present constituencies of Ynys Mon, Caernarfon, Conwy, Meirionnydd nant Conwy, Clwyd North West, and Clwyd South West, might be converted into a six-member constituency of 'Conwy and Clwyd'.

The process of calculating precisely which candidates have won under the STV is a complex and sophisticated business. So far as the voter is concerned, he or she is simply asked to mark on the ballot paper his or her preferences by placing numbers 1, 2, 3, etc. against the candidates' names (see the sample ballot paper on page 372). What is important under this system is for a 'quota' (in Ireland, known as the 'droop quota') to be calculated in advance, which, for example, in a five-member constituency would be roughly equivalent to one-sixth of the votes cast, and the eventual results are decided by reference to successful candidates reaching this quota of votes, and a method of transferring second, third, etc., preference votes among all the candidates in successive counts until the required number of successful candidates as MPs is attained. This transfer of votes is always likely to be necessary, not least because the reputation or standing of one of each party's candidates will generally be higher among the party's supporters than other candidates who are possibly less well known, and so the most popular party figure will probably have attracted the lion's share of the total first preferences. There may be said to be three stages in the whole process of electing candidates under STV, which may involve as many as eight or more separate counts by the returning officer and his or her staff.

Stage one

After the close of the poll, each returning officer will work out the quota for his or her constituency. The precise formula of the quota is:

$$\frac{\text{Total ballot}}{\text{Total seats} + 1} + 1 \quad \text{or} \quad \frac{b}{s+1} + 1$$

So if 240 000 electors voted, and there were five MPs to be returned, the quota would be 40 001. Any of the candidates polling this quota or more is elected.

Stage two

If fewer than five candidates are elected at stage one, then a transfer of second preferences from the winners' ballot papers will take place. The candidates who were marked second on the winners' ballot papers therefore receive more votes, not at their full value, but scaled down by a fraction depending upon the sizes of the surplus. The precise fraction to be used by the returning officer and multiplied against the number of votes for each of the candidates nominated as a second preference would be,

$$\frac{\text{Votes for a candidate} - \text{Quota}}{\text{Votes for that candidate}} = \frac{v - q}{v}$$

So if A received 60 001 first preference votes, and the quota is 40 001, then 20 000 votes – or one-third of the value of each of his or her second preferences – can be redistributed to other candidates. This transfer begins with the top-scoring winner, and is then repeated for all other winning

Specimen Ballot Paper: the single transferable vote

VOTING PAPER

Election of 5 members

Mark your first preference candidate "1" in the box next to the name [1], your second preference candidate "2" [2], and so on, up to a maximum of "14". You may number as many or as few as you wish.

A Conservative Party	B Labour Party	C Liberal Democrat	D Green Party	E Natural Law Party
☐ BOTTOMLY Virginia	☐ DOBSON Frank	☐ HUGHES Simon	☐ LAWSON Richard	☐ ARGYLE Jacqueline
☐ WATTS John	☐ HARMAN Harriet	☐ GIFFORD Zerbanoo		
☐ HENNESSY Tony	☐ KHABRA Piara	☐ MARQUAND Charles		
☐ BOWDEN Gerry	☐ JOHNSON Yvonne	☐ BARING Susan		

candidates who have passed the quota and been elected. Where second preference votes are for candidates who have already passed the quota, they are ignored, and the candidate who is marked as third preference receives them (or if the third preference has already won, then whichever next preference down the order on the ballot paper who has not yet reached the quota).

Stage three

If stage two fails to produce five winning candidates, then a different process begins, of eliminating the lowest-ranking candidate, and spreading second or next preferences around the other candidates. This is repeated, working up from the bottom of the list of candidates, until the required number of winners is deemed to have reached the quota. In the rare event of the elimination process itself failing to produce the requisite number of winning candidates, then the candidates falling below the quota who have won the highest number of votes are none the less declared elected.

The STV method of elections has been used in the Republic of Ireland since 1922, and in a few other representative assemblies including Malta (since 1921) and the Australian Upper House (since 1949). It was used nationally in Britain for electing the university parliamentary seats between 1918 and 1948, and is used at the time of writing in Northern Ireland for elections to the European Parliament. It has been the most favoured model of the twentieth century among reformers as a proposal for securing greater proportional representation in Britain, and, indeed, in 1954 David Butler referred to it as being 'the only system seriously advocated in Britain'.[11] Certainly, in terms of party politics, the Liberal Party (now the Liberal Democrats) have in the post-Second World War period consistently supported the introduction of STV over alternative models of electoral reform. The most direct consequence of STV is to make the great majority of votes count towards the parliamentary representation of the constituency, so that the large numbers of 'wasted votes' produced under the first-past-the-post system are minimised. Similarly, there is little doubt that STV tends to produce a high degree of proportionality between national votes and party representation, and the larger the number of seats within each constituency, the greater the representative proportionality becomes. In the case of the Republic of Ireland in the 1987 and 1989 elections, the two major parties' presence in their parliamentary assembly, Dail Eireann, were very close to their national level of support compared to British elections: Fine Gael polled 27.1 per cent of the votes and received 30.3 per cent of the seats in 1987, and 29.3 per cent and 33.3 per cent respectively in 1989; Fianna Fail polled 44.1 per cent of the vote for 49.1 per cent of the seats in 1987, and 44.1 per cent and 46.7 per cent respectively in 1989. STV does not purport to be completely proportional, but much more so than first-past-the-post can ever achieve. STV's level of proportionality is tempered by retaining constituencies (albeit very large ones, as would be the case if applied in Britain) and its scheme of preferential voting. It has been claimed that preferential voting allows voters for one of the major parties to indicate which of the minor parties is the most favoured junior coalition partner, if no overall majority is obtained. At the 1973 Irish election, Fine Gael and Labour agreed a coalition deal in advance of polling, and urged their respective supporters to support this pact by supporters of each nominating the other party as their second preference.

Another distinctive feature of STV is that it allows voters to choose between the different candidates belonging to the same party. In other words, if you are a Labour Party supporter in a five-member parliamentary constituency, and the local party association selects Tony Blair, Robin Cook, Tony Benn, Dennis Skinner, and somebody else you have never heard of, you are effectively being asked whether you prefer one candidate and his or her personal politics over the other. In this example, some potential Labour voters will be attracted to the more moderate line of the party leadership represented by Messrs Blair and Cook, and be put off by the socialist radicalism of Messrs Benn and Skinner, or vice versa. This aspect of STV is, in fact, highly controversial, and goes to the heart of the role that should be played by local party associations in the political process. There were many complaints by Labour politicians at the start of the 1980s, especially from those who later broke away to form the Social Democratic Party, that some local parties had become unrepresentative left-wing caucuses wielding an excessive degree of power over MPs and candidates, effectively dictating to voters for whom they should vote, and often fielding candidates who did not typify mainstream political views sufficiently attractive to gain the support of most local voters. Indeed, the SDP, several of whose members had formerly had difficulties with their local parties when within the Labour Party, saw the weakening of the authority of local party associations over constituency representatives as a very welcome feature of STV. Dr David Owen, former leader of the SDP, wrote:[12]

One advantage of choosing the single transferable vote is that it is a preferential system; the quality and views of the candidates are of considerable importance, and the voter can discriminate between candidates of a particular party or between parties. For example, traditional Labour supporters could drop a militant Labour candidate from their selection, and a traditional Conservative voter could drop a Monday Club right-wing Conservative candidate . . . Critics of preference voting see it as undermining the authority of the party, encouraging individualism and reducing the power of the party whip. For many people this will be an advantage rather than a disadvantage.

A similar point about preferential voting has been elaborated by some to argue that a beneficial consequence of introducing STV into British elections would be to establish what was effectively a system of primary elections upon our candidates, and one, in fact, that would be superior to the model best known in the USA. Vernon Bogdanor, an Oxford University Reader in Government, has argued this as follows:[13]

> Each party is represented by the candidate or candidates whom the voters most favour. STV, it will be seen, combines a general election, in which there is a choice between parties, with a *primary election,* in which there is a choice between candidates. Moreover, the primary election, which is an intrinsic part of STV, is superior to a separate primary election for two reasons.
>
> The first is that where a separate primary is held, as in the United States, the winner of the primary becomes the party's sole nominee. Supporters of other candidates, therefore, have to vote for a candidate who is not their first preference. Under STV, by contrast, the minority is not disenfranchised. In a multi-member constituency voters can still support a candidate who may not be the first choice of their party and can hope that he may win with the support of uncommitted voters or transfers from candidates of other parties.
>
> Secondly, a primary election is open only to dues-paying or registered party members, and not to the electorate as a whole. Under STV, on the other hand, the primary election is open to every elector who chooses to vote. Instead of going to the expense of organising a separate primary election, the voter participates in the primary simply by taking part in the election itself.

From calculations of what might have been the result of the 1992 general election if it had been held under the STV system, it is clear that there would have been a major political gain for the centre party, the Liberal Democrats. According to the research of the Public Policy Group at the London School of Economics, the Conservative Party would have won 256 seats instead of 335; Labour would have won 250 instead of 271; the nationalist parties would have gained 20 seats between them instead of 7; and the Liberal Democrats would have won 82 extra parliamentary seats to add to the 20 it won under first-past-the-post, which would have brought its total representation under STV to 102 MPs.[14] These projected results also show clearly that STV in 1992 would have produced a very definite hung Parliament, with the Liberal Democrats acting as power-brokers between the two major political parties. With the level of seats won by the Conservative and Labour parties being fairly close, and with the Liberal Democrats polling over a hundred MPs, the pressure for a coalition government would have been very great indeed.

The additional-member system

The additional-member system contains two methods of election, aiming to combine the advantages of single member constituencies and proportionality. It would retain the British single-member, first-past-the-post constituency elections for electing half of the MPs at Westminster, but the other half would be elected from national or regional lists of party candidates. For the voter, this system is straightforward. On polling day, voters are asked to enter two crosses on their ballot paper: the first one is for the candidate whom they support as their constituency MP; and the second vote is for their preferred political party (see below). Both count as separate

Specimen ballot paper: the additional-member system

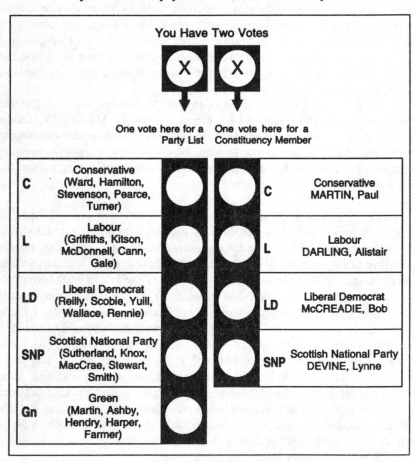

votes. The first vote would be taken to calculate the winning constituency MP exactly as is done at present. The second vote would count towards the number of MPs who are elected from the party lists. If the present number of 651 MPs was retained, then 326 might be constituency MPs, and the other 325 party list MPs. At general elections, each political party could field one candidate in each of the constituencies, and in addition the party through its regional offices might prepare lists totalling 325 selected party candidates. The level of voter support for each of the parties would determine how far down each of the party lists candidates would be declared as being returned as MPs.

It is important to realise that the object of the additional-member system is to compensate for such disproportionality as occurs from the constituency first-past-the-post elections. It does not determine who has won among the party list candidates as an isolated process, simply by allocating additional MPs from the party lists according to the percentage of votes cast for each party, but it does so by reference to the number of seats that have already been won in the constituency elections. The returning officers must therefore first calculate the results of the constituency elections. If one party's candidates in the constituencies have polled disproportionately few seats, considering its overall level of electoral support, then it will be compensated by being allocated more or 'additional' seats from the party lists of candidates than another party which gained a disproportionately high number of constituency MPs. The returning officers must calculate how many of the 651 MPs should be, respectively, Labour, Conservative, Liberal Democrat and so on, in terms of proportionality to total votes cast towards the party lists, and then the actual number of constituency MPs belonging to each party is deducted from that figure. If one party exceeds its proportionality quota, it is allowed to keep the extra MPs.

The exact details of the additional-member system can be tailor-made to suit the indigenous conditions of a country. One important variant is whether the party lists are drawn up and voted on nationally or regionally. In Germany, where this system is currently used, it is adopted regionally. It would be natural to operate the party lists regionally in Britain also, especially as there are distinctive parties operating at a regional level, notably the Scottish National Party and Plaid Cymru. Another variable is the threshold at which minor or fringe political parties are permitted to be allocated any additional seats: in Germany, a party must poll a minimum of 5 per cent of the total second votes in the country, or else win at least three seats by first votes in constituencies. In both theory and practice a balance must be struck by the founding fathers of an electoral system between the generally-perceived desirability or otherwise of excluding ultra-extremist parties and including minority or single-issue representation. This section has assumed that the number of party list or 'additional' members would constitute half of the House of Commons, similar to the way that the system operates in Germany, but the precise figure could be different, perhaps numbering a third of all MPs, or a specified number such as 160, as recommended in 1976 by a Hansard Society Commission chaired by the Conservative peer Lord Blake.[15] However, it is generally accepted that the additional-member system operates best when there are equal numbers of constituency and party list MPs, and this was the recommendation of the Institute for Public Policy Research, in its detailed programme of constitutional reform published in 1991.[16] Finally, it should be noted that the additional-member system was recommended in 1992 by the Labour Party's working party on electoral systems, chaired by Raymond Plant, as the device for composing a new Scottish Parliament (an election manifesto commitment of Labour in 1992):[17]

> The working party concludes that it would be appropriate to adopt a form of additional-member system for elections to the Scottish Parliament. There should be a clear constituency link. We have not formed a view on the proportion of constituency members and additional members. However, we are of the opinion that the constituency members would be likely to constitute the majority in the new Parliament. They should be elected on a first-past-the-post basis. The additional members would ensure a broader overall representation in Parliament and should be elected through a system drawn upon on something other than a Scotland-wide list. We believe that this would strike the best balance between a desire for proportionality and the need for proper representation of geographical communities.

The additional-member system has the great advantage of building on the first-past-the-post system with which voters are familiar. While halving the number of constituency MPs would involve doubling the size of each particular constituency, the scale of such an increase is not such that the existing constituency–MP link would be altered significantly. Yet at the same time, this particular method of election accords very closely with the principle of proportional representation.

So what degree of proportionality would have been the result if the 1992 general election had been conducted under the additional-member system? The research of the Public Policy Group on this question, undertaken on the day following the election, involved asking a representative sample of 9 600 respondents how they would have cast their two votes under this system, so that the degree of divergence between the same person voting for one political party and a constituency candidate belonging to another party would be taken into account.[18] Almost nine out of ten respondents did, in fact, vote for both list and constituency candidates belonging to the same political party, but 10 per cent distinguished between the two categories of MP, allowing for tactical voting where the constituency candidate of their favoured party had no chance of being elected. Their results showed that more Conservative and Labour voters support the Liberal Democrats as constituency candidates than as party list MPs. This projected result for the 1992 general election under the additional-member system proceeded on the basis of the House of Commons being composed of half constituency and half party list MPs, the party lists being drawn up within thirteen regions of Great Britain. It concluded that the Conservative Party would have won 268 seats (instead of 336), Labour 232 (instead of 271), the nationalist parties 18 (instead of 7), and the Liberal Democrats 116 (instead of 20). The level of representative proportionality, therefore, between total votes cast and party seats won was very high.

The table below shows how the different electoral systems described above would have affected the 1992 general election result.

How different electoral systems would have affected the 1992 General Election result (number of MPs and their percentage in the House of Commons)

	Actual result	*Alternative vote*	*Supplementary vote*	*Single transferable system*	*Additional-member system*
Conservative	336 MPs	325 MPs	304 MPs	256 MPs	268 MPs
41.9% total vote	51.6%	49.9%	46.7%	39.3%	41.1%
Labour	271 MPs	270 MPs	271 MPs	250 MPs	232 MPs
34.4% total vote	41.6%	41.5%	41.6%	38.4%	35.6%
Liberal Democrat	20 MPs	30 MPs	49 MPs	102 MPs	116 MPs
17.8% total vote	3.1%	4.6%	7.5%	15.7%	17.8%
SNP/PC	7 MPs	9 MPs	10 MPs	20 MPs	18 MPs
3.5% total vote	1.1%	1.4%	1.5%	3.1%	2.8%

Table 8.2[19]

The electoral systems of Europe

Electoral systems can be classified in a number of ways, and even within one general model of an electoral system there can be several important differences on points of detail. A short description of the different methods of election used for the principal (or 'lower') House in each of the Parliaments of states belonging to the European Union is given on page 381. In approaching an understanding of European electoral systems, it may be useful to draw some major distinctions that may be made. One is that some countries adopt single-member constituencies (the United Kingdom, France and Germany, for example), whereas others have multi-member constituencies (that is, larger geographical units, each returning several MPs who are declared winners by a returning officer using some statutory quota for weighting votes between the candidates or parties). Within the European single-member systems, there is the first-past-the-post method (used for electing all MPs in the United Kingdom, three-quarters of all MPs in Italy, and half of all MPs in Germany) and the second ballot method of elections (which is used in France). The second ballot method only permits a candidate to win in the first round of voting if he or she wins an absolute majority of votes. Failing this, a limited number of candidates (depending on their level of support in the first round) go forward to a second ballot, which will produce the final result on a first-past-the-post basis. As discussed earlier in this chapter, the election of the French President operates in a similar way, but with only the two candidates gaining the greatest number of votes in the first round going through to the second ballot. The alternative vote, a serious contender for introduction into Britain at various times this century (as described above) is not used in any EU country.

Another major distinction to be made concerns those countries with large multi-member constituencies. In just one of those European states (the Republic of Ireland) the voter indicates a choice (or rather, a preferential list of choices) between the particular individuals standing as party candidates. This is the STV method, a basic electoral model invented in Britain in the nineteenth century and described earlier in this chapter. In other EU countries with multi-member constituencies (notably Belgium, Denmark, Germany, Greece, Luxemburg, the Netherlands, Portugal and Spain), electors effectively cast their vote for a political party by way of a list system. As already explained when considering the additional-member system, list systems achieve a high degree of proportional representation between popular votes cast for a party and the number of party MPs who are returned to Parliament. List systems operate in a number of different ways. In Italy and Germany, as we have seen, only one-quarter and one-half respectively of all MPs are elected under a list system (the rest being constituency MPs elected under a first-past-the-post method). Generally, the party lists operate within each constituency, although in the Netherlands the whole country is treated as one constituency. Some countries have constituencies that resemble the different regions of the state, such as in Portugal where twenty-two constituencies each return between three and fifty-six MPs from regional party lists, or in Denmark, where nineteen constituencies each return between two and twenty-one MPs from regional lists. It is usual for voters to exercise their party preference by making a cross against their choice of candidate on the party lists.

Britain is remarkable within the EU for having an electoral system that is so distortional in terms of proportionality between parliamentary

European electoral systems
(Lower Houses of Parliament in European Union states)

Country	Total MPs	Constituencies		Electoral system
		Number	MPs in each	
Belgium	212	30	2–34	Party list PR (choice of one candidate)
Denmark	179	19	2–21	Party list PR (choice of one candidate)
France	577	577	1	Second ballot (majority)
Germany	656	328	1	Additional-member system (single member first-past-the-post, corrected by party list PR)
Greece	300	56	1–32	Party list PR (choice of 1, 2 or 3 candidates)
Ireland	166	41	3, 4 or 5	Single transferable vote
Italy	630	483	1–13	Mixed largely majoritarian (first-past-the-post and party list PR)
Luxemburg	60	4	7–23	Personal voting, with parties awarded seats in proportion to its candidates' votes
Netherlands	150	1	150	Party list PR (choice of one candidate)
Portugal	250	22	3–56	Party list PR (no choice of candidate)
Spain	350	52	3–33	Party list PR (no choice of candidate)
United Kingdom	651	651	1	First-past-the-post (simple majority)

Table 8.3[20]

representation and votes cast. The degree of proportional representation produced by any electoral system is most usually measured by political scientists in terms of what is called 'deviation from proportionality', which indicates the percentage variance between the number of seats won by MPs of a party and the number that would have been won under a purely proportional system. An analysis of European electoral systems conducted by Professor Patrick Dunleavy for his inaugural lecture at the London School of Economics in 1991, showed very clearly that the United Kingdom in the mid-1980s had the greatest deviation and most disproportional representation of any electoral system operating in Europe (see overleaf).[21]

There can be little doubt that, assuming an 'ever closer union' between the European states (even if conducted with greater subsidiarity of decision-making affecting local or regional areas), pressure will grow from different

Deviation from proportionality in European electoral systems

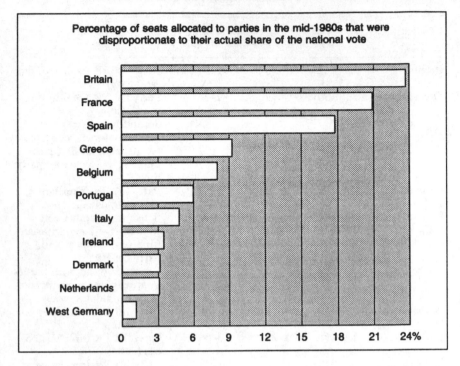

Percentage of seats allocated to parties in the mid-1980s that were disproportionate to their actual share of the national vote

quarters within the EU for Britain to adopt a more proportionally representative electoral system in line with her European partners. It is extremely likely that very soon there will be a serious attempt to adopt a standard electoral system that applies across the whole EU, for the election of MEPs to the European Parliament (instead of, at the time of writing, leaving each individual member country to decide how MEPs from its territory are to be elected). Having different electoral systems operating within the European Parliament renders its character somewhat chaotic in terms of representing shades of political opinion across Europe. And it seems almost certain, given that the great majority of other EU countries have proportional systems, that the uniform system to be selected by EU partners will be one that embraces the principle of proportional representation. Once such a system is adopted for one part of Britain's political structure, it may be that it will act as a 'Trojan horse' to galvanise pressure for proportional representation for its other parts, and ultimately the House of Commons. The future of the EU may hold the key to the debate in Britain over whether or not to adopt proportional representation.

POLICIES OF THE POLITICAL PARTIES ON ELECTORAL REFORM

For many people in Britain, the term 'proportional representation' has a novel ring to it. It is often associated with the thinking of the Liberal Democrats (and their predecessors, the Liberal Party and the Social Democratic Party) who since the 1970s have presented it prominently during general election campaigns as one of their foremost party policies. However, proportional representation is a very old political issue in Britain. Different electoral systems, including STV, were worked out in great detail by politicians and theorists in the nineteenth century.[22] The English lawyer, Thomas Hare, published an explanation in his *Treatise on the Election of Representatives, Parliamentary and Municipal* in 1859 of how STV system operated; and his support for STV, together with an attack on the defects of the existing electoral system in Britain, was in the 1860s supported by the MP and philosopher, John Stuart Mill. Mill attempted unsuccessfully to introduce into the Reform Act of 1867 clauses embodying STV, and a few years later, in 1872, the first detailed draft legislation on the issue appeared, when a group of MPs including Auberon Herbert and Thomas Hughes presented their Proportional Representation Bill to the Commons, which was defeated eventually after a lengthy second reading debate.[23] This was followed by many other attempts by backbench MPs to secure parliamentary passage of electoral reform by way of Private Members' Bills, such as the Parliamentary Elections Bill 1908.[24] Throughout the twentieth century, proportional representation has been discussed regularly by politicians of all parties at Westminster, and by lawyers and political scientists of all political persuasions in the media and at our universities. Proportional representation is not a recent controversy, therefore, nor one of fringe or mere academic interest, nor a policy that can be claimed as the personal possession of any single political party in modern times. On two separate occasions since the First World War, the single transferable vote or the alternative vote have narrowly missed being voted through Parliament. In both 1918 and 1931, the House of Commons voted to replace first-past-the-post voting, but the legislation to give effect to its decision was stymied by political intrigue and the House of Lords. In the parliamentary proceedings of 1917 prior to the Representation of the People Act 1918, a cross-party Speaker's Conference had recommended adoption of STV.[25] The Commons, after a lengthy debate, in which the former Liberal leader and Prime Minister, David Lloyd George, opposed proportional representation, narrowly rejected STV by eight votes – but supported instead an amendment to introduce the alternative vote. This was vetoed by the House of Lords, who restored the Speaker's Conference's recommendation of STV in the Bill, and after the issue had gone backwards and forwards between the two Houses five times, the *status quo* of first-past-the-post succeeded by default. Later, in 1931, the Labour government presented and secured passage of an Electoral Reform Bill through the Commons which would have introduced the alternative vote into parliamentary elections, but this was rejected by the House of Lords and shortly afterwards the government resigned because of the economic crisis in August 1931 and the Bill had to be abandoned. From a cynical perspective, it is hardly surprising that the Liberal Democrats have latterly been the most vociferous supporters of electoral reform, because as the contemporary third party in British politics their candidates have the most to lose under first-past-the-post voting. On polling day in 1992, it took just 41 947 citizens' votes to elect each of the Conservative Party's 336 MPs, and 42 646 votes to elect each of Labour's 271 MPs, but it required a massive 299 922 votes to count towards each of the Liberal Democrats' 20 MPs who were successful in that election. Coming in at second or third place, even with a level of support of over 10 000 votes, counts for nothing towards the party's overall level of parliamentary representation.

As with most public issues that have some moral or constitutional aspect to them, the attitudes of today's politicians at Westminster towards electoral reform does not conform entirely to party lines. Over the period since the Second World War, the formal policies of the leaderships of the two main parties, Conservatives and Labour, have been to retain the existing first-past-the-post system and therefore opposed to electoral reform. But there are a considerable number of supporters of proportional representation to be found within the Conservative and Labour parties, including organised lobby groups within each party, notably the Conservative Action for Electoral Reform group, and the Labour Campaign for Electoral Reform. Meanwhile, the official policy of the Liberal Party, today the Liberal Democrats, has consistently in recent decades supported adoption of STV. How, then, were the policies of each party towards proportional representation displayed and presented to the British public at the 1992 general election?

The Liberal Democrats

The Liberal Democrats have pledged themselves unequivocally to electoral reform and the introduction of the STV system. Furthermore, believing a hung Parliament to be a very possible outcome at the 1992 general election, their leader, Paddy Ashdown, publicly stated that the acceptance of proportional representation by either of the other two parties within the first year of the new Parliament would be the price demanded by Liberal Democrat MPs for supporting them in a coalition government or under some pact in the House of Commons whereby they would agree not to vote against the government in a No Confidence motion.

The election manifesto of the Liberal Democrats, entitled *Changing Britain for Good*, promised to 'Bring in fair votes. We will introduce proportional representation for all elections at local, national and European levels. We propose the single transferable vote, by which electors cast their votes in multi-member constituencies based on natural communities.' Claiming that 'Liberal Democrats, alone in British politics, recognise that unless we change Britain's system of government, we cannot change Britain's future', the manifesto condemned 'our current "winner takes all" system of voting' for many faults, including being 'unfair, unstable and divisive'. It stated:

> Government by minority is usually bad government . . . Fair votes will make every elector's vote count. It will increase citizens' control over their elected representatives, by abolishing safe seats. It will eradicate the power of the extremist minority in political parties. It will lead to a better choice of candidates and ensure that more women and candidates from minority ethnic communities are elected. Above all, it will reduce tit-for-tat politics and introduce much greater stability into government.

In speeches around the country during the election campaign, the Liberal Democrat leader, Paddy Ashdown, addressed in dramatic terms the issue of electoral reform. For example, at a party rally in Eastbourne on 2 April, he attacked a 'discredited system which now debases the very idea of democracy . . . The voting system lies like a dead hand stopping progress'. He added that the other parties' claims about first-past-the-post voting producing a desirable system of 'strong government' amounted to 'the strength of a gang of playground bullies to grab their Buggins' turn to do whatever they like'. This was arrogant government, he said, which 'told people they wasted their votes and which swung from one extreme to the other with no consensus or continuity',[26]

Further discussion of current Liberal Democrat policy on proportional representation was to be found in the report of its working group on constitution reform, chaired by the former SDP leader, Robert Maclennan, which had been endorsed by the party conference and formed part of the Liberal Democrat policy programme at the 1992 general election. This report elaborates on the Liberal Democrats' proposals for constitutional reform generally, with its section on the subject of electoral reform declaring:[27]

> Electoral reform is the cornerstone of Liberal Democrats' constitutional agenda; the essential prerequisite for revitalising our democracy. We would introduce a bill to apply proportional representation to all elections . . . [and] of all available systems, the best able to meet [our] goals is the single transferable vote system in multi-member constituencies

of between two and seven members . . . The present first-past-the-post system is blatantly unfair and undemocratic.

The Conservative Party

There was nothing at all on the subject of the electoral system in the Conservative Party's manifesto, entitled *The Best Future of Britain*, apart from a promise to keep the working methods of Parliament under review and 'the need to attract more women to stand for election'. However, the Conservative Campaign Guide, published in 1991, gave an account of the Conservative view on proportional representation. This was one of firm and definite opposition to proportional representation, although it did recognise that in some quarters of the party 'discussions continue about the relative merits of systems'. It explained that, 'Traditionally most people in the Conservative Party have attached overriding importance to ensuring that the electoral system provides stable Parliaments with secure government, and maintains the link between MPs and their constituents. The present first-past-the-post system meets those requirements. It is hard to see how any system of PR could do so.' Proportional representation was criticised in the following way:[28]

(1)   It would create a series of hung Parliaments, leading to instability which could draw the Crown into party politics.
(2)   Minority groups with only a marginal political following could determine which major party held power and extract concessions (which were not in the public interest) in return for their support.
(3)   Governments would be determined not by the votes of the electorate, but by deals struck between political factions. Voters would not know which policies their party would have to drop, adapt or adopt in order to take office.
(4)   MPs would no longer be so closely involved with their constituents or represent a particular geographical area. Some systems of PR cut this link completely.

Constitutional reform in general assumed a high profile during the 1992 general election campaign, and the Conservative Prime Minister, John Major, together with his Cabinet colleagues, gave a robust defence of the political system against fundamental change. Proportional representation itself as an electoral issue achieved greater prominence than at any time since the 1930s, even more than the Liberal/SDP Alliance managed to achieve in the 1980s, as a direct result of Labour's declared policy of keeping an open door on the issue and its intention to establish an independent commission on the electoral system if it won the election. The Conservative Party had to respond, but its strategists believed that they could make political capital out of the fact that Labour could easily be made to look as if it did not have a policy of its own on the issue. In fact, Labour had realised this earlier, and warned in its policy review document, *Meet the Challenge, Make the Change*, which had been approved by the party in 1989, of the dangers to itself of being associated with proportional representation. The review had said that, 'Talk of proportional representation or any alternative voting system would cause the electorate to question our resolve, our commitment, and our confidence.'[29]

What prompted Conservative campaign planners to encourage members of its leadership to engage prominently in public debate on proportional representation, therefore, was the tactical assessment that Labour's policy of saying that if they were elected to government they would set up an all-party inquiry under Professor Raymond Plant to look into the issue, would look weak by comparison. Conservatives aimed to present themselves to the electorate as having a clear vision of strong government, and they would argue that the Liberal Democrats – like proportional representation itself – was all about coalitions and compromises, and a vote for Liberal Democrat candidates was tantamount to a vote for a Labour government, with Liberal Democrats sustaining Labour in some sort of coalition or pact. John Major and other senior Conservative figures projected a very clear message of rejection and condemnation of proportional representation during the 1992 election campaign. John Major publicly stated that he would resign politics rather than accept either proportional representation or a coalition deal with the Liberal Democrats.[30] In the last week before polling day, he prominently declared on more than one occasion:[31]

I do not favour proportional representation. I will not introduce proportional representation. There are no circumstances in which I will introduce proportional representation, and I hope that is entirely clear.

The Labour Party

The Labour Party went into the 1992 general election campaign armed with a policy commitment in its manifesto, which was called *It's Time to Get Britain Working Again*, that:

We will continue to encourage a wide and well-informed public debate on the electoral system. The working party on electoral systems which we established in opposition under the distinguished chairmanship of Professor Raymond Plant will continue its work with an extended membership and enhanced authority and report to the next Labour government.

Labour policy, then, was neutral on the subject of proportional representation. However, the party leadership's willingness even to consider reform of the first-past-the-post system for elections to the House of Commons has been a highly significant development in the proportional representation debate. For at no time since the 1930s has the Labour Party supported electoral reform, and throughout the period down to the 1990s it consistently rejected any proposals to reform the present electoral system.

The 1992 election came at a time when the Labour Party was undergoing a surge of interest in many matters of constitutional reform. The comprehensive policy review launched by the then Labour leader, Neil Kinnock, immediately after the 1987 election defeat, led to a new programme of Labour policies contained in the document *Meet the Challenge, Make the Change*, published and approved by the Party Conference in 1989. This new programme for a future Labour government laid down the framework for wholesale modernisation of the British system of government, including reform of the House of Lords, freedom of information, and devolution measures for a Scottish Parliament and regional assemblies in England and Wales. Electoral reform was not part of this policy review, but by the time it was completed a substantial movement had emerged within the party that supported proportional representation and wished to see the party debate the issue. There are many long-standing supporters of electoral reform within the Labour Party, including many MPs, for example, Robin Cook, Ann Clwyd, Giles Radice, Jeff Rooker, Dale Campbell-Savours and Joe Ashton, and other prominent figures outside Westminster, including academics such as Professor Bernard Crick and trade union figures such as the National Union of Miners' president, Arthur Scargill. The reasons for the rising level of Labour support for electoral reform are diverse, but there can be no doubt that there is a new, younger generation of Labour members who see a new voting system as part of a general modernisation of the country. Throughout 1990 and 1991, national opinion polls consistently indicated that a clear majority of Labour supporters favoured changing the electoral system to one of proportional representation.[32] Furthermore, Labour's attention to the issue of proportional representation has been galvanised not simply by the party's current interest in constitutional reform, but also by reflection upon the succession of crushing electoral defeats it has suffered. It has been accepted by many that fragmentation of the Left in British politics, between Labour and Liberal Democrat support, has allowed the Conservative Party to remain in government and implement policies to which Labour is utterly opposed. For some, leadership of a coalition or minority government might be better than no share in government at all, but neither does proportional representation preclude an overall majority in the Commons if a party can succeed in gaining a majority of the popular vote.

In 1990, Labour's National Executive Committee established a working party on electoral systems under the chairmanship of Professor Raymond Plant. The original terms of reference of the working party did not in fact extend to the House of Commons, and were limited to which voting system was appropriate for elections to the European Parliament, the proposed new second chamber, the proposed Scottish Parliament, and the proposed regional assemblies for England and Wales. However, it was a widely-held view at the October 1990 Party Conference held in Blackpool, that elections to the House of Commons should be included in the work of the Plant committee, and a motion put forward to this effect was carried by a majority of 2 766 000 votes to 2 557 000, despite the impassioned opposition of the then deputy leader and Home Affairs spokesman, Roy Hattersley. Prior to the 1992 general election, only an interim paper had been produced by the Plant working party, simply giving an analysis of the issues and questions involved, and inviting comments and views. During the 1992 general election campaign, Neil Kinnock elaborated on the function of the working party to say that it would be converted into a formal government inquiry, possibly a Royal Commission, if Labour won the election, and its membership would be widened to include members from outside the Labour Party, including business, trade unions, churches, and members of other political parties.[33] He went on to state publicly that, after this Commission had completed its work and presented its recommendations, the Labour government would respond by determining its own policy on the matter, which it would then lay before the electorate at the next general election. Mr Kinnock's view was that in any event an electoral mandate would be required to make such an 'irreversible and significant' change to the future of our political democracy.[34] He said that whilst he did not exclude the possibility of a referendum on proportional representation, a general election with the policy proposals contained within the government's manifesto might be the way of proceeding which was most consistent with British constitutional traditions.

Labour Party policy on proportional representation during the 1992 general election campaign, therefore, was generally muted and neutral. Some of the known supporters of electoral reform pressed their case, including Robin Cook who at a press conference five days before the election said,[35]

> I wish we had had proportional representation for the elections of 1983 and 1987. We would not then have had the abuse of power of the past decade that gave us the poll tax and opted-out hospitals in defiance of the wishes of the great majority of the British people. I also strongly take the view that Labour should, as the majority government we are going to be, not simply implement Labour's programme but also change the constitution so that never again can our opponents abuse the levers of power in the way they have done.

Not surprisingly, many voters and virtually all the media wanted to know Neil Kinnock's own personal view on electoral reform, since as Prime

Minister he would have the final power over what would be done. However, in media interviews he refused to give his personal opinion on the issue, saying that he had formed a view about proportional representation, but was not disclosing it because he wanted to allow an open debate on the matter and did not want to compromise the outcome of the Plant inquiry. It was only after the election and his resignation as party leader, that he was prepared to reveal his own personal views in a television interview in December 1992. Asked by David Dimbleby whether he would now say whether or not he supported proportional representation, he said: 'Yes, I support electoral reform. My only further deliberation is what form it should take.'[36]

When the Plant working party produced its final report in April 1993, it recommended adoption of the supplementary vote system for elections to the Commons. The report said:[37]

> While there was a clear majority in favour of some form of change from the present system, there was also a clear majority in favour of a single-member constituency majoritarian system. Both the alternative vote and the supplementary vote would represent a change retaining these features. Between the two, there was, though, a clear preference for the supplementary vote; and accordingly, this is the majority recommendation of the working party.

At first sight this appeared to be a set-back for those within the Labour Party who supported proportional representation, because the supplementary vote system (described above at pages 368–9), being a majoritarian system, would have no real impact upon the electoral process in terms of the principle of proportionality. However, there had evidently been a significant division of opinion within the working party, not surprisingly since the selection of members had been intended to cover all shades of opinion on the matter. The views of some particular members was well-known, ranging from Margaret Beckett's outright opposition to electoral reform (made vocal during her campaign for the deputy leadership in June 1992) to Jeff Rooker's long-standing, enthusiastic support for electoral change embracing proportional representation.[38] The Labour leadership's measured response to the Plant Report's conclusion on the electoral system for the Commons was not to endorse the specific recommendation it made, or lay the recommendation before the Party Conference for adoption as party policy, but instead simply to welcome the document as part of a continuing consultative process within and beyond the party.

Immediately after the National Executive Committee had met to consider the matter, the then Labour leader, John Smith, delivered a public statement which contained a proposal for a referendum on the future of the electoral system. His public statement declared:[39]

It is a matter of such constitutional significance that it should be for the people to decide. Any decision on the retention or change of the electoral system for the House of Commons must carry the demonstrable consent of the public. That is why I firmly believe that the final decision on this issue must be taken by means of a referendum and why I propose that such a referendum be held during the first Parliament of the next Labour government.

This, then, was a highly significant new direction for Labour to follow. Apart from the moral, democratic case for a referendum, as a matter of party self-interest it is seen as a useful device for resolving an issue which rouses passionate, conflicting views within the party. John Smith's initiative was widely welcomed by Labour members, and at the 1993 annual conference a resolution was passed supporting it as party policy.[40] In 1994, Tony Blair, the present Labour leader, equally made it quite clear that, 'I fully support the party's commitment to a referendum on the issue of the electoral system for the Commons.'[41]

THE RHETORIC OF THE DEBATE

This chapter now seeks to illustrate some of the principal forms of argument that have been adopted in the controversy over proportional representation in recent times, and identify some of the leading commentators, politicians and writers who have acted as protagonists in the debate.

Arguments in resistance to proportional representation

Defence of the existing system against reform has been conducted regularly at an emotive level, relying heavily upon intuitive, conservative and patriotic sentiments. It is commonly argued by opponents of reform that experience rather than logic, and practice rather than theory, is what matters in the construction of constitutional affairs. The genius of the British political system, it is argued, has been that it is geared to the real world. Much of the reasoning against proportionality in British parliamentary representation has therefore been phrased in terms of history and experience. Ramsay Muir characterised the opposition to electoral reform as follows:[42]

The argument for some system of proportional representation is in theory unanswerable: it is the natural corollary of democracy. But many people, especially English people, have a healthy distrust of logic in human affairs. They rightly insist that it is the practical working of institutions that matters, rather than their logical perfection; and when elaborate schemes of proportional representation are put before them, they have instinctive misgivings that the indirect and unpredictable consequences of such a change may be dangerous; may upset the whole working of our system of government, and lead us into chaos. Even when they are told that various forms of proportional representation have been tried, with more or less success, they rightly maintain that foreign experience is no sound guide for this country, with its old, customary, slowly developing institutions; and rightly demand that any proposed electoral system shall be justified, not merely by logic, but by a searching analysis of the way in which it would work in our conditions.

There is, of course, a whole range of other British public institutions which are explicable only in terms of history, and are similarly very difficult to justify in terms of democratic principle or logic (the House of Lords being perhaps the most glaring example).

One of the primary ways in which defenders of first-past-the-post voting articulate their case is to present the system as being something familiar and normal to the British people, and one that has served them well over a very long period of their history. It is viewed as part of their national heritage, and something essentially British, which no other European country possesses. The argument then often proceeds to suggest that other European countries' political systems are rather eccentric. Alternatively, it is suggested that the affairs of a particular European state are in a mess precisely because they have an electoral system with proportional representation and not one of first-past-the-post like Britain's. Italy – because its federal system of politics is most fragmented – is cited with monotonous regularity by opponents of electoral reform as an illustration of what proportional representation would mean in Britain, with Israel, Belgium and the Republic of Ireland featuring strongly as further examples of how the British should definitely not conduct their affairs. Sometimes, opponents of electoral reform have alleged that the single transferable vote or additional-member systems are not really systems of proportional representation at all, and thereby have no higher claim for democratic authority than the British system. The idea of politicians from minority parties being appointed ministers in a coalition, as often happens in Germany, is portrayed as being thoroughly undemocratic and anathema to British tradition. A recent example of such sentiments came from the former Education Secretary John Patten, when giving his 1991 Swinton Lecture to the Conservative Political Centre, entitled 'Political Culture, Conservatism and Rolling Constitutional Change':

Electoral reform – in the form of proportional representation – does not really hold out what [its supporters] believe it to offer. No electoral system – there are over 300 to choose from, I'm told – can ever offer exact proportionality. The seductively fair-sounding principle of 'proportionality' is always automatically compromised as a result before you start. Where the system most favoured by recent reformers – the single transferable vote (STV) – is in operation at a national level elsewhere, for example (principally Malta and the Republic of Ireland), it has managed to produce parties winning a majority of seats on a minority of the votes!

And what do other PR systems produce? In what was West Germany, a party which gets little more than 5 per cent of the votes cast, regularly gets four of its members in the Cabinet, while the second largest party in the country has no such representation. In Italy, their system has proved so problematic that Italians have recently voted overwhelmingly during a referendum – in a remarkably high turn-out (62.5 per cent) – for a change to the existing arrangements, restricting from four to one the number of preferences that can be expressed on the ballot paper – the existing system having lent itself to a significant degree of corruption, I read.

Benjamin Disraeli opposed proportional representation on the grounds that, 'It would allow crotchety old men into the House – an inconvenience we have hitherto avoided.' This same argument today tends to take the form of ominous warnings about proportional representation letting a lunatic fringe of dangerous extremists into the Commons. The spectre of extremism in other European countries being transported here by proportional representation regularly featured in the debate in recent years. The rise to power of Adolf Hitler in the 1930s under a proportional party list system has been alluded to. So too have the successes of the National Front in France, where the party managed to gain one MP in 1988 after polling 9.7 per cent of the national vote. This inflammatory line of oratory seems to suggest that the phenomenon of political fanaticism is somehow linked to the electoral laws of a country rather than to more obvious factors such as the frailty of a country's national identity, its poor economic condition, or its own indigenous social and political culture. John Major, the Prime Minister at the time of writing, has said, 'Some sorts of proportional representation would let in very tiny minorities with extremely unrepresentative views – the National Front, yes, the Communist Party, yes – all alien to the way our Constitution has run for over 200 years.'[43] Similarly, Kenneth Baker, during his term as Home Secretary, when his ministerial responsibilities included those for Britain's electoral affairs, warned:[44]

Proportional representation has helped the fascists to march again in Europe. It is a terrible warning to us about what could happen if we threw away our system of first-past-the-post elections. That is what Mr Ashdown wants to do. It is what Mr Kinnock is prepared to do as the price for power. If proportional representation turned out to have the same results in Britain, it would be a pact with the devil.

Another favourite argument of opponents to reform is to state that first-past-the-post voting produces 'strong government' by a single party whereas proportional representation produces coalitions of parties in office, which leads to 'weak government'. It is well known that proportional representation would make coalition government more likely in Britain, in so far as one party would generally need to win the electoral backing of over 50 per cent of national votes cast to be able to form a government by itself alone.

Electoral majorities have been won by single parties in British political
history, but none of the parties individually since before the Second World
War has won that measure of popular support. Whether or not coalition
government is indeed tantamount to weak government is a point of serious
dispute between protagonists in the electoral reform debate. But in the
unequivocal view of the former Conservative Party chairman and Cabinet
minister, Norman (now Lord) Tebbit:[45]

> Just ask yourselves, would a government without a majority [of seats in
> the Commons] – the Neil and Paddy show – have been able to take the
> decisions needed to have thrown the army of the fascist Argentinian
> dictator out of the Falklands . . . Let's have no truck with the nonsense
> call for a return to the Lib-Lab pact. Let's rule out a hung Parliament.

The political process of negotiation and discussion between parties – an
essential ingredient of coalitions – is portrayed by opponents of electoral
reform as a weakness. John Major has said that proportional representation
would 'drain authority from the Westminster Parliament' and lead to
minority governments formed by 'backstage deals' in 'smoke-filled
rooms'.[46] 'Proportional representation is all about horse-trading', says the
Daily Telegraph.[47] Similarly, in the view of Roy Hattersley, a Labour
opponent of reform, 'With proportional representation and the inevitable
hung Parliament it produces, the people vote first and then the politicians
huddle together afterwards to decide what policies they are going to
introduce in Parliament.'[48] Sir Ivor Jennings, the constitutional lawyer, put
a similar point metaphorically when he wrote:[49]

> A system of bargaining would then be necessary. Each party would drive
> its engine to the junction and the drivers would adjourn to the signal-box
> to debate at length in what order they should cross the points. If the meat
> went first the coal would go home and the people would have raw meat
> for lunch, or more probably, nothing.

To the minds of most opponents of reform, coalitions are essentially
unstable. According to a Conservative Political Centre pamphlet in 1982,
'Why Electoral Change: The Case for PR Examined' by Sir Angus Maude
and John Szemerey:[50]

> Minority government and coalitions are conducive to unstable and weak
> government. There is often a long period after elections without a
> government, as the parties haggle over policies before arrangements
> between the potential partners are finalised. Experience from countries
> which have coalitions suggests that coalition partners, particularly
> minority parties, frequently withdraw backing from governments faced
> by a downturn in the economy or the need to take unpopular measures.
> The examples of Italy and Belgium support this view.

Or, as a leading article of the *Daily Telegraph* put it recently:[51]

> A vote for proportional representation . . . is not a vote for fairness, but
> for injustice; not a vote for stability, but for political chaos. Take the
> example of Belgium, where . . . proportional representation has created a
> political culture of backstairs deals and perpetual campaigning. Take the
> example of Italy, where proportional representation has created
> permanent instability, with a series of coalition governments that have
> had to depend on several minor parties whose influence has been out of
> all proportion to their success in the polls.

The degree of influence that junior coalition parties might be able to
exercise in government is particularly criticised by opponents of reform. It is
argued that under the guise of giving fair representation, proportionality in
fact gives to the smallest of the three parties the greatest power to determine
the nature of each government.[52] Many European countries, John Major
has publicly argued, are saddled with a 'tiny coalition tail dragging down the
majority party and imposing policies that nobody wants'.[53] In the view of
Jack Straw, a Labour opponent of reform, proportionality 'is about giving
parties who get the least number of votes the most power – it's very clever'.[54]
Along similar lines, the Conservative MP Graham Riddick argued in a
House of Commons' debate on constitutional reform in 1991:[55]

> In some cases, and Israel is a classic case, very small minority parties are
> given enormous power – I would say disproportionate power. That in
> itself can tie the hands of the majority party. Either that can happen or,
> alternatively, chaos reigns. Italy is now on to its 30th, 40th or 50th
> government since the last war. That is no recipe for good government.
> The other possibility with proportional representation is a weak
> coalition government, in which the weakest – the lowest common
> denominator – decide government policy. That is because consensus has
> to be reached. I believe therefore that weak government could come about.

Opponents of electoral reform regularly maintain that if the social and
economic conditions of Britain need a radical solution (as is generally
claimed to be the case by all politicians) then the the brand of radicalism
they represent will be obstructed or neutralised by proportional representation. This, again, tacitly assumes that a majority of voters will never vote for
a single party, and that proportional representation will mean a virtually
continous programme of 'moderate' public policies being pursued by
government. Roy Hattersley has articulated this line of argument
memorably, as follows:[56]

> Proportional representation prevents the radical change which this party
> supports and on which this party campaigns. That's why it's so popular
> with the soggy middle ground.

It is most certainly true that the current electoral system allowed a radical Conservative government throughout the 1980s to effect a great many fundamental changes to Britain's social and economic life. At three successive elections this particular brand of radicalism was opposed by around 57 per cent of voters, but none the less the British electoral system converted these votes into huge overall Conservative majorities in the Commons. Currently all three main parties view their own policy programmes as being the most radical for the country, but a majority of voters agreed with none of them at the 1992 general election.

A personal target for a great deal of the criticism of proportional representation has been directed at the Liberal Democrats and their support for STV. It is routinely alleged that Liberal Democrat arguments in support of reform are in reality a less-than-honest attempt to gain more parliamentary seats for themselves. So, for example, under the title, 'Behind the Self Righteous Mask', a Conservative Party research department paper in 1991 argued that, 'The [Liberal Democrats'] adoption of proportional representation is motivated by the natural self-interest of politicians frustrated by their political impotence; in proportional representation, they are advocating what they perceive as an instant route from permanent opposition to a permanent role in government.'[57] The Maude–Szemerey Report for the Conservative Political Centre in 1982 described the Liberal rationale for STV as 'a fiddle in sheep's clothing',[58] and during the 1992 election hustings, the Prime Minister, John Major, proclaimed: 'We are going to show up their proportional representation campaign for the sham it is.'[59] The Conservative, Graham Riddick, suggested during House of Commons' debate that:[60]

> The truth is that [the Liberal Democrats and SDP] advocate proportional representation because [they] believe it to be the surest way to get a taste of power.
>
> It is revealing that the Right Hon. Member for Plymouth, Devonport (Dr David Owen), Lord Jenkins of Hillhead, Shirley Williams and others – and perhaps, for all I know, the Hon. Member for Caithness and Sutherland (Robert Maclennan) – showed little interest in proportional representation when they were members of the Labour Party, but they showed great interest in it once they switched parties and became part of the Alliance. It was not always thus.

The STV system advocated by Liberal Democrats is regularly targeted for criticism upon the grounds that it is too complex for ordinary voters to understand.[61] Unquestionably, first-past-the-post is simple for voters to follow, and STV is easily the most complicated of any version of proportional representation. However, Liberal Democrats vehemently dismiss this view, and maintain that all voters have to understand is that they mark their order of preferences against candidates' names on their ballot paper. A party political broadcast for the SDP, delivered by the comedian John Cleese in 1985, responded to this criticism, with Mr Cleese saying, 'Well yes, if the voter can't count up to five, you'll find it pretty bewildering.' Those who oppose STV, however, argue that this misses the point about how desirable or otherwise it is for the voter actually to understand the process whereby the winners in the multi-member constituencies are calculated. Whereas Liberal Democrats maintain that it is sufficient for the returning officer to understand the mathematical calculations of how votes are translated into seats, the recent Plant Report for the Labour Party has said,[62]

> Is a democracy secure if the average voter cannot explain the mechanism at work between his or her casting a vote and the eventual result? It does not bode well for the claims that proportional representation increases political knowledge if the system is so complex that the link between voting and representation ultimately is usually only understood by officials.

Arguments in support of proportional representation

The *Economist* magazine in 1991 characterised the British political system by saying:[63]

> It ain't broke, but like much of British industry in the 1970s, its proper place is in a museum. It does not need to be fixed; it needs to be replaced.

There is at present a widespread movement across the political spectrum which supports a systematic modernisation of Britain's antique and antiquated constitution, with electoral reform taking a central role in helping to improve the quality of British democratic and political life. Most proponents of proportional representation tend to take the view that it is not just the electoral system to the Commons, but the British system of checks and balances upon government as a whole which is now in need of an overhaul. Since the 1960s, a steady stream of constitutional speeches and literature in Britain has become increasingly vociferous, criticising the polarisation of political power in the hands of party leaders in government, and this has become ever stronger with the massive growth in government activity over the twentieth century. Lord Hailsham, the former Lord Chancellor, struck a powerful chord in the 1970s with warnings that Britain's political system was drifting into what was in effect an 'elective dictatorship'.[64] On the role of electoral reform within the political system, he wrote in his book *The Dilemma of Democracy*,[65]

> I would certainly prefer almost any system of electoral reform to the prospect of elective dictatorship in any form, but particularly one based on first-past-the-post voting . . . It is amply established that our present

system of voting can install in office a government representing no more than a minority of those who voted, and perhaps no more than a quarter of the total electorate, and that the whips and the guillotine [a parliamentary device to curtail opposition debate] combined can drive through the House of Commons almost any legislation acceptable to the majority virtually without discussion, and without the minimum delay necessary to give public opinion a chance to make its weight felt. It is also clearly established since the war that the prerogative of dissolution in the hands of a skilful Prime Minister can manipulate the timing of an election to give a better than even chance on the present system of voting of perpetuating his rule. To give a single chamber elected by this means unlimited powers, not even trammelled with the vestigal rights of delay now remaining in the hands of the present House of Lords, would be in fact to establish an elective dictatorship, based on minority rule, since the House of Commons, elected by this manner, would have neither legal nor political limits imposed upon it.

A number of other prominent Conservatives have joined in the electoral reform debate, adopting views of a similar nature to Lord Hailsham's. Lord Home, formerly Sir Alec Douglas-Home, who was Prime Minister in the early 1960s, has said:[66]

A party can be elected on a minority vote, and in spite of that gain a parliamentary majority, and use it to force down the throats of the electorate policies which the majority do not approve. This is a caricature of democracy. It was never meant to be like that. Mr Solzhenitsyn has called it the 'strangled silence' of the majority.

Sir Ian Gilmour, a prominent MP until 1992 and a Cabinet minister in Margaret Thatcher's first Cabinet in the early 1980s, argued in a lecture he gave in 1982 that it was clearly undesirable that two diametrically opposed parties, Labour and Conservative, should alternate in government, tearing the country apart and doing untold damage to the economy. 'And if we are going to have full-blooded socialism . . . it should be the result of the wishes of a majority of the electorate and not the result merely of the wishes of a minority and of the quirks of the electoral system.'[67] Later in 1983, at a press conference to launch the Campaign for Fair Votes, he commented on the result of the 1983 election, in which the Liberal/SDP parties polled 25.4 per cent of the national votes but through the electoral system received only 3.5 per cent of the seats in the Commons, by saying that the result was 'plainly indefensible' and that 'the present system, as long as there are three parties, is likely to lead to very bizarre results, which cannot really be justified'.[68] Along similar lines were the sentiments of Chris Patten, the Conservative Party chairman at the time of the 1992 general election, who wrote in a pamphlet entitled *The Tory Case* published in 1983 (before his appointment as a government minister):[69]

The present system cheats the majority of voters of what they want . . . Conservatives believe in defending our liberties and sustaining efficient government. Electoral reform, as Sir Winston Churchill accepted, provides the best way of doing both those things . . . Limiting government's capacity to do harm, while strengthening its ability to do good, through a reform in the voting system, provides the best chance of safeguarding our constitution and accomplishing the other national objectives of Conservatism. We should take it.

An argument often used by Conservative reformers, and sometimes taken up by industrialists, is that the present system tends to produce wild swings in government policy, with Conservatives and Labour adopting very different strategies in social policy, and consequently making medium and long term financial and business planning more difficult. By contrast, it is believed that proportional representation would be conducive to greater continuity in public policy, with less drastic U-turns or policy reversals. Such assertions are currently less in evidence, as a result of the unprecedented success of the Conservative Party in winning four elections in succession and remaining so long in office, but a good example in 1980 was provided by Lord Caldecote, in a pamphlet entitled *Industry Needs Electoral Reform*:[70]

The great disadvantage of the present electoral system from the industrial point of view is that it produces drastic and exaggerated changes in policy at intervals which are far too short to enable industry to plan and operate efficiently. There is a mismatch between the long lead times necessary for investment and development in complex modern industry and the 180 degree reversals of policy which occur at relatively short intervals when the government changes.

I firmly believe that electoral reform will benefit industry in three ways. First: it will strengthen the moderate view in government and the influence of those who prefer consensus and consistency of government policy. Second: it will give to genuinely majority governments the legitimacy and support for necessary and difficult decisions. Third: it will produce few but more carefully considered laws, making it easier for industry to get on with our real task of wealth and job creation.

The impact of the present electoral system on the nature and working of British political parties is the subject of diverse views. A direct tendency of the first-past-the-post system is to produce the least number of parties in the House of Commons: whatever the voting pattern, the usual result is for one party to receive an overall majority of seats, a second party to secure a substantial number of seats and form the opposition, and all other parties to be squeezed out of any substantial presence in the Commons. This 'two-party system' inherent in Britain's political structure as a direct consequence of the electoral system has naturally been portrayed negatively by third parties, notably the Liberal Democrats, but also by many academics, such as the Oxford professor, S. E. Finer, who have coined the terminology of 'adversary politics' to criticise the electoral system. Here, the system is attacked on the grounds of making the parties too inward-looking and insular in their political outlook. It has been said that parties nowadays only ever really talk to themselves – never to one another, unless it is to oppose what is being said. A two-party system is also conducive to each party seeking to emphasise their differences from one another, and this is reflected in the fact that Conservative and Labour leaders tend to be selected from the outside wing of their parties instead of the more moderate wing. According to Professor Finer:[71]

> The government of the day, whichever of the two party-complexions it may be, is unduly influenced by the extremists in its ranks. In office, each party has to reach some compromise between its right and left wings, in order to preserve its unity in the face of the opposition. But this compromise 'centre' position reached by either of these parties is far removed from the central attitude of Parliament as a whole and to an even more considerable degree, from that of the electorate as a whole.

Across the broad party political spectrum that supports proportional representation, it is natural that particular political groups give greater emphasis to some political arguments for electoral reform which are of special concern to them over others, and that in their oratory and writings they take pains to distance themselves from being associated with politicians of other parties, or other political persuasions, who hold very different views about politics and society. On the left wing of socialist politics, there are those who scorn constitutional reform as a social irrelevancy – 'a liberal game, like Scrabble' – and label those who participate in the game as belonging to the 'chattering classes'. But there are some prominent members of the socialist left who have argued strongly in support of reform. The National Union of Mineworkers' president, Arthur Scargill, for example, has said:[72]

> Proportional representation is a fundamental socialist concept. No socialist seriously committed to democratic, accountable representation can advocate any other electoral system. My argument, however, is completely different from that put by the SDP/Liberal Alliance.
>
> I see it not as a device for compromise and coalition but as the exact opposite: a means of polarising political views around alternative programmes and class approaches, of clarifying the fundamental contradictions within capitalism and exposing the class nature of this society, thus involving more and more people in the struggle to transform it.
>
> If the Labour Party were to receive 51 per cent of the votes at the next general election, it is sensible, logical and democratic that Labour should acquire 51 per cent of the seats available in Parliament. But those who

oppose proportional representation turn their backs on both logic and democracy. Instead, they argue for a system so daft and dangerous that it enabled the Tories to be elected on a minority vote not only in 1979 and 1983 – but back in 1951 when they polled fewer votes than the Labour Party. How can socialists advocate such an unrepresentative system?

Another prominent figure of the socialist left, belonging to the New Left school of radicalism, is the political sociologist, Robin Blackburn, famous for his involvement in student activism in the 1960s, and now editor of the journal *New Left Review*. Describing the British constitution as 'an ungainly, dilapidated, half-refurbished Victorian pile threatened by the simultaneous onslaught of subsidence, storm damage, woodworm and dry rot', he is concerned that the existing electoral system effectively excludes a genuinely socialist programme.[73] He argues that it has allowed the Labour Party a monopoly of representation of the left in British politics, and operates against the interests of radicals within the party and/or the emergence of a separate New Left or Socialist Party:

> While proportional representation would certainly make it easier for a New Left Party to secure electoral representation, this would not weaken the overall representation of the left in a truly proportional system, but merely put Labour in a less inflated position, and one in which it might be pulled to the left than the right. It should not be forgotten that past Labour governments have, in political terms, always been coalitions under the structural domination of the right . . . . Britain's first-past-the-post system has long seemed convenient to Labour because it offered it the possibility of forming a government on a plurality of the vote – and because it has given it a monopoly of the representation of the left. Yet in its origins and operation, the British system of representation has always encouraged a species of corporate bourgeois politics, geared to representing already existing interests and working to exclude radical critiques or alternatives.

Not surprisingly, many of the strongest protestations in the electoral reform debate has come from those suffering disproportionately under first-past-the-post voting, and also those who care most passionately about minority representation. Some of the language used today is, in fact, fairly mild compared to that of many decades ago. Thus, for example, Professor Ramsay Muir in 1930 dramatically declared:[74]

> Our method of election is in the highest degree unjust, unsatisfactory and dangerous . . . The fair representation of minorities is essential not only for their own protection, but for the well-being of the whole. Representative government is a dangerous system unless there is representation of all . . . Nobody ought to be disfranchised, as a majority are in practice today. Every elector ought to be able to feel that

his vote has directly contributed to the election of somebody who represents his view, and to the shaping of national policy.

The Liberal Democrats' and their predecessors' style of argument has been equally dramatic. In the early 1980s the Social Democratic/Liberal Party Alliance adopted slogans about 'breaking the mould' of British politics. The first two paragraphs of the 'Twelve Tasks for Social Democrats' policy statement, issued in 1981, declared commitments to,

(1) Breaking the Mould:
Britain needs a reformed and liberated political system without the pointless conflict, the dogma, the violent lurches of policy and the class antagonisms that the two old parties have fostered.
(2) Fair Elections:
The present 'winner takes all' system of electing MPs is unfair to the voters . . . We need a sensible system of proportional representation in which every vote really counts.

Similar assertions were developed in a Liberal/SDP Alliance Commission on Electoral Reform Report in 1982, which read:[75]

Since the war, no party and hence no government has achieved 50 per cent of the vote. This is particularly dangerous at a time when both Conservative and Labour parties (partly as a consequence of the electoral system) have become more extreme. An alternation of 'strong governments' put into power by a minority of the voters may now lead to each government putting through extremist measures which are desired by only a minority of the voters, and which the next government will then do its best to reverse (unless they are irreversible) whilst at the same time putting through extremist measures of its own which again are desired by only a minority of the voters . . . The first-past-the-post system encourages governments to believe that their policies enjoy widespread support even though they may be endorsed by only a fraction of the electorate. Governments claim that they enjoy a 'mandate' to implement their programmes, frequently drawn up by party activists whose enthusiasm may not be shared by the whole party let alone by the electorate as a whole. Yet voters are deemed to agree with every item on the party manifesto, and governments spend their first year or two in office frantically implementing the more doctrinaire elements in their programme; although, often in their last two years in office are spent in an equally frantic attempt to repair the damage.

Recent public statements by Liberal Democrats continue to elaborate on these themes, together with others borrowed from members of different parties. For example:[76]

The elective dictatorship of a single party has assumed virtually absolute control, subject to none of the checks and balances integral to most other democratic constitutions . . . . Liberal Democrats and our predecessor parties have consistently argued the case for proportional representation into British elections. Our prime concern is to remove the distortions and unfairness of the present system . . . . Electoral reform would transform British politics. It would become impossible for a party to claim a mandate to govern on a minority of the vote.

Despite some party political posturing to the contrary, there is in substance now a great deal of common ground between electoral reformers within the different political parties. Thus the Labour Campaign for Electoral Reform believes that:[77]

Many previous justifications for electoral reform have tended to come from Liberals seeking a back way in for whatever brand of centre party policies is current at the time. But electoral reform is now associated with a broader view of politics, with an idea about what sort of government we in the Labour Party want to see. It is associated with the achievement of sustainable social progress – not surprisingly a perspective which is informed by the experience of our European sister parties . . . The present system has allowed the corruption of democracy in the UK. It is an obstacle to the constitutional and democratic changes which Labour has identified as necessary to respond to the needs of the British people in the twenty-first century.

The single most powerful argument that unites electoral reformers of all parties is the principle of equal rights for all citizens to a share in the system of political representation. In its section on 'The Fair Value of a Vote', the Plant Report for the Labour Party cited John Stuart Mill's well-known passage from his *Considerations on Representative Government*:

In a really equal democracy, every or any section would be represented, not disproportionately, but proportionately. A majority of the electors would always have a majority of the representatives; but a minority of the electors would always have a minority of the representatives. Man for man they would be as fully represented as the majority. Unless they are, there is not equal government, but a government of inequality or privilege . . . contrary to all just government, but also above all, contrary to the principle of democracy, which professes equality as its very root and foundation.

THE CASE FOR THE ADDITIONAL-MEMBER SYSTEM

Having surveyed the general types of argument that are employed in the proportional representation debate in Britain, this chapter now turns to the author's own conclusions on the subject. The remainder of the chapter will put forward the author's detailed reasons for supporting proportional representation over first-past-the-post voting, and for his preference for the additional-member system over other systems for electing MPs to the House of Commons.

First, it is important to identify and be clear about the precise criteria upon which the electoral system is being evaluated. These fundamental criteria are summarised below, and reference to them is made in the case for reform of the electoral system which follows. It should be emphasised at the outset as being axiomatic that just as there is no ideal constitution for all countries, equally there is no ideal model electoral system for all representative assemblies. The method of election employed in composing the House of Commons must match Britain's own indigenous political structure and traditions, and seek to improve the efficiency of its system of parliamentary democracy.[78]

Criteria for a new electoral system in Britain

(1) Proportionality

There should be a close correlation between the level of total votes cast for a political party, and its proportion of seats won in the House of Commons.

The electoral system should not produce the result, or should strongly tend against doing so, that one political party wins an overall majority of seats in the House of Commons without that party winning a majority of total votes cast at the election.

(2) Representation of local communities

There should be direct representation of local communities in the House of Commons, with every voter having access to a particular person representing him or her, and local representatives being accountable to the local electorate.

(3) Representation of minorities

The House of Commons should fairly represent the composition of British society, and should facilitate the representation of its different ethnic and cultural interests.

The electoral system should not unfairly discriminate against minorities representing sizeable bodies of political opinion.

(4) Citizen participation

The electoral system should encourage citizen participation; it should allow citizens as voters a genuine party political choice; and the vote of every citizen should be reflected in the election's outcome.

(5) Popular credibility

The British people should understand and approve of the electoral system in which they are voting, and should support the particular way in which it translates votes into parliamentary seats.

(6) Effective government

The electoral system must be capable of producing an efficient and effective Executive, headed by a Prime Minister who commands the confidence of the House of Commons, and a Cabinet system of government.

(7) Effective political parties

Political parties are essential to popular participation in politics and the organisation of public opinion, and the effect that the working of any electoral system has on the local or national performance of the parties should be taken into account.

(8) An effective House of Commons

The efficiency with which the House of Commons performs its functions of shaping our national legislation and holding the Government to account depends upon the quality of its representative character, and a criterion of paramount importance in considering any new electoral system is the impact it will have upon the effectiveness of the Commons' parliamentary work.

Relative advantages and consequences of proportional representation and the additional-member system

The most suitable method of election for the House of Commons is the additional-member system, which retains the virtues of the existing constituency system while adding a greater degree of proportionality into the composition of the Commons. As seen,[79] it achieves this by allocating seats partly through single-member constituency elections as at present, and partly through additional seats being awarded to the political parties by reference to the proportion of total votes received by each. Most countries in Western Europe have adopted some variety of this method of parliamentary election,[80] and it represents the simplest way of balancing the various democratic factors involved.

The MP-constituency link

One fundamental of any new British electoral system must be to retain the present close link between each constituency and its MP. It is essential to retain the political advantages of Britain's system of local representation, with MPs being responsive to local opinion and representing local interests in the Commons, and individual citizens being able to call on their constituency MP's services, particularly in the field of injustices by adminstrative bodies.

It is here that the problem lies in adopting STV in Britain. To secure its objective of greater proportional representation, STV operates on the basis of each constituency returning between three and seven MPs, together representing a balanced ticket of voting preferences within that constituency. But if a constituency is to return five MPs, this means increasing the electoral size of constituencies from the existing number of about 60 000 voters to 300 000, and reducing the number of constituencies from 651 to 130. Under such circumstances, the ordinary citizen's sense of political community or identity with such a huge area and large number of people would be seriously impaired and, perhaps more importantly, the personal link between MPs and their constituents, to which MPs at present attach very great importance, would be lost. When reform of the electoral system was last seriously considered by a Speaker's Conference in the late 1960s, it rejected adoption of STV (by 19 votes to 1), principally on these grounds.[81] Similarly, in responding to the Speaker's Report, the then Home Secretary, James Callaghan (later to be Prime Minister) gave this constituency factor as his own major objection to the STV electoral system:[82] 'All of us who have experience of this link attach very great value to it. It is difficult enough now in all conscience to get to know 50 000 or 60 000 electors and it would be obviously impossible to get to know 300 000 electors . . . That to me is the beginning of the major objection.'

For the same reason, no country in the world with a population as large as that of the United Kingdom employs STV. It is more suitable in the Republic of Ireland, for example, where a much smaller population allows for the 166-seat Dail to be composed from 41 constituencies, each returning between three and five MPs, but maintaining a constituency voting population of about 55 000. Retaining a similar size of constituency as in Britain at the present time under STV is completely unrealistic; it would mean expanding the composition of the House of Commons to the wholly untenable number of about 2 000 MPs. The main alternative electoral system for achieving proportional representation – the additional-member system – is therefore far preferable from this point of view. If even as many as half of the MPs at the House of Commons were elected under party lists according to the additional-member system, it would still only involve constituencies rising to around 120 000 electors which, while being an undesirable increase in size *per se*, is considerably more manageable than around 300 000, and should be regarded as being an acceptable compromise to be set against the very great benefits of proportionality that the additional party list MPs would bring.

The quality of government

The argument that there should be a close relationship between the level of popular votes cast for a political party at a general election and its proportion of seats won in the House of Commons is, in principle, undeniable. The outcome of democratic elections should reflect accurately the political preferences of the voting public at large. It is true, none the less, that the desirability of proportionality has to be balanced against other political criteria expected of the electoral system, particularly allowing for constituency and regional factors, so that there is always likely to be some divergence between the levels of votes and seats expressed in terms of party preferences. There is nothing wrong as such with the electoral system producing some small degree of bias towards a particular party that performs better than others across the country, thereby having a greater claim for political authority than others, but the tolerance of any such disproportionality should not be so great that it allows a single party to gain an overall majority in Parliament and be elected to office without that party winning a majority of popular votes cast at a general election.

The additional-member system will not preclude single party government in Britain. If there is the necessary level of electoral support, the Labour Party or the Conservatives will certainly be able to govern in their own right. In several European countries with proportional representation, single parties have achieved their own electoral mandates from over 50 per cent of the voting population, including instances in Sweden, Germany, Portugal, Spain and Ireland. What adoption of the additional-member system will preclude, however, is one party, in isolation from others, claiming a false mandate on the electoral authority of substantially less than half of the votes cast in a general election, and then being in a position to wield unlimited governmental and legislative power for a period of up to five years. It will preclude huge parliamentary majorities produced from little more than 40 per cent of the popular vote pursuing national policies which are actively opposed by the majority of the population, and remove the potential of central government to enact wholly unacceptable legislation such as the poll tax in 1988 (which eventually had to be abandoned) or the abolition of the capital's regional government (the Greater London Council), to which over 70 per cent of Londoners were opposed in 1984, without even holding a local referendum.

Any electoral system can throw up circumstances in which no single party has an overall majority, and this includes not only methods of proportional representation but also Britain's first-past-the-post system. There have been several cases of general elections producing no overall majority for any one party in twentieth-century British politics – it happened in 1910, 1923, 1929 and 1974. Tiny majorities of less than ten seats were produced by the general elections of 1950 and 1966. Perhaps most significant of all, the instinctive reaction of Britain's political culture in times of national crisis has been to embrace coalitions between parties as the most efficient way to manage the crisis, rather than to lurch towards a more dictatorial form of single-party government, as has been the case elsewhere. Coalitions drawn from across the political parties were formed to meet the financial and political crisis between 1931 and 1935, to meet the challenge of war during 1915–18, and again in 1940–5, and to join together in the task of national reconstruction between 1918 and 1922 following the First World War. To suggest that coalition government in Britain is either unknown or alien to its political culture is patently not true. The superficial appearance of Britain's adversarial form of political discourse disguises the reality that British political parties possess a more deeply ingrained consensus regarding the fundamentals of national life than do the great majority of countries in the Western world. Few individual politicians will admit to this publicly, for the simple reason that party electioneering places a premium upon emphasising the differences, rather than the similarities, between the parties.

Proportional representation is lambasted regularly by opponents for being equivalent to coalition government, which is then portrayed as being essentially weak and unstable. The truth is, however, that the likelihood or otherwise of coalitions is a distraction from the central issues involved, and much of the discussion on this important subject of electoral reform unhelpfully revolves around the meaning of the term 'strong government', antagonists drawing upon whatever comparison abroad best serves the purposes of their argument, from Germany's acknowledged success in its economic management of the country under the additional-member system, to Italy's crisis in federal affairs and fragmentation of political parties under a mixed majoritarian and list system. In general, many believe that single-party government is preferable to coalitions but this does not mean that coalitions are intrinsically ineffective or inefficient. Political circumstances vary, and under some conditions single-party rule may be preferable. But under other conditions – including where (a) no single party has anything like the support of a majority of the country for its programme; or (b) a grave national crisis requires two or more of the parties to co-operate; or (c) it is clear (and evident from public opinion) that none of the parties is fit to govern on its own – then coalition government is likely to be the popular choice and the most effective form of government.

It is obvious that party politicians prefer to get their own way, and especially when in government will prefer to avoid measures such as proportional representation that make a process of compromise or negotiation a greater possibility than at present. But it is equally obvious that politicians will work with one another if circumstances so dictate. All political parties contain a broad spread of opinion, with their own gradients from left to right that can overlap party barriers (it is sometimes possible to imagine that some politicians of one party might find it easier to work with some personalities from another party rather than their own colleagues). The experience of local authorities is useful to observe in this context, for it very often happens that there are hung councils following local elections. Opponents of proportional representation claim that coalitions mean secret deals between parties in 'smoke-filled rooms', in which the distinctive policies of two or more parties are bargained away. But in practice the necessity for agreement between Labour and Liberal Democrats on hung councils at the beginning of the 1990s, as in Avon, Cambridgeshire, Hertfordshire and Humberside County Councils, brought about constructive and public debates about their differences, certainly, but also about how best to secure their common aims. For a great many Labour supporters this is far preferable to not being in government at all.

Objective assessments from across the political spectrum, including from the Conservative peer Robert Blake (in the Hansard Report on Electoral Reform in 1976), and from the Labour peer Raymond Plant (in his interim Report on Electoral Systems in 1991), both refute the suggestion that coalition governments are necessarily weak and unstable. In Lord Blake's view:[83]

Even if reform means that coalitions become more frequent, we do not see this as a major objection, as long as the system prevents a multiplicity of small parties. Political parties will still be answerable to the electorate. The avoidance of flagrant minority rule is, we believe, more important than any disadvantages which coalitions may have. Alternating single-party governments have during the last few years produced a series of abrupt and unsettling reversals of policy. An electoral system which makes this less likely might well be advantageous . . . We are aware of the view that any system which may lead to coalitions may also give power to a minority party to determine the complexion of a government after a general election. It is said that this choice will be made, not by the electors, but by politicians in backstage bargains and wheeler-dealing in 'smoke-filled rooms'. We are not much impressed by this argument, because such a situation might well occur under our present electoral system anyway – indeed it did in February 1974. It may be better to have visible coalitions between parties than to have invisible ones between sections of one party. Furthermore, representative democracy does, by definition, entail rule by elected representatives on behalf of those whom they represent: Parliament can even lead the country into war without reference to the electorate. A general election does not take the form of a referendum, and those who cling to a system under which in three of the last 13 general elections governments have been formed by parties with fewer popular votes than the runners-up, can hardly argue that the voters choose the governments now. Nor is it obvious that a decision to join or not to join a major partner in a coalition must be taken in 'smoke-filled rooms'. A party could convene a conference after an election or it could announce its stance in advance.

And Lord Plant's conclusion is:[84]

We have surveyed the evidence about government stability and there is evidence to suggest that European countries with proportional representation electoral systems do not suffer markedly more instability than governments elected by first-past-the-post in the United Kingdom. Of course, there are exceptions, but these are not confined to the former, since in Britain there was some degree of instability between 1964–66, 1974 and 1977–79 under first-past-the-post.

The House of Commons

The dual role of general elections in the British political structure means that the same electoral system determines not only the composition of the government, but also – most directly – the composition of the House of Commons. There may be a theoretical case for saying that two different electoral processes should operate, one to decide whose party leader should be Prime Minister, and another to elect representatives in the Commons – after all, Parliament and government are performing two entirely different functions. But the Queen is Britain's Head of State, not an elected President, and the constitution does not give her any powers that are other than purely ceremonial, in contrast to, say, the American or French Presidents, who are elected directly by the people, by a separate electoral process from that composing Congress and the National Assembly, and whose offices hold real Executive power. While Britain retains its parliamentary system of government, with the Prime Minister – the 'Head of the Queen's Government' – and other government ministers sitting in the House of Commons and being directly accountable to the House, the same method of elections must decide both outcomes.

Proportional representation is even more important as an issue affecting the House of Commons than it is for determining the government. Constitutionalists will always tend to see the composition of the House of Commons as being of paramount importance, rather than how individuals are selected to manage government departments; whereas businessmen tend to regard who is managing the national economy as much more important than who is sitting on the backbenches of Parliament. The most cost-and-time-efficient form of government might be a dictatorship (which may explain why so many commercial companies are run along authoritarian lines); but managerial efficiency in running the British state must be balanced against the requirements of a political democracy. The ideals of government by discussion and government by consent – together with the constitutional protection of the British citizen's rights and freedoms – depend upon an efficient and effective working of a representative House of Commons.

The primary functions of the House of Commons are to make laws for the peace, order and good government of the United Kingdom, and to hold the government of the United Kingdom to account. The Commons' performance of these two fundamental tasks of legislation and scrutiny of public administration relies upon the House being composed in such a way that it genuinely reflects public opinion within the country. That the quality of British national legislation and its public acceptance will suffer if Parliament is unrepresentative should be self-evident in a democracy. The House of Commons should not be in a position – because of the vagaries of a distorted electoral system – to be able formally to legitimise legislative measures upon which there exists a substantial majority of opinion in opposition. The role of British MPs with respect to the scrutiny over all that goes on in the vast machinery of central government is constitutionally of very great importance. It is their duty to seek justifications and answers from ministers for the policies they pursue and the administrative actions they take, and to act as an effective watchdog over the government machine in Whitehall. MPs must act collectively, in Lloyd George's phrase, as 'the sounding board of the nation'. They must make sure that government ministers are constantly confronted by, and made responsive to, public opinion. In short, they must serve as an accurate reflection of local, regional and national opinion of the ordinary men and women throughout Britain who have elected them into office.

Consideration is now given to three selected examples of how the existing first-past-the-post electoral system adversely impinges upon the constitutional performance of the House of Commons. These concern, first, the domination of the House of Commons' Select Committee system by the party in government; second, the demographic distortion in how political opinion in the different regions of Britain is reflected in the Commons: and third, the low level of representation of women and ethnic minorities in the Commons. In each of these three respects, it will be argued that proportional representation and adoption of the additional-member system would significantly improve the representative quality and functional efficiency of the House of Commons.

A case study on the working of the Commons: Select Committees

The present House of Commons' Select Committee system was established in 1979 (following Richard Crossman's experimental committees first introduced in the 1960s), with the express purpose of facilitating the work of MPs in scrutinising the work of government departments and holding ministers to account for their decisions, policies and general efficiency in Whitehall.[85] Their formal terms of reference are 'to examine the expenditure, administration and policy of the principal government departments . . . and associated public bodies' of British central government.[86] Each Committee initiates its own inquiries, and publishes reports. The introduction of the Select Committee system was part of a deliberate initiative aimed at redressing the balance of power between the House of Commons and the Executive. Thus, when presenting the 1979 Select Committee system for parliamentary approval, the then Leader of the House, Norman St John Stevas, explained that the Committees were designed for a 'more effective means of controlling the Executive', and said,[87]

> We believe . . . the coherent and systematic structure of Select Committees . . . to be a necessary preliminary to the more effective scrutiny of government and the wider involvement that Hon. Members on both sides of the House have sought for many years. It will provide opportunity for closer examination of departmental policy . . . It will also be an important contribution to greater openness in government, of a kind that is in accord with our parliamentary arrangements and our constitutional tradition.

At the time of writing, the number of Select Committees has risen to sixteen, dealing with the departments of Agriculture, Defence, Education, Employment, Environment, Foreign Affairs, Health, Home Affairs, National Heritage, Science and Technology, Scottish Affairs, Trade and Industry, Transport, Treasury and Civil Service, and Welsh Affairs.

The Committees have had a considerable degree of success in drawing the attention of the House and the public to the way the government is handling a wide range of important national issues – even if the Leader of the House of Commons (a government Cabinet minister) rarely allows time for MPs to debate the Committees' reports' findings and recommendations. None the less, the process of examination and questioning of witnesses and advisers in the course of the Select Committees' inquiries have in themselves attracted a great deal of parliamentary and public attention. Especially since television broadcasting of British parliamentary proceedings was introduced in 1988, Select Committees have assumed a high public profile, and ministers and civil servants treat their inquiries with great respect. It is probably true that alongside Prime Minister's Question Time on Tuesdays and Thursdays, and a handful of major debates in the chamber each year, such as those regarding the Maastricht Treaty, for most people the televised broadcasting of the proceedings of Select Committees has become the most interesting and illuminating form of parliamentary work. Many will vividly recall the sessions in which the Treasury and Civil Service Committee questioned Norman Lamont (then Chancellor of the Exchequer) on the withdrawal from the exchange rate mechanism of the European Monetary System in 1992, and Robin Leigh-Pemberton (then Governor of the Bank of England) on the closure of the Bank of Commerce, Credit and Industry in 1991; and, similarly, when the Social Security Committee sought to elicit answers from the Maxwell brothers during the course of its inquiry into private pension funds in 1992.

The conduct of the Select Committee inquiries may involve the detailed questioning of anyone whom Committee members believe can assist their work, and ministers and civil servants are generally an essential source of information at some point in each inquiry. In theory, the power of the House of Commons, which may be delegated to its committees, is unlimited. Yet a grey area exists between this absolute right of parliamentary committees to demand any information they require for the purposes of their inquiries, and the extent and application of Crown privilege, which is utilised by politicians in office to claim public interest immunity and which has never properly been rationalised or clarified. So far as civil servants are concerned, the ministers of the British government maintain that it is they (not civil servants) who are responsible to Parliament, and so they will decide who from their departmental staff, if anyone at all, can or will appear before a Committee. It was by this political means, for example, that Margaret Thatcher's press secretary, Bernard Ingham, famously avoided being questioned about the leak to newspapers of the Solicitor-General's letter during the Westland Affair in 1986.[88] The attendance and manner of response by civil servants to Select Committees is regulated not by any parliamentary code or law decided by the Commons or its Select Committees, but instead by the government itself, in an internal Cabinet Office circular known as the Osmotherly Rules (the existence and contents of which were an official secret until 1992). This memorandum declares, 'The general principle to be followed is that it is the duty of officials to be as helpful as possible to Committees, and that any withholding of information should be limited to reservations that are necessary in the interests of good government or to safeguard national security', but then precludes many matters that might be of interest to the Committees by defining 'good government' to include: interdepartmental exchanges on policy issues; civil service advice to ministers; the level at which decisions were taken and the manner in which a minister consulted his colleagues; and questions 'in the field of political controversy'.

This brings us to the crucial question of how Select Committees are composed, and how the adoption of the additional-member system would improve the quality of their work. Currently, each Committee comprises eleven MPs, formally appointed by the House of Commons itself. As with all Commons' committees, the political balance in the membership of each Select Committee reflects the respective party strengths within the House as a whole. This means that a party in government with a majority of seats in the Commons (even when founded upon a minority of electoral support such as the Conservative government's 41 per cent in the 1992 general election) always has a built-in majority of its own party members on each Select Committee. Thus the most inappropriately composed departmental Select Committee of all at present is the Committee for Scottish Affairs. At the 1992 general election, electors within the 72 parliamentary constituencies of the region of Scotland expressed their political preferences as follows:

49 Labour MPs	(39% of the total vote)
11 Conservative MPs	(25.7% of the total vote)
3 Scottish Nationalist MPs	(21.5% of the total vote)
9 Liberal Democrat MPs	(13.1% of the total vote)

Yet this specialist Commons' Select Committee charged with supervising Scottish affairs is composed of:

6 Conservative MPs	(4 from Scottish constituencies – 1 of whom is unique in being simultaneously a member of another Select Committee; and 2 from England – at Bournemouth and Woodspring)
3 Labour MPs	(All from Scottish constituencies)
1 Scottish Nationalist MP	(From Scottish constituency)
1 Liberal Democrat MP	(From Scottish constituency).

This gross distortion of Scottish political interests reflected on the Committee illustrates very clearly the unsatisfactory extent of Executive control and political misrepresentation endemic within the existing electoral and parliamentary system, which damages the authority and credibility of the Select Committees generally. Nominations on precisely which members of the Commons might be suitably qualified to sit on which Commons' committee are prepared by a Selection Committee, which itself is composed in proportion to party strengths in the House, and whose precise members are chosen through negotiations between the government and opposition party whips. Thus the Selection Committee composed on 11 May 1992 following the 1992 general election had nine members, comprising five Conservative MPs, three Labour MPs, and one Liberal Democrat. Furthermore, 'the Government always have the Chair of the Committee of Selection', in the words of the present incumbent, Sir Marcus Fox (who also happens to be the Chairman of the 1922 Committee, the body which comprises all backbench Conservative MPs).[89] Sir Marcus Fox has recently stated that the Selection Committee's choice of people to sit on the Select Committees is guided by three principles:[90]

(1) That the government should have a majority on each Select Committee;

(2) That the overall number of members from each party nominated by the Committee of Selection to Select Committees should reflect the party strengths in the House as a whole; and

(3) That no ministers, whips, personal private secretaries or principal opposition spokesmen should be considered.

The Select Committees are reconstituted after each general election. The way in which committees were composed in 1992 illustrates the real extent to which the government whips are now controlling a ruling majority on each committee's membership. In 1990, Norman St John Stevas (now Lord St John of Fawsley) had complained:[91]

> Having looked at the way the system has operated over these past few years, I would say that the influence of the whips has increased, is increasing, and certainly ought to be diminished.

However, in 1992, with the results of the general election leaving the Conservative government with a slender majority of just 21 MPs, leaving it far more vulnerable than before to internal Commons' dissent, the potency of the Select Committees to act as a source of criticism of government ministers and policy stung the government's whips into greater efforts than ever before to control the composition of the Committees. Selected individual MPs whose criticisms the government feared found themselves ousted from the positions they held prior to the general election. The Conservative backbencher, Nicholas Winterton, who, as chairman of the Heath Select Committee's inquiry into National Health Service Trusts hospitals in 1991, had been responsible for some fierce criticism of ministers, was one such victim. The process whereby he was removed involved a new 'rule' (as it was reported in the press)[92] being invented whereby an MP might not sit on the same Committee for longer than a limited period, stated to be the duration of two consecutive Parliaments. In fact, no such rule exists nor has ever done so: it was purely a declaration by Sir Marcus Fox, the Conservative Selection Committee Chairman, of what the Conservative majority on the Selection Committee was going to do. Only the House of Commons itself has the authority to lay down such a rule to control its own procedures. As Sir Terence Higgins later commented in the Commons:[93]

> It is wrong that this rule should have been announced to the media rather than to the House of Commons. However, it is not surprising that is so, because there is no such rule. The device has been invented at the last minute to justify a series of selections.

It would appear that the Selection Committee's choice of MPs whom they nominated to sit on the Select Committees simply adopted those names which were given to them by the party whips (acting in consultation with their party leaderships). The whips tendered the names to the Selection Committee's Chairman in a list via their party members sitting on the Committee. As a result, the deliberations of the Selection Committee in July 1992 to decide the entire composition of all sixteen departmentally-related Select Committees took just fifteen minutes. The comment on this process by the solitary Liberal Democrat member on the Selection Committee, Archie Kirkwood, was that, 'It is the Executive through the whips who come along with the names. That is exceptional, wholly wrong, disreputable and objectionable.'[94] Finally, when the motion was put forward for the House of Commons to approve the names given by the Selection Committee, the government's majority in the Commons ensured their rubber-stamping. The formal votes in the Commons on the nominations took place almost exactly at midnight on 13 July. Although there is a convention against three-line whips being issued to backbenchers on selection issues, Westminster lobby correspondents in the press reported that the Conservative Chief Whip had instructed all ministers and parliamentary private secretaries – the 'payroll vote' – to attend the debate to ensure its passage.[95] Even Cabinet ministers and Prime Minister John Major, himself, were present to vote and see that the government secured the Select Committee memberships it wanted.

This degree of government control over the composition of the Select Committees – whose job it is to scrutinise and act as a watchdog on the government – has proved to be a source of considerable parliamentary concern. As Labour's Frank Field has commented, 'On some issues it is necessary to take a view for the House of Commons itself, rather than a strict party view.'[96] MPs in the past have successfully fought off attempts to have Speakers foisted on them who represented the government's choice, rather than a result of the consensus of backbench opinion,[97] and similar efforts must be made in protection of the Commons' privileges with respect to the Selection Committee and the increasingly important offices of membership (and especially Chairmanship) of Select Committees. A prerequisite, then, for any improvement in the composition of Select Committees is that following the next general election, backbench MPs of all parties should bring pressure to bear upon the Committee of Selection to act as a genuine agency of the House, and not as a mere cipher for the will of government ministers. As the Conservative MP, Sir Terence Higgins, has commented, 'It is wrong that the whips should become involved, as they have increasingly become involved in the past ten years, in the question of who is selected to serve on the Committees . . . It is important that the [Selection] Committee should act as a Committee of the House, representing all parts of the House.'[98]

Even where a single party might win over half the popular votes cast at a general election and form a government with an overall majority of seats in the House of Commons, they should not seek to impose their nominees upon a Selection Committee that exists constitutionally to represent the interests of the House of Commons. Still less should a government seek to do so when it has received only 41 per cent of the country's support. The additional-member system of elections to the Commons would result in a more legitimate balance of political opinion represented in the membership of each Select Committee, in direct reflection of the proportional representation on which the House of Commons itself had been composed at the previous general election. Where no overall majority of votes at an election produced an overall majority of seats for one party and outright single-party government, then whether or not a minority or coalition was formed in government, the work of Select Committees would be performed by MPs drawn proportionately from across the political parties. No single party could dominate these specialist bodies that are set up by the House to scrutinise in detail the activities of the Executive. A proportional balance of political opinion between parties on the Select Committees would give each a far greater strength to assert the legitimacy of their work, to protect it from undue influence by the government.

That the political composition of the Select Committees does directly affect the quality and manner of their work goes without saying. It is particularly transparent whenever a Select Committee inquiry leads into the examination of administrative conduct that might prove embarrassing to the party in government. It has become a political fact of life that in any confrontation – and the more controversial the episode the more likely it is to be the case – the majority on Select Committees have chosen to back down rather than to see their own party leaders in office politically embarrassed and therefore likely to lose votes for the party. On virtually every occasion in recent years when a Select Committee has attempted to discover the facts lying at the root of some controversy or scandal within Whitehall (such as the question of who authorised the leak of the Solicitor-General's letter during the Westland Affair in 1986; or what precisely was the extent of the government's knowledge about the level of salmonella poisoning in eggs being sold around the country in 1988; or about military decisions taken during the Falklands War, notably the Belgrano Affair in 1982) the Select Committee in question has always decided to accept rather than to challenge the government's assertion that ministers have the prerogative to refuse to answer certain questions or to allow certain civil servants to be examined, on the basis that it would be 'contrary to the public interest'.[99] The Congressional Committees in the United States would not tolerate the level of obstruction that is currently regularly encountered at Westminster.

The composition of the House of Commons should reflect the political views of the electorate, and Select Committees should reflect the political views and special interests in the Commons. A reform involving proportional representation, combined with a guarantee that MPs will be allowed to choose their own preferred colleagues to serve on Select Committees, would improve substantially the effectiveness of the Committees to perform the important work for which they were established.

The demographic factor

An overview of the political geography of Great Britain (see page 418) immediately reveals one very damaging aspect of the present electoral

Political map of Great Britain, 1992

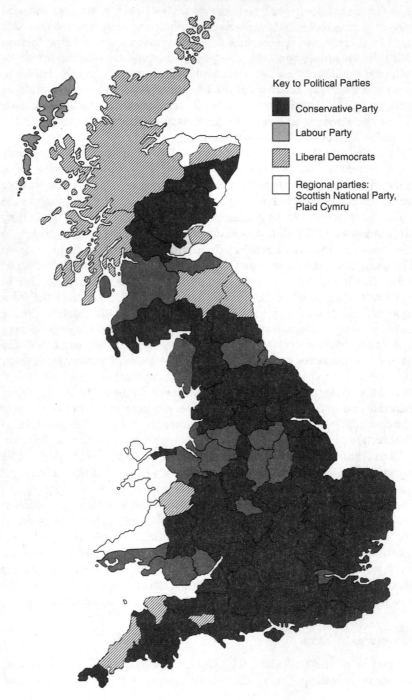

Key to Political Parties

Conservative Party

Labour Party

Liberal Democrats

Regional parties:
Scottish National Party,
Plaid Cymru

system, which is the chronic polarisation of Conservative and Labour party representation between the South and North of the country, between the different regions, and between the countryside and the metropolitan centres. Under existing electoral arrangements, Conservative MPs virtually monopolise the parliamentary representation of the non-metropolitan areas of England, where the Conservative Party's highest level of electoral support traditionally lies (with either none, or only a handful, of Labour MPs being returned to Westminster to represent opinion in those parts of the country); and similarly, the Labour Party tends to dominate the representation of the most highly populated regions and concentration of parliamentary constituencies within Scotland and Wales, and the inner cities of England. This geographical polarisation of party representation at Westminster is a direct product of the first-past-the-post method of voting. The additional-member system would ensure that political preferences and opinions throughout all parts of the country were properly represented in the House of Commons, and also inside each party capable of forming a government.

A huge degree of deviation from proportionality is to be found within most of the different regions of Great Britain. Nationally across the country the level of deviation from proportionality (being the percentage variance between the number of seats won by MPs of a party and the number that it would have won under a purely proportional system) was 16.5 per cent in the 1992 election. This figure is bad enough in comparative terms, but becomes far worse when one realises that it is, in fact, an average aggregate,

Regional deviation from proportionality in 1992

Region	Deviation from proportionality (%)	Percentage share of votes				Percentage share of seats			
		Con.	Lab.	Lib. Dem.	Other	Con.	Lab.	Lib. Dem.	Other
South East	43	55	21	23	1	97	3	0	0
Strathclyde	33	27	38	15	20	17	71	13	0
East Scotland	33	27	38	15	20	17	71	13	0
East Anglia	32	51	28	20	2	80	15	0	0
South West	32	48	19	31	2	80	8	13	0
North	30	33	51	16	1	17	81	3	0
Wales	23	29	50	12	9	16	71	3	11
London	21	45	38	15	2	63	46	1	0
East Midlands	20	47	37	15	1	67	33	0	0
Yorkshire	19	38	44	17	1	37	63	0	0
Highlands	17	34	19	21	26	31	13	0	19
West Midlands	16	45	39	15	2	50	50	0	0
North West	15	38	45	16	2	37	60	3	0

Table 8.4[100]

and is only prevented from being far worse because of the gross imbalance towards one political party in one part of the country being set against the gross imbalance towards the other major party in another part. In the South East of England, for example, the level of deviation from proportionality is as high as 42 per cent, and in Strathclyde it stands at 33 per cent. 'Fair' or 'proportional' political representation at Westminster of community interests and public opinion existing within these parts of the country, this most certainly is not. Under the British electoral system as it now operates, the parliamentary representation of the real political preferences of voters living in some parts of the country is massively distorted.

The political consequences of the way in which the first-past-the-post electoral system operates in regional terms are of some considerable importance. What matters for a great many people is how effective their vote is within the area they live and work, be it problems or concerns directly related to London, Strathclyde or Wales. Yet within such areas there are literally millions of 'wasted votes' of disenfranchised voters, left without a voice in Parliament. Similarly, the political parties are encouraged to be most responsive to where their local and regional power bases lie, and less sensitive to the social concerns of those areas where they have no MPs and under the first-past-the-post voting little prospect of doing so. Under such a system,[101]

There will be a danger that the political parties will be excessively influenced by the interests of the large cities of the north, and insensitive to the needs of commuter suburbs or agricultural areas. The Conservatives, on the other hand, may be insensitive to the economic and human problems associated with the decay of older industries, and the run-down of the inner cities. The present Conservative government is often accused of a lack of awareness of industrial problems and of the human costs of unemployment. This is hardly surprising since following the 1979 election it held only 7 out of the 51 parliamentary constituencies in Bradford, Glasgow, Hull, Leeds, Liverpool, Manchester, Newcastle and Sheffield.

The electoral system thus encourages a class and regional polarisation of politics by emphasising divisive factors far more than the feelings of the electorate warrant, while issues which cannot be fitted into the class alignment of politics are underplayed or ignored.

This electoral system thus makes the country – as reflected in Parliament – look more divided than it actually is; it overemphasises the divisive factors in society, and underplays the strong feelings of national unity which still exist. It thus militates against the idea of 'One Nation'. It is a barrier to both national unity and to good government.

This very important demographic factor in the British voting system therefore requires the greater representative proportionality of any reform to be directed towards regional and community areas. The solution is to ensure that the additional-member system adopted for the United Kingdom makes its assessments about proportionality at regional and community level. This means that the party lists of candidates, from which additional members will be elected to Parliament in proportion to votes cast, should be drawn up at regional level. Another important reason for preferring regional party lists is that if a national system of lists applied, those parties who only operated at a regional level (such as the Scottish National Party and Plaid Cymru) would not pass the legal threshold that is generally applied in list or additional-member systems of election (which is, for example, 5 per cent in Germany). For the purposes of allocating party list MPs in this way, the United Kingdom might be divided up into fifteen electoral areas, as shown on page 421. The calculation, for illustration purposes, adopts the proposal for a 500-member House of Commons, being composed of 50 per cent constituency MPs and 50 per cent party list MPs.

500-seat House of Commons under the additional-member system
using regional party lists

	Region	Electorate	Shares	House of Commons
01	Northern	2 001 807	4.63	12
02	North West	5 219 626	12.08	30
03	Yorkshire	3 729 670	8.63	22
04	West Midlands	3 942 925	9.13	23
05	East Midlands	2 575 795	5.96	15
06	Central	2 008 846	4.65	12
07	East Anglia	2 663 392	6.16	15
08	London	5 120 379	11.85	30
09	South East	2 240 707	5.19	13
10	South Central	2 999 691	6.94	17
11	Wessex	2 391 080	5.53	14
12	South West	1 114 761	2.58	6
13	Wales	2 151 352	4.98	12
14	Scotland	3 953 497	9.15	23
15	Northern Ireland	1 089 160	2.52	6
Total		43 202 688	99.98	250

Table 8.5[102]

The representation of minorities and women

The case for proportional representation rests on the belief that the House of Commons should represent a proper balance of public opinion within itself in order to fulfil effectively its constitutional functions. In so doing, the electoral system should not only determine the level of political support for the parties as between their specific policies or policy packages; it should also determine more accurately the attitudes, characteristics and style most favoured by ordinary people within Britain. It is the attitudes and personalities of politicians towards the way they exercise their power in government that is potentially most damaging and corrupting in politics and society at large or, conversely, most capable of encapsulating the values and aspirations of ordinary men and women within the country and giving the brand of leadership that most people want.

One important aspect of this is that the composition of Parliament should represent the outlook and voice of cultural and ethnic minorities living within the country. The major parties may be able to incorporate such minority representation of outlook within the body of their MPs at Westminister, but only if there are enough successful parliamentary candidates who belong to such a social group. The racial characteristics of a particular candidate may be irrelevant to his or her politics, and may be irrelevant to voters who choose to vote for or against him or her. And some racial minorities, notably Jews, have tended to have a higher number of members as MPs than there are proportionately members within the country at large. But research indicates clearly that the Asian community is at least as likely to want to vote for an Asian rather than a white candidate, and there is good reason to suppose this is so in respect of several other ethnic minorities; also in the case of a community containing a large number of black people. As Professors Richard Rose and Ian McAllister have said in their book *The Loyalty of Voters,* 'The important point for a voter is to support the party that best expresses his or her outlook. The outlook may be shaped by the current performance of the parties, or it may reflect durable socio-economic interests or family loyalties learned in early childhood. Even in the absence of parties, electors may still vote expressively, using ethnicity, gender or religion of candidates to identify the candidate who best represents an individual's outlook.[103]

The level of success of MPs belonging to ethnic minorities entering the House of Commons has been poor. As observed in Chapter 5, only twenty-three such candidates were selected in 1992, of whom only six (including four incumbent MPs) were elected.[104] Prior to the previous election in 1987, there had never been a black MP in the Commons, nor an Asian MP since 1929. There is no doubt that Britain's first-past-the-post electoral system badly aggravates this under-representation of cultural minorities. While they may constitute a substantial (yet still a minor) part of the community within a constituency, similar outlook factors appealing to the white Christian majority in practice tend to promote the selection of white candidates. In constituencies where there is a negligible black or Asian community, the electoral prospects of a black candidate have not been good: the 39-year-old black barrister, John Taylor, who stood as a Conservative candidate in Cheltenham in the 1992 election suffered a collapse of the Conservative majority of 4896 in that constituency and a victory for the

Liberal Democrats.[105] One root of the problem is that constituencies returning one MP will always tend to market its appeal towards the majority, whereas under the systems of proportional representation involving either party lists (such as the additional-member system) or multi-member constituencies (such as STV) each party can field a 'slate' of candidates up to the number of MPs to be returned, and in so doing, it is always likely that the party will want to field a balanced ticket of candidates that appeal to the broad composition of the local electorate. The other, more fundamental, root of the problem is simply that there is no mechanism for proportional representation across Britain, or any region, whereby the large number of 'wasted' votes from culturally homogeneous minorities towards candidates who belong to those social groups can count towards any parliamentary representation at all.

The fact that a disproportionately low number of MPs at Westminster are women is not unassociated. Chapter 5 has already commented on the overwhelming male culture of the House of Commons, and inside government as a whole. It was seen that Britain's 91:9 ratio of men to women in the Commons is one of the worst, and most disproportionate, of the population within the European Union. Yet the ideals that British political leaders proclaim about the modern egalitarian society in Britain, together with sexual equality and equal opportunities, have patently failed to confront the institutionalised procedures and dynamics of a political system that so obviously serves to disadvantage women from entering political life. It was observed in the earlier chapter on candidates that all empirical research on electoral systems has shown that proportional representation favours the election of women, and that the first-past-the-post, single-member method of elections in practice worked against the prospects of women in their thirties, forties and fifties seeking and gaining membership of the Commons. The Plant Report was rather less than unequivocal on this important factor in determining a new electoral system, rather weakly concluding that, 'While it may be the case that more proportional systems are an enabling condition, the most recent academic analysis shows that they are neither necessary nor sufficient conditions.'[106] Undoubtedly, as argued earlier in this book, other aspects of British political culture operate against women entering political life – such as the timetable, atmosphere and facilities at Westminster – and need to be changed.[107] But many of these other conditions are simply a reflection of the existing predominantly male character of politics and government in Britain: the reality is that in order to change this culture to a more equal balance between male and female concerns, proportional representation is now virtually a prerequisite.

A strong reason for preferring the additional-member system over other electoral systems is the simplicity with which an equal and fair representation of women, and also ethnic minorities, can be achieved.

Political parties committed to sexual equality, and to promoting the political prospects of ethnic and black candidates within their party, will ensure their party lists contain a properly balanced range of candidates. For this reason, the recommendation of the Hansard Society that additional members should be drawn from all the 'best losers' across the 651 constituency elections in the United Kingdom should be rejected (and in addition, 'best loser' MPs could too easily be labelled as political rejects, demeaning the whole nature and purpose of the party list MPs, which is to buttress the democratic credibility of the House of Commons). The lists of additional candidates should be prepared by the political parties themselves, and although it would be for each party to decide on their own selection procedures, it is likely that each party would constitute for the purpose of drawing up the lists in advance of each general election a special selection committee comprising a representative from each constituency affected and one or two national delegates.

Political and legal implementation

Electoral reform and party politics

During a parliamentary debate on electoral reform in the 1930s, Labour's Clement Attlee, then Leader of the Opposition, told the Commons:[108]

I find that all parties, possibly we ourselves, tend to adopt the electoral system which suits their political position in any country for the time being. Minority groups naturally ask for the system that suits them, and majority groups probably have a dangerous tendency to squeeze out minorities. You get a party that thinks it is going to run second on the poll out of three and find it very keen on the alternative vote. On the other hand, the party which runs third moves away from the alternative vote and decides that its only chance is in proportional representation . . . I have never concealed the point that I dislike the system, although I am perfectly willing to admit that some 20 years ago, when our party were in an even worse position than the Liberal Party, I thought there might be something in proportional representation.

The political implementation of electoral reform will require (a) its adoption by one of the two major political parties as official policy prior to a general election, and/or (b) the willingness and sufficient commitment by the party in government to refer the question of electoral reform to the final decision of a popular referendum. There is a perennial problem here, reflected in Clement Attlee's words, that party politicians tend to view electoral arrangements – indeed constitutional arrangements in general – as a theoretical matter, largely to be construed according to how those arrangements will facilitate or obstruct their ability to do the things they want to do when they are in governmental office. By and large politicians have always had to be driven to accept limitations upon their power, and whilst there is a real prospect of a party gaining an overall majority at the next election, it will always be an uphill struggle persuading politicians of the benefits of a different electoral system that makes achieving an overall majority a less easy proposition. There is little prospect of the Conservative Party leadership espousing electoral reform (although, as seen,[109] there are Conservative supporters of reform) so it is upon the Labour Party that the prospects for reform depend. The Labour Party, as seen,[110] is consulting widely on the future of the electoral system, and has promised a referendum on the issue if elected to government. Whether either as a result of its own internal policy-making favouring change or because a popular majority backs electoral reform in a referendum, it will remain important that the party as a whole chooses to support reform not for reasons of political self-interest (or not only for reasons of political self-interest) but for reasons of constitutional principle and because it believes in the political desirability of reform. Without this principle and belief, the party's commitment to reform and/or a referendum could easily evaporate once in office. The case for electoral reform, therefore, must continue to be put, and those who advocate proportional representation must seek to persuade and carry the broad support of the party as a whole.

The role of Liberal Democrats in this respect must be to give constructive support in the debate. There is negligible likelihood in the foreseeable future of them being elected to government to implement electoral reform themselves, and meanwhile their arguments are always likely to be most tainted by the suspicion of self-interest. As Tony Banks MP has put it,[111]

> I believe that the principle of proportional representation is coming into favour in the country. It is coming into favour within the Labour Party. There is still some way to go, but its day has arrived. However, the idea of proportional representation comes better from one of the major parties, Conservative or Labour, than it does from the Liberal Democrats. When that party makes the proposal one can accuse it of being self-seeking, as it knows that proportional representation is the only way in which it can increase its level of representation. When the proposal comes from the Conservative or Labour Party, however, there is no self-seeking motivation. It means that those parties are making a genuine attempt to address the democratic argument and to try to find a way in which to achieve greater fairness within our electoral system.

The policy of Liberal Democrats must be to address their arguments and views towards Labour's debate on electoral reform, explaining their reasons for supporting the particular system to which their party is wedded, but not so as to exclude the possibility of supporting a different scheme for greater proportional representation which might be adopted by the Labour Party. Greater proportionality might prove a common goal, and any new system towards this end will benefit Liberal Democrats perhaps more than any other political party.

Popular support and the referendum

The criteria for a democratic electoral system include that the British people understand and approve of the electoral system in which they are voting, and support the particular way in which it translates votes into parliamentary seats. Clearly, the popularity of proportional representation is a very important component in the political implementation of reform, to convince politicians of the desirability of electoral change, for the sake of the credibility of the political system, and because any fundamental change in our democratic process should have the backing of a majority in the country. There is good reason to suppose that the necessary majority in popular opinion behind some form of electoral change already exists. On virtually every occasion that public opinion has been tested by professional market researchers since the early 1980s, a majority has favoured the principle of proportional representation. In a 9 600 voter survey after the 1992 general election, an ICM poll found that 57 per cent of voters agreed that Britain 'should adopt a new voting system that would give parties seats in Parliament in proportion to their share of the vote', with 29 per cent disagreeing.[112] In May 1991, another ICM poll found that 60 per cent said that they were 'in favour of a change in the voting system so that the number of MPs in the Commons more closely mirrors the actual vote each party receives at the general election', with 18 per cent against.[113] In 1986, a Marplan poll showed that 49 per cent of respondents agreed that 'proportional representation should be introduced for elections to Parliament', with 14 per cent disagreeing (and 37 per cent undecided).[114] And in 1982 another Marplan poll showed that 65 per cent of people replied that it would be good for the country when asked 'whether it would be good or bad to adopt an alternative to the present voting system which would give each party seats in the Commons in direct proportion to the share of the votes it had taken at an election', with 18 per cent responding that it would be bad.[115] Opinion polling can never be wholly relied upon for its scientific accuracy in testing the strength and breadth of people's feelings, but it can confidently state that, at the very least, public opinion is not antagonistic to electoral reform. There is, in fact, now every indication to suggest that most people around the country are both interested by, and supportive of, the claims made for proportional representation.

The political implementation of electoral reform must be preceded by a major national debate, led by a commission of inquiry. This preceding commission might take the form of a Speaker's Conference on Electoral Law (a traditional parliamentary practice for the review of electoral affairs), which would be composed of MPs and operate within Westminster. One advantage of such a conference would be to focus the attention of representatives of the political parties upon whether common agreement could be reached or negotiated on possible reform. However, it would be preferable for a Royal Commission on the Electoral System to be established, with a membership drawn predominantly from the political parties but also comprising figures from outside politics, including industry, trade unions, education and the media. The advantage of a Royal Commission would be that it would engage in a deeper and more comprehensive examination of the subject, publishing a substantial report from the evidence it had received, and generate greater public discussion. One possible disadvantage might be the length of time taken in its deliberations, making reform unlikely within the lifetime of the Parliament in which it was set up. Whatever form of public inquiry was conducted, the government of the day should finalise its legislative proposals only after it had secured the moral backing of the electorate, either in the form of a referendum or else by including its recommended policy in the party's manifesto at the next general election.

A useful precedent for the United Kingdom on how to conduct a referendum over proportional representation comes from recent experience in New Zealand. A Royal Commission on the Electoral System, established by the New Zealand Labour government, held a wide-ranging inquiry into electoral reform leading to a report being published in 1986, including a recommendation for a change from first-past-the-post voting to the 'mixed member proportional' system (similar in operation to the additional-member system). The question of electoral reform was then put to the electorate in a referendum – or 'preferendum' as it has been called – held on 19 September 1992 in order to establish, first, the extent of public opinion for and against changing the electoral system, and second, the relative preferences between five different electoral systems (among them STV, the alternative vote, and the mixed member proportional) within the body of those persons who supported change. In the event, an overwhelming majority supported change, with over two-thirds of those persons favouring the mixed member proportional system. Then, on 6 November, 1993, a second referendum was held, putting a straight choice to the electorate between the first-past-the post and mixed member proportional systems. This second referendum, held simultaneously with the date of a general election, produced a popular majority in support of the mixed member proportional system, which has since been established as New Zealand's new electoral system.[116] If the Labour Party in the United Kingdom wins the next general election and takes office, then assuming it proceeds to carry out its promise to launch a national debate on the question of electoral reform, it might well decide to follow the procedures successfully adopted in New Zealand, both for publicly inquiring into and reporting on the subject, and for finally determining the matter by use of referendums.

Conclusions and consequential changes

There is now a powerful and popular case for proportional representation in the United Kingdom, and for choosing the additional-member system as the most suitable method of electing MPs to the House of Commons in the twenty-first century. There is no universal, perfect method of elections for use by all representative assemblies, and a preference for one type of electoral system over another in Britain is ultimately a question of political judgement. That judgement must take into account political and administrative practicalities, opinion within and across the political parties, public opinion across the different parts of the country, and the principles and traditions upon which we wish to found any new system for the future. Both the alternative vote and its variant, the supplementary vote system, are majoritarian systems, not designed for achieving a close proportionality with the views of the electorate. The single transferable vote has many undoubted advantages over the existing system, and works well in terms of proportionality, but would undermine the traditional constituency basis of political representation in the United Kingdom. It is the additional-member system which combines best the virtues of Britain's existing constituency system while adding a very high degree of proportionality into the composition of the Commons.

The form of proportionality that the additional-member system should operate in this country is at a community and regional level, with the United Kingdom being divided into fifteen regional, electoral areas for the purpose. Each political party should be allowed to decide for itself its own internal procedures for drawing up the party lists in each of the regional areas. The precise number of additional seats should constitute half of the membership of the House of Commons. Research indicates that if the proportion of additional members is any less than half (such as the quarter of seats proposed by Lord Blake's Hansard Report on Electoral Reform in 1976) the degree of proportionality achieved is markedly impaired. According to research by Professor Patrick Dunleavy, if the 1992 general election had been conducted under the additional-member system with only a quarter of seats drawn from party lists, then in some areas where support for one party was high (such as for the Conservatives in East Anglia and the South East) that party would have won 75 per cent of the parliamentary seats upon less than 50 per cent of the vote.[117] A method using equal numbers of constituency and party list MPs has operated successfully in Germany, and was recommended in the Institute for Public Policy Research's project on constitutional reform.[118] Its two-vote ballot paper (one for the preferred constituency candidate, and one for the preferred political party) is easy to use and translate into seats. It would also ensure equal status of both kinds of parliamentary member in the House of Commons. The division of political responsibility between constituency and party list MPs would be a matter for each political party to decide for itself, but it would be natural for constituency MPs to give primary attention to the representation of their constituents and local party, and for party list MPs to devote their work outside Westminster to the national and regional work of the party on matters such as policy formulation. In terms of the political implementation of this reform proposal, however, if it might smooth general political acceptance of the scheme as a whole, the numbers of additional members might be phased in: a quarter or a third of the House being elected in this way at the next general election, with a commitment to equal membership at the subsequent election.

A number of consequential changes will be required when electoral reform comes. The two most direct constitutional changes needed will be the statutory regulation of the dissolution of Parliament and the appointment of the Prime Minister. Situations where no single party commands an overall majority in Parliament will become more likely, and instead of relying upon the Queen's prerogative to adjudicate upon competing claims between the political parties for office or to have an election, these matters should be expressly provided for in Britain's constitutional law, reserving any discretion to decided by motions in the House of Commons. An earlier chapter in this book, on the timing of general elections, has already suggested a detailed statutory framework for fixed Parliaments setting out the circumstances in which early elections can be called.[119] On prime ministerial appointment, some statutory provision recognising in law the office of Prime Minister (which is at present a pure creature of *de facto* political practice, carrying on the business of government in the name and place of the Queen) would be desirable, to be followed by the simple provision that, 'The Prime Minister shall be elected by the House of Commons from among its members.'

Drafting the legislation

The legal drafting of a new electoral system in Britain founded upon the additional-member system and the details recommended in this chapter might be as follows. A separate part of the Act could establish the new 250 or so constituencies; create the new Electoral Commission (recommended in chapter 4); and provide the new election rules relating to numbers and electoral quotas within the constituencies (also as recommended in chapter 4). The Act would further need to create, and provide for the boundary review of, the fifteen or so electoral regions for the purposes of allocating additional members on a party list basis. The particular part of the Act establishing the additional-member system itself might read as follows:[120]

REPRESENTATION OF THE PEOPLE BILL

Method of Election to the House of Commons

1. At each general election one member shall be returned for each constituency, and at each such election, and in any by-election, for the House of Commons, the candidate who has secured the largest number of votes in a constituency shall be declared elected.

2. At each general election, additional members equal in number to the number of constituencies shall be declared by the returning officer for each electoral region in accordance with sections 3 and 4 below.

3. At each general election following the results of all the constituency elections having been declared, as soon as practicable after the returning officer for each electoral region shall –

    (a) compare the votes cast for each political party contesting the election in that electoral region with the number of constituency seats won in the House by that party across the region; and

    (b) declare the number of additional members in the House for each political party, in order that the proportion of the seats held by that party in the House in respect of that electoral region corresponds as closely as possible to the proportion that the votes cast for that party in the electoral region bear to the total votes cast there.

4. No additional member of the House of Commons in respect of any electoral region shall be declared for any political party for which the number of votes cast in that region in respect of that House is less than 5 per cent of the total of all such votes.

Appendix 1:
Electing the Party Leader

THE LEADERSHIP ELECTION RULES OF THE POLITICAL PARTIES

The Conservative, Labour and Liberal Democrat parties each have their own particular system for electing or removing their party leaders. The latest versions of each parties' respective procedures controlling these elections are given below. There has only ever been one party leader who has been forcibly removed under the party's leadership election rules whilst holding office as Prime Minister, and that was Margaret Thatcher in November 1990.[1] As a consequence she was politically obliged to resign as Prime Minister. And since 1945 there has been only one party leader to be forcibly removed under the leadership rules whilst serving as Leader of the Opposition, this being Edward Heath in 1975 (who was ousted in the contest by Margaret Thatcher). All other leaders of the Conservative and Labour parties, whether in government or opposition, have voluntarily resigned their position. With the single exception of Harold Wilson, who freely stepped down as Labour leader and Prime Minister in 1976, the reasons for other departures have been either a general election defeat (as with Labour's Clement Attlee in 1955, James Callaghan in 1980 and Neil Kinnock in 1992, and the Conservatives' Sir Alec Douglas-Home in 1964) or else the physical reasons of ill-health (as with the Conservatives' Sir Winston Churchill in 1955, Sir Anthony Eden in 1957 and Harold Macmillan in 1963) or death (Labour's Hugh Gaitskell in 1963 and John Smith in 1994). The Conservatives have only had formal party leadership election rules since 1965: previously leaders 'emerged' after a period of consultation and negotiation (generally with Buckingham Palace acting as broker if the party leader was Prime Minister, as in 1957 and 1963). Across all the parties, therefore, even allowing for a number of unsuccessful challenges to incumbent leaders (such as Tony Benn's challenge to Neil Kinnock in 1988 and Sir Anthony Meyer's against Margaret Thatcher in 1989), contests to replace or remove party leaders have not taken place with any great frequency over the past 50 years of British politics.[2]

The Conservative Party

PROCEDURE FOR THE SELECTION OF THE LEADER
OF THE CONSERVATIVE PARTY

Timings of Elections and General Responsibilities

1.   If the position of Leader of the Party is vacant, an election shall be held as early as possible.

2.   Otherwise there shall be an election in the House of Commons beginning within 28 days of the opening of each new Session of Parliament (except that in the case of a new Parliament the election shall be held not earlier than three months or later than six months from the date of assembly of that Parliament) provided that the Chairman of the 1922 Committee is advised in writing by not less than 10 per cent of the members of the Parliamentary party that they believe such an election to be necessary.

On receipt of such advice, which must reach him within 14 days of the opening of a new Session or within three months of the start of a new Parliament, and without disclosing the names of any of the signatories, the Chairman shall inform the Leader of the Party that an election is required, and together they shall determine the actual date. Otherwise the Chairman will declare that the Leader of the Party has been returned unopposed for a further term.

3.   The Chairman of the 1922 Committee will be responsible for the conduct of all ballots and will settle all matters in relation thereto.

Nominations and List of Candidates

4.   Candidates will be proposed and seconded in writing by Members of the House of Commons in receipt of the Conservative Whip. The Chairman of the 1922 Committee and scrutineers designated by him will be available to receive nominations. Each candidate will indicate on the nomination paper that he is prepared to accept nomination, and no candidate will accept more than one nomination. The names of the proposer and seconder will be published by the scrutineers. Nominations will close by noon on a Thursday five days before the date of the First Ballot.

5.   If only one valid nomination is received, the Chairman of the 1922 Committee shall declare this person elected. If more than one valid nomination is received, the Chairman of the 1922 Committee and his scrutineers will publish a list of the valid nominations and immediately transmit a copy to the two Vice-Chairmen of the 1922 Committee, the Chief Whip in the House of Commons, the Chairman of the National Union, the

Chairman of the Executive Committee of the National Union, the President of the Scottish Conservative and Unionist Association, the Chairman of the Party, the Chairman of the Party in Scotland, the Chairman of the Association of Conservative Peers, the Chief Whip in the House of Lords, and the Leader of the Conservative Members of the European Parliament.

Procedure for Consultation

6. During the period between the close of nominations and the date of the First Ballot it shall be the responsibility of the constituency Association in each constituency which is represented by a Conservative Member of Parliament to ascertain, in conjunction with the Member, the views of their membership regarding the candidates by the most effective means available.

7. The Chairman of the Association of Conservative Peers and the Chief Whip in the House of Lords will make such arrangements as appropriate to obtain the views of Peers in receipt of the Conservative Whip.

8. The Leader of the Conservative Members of the European Parliament will obtain the views of MEPs in receipt of the Conservative Whip.

9. In order that all sections of the Party shall be consulted, Area Chairmen of the National Union will obtain the opinions of constituency associations, through their Chairmen and report their findings to the Chairman of the National Union and the Chairman of the Executive Committee of the National Union. In Scotland the Area Chairmen will similarly consult and report to the President of the Scottish Conservative and Unionist Association. They will also report to Conservative Members of Parliament within the area of their responsibility the views of constituencies not represented by a Conservative Member of Parliament.

10. The Chairman of the Association of Conservative Peers, the Chief Whip in the House of Lords, the Leader of the Conservative Members of the European Parliament, the Chairman of the National Union and the Chairman of the Executive Committee of the National Union, together with the President of the Scottish Conservative and Unionist Association, will on the Monday attend a meeting of the Executive Committee of the 1922 Committee for the purpose of conveying to them the collective views of the Peers in receipt of the Conservative Whip, the Members of the European Parliament in receipt of the Conservative Whip, the National Union and the Scottish Conservative and Unionist Association respectively. Each will be invited to bring a brief note summarising the views of those consulted.

11. It shall be the responsibility of the Chairman and other members of the 1922 Executive Committee to ensure that these views are available to Members of the House of Commons in receipt of the Conservative Whip.

PART II – CONDUCT OF THE ELECTION

First Ballot

12.   The First Ballot will be held on the Tuesday immediately following the closing date for nominations. For this ballot the scrutineers will prepare a ballot paper listing the names of the candidates and give a copy for the purpose of balloting to each Member of the House of Commons in receipt of the Conservative Whip.

13.   For the first ballot each voter will indicate one choice from the candidates listed.

14.   Where any Member is unavoidably absent from the House on that day for any reason acceptable to the scrutineers, the Chairman of the 1922 Committee shall make appropriate arrangements for the appointment of a

15.   The ballot will be secret and neither the names of those who have voted for a particular candidate nor the names of those who have abstained from voting shall be disclosed by the scrutineers.

16.   If, as a result of this ballot, one candidate both (i) receives an overall majority of the votes of those entitled to vote and (ii) receives 15 per cent more of the votes of those entitled to vote than any other candidate, he will be elected.

17.   The scrutineers will announce the number of votes received by each candidate, and if no candidate satisfies these conditions a second ballot will be held.

Second Ballot

18.   The Second Ballot will be held on the following Tuesday. Nominations made for the First Ballot will be void. New nominations will be submitted by the Thursday, under the same procedure and with the same arrangements for consultation as described in paragraphs 4–11 for the First Ballot, both for the original candidates if required and for any other candidates .

19.   The voting procedure for the Second Ballot will be the same as for the First, save that paragraph 16 shall not apply. If, as a result of this Second Ballot, one candidate receives an overall majority of the votes of those entitled to vote, that candidate will be elected.

Third Ballot

20.   If no candidate receives an overall majority, any candidate may withdraw his or her name by advising the Chairman of the 1922 Committee to that effect before 6pm the following day. Of those then remaining, the

two candidates who received the highest number of votes at the Second Ballot will go forward to a Third Ballot on Thursday.

21.   The candidate receiving a majority of votes cast in this Ballot will be elected .

22.   Should this Ballot result in a tie, and unless the two candidates are able to inform the Chairman of the 1922 Committee that they shall have resolved the matter between themselves, a Fourth Ballot shall be held on the Tuesday following.

Party Meeting

23.   When an election results in the return of a new Leader of the Party, the candidate thus elected will be presented for confirmation as Party Leader to a Party meeting constituted as follows:

Members of the House of Commons in receipt of the Conservative Whip
Members of the House of Lords in receipt of the Conservative Whip
Members of the European Parliament in receipt of the Conservative Whip
Adopted Parliamentary Candidates
Members of the Executive Committee of the National Union not already
   included in the above categories.

The Labour Party

LABOUR PARTY RULE BOOK

CONSTITUTIONAL RULES, Clause VI

1.   There shall be a leader and deputy leader of the Labour Party who shall be *ex-officio* leader and deputy leader of the Parliamentary Labour Party.

2.   The leader and deputy leader of the party shall be elected and/or re-elected from amongst the Commons members of the Parliamentary Labour Party at a party conference . . . . and with the provision as may be set out in the procedural rules for the time being in force.

PROCEDURAL RULES, Rule 5: Election of Leader and Deputy Leader

1.   (a)   The Leader and Deputy Leader of the party shall be elected separately in accordance with rule 5(2) unless 5(30) applies.
(b)   In the case of a vacancy for Leader or Deputy Leader each nomination must be supported by 12.5 per cent of the Commons members of the Parliamentary Labour Party. Nominations not attaining this threshold shall be null and void.

(c)   In the case where there is no vacancy, nominations should also be sought on an annual basis. Each nomination must be supported by 20 per cent of the Commons Members of the Parliamentary Labour Party to be valid. Nominations not attaining this threshold shall be null and void.

(d)   Affiliated organisations, constituency parties and Labour Members of the European Parliament may also nominate for each of the offices of Leader and Deputy Leader; all nominees must be Commons members of the Parliamentary Labour party.

(e)   Nominees should inform the General Secretary of the acceptance or otherwise of their nomination within two clear weeks before the commencement of the procedures of voting set out in rule 5(2). Unless consent to nominate is received, nominations shall be rendered null and void. Valid nominations shall be printed on the agenda of Annual Conference, or together with ballot documentation under rule 5(3) together with the names of the nominating organisations and Commons Members supporting the nominations.

(f)   Nominees who do not attend the party conference shall be deemed to have withdrawn their nominations unless they send to the secretary on or before the date on which the conference opens an explanation in writing of their absence, satisfactory to the Conference Arrangements Committee.

2.   (a)   Voting in the election of Leader and Deputy Leader will take place so that the results are declared at annual conference, unless a vacancy occurs under section 5(3) of these rules, in which case the timing of the ballot will be as determined by the National Executive Committee.

Voting shall take place consecutively in three sections as follows:

(i)   Section 1 shall consist of Commons Members of the Parliamentary party and Members of the European Parliamentary Labour Party. Each such member will be entitled to one vote in each ballot held under this section in the election.

(ii)   Section 2 shall consist of the vote of all individual members of the party, on the basis of one member one vote. This ballot shall take place on a national basis and shall be counted and recorded as an aggregate vote broken down by constituency parties.

(iii) Section 3 shall consist of those members of affiliated organisations who have indicated their support of the Labour Party and that they are not members or supporters of any other party or otherwise ineligible to be members of the Labour Party. Voting shall take place under the procedures of each affiliated organisation, but voting will be on a one person one vote basis, recorded by affiliated organisations and aggregated for a national total. The ballot paper shall provide for the declaration of support and eligibility required under this rule if no prior declaration has been made.

(b) The votes of each nominee in each section shall be calculated as a percentage of the total votes cast in that section and shall then be apportioned in the following manner:

Section 1: Parliamentary Labour Party and European Parliamentary Labour Party – one third;
Section 2: Individual members of the Labour Party – one third;
Section 3: Members of affiliated organisations – one third.

(c) The votes proportioned as provided in Rule 5(2)(b) above shall be totalled, and the candidate receiving more than half of the votes so apportioned shall be declared elected. If no candidate reaches this total on the first ballot, further ballots shall be held on an elimination basis.

(d) (i) Subject to sub-paragraph (ii) below, when the parliamentary Labour Party is in opposition in the House of Commons the election of the Parliamentary Leader and Deputy Leader shall take place at each annual party conference.

(ii) When the party is in government and the party leader is prime minister, the election shall take place only if requested by the majority of the party conference on a card vote.

(iii) Subject to paragraph 5(3) below, in any other circumstances an election shall only be held when a vacancy occurs. (e) The votes cast for each nominee in each section, recorded as prescribed, shall be made available as soon as possible.

3. (a) When the party is in government and the party leader is Prime Minister, and the party leader for whatever reason becomes permanently unavailable, the Cabinet shall in consultation with the National Executive Committee appoint one of its members to serve as party leader until a ballot under these rules can be carried out.

(b) When the party is in government, and the Deputy Leader becomes Party Leader under Clause 5(a) and for whatever reason the Deputy Leader becomes permanently unavailable, then the Cabinet in consultation with the National Executive Committee shall appoint one of its members to serve as Deputy Leader who shall hold office until the next party conference. Alternatively, the Cabinet or Parliamentary Committee, in consultation with the National Executive Committee, has the power to leave the post vacant until party conference.

(c) When the party is in opposition and the Party Leader for whatever reason becomes unavailable, the Deputy Party Leader should automatically become Party Leader on a pro-tem basis. The NEC shall decide whether to hold an immediate ballot as provided for under rule 5(2) or to elect a new Party Leader at the next annual conference to the party.

(d) When the party is in opposition and the Leader and Deputy Leader for whatever reason both become permanently unavailable, the National

Executive Committee shall order postal ballot as provided for under these rules. In consultation with the Parliamentary Committee they may choose to appoint a member of the Parliamentary Committee to serve as Party Leader until the outcome of that ballot.

The Liberal Democrats

THE CONSTITUTION OF THE SOCIAL AND LIBERAL DEMOCRATS

Article 10: The Leader

1.   The Leader of the Party shall be elected by the members of the Party in accordance with election rules made pursuant to Article 8.5.*

2.   An election for the Leader shall be called upon:
   (a)   the Leader asking for an election;
   (b)   the death or incapacity of the Leader;
   (c)   the Leader ceasing to be a Member of the House of Commons (other than a temporary cessation by reason of a dissolution);
   (d)   the receipt by the President of the resignation of the Leader or of a declaration of intent to resign upon the election of a new Leader;
   (e)   a vote of no confidence in the Leader being passed by a majority of all Members of the Parliamentary Party in the House of Commons;
   (f)   the receipt by the President of a requisition submitted by at least 75 Local Parties following the decision of a quorate general meeting; or
   (g)   the second annivesary of the preceding general election being reached without an election being called under any of paragraphs (a) through (f), provided that:
      (i)   in exceptional circumstances, the Federal Executive may postpone such an election for no more than one year by a two-thirds majority of those present and voting; and
      (ii)   this paragraph (g) shall not apply if the Leader is a member of the Government.

3.   Upon election, the Leader shall hold office until death, incapacity or resignation or the completion of an election called under this Article.

4.   Upon the calling of an election, the Federal Executive shall publish a timetable for nominations, withdrawals, despatch and receipt of ballot papers and the holding of ballots and shall appoint a disinterested person or body to receive and count the ballot papers.

5.   Nominations must be of a Member of the Parliamentary Party in the House of Commons, who must be proposed and seconded by other such Members and supported by 200 members in aggregate in not less than 20 Local Parties (including, for this purpose, the Specified Associated Organisations representing youth and students as provided by Article 13.8) following the decision of a quorate general meeting and must indicate acceptance of nomination.

* Note.   Article 8.5 reads: 'The Federal Executive shall have power, after appropriate consultations and subject to ratification by the Federal Conference, to make and from time to time vary rules as to membership, elections and such other matters as it may consider necessary or desirable to give effect to or supplement the provisions of this Constitution. Any election rules must provide for elections to be by Single Transferable Vote and secret ballot.'

Notes and References

1.   Robert Blackburn, 'Margaret Thatcher's Resignation as Prime Minister', Ch. 3 in Robert Blackburn (ed.), *Constitutional Studies* (1992); Rodney Brazier, 'The Downfall of Margaret Thatcher', *Modern Law Review* (1991), p. 471.
2.   See R. M. Punnett, *Selecting the Party Leader: Britain in Comparative Perspective* (1992); for statistics on party leaders, D. and G. Butler, *British Political Facts 1900–85* (1986), in Part II; and on the changes made to the Conservative Party rules following the resignation of Margaret Thatcher, R. K. Alderman, 'Electing the Leader of the Conservative Party: Revision of the Rules', *Public Law* (1991), p. 30.

Appendix 2: By-Elections

A by-election takes place in a constituency whenever a vacancy occurs in the House of Commons. The reasons for a vacancy include the death of an MP, an MP's acceptance of a disqualifying office, some other legal disqualification applying (e.g. bankruptcy or mental illness),[1] or an Election Court's declaration that the election or return of an MP was void.

The procedure that sets off the by-election campaign and determines the date for polling in the constituency is a motion being passed in the House of Commons calling upon the Speaker to make out his warrant for the issue of a writ of election. The general principle at Westminster is that this motion should be put forward within three months of the vacancy arising,[2] and that within this period the party whose member held the seat is entitled to control the motion's precise timing. Any MP may put forward the motion, but the usual practice is to leave the initiative to the Chief Whip of the party to which the outgoing MP belonged.[3] If the vacancy occurs at a time when the Commons stands prorogued or adjourned, the Speaker is empowered without the authority of the House to make out his warrant for the election writ to be issued.[4] After the Speaker's warrant has been duly delivered to the Clerk of the Crown in Chancery (which is part of the Lord Chancellor's Department, housed at Westminster in the House of Lords), the Clerk will as soon as practicable issue a writ of election and have it delivered to the returning officer for the constituency where the parliamentary vacancy has arisen.[5] The procedural stages down to polling day are similar to those for a general election, except that the returning officer is permitted some discretion in matters as to time concerning the delivery of nomination papers and the date set for polling day. The last day for delivery of nomination papers is fixed by the returning officer and must be a date not earlier than the third day after his publication of the notice of election, nor later than the seventh day after his receipt of the writ of election. The precise date for polling day in the by-election is fixed by the returning officer, and must not be earlier than the ninth day nor later than the eleventh day after the closing date for delivery of nomination papers. Thus polling day at a by-election will be between seventeen and nineteen working days following the issue of the writ of election from the Clerk of the Crown in Chancery.

The frequency of by-elections varies a great deal, but the average in recent decades has been around 6 per year.[6] During the four years of the last Parliament, 1987–92, 24 by-elections were fought in total. The most common reason for a by-election is the death of an incumbent MP. Between 1832 and 1987 a total of 1 190 MPs died in service, with the death rate of MPs (along with their average age) declining in recent times.[7] The other major causes for by-elections are an MP's resignation from office or an MP's disqualification from membership of the Commons. As seen, technically MPs cannot resign their membership of the House of Commons but in effect they can arrange to do so by accepting one of the fictional offices of Bailiff or Steward of the Chiltern Hundreds or the Manor of Northstead.[8] MPs most commonly resign either to accept a prestigious public office outside Westminster politics, as when Sir Leon Brittan became a European Commissioner in 1988, or otherwise for reasons of disenchantment with politics, combined perhaps with the offer of better-paid, commercial employment. The acceptance by an MP of a peerage has remained another cause for by-elections over the past two decades, occurring particularly as a result of Cabinet re-shuffles where a senior government minister is effectively retired by the Prime Minister from centre-stage politics but offered a top honour and a role to play in the Lords instead. This happened to William Whitelaw in 1983 and David Waddington in 1991, in both cases retiring Home Secretaries becoming Leaders of the House of Lords.

By-elections are often sensational political events, especially if the candidate for the party formerly holding the seat is defeated.[9] By contrast to voting intentions gauged by opinion polls, they are tangible, real tests of public opinion on the level of electoral support enjoyed by the respective parties. However, it is well known that by-elections often produce much wilder swings for or against the government than occurs at a general election on a national scale.[10] None the less the result will be claimed by members of the winning party as proof of public support for themselves and their policies, and the press will project what the result might mean if a general election was held in the near future. Where a by-election takes place during a period of government unpopularity and the government party candidate loses, especially if it was formerly held by one of their MPs, then this can and will be used by the opposition to embarrass government ministers' claims to be acting in the public interest and passing legislation with the country's support behind them. For many reasons, therefore, the national party campaigning machines and the national press will be especially focused and concentrated on the individual candidates' performance and the particular constituency at a by-election, quite unlike the local contest fought at a normal general election. Whilst the absence of any expenditure limit on national campaigning expenses incurred by the parties continues to apply in by-election campaigns as in general election campaigns, the individual candidates at by-elections are permitted to incur a higher level of local campaign expenses than at a general election. The present limit is a lump sum of £18 572 (instead of £4 642 at a general election) plus a sum equivalent to 20.8p in county constituencies and 15.8p in borough constituencies for every registered elector (instead of 5.2p and 3.9p respectively at a general election).[11]

The political significance of by-elections may be larger than just morale and propaganda victories for one party or another. The long-term cumulative effect of a succession of by-election losses for a government that has been elected to office at the previous general election with only a slender majority of seats in the Commons may prove disastrous. In the 1970s the Labour government won an overall majority of three seats at the October 1974 general election, but then lost seven seats at by-elections over the following years, which led directly to the Lib–Lab pact in 1977–78 and finally the collapse of the government itself in spring 1979 following its defeat in a No Confidence motion in the Commons tabled by the opposition leader Margaret Thatcher. The slender overall majority of 21 Conservative seats won by John Major's government in 1992 may prove sufficient numerically to withstand a run of by-election losses over a four or even five year parliamentary term. In such a situation however, the potential for disruption to government business by groups of government backbenchers opposed to individual items of government policy makes it all the more likely that a Prime Minister will be prepared to call a general election at the earliest possible moment when he believes he can win the election and significantly increase his party's overall level of parliamentary representation.

Notes and References

1. On disqualifications from membership of the House of Commons, see ch. 5 above, especially pp. 160f.
2. This period was recommended by the Speaker's Conference in 1973, Cmnd 5500. It has been breached on at least four occasions since.
3. On occasions when MPs other than the Whips have put forward the motion, see J. A. G. Griffith and M. Ryle, *Parliament* (1989), pp. 193, 403.
4. See Erskine May, *Parliamentary Practice* (21st edn, 1989), p. 19.
5. On the timetable, see Representation of the People Act 1983, Schedule 1: Parliamentary Election Rules, especially r. 1.
6. For historical statistics, see D. & G. Butler, *British Political Facts 1900–1985* (6th edn, 1986), p.141.
7. See F. W. Craig, *British Electoral Facts 1832–1987* (5th edn, 1989), p. 59.
8. See Ch. 5 above, p. 165.
9. Historically, by-elections have sometimes been uncontested, although there have been no such occasions now since the 1951–55 Parliament. During the two world wars this century, the three main parties observed a truce by nominating candidates only for seats which they had previously held. See F. W. Craig, *British Electoral Facts 1832–1987* (5th edn, 1989), p. 17.
10. See my comments at p. 28, and for statistics F. W. Craig, *Chronology of British Parliamentary By-Elections* 1833–1987 (1987).
11. See Ch. 6 above, pp. 282–3, and Representation of the People (Variation of Limits of Candidates' Election Expenses) Order 1994.

Appendix 3: Rules for Redistribution of Seats

[from the Parliamentary Constituencies Act 1986]

The Rules

1. (1) The number of constituencies in Great Britain shall not be substantially greater or less than 613.

(2) The number of constituencies in Scotland shall not be less than 71.

(3) The number of constituencies in Wales shall not be less than 35.

(4) The number of constituencies in Northern Ireland shall not be greater than 18 or less than 16, and shall be 17 unless it appears to the Boundary Commission for Northern Ireland that Northern Ireland should for the time being be divided into 16 or (as the case may be) into 18 constituencies.

2. Every constituency shall return a single member.

3. There shall continue to be a constituency which shall include the whole of the City of London and the name of which shall refer to the City of London.

4. (1) So far as is practicable having regard to rules 1–3

    (a) in England and Wales,

       (i) no county or any part of a county shall be included in a constituency which includes the whole or part of any other county or the whole of part of a London borough,

       (ii) no London borough or any part of a London borough shall be included in a constituency which includes the whole or part of any other London borough,

    (b) in Scotland, regard shall be had to the boundaries of local authority areas,

    (c) in Northern Ireland, no ward shall be included partly in one constituency and partly in another.

(2) In sub-paragraph (1)(b) above 'area' and 'local authority' have the same meanings as in the Local government (Scotland) Act 1973.

5. The electorate of any constituency shall be as near the electoral quota as is practicable having regard to rules 1 to 4; and a Boundary Commission may depart from the strict application of rule 4 if it appears to them that a departure is desirable to avoid an excessive disparity between the electorate

of any constituency and the electoral quota, or between the electorate of any constituency and that of neighbouring constituencies in the part of the United Kingdom with which they are concerned.

6.   A Boundary Commission may depart from the strict application of rules 4 and 5 if special geographical considerations, including in particular the size, shape and accessibility of a constituency, appear to them to render a departure desirable.

General and Supplemental

7.   It shall not be the duty of a Boundary Commission to aim at giving full effect in all circumstances to the above rules, but they shall take account, so far as they reasonably can –

(a)   of the inconveniences attendant on alterations of constituencies other than alterations made for the purposes of rule 4, and

(b)   of any local ties which would be broken by such.

8.   In the application of rule 5 to each part of the United Kingdom for which there is a Boundary Commission –

(a)   the expression 'electoral quota' means a number obtained by dividing the electorate for that part of the United Kingdom by the number of constituencies in it existing on the enumeration date,

(b)   the expression 'electorate' means –

(i)   in relation to a constituency, the number of persons whose names appear on the register of parliamentary electors in force on the enumeration date under the Representation of the People Acts for the constituency,

(ii) in relation to the part of the United Kingdom, the aggregate electorate as defined in sub-paragraph (i) above of all the constituencies in that part,

(c) the expression 'enumeration date' means, in relation to any report of a Boundary Commission under this Act, the date on which the notice with respect to that report is published in accordance with section 5(1) of this Act.

Note. Section 5(1) of the Act reads: 'Where a Boundary Commission intend to consider making a report under this Act they shall, by notice in writing, inform the Secretary of State accordingly, and a copy of the notice shall be published (a) in a case where it was given by the Boundary Commission for England or the Boundary Commission for Wales, in the *London Gazette*, (b) in a case where it was given by the Boundary Commission for Scotland, in the *Edinburgh Gazette*, and (c) in a case where it was given by the Boundary Commission for Northern Ireland, in the *Belfast Gazette*.'

Notes and References

1 Introduction: British Parliamentary Democracy

1. *Thoughts on the Constitution* (1947), pp. 20–1.
2. See C. B. Macpherson, *The Life and Times of Liberal Democracy* (1977); A. H. Birch, *Representative and Responsible Government* (1964); J. Lively, *Democracy* (1975); R. Barker, *Political Ideas in Modern Britain* (1978).
3. *The Politics* (translated by Ernest Barker, 1948), p. 128.
4. Generally, see M. J. C. Vile, *Constitutionalism and the Separation of Powers* (1967).
5. See R. Brazier, *Constitutional Practice* (1988), ch. 4, especially pp. 49–50.
6. Contained within the preamble to the Parliament Act 1911. Generally on the constitutional working of the House of Lords, see Sir I. Jennings, *Parliament* (2nd edn, 1970), ch. XII; J. A. G. Griffith and M. Ryle, *Parliament* (1989), ch. 12; D. Shell, *The House of Lords* (2nd edn, 1992).
7. As at 11 June 1994.
8. Under the terms of the Parliament Acts 1911 and 1949. On passage of the War Crimes Bill, see D. Shell, *The House of Lords* pp. 251–2.
9. See Sir I. Jennings, *Cabinet Government* (3rd edn, 1959), ch. XII; R. Brazier, *Constitutional Practice* (1989), ch. 8.
10. See A. V. Dicey, *The Law of the Constitution* (1959), ch. 1; A. W. Bradley and K. D. Ewing, *Constitutional and Adminstrative Law* (11th edn, 1993), ch. 5.
11. See B. Crick, *The Reform of Parliament* (1964), p. 19; and on proportional representation, Chapter 8 below.
12. See P. Norton, *The Constitution in Flux* (1982), ch. 11; V. Bogdanor, *The People and the Party System* (1981), pts I & II.
13. Quoted in S. D. Bailey (ed.), *The British Party System* (2nd edn, 1953) at p. v. On the political work and functions of parties, see Sir I. Jennings, *Party Politics* (3 vols, 1960, 1961, 1962); R. Rose, *The Problem of Party Government* (1974), and *Do Parties Make a Difference?* (1980); S. E. Finer, *The Changing British Party System 1945–79* (1980); S. Ingle, *The British Party System* (1987).
14. Report of the Committee on Financial Aid to Political Parties (1976), Cmd 6601, p. 53. This report is commonly known, and referred to elsewhere in this book, as the 'Houghton Report' (after the Committee's chairman, Lord Houghton).
15. See Robert Blackburn, 'Margaret Thatcher's Resignation as Prime Minister', in Robert Blackburn (ed.), *Constitutional Studies* (1992), ch. 3.
16. See below, Appendix A.
17. *The Dilemma of Democracy* (1978), p. 37.
18. See below, pp. 283f.
19. The main parties do, however, publish voluntarily some annual information about their finances: see below, pp. 313f.
20. See below, pp. 36–7.
21. Article 4, The Constitution of the Fifth French Republic.
22. Article 21, Basic Law; and, for example, especially the Law on Political Parties 1967.

445

23. On the history of these parties, see H. Pelling, *A Short History of the Labour Party* (3rd edn, 1968); R. Blake, *The Conservative Party from Peel to Thatcher* (1985); C. Cook, *A Short History of the Liberal Party 1900–1987* (1989).

24. On the structure of the Conservative Party, see P. Norton and A. Aughey, *Conservatives and Conservatism* (1981); Conservative Party, *Rules and Standing Orders of the National Union of Conservative and Unionist Associations.*

25. Clause IV, Party Objects (1), contained within the party's constitution. On the structure of the Labour Party, see S. Barker, *How the Labour Party Works* (1971); Labour Party, *Constitution and Standing Orders of the Labour Party,* and the annually produced *Rule Book.*

26. *Constitution of the Social and Liberal Democrats* (1988).

27. D. Butler and D. Kavanagh, *The British General Election of 1979* (1980), p. 199.

28. Generally, see R. M. Punnett, *Front-Bench Opposition* (1973); J. A. G. Griffith and M. Ryle, *Parliament* (1989), ch. 9.

29. Sir I. Jennings, *Parliament* (2nd edn, 1957), p. 168.

30. Sources: House of Commons Information Office; F. W. Craig (ed.), *British Electoral Facts 1832–1987* (5th edn, 1989); and D. and G. Butler (eds), *British Political Facts 1900–1985* (6th edn, 1986).

31. *Parliamentary Government in England* (1938), p. 15. See further, W. J. M. Mackenzie, *Free Elections* (1958); S. E. Finer, *Comparative Government* (1970), esp. ch. 9; D. Butler, H. R. Penniman and A. Rannay, *Democracy at the Polls* (1981).

2   The Timing of General Elections

1. The Septennial Act 1715 as amended by section 7 of the Parliament Act 1911.

2. On the prerogative generally, see S. de Smith and R. Brazier, *Constitutional and Adminstrative Law* (6th edn, 1989), ch. 6; E. C. S. Wade and A. W. Bradley, *Constitutional and Administrative Law* (11th edn by A. W. Bradley and K. D. Ewing, 1993), ch. 12; R. F. V. Heuston, *Essays in Constitutional Law* (2nd edn, 1964). On the summoning and dissolution of Parliament, see Robert Blackburn, *The Meeting of Parliament* (1990). Early classic works on on the prerogative are Sir W. Blackstone, *Commentaries on the Laws of England* (5th edn, 1773), book I, ch. VII; J. Chitty, *The Prerogatives of the Crown* (1820); Sir W. Anson, *The Law and Custom of Parliament*, vol. II: The Crown, (3rd edn, 1907), ch. I.

3. Eight Bills for this purpose were introduced by Keir Hardie or Sidney Buxton between 1889 and 1903.

4. House of Commons Debate, 21 February 1911, col. 1749.

5. See pp. 53f.

6. [1984] 3 All ER 935 at 937.

7. See p. 16.

8. See p. 50.

9. See Representation of the People Act 1983, Schedule 1: Parliamentary Election Rules (commonly known as and referred to elsewhere in this book as the 'Election Rules').

10. Source: F. W. Craig (ed.), *British Electoral Facts 1832–1987* (5th edn, 1986), p. 152.

11. Generally, see G. Marshall, *Constitutional Conventions* (1984), ch. III; R. Blake, *The Office of Prime Minister* (1975), pp. 58f.; Harold Wilson, *The Governance of Britain* (1976), pp. 37f.

12. *Fifty Years of Parliament* (1926), vol. II, p. 194.
13. *Constitutional and Administrative Law* (6th edn, 1989), p. 166.
14. *The King, the Constitution, the Empire and Foreign Affairs: Letters and Essays 1936–37* (1938), p. 42.
15. *Ibid.*, p. 41.
16. *The Governance of Britain* (1976), p. 38.
17. *Ibid.* However in his book *The Labour Government 1964–70* (1971) (for example, on p. 201), he records that he took colleagues' advice before deciding the 1970 date of election, which he lost.
18. *Upwardly Mobile* (1988), p. 203.
19. See for example, his Crown Prerogatives (House of Commons Control) Bill 1988, HC [1987–88] 117.
20. On p. 36.
21. BBC Radio 4, 'Jewel in the Crown', 6 April 1989.
22. Quoted in R. Leonard, *Elections in Britain* (1968), p. 5.
23. (2nd edn, 1957), pp. 414–5.
24. On opinion polling generally, see pp. 297f.
25. London Weekend Television News, 7 June 1991.
26. *The Dilemma of Democracy* (1978), p. 191.
27. (1954), p. 193.
28. (1971), p. 200.
29. The question of whether the Queen might ever exercise a personal discretion to refuse the Prime Minister a dissolution – in circumstances where there is no breach of an established convention by the Prime Minister – is considered on pp. 58f.
30. See further on p. 291.
31. HC Deb., 11 May 1987, col. 21.
32. HC Deb., 9 May 1983, col. 631.
33. HC Deb., 29 March 1979, cols. 631–9.
34. On the preparation and issue of the Proclamation, see Robert Blackburn, *The Meeting of Parliament* (1990), p. 44.
35. However, the Royal Proclamation of 16 March 1992 was never published because of an administrative oversight of not sending a copy to the printers.
36. There is, however, one bogus precedent for Parliament being able to do so. In 1689, the 'Convocation Parliament' convened itself under the auspices of William of Orange, after King James II had been forced to flee the country. This assembly proceeded by way of legal fiction to proclaim the abdication of King James and the enthronement of King William and Queen Mary, and then retrospectively legitimised itself as a Parliament nothwithstanding that no proper writs of summons had ever been issued.
37. *The Labour Government 1964–70* (1971), p. 215.
38. See J. de Lolme, *The Constitution of England: or, An Account of the English Government* (4th edn, 1790), pp. 414–5.
39. Schedule 1, rule 5.
40. Schedule 2, para. 4.
41. Schedule 4, para. 68.
42. Generally see Robert Blackburn, *The Meeting of Parliament* (1990), pp. 56–7. The ancient common law rule was that on the death of a monarch, Parliament automatically dissolved and awaited being called into existence once more by the new King or Queen.
43. The House of Lords' capacity to hold up government legislation approved by the Commons is, with this single exception of prolongation Bills, limited to a delaying power of twelve months, after which the Bill can be presented for the

royal assent and pass into law. See Parliament Acts 1911 and 1949, and Erskine May, *Parliamentary Practice* (21st edn 1989, by C. J. Boulton), ch. 30.

44. For a work of reference on comparative parliamentary practice, see Inter-Parliamentary Union, *Parliaments of the World* (2 vols, 1986).

45. HC Deb., 26 October 1943, col. 109.

46. Respectively, the Parliament and Registration Act 1916; Parliament and Local Elections Act 1916; Parliament and Local Elections Act 1917; and Parliament and Local Elections Act (No. 2) Act 1917.

47. Respectively, the Prolongation of Parliament Act 1940; Prolongation of Parliament Act 1941; Prolongation of Parliament Act 1942; Prolongation of Parliament Act 1943; and Prolongation of Parliament Act 1944.

48. HC Deb., 26 October 1943, Col. 109.

49. A model for reform is contained within Institute for Public Policy Research, *A Written Constitution for the United Kingdom* (1993).

50. *Ibid.*

51. For example, Fixed Parliaments Bill [1986–87] 64.

52. *Reform of the Constitution* (1970), p. 52.

53. Lord Holme, HL Deb., 22 May 1991, col. 245.

54. See p. 20.

55. *Elective Dictatorship* (1976), pp. 8–9.

56. 19 May 1991.

57. *The Times*, 25 September 1990.

58. *Independent*, 17 February 1991.

59. *Observer*, and see *British Public Opinion* (April 1991), p. 7.

60. *Independent*, 1 March 1991.

61. *Independent*, 15 June 1991.

62. *New Statesman*, 9 August 1991.

63. HL Deb., 22 May 1991, cols. 244–5, Lord Holme.

64. HC Deb., 17 May 1991, col. 577.

65. Vol. II: The Crown, (3rd edn, 1907), Part I, p. xxvi.

66. *The Governance of Britain* (1914), p. 110.

67. *London Standard*, 24 July 1985; *The Times*, 25 July 1985.

68. *The Privileges and Rights of the Crown* (1936), p. 64.

69. Tony Benn, *Arguments for Democracy* (1981), p. 31.

70. See, for example, J. P. Mackintosh, *The British Cabinet* (3rd edn, 1959); R. H. S. Crossman, *Inside View: Three Lectures on Prime Ministerial Government* (1970).

71. *The Dilemma of Democracy* (1978), pp. 192–3.

72. *The English Constitution* (1867, Fontana edn 1963), p. 111.

73. *Cabinet Government* (3rd edn, 1959), p. 394.

74. Gresham College Lecture, 3 July 1984; letter to *The Times*, 27 February 1984.

75. Letter to *The Times*, 2 May 1950. Lascelles' identity was widely known but only later officially confirmed in J. Wheeler-Bennett's authorised biography, *George VI: His Life and Reign* (1958), p. 775.

76. On the possible appointment of Prince Charles, see *The Times*, 4 May 1981.

77. V. Bogdanor, *No Overall Majority* (1986), p. 21.

78. *Guardian*, 12 September 1985; and, generally, see Robert Blackburn, *The Meeting of Parliament* (1990), pp. 69–71.

79. p. 43.

80. See p. 50.

81. See p. 19.

82. See, for example, the Bill proposed by Austin Mitchell in 1983 for a four-year fixed term subject to earlier dissolution 'if a majority of the House votes for an earlier dissolution': HC Deb., 9 March 1983, col. 841.

83. Basic Law, Art. 39 (Assembly and Legislative Term).
84. For the prerogative immunity of the Crown from judicial process, see S. A. de Smith and R. Brazier, *Constitutional and Administrative Law* (6th edn, 1989), pp. 133f.
85. The form of draft legislation proposed draws upon work of the Institute for Public Policy Research, *A Written Constitution for the United Kingdom* (1993) of which Robert Blackburn was co-author of the Parliament section.

3 The Electorate: Voters and Voting

1. *Reflections on the Revolution in France* (1790, Penguin edn, 1968), p. 141.
2. (1867; Fontana edn, 1963), pp. 62, 78 and 277.
3. For works of reference on British electoral history, see Sir Ivor Jennings, *Party Politics*, vol. I: Appeal to the People (1960); F. W. Craig (ed.), *British Electoral Facts 1832–1987* (1988).
4. A. J. Allen, *The English Voter* (1964), pp. 10–11.
5. Quoted in H. J. Hanham, *The Nineteenth Century Constitution* (1969), p. 280.
6. D. Fraser, *The Evolution of the British Welfare State* (1973), p. 164. Generally, see A. F. Havighurst, *Britain in Transition* (4th edn, 1985), ch. 5; and M. Pugh, *Women and the Women's Movement in Britain* 1914–59 (1992), especially ch. 6.
7. HC Deb., 28 March 1917, cols. 492–4.
8. Cd 8432.
9. HC Deb., 22 May 1917, col. 2135.
10. *Fifty Years of Parliament* (vol. II, 1926), p. 125.
11. Representation of the People Act 1949.
12. For statistics on the number of business voters, see D. and G. Butler, *British Political Facts 1900–85* (1986), p. 147.
13. HC [1982–3] 63.
14. HC [1990–1] 161.
15. *We the People: Towards a Written Constitution* (1990).
16. HC Deb., 9 January 1985, col. 787.
17. Representation of the People Act 1983, s(1)(a) and ss. 4 and 5.
18. The recommended standard form being known as 'Form A'.
19. Source: Hansard Society, *Our Parliament* (6th edn, 1964, by S. Gordon), pp. 50–1.
20. Source: Office of Population Censuses and Surveys, *1992 Electoral Statistics* (HMSO, 1992, Series EL No. 19), p. 1.
21. [1970] 2 QB 463 at 475.
22. *Independent*, 25 March 1992.
23. Chris Husbands, quoted in *Times Higher Education Supplement*, 3 April 1992.
24. See, for example, P. Pulzer, *Political Representation and Elections in Britain* (3rd edn, 1975), pp. 102–12; J. Blondel, *Voters, Parties and Leaders* (1965), chs 2 and 3.
25. Abolition of multiple registration was recommended in the Reports of both the Speaker's Conference on Electoral Law 1973–4 and the House of Commons Home Affairs Committee on the Representation of the People Acts [1982–3] 32.
26. HC [1982–3] 32–I, pp. xiv–xix.
27. HC Deb., 27 June 1984, Vol. 62, cols. 1030–1.
28. *1992 Electoral Statistics* (Series EL no. 19), p. 1.
29. *Agenda for Change* (1991), pp. 21–2.
30. See Home Office memorandum of evidence to the Home Affairs Committee on the Representation of the People Acts, [1982–83] 32, vol. 2, pp. 1f.

31. Quoted *ibid.*, p. 2.
32. Excluding Irish citizens and minors.
33. (4th edn), vol. 15, para. 410; and vol. 35, para. 802.
34. *Observer,* 12 June 1983. See also P. Hughes and S. Palmer, 'Voting Bishops', *Public Law* (1983) p. 393.
35. *Observer,* 12 June 1983.
36. HL Deb., 29 June 1983.
37. Letter to author, 5 November 1986.
38. s. 3, and ss. 173 and 160, respectively.
39. Generally, see *Parker's Conduct of Parliamentary Elections* (1983 edn, by R. J. Clayton), p. 166.
40. s. 7.
41. Representation of the People Act 1983, s. 1(3).
42. s. 9.
43. See p. 73.
44. s. 10.
45. Report of the House of Commons Home Affairs Select Committee on the Representation of the People Acts [1982–3] 32, vol. II, pp. 203f.
46. *Ibid.*, vol. I, p. vi.
47. *Ibid.*, vol. II, p. 23.
48. These are collected together in *Schofield's Election Law* (1984 edn by A. J. Little, revised issue no. 15, 1993), Appendix C: Circulars and Memoranda.
49. M. and S. Pinto-Duschinsky, *Voter Registration: Problems and Solutions* (1987), p. iii.
50. OPCS, *Compiling the Electoral Register 1990* (1991, by Mary Hickman), p. 17, and ch. 4 generally.
51. s.29.
52. Home Office Circular RPA 347, Practice Note 3: reproduced in *Schofield's Election Law, op. cit.,* Appendix C: 543.
53. See OPCS, *Electoral Statistics* (EL Series); and reports in *Observer,* 16 February 1992, and *Independent,* 25 March 1992.
54. *Richmond Borough Herald,* 15 April 1992.
55. From Hansard Society, *Agenda for Change* (1991), p. 84.
56. *Ibid.,* p. 61.
57. Representation of the People (Amendment) Bill [1992–3] 17; on which, see HC Deb., 12 February 1993, vol. 122, cols. 1207f.
58. See pp. 358f.
59. Representation of the People Act 1983, Schedule 1: Parliamentary Election Rules (the 'Election Rules'), r. 28(1).
60. Schedule 2, Form E.
61. For spoilt ballot statistics, see F. W. Craig, *British Electoral Facts 1832–1987* (1988), p. 172.
62. r. 41.
63. r. 47(2).
64. See D. Pannick, 'Making Your Mark', *The Times,* 9 April 1992.
65. The form of ballot paper shown on page 90 is an example, which modifies the statutory illustration given in the Representation of the People Act 1983, Schedule 1, to indicate descriptions of parties.
66. ss. 101, 102.
67. Letter from David Prout, *Independent,* 16 April 1992.
68. See p. 104f.
69. *Op. cit.* pp. 46.
70. s. 6.

71. See D. Butler and D. Kavanagh, *The British General Election of 1992* (1992), p. 244.
72. 1985 Act, s. 6(6).
73. 1985 Act, s. 7.
74. See *Parker's Conduct of Parliamentary Elections, op. cit.*, p. 202.
75. Representation of the People Regulations 1986, reg. 69. Late applications because of ill-health must be received before noon on the sixth day before the poll.
76. *Ibid.*, regs. 90–92; and Election Rules, r. 45.
77. Generally, see I. Crewe, *British Electoral Behaviour 1945–1987* (1989); A. Heath, R. Jowell and J. Curtice, *How Britain Votes* (1985); D. Butler and D. Stokes, *Political Change in Britain* (2nd edn, 1974).
78. *British General Elections since 1945* (1989), p. 60.
79. *Political Representation and Elections in Britain* (3rd edn, 1975), pp. 112–3.
80. See Table 3.3.
81. See p. 99.
82. Source: MORI.
83. See D. Butler and D. Kavanagh, *The British General Election of 1983* (1984), p. 282.
84. For weather conditions during previous elections, see F.W. Craig, *British Electoral Facts 1832–1987* (1988), p. 157.
85. p. 84. See further below, p. 233.
86. See F.W. Craig, *op. cit.*, p. 54.
87. *Op. cit.*, pp. 124–5.
88. *Voters, Parties and Leaders* (1965), p. 71.
89. HC Deb., 9 March 1983, vol. 38, col. 841.
90. Election Rules, r. 44.
91. *Ibid.*, r. 47.
92. *Ibid.*, r. 48.
93. *Guardian*, 25 January 1993.
94. Report of the House of Commons Select Committee on Home Affairs on Electronic Counting Methods, [1991–2] 49.
95. Election Rules, r. 46.
96. *Ibid.*, r.49.
97. H.F. Rawlings, *Law and the Electoral Process* (1988). For full titles of *Parker* and *Schofield*, see Notes 39 and 48 above.
98. *Morgan* v. *Simpson* [1975] QB 151 at 161/2.
99. Election Rules, r. 18.
100. *Ibid.*, r. 31.
101. *Ibid.*, r. 32.
102. *Re: South Newington Election Petition* [1948] 2 All ER 503. See above, pp. 89–91.
103. See correspondence on the subject in the *Independent*, 14, 16 and 21 April 1992.
104. See pp. 101–2.
105. Election Rules, r. 55.
106. *Ibid.*, r. 57. In Scotland the documents are stored by the Sheriff's Clerk for each court district (r. 58), and in Northern Ireland by the Clerk of the Crown for Northern Ireland (r. 59).
107. *Ibid.*, r. 56.
108. For the recent problem in Northern Ireland, see H.F. Rawlings, *op. cit.*, p. 214.
109. Such identification has been required in Northern Ireland elections since 1985: generally see R.J. Clayton (ed.), *Parker's Conduct of Parliamentary Elections* (1992), pp. 243–4.

110. p. 78.
111. (1910 edn), p. 300.
112. Figures from F. W. Craig, *British Electoral Facts 1832–87* (5th edn, 1989), p. 66; and House of Commons Information Office.
113. State of the Nation poll, 1991.
114. HC [1982–3] 32–II, p. 106.
115. *Ibid.*, p. 244.

4 Parliamentary Constituencies

1. Source: Office of Population Censuses and Surveys, *Electoral Statistics 1992* (HMSO, 1992, Series EL No. 19), p. 2.
2. HC Deb., 15 June 1992, col. 684.
3. Report of the House of Commons Home Affairs Committee on Redistribution of Seats, [1986–7] 97–I, p. vi.
4. *A Written Constitution for the United Kingdom* (1993), ch. 6.
5. See *Here We Stand: Proposals for Modernising Britain's Democracy* (1993), p. 60.
6. HC [1985–6] 120, which did not proceed beyond a formal first reading.
7. HC Deb., 8 March 1991, col. 635.
8. See Sir I. Jennings, *Party Politics*, vol. I: *Appeal to the People* (1960), ch. 1.
9. See the report by R. Mortimore, *Probable Political Effects of the Boundary Review in England* (1992), and S. Baxter, 'The Draughtsman Cometh', *New Statesman and Society*, 15 May 1992.
10. Fergus Montgomery, HC Deb., vol. 70, col. 263.
11. On the constitution of the Commissions, see Schedule 1 of the Parliamentary Constituencies Act 1986.
12. HC Deb., 15 June 1992, vol. 209, col. 669.
13. Generally, see P. Laundy, *The Office of Speaker* (1964); and J. A. G. Griffith and M. Ryle, *Parliament* (1989), pp. 141–9.
14. See p. 143–5.
15. HC Deb., 15 June 1992, col. 671.
16. HC Deb., 2 March 1983, col. 269.
17. A boundary commissioner or assistant commissioner is one of the disqualifying offices listed in Schedule 1, Part III of the 1975 Act.
18. See Report of the House of Commons Home Affairs Committee on Redistribution of Seats, [1986–7] 97–I, p. 93.
19. Schedule 1, para. 4.
20. s. 1(2).
21. Schedule 1, para. 6.
22. Edmund Marshall, HC Deb., 1 March 1983, vol. 38, col. 159.
23. The Report of the Home Affairs Committee on Redistribution of Seats, HC [1986–7] 97–I, p. 93.
24. *Ibid.*
25. *Ibid.*
26. *Ibid.*
27. *Ibid.*
28. Reproduced in Appendix 3.
29. Figures from R. Waller, 'The 1983 Boundary Commission: Policies and Effects', *Electoral Studies* (1983), p. 204.
30. Report of the Boundary Commission for England (1983), Cmnd 8797–I, p. 6.
31. See pp. 146f.

32. Figures from R. Waller, 'The 1983 Boundary Commission: Policies and Effects', *Electoral Studies* (1983), p. 204.
33. HC Deb., 1 March 1983, col. 144.
34. Report of the Boundary Commission for England (1983), Cmnd 8797–I, p. 9.
35. Edmund Marshall, HC Deb., 1 March 1983, vol. 38, col. 163.
36. See pp. 140f.
37. See pp. 146f.
38. On publication requirements concerning the Commissions' intention to proceed, see Parliamentary Constituencies Act 1986, s.5.
39. See pp. 134f.
40. Report of the Boundary Commission for England (1983), Cmnd 8797–I, p. 1.
41. Edmund Marshall, HC Deb., 1 March 1983, col. 162.
42. *Op. cit.*, p. 5. More recently, a newsletter has been circulated by the Boundary Commissions to MPs indicating their intentions to proceed and their estimated completion date: see HC Deb., 15 June 1992, col. 699.
43. HC Deb., 2 March 1983, col 265.
44. *Op. cit.*, p. 7.
45. *Op. cit.*, p. 3.
46. Generally, see ss. 5 and 6.
47. s. 5(2).
48. s. 6(1) and (2).
49. s. 6(3).
50. Merlyn Rees, HC Deb., 2 March 1983, col. 267.
51. pp. 121–2.
52. *Op. cit.*, p. 4.
53. 'The 1983 Boundary Commission: Policies and Effects', *Electoral Studies* (1983), p. 197.
54. Generally see Erskine May, *Parliamentary Practice* (21st edn 1989, by C. J. Boulton), pp. 542f.
55. s. 4(2).
56. Cmnd 4040 (1969).
57. s. 3(5).
58. *Times Law Reports,* 20 October 1969.
59. See the Bill of Rights 1689, art. 8, on which a leading authority is *Bradlaugh* v. *Gossett* (1884) 12 QBD 271; and generally S. de Smith and R. Brazier, *Constitutional and Administrative Law* (6th edn, 1989), ch. 14 and p. 324.
60. HC Deb., vol. 791, col. 428.
61. *Ibid.*, cols. 453–66.
62. HC Deb., 15 June 1992, col. 671.
63. Generally, see H. W. R. Wade, *Administrative Law* (6th edn, 1988), ch. 2.
64. s. 4(7).
65. [1983] 1 QB 600.
66. [1955] 1 Ch 238.
67. Pages 615/6.
68. See H. W. R. Wade, *op. cit.*, pp. 14–15.
69. [1948] 1 KB 223 at 230.
70. [1983] 1 QB 600 at 626.
71. T. C. Hartley and J. A. G. Griffth, *Government and Law* (2nd edn, 1981), p. 326.
72. See for example Lord Hailsham's remarks in *Re W (An Infant)* [1971] AC 682 at 700.
73. [1983] 1 QB 600 at 636.
74. *Ibid.*, pp. 636–7. It should be noted that Lord Donaldson did say that if ever there was evidence that the Commission had decided upon a rigid, fixed policy

of never crossing existing borough or metroopolitan district boundaries, that would constitute an unlawful fetter and abuse of their statutory discretion, and accordingly the Commission would be misdirecting themselves in law such that their recommendations might be quashed by the court: *ibid.*, 631.

75. *Op. cit.*, 616.
76. *Op. cit.*, 251.
77. See below, pp. 290, 358–60, 429.
78. Merlyn Rees, HC Deb., 2 March 1983, col. 268.
79. 15 December 1954, col. 1920.
80. 15 June 1992, col. 694.
81. HC Deb., 1 March 1983, cols. 161–2.
82. 'The 1983 Boundary Commission: Policies and Effects', *Electoral Studies* (1983), p. 200.
83. 1 March 1983, cols. 146–7.
84. See pp. 151f.
85. See p. 117.
86. See p. 124f.
87. Boundary Commissions Act 1992, s. 2(2).
88. Under s. 2(3) the 1992 Act, the Commissions' Reports must be completed within 8 to 12 years of their previous ones (replacing the previous provision in the Parliamentary Constituencies Act 1986 for completion between 10 to 15 years).
89. See pp. 151f.
90. See Report of the House of Commons Home Affairs Committee on Redistribution of Seats, [1986–7] 97–I, p. viii; and also Report of the Boundary Commission for England (1983), Cmnd 8797–I, p. 76.
91. See p. 131.
92. Edmund Marshall, HC Deb., 2 March 1983, Col. 259.
93. HC Deb., 1 March 1983, col. 144.
94. *Ibid.*, col. 192.
95. Martin Flannery, 2 March 1983, cols. 296/7.
96. HC.Deb., 1 March 1983, cols. 146–7.

5 Parliamentary Candidates

1. The returning officer may, however, hold a nomination paper to be invalid where the candidate is disqualified under the terms of the Representation of the People Act 1981: see p. 164.
2. On the Election Court, see p. 275.
3. *Re Parliamentary Election for Bristol South East* [1964] 2 QB 257.
4. s. 3.
5. s. 3.
6. s. 52(6) and schedule 7 of the 1981 Act. On persons who are Commonwealth citizens see s.37 of the Act, and, generally, A. Dummett and A. Nicol, *Subjects, Citizens, Aliens and Others* (1990); and S. Juss, *Immigration, Nationality and Citizenship* (1993).
7. See pp. 167f.
8. This disqualification is derived from the common law. The holders of peerages of Ireland are not disqualified: Peerage Act 1963, s.5.
9. See pp. 185f.
10. s. 141.
11. See para. 2.02.05.
12. p. 50.

13. See, especially, ss. 158, 159 and 160.
14. See Erskine May, *Parliamentary Practice* (21st edn, 1989, by C.J. Boulton), pp. 112–3.
15. See letter by Colin Smith, published in the *Guardian*, 8 November 1982.
16. See pp. 170f.
17. HC [1986–7] Bill 157, on which see HC Deb., 12 May 1987, Cols. 182–184.
18. *Op. cit.*, pp. 50–1. See further, below p. 185.
19. [1899] 1 QB 852.
20. p. 858.
21. Now contained in rr. 17(2) and 50(2) of the Election Rules.
22. p. 858.
23. 10 March 1623, C.J. (1547–1628) 681, and see Erskine May, *Parliamentary Practice*, pp. 40–41.
24. Schedule 2, para. 2.
25. *Diaries of a Cabinet Minister*, vol. III (1977), p. 92.
26. *The Times*, 25 July 1968.
27. D. and G. Butler, *British Political Facts 1900–85* (1986), p. 184.
28. See P. Norton, 'The Qualifying Age for Candidature in British Elections', *Public Law* (1980), p. 66.
29. [1984–5] Bill 155, whose supporters in the Commons included David Amess and Jeremy Hanley.
30. Report from the House of Commons Select Committee on Offices or Places of Profit under the Crown [1940–1] 120, p. xiv.
31. s. 1(1)(b).
32. s. 3(3).
33. s. 1(1)(c).
34. Defined in s. 1(3) of the Act, read with s.225 Army Act 1955 and s. 223 Air Force Act 1955.
35. See D. Leonard, *Elections in Britain* (1968), pp. 64–5
36. Respectively, s. 1(1)(a) and Part I of Schedule I, and s. 1(1)(d).
37. s. 1(1)(e).
38. See HC Deb., 22 July 1985, Col. 801.
39. *Ibid.*
40. s. 2.
41. See R. Brazier, *Constitutional Practice* (1988), ch. 4.
42. There have been occasions where ministers have been allowed a free vote over major policy issues, notably during the 1975 referendum campaign on membership of the European Community. Generally, see G. Marshall, *Constitutional Conventions* (1984), ch. IV.
43. On the feelings of Lord Callaghan see Tony Benn, *Conflicts of Interest: Diaries 1977–80* (1992); and of John Major see *Guardian*, 26 July 1993.
44. Schedule 2.
45. 1900–80 figures from D. and G. Butler, *British Political Facts 1900–1985* (1986), p. 82.
46. HC [1940–1] 120 (1941), p. xx.
47. See P.G. Richards, *The Backbenchers* (1972), chs. 3 and 11.
48. On the old law which disqualified MPs who accepted an office of profit under the Crown, dating from a statute in William III's reign, see Report of the House of Commons Select Committee on Offices or Places of Profit under the Crown, [1940–1] 120; and Sir T. Erskine May, *The Constitutional History of England* (1912 edn by Francis Holland), vol. III, pp. 85–6.
49. Report of the House of Commons Select Committee on Offices or Places of Profit under the Crown, *ibid*, p. xix.

50. *Ibid.*, p. xx. See also, above p. 165.
51. For general histories containing accounts of religious disabilities, see Sir W. Anson, *The Law and Custom of the Constitution* (vol. I, 5th edn, 1922); F. W. Maitland, *The Constitutional History of England* (1908); T. F. T. Plucknett (ed.), *Taswell-Langmead's English Constitutional History* (11th edn, 1960); Sir Thomas Erskine May, *Constitutional History*; D. L. Keir, *The Constitutional History of Modern Britain 1485–1937* (2nd edn, 1943); G. B. Adams, *The Constitutional History of England* (1921).
52. See s. 1(3) of the 1978 Act; and Erskine May, *Parliamentary Practice* (21st edn, 1989, by C. J. Boulton), pp. 229–31.
53. s. 5(2) and (3).
54. Author's italics in this and the following statutory extracts.
55. *In re MacManaway and In re The House of Commons (Clergy Disqualification) Act 1801* AC [1951] 161 at 178.
56. Paraphrased by the Attorney-General, Sir Hartley Shawcross, during the MacManaway case, *ibid.*, at 164.
57. ss. 1 and 2(4).
58. Report of the House of Commons Select Committee on Clergy Disqualification, [1951–2] 200, p. 26.
59. *Ibid.*, pp. 31 and 27.
60. Extract from long title and ss. 3 and 4.
61. See pp. 159–60.
62. *Op. cit.*, p. v.
63. Mr W. S. Wigglesworth, at p. 23.
64. Mr James Randall Philip, at p. 40.
65. Most Rev. Edward Myers; his view summarised by the Committee Chairman at p. 45.
66. HC [1985–86] Bill 87 (not printed); and HC Deb., 19 February 1986, vol. 92, col. 324.
67. *Guardian* and *London Daily News*, 23 June 1987.
68. Report of the House of Commons Select Committee on Clergy Disqualification, [1951–2] 200, p. 23.
69. *Ibid.*, p. 56.
70. Report of Proceedings, p. 797. The Private Members' Motion was moved by the Archdeacon of Derby.
71. See P. G. Richards, *The Backbenchers* (1972), ch. 1; J. Blondel, *Voters, Parties and Leaders: The Social Fabric of British Politics* (1963), especially ch. 5; P. Pulzer, *Political Representation and Elections in Britain* (3rd edn, 1975), especially pp. 70–77.
72. From D. Butler and D. Kavanagh, *The British General Election of 1992* (1992), p. 224.
73. From D. and G. Butler, *British Political Facts 1900–85* (1986), p. 179.
74. From D. Butler and D. Kavanagh, *op. cit.*, p. 226.
75. *Voters, Parties and Leaders* (1963), p. 133.
76. From D. Butler and D. Kavanagh, *op. cit.*, p. 221.
77. From D. and G. Butler, *op. cit.*, p. 249.
78. Tam Dalyell, quoted in *Independent*, 14 July 1992. On the debate over the parliamentary timetable generally, see Report from the Select Committee on Sittings of the House (chaired by Michael Jopling MP), HC [1991–92] 200.
79. Except, in the case of the Labour Party, where an all-women short list is imposed under the Conference decision in 1993. See below, pp. 211–13.
80. Quoted in *Labour Research*, January 1992, p. 16.
81. ICM/Guardian Poll in 1991 cited *ibid.*

82. *Women at the Top* (1990), p. 31.
83. NOP poll, see *Independent*, 'Does Sex Matter in the Polling Booth', 18 March 1992.
84. 'A Woman's Place is in the House, or Is It?', *Times*, 13 April 1983.
85. *Spectator*, 4 July 1992, pp. 17–18.
86. *Women in the House* (1979), pp. 12–13.
87. See the statistics and tables given in Hansard Society, *Women at the Top* (1990).
88. 'Why More is Not Enough', *Guardian*, 14 April 1992.
89. *Op. cit.*, p. 18.
90. HC Deb., 21 January 1992, cols. 185/6.
91. *Ibid.*, col. 186.
92. HC [1990–1] Bill 161.
93. *A Future for Socialism* (1991), p. 55.
94. Labour Party, *Rule Book 1993–94* (1993), Selection Procedure for Parliamentary Candidature, 9(4)(f), p. 56.
95. Labour Party, *Record of Decisions* (1993, 92nd Annual Conference), Resolution 417, p. 21.
96. BBC 1, 'On the Record', 21 November 1993.
97. See 'Does Labour's Policy on Women Break the Law?', *Times*, 9 November 1993.
98. *Op. cit.*, 1(6) and (7), p. 52.
99. See Labour's 1992 election manifesto, p. 24.
100. Ch. 8, especially pp. 376f. and 403f.
101. See Institute for Public Policy Research, *A Written Constitution for the United Kingdom* (1993), para. 63:2.
102. See Hansard Society, *Women at the Top* (1990), p. 31.
103. See Conservative Party, *Notes on Procedure for the Adoption of Conservative Party Candidates in England, Wales and Northern Ireland* (1990); Liberal Democrats, *Constitution of the Social and Liberal Democrats* (1988), Article 11; and *Rules for the Selection and Adoption of Prospective Parliamentary Candidates in England* (1988); Labour Party, *Rule Book 1993–94* (1993), 'Selection Procedure for Parliamentary Candidature'. Useful commentaries are M. Rush, *The Selection of Parliamentary Candidates* (1969); A. Ranney, *Pathways to Parliament* (1965); P. Paterson, *The Selectorate* (1967); and A. Jones, *The Reselection of MPs* (1983).
104. On special provisions concerning women, see pp. 211–12.
105. See Labour Party, *Rule Book, op. cit.*, para. 12.
106. The motion was only narrowly passed, with 48.926 per cent for and 48.127 per cent against.
107. Constitutional Rules, cl. X(2).
108. *Op. cit.*, p. 6
109. *Rule Book, op. cit.*, para. 9(4)(d).
110. *Op. cit.*, p. 6.
111. 'Government by Greengrocer', *New Statesman*, 5 February 1965.
112. See Representation of the People Act 1983, Schedule 1: Parliamentary Election Rules, rr. 6–17.
113. On the history of the deposit, see J. F. S. Ross, *Elections and Electors* (1955), pp. 224f.
114. From F. W. Craig, *British Electoral Facts 1832–1987* (5th edn, 1989), p. 82.
115. Report of the House of Commons Home Affairs Committee on the Representation of the People Acts, [1982–3] 32–II, pp. 211 and 316.
116. See G. Hand, J. Georgel and C. Sasse (ed.), *European Electoral Systems Handbook* (1979).

117. Memorandum of evidence by Mr P. Gould to the House of Commons Home Affairs Committee on the Representation of the People Acts, *op. cit.*, p. 340.
118. HC Deb., 10 December 1984, col. 789.
119. Oral evidence, Report of the House of Commons Home Affairs Committee on the Representation of the People Acts, *op. cit.*, p. 211.
120. Home Office memorandum of evidence, *ibid.*, p. 14.
121. A separate problem is where candidates are nominated with names and/or party descriptions which confuse the voters. For example, a 'Roy Jenkins' (who had changed his name) stood with the description of 'Social Democratic Party' (which he claimed to have founded months before the SDP broke away from Labour) against Roy Jenkins, then leader of the SDP, in the 1982 Glasgow Hillhead by-election (the SDP leader won). A worse instance came in 1994, when a 'Literal Democrat' candidate stood in a European parliamentary election, and polled over 10 000 votes, with the real Liberal Democrat losing to the Conservative candidate by 800 votes. In the Literal Democrat case (*Sanders and Another* v. *Chichester and Another*, QBD 11 November 1994), the Election Court ruled that the nomination and ballot papers had been valid, and refused to order a fresh election. The remedy for this mischief is the introduction of a legal requirement that the description of a candidate should be 'true, fair and not confusing'. This improvement in our election law can be effected simply by a short amending bill (or a clause being added to some other legislation on electoral affairs which is passing through Parliament), modifying the existing legislative provision on nomination of candidates in rule 6(3), Schedule 1, Representation of the People Act 1983.
122. Report of the House of Commons Home Affairs Committee on the Representation of the People Acts, *op. cit.*, p. 212.
123. *Ibid.*
124. Quoted *ibid.*, p. 337. The book's author was G. Thayer.
125. HC Deb., 10 December 1984, col. 789.
126. *Ibid.*
127. Government Reply to the First Report from the Home Affairs Committee (Session 1982–3, HC 32), Representation of the People Acts, Cmnd 9140 (1984), p. 21.
128. Nuffield College, Oxford seminar, see P. Kellner, *Times*, 21 March 1984.
129. P. Kellner, *ibid.*

6 Election Campaigns: Publicity and the Media

1. 'Democracy in Danger', *Dispatches*, Wide Vision Productions for Channel Four Television, 18 March 1992.
2. On the legal obligations upon broadcasting companies, see pp. 252f.
3. (1908), pp. 83–4. See above, p. 99.
4. Broadcasting Act 1990, s. 8(2)(a)(ii), which states that a television broadcasting service 'must not include any advertisement which is directed towards any political end'.
5. See note 1 above.
6. Clause 5.
7. See J. Antcliffe, 'Politics of the Airwaves', *History Today* (March 1984), pp. 5–6.
8. On the history of broadcasting, see A. Briggs, *The History of Broadcasting in the UK* (4 vols., 1961–79); J. Curran and J. Seaton, *Power without Responsibility: The Press and Broadcasting in Britain* (4th edn, 1991), part II.
9. For the BBC's duty of impartiality, see pp. 252f.

10. For the independent TV companies' duty of impartiality, see pp. 255f.
11. But see the aide-memoire published in G. W. Goldie, *Facing the Nation* (1977). Generally, see BBC, *Fairness and Impartiality in Political Broadcasting* (1987), ch. 3; C. R. Munro, *Television, Censorship and the Law* (1979) and 'Party Politicals – who says they are legal and why?', *The Times*, 12 February 1982; A. Boyle, 'Political Broadcasting, Fairness and Administrative Law', *Public Law* (1986), p. 562; A. Smith, *Television and Political Life* (1979).
12. See A. Boyle, 'Political Broadcasting' p. 580. No agreement has been made for normal party political broadcasts in the region outside election times.
13. A term employed by A. Boyle, *ibid.*
14. Bearing some analogy with judicial reluctance to interfere with the discretion of the boundary commissioners over redistribution of parliamentary seats, see above pp. 137f. Generally, see H. W. R. Wade, *Administrative Law* (6th edn, 1988), ch. 12.
15. Quoted in J. Antcliffe, 'Politics of the Airwaves' p. 7.
16. D. Butler and D. Kavanagh, *The British General Election of 1983* (1984), p. 148.
17. *Independent*, 28 March 1992.
18. A. Smith, *Television and Political Life* (1979), p. 18.
19. 4–10 April 1992.
20. D. Butler and D. Kavanagh, *The British General Election of 1987* (1988), p. 154.
21. The articles were written by David Smith for *The Sunday Times*, and the extracts reproduced with kind permission are from the editions published on 8 and 22 March 1992:© Times Newspapers Ltd, 1992.
22. *Independent*, 13 March 1993.
23. Royal Charter for the continuance of the British Broadcasting Corporation, Home Office (1981), Cmnd 8313.
24. Clause 3(a).
25. Clause 3(e).
26. Licence and Agreement Dated the 2nd Day of April 1981 Between Her Majesty's Secretary of State for the Home Department and the British Broadcasting Corporation, Cmnd 8233.
27. Clause 13(7).
28. Clause 13(2).
29. BBC, *Guidelines on Factual Programmes* (1989), section 21, 1.
30. BBC, *Fairness and Impartiality in Political Broadcasting* (1987), p. 8.
31. *Ibid.*, p. 8.
32. BBC, *Guidelines on Factual Programmes* (1989), section 21, 1.
33. Lecture given on the 125th anniversary of the Methodist Recorder at the Wesley Chapel, 24 October 1986 (extract published in *Observer*, 16 October 1986).
34. s. 6(1).
35. s. 6(3)–(7).
36. p. 19.
37. p. 20.
38. See BBC, *Guildelines for Factual Programmes* (1989), section 18.
39. Letter supplied by BBC Political Office.
40. See p. 236f.
41. *Independent*, 15 January 1992.
42. *Ibid.*
43. *Ibid.*
44. s. 92 as amended by Schedule 20 of the Broadcasting Act 1990.
45. Tim Pitt, manager of BBC Radio Sheffield, in *The Times*, 25 March 1985.

46. Or at the dissolution of Parliament, if no earlier announcement is made: s. 93(2)(a).
47. This restatement of the effect of s.93 comes from the BBC's guidelines on the subject issued at the time of the 1992 Election.
48. [1979] 3 All ER 80.
49. *Ibid.* at 82(j) to 83(b).
50. Margaret Douglas, submission to Report of the International Press Institute, 'Potholes on the Campaign Trail' (1992), p. 8.
51. Generally, see P. Birkenshaw, *Freedom of Information* (1988).
52. *Commentaries on the Laws of England,* vol. 4 (1770), pp. 151–2.
53. Adapted from D. Butler and D. Kavanagh, *The British General Election of 1992* (1992), pp. 181–2.
54. MORI and D. Butler and D. Kavanagh, *ibid.,* p. 190.
55. 27 April 1979, and see D. Butler and D. Kavanagh, *The British General Election of 1979* (1980), pp. 259–60.
56. 'Fleet Street: Its Bite on the Ballot', *New Socialist,* January (1985), p. 25.
57. 'Hard News' series, Channel Four Television, 26 April 1992.
58. Quoted in D. Butler and D. Kavanagh, *The British General Election of 1992,* p. 208.
59. 'Hard News' series, Channel Four Television, 3 May 1992.
60. *Ibid.*
61. On political advertisements see pp. 287f., and on the publication of opinion polls see pp. 297f.
62. Source: *Independent,* 27 February 1992.
63. Generally, see Representation of the People Act 1983, ss. 67–71 and s. 158.
64. See pp. 281f.
65. 4 O'M. and H. 76 at 82/3 per Field J.
66. D. Butler, *British General Elections since 1945* (1989), p. 112.
67. s. 67(2) and s. 70.
68. See s. 158.
69. s. 69.
70. National Executive Committee paper, March 1993.
71. s. 113.
72. s. 115.
73. s. 114.
74. s. 107.
75. See s. 159.
76. s. 167.
77. s. 164.
78. *R. v. Local Government Election Commissioner, ex parte Mainwaring and Another*; *R. v. Same, ex parte Harris, Times,* 21 January 1991.
79. Quoted in D. Butler and R. Rose, *The British General Election of 1959* (1960), p. 280.
80. Schedule 1. See further, C. Tapper, *Computer Law* (4th edn, 1989), and on the civil rights issues involved, P. Sieghart, *Privacy and Computers* (1977).
81. D. Butler, *British General Elections since 1945* (1989), p. 112.
82. s. 95.
83. s. 91.
84. Generally see D. Butler and D. Kavanagh, *The British General Election of 1992,* pp. 233–7.
85. s. 109.
86. s. 111.
87. s. 108.

88. s. 109.
89. s. 101 causes any such hiring of public vehicles (for example, taxis, buses) to be an illegal hiring. See also s. 102, making the hiring of any transport facilities for voters an illegal practice. An exception lies in s. 105, which provides that hiring sea travel for voters who are unable to reach their polling station without crossing the sea is allowed as an election expense.
90. Under a formula provided for within s. 76 (as amended by s. 6(1)(b) of the Representation of the People Act 1989), and see the Representation of the People (Variation of Limits of Candidates' Election Expenses) Order 1994.
91. [1952] 1 All ER 697.
92. *Times*, 19 October 1951, p. 11.
93. See D. Butler and D. Kavanagh, *The British General Election of 1992*, p. 41.
94. On the drafting of the manifestos, see *ibid.*, pp. 92–4 and 106–8.
95. Broadcasting Act 1990, s. 8(2)(a)(ii); see Note 4 above.
96. *Independent*, 7 April 1992.
97. *Media Week*, 20 March 1992.
98. D. Butler and D. Kavanagh, *The British General Election of 1992*, p. 205.
99. Tony Brignull, *Guardian*, 5 February 1992.
100. D. Butler and D. Kavanagh, *The British General Election of 1992*, p. 116.
101. *Independent*, 20 March 1992.
102. (8th edn, 1988).
103. pp. 142–6 and 358–60.
104. International Press Institute, 'The Potholes on the Campaign Trail' (1992), p. 5.
105. *Ibid.*, p. 19.
106. *Ibid.*, p. 20.
107. *Ibid.*, p. 11.
108. *Ibid.*, p. 18.
109. See comments of Peter Emery, in 'Democracy in Danger', *Dispatches*, Wide Vision Productions for Channel Four Television, 18 March 1992.
110. D. Butler and D. Kavanagh, *The British General Election of 1992* , p. 155.
111. 'Democracy in Danger', *op. cit.*
112. *Ibid.*, and see D. Butler and D. Kavanagh, *The British General Election of 1983*, p. 167.
113. On these episodes, see D. Butler and D. Kavanagh, *The British General Election of 1992*, pp. 172–3.
114. 'Power to the People', *Times* leading article, 9 April 1992.
115. HC Deb., 12 March 1992.
116. 'Democracy in Danger', *op. cit.*
117. See I. Crewe, 'Saturation Polling, the Media and the 1983 Election', in I. Crewe and M. Harrop (eds), *Political Communications: The General Election Campaign of 1983* (1986), p. 236.
118. See D. Kavanagh, 'Private Opinion Polls and Campaign Strategy', *Parliamentary Affairs* (1992), p. 518.
119. *Independent on Sunday*, 8 March 1992.
120. *Observer*, 22 March 1992.
121. Source: MORI, *British Public Opinion*, April 1992, p. 26, and D. Butler and D. Kavanagh, *The British General Election of 1992*, p. 136.
122. For opinion polling statistics, see F. W. Craig (ed.), *British Electoral Facts 1832–1987* (5th edn, 1989), pp. 101–13, and D. and G. Butler (eds.), *British Political Facts 1900–1985* (6th edn, 1986), pp. 254–65.
123. From I. Crewe, 'A Nation of Liars? Opinion Polls and the 1992 Election', *Parliamentary Affairs* (1992), p. 475.

124. For example, A. King, 'Why Did They Get It Wrong?', *Daily Telegraph*, 11 April 1992; D. Kavanagh, 'Spirals of Silence, *Guardian*, 21 April 1992; I. Crewe, 'A Nation of Liars? Opinion Polls and the 1992 Election'; and generally, D. Butler and D. Kavanagh, 'The Waterloo at the Polls', ch. 7 in *The British General Election of 1992.*

125. Report of the Market Research Society Inquiry into the 1992 General Election Opinion Polls, June 1992 ('MRS Report').

126. ICM Research, Results of Recall Interviews Conducted after the 1992 General Election, May 1992,

127. See, for example, MRS Report, p. 3.

128. *Ibid.*, p. 14.

129. *Ibid.*, p. 7.

130. See p. 100.

131. Quoted in D. Kavanagh, 'Spirals of Silence', *op. cit.*.

132. From D. Butler and D. Kavanagh, *The British General Election of 1992*, p. 201.

133. Quoted in P. Kellner, 'How polls can be poles apart', *Observer*, 29 May 1983.

134. 1989, sections 18 and 46.

135. *Guardian*, 2 April 1992.

136. Final Report of the Conference on Electoral Law (1968), Cmnd 3550.

137. HC [1986–87] Bill 88.

138. HC Deb., 24 February 1987, col. 164.

139. *Ibid.*, col. 165.

140. *Ibid.*, col. 166.

141. Hansard Society, *Agenda for Change* (1991), ch. 6.

142. Committee on Parliamentary and Public Relations, Information Report on Public Opinion Polls, 29 August 1985, doc. 5449.

7   The Financial Affairs of the Political Parties

1. D. Butler and D. Kavanagh, *The British General Election of 1992* (1992), p. 260.

2. Figures from the parties' accounts, 1991 and 1992; and M. Pinto-Duschinsky, in Hansard Society, *Agenda for Change* (1991), p. 107.

3. See pp. 328–9. The accounts published in autumn 1993 have been expanded into a fuller, 20-page glossy report, with a chairman's statement, general review of the year, and greater explanation of accounting policies and notes to the accounts (though there is no further breakdown of the Income and Expenditure Account, which fits on to one page).

4. Labour Party memorandum of evidence to the House of Commons Home Affairs Committee, 28 May 1993.

5. Generally, see M. Pinto-Duschinsky, *British Political Finance 1830–1980* (1981); K. D. Ewing, *The Funding of Political Parties in Britain* (1987).

6. Generally see R. Miliband, *Parliamentary Socialism* (1972); H. Pelling, *A History of British Trade Unionism* (3rd edn, 1976).

7. [1910] AC 87.

8. ss. 71, 73 and see chapter VI of the Act generally.

9. s. 72.

10. *Guardian*, 1 July 1993.

11. *Ibid.*

12. 'Who Paid for the Tory Victory?', *Labour Research*, July 1993, p. 13.

13. Labour Party memorandum of evidence to the House of Commons Home Affairs Committee, 28 May 1993.

14. Conservative Party memorandum of evidence to the House of Commons Home Affairs Committee, 26 May 1993.
15. Schedule 7, para. 3 to 5.
16. Sources for the following figures and data are 'Who Paid for the Tory Victory?', pp. 11–13; *Company Donations to the Conservative Party and other Political Organisations*, Labour Party Information Paper No. 90 (1990); *Business Age*, May 1993, p. 40; HC Deb., 22 June 1993, cols. 197–8.
17. 'Who Paid for the Tory Victory?', p. 13.
18. *Ibid.*, p. 11.
19. For example, Charter Movement Party Accounts Scrutiny Committee, *Called To Account*, May 1993, and p. 328.
20. See, for example, 'Funding the Tories', *Observer*, 20 June 1993; 'Tory Money', *Business Age*, May 1993; *Sunday Times*, 20 and 27 June 1993.
21. *Ibid.* and see HC Deb., 22 June 1993, col. 175.
22 *Ibid.* and M. Linton, *Money and Votes* (1994), p. 66.
23. HC [1992–93] 726, [1993–94] 301.
24. Hb Deb., 22 June 1993, col. 175.
25. *Ibid.*, cols. 192 and 196.
26. May 1993, p. 40.
27. *Guardian*, 29 and 30 April 1993.
28. Conservative Party memorandum of evidence to the House of Commons Home Affairs Committee, 26 May 1993.
29. BBC1 television programme, 'Panorama': 'Who Pays for the Party?', 8 October 1990.
30. BBC television interview, 27 June 1993; *Guardian*, 28 June 1993.
31. HC Deb., 22 June 1993, col. 194.
32. *Ibid.*, col. 186.
33. Generally, see M. De la Noy, *The Honours System: Who Gets What and Why* (1991); J. Walker, *The Queen Has Been Pleased* (1986).
34. HC Deb., 22 June 1993, col. 176.
35. Labour Party memorandum of evidence to the House of Commons Home Affairs Committee, 28 May 1993.
36. See COI, *Honours and Titles* (1992), App. 6; De la Noy, *op. cit.*, ch. 6.
37. HC Deb., 22 June 1993, col. 259.
38. 13 June 1992.
39. 'Honours that Carry a Whiff of Corruption', *Observer*, 23 December 1990.
40. HC Deb., 22 June 1993, col. 209.
41. Examination of witnesses, 16 July 1993; and see further HC Deb., 22 June 1993, col. 208.
42. See Council of Europe Parliamentary Assembly, *Financing of Political Parties: A Cornerstone of Pluralist Democracies*, Doc. 6072 (1989).
43. The Law on Political Parties 1967, section VI.
44. Canada Elections Act 1985, s. 44.
45. Commonwealth Electoral Act 1918 (as amended), s. 314.
46. On the disclosure of MPs' financial interests, see J. A. G. Griffith and M. Ryle, *Parliament* (1989), pp. 55ff; and Erskine May, *Parliamentary Practice* (21st edn 1989, by C. J. Boulton), pp. 384–90.
47. HC Deb., 22 June 1993, col. 256, and see Labour Party, Charter for Party Political Funding.
48. Quoted in HC Deb., 22 June 1993, at col. 209.
49. *Ibid.*, col. 263.
50. Conservative Party memorandum of evidence to the House of Commons Home Affairs Committee, 26 May 1993.

51. HC Deb., 22 June 1993, col. 238.
52. *Ibid.*, col. 219.
53. Charter Movement Party Accounts Scrutiny Committee, *Called to Account: A Report on Conservative Party Central Funds*, May 1993.
54. Quoted in HC Deb., 22 June 1993, at col. 254.
55. *Ibid.*, col. 231.
56. *Ibid.*, col. 188.
57. *Ibid.*, col. 227.
58. *Ibid.*, col. 212.
59. *Ibid.*, col. 220–1.
60. Hansard Society, *Paying for Politics* (1981); K. D. Ewing, The *Funding of Political Parties in Britain* (1987); D. Oliver, 'Fairness and Political Finance: The Case of Election Campaigns', ch. 8 in Robert Blackburn (ed.), *Constitutional Studies* (1992).
61. ICM poll in *Guardian*, 9 June 1993.
62. Robin Cook, HC Deb., 22 June 1993, col. 260.
63. Conservative Party memorandum of evidence to the House of Commons Home Affairs Committee, 26 May 1993.
64. *Ibid.*, col. 238.
65. See, for example, Labour Party memorandum of evidence to the House of Commons Home Affairs Committee, 28 May 1993.
66. HC Deb., 22 June 1993, col. 261.
67. See Council of Europe Parliamentary Assembly, *Financing of Political Parties: A Cornerstone of Pluralist Democracies*, Doc. 6072 (1989).
68. Schedule 7, para. 3 to 5.
69. BBC1 television, 'Panorama': 'Who Pays for the Party?', 8 October 1990.
70. K. D. Ewing, *The Funding of Political Parties in Britain*, ch. 2.
71. *Company Donations to Political Parties* (1985), pp. 20–1.
72. Labour Party memorandum of evidence to the House of Commons Home Affairs Committee, 28 May 1993.
73. *Company Donations to Political Parties* (1985).
74. HC Deb., 25 October 1989, col. 883.
75. HC Official Report, Standing Committee D, 16 May 1989, c.8.
76. HC [1989–90] Bill 98.
77. See pp. 233f.
78. s. 91. See above, p. 279.
79. s. 95.See above, p. 278.
80. HC Deb., 4 November, 1993, col. 615.
81. For these political donations to be exempt from death duties under the terms of the Inheritance Tax Act 1984 (s. 24(1) as amended by s. 137 Finance Act 1988) the party in question must have had at least two of its members elected to the House of Commons at the last general election, or one member elected and all its candidates receiving in total not less than 150 000 votes.
82. See p. 222f.
83. See Council of Europe Parliamentary Assembly, *Financing of Political Parties*.
84. Report of the Committee on Financial Aid to Political Parties (Houghton Report) (1976), Cmd. 6601; Hansard Society Commission, *The Financing of Political Parties: Paying for Politics* (1981); House of Commons Home Affairs Committee, *Funding of Political Parties* [1993–4] 301, Minutes and Memoranda of Evidence [1992–93] 726.
85. Houghton Report, p. 78.
86. *Ibid.*, p. 81.
87. *Ibid.*, p. 78.

88. Conservative Party memorandum of evidence to the House of Commons Home Affairs Committee, 26 May 1993.
89. HC Deb., 22 June 1993, col. 194.
90. Conservative Party memorandum of evidence to the House of Commons Home Affairs Committee, 26 May 1993.
91. (1981), p. 31.
92. *Ibid.*, p. 295.
93. *Ibid.*, p. 292.
94. *Ibid.*, p. 296.
95. Houghton Report, p. 79.
96. HC Deb., 22 June 1993, col. 263.
97. *Ibid.*, col. 211.
98. Houghton Report, p. 54.
99. *Ibid.*
100. *Paying for Party Politics: The Case for Public Subsidies* (1975), p. 9.
101. Labour Party memorandum of evidence to the House of Commons Home Affairs Committee, 28 May 1993.
102. *Paying for Politics* (1981), p. 12.
103. *Ibid.*, p. 33.
104. *Ibid.*, p. 35.
105. See p. 317–18.
106. Houghton Report, p. 53.
107. Council of Europe Parliamentary Assembly, *Financing of Political Parties*, p. 4.
108. Report of the Committee on Financial Aid to Political Parties (Houghton Report) (1976), Cmd. 6601.
109. Four of the twelve members of the Committee opposed state aid and dissented.
110. Reimbursement of candidates at local government elections was also included in the Houghton recommendations, and the Report similarly envisaged that the scheme would eventually extend to European Parliament elections.
111. See p. 337.
112. *Paying for Politics* (1981).
113. *Ibid.*, pp. 38–9.
114. p. 147.
115. Report of a Commission of Inquiry into the Finances, Organisation and Political Education of the Party (1980), p. 16, quoted *ibid.*, p. 130.
116. p. 56. See also Labour's election manifesto, 1992, p. 25.
117. See, for example, *We the People: Towards a Written Constitution* (1990), pp. 9–10.
118. See Labour Party memorandum of evidence to the House of Commons Home Affairs Committee, 28 May 1993; Larry Whitty's examination by the Committee, 23 June 1993; Report of the House of Commons Home Affairs Committee on the Finances of Political Parties, [1993–94] 301, and Minutes and Memoranda of Evidence [1992–93] 726.
119. Being half of the £5m maximum which, under another of its proposals, it would place upon each party's allowable national election expenditure.
120. See G. Hand, J. Georgel and C. Sasse (eds), *European Electoral Systems Handbook* (1979); Council of Europe Parliamentary Assembly, *Financing of Political Parties*.
121. ICM poll, *Guardian* 9 June 1993.
122. See, for example, Labour Party memorandum of evidence to the House of Commons Home Affairs Committee, 28 May 1993, section IV; Liberal

Democrats, *Here We Stand: Proposals for Modernising Britain's Democracy* (1993), p. 14.
123. HC [1989–90] Bill 98.
124. Submission from the Conservative Party, Appendix A in Hansard Society, *Agenda for Change* (1991), p. 76.
125. *Ibid.*, pp. 4 and 40.
126. *Ibid.*, p. 41.
127. *Paying for Politics* (1981), p. 41.
128. Figures from party accounts, and M. Pinto-Duschinksky, in Hansard Society, *Agenda for Change* (1991), p. 109.
129. HC Deb., 22 June 1993, cols. 246–7.
130. See Council of Europe Parliamentary Assembly, *Financing of Political Parties*.
131. ICM poll, *Guardian* 9 June 1993.
132. See pp. 360–1.
133. s. 75.
134. *R. v. Tronoh Mines Ltd and Others* [1952] 1 All ER 697, and see pp. 284–5.
135. See p. 330.
136. pp. 332f.
137. p. 142.
138. The Australian Electoral Commission does not, however, have responsibility for reviewing the boundaries of constituencies.
139. Quoted in Hansard Society, *Agenda for Change* (1991), p. 69.
140. Now consolidated in the Trade Union and Labour Relations (Consolidation) Act 1992.
141. Respectively, Institute for Public Policy Research, *A Written Constitution for the United Kingdom* (1993); and Labour Party memorandum of evidence to the House of Commons Home Affairs Committee, 28 May 1993.
142. Elections Finances Act, SM 1980.

8 Arguments about Proportional Representation

1. Sir I. Jennings, *Cabinet Government* (3rd edn, 1959), ch.1, and *The British Constitution* (5th edn, 1966), ch. 1.
2. *How Britain is Governed* (1930), p. 171.
3. *Constitutional Fundamentals* (1980), p. 10.
4. Sources: F. W. Craig, *British Electoral Facts 1832–87* (5th edn, 1989), pp. 52–3, D. and G. Butler (eds), *British Political Facts 1900–1985* (6th edn, 1986), and House of Commons information office.
5. On the history of electoral reform attempts, see D. Butler, *The Electoral System in Britain since 1918* (2nd ed, 1962); V. Bogdanor, *The People and the Party System* (1981).
6. P. Dunleavy, H. Margetts and S. Weir, *Replaying the 1992 General Election* (LSE Public Policy Paper No. 3, 1992).
7. Labour Party, *Report of the Working Party on Electoral Systems* (1993) ('Plant Report').
8. *Independent*, 21 April 1993.
9. See G. Goguel, *Chroniques Electorales: la Cinquieme Republique apres De Gaulle* (1983); A. Cole and P. Campbell, *French Electoral Systems and Elections* (3rd edn, 1989).
10. *Electoral Reform: Fairer Voting in Natural Communities* (1982).
11. *The Electoral System in Britain since 1918* (2nd ed, 1962), p. 184.
12. D. Owen, *A United Kingdom* (1986), p. 53.
13. *What is Proportional Representation?* (1984), p. 90.

14. P. Dunleavy, H. Margetts and S. Weir, *Replaying the 1992 General Election*.
15. The Report of the Hansard Society Commission on Electoral Reform (1976).
16. Institute for Public Policy Research, *A Written Constitution for the United Kingdom* (1993).
17. See Labour Party, *Second Interim Report of the Working Party on Electoral Systems* (1992), appendix 2, p. 17. This recommendation was endorsed by the Party's National Executive Committee, and appeared in Labour's 1992 election manifesto at p. 23.
18. P. Dunleavy, H. Margetts and S. Weir, *Replaying the 1992 General Election*.
19. Based on calculations of P. Dunleavy, H. Margetts and S. Weir, *ibid.*, and (on the supplementary vote) of Dale Campbell-Savours, *Independent*, 21 April 1993.
20. Amended table from E. Lakeman, *Twelve Democracies* (4th edn, 1991), p. 32.
21. *Democracy in Britain: A Health Check for the 1990s* (LSE Public Policy Paper, 1991).
22. Generally, see V. Bogdanor, *The People and the Party System* (1981); J. Hart, *Proportional Representation: Critics of the British Electoral System 1820–1945* (1992); D. Butler, *The Electoral System in Britain since 1918* (2nd ed, 1962); M. Pugh, *The Evolution of the British Electoral System 1832–1987* (1988).
23. 1872, Bill 67; HC Deb., 10 July 1872, col. 890.
24. Parliamentary Elections Bill 1908, 74. See also Parliamentary Elections (Alternative Vote) Bill 1910, 101; Parliamentary Elections Bill (Alternative Vote) Bill 1910, 216; Alternative Vote in Democratic Elections 1974–5, 178.
25. Report of the Speaker's Conference on Electoral Reform, Cd 8463.
26. *Times*, 3 April 1992.
27. *We the People: Towards a Written Constitution* (1990), pp. 7–9.
28. pp. 509–13.
29. p. 65.
30. *Sunday Times*, 5 April 1992.
31. *Guardian*, 3 April 1992.
32. For exmple, MORI poll, *Independent*, 26 September 1990; NOP poll, *Independent*, 24 May 1991.
33. Party press conference, 2 April 1992.
34. BBC2 Television 'Newsnight', 3 April 1992.
35. *Independent*, 6 April 1992.
36. BBC2 Television, 5 December 1992.
37. Labour Party, *Report of the Working Party on Electoral Systems* (1993), p. 38.
38. For example, see Margaret Beckett's comments reported in *Independent*, 15 June 1992; Jeff Rooker's article on electoral reform, *Independent*, 6 October 1990.
39. Press Release, 19 May 1993.
40. The 1993 Labour Party conference passed the following resolution (45.491 per cent For, and 42.021 per cent Against): 'Conference welcomes the report of the Plant Commission and congratulates it on its thorough review of electoral systems . . . Conference favours constituency representation for the House of Commons and supports the commitments of John Smith, Leader of the Labour Party, for a referendum on the issue of electoral reform for the Commons.' (Record of Decisions, composite 31, at p. 33.)
41. Tony Blair, *Leadership Election Statement: Change and National Renewal* (1994), p. 17
42. *How Britain is Governed* (1930), p. 177.
43. *Sunday Times*, 5 April 1992.
44. *Guardian*, 7 April 1992. See the reply of V. Bogdanor to Mr Baker's attack, 'The Public Relations of PR', *Guardian* 17 April 1992.

45. *Independent*, 25 March 1992.
46. *Independent on Sunday*, 15 March 1992.
47. 4 April 1992.
48. Labour Party Conference debate, 2 October 1987.
49. *Parliament* (2nd edn, 1957), pp. 142–3.
50. p. 46.
51. 4 April 1992.
52. See A. Cooke, 'Proportional Representation', Conservative Research Department Paper, *Politics Today* (1983) no. 15, p. 285.
53. *Guardian*, 2 January 1992.
54. *Tribune*, 20 December 1985.
55. HC Deb., 17 May 1991, col. 573.
56. Labour Party Conference debate, 2 October 1987.
57. 'Proportional Representation', A Conservative Research Department Paper, *Politics Today* (1991) no. 12, p. 218.
58. Sir A. Maude and J. Szemerey, *Why Electoral Change? The Case for P.R. Examined* (1982), p. 35.
59. *Independent on Sunday*, 15 March 1992.
60. HC Deb., 17 May 1991, col. 571.
61. See pp. 370f.
62. (1991), pp. 30–1.
63. 11 May 1991.
64. *Elective Dictatorship* (Richard Dimbleby lecture, 1976).
65. (1978), pp. 187–8.
66. Lord Home, *The Way the Wind Blows: An Autobiography by Lord Home* (1976), p. 282.
67. John Mackintosh lecture 1982.
68. *Times*, 21 July 1983.
69. Quoted in P. Kellner, 'Electoral Reform: No Longer a Tory Taboo?', *Independent*, 13 March 1992.
70. Extract in *Times*, 10 November 1980.
71. S. E. Finer (ed.), *Adversary Politics and Electoral Reform* (1975), p. 12.
72. 'PR Pluses', *Guardian*, 17 October 1985.
73. Robin Blackburn, 'The Ruins of Westminster', *New Left Review* (1992), no. 191, pp. 5, 9 and 15.
74. *How Britain is Governed* (1930), pp. 168 and 178.
75. p. 3.
76. *We the People: Towards a Written Constitution* (1990), pp. 7–9.
77. Submission to the Labour Party Working Party on Electoral Systems (1991) p. 8.
78. See also the criteria adopted by the Hansard Society, *Electoral Reform* (1976), p. 26; Institute for Public Policy Research, *A Written Constitution for the United Kingdom* (1993), p. 224.
79. See pp. 376f.
80. See pp. 379f.
81. Conference on Electoral Law (1968), Cmnd 3550.
82. HC Deb., 14 October 1968, col. 43.
83. pp. 46 and 24.
84. pp. 9–10.
85. Generally, see Erskine May, *Parliamentary Practice* (21st edn, 1989, by C. J. Boulton), ch. 24; J. A. G. Griffith and M. Ryle, *Parliament* (1989), ch. 11.
86. Standing Orders of the House of Commons (Public Business), 1991, S.O. 30.
87. HC Deb., 25 June 1979, col. 49.
88. See D. Woodhouse, *Ministers and Parliament* (1994), ch. 10 and p. 208.

89. HC Deb., 13 July 1992, col. 916.
90. Report of the House of Commons Select Committee on Procedure, *The Working of the Select Committee System*, [1989–90] 19–1, para. 176.
91. *Ibid.*, para. 172.
92. For example, *Observer*, 12 July 1992.
93. HC Deb., 13 July 1992, col. 921.
94. *Ibid.*, col. 923.
95. *Independent*, 14 July 1992.
96. HC Deb., 13 July 1992, col. 918.
97. See J. A. G. Griffith and M. Ryle, *Parliament* (1989), pp. 142–3; J. Kingdom, *Government and Politics in Britain* (1991), pp. 269–70.
98. HC Deb., 13 July 1992, Col. 921.
99. See G. Drewry, 'Select Committees and Back-bench Power', ch. 6 in J. Jowell and D. Oliver (eds.), *The Changing Constitution* (2nd edn, 1989); R. Brazier, *Constitutional Practice* (1988), pp. 188–190; D. Woodhouse, *Ministers and Parliament* (1994), ch. 10; J. Kingdom, *Government and Politics in Britain* (1991), p. 300.
100. From P. Dunleavy, H. Margetts and S. Weir, *Replaying the 1992 General Election* (LSE Public Policy Paper No. 3, 1992), p. 3.
101. Liberal/SDP Alliance Commission, *Electoral Reform* (1982), pp. 5–6.
102. From Institute for Public Policy Research, *A Written Constitution for the United Kingdom* (1993), p. 226. The figures are based on 1987 electoral statistics.
103. Quoted in the Plant Report, *op. cit.*, p. 27.
104. See D. Butler and D. Kavanagh, *The British General Election of 1992*, p. 220.
105. See *ibid.*, pp. 218–19 and 338–9.
106. p. 57.
107. See pp. 205f.
108. HC Deb., 6 December 1933, col. 1744.
109. See pp. 397f.
110. See pp. 387f.
111. HC Deb., 17 May 1991, col. 603.
112. *Guardian*, 11 June 1992.
113. *Independent*, 24 May 1991.
114. *Guardian*, 19 September 1986.
115. *Guardian*, 20 February 1982.
116. See New Zealand Royal Commission on the Electoral System, *Towards a Better Democracy* (1986); New Zealand House of Representatives Electoral Law Committee, *Inquiry into the Report of the Royal Commission on the Electoral System* (1988). At the 19 September 1992 referendum, 84.7 per cent of those voting supported change, with 70.5 per cent of those persons favouring the mixed member proportional system. At the 6 November 1993 referendum, 53.8 per cent voted for the mixed member Proportional system, and 46.2 per cent voted to keep the first-past-the-post system.
117. P. Dunleavy, H. Margetts and S. Weir, *Replaying the 1992 General Election* (LSE Public Policy Paper No. 3, 1992), pp. 6/7.
118. *A Written Constitution for the United Kingdom* (1993), ch. 8.
119. See pp. 61f.
120. The form of draft legislation proposed draws upon work of the Institute for Public Policy Research, *A Written Constitution for the United Kingdom* (1993), to which Robert Blackburn was a contributor.

Select Bibliography

Alderman, G., *British Elections: Myth and Reality* (1978).

Allen, A. J., *The English Voter* (1964).

Amery, L. S., *Thoughts on the Constitution* (1947).

Aristotle, *The Politics* (1948 ed., trans. by Barker, E.).

Bagehot, W., *The English Constitution* (1867; with Introduction by Crossman, R. H. S., 1963).

Ball, A. R., *British Political Parties: The Emergence of a Modern Party System* (2nd ed., 1987).

Barker, R., *Political Ideas in Modern Britain* (1978).

Benn, T., *Arguments for Democracy* (1981).

Birch, A. H., *The British System of Government* (9th ed., 1993).

Birch, A. H., *The Concepts and Theories of Modern Democracy* (1993).

Birch, A. H., *Representative and Responsible Government* (1964).

Blackburn, R., *The Meeting of Parliament: A Study of the Law and Practice relating to the Frequency and Duration of the United Kingdom Parliament* (1990).

Blackburn, R. (ed.), *Constitutional Studies* (1992).

Blackburn, R. (ed.), *Rights of Citizenship* (1993).

Blake, R., *The Conservative Party from Peel to Thatcher* (1985).

Blondel, J., *Voters, Parties and Leaders: The Social Fabric of British Politics* (1965).

Blondel, J., *Comparative Government* (1990).

Bogdanor, V. and Butler, D. (eds), *Democracy and Elections* (1983).

Bogdanor, V., *Multi-Party Politics and the Constitution* (1983).

Bogdanor, V., *The People and the Party System* (1982).

Bogdanor, V., *What is Proportional Representation?* (1984).

Brazier, R., *Constitutional Practice* (1988).

Brazier, R., *Constitutional Reform* (1991).

Briggs, A., *The History of Broadcasting in the UK* (4 vols: 1961-79).

Butler, D., *The British General Election of 1951* (1952).

Butler, D., *The British General Election of 1955* (1955).

Butler, D. and Rose, R., *The British General Election of 1959* (1960).

Butler, D. and King, A., *The British General Election of 1964* (1965).

Butler, D. and King, A., *The British General Election of 1966* (1966).

Butler, D. and Pinto-Duschinsky, M., *The British General Election of 1970* (1971).

Butler, D. and Kavanagh, D., *The British General Election of February 1974* (1974).

Butler, D. and Kavanagh, D., *The British General Election of October 1974* (1975).

Butler, D. and Kavanagh, D., *The British General Election of 1979* (1980).

Butler, D. and Kavanagh, D., *The British General Election of 1983* (1984).

Butler, D. and Kavanagh, D., *The British General Election of 1987* (1988).

Butler, D. and Kavanagh, D. (eds), *The British General Election of 1992* (1992).

Butler, D., *British General Elections since 1945* (1989).

Butler, D., *The Electoral System in Britain since 1918* (2nd ed., *1962*).

Butler, D., *Governing Without a Majority: Dilemmas for Hung Parliaments in Britain* (2nd ed., 1986).

Butler, D. and G., *British Political Facts 1900–94* (7th ed., *1994*).

Butler, D., Penniman, H. R. and Ranney, A., *Democracy at the Polls* (1981).

Butler, D. and Ranney, A. (eds), *Electioneering, A Comparative Study of Continuity and Change* (1992).

Butler, D. and Stokes, D., *Political Change in Britain: The Evolution of Electoral Choice* (2nd ed., 1974).

Committee on Financial Aid to Political Parties (Houghton Report) (1976), Cmd 6601.

Constitutional Reform Centre, *Company Donations to Political Parties: A Suggested Code of Practice* (1985).

Constitutional Reform Centre, *No Overall Majority: Forming a Government in A Multi-Party Parliament* (1986, by Bogdanor, V.).

Cook, C., *A Short History of the Liberal Party 1900–92* (4th ed, 1993)

Council of Europe Parliamentary Assembly, *Financing of Political Parties: A Cornerstone of Pluralist Democracies* (1989) 6072.

Craig, F. W., *British Electoral Facts 1831–1987* (5th ed. 1989).

Craig, F. W., *British General Election Manifestos 1900–1987* (3rd ed., 1989).

Craig, F. W., *British General Election Manifestos 1959–1987* (1990)

Craig, F. W., *British Parliamentary Election Results 1885–1918* (2nd ed., 1989).

Craig, F. W., *Chronology of British Parliamentary By-Elections 1833–1987* (1987).

Crewe, I. and Harrop, M. (eds), *Political Communications: The General Election Campaign of 1983* (1986).

Crewe, I, and Harrop, M. (eds), *Political Communications: The General Election Campaign of 1987* (1989).

Crewe, I., *British Electoral Behaviour 1945–1987* (1989).

Crewe, I., Day, N. and Fox, A., *The British Electorate 1963–87: A Compendium of Data from the British Election Studies* (1991).

Crick, B., *The Reform of Parliament* (1964).

Curran, J. and Seaton, J., *Power without Responsibility: The Press and Broadcasting in Britain* (4th ed., 1991).

De la Noy, M., *The Honours System: Who Gets What and Why* (1991)

De Smith, S. A. and Brazier, R., *Constitutional and Administrative Law* (6th ed., 1989, by Brazier, R.).

Denver, D. and Hands, G., *Issues and Controversies in British Electoral Behaviour* (1992).

Denver, D., Norris, P., Rallings, C. and Broughton, D. (eds), *British Elections and Parties Yearbook 1993* (1993). The *British Elections and Parties Yearbook* is published annually.

Dicey, A. V., *The Law of the Constitution* (10th ed., 1985).

Dunleavy, P. and Husbands, C., *British Democracy at the Crossroads: Voting and Party Competition in the 1980s* (1985).

Dunleavy, P., *Democracy in Britain: A Health Check for the 1990s* (LSE Public Policy Paper, 1991).

Dunleavy, P., Margetts, H. and Weir, S., *Replaying the 1992 General Election* (LSE Public Policy Paper, 1992).

Emden, C. S., *The People and the Constitution* (2nd ed., 1956).

Erskine May, *Parliamentary Practice* (The Law, Privileges, Proceedings and Usage of Parliament) (21st ed, 1989, by C. J. Boulton).

Ewing, K. D., *The Funding of Political Parties in Britain* (1987).

Finer, S. E. (ed.), *Adversary Politics and Electoral Reform* (1975).

Finer, S. E., *The Changing British Party System 1945–79* (1980).

Forsey, E. A., *The Royal Power of Dissolution of Parliament in the British Commonwealth* (1943).

Gallagher, M., Laver, M. and Mair, P., *Representative Government in Western Europe* (1992).

Garrett, J., *Westminster: Does Parliament Work?* (1992).

Graham, B. D., *Representation and Party Politics* (1993).

Griffith, J. A. G. and Ryle, M., *Parliament: Functions, Practice and Procedures* (1989).

Hailsham, Lord, *Elective Dictatorship* (1976).

Hailsham, Lord, *The Dilemma of Democracy* (1978).

Hand, G., Georgel, J. and Sasse, C. (eds), *European Electoral Systems Handbook* (1979).

Hanham, H. J., *Elections and Party Management: Politics in the time of Disraeli and Gladstone* (rev. ed 1978).

Hanham, H. J., *The Reformed Electoral System in Great Britain 1832–1914* (1971).

Hansard Society Commission, *Election Campaigns: Agenda for Change* (1991).

Hansard Society Commission, *Electoral Reform* (1976).

Hansard Society Commission, *The Financing of Political Parties: Paying for Politics* (1981).

Hart, J., *Proportional Representation: Critics of the British Electoral System 1820–1945* (1992).

Heath, A., Jowell, R. and Curtice, J., *How Britain Votes* (1985).

Hood Phillips, O., *Constitutional and Administrative Law* (7th ed 1987, by Hood Phillips, O. and Jackson, P.).

Hood Phillips, O., *Reform of the Constitution* (1970).

House of Commons Home Affairs Committee, *Funding of Political Parties* [1993–94] 301. Minutes and Memoranda of Evidence, [1992–93] 726.

House of Commons Home Affairs Committee, *Redistribution of Seats* [1986–87] 97.

House of Commons Home Affairs Committee, *Representation of the People Acts* [1982–83] 32.

Ingle, S., *The British Party System* (1987).

Institute for Public Policy Research, *A Written Constitution for the United Kingdom* (1993).

Institute for Public Policy Research, *Money and Votes* (1994, by Martin Linton).

Inter-Parliamentary Union, *Electoral Systems: A World-wide Comparative Study* (1993).

Inter-Parliamentary Union, *Parliaments of the World* (1986).

Jennings, Sir I., *Cabinet Government* (3rd ed., 1959).

Jennings, Sir I., *Parliament* (2nd ed., 1957).

Jennings, Sir I., *Party Politics* (3 vols: 1960, 1961, 1962).

Jennings, Sir I., *The British Constitution* (5th ed., *1966*).

Jones, A., *The Reselection of MPs* (1983).

Kavanagh, D., *Constituency Electioneering in Britain* (1970).

King, A. (ed.), *Britain at the Polls 1992* (1992).

Kingdom, J., *Government and Politics in Britain* (1991).

Labour Party, *Report of the National Executive Working Party on Electoral Systems* (Plant Report) (1993); Interim Report (1991).

Lakeman, E., *Twelve Democracies: Electoral Systems in the European Community* (4th ed., 1991).

Laski, H. J., *A Grammar of Politics* (1925).

Laski, H. J., *Parliamentary Government in England* (1938).

Laski, H. J., *The Position of Parties and the Right of Dissolution* (Fabian Tract, 1924).

Leonard, R., *Elections in Britain Today* (2nd ed., 1991).

Leonard, R., *Paying for Party Politics: The Case for Public Subsidies* (1975)

Liberal Democrats, *We the People: Towards a Written Constitution* (1990)

Liberal/SDP Commission, *Electoral Reform: Fairer Voting in Natural Communities* (1982).

Lijphart, A., *Electoral Systems and Party Systems: A Study of Twenty-Seven Democracies 1945–1990* (1994).

Lively, J., *Democracy* (1975).

MacDonald, B., *Broadcasting in the United Kingdom: A Guide to Information Sources* (1993).

MacKenzie, W. J. M., *Free Elections* (1967).

Mackie, T. and Rose, R., *The International Almanac of Electoral History* (3rd ed., 1990).

Macpherson, C. B., *The Life and Times of Liberal Democracy* (1977)

Maitland, F. W., *The Constitutional History of England* (1908).

Markesinis, B. S., *The Theory and Practice of Dissolution of Parliament: A Comparative Study* (1972).

Marshall, G., *Constitutional Conventions* (1984).

Maude, Sir A. and Szemerey, J., *Why Electoral Change? The Case for P.R. Examined* (1982).

McCallum, R. and Readman, A., *The British General Election of 1945* (1947).

McKenzie, R., *British Political Parties* (3rd ed., 1963).

MORI/Rowntree Trust, *State of the Nation Poll 1991* (1991).

Munro, C. R., *Television, Censorship and the Law* (1979).

New Zealand House of Representatives Electoral Law Committee, *Inquiry into the Report of the Royal Commission on the Electoral System* (1988).

New Zealand Royal Commission on the Electoral System, *Towards a Better Democracy* (1986).

Nicholas, H., *The British General Election of 1950* (1951).

Norris, P., *British By-Elections: The Volatile Electorate* (1990).

Norton, P. and Aughey, A., *Conservatives and Conservatism* (1981).

Norton, P., *The Constitution in Flux* (1982).

Oliver, D., 'Fairness and Political Finance: The Case of Election Campaigns', in Blackburn, R. (ed.), *Constitutional Studies* (1992).

Parker, F. R., *Conduct of Parliamentary Elections* (1983 ed. by R. J Clayton).

Paterson, P., *The Selectorate* (1967).

Pelling, H., *A Short History of the Labour Party* (10th ed., 1993).

Pinto-Duschinsky, M. and S., *Voter Registration: Problems and Solutions* (1987).

Pinto-Duschinsky, M., *British Political Finance 1830–1980* (1981).

Pinto-Duschinsky, M., 'Trends in British Party Funding 1983–87', *Parliamentary Affairs* (1989).

Plant, R., 'Criteria for Electoral Systems: the Labour Party and Electoral Reform', *Parliamentary Affairs* (1991).

Pugh, M., *Electoral Reform in War and Peace 1906–18* (1978).

Pugh, M., *The Evolution of the British Electoral System 1832–1987* (1988).

Pugh, M., *Women and the Women's Movement in Britain 1914–59* (1992).

Pulzer, P., *Political Representation and Elections in Britain* (3rd ed., 1975)

Punnett, R. M., *Selecting the Party Leader: Britain in Comparative Perspective* (1992).

Radice, L., Vallance, E. and Willis, V., *Member of Parliament* (1987).

Ranney, A., *Pathways to Parliament: Candidate Selection in Britain* (1965).

Rawlings, H. F., *Law and the Electoral Process* (1988).

Reeve, A. and Ware, A., *Electoral Systems: A Comparative and Theoretical Introduction* (1992).

Richards, P. G., *The Backbenchers* (1972).

Robertson, G. and Nicol, A., *Media Law: The Rights of Journalists and Broadcasters* (2nd ed. 1990).

Rose, R., *Do Parties Make a Difference?* (1980).

Rose, R., *The Problem of Party Government* (1974).

Ross, J. F. S., *Elections and Electors: Studies in Democratic Representation* (1955).

Ross, J. F. S., *Parliamentary Representation* (1943).

Rule, W. and Zimmerman, J. F. (ed.), *Electoral Systems in Comparative Perspective: Their Impact on Women and Minorities* (1994).

Rush, M., *The Selection of Parliamentary Candidates* (1969).

Schofield, N., *Election Law* (1984 ed., by A. J. Little).

Seaton, J. and Pimlott, B., *The Media in British Politics* (1987).

Smith, A., *Television and Political Life* (1979).

Vallance, E., *Women in the House: A Study of Women Members of Parliament* (1979).

Vile, M. J. C., *Constitutionalism and the Separation of Powers* (1967).

Wade, E. C. S. and Bradley, A. W., *Constitutional and Administrative Law* (11th ed. 1993, by Bradley, A. W. and Ewing, K. D.).

Wade, H. W. R., *Constitutional Fundamentals* (1980).

Walker, J., *The Queen Has Been Pleased: The British Honours System at Work* (1986).

Waller, R., *The Almanac of British Politics* (4th ed., 1991).

Watkins, A., *A Conservative Coup: The Fall of Margaret Thatcher* (1991).

Wilson, H., *The Governance of Britain* (1976).

Wood, A. and R. (eds), *The Times Guide to the House of Commons: April 1992* (1992). A *Times Guide* is published after every general election.

Worcester, R., *British Public Opinion: A Guide to the History and Methodology of Public Opinion Polling* (1991).

Young, A., *The Reselection of MPs* (1983).

Index